W9-BYY-816

Thinking: Its Nature
and Development

Thinking: Its Nature and Development

JOHN RADFORD
and
ANDREW BURTON

*Department of Psychology,
North East London Polytechnic*

JOHN WILEY & SONS

London . New York . Sydney . Toronto

Library of Congress Catalog card No. 73-8197

ISBN 0 471 70476 8 Cloth bound
ISBN 0 471 70475 x Paper bound

Made and printed in Great Britain by
The Garden City Press Limited
Letchworth, Hertfordshire SG6 1JS

Preface

Our book began, as so many do, as a series of lectures which were given first by J.K.R. and later by A.B. In writing, we have retained a personal approach. When the lectures started (in 1965) and even when the book began as an idea (in 1968), 'Thinking' was only just re-emerging as a respectable topic for psychological study; and there was, in our view, no good general text. By the time we finished writing, several had appeared. We have perhaps included a wider range of material than some texts, and a good deal of personal opinion. The book is, on the whole, what we set out to present, our course on Thinking—not complete or final: such a thing is never possible; but this area of knowledge as we see it now.

It might seem odd to have the occasional use of 'I' in a book of joint authorship. The final version of the manuscript was prepared by A.B., but initially sections of the book were drafted independently. 'I' therefore means one or the other of us although the book as a whole is in every sense a joint effort. In general however, J.K.R. wrote the first part of each chapter, while the *Focus* sections were written by A.B., except Chapters 3 and 10. J.K.R. also contributed a good deal of whimsy, most of which A.B. succeeded in banishing. The Bibliography was prepared by A.B. with the welcome assistance of Patrick Downes and Pete Hair.

We should like to acknowledge gratefully the help, in various ways, of the following: Esme Burton; George Butterworth; Pete Hair; Elizabeth Valentine; and, as a reviewer, Peter Wason provided much valuable comment. We also owe much to discussions with numerous other colleagues and students. Without the latter, we might have finished sooner; on the other hand, we probably would never have started. The secretarial and technical staff of our Department ungrudgingly produced many duplicated versions of notes. Miss Valerie Campling typed most of the final version with remarkable speed and accuracy.

JOHN K. RADFORD
ANDREW BURTON

London, February 1973

Contents

1

Concept Identification

DEFINITIONS

This is one of the areas of investigation, where much of what has been done has been summarized so neatly and concisely that it is difficult to avoid merely copying the first author's account. In this case L. E. Bourne (1966) in his monograph *Human Conceptual Behaviour*, has analyzed many of the issues and experiments so well that his book is the obvious starting point for our account of this area. Also Bourne *et al.* (1971) review work published since this date. We shall, however, comment on what he says, make a different selection of material; and discuss the theoretical questions, and what seems to us to be the most important pieces of experimental work, in much more detail. 'As a working definition', Bourne says, 'we may say that a concept exists whenever two or more distinguishable objects or events have been grouped or classified together and set apart from other objects on the basis of some common feature or property characteristic of each.' This indicates that in studying concepts, psychologists are interested in the ways in which organisms classify or categorize stimuli. They are less interested, as a rule, in a close linguistic analysis of the concept of concepts, as a philosopher might be. A 'working definition' is quite satisfactory: it simply, in this case, points to the general area to be studied. Psychologists sometimes venture on definitions which would almost certainly be subject to attack by a linguistic philosopher: for example, the suggestion that concepts '... are meaningful words which label classes of otherwise dissimilar stimuli' (Archer, 1964). This sort of approach seems less helpful, first of all because I would not agree that a concept can be a word—a word, at most, can *stand for* a concept. Then it is not clear what is meant by 'otherwise dissimilar'. Presumably this means that the stimuli are alike in one or more respects and unalike in others. But just what are these respects? And how do you define likeness? This is only obvious in rather simple cases, like having four legs. It is not at all obvious in the case of abstract qualities like unselfishness, or intelligence. And even apparently obvious concepts like blue or yellow can give rise to disagreement (see *Language and Thought*). Then thirdly, Archer's definition would rule out non-verbal organisms; and while we can argue over what it means to say that a rat has a concept of triangularity, no one would question that rats can learn to classify triangles differently from circles, and will jump to a door marked with any triangle when it has always had food behind it. And it is just this business of classifying that seems to be an important characteristic of organisms, and which we want to investigate. It is this characteristic about which one might expect experiments on concepts to tell us something. Bourne's 'working definition'— which is as we have seen an *ostensive* definition, i.e. just points to examples —has the further advantage, for the psychologist, of leading to objective measurements. For we can count the number of times a subject responds in particular ways, viz. by classifying certain stimuli together.

We should notice here that we meet immediately one of the most important problems in psychology: the relationship between the laboratory experiment and real life. In their attempts to exercise control over their subject matter, psychologists constantly risk the accusation of artificiality, or of throwing out the baby with the bath water. Some of the solutions to this will appear in due course. Here, let us just point out that while it is obviously true that in everyday life we are constantly classifying people, objects, and events, the process is obscured by many variables, such as experience, intelligence, motivation, and so on. The typical laboratory situation, on the other hand, is usually highly abstract, so that what we have is simply a subject classifying certain very circumscribed stimuli, such as playing cards (which are, indeed, one of the psychologist's great standbys—Robert Phillips, 1969, has devised an entire first year laboratory course using nothing else).

Kendler (1964) takes this classifying of stimuli as his starting point in a discussion of the ways in which psychologists consider concepts. He suggests three approaches. The first is to regard them as associations: associations between *stimuli* which are dissimilar in some respects, and a common *response*. Suppose we give our subject a pack of playing cards, and simply ask him to sort them in any way that occurs to him. The most likely ways are by colour or by suit. Then we could simply say that he shows the existence of a set of S–R associations: stimulus, any of the black cards; response 'put it on the black pile'. But it is pretty obvious that a subject cannot actually have learned such a set of associations, each one separately. A strict S–R analysis would have to show that the subject had been reinforced at least once for correctly responding to every single black card. This is unlikely to have happened; and presumably even a subject who had never seen playing cards before could sort them into colours. Kendler therefore suggests a second way of considering concepts, namely as mediating processes of some kind. These could be something like ideas or principles, or rules, or strategies, such as 'all the black ones go together'. In the case of the subject with his playing cards, this may seem obvious; one would probably say something like this to oneself, perhaps not very explicitly. But it is not obvious when, as not uncommonly happens, a subject can respond correctly but cannot state the rule when asked. I found this in an (unpublished) experiment in which subjects had to choose one of a set of diagrams on each page of a booklet, and below it write down their reasons for choosing. On the back of each page the subject was given the answer, correct according to the rule I had decided. Some subjects got to where they could choose correctly every time, but their stated reasons were quite wrong. So how could they choose right? Similarly, subjects such as animals or preverbal children can master similar situations, but obviously cannot state how they do it: they cannot, therefore, have a verbal rule. So perhaps one should consider, thirdly, some *response* to be the important element, but of a more general kind. There could be an implicit response, usually but not necessarily verbal, to each stimulus—'black', for example—which in turn serves as the stimulus for the correct response of sorting. Or there could be some kind of observing or attending response, the response of noticing the relevant part of the stimulus (colour) and ignoring the rest. This would be rather like Harlow's 'error factor theory' (see *Problem Solving*). And it raises the whole question of attention, a very important and current topic, which we must discuss in more detail later. Each of these approaches distinguished by Kendler has been developed by various investigators.

Another distinction which both Kendler and Bourne make, and which is a fundamental one, is between cases where the subject is learning to classify for the first time, and cases where he merely has to discover which of several ways of classifying, with which he is already familiar in principle, is correct. The first sort is more common in childhood: for example, learning to distinguish dogs and cats, or to use words like 'honesty' correctly. But it is quite common to go on acquiring new concepts throughout life, particularly when studying any new subject. 'Inhibition', for example, is a new concept at the beginning for most students of psychology. To digress, psychology students often have particular difficulty with new concepts, because so many of the words that stand for them mean something rather different for them in everyday life. An 'inhibited' person is a far cry from the inferred neurophysiological process of 'inhibition' described by Pavlov. To digress further, the ability to acquire new concepts can perhaps be preserved deliberately, and is a mark of an active mind. My great-aunt was over ninety when she acquired the concept of 'hippy'. More relevantly, perhaps, *changes* in concepts—classifying and reclassifying—have been thought to be fundamental to creative thinking (see references to Schon 1963 and to Gordon 1961). The process of acquiring *new* concepts Kendler refers to as *concept acquisition.* Bourne uses the word *formation.* The latter seems preferable, and work on it is discussed separately under the heading of *The Geneva School.* Card sorting is a standard laboratory example of the other process, which Kendler calls *identification,* and Bourne *utilization.* I use Kendler's word, because so many of the experiments constitute a sort of guessing game. In everyday life, devising a new filing system is something

4

like it; but there, there is no criterion for correctness imposed from outside. Nor would the task of the office boy learning the system exactly correspond to the laboratory experiment, since he is usually *told* what to do. In the laboratory, the traditional procedure has been that the experimenter decides upon a rule, which the subject has to discover. Sometimes the experimenter gives him a list of objects (or words, pictures, diagrams, etc.), telling him in each case whether it is or is not an example or positive instance; sometimes the subject can pick out objects in turn from a display, and ask about each. The first way has been called a *reception* procedure, and the second a *selection* procedure. Perhaps the nearest example in real life is the rather pointless game sometimes called 'My aunt's going to Africa'. For those who do not know it, one player decides privately on a rule about the things his aunt will take. He says 'My aunt's going to Africa, and she is taking a teacup and some tea, and a toy train.' Subsequent players offer other likely articles according to the rule they guess to be in operation—as it might be, articles beginning with 't'. This may seem trivial, but it is in fact difficult to think of any more serious situation closely resembling the typical laboratory one. So much the worse, you may say, for the laboratory.

THEORETICAL APPROACHES

Now it is important also to notice a difference in theoretical approach, which runs through most of the study of thinking, and which we shall meet again and again, but which is particularly important here. Anderson (1965) describes this as the difference between a behaviourist and a cognitive orientation. The first stresses, as we have so far done, the making of a common response to a class of stimuli; the other is more interested in supposed or inferred events within the organism. Actually, of course, such events can only be inferred from observation of responses or other behaviour; and on the other hand the strict observers of behaviour have been forced to talk about what goes on inside as well. It just so happens that experimental work on concept identification largely stems, as H. Kendler (1964) points out, from a background of stimulus—response theory, with a gradual move towards the incorporation of cognitive variables which common sense, as it seems today, would have included from the start. It all goes back, of course, to J. B. Watson and his attempt to make psychology respectable by studying only behaviour. Actually psychologists had been studying behaviour for years before Watson launched his 'manifesto', as Woodworth calls it, in 1913. But Watson had a vision of a new sort of psychology: he decided 'either to give up psychology or else to make it a natural science' (Watson, 1924). This involved rejecting the study of anything that could not be observed. In general, this is quite a good piece of scientific advice. Science does depend on observations that can be checked by others. With missionary zeal, however, Watson ruled out a lot of phenomena, such as all conscious experiences, which psychology surely must take into account. And he went on to suggest that not only was behaviour the only thing that could be studied; it was all that the psychologist could talk about. This was a naïve view of science, which certainly does not correspond to the other natural sciences. You cannot see gravity. In other ways Watson's psychology was surprisingly old fashioned. He took over from the classical German psychology of Wundt the idea that the task of psychology was to analyse its subject-matter into some kind of basic elements or units, and then show how these combined to give complex behaviour. Whereas Wundt, however, thought that the units were bits of conscious experience, Watson adopted the reflex, and believed that Pavlov's recent work on conditioning showed how these were built up in the course of development. Hence his famous experiment in which the wretched child Albert was made to be afraid of the white rabbit by a loud noise; this showed in principle, Watson thought, how the complex emotion of fear came about. Aldous Huxley's *Brave New World* was of course dependent upon Watson's conditioning principles. Watson's ideas now seem in many ways naïve. They are important, because they profoundly influenced, even dominated, so much of psychology for so long, and even now many of his assumptions are implicit in current work. Watson had his own theory of thinking, which we discuss under *Language and Thought*. Here, we are more concerned with his general ideas. In the first place, there is the assumption that the physical sciences provide the best model for psychology. Psychologists ought to produce a sort of physics or chemistry of behaviour. The attraction of these sciences has no doubt been their enormous success in giving control over the environment. For Watson, psychology's 'theoretical goal is the prediction and control of behaviour'. The point here is not that physics is *necessarily* the wrong model for psychology (although I believe it is); but that a very different account emerges if one takes a different model, as will be apparent when we discuss the biologically oriented approach of Piaget. If one science is to be taken as a model at all, this should be done with an awareness of the assumptions involved.

More specifically, Watson's ideas, developed and extended by others, led directly to what Kendler describes as three orienting attitudes. There is the assumption that behaviour can be adequately represented in terms of sets of stimulus—response associations, even though these have to be very complex. This is a more sophisticated version of Watson's idea that behaviour actually is composed of such associations. Then there is the belief in the general value of the behaviouristic approach—more objective, more scientific, ultimately more productive. And there is the assumption that, specifically, stimulus–response theories formed to account for, and supported by evidence from, experiments on conditioning and discrimination, are useful for more complex behaviour. Developing this point, Kendler says: 'The main difference between the typical experimental methodology used by S–R psychologists to study discrimination learning and concept learning is that in the former situation single stimulus events are discriminated from each other, while in the latter situation classes of stimuli are discriminated.' Taking this line, T. S. Kendler declares: 'Concept formation is taken to imply the acquisition or utilization, or both, of a common response to dissimilar stimuli.' It is this approach that has inspired the greatest number of experiments.

But we must note as well, as we have already briefly done, the existence of a more cognitive theoretical approach, characterized by Ausubel (1963): 'Existing cognitive structure... is the major factor influencing the learning and retention of meaningful new material.' As we shall see, this line has gradually come more into prominence, a development which appears particularly clearly in the work of J. S. Bruner (see the discussion of his 1956 book *A Study of Thinking* below, and compare with his later work described under *Development and Culture*). Indeed in recent years a whole school of 'cognitive psychology' has sprung up. However this should not be thought of as a direct opposite to Behaviourism. It is rather a matter of interest in the internal processes of the organism, especially 'mental' processes which had been neglected for so long, together with a willingness to speculate about unobservables. The cognitive psychologists do not have a Watsonian dogmatism that we *must* proceed in such a way and no other. And as far as thinking is concerned, we are moving more and more towards an eclectic position in which evidence and ideas are accepted without too many prejudices intervening. As Dienes and Jeeves (1965) say: 'It is difficult to draw a line between what we term thinking and what is usually described as learning, especially when what is being learnt is a set of concepts or structures.' Nevertheless an awareness of the main historical traditions is one of the most useful aids to making sense of what seems at first sight an undifferentiated flood of experimentation.

Now another difference of approach which we can see, also pointed out by Bourne (1966) is that in considering the processing of information it is possible to regard the organism either as a passive recipient of stimuli, or as an active searcher, a maker and tester of hypotheses, a user of strategies or plans. The first view fits in with a general behaviouristic approach, the organism being regarded as a sort of machine which does nothing of itself. But the second view seems to accord better with common sense. For surely it is normal experience, when faced with any puzzlement, to seek some increased information. There is hardly ever the impression that we just sit passively waiting, like an adding machine, for information to be fed in. And that is not the impression we get, either, from watching children or even animals. Of course, it is not as simple as this makes it sound, either. It is, probably, in general the most rational or effective thing to do, to seek more information. But there are plenty of situations in which we do not do the most rational thing. Many of these were described long ago by Freud; and others, more recently, by Festinger, who has shown some of the ways in which, when information conflicts, it can be subtly modified to relieve the situation or in his terms reduce cognitive dissonance. To discuss this here would lead us too far afield, but both rational and irrational techniques are clearly active.

A slightly different point—it is curious how appealing are the most far-fetched and fantastical belief systems. To list these outside the psychological field might offend some worthy persons, but everyone will be able to think of examples, in which some doctrine is tenaciously adhered to apparently without a shred of evidence, or even in flat contradiction of the facts. It is as though anything that helps us to make some kind of order of the world is better than nothing. In my view, too little attention has yet been paid to a fundamental need to master the environment by means of intellectual processes. It is true that both Freud and Piaget have devoted much time to the notion, in different ways; but for most psychologists it perhaps smacks too much of 'instinct'. What I mean is something more than 'curiosity' as described by Butler, Berlyne, and others. Consider the fascination of being 'in the know'—even when the know is shared by another few million newspaper readers or television viewers. Another aspect, which brings us back to Behaviourism, is the attraction of a sort of reductionism. 'Of course, these international financiers are all Jews'; 'All our behaviour is really reflexes, isn't it?' Some kind of classifying or categorizing system is needful: and this is perhaps the real justification for studying the admittedly artificial concepts of the laboratory. But still the guessing game technique seems subject to criticism.

Returning from this detour, and embarking immediately on another, a further point that arises from Bourne's dichotomy between the active and the passive organism is that the latter can be seen as operating *inductively*—which is precisely the view of scientific method advocated by the stricter behaviourists, most explicitly by B. F. Skinner. Sir Karl Popper has devoted much of his life to slaying the dragon induction, but has never finally succeeded, as it still raises its head despite his knock-down arguments. He points out that a strict inductive method, according to which the scientist simply records all the facts about everything, with complete objectivity and impartiality, and waits for a general principle or law to emerge, is actually impossible. Some decision must be taken as to which aspects of the environment will be recorded, and in what order. Indeed the job of a scientist can rather be seen as deciding on a system for ordering the world, and modifying it in the light of experience, so that it gradually becomes more comprehensive. And even if this were not so, when would a completely impartial cataloguing ever be complete? Now exactly the same arguments can be applied to any organism trying to make sense of its environment; and, more trivially perhaps, to a subject faced with a concept identification task. Here, the experimenter has carefully arranged things so that the subject is presented with an exactly circumscribed set of stimuli (rather as if God provided scientists with enormous stamp albums). But the experimenter still has no way of determining which stimuli, or which aspects of the stimuli, the subject will record and take account of. So *attention* comes into it once more (see our *Focus* topic).

SORTING OUT THE EXPERIMENTS

To go back once more to Bourne's classification, one of the most useful things he has done is to distinguish between two sorts of *elements* of which concept situations can be composed. These he terms *attributes* and *rules*. *Attributes* are particular values of stimulus dimensions. Take the example of playing cards. These can be classified along three dimensions: colour, suit, value. There are no other dimensions belonging to playing cards as such. These three dimensions have respectively two, four and thirteen values each. Any card, or any set of cards, can be specified exactly by reference to these dimensions only (e.g. the black cards; the aces; the red queens; etc.). Thus a concept identification problem could be described in terms of a selection of these values, e.g. what the subject is looking for might be spades, or red court cards, or aces. *Rules* on the other hand are principles for grouping some stimuli together as distinct from others. Using cards again, such a rule might be 'all the odd numbers', or, given that the subject was presented with a series of pairs, 'the higher value in each pair'.

Based on his discussion, Bourne presents a scheme for classifying research and theory on concepts, as shown in Table 1.1.

Table 1.1—Possible scheme for classifying research and theory on concepts. (From Lyle E. Bourne, Jr., Human Conceptual Behavior *(1966). Copyright © Allyn and Bacon, Inc., Boston, Mass. Used by permission.)*

		Type of behaviour	
		Learning	Utilization
Problem element	Attribute	1. Perceptual learnings, labelling.	2. Concept identification, sorting tasks.
	Rule	3. Formation of learning sets, positive transfer based on rules.	4. Rule identification, problem solving.

Here we must pause to explain what sorts of situations are understood by the items in each cell.

1. Perceptual learning, labelling. By this is meant cases where the subject has to learn a name for a set of stimuli. For example, a child learns to call some animals dogs, and not others; a biology student learns to label, say, molluscs correctly. This is what we have called earlier concept *formation*.

2. Concept identification, sorting tasks. These are the cases where there is a

set of possible classifications, and the subjects taks is to find the correct one. 'Correct' in the experimental situation means 'defined as correct by the experimenter'.

3. Formation of learning sets, positive transfer based on rules. Learning sets are in fact an example of such transfer. The term (LS for short) is due to H. F. Harlow (1949, 1959) etc., who studied discrimination learning in, at first, rhesus monkeys. The traditional experiment had been to present the subjects with two objects, under one of which a food reward was hidden. After a number of trials, varying of course from subject to subject, the correct response would be learned. The variation which Harlow introduced was to present the objects for a fixed number of trials, say five; and then, whether or not any learning had occurred, replace them by two others, also presented for five trials and then replaced, and so on. It might have been expected, since the subject never had enough trials to learn any one problem, that no learning would occur. This was not so. After a large number of problems, perhaps a hundred, the monkeys were able to solve new problems in one go, as it were. That is, on presentation of objects X and Y, if the rewarded object was chosen on Trial 1, the monkey stuck to it; if he chose the wrong object on Trial 1, he immediately corrected himself on Trial 2. In other words, the subject seemed to have *learned to learn*, as Harlow put it; or to have learned a rule or strategy, expressed by Levine (1959, 1963) as Win Stay, Lose Shift (WSLS). In a variant of the procedure, the subject learned to pick the odd one out of three stimulus objects. The procedure has been used with many other species since, including humans (children and mental defectives), and interestingly enough performance in these situations correlates approximately with position on the phylogenetic scale. One criticism of the reported experiments is that there is no specification of the degree of similarity between problems, obviously a critical variable where transfer is involved. Each problem was composed of items randomly selected from a 'population of miscellaneous objects'—one wonders if this produced the homogeneity common in laboratory populations. However, this procedure exemplifies what Bourne means by learning a rule.

4. Rule identification, problem solving. Bourne seems to mean here only a limited class of problems, since he says that experimental studies are rare. He quotes Maier's (1930, 1931) designs in which a subject had, for example, to tie together two strings hanging from the ceiling, but too far apart for him to reach both at once. The solution is to make an unusual use of a pair of pliers, as a pendulum bob to set one string swinging (see *Problem Solving*). To me, these problems have a strong perceptual element, since it is necessary to 'see' the objects as something else. I do not really see where the rule identification comes in, and I should have thought a better example might be chess, where in any situation all the possible moves are, or can be, known. And another case of this sort, of which Bourne seems unaware, is a procedure devised by Wason (1960). He gave subjects three numbers, say 2, 4, 6, and asked them to

discover the rule which made them a series. They could obtain further information by suggesting additional sets of three numbers, when Wason would tell them if they were right or wrong. The rule was in fact 'ascending numbers', which many subjects found very hard to get, expecting something more complex. In fact, for frustrating subjects this procedure is about as good as Peterson's mental mazes (see *Problem Solving*). Try them. The point, however, is that there is a set of mathematical relationships known to the subject and his job is to hit on the correct one.

Bourne stresses that these distinctions are ideal rather than actual. In any laboratory situation, to say nothing of real life, it is almost impossible to distinguish between learning and use, or rules and attributes, as we have already seen. Similarly, one cannot distinguish sharply between experiments on concepts and experiments on, for example, learning or problem solving.

This is perhaps a useful place at which to bring out a most fundamental point, which students often have difficulty in understanding. It is that the division of material within Psychology is largely an arbitrary matter—perhaps more so than in some other disciplines. The division of knowledge into disciplines is in any case only done for convenience of timetables, examinations, textbooks, and the like. Who can say where history, economic history and economics exactly have their common boundaries? The important point is that one cannot say in advance that no useful knowledge will come from any particular area, or that even the most unlikely studies will not eventually join up. Until Norbert Wiener invented cybernetics, the science of control mechanisms, no one had thought to group together brains, committees, and guided missiles. Psychology is a group of enquiries concerned with behaviour and experience, and the psychologist can, indeed must, say with Molière, 'je prends mon bien où je le trouve'. At the same time in some disciplines we do find a fairly natural division of subject matter: history does have a chronological sequence, geography a spatial order. In psychology this is less clear. It is partly that any aspect of behaviour can interact with any other, for example emotion and perception; and partly that the labels are arbitrary and not generally agreed. But one cannot talk about everything at once, and we find it useful in this book to preserve a traditional framework.

SOME EXPERIMENTS

We had now better look at some of the experiments usually filed under the heading of *Concepts*, and first some of the more classical ones. Clark L. Hull in 1920 claimed that 'the functional and quantitative aspects of the problem of the evolution of concepts remain almost untouched'. Hull was a fairly devout Behaviourist, extremely influential for a time, who departed radically from the Watsonian doctrine by postulating a complicated system of intervening variables within the organism to account for the relationship of R–S. They failed to do so, and Hull's theory was left like some abandoned temple, a wonder to later travellers who are prepared to trudge through the deserts of maze learning. However, in this early experiment, Hull used a series of packs of twelve cards, each bearing a Chinese ideogram or character. In each pack, each ideogram had a particular element embedded in it, these elements being repeated across the series of packs (see Figure 1.1). The cards were presented sequentially, the

Figure 1.1. Some of the Chinese characters used by Hull (1920)

experimenter naming each one with a nonsense name. The subject's task was to learn to anticipate, so as to say the name before the experimenter did. This was thus an example of a *reception* procedure, since subjects were simply presented with the stimuli by the experimenter; they had no choice as to which they dealt with. Subjects were subsequently asked to draw the characteristics which were required for an ideogram to be given its name. This they were unable to do, even when they had learned to use the name correctly. Hull's subjects were (experimentally) naïve students, and he reports: 'Ordinarily they regarded the work as a kind of memory experiment and were mainly interested in making a good score.' Not one suspected that it had anything to do with concepts, and: 'When informed of this at the end of the experiment they never failed to express more or less astonishment.' As well they might. It is a delightful picture: the brilliant young psychologist, and his strings of astonished students. This obviously *is* 'a kind of memory experiment'. Osgood (1953) criticized it as being merely a study of labelling, not concepts at all. But this is unfair. On

Bourne's classification, Hull's experiment comes in cell 1, learning of attributes. Smoke (1933) also criticized Hull, claiming that the important factor in concept formation was some common perceptual organization or pattern among the stimuli—not a common *element* as Hull had said. Here we see the influence of Gestalt psychology contrasted with the elementism of Behaviourism. Smoke used figures, in which the criteria for classification were rules like 'triangle with a line at right angles to the shortest side' or 'circle containing one dot'. Subjects saw a series of such figures in a memory drum, and learned to name them with some rather splendid names such as 'zum', 'woz' or 'pog'. Smoke's conclusions were in line with the cognitive line of theory which we shall gradually see emerging:

> '1. The process of concept formation appears to involve grouping. The learner tends to envisage certain stimulus patterns as constituting a group to which any given stimulus pattern does or does not belong.
> 2. Insightful behaviour seems to be present in at least some instances of concept formation.
> 3. Concept formation, like most "thinking", appears to involve the formulation, testing and acceptance or rejection of hypotheses . . .
> 4. One may have a concept and yet be quite unable to give an accurate verbal formulation of it. . . .'

Osgood (1953) attacked Smoke's procedure also, on the grounds that many instances of concepts have no perceptual characteristics in common, e.g. clothing, or nations. He argued: 'It would seem that the only essential condition for concept formation is the learning of a common mediating response (which is the meaning of the concept) for a group of objects or situations, identical elements and common perceptual relations merely facilitating the establishment of such mediators.' We can illustrate Osgood's view with an experiment by Reed (1946). Subjects were shown cards containing four words (e.g. club, picnic, reaches, beer). The experimenter spoke a nonsense syllable on each presentation which the subject had to learn to anticipate. On each card only one word was relevant, and the word was one of a class. For example, every BEP card bore the name of a vegetable, but a different vegetable each time. So the subject's task was first to distinguish which of the words was relevant, viz. the vegetable word, and then to associate BEP with these. Osgood calls 'vegetables' a mediating response. This is rather an odd experiment: it is not clear what is the point of the second part. Possibly it is a case of following an experimental tradition, namely that of nonsense syllable learning. Without the nonsense syllable, it would be a perfectly acceptable concept identification experiment. Indeed, Reed himself defined a concept as any word or idea standing for any one of a group of things. I suppose he wanted to introduce *learning* into it somehow. Thus the design is a very good example of Bourne's point about the overlap between different 'ideal' paradigms. The same thing is apparent in Osgood's discussion, for he seems to regard both these experiments, and those of Piaget, whom he accords the brief mention customary at that time, as all on some general process of concept formation. One other piece of work of this period that is customarily mentioned is that of Edna Heidbreder (1946). She had her subjects learn nonsense names for groups of pictures having something in common. The variation she introduced was that what they had in common was *either* concrete *or* spatial *or* numerical. That is, the name might apply, e.g. to any picture of a house, or to any circular form, or to any set of three things. Heidbreder reported that concrete concepts were most easily identified, while abstract were hardest. Heidbreder's approach shows a behaviourist influence:

> 'A subject is said to "use" a concept whenever, during the course of an experiment, he produces behaviour meeting accepted criteria. The criteria themselves are a set of specifications for identifying behaviour which can be made intelligible to any observer if and only if he, the observer, supposes that the subject is reacting to those characteristics of a situation to which the concept in question refers.'

These early experiments have been described partly to illustrate the experimental biases previously mentioned, and partly to show the context from which the first major piece of work emerged, namely that of Bruner, Goodnow, and Austin (1956).

SOME THEORIES

First, however, let us develop a little further the matter of theoretical orientation by showing some of the main theories of conceptual behaviour that have emerged. Once again we are indebted to Bourne for an ordering of the material. Taking first the general S–R associationistic approach, we can distinguish *mediated* and *non-mediated* theories. Hull's experiment illustrates a non-mediated theory. Concept formation is conceived of as essentially a discrimination process, involving the learning of a certain response to a stimulus element common to a number of stimulus patterns. A very similar view is taken by Skinner (1953) who attempts to account for conceptual, as for all other, behaviour, by describing its history of reinforcement. The response 'round' has always been reinforced (i.e. approved, understood, etc.) when made in the presence of round objects. The usual process of generalization accounts for our ability to make the correct response to new instances. The explanatory status of operant conditioning has never been clear, especially when applied to real-life situations in which the existence of a history of reinforcement is only a likely supposition, not a proved fact. And even if 'round' has been reinforced, it does not follow that this is sufficient to account for its correct use, still less its novel use. It might even be argued that generalization is itself not an explanation, but a phenomenon requiring explanation. Harlow's account of his learning set experiments can be classed here also, for it was in terms of the gradual suppression or inhibition of *error factors*, or tendencies to respond to inappropriate cues (such as the position of objects). Eventually all that is left is a tendency to respond to the appropriate cues, i.e. those characteristics of the correct object that distinguish it from the other. But error factor theory seems to have won little support or acceptance, and other interpretations are possible and perhaps more plausible (e.g. in terms of hypothesis testing, or in terms of learning a strategy common to all the problems).

Even within a strictly behaviouristic framework, however, theorists have been led to postulate mediating processes, and probably the first to do so was Hull (1930). In the simplest version this was an attempt to describe what processes inside the organism link the Stimulus to the Response. Hull postulated that external stimulation must produce some kind of internal reaction, which in turn produces internal stimulation, which triggers off the observed Response. Diagrammatically this can be shown in Figure 1.2(a).

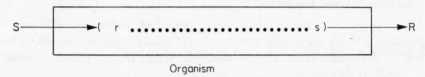

Organism

Figure 1.2(a). (Reproduced from C. E. Osgood, *Method and Theory in Experimental Psychology* (1953), by permission of Oxford University Press, New York)

In the case of concepts, there is a set of Stimuli, each slightly different, which elicit a common Response. This can be expressed as in Figure 1.2(b).

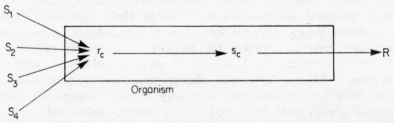

Organism

Figure 1.2(b). (Reproduced from C. E. Osgood, *Method and Theory in Experimental Psychology* (1953), by permission of Oxford University Press, New York)

Reed's experiment described above also illustrates this approach. Some more sophisticated attempts have been made to investigate the notion of mediating processes, a good example being that of Kendler and Kendler (1962). They had their subjects solve two concept problems in succession. The second problem differed from the first in one of two ways, termed a reversal or non-reversal shift. Suppose that the stimuli are cards with figures which can be either squares or triangles, and either red or green. In Problem 1, S has to group the red figures together as concept A, and the green as concept B (or as 'right' and 'wrong'). Then in Problem 2 a *Reversal* Shift would have the subject reclassify red figures as B, and green as A. A *Non-reversal* Shift has him change to classifying squares as A, and triangles as B, as can be seen from Figure 1.3.

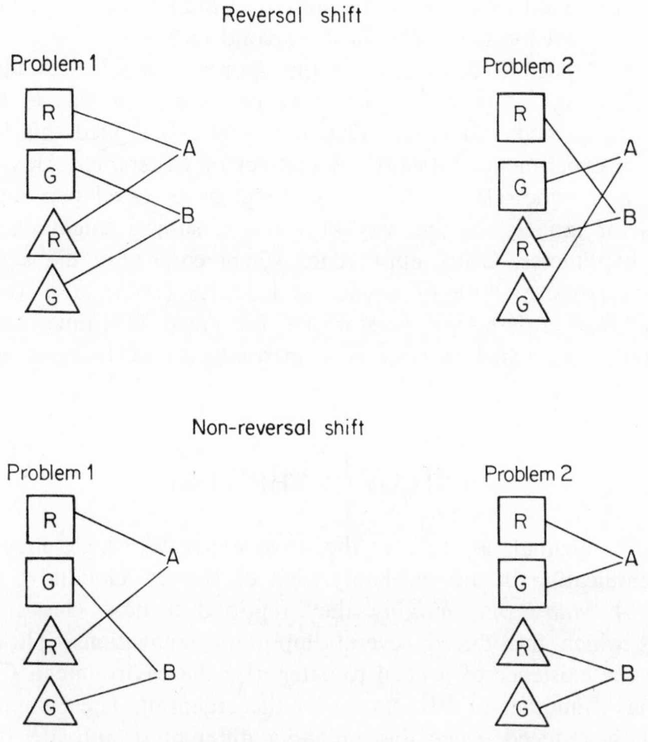

Figure 1.3. Schematic representation of reversal and non-reversal shifts. (H. H. Kendler and T. S. Kendler (1962), 'Vertical and horizontal processes in problem solving,' *Psychol. Rev.*, **69**, 1–16. Copyright 1962 by the American Psychological Association, and reproduced by permission)

The point of all this is that in the Reversal Shift, the subject has to relearn all his associations—each Stimulus that was formerly A is now B; whereas in the Non-reversal Shift half the associations remain correct (red squares are still A, red triangles are still B). The Kendlers found that Reversal Shifts are easier for children and non-human subjects.

They argued that the latter depend on associative links, the former on some form of mediating process. This they think is probably verbal, a conclusion supported by Goss (1964) reviewing some similar experiments. In a further experiment, Kendler, Kendler and Marken (1970) used undergraduate students as subjects. The subjects learned to discriminate words from two conceptual categories. Then a reversal shift took place, so that subjects had to reverse their responses. But for one group, new words from the same conceptual categories were substituted. Subjects learned to sort these new words just as quickly as they could reverse their sortings of the old words. This was taken as evidence that a cue from a mediated response, acquired in the first half of the experiment, was what controlled the behaviour in the second half.

In contrast to such S–R theories is the approach which sees the organism as actively seeking information. One way of expressing this is to say that hypotheses are formed and tested. Krechevsky (1932) argued this from simple discrimination experiments with rats. A number of writers, e.g. Hovland (1952); Hunt (1962); Levine (1959); Restle (1962), have developed mathematical descriptions, or models, of the way in which a subject might choose among a stock of hypotheses. Other approaches which emphasize the active seeking and manipulation are those of Dienes and Jeeves (1965), and Wason (1960, 1968). This, however, is taking the story too far ahead. It is time now to discuss an important book which was largely instrumental in bringing about these developments.

A STUDY OF THINKING

The most influential, as well as the most extensive, single investigation of concept identification is still, probably, that of Bruner, Goodnow, and Austin (1956). In *A Study of Thinking* they reported a now classical series of experiments which introduced several important innovations. They began by arguing for the existence of a need to categorize the environment. Categorizing, they said, has a number of advantages for the organism. The complexity of the environment is reduced, since discriminably different stimuli are treated as if equivalent. Categorizing is 'the means by which the objects of the world about us are identified'. Categorizing reduces the need for constant learning, since new objects can be identified according to whether or not they possess relevant characteristics. Categorizing provides direction for instrumental activity, because if one knows in what class an object falls, one also tends to know what to do about it (hot—don't touch; liquid—don't spill, etc.). And categorizing of individual items opens the way to dealing with classes of events, which is essential for abstract thinking. Thus the aim of Bruner *et al.* was to investigate experimentally this fundamental operation. They went so far as to say: 'the case can be made that all cognitive activity depends upon a prior placing of events in terms of their category membership'. It is evident that this refers to what we have called concept *formation*, rather than identification, and it is therefore surprising to find that the experiments that Bruner *et al.* actually carried out were of the 'guessing game' type. This might be understood, if it were assumed that the real world is already conveniently divided up into dimensions and attributes, and some *deus ex machina* were setting us all problems and telling us when we solved them. But this is exactly the opposite of what Bruner *et al.* think, for they say: 'the categories in terms of which we group the events of the world around us are constructions or inventions'. This of course is really a philosophical rather than a psychological argument, and it does not affect the experimental procedures and findings. It is of interest, though, in view of Bruner's later preoccupation with the development of conceptual thought in different cultures, and the extent to which these produce different categories (see *Development and Culture*). Here, however, he was concerned only with identification or attainment, defined as 'the search for and testing of attributes that can be used to distinguish exemplars from non-exemplars of various categories'.

It is useful here to give a fairly lengthy quotation, since it expresses the essence of the whole book.

'Let us take as an example of concept attainment the work of a physicist who wishes to distinguish between substances that undergo fission under certain forms of neutron bombardment from substances that do not. Note that our physicist does not have to form the concepts "fissile" and "non-fissile". The essence of his problem is to determine what qualities are associated with fissile and non-fissile substances and eventually to determine which substances will be fissile and which ones non-fissile by means short of neutron bombardment. This kind of problem is hardly unique. The child seeks to distinguish cats and dogs by means other than a parent's say-so; the Army psychiatrist seeks out traits that will predict ultimate adjustment to and performance in the Army. All such tasks can be stripped down to the following elements:

1. There is an array of *instances* to be tested, and from this testing is to come the attainment of the concept. The instances can be characterized in terms of their *attributes*, e.g. colour, weight per volume, and in terms of attribute *values*, the particular colour, the particular weight per volume, etc.

2. With each instance, or at least most of them once the task is underway, a person makes a tentative prediction or *decision* whether or not the sample before him is, say, fissile, and before he is through with his task there will be a number of such decisions to be made.

3. Any given decision will be found to be correct, incorrect, or varyingly indeterminate; i.e. whatever the decision, the instance will turn out to be fissile, non-fissile, or indeterminate. We refer to this as *validation* of a decision, the major source of information about the relevance of cues exhibited by an instance for its category membership.

4. Each decision-and-test may be regarded as providing potential *information* by limiting the number of attributes and attribute values that can be considered as predictive of the fissibility of substances.

5. The sequence of decisions made by the person en route to attaining the concept, i.e. en route to the discovery of more or less valid cues, may be regarded as a *strategy* embodying certain *objectives*. These objectives may be various in kind but in general one may distinguish three kinds of objectives: (a) to maximize the information gained from each decision and test

of an instance; (b) to keep the cognitive strain involved in the task within manageable or appropriate limits and certainly within the limits imposed by one's cognitive capacity; and (c) to regulate the risk of failing to attain the concept within a specifiable time or energy limit and to regulate any other forms of risk consequent to making a decision and testing it. A sequence of decisions or a strategy may be evaluated in the light of these objectives whether the subject "intends" these as his objectives consciously or not. Strategies are not here considered as conscious or deliberate behaviour sequences. Whether or not the subject is conscious of the strategy he is employing and can tell you its objectives is an interesting but not a critical datum.

6. Any decision about the nature of an instance may be regarded as having consequences for the decision-maker. Whether the instance is called fissile or non-fissile and whether it turns out on test to be one, the other, or indeterminate, there are consequences to be considered—sometimes grave, sometimes not. A given wrong decision may mean one's job and one's contract, a right one (e.g. coding a fissile instance correctly) may mean a new grant, etc. The set of consequences following upon each decision and each outcome we refer to as the *payoff matrix* of a decision, and the relevant consequences reflect the objectives of the strategy and the over-all task.'

Several comments can be made on this. The first is that while the physicist's task may not be unique, it is surely only a part of what a scientist does by way of classification. Creative scientific work consists largely in *discovering* or *devising*, new categories by which to order the phenomena; and routine work, on the other hand, involves a great deal of sorting into already known categories (which is what our physicist's task seems to have become by paragraph 6). Secondly, still less does this task subsume other sorts of classifying. While it may be true that both the physicist and the child face the same sort of task, inasmuch as they are faced with an array (or sequence) of instances and must discover how to classify them, there is no real reason to think that the situations are effectively the same. The physicist may well set out deliberately to classify, test, etc.; the child probably does not, not having reached the stage of formal operations, in Piaget's terms, or not having developed mediating processes on the Kendler view. The next point is that the analysis above slips from description to interpretation. Specifically in paragraph 5, while it is true that 'the sequence of decisions may be regarded as a strategy', it is not clear that it *must* be. Actually it is not clear what a strategy *is*, but presumably it is something other than a random sequence. But the existence of order in the sequence of responses can only be established empirically, not *a priori*. It is precisely because we do not *know* whether a subject's responses are orderly that we need experiments. A fourth point concerns consciousness of the strategy. This is 'not a critical datum'. Critical to what? It is true that the experimenter may be able to discern order in a subject's responses without knowing whether the subject is aware of such an order. Also, the subject may quite possibly respond systematically without being aware that he is doing so. But the subject's consciousness—his conscious easoning process, if you like—is surely very likely to be important in determining whether there is order in his responses, or not; and if there is, what form it akes. At least in the case of adult humans, subjects are highly unlikely to approach any experimental task, or indeed any new or puzzling situation, without very quickly making some sort of decision about how to deal with it. Bruner *et al.* elsewhere criticized the early investigators who as it were slipped a concept experiment over on subjects under the guise of a memory task. But it seems somewhat similar to ignore the question whether subjects have a deliberate plan, and then—surprise—discover one from what they do. 1956 seems a milestone on the long trek back from behaviourism, when consciousness, once forbidden, can be 'interesting' but not yet 'critical'.

Nevertheless the inference of strategies from observed behaviour and verbal reports was one of the main achievements of Bruner *et al.*, and to these we must now turn. We must first explain that the typical stimulus materials used were sets of cards bearing figures representing all possible combinations of a number of dimensions (or attributes), each having several values. For example: shape (square, circle, or cross); colour (red, green, or black); number (single, double or triple); border (one, two, or three). (See Figure 1.4.) A concept would be defined as specific values of selected attributes, e.g. 'all red figures', or 'black circles'. These are *conjunctive* concepts, defined by the joint presence of the relevant values. Bruner *et al.* also examined *disjunctive* concepts, defined by the presence of any of a specific set of attributes, e.g. three red circles or any constituent thereof: three figures, red figures, circles, three red figures, red circles, or three circles. A third sort of concept is *relational*, e.g. cards with fewer figures than borders. This discussion will be confined to conjunctive concepts as these are easier to understand. Before describing some strategies, I would say the precise nature of these is less important than their existence.

In Bruner's experiments, the complete set of cards was presented to a subject in an orderly array, as in Figure 1.4. The nature of the task was explained to the subject, viz. that he had to identify a rule which the experimenter had formulated, and according to which he called some cards correct and others incorrect. In a selection procedure or paradigm, the subject was allowed to ask about successive cards in any order he chose; in a reception *procedure*, the experimenter pointed to cards in a fixed order. The subject could make a guess at the concept after each instance. Thus the data consisted of the subject's series of choices and suggested concepts (hypotheses) in the selection procedure; in the reception procedure, his hypotheses only. Thus one difference from earlier experiments was in allowing the subject to select information. Another lay in taking subjects' speculations, i.e. their hypotheses, about the situation, as basic data, making a clear break with the strictly behaviouristic tradition. A third one was the inference from subjects' behaviour of *strategies*. In one sense these can be considered simply as rules for dealing with information. They are rules which could be worked out by the experimenter just considering the situation. He knows

20

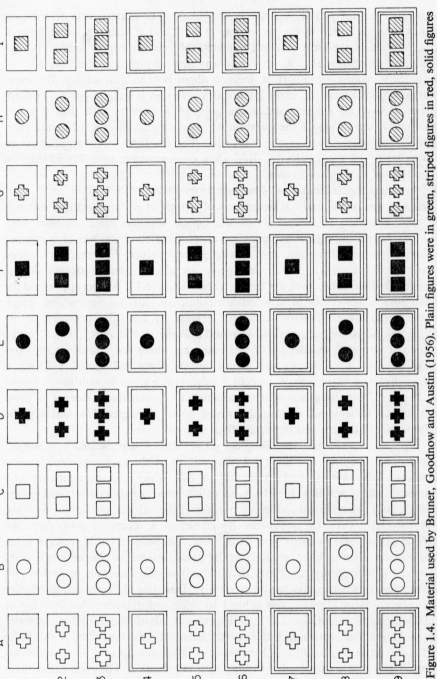

Figure 1.4. Material used by Bruner, Goodnow and Austin (1956). Plain figures were in green, striped figures in red, solid figures in black. (Reproduced from J. S. Bruner, J. J. Goodnow and G. A. Austin, *A Study of Thinking* (1956), Wiley, New York)

the solution, and therefore knows what sequence of guesses the subject ought to make to reach the solution most efficiently. Before discussing the strategies, let us give examples. Take the reception procedure. There are two general ways of going about the task, according to Bruner, depending on whether the subject takes as his initial hypothesis all the attributes of the first positive instance, or only one. It is obvious that every successive instance will be either *positive* or *negative* (correct or incorrect). It can also be *confirming*, i.e. consistent with the subject's hypothesis, or *infirming*. Two main strategies can then be described, as shown in Table 1.2.

Table 1.2—*Focusing and scanning strategies.* (*Reproduced from J. S. Bruner, J. J. Goodnow and G. A. Austin*, A Study of Thinking (*1956*), *Wiley, New York.*)

1. Wholist or focusing (S takes first positive instance as initial hypothesis (H)).

	Positive instance	Negative instance
Confirming	Maintain H	Maintain H
Infirming	Take as new H what old H and new instance have in common.	Impossible unless one has mis-reckoned. If so, change hypothesis on the basis of memory of past instances.

2. Partist or scanning (the subject takes one aspect of first positive instance as initial hypothesis).

	Positive instance	Negative instance
Confirming	Maintain H	Maintain H
Infirming	Choose H not previously infirmed.	Choose H not previously infirmed.

What do these mean as descriptions of a subject's thinking? Let us suppose the concept is 'black circles', and that the experimenter gives his subject the series of cards shown below. Then it is as if a 'wholist' subject thought thus: (E, the experimenter; S, the subject).

E: Card E1 is positive.

S: (thinks): Maybe the concept is 'one black single-bordered circle'.
   (says): Is the concept 'one black single-bordered circle'?

E: No. Card A3 is negative.

S: (thinks): Well, that doesn't help me; the concept could still be what I said.

E: Card E3 is positive.

S: (thinks): That means it must be more than one circle—maybe 'black single-bordered circles'.

E: Card E9 is positive.

S: (thinks): Well, all that the three positive examples have in common is that they all have black circles. Borders can't have anything to do with it; the number of circles can't either.
(says): Is the concept 'black circles'?

E: Yes.

In this example, which is *not* an actual protocol, Card A3 is a negative confirming instance; Cards E3 and E9 are positive infirming instances. The subject deals in a 'wholist' way with each of them. Had he been a partist, he would have made as his first hypothesis one aspect of Card E1—say, 'single border'. Then A3 is a negative infirming instance, so S must go back to Card E1 and choose another possibility: say, 'single figure'. But the next instance, E3, is positive—a positive infirming instance. So once more he goes back to E1 and chooses again. Suppose he now chooses 'black', the next instance, E9, being positive confirming, allows him to maintain his hypothesis—and so he goes on. It turns out that in general the wholist strategy is more efficient, as may be apparent from this example. First, in the partist method you have to remember each of the guesses you have made and which have been proved wrong. Otherwise you will waste time rechecking some of them, especially if the task is a complex one. By the wholist strategy, the hypothesis you are currently holding acts as a summary of what you have done so far, since it consists in what the positive instances have had in common. Secondly, the wholist strategy means that negative infirming instances are never met with; and these are the hardest to make use of. Indeed it is a general finding that negative information is harder to use, as P. C. Wason, among others, has shown in a series of experiments (see *Problem Solving: Negative Information*). It is illustrated in Table 1.3 by some of Bruner's data showing how subjects dealt with various sorts of instances

Table 1.3—Analysis of responses according to subjects' conformity to original strategy. (Reproduced from J. S. Bruner, J. J. Goodnow and G. A. Austin, A Study of Thinking (1956), Wiley, New York.)

| Instances | Original strategy | |
	1. Wholist	2. Partist
PC	54%	66%
NC	61	52
PI	54	50
NI	10	26

(either Positive (P) or Negative (N) and either Confirming (C) or Infirming (I), after starting with either a wholist or a partist hypothesis. From this it emerges that somewhere between a half and two-thirds of responses continue to conform to the strategy with which the subject started (see Table 1.3 above), except for the negative infirming cases, where both strategies more or less collapse. So a subject who begins with the wholist strategy maintains his hypothesis on 54 per cent encounters with PC instances but follows the 'ideal' strategy 'change hypothesis on the basis of memory of past instance' only on 10 per cent encounters with NI instances. These figures also stress that the strategies as described above are *ideal* only; they are plans that subjects *could* follow consistently.

If the experiment uses a selection procedure, the possible strategies vary somewhat, since the subject is free to select which cards he thinks will help him to solve the problem. Bruner *et al.* describe four strategies in this situation.

1. *'Simultaneous scanning* ... consists in essence of the person using each instance encountered as an occasion for deducing which hypotheses are tenable and which have been eliminated.' This is a very difficult strategy, since it involves remembering all that has gone before, and at the same time working out all the consequences of choosing any potentially relevant card.

2. *'Successive scanning* ... consists in testing a single hypothesis at a time.' The subject has to remember which hypotheses he has already tested, but at each choice he only has to work out the relevance of cards to one hypothesis, not all possible hypotheses as in simultaneous scanning.

3. *'Conservative focusing* ... may be described as finding a positive instance to use as a focus, then making a sequence of choices each of which alters but one attribute value of the first focus card and testing to see whether the change yields a positive or a negative instance.' This is a relatively economical strategy, because the subject can disregard the question of possible hypotheses, and concentrate on testing attributes of a known positive instance.

4. *'Focus gambling* ... The subject uses a positive instance as a focus and then changes *more than one* attribute value at a time.' This is a more risky strategy, since if the gamble does not succeed, one has learnt nothing about which values are relevant. Using this technique, luck may make the task shorter or longer.

We must now comment on this notion of 'strategies' as used by Bruner *et al.* Anderson (1965) has pointed out that the *status* of a strategy is far from clear. It is not obvious whether S is supposed to be able to state the strategy, at least to himself; or whether there exists, as it were, a stateable rule within a subject but not accessible to himself; or whether it is only *as if* he had such an internal plan. Bruner's statement on this matter is as follows: 'What psychological status shall we afford the construct of a strategy? ... they are not necessarily deliberate and conscious forms of behaviour, decided upon in advance by subjects and then put into operation.... The concept of strategy has, we should say, a kind of middling status. It is not a construct in the grand manner such as *libido* or *habit strength*, for it is in no sense proposed as an "explanation" of the behaviour from which it is inferred. It is, rather, a description of extended sequences of behaviour, a description that is also evaluative in the sense that it proposes to consider what the behaviour sequence accomplishes for the organism in terms of information getting, conservation of capacity and risk regulation.' The modest disclaimer of explanation, with or without quotation marks, does not entirely answer Anderson's objection, for it is still not clear in whose head, as it were, the strategy exists. If it is just the experimenter's shorthand for saying that a subject behaves in an orderly rather than a random way, then it seems an odd and perhaps misleading use (since 'strategy' usually refers to a deliberate plan of some kind). If the strategy, on the other hand, is something that a subject works to, or responds as a result of, then it *is*, partly at least, an explanation.

Bruner, Goodnow, and Austin certainly reported as their 'first principal finding... that it is possible to describe and evaluate strategies in a relatively systematic way.' Despite the ambiguities discussed above, I agree with this claim. Perhaps the historical importance of the work was its contribution to dragging Behaviourism, kicking and screaming, into the second half of the twentieth century—even if the authors were not quite sure what they were doing. Of one strategy they say dubiously 'our intelligent subjects employ it (if such a voluntaristic word as "employ" is appropriate here)'. Their second major finding is that it is possible to demonstrate the effect of relevant conditions upon measurable aspects of categorizing strategies. This is really, as the authors say, an advance in experimental design rather than a result in the usual sense. There are also three more general findings. The first is the tendency for subjects to fall back on cues that have been useful in the past, regardless of whether they are relevant to the present situation, or indeed of whether the situation in which they were once useful was analogous to the present one. This could of course be regarded as a matter of reinforcement. Another general finding is the difficulty of using negative or indirect information. And a third is a tendency to find conjunctive concepts easier than others, and to use strategies appropriate to them even when the task involves disjunctive concepts.

We see, therefore, some of the ways in which *A Study of Thinking* marked an advance in the investigation of concept identification. Apart from what has just been said, we should note the emphasis on the active subject—exemplified by the use of selection procedures; the willingness to postulate intervening variables of a relatively new sort, even though their status is not quite clear; and the largely successful attempt to objectify the experimental tasks by exact specification of attributes and values.

AFTER BRUNER, GOODNOW, AND AUSTIN

It is probably fair to say that practically all work on concepts since 1956 has been influenced in some measure by the book we have just discussed. As is true of psychology generally, the publication rate has increased very rapidly, and a sizeable volume would be needed merely to summarize the work in each area. However, we may usefully select four main lines of activity for discussion. There is first the large number of studies intended to elucidate one or more of the many variables in the experimental procedures of Bruner *et al.* Then there are the mathematical models mentioned earlier. The last two lines are more closely associated with the work of individuals. Dienes and Jeeves have tried to integrate important features of Bruner's work into an older tradition represented by Bartlett. And Wason and coworkers have presented a newer approach under the heading of 'reasoning'. In terms of the behaviourist–cognitive dichotomy which we discussed at the beginning, one could say that all these approaches involve a fusion of behaviourist procedures with a willingness to accept cognitive intervening variables. It will be seen in what follows how far the procedures used fit into Bourne's classification of types of behaviour and problem elements.

First, then, the variations on a theme. These studies while numerically the largest, are perhaps the least important of the four lines. It will be obvious on considering the procedures of Bruner *et al.* that they suggest a host of variables that might be investigated: for example, relative complexity or simplicity of the concept, the amount of relevant or irrelevant information available, the order or pattern in which the stimuli are presented, the amount and training of feedback to the subject, and so on. Bourne (1966) lists some forty classes of variable that have been investigated. But the theoretical interest of these seems to me to be small. It is fairly obvious that a subject will find that a greater burden on memory will make a task more difficult: and while it is a definite addition to our knowledge to learn more about the conditions under which this happens, it appears to tell us rather little of great theoretical or practical importance. Perhaps eventually these painstaking accretions will yield a further breakthrough: at this time, let us illustrate the work by a paper of Siegel (1969).

'Three sets of 64 stimuli were used; all the sets had identical amounts of information, but differed in the form in which this information was presented in each set. The stimuli of Set 1 consisted of one figure varying in six binary dimensions: shape (rectangle or triangle), color (red or green), size (large or small), number (one or two), striations (absent or present), and orientation (upright or tilted). The stimuli of Set 2 consisted of two figures, a rectangle and a triangle, each of which varied in three bi-leveled dimensions: striations, color, and size. . . . The stimuli of Set 3 consisted of a rectangle, circle, and triangle, each of which varied in two bi-leveled dimensions: color and striations. . . . For each set of stimuli, problems of three different complexities varying in the number of relevant dimensions (one, two, or three)

2—T * *

were used. (Results)... A latin-square analysis of these data indicated a significant effect of form of information, a significant effect of amount of information, and a significant interaction between these two variables.... The more complex problems (two and three relevant dimensions) were significantly easier for subjects to solve in Set 1 than in Sets 2 and 3. Thus, form of information is an important determinant of concept attainment performance and so subjects experience greater difficulty in solving problems when the information is contained in two or three figures than when it is contained in one figure.'

This leaves me with a feeling of 'So what?'—as do the many other excellently competent papers of which this is, I think, a fair sample.

The mathematical approaches, in my view, are potentially more interesting; although in practice perhaps little has been achieved beyond a new description of parameters. For example, Bourne and Restle (1959) '... reported an attempt to extend a theory of discriminative learning so as to analyse the process of identifying concepts. We have drawn on two sources: (a) theoretical analyses of animal and human learning in simple discrimination problems...; and (b) the procedures of concept-identification experiments. The analysis arises from the assumption that concept identification is a slight complication of discrimination learning. We have employed a theory which states that discrimination learning involves two processes—conditioning relevant cues and adapting irrelevant cues.' Then, on the assumption that the dimensions defining the stimuli can be regarded as equivalent to sets of cues, the same sorts of calculation can be made as Estes (1964), for example, has presented for learning situations. This enables predictions to be made, for example, that the cues from various dimensions will be additive, and that stimulus traces will decay exponentially. These predictions were confirmed. But as the authors say, 'there is a looseness in the tests of theoretical points which we have not been able to prevent. Our procedure has been to estimate parameters (in this theory the measurement of certain sets of cues) from part of the data of an experiment, and then use the theory to predict statistics of the rest of the data.' But 'the theoretical predictions depend on estimates of parameters... Furthermore, to obtain specific predictions we have inserted several special assumptions...' So what has really been done is to take whatever values are known mathematically, guess some more, and calculate with these sets of figures. This is like making a model of the whole process from what is known of part of it. Models will be discussed in more detail elsewhere.

Let us rather turn here to the third line of development, that of Dienes and Jeeves (1965, *Thinking in Structures*). They reported a series of experiments deriving from the ideas both of Bruner, Goodnow, and Austin, and of Sir Frederic Bartlett. As they put it, Bartlett (*Thinking*, 1958) had studied the whole process of thinking and Bruner *et al.* its parts. 'In this study, it is hoped that the whole is being considered through the detailed ways in which its parts are put together.... We shall be concerned with the study of the emergence of models, structures, in terms of which we think.' More specifically, they wished to examine 'the problem of how human beings evolve mechanisms or schemata by means of which they evaluate the mass of stimuli in the environment, making "sense" of those in such a way as to enable them to predict events with a very high degree of probability'. In the experiments, the subject was provided with a small set of cards (two or four), and faced a sheet of hardboard with a window in it. His task was to observe a card in the window, present one of his cards, and observe which card the experimenter presented in return. It was explained that the experimenter would play according to strict rules, and the subject had to predict the experimenter's behaviour. Subsequently he was asked about his reasoning. The subjects were children of around 10 years of age, and a number of adults. The rules according to which the experimenter played were those of various types of mathematical groups. The simplest was that with two elements (cards) only, for which the rules are:

Let (a) and (b) denote the elements. Then:
1. (a) + (a) gives (a)
2. (a) + (b) gives (b)
3. (b) + (a) gives (b)
4. (b) + (b) gives (a)

Dienes and Jeeves distinguished from their results three basic modes of tackling this problem. *Memory subjects* simply tried to memorize each combination of cards as it occurred, so as to be able to predict correctly when it occurred again. One the other hand the most sophisticated approach was to conceive of the card played as in some sense *operating on* the card in the window so as to alter it (or not). An intermediate degree of sophistication was shown by Ss who appeared to think of the game as split up into two sub-wholes or *patterns*: one where the card in the window and the card played were the same (1. and 4. above), the other where they were different (2. and 3. above). In more advanced games with four or eight cards variations of these evaluations of the situation became apparent.

These evaluations, as Dienes and Jeeves call them, were derived from the subjects' remarks. The authors also tried to determine how far the evaluations corresponded to the actual sequences of cards played—for example, whether subjects who expressed the *operator* principle systematically played a card so as to check out its operational properties. But the results of this enquiry are not clear. A third aspect of the data concerned subjects' *explanations*, which could be classified as mathematical, scientific, or imaginative. The mathematical and scientific explanations ranged from vague gropings to accurate accounts; mathematical accounts agreed with the rules devised by the experimenter, scientific ones expressed the same rules by analogies (such as the theory of magnetism). Imaginative explanations were sometimes very ingenious; with different cards representing Love and Death, or other abstract ideas. Finding similar fantasies myself once in some concept experiments I termed them *notions*; but it was not clear from my experiments, nor from those of Dienes and Jeeves, how they interact with reasoning or with actually obtaining the solution.

Dienes and Jeeves present two general sorts of comments on their work. They quote a remark by Bartlett (1961) to the effect that Bruner *et al.* neglected the study of tactics of thinking in favour of strategies. Dienes and Jeeves believe that their work makes a start on this closer sort of analysis. Secondly they stress the educational implications. Their main point here seems to be that subjects can handle mathematically-based situations (and find them fascinating games) without formal mathematical training—which may indeed even be a handicap. There are several interesting comparisons, to be made here, for example with the work of Wertheimer (see *Problem Solving*) and of Piaget (see *The Geneva School*).

This interesting little series of experiments raised the important, if often ignored, question, of just *why* experiments are done at all. Three common sources of new experiments occur to me, all of them exemplified here. One source is obvious previous work—in this case, that of Bartlett and of Bruner, as stated above. The second is an often vaguer idea of what might turn out to be useful, this often being derived from an author's particular personal interests. Here, this is apparent in the choice of mathematical groups, which were selected partly because they 'have the advantage of providing mathematical learning situations, the results of which might be used to predict how learning would take place in other similar mathematical learning situations'. This *might* be so; but this is really just an expression of interest, particularly since the authors later argue that children, at least, are *not* given mathematics of this type.

The third source concerns the assumptions about how best to investigate psychological processes, in the present case thought processes. Dienes and Jeeves are to be congratulated on being most explicit here, and we shall quote their whole paragraph.

'The question to which we wanted to find at least a partial answer was "How do we sort out the apparent chaos of our environment into anything like order?" Experimentally speaking, we may assume that the order is our own fabrication and then the problem of finding how we fabricate these regularities becomes a problem in experimental psychology and not in philosophy. To study the process it is necessary to establish some experimental chaos, that is a situation which is almost bound to appear chaotic to a subject upon a first encounter. Ways must be provided for the subject to sort out this chaos, enabling him to work a model which has predictive value. When the subject has worked out a model which has 100 per cent predictive value he has sorted out the chaos, and has fabricated the order, according to which he evaluates and predicts events. In order to approximate our situation to a real one, we should give the subject a reasonable choice of strategies in the sorting out process, yet the choices must be provided in an experimentally-controlled way, so as to make the results of the sorting by different subjects comparable. It is also necessary that every subject should be in the same position with regard to the task. The only way to satisfy this condition is to construct a task which no subject is likely to come across, and one involving a chaos that cannot be sorted out by well-worn strategies. In order to study developmental differences, it is also desirable to construct tasks which children can sort out and which are at the same time not trivial for adults. Situations involving mathematical groups are the most likely to satisfy all the above conditions.'

The clarity of this makes it seem at first sight eminently reasonable. But it does, of course, involve a whole set of assumptions. Setting aside the philosophical question, is there experimental evidence for 'apparent chaos'? Can experimental chaos ever be the same as real chaos? Why must the experimenter *give* his subject a choice of strategies—does God or nature do so? How can every subject possibly be in the same position with regard to the task?—unless they are reared for this especial purpose. The potential importance of individual differences in background appears from the subjects' explanations mentioned above, for where did these originate? It is not at all clear that developmental differences can best, or at all, be studied by using one task—as with a standard intelligence test, all we may be showing is what subjects at some age *cannot* do. Even the choice of mathematical groups, apparently such neutral material, is open to question, for if Piaget is right, an implicit understanding of such groups underlies adult thinking, and thus they may not at all satisfy the specified conditions. In general, the assumptions suggest what may be called the paternalistic approach to experimentations: the experimenter should set his subject a task, not too hard, yet not too easy, giving him a little help but not too much. I think this derives partly from the 'objective' approach of Behaviourism, and partly, here, from Bartlett's rather narrow view of thinking, corresponding roughly to 'reasoning'. But both these are open to question. It is now fairly clear that the complete objectivity desired by Watson is impossible; and it is fairly clear that even were it possible, it would not be the only useful approach.

Now, more briefly, for the fourth line of activity, the work of Peter Wason and his colleagues. Wason's work is relevant to several aspects of thinking, so we shall have occasion to discuss it elsewhere also. The relevant part of his work here is that which we mentioned as an example of Bourne's fourth category of experiments, 'rule identification'. Wason is interested in *reasoning*, both inductive, as here, and deductive, which we shall discuss under the heading of *Problem Solving*. Wason (1968) published a follow-up study to his 1960 paper mentioned earlier. He began by stressing that 'unlike most concept attainment tasks the point was not to see whether the subjects discovered the rule. The point was to see how they behaved when their hypotheses had been corroborated by confirming evidence.' In the original experiment subjects had to discover the rule connecting three numbers, which was in fact 'ascending order', by means of generating further sets of three. The experimenter told the subject in each case whether his set obeyed the rule or not. Subjects also wrote down their reasons for choosing each set, and made guesses at the rule when they were confident. In one variation of the procedure, subjects were started off with a series which they were told did *not* obey the rule. In another, by Jonathan Penrose (incidentally British chess champion for many years), subjects were given an instance of a class of which the experimenter was thinking, and had to work out the class. For example, they were told 'a Siamese cat', and had to reach the class 'living things'. These tasks have three important features. One is that the correct rule cannot be proved by generating instances; but any incorrect hypothesis can be disproved. Secondly, an endless series of examples exemplifying any hypothesis can be produced. Thirdly, the subject is not presented with a stimulus array, but has to produce his own instances of any possible rule. (But numbers are fairly readily available to most people.) Now while some subjects hit upon the correct rule quite easily, many did not: and the difficulty seemed to lie in being unable to reject the hypotheses they had thought of. The way to do this, of course, is not to think of examples which would confirm the hypothesis, but examples which would *disprove* it. It is apparently *negative proof* that subjects find so hard to use. This is of general interest in view of Popper's argument that an essential feature of scientific progress is the generation of disprovable hypotheses. Wason argues '... the fixated, obsessional behaviour of some of the subjects would be analogous to that of a person who is thinking within a closed system—a system which defies regulation, e.g. existentialism and the majority of religions'. The question of negative information is one to which we must return later.

SOME REMARKS

Experiments on concept identification continue to occupy many psychologists. Why should we be interested in these elaborate, or trivial, guessing games?

We might first consider what thinking is. Bartlett, as we have seen, tended to restrict his definition to 'reasoning'. Hebb's (1949) view has, rather, been in terms of that which is concerned with the ability to act independently of the environment. Another view would be that the essential feature is representation of the external world. It is with this aspect that Bruner has become increasingly concerned. Perhaps one of the widest views would be to subsume under 'thinking' all that goes on between input and output. This of course raises further problems of definition. We do not want to suggest that because we have a word 'thinking', there must exist one neat process, or set of processes, corresponding to our word. It is, rather, a question of where we can draw a loose boundary around the subject matter we are to study. We favour a fairly widespread, as well as fairly flexible, boundary line in this book. Somewhere within this line we find the activity of classifying. An old examination question used to be 'Man is a classifying machine. Discuss'. This I would file under the heading of 'Thinking'. However, all organisms must classify stimuli, in the sense that they must make the same response to stimuli differing from each other along one or more dimensions, even if only slightly. For example, every organism must classify incoming stimuli as edible or inedible. The higher up the phylogenetic scale the organism is, it would seem, the greater the number of categories that can be used, the more new categories can be added, and the less tied the responses are to stimuli. A male stickleback could be said to have a concept of the female of his species, in that he is able to classify some groups of stimuli as such, and with a good degree of success. But, as we know, he can be rather easily deceived by an experimenter with a model of a distended red belly. He has a built-in tendency to respond to certain dimensions which are usually, but not essentially, related to femaleness. When these dimensions become irrelevant, the stickleback cannot switch to others which are relevant. A similar difficulty is experienced by humans who think in a rigid or prejudiced way. The ability to switch concepts is essential to scientific and creative thinking, as has been stressed, for example, by Wason, and by Schon. Experiments on human concept identification have attempted to show how this classifying is done at what we consider the top of the phylogenetic scale. But in my view much of what has been done has been less revealing than might have been hoped, due to the insistence on artificial conditions. Bruner's situation, for example, is rather that of the stickleback, but rather unlike those we meet in everyday life. This is because what we are usually faced with, is deciding whether a given instance is, or. is not, an example of a concept which we already know. Most of these decisions are rather easy: one does not have much difficulty in classifying organisms as cats or dogs, or even boys or girls. Where there is a difficulty, it may be due to lack of information. For example, a bomb disposal expert trying to decide on the type of a bomb of which he can only see part. Or it may be due to not knowing what are the dimensions and values that are important. This is typical of many teaching situations, and not just formal ones. Much of what any student has to learn is how to classify. But when in doubt, he asks. And the teacher's reply is in terms of pointing out the relevant dimensions, and helping the student to recognise them. For example, a student might refer to *Pickwick Papers* as a picaresque novel, having heard that word applied to *Tom Jones* and *Moll Flanders*. He thinks that all are long rambling stories with the central characters roaming the world in search of adventure. So they are; but the teacher will point out that *picaresque* is defined as 'dealing with the adventures of rogues', and that no one (except perhaps Serjeant Buzfuz) would apply that word to Samuel Pickwick.

These differences may mean that the experimental findings reported may not be of general applicability. Wetherick (1969) for example, argues that the strategy that is best in a Bruner-type situation may be inefficient, or even impossible, in real life. And it may be that experimenters have not yet really started to deal with the most important real situations. Be that as it may, we can note some trends in the study of concept identification that are to a certain extent typical of recent psychology as a whole. The organism is now presumed to be active rather than passive; it seeks information and does not just wait passively to have it fed in. Similarly, it is allowed to have some sort of internal structure before the experimenter gets to work on it, and is not just a blank slate. Interest tends to be in cognitive rather than purely behavioural variables. And we are, perhaps, moving towards more interest in real-life situations. As a matter of fact, the relationship between real-life and experiment is one of the most important and most intractable in psychology. In general, there would seem to be three main sorts of approach to the problem. One method is to observe real situations, hoping not to disturb them, and hoping that the natural course of events will enable one to assess the effects of important variables. A second way is to carry the real situation into the laboratory, tolerating and trying to offset artificiality for the sake of control. And third, one can try to guess what are the variables important in the real situation, so that they can be studied as it were in the abstract. Concept identification experiments have so far nearly always fallen in the last group.

FOCUS: CONCEPTS AND ATTENTION

Earlier the point was made that an experimenter has no real control over which stimuli, or aspects of the stimuli, his subjects will take account of in a concept identification task. This of course is tantamount to admitting that we do not always know what steps a subject has gone through in arriving at the identification of the concept in question. Even if we painstakingly enumerate the dimensions along which the stimuli vary before the experiment begins, there is no guarantee that the subject will use this information effectively during the course of the experiment. Moreover some attributes may be more noticeable than others—Trabasso and Bower (1968) speak of a 'hierarchy of cue weights' in this connection. An additional complicating factor is that it is extremely difficult to establish equality of dimensional discriminability. As we shall see in a moment there are experimental procedures which help us to check a subject's progress and to discover the actual stages which he has passed through. But in any event, it is difficult to avoid reference to the concept of attention, a concept which has lately aroused a good deal of interest in Psychology. Much of the relevant material would probably normally be filed under the heading of 'discrimination learning' rather than 'concept identification', since interest in attention arose in part of the 'all or none' versus 'incremental' learning controversy of the 1930's and later; and thus the work to be considered stems from a different experimental tradition even though the two situations have much in common.

Attention has been defined in many ways—Meldman (1970) lists twenty-six definitions, many of which are vague and imprecise. Recently however it has been the selective aspects that have been emphasized (Berlyne, 1960; Broadbent, 1958). Assuming an organism has a limited capacity for processing information from the environment, certain aspects of incoming information must be selected for processing or analysis at the expense of others. Within the context of animal discrimination learning experiments Lashley (1938) argued that: 'A definite attribute of the stimulus is "abstracted" and forms the basis of the reaction; other attributes are either not sensed at all or are disregarded.' However, a contrary view had been expressed earlier by Spence (1936) working within a traditional Hullian framework. 'If a subject approaches a stimulus complex and is rewarded, then all stimulus components affecting his sensorium at the initiation of this approach response receive an increment in their association to this approach response.'

A formidable body of experimental work, most of it conducted with animals as subjects has accumulated from the many attempts which have been made to settle this dispute one way or another. Much of this work is of theoretical and practical importance to the study of concept identification, and although it is not our intention to give a comprehensive account of this research, a few examples are necessary, and should be sufficient to indicate the typical modes of approach and general trend of results in this field.

Sutherland and Mackintosh (1964) used the 'redundant relevant cue' paradigm to investigate simultaneous 2-choice discrimination learning in rats. Animals were trained on a white vertical rectangle (WV) versus a black horizontal (BH) discrimination. Here both the orientation and brightness dimensions are relevant, since the discrimination can be learned using either or both cues; but both dimensions are also redundant, since vertical rectangles are always white and horizontal ones always black; and vice versa. Following training the rats were given test trials on single cues by holding constant the value of the alternative dimension: i.e. the test for orientation would be BV versus BH and WV versus WH; and for brightness BV versus WV and BH versus WH. Percentage correct transfer scores for the two test series were correlated, a correlation of -0.42 being obtained. Sutherland and Holgate (1966) repeated the experiment and obtained a correlation of -0.56. From these results it can be concluded that the more the rat attends to and learns about a particular cue or dimension, the less it will learn about the other cue(s); i.e. the more it learns about brightness the less it learns about orientation, and vice versa.

Comparable results have come from experiments using human subjects. Suchman and Trabasso (1966) had children sort cards in which both dimensions were relevant and redundant. After attaining criterion, two single cue sorting tests were administered. An analysis by correlation of the errors on these two tasks revealed a correlation of -0.38, indicating that one or the other had tended to dominate while the subject was attaining criterion. However it should also be noted that 32 per cent of subjects made no errors on either single cue test showing that they had attended to and learned both cues.

These few studies can be taken as representative of the general trend of results in this field, and it can be concluded therefore that although some subjects do learn both cues the more frequent outcome is for one to dominate. However, in addition to permitting such a conclusion, the research we have briefly considered can be said to have led to the development of formal attentional models and theories of discrimination learning and concept identification (e.g. Lovejoy, 1965; Sutherland, 1959, 1964; Trabasso and Bower, 1968; and Zeaman and House, 1963).

These models and theories have many common properties. The fundamental assumption is that patterns are broken down into their constituent parts by 'feature analysers' sensitive to variations in, for example, orientation, brightness, shape, etc. In the discrimination learning situation one or more of these analysers may be selected and the stimuli scanned for the presence or absence of the features in question. The output from the analysers is then correlated with the reinforcement which is received as a result of responding to one of the stimuli. The models vary in their formulations of the exact way in which this is supposed to occur, but these operations are usually specified in some form or other.

Let us consider briefly the model proposed by Trabasso and Bower (1968). In addition to the usual operations of feature analysis etc., this model incorporates a 'search' and a 'test mode'. In the former the subject decides which attributes to select and attaches classificatory responses to their values, depending on the information given him by the experimenter. Following the selection of this 'focus sample', the subject is said to move into the test mode on the next trial in order to test out the 'hypotheses' contained in the focus sample. The authors describe this stage of the model thus:

> 'This consists in classifying each subsequent stimulus pattern according to the hypotheses in the current focus sample, and evaluating the feedback or reinforcement obtained. When a response is correct or reinforced, hypotheses in the focus that dictated that response are retained whereas those that indicated the opposite (error) response are eliminated from the focus at that moment.... When a response is in error, the sample focus is given up and the search made is reactivated. A new sample focus is selected and the testing operations proceed on it. The alternation of search sample-then-test goes on until an errorless solution is obtained.'

Trabasso and Bower go on to report a number of experiments designed to test the adequacy of their model. One experiment set out in part to test a prediction made by the model that the subject does not add new cues to his sample focus on trials when he responds correctly. This is especially relevant since it provides an interesting parallel to Wason's (1960) findings mentioned elsewhere. Wason found subjects unwilling to generate instances which were inconsistent with their own hypothesis as to what rule the experimenter had in mind. In Trabasso and Bower's experiment subjects were required to learn to classify cards into two categories by naming them Alpha and Beta. The cards differed along five dimensions, only one of which was relevant (i.e. the others were correct only on a chance basis). Subjects were told that after a while they would learn a rule which would enable them to classify every card correctly. After the subject had reached a criterion of ten consecutive correct responses and without a break one of the initially irrelevant cues was made relevant and redundant for the next thirty-two trials. This was followed by a test series which examined the learning of the previously irrelevant cue. For another group the cue which was to be made relevant and redundant was only introduced after the initial learning criterion had been attained. A third group simply learned the discrimination from the outset with the two cues relevant and redundant.

The model predicts that no learning of the initially irrelevant cue should take place; although in the case of the second group the introduction of novelty itself may be sufficient to attract attention (Sokolov, 1963). The results showed that where the added, redundant, cue had been irrelevant during training, *no* subjects ($N = 270$) learned its relevance; but when the added redundant cue was *novel*, about 8 per cent of subjects did so. A second major finding was that the third group learned in an 'all-or-none' fashion—they solved either with one cue or with the other or with both, that is, some subjects did attend to both cues but there was no evidence of partial learning of either.

Now the fact that in normal circumstances a subject does not add new cues to his focus sample provides a link with Wason's findings. In Trabasso and Bower's situation the subject is quite satisfied to classify each card according to the information he gets from one cue, providing that he has been successful with previous cards. And of course this is the most economical strategy to adopt—if a sorting principle works, it works. Even if half a dozen cues were relevant and redundant a subject would not be 'wrong' in any sense to classify the cards according to a principle which involves only one. What *would* be wrong however is the assumption that the principle being used is necessarily the only possible one. And here is the link with Wason. In the Wason situation the issue is not simply whether a subject's hypothesis 'works' (which it may well do), but whether it is correct according to the experimenter. A strategy which is suitable in the Trabasso and Bower situation therefore becomes quite inappropriate if adopted in the Wason situation despite the apparent similarity of the two.

Attention models of discrimination learning and concept identification can also be said to provide useful and perhaps desirable alternatives to the 'mediation' models of, for example, Kendler and Kendler. As mentioned earlier these workers infer the presence of covert mediating processes from the fact that reversal shifts are executed in favour of non-reversal shifts. This interpretation has often been subject to critical attack from various quarters (e.g. Slamecka, 1968; Wolff, 1967). In fact the Kendlers argued recently that much of this criticism is unwarranted, since it stems from either ignorance or mis-understanding (Kendler and Kendler, 1962). (See also *Language and Thought: Verbal Mediation.*) Attention models do not really provide explanations which run counter to theories like those of the Kendlers. But they do constitute a more sophisticated and more fertile conceptual approach to discrimination learning and concept identification. And, as we shall see in a moment, they are able to handle data which would prove embarrassing for any simple mediation theory.

Eimas (1967, 1969) has used the 'optional shift' paradigm, a procedure similar to that of Trabasso and Bower, to study discrimination learning in young children and college students. In this situation subjects are trained to criterion on a 2-choice discrimination in which one dimension is relevant and one irrelevant. After attaining criterion, both dimensions are made relevant and redundant, and the reinforcement contingencies along the previously relevant dimension are reversed. For instance the initially relevant dimension could be size, 'large' being positive and 'small' negative. The irrelevant dimension could be colour, the particular values being black and white. 'Optional shift' refers to the fact that after criterion the situation is altered such that both 'small' and 'black' become positive and 'large' and 'white' negative.

Now a subject can solve the optional shift by executing a reversal *or* an extradimensional shift. That is, he can choose the small black figure either because it is small (reversal shift) or because it is black (extra-dimensional shift). In terms of attention theory the subject has 'switched in' a new analyser (colour) in the extradimensional shift; but has kept the same one 'switched in' in the reversal shift. The nature of the solution chosen by the subject is deter-mined by giving test trials on one dimension only after the optional shift discrimination has been learned. (See Figure 1.5.)

Eimas was interested in the effect of two variables on optional shift behaviour —the effect of overtraining on the initial discrimination; and the effect of training with a *variable* irrelevant dimension as opposed to a constant irrelevant dimen-sion (see Figure 1.5). Overtraining is assumed to increase the probability of attending to the initially relevant dimension (i.e. it 'stamps in' one analyser), and consequently the likelihood of a reversal shift being executed. Constant irrelevant training however should decrease the number of reversal shifts since the sudden introduction of the black figure will make the colour dimension novel andy consequently a strong determinant of attention.

Taking the results of the two studies together it can be concluded that, as predicted, both overtraining and training with variable irrelevant stimuli produce more reversal shifts. Another significant finding was that there was no 'developmental' effect such as has been reported by the Kendlers—although adults did make more reversal shifts than children the difference did not reach significance. However in the 1967 study there was a small developmental effect with second grade children compared with fourth grade, but only after constant irrelevant training. On the basis of these results Eimas argues that whereas the

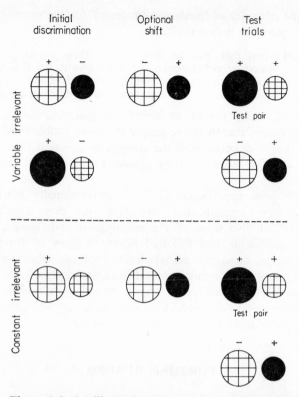

Figure 1.5. An illustration of one set of stimuli and reinforcement patterns for each type of irrelevant stimulation during the initial discrimination. For convenience, cross-hatching has been used in place of grey. (Reproduced from P. D. Eimas (1967), 'Optimal shift behaviour in children as a function of overtraining irrelevant stimuli and age', *J. Exp. Child Psychol.*, **5**, 332–340 by permission of Academic Press, Inc., New York)

Kendlers have stressed the importance of developmental variables, there are also a number of important non-developmental variables, such as these stimulus and training factors, which need to be taken into account in interpreting reversal shift behaviour. And, as we have seen, these can be handled quite neatly by an attention model—even developmental effects themselves can be dealt with by postulating more sensitive novelty-detecting mechanisms in very young children (not on the face of it, an implausible assumption) than are found in older children and adults. It is worth noting in this context that other workers (e.g. Tighe and Tighe, 1966) have also questioned the 'developmental' effect and in consequence the necessity of 'mediating processes' for the execution of reversal shifts. We can agree with Bolton (1972):

> 'The implication that may be drawn from these studies is, not that concept-shift behaviour is independent of development, but that it is necessary to specify more accurately than hitherto which developmental variables are operative under different circumstances and at different ages.'

And finally Slamecka (1968), reviewing the literature on shift paradigms, concludes despairingly that there are simply too many problems of interpretation and that we should dispense with the designs in question (viz. reversal shift, etc.). If such a policy were generally agreed, there would doubtless be many a sigh of relief.

We see here how experiments in fields conventionally labelled 'problem solving' and 'concept identification' are often very close together. Work on attention brings out also some of the assumptions underlying even the more sophisticated experiments that followed after the work of Bruner, Goodnow and Austin. One of these has perhaps been, that the subject will react in a predictable and as it were standard way to standard instructions. If the dimensions used are carefully explained, subjects can then be assumed to be in a controlled experimental situation. Common sense suggests that this is not necessarily so, and 'attention' experiments bear this out.

FURTHER READING

Bolton, N. (1972). *The Psychology of Thinking*. Methuen.
Bourne, L. E. (1966). *Human Conceptual Behaviour*. Allyn and Bacon.
Bruner, J. S. *et al.* (1966). *A Study of Thinking*. Wiley.
Kendler, H. H. (1964). 'The concept of the concept', in Melton, A. W. (Ed.) *Categories of Human Learning*. Academic Press.

2

Problem Solving

LINES OF INVESTIGATION

Davis (1966) reviewing an extensive literature, remarks that: 'Research in human problem solving has a well-earned reputation for being the most chaotic of all identifiable categories of human learning.' With this encouraging start, we should consider what the category contains: '... virtually any semi-complex learning task which does not clearly fall into a familiar area of learning can safely be called "problem-solving",' says Davis. Repetition of the word 'learning' alerts us to the fact that, as in other areas, there is more than one line of investigation. In practice, we suggest that it would be more useful not to build into a definition the assumption that this activity should be grouped with learning. Rather, we could say that when psychologists investigate problems, they are concerned with any situation in which the end result cannot be reached immediately. Looked at in this way, it will be seen that many of the concept identification puzzles, as devised by Bruner or Wason, constitute problems. And we have in fact stressed that there is no clear boundary between the two. But we have also said that concept identification tasks commonly require a subject to make one response to a set of stimuli differing in some respect. While this is often something that cannot be done at once, and so constitutes a problem in our terms, 'Problem Solving' is usually taken to cover other situations also. Thorndike (1898) and later Guthrie (see e.g. 1952) carried out well-known experiments in which cats had to escape from boxes: these were 'semi-complex learning situations', in which both stimulus and response were essentially the same on each trial. Problems posed by theorists with a 'Gestalt' influence have often been 'one-off' situations in which a set of stimulus elements have to be manipulated into a new form. The classical problems of Köhler, of Maier, and of Duncker, have been of this type. So have many of the problems incorporated in traditional intelligence tests. Irving Maltzman has given subjects a task in which they have to make a series of different responses to the *same* stimulus (see *Creative Thinking*). He did this in order to investigate creative thinking; and J. P. Guilford has said that creative thinking can be equated essentially with problem solving. We do not agree with this, as will appear later; but it is convenient to group the topics Concepts, Problems, Creativity consecutively. Note also the simple but important point that a situation that constitutes a problem for an animal, or a child, may not do so for an adult. Indeed, even between adults, wide differences will obviously appear. Another point is that whether we take the wider definition we have suggested, or a narrower one such as that of Davis, subhuman organisms are clearly included. While we are really concerned here with humans, some of the theoretical orientations, and some of the experimental findings, that are relevant, come from work with animals.

At the present time, four main streams of thought—or better, perhaps, bodies of work—about problem solving can be distinguished. Two of these are already familiar: the learning theory/stimulus–response approach, and the cognitive/ Gestalt line. The other two can be called computer/mathematical and psychometric respectively. This division of subject-matter is suggested by, among others, Forehand (1966).

DYNAMICS OF THINKING

Both Behaviourism and Gestalt psychology were to a large extent reactions against the classical Wundtian *psychology of content*. Wilhelm Wundt, 'the senior psychologist in the history of psychology', Boring calls him, was one of the army of indefatigable nineteenth century German scientists whose works advanced inexorably like some glacier, crushing all opposition by sheer weight. Boring worked out that Wundt averaged one published word every two minutes, day and night, throughout the sixty-eight years of his active career. Wundt was quite clear that psychology should be an experimental science—his laboratory at Leipzig is usually considered the first—and he was also quite certain what should be the subject-matter of this science. It was *immediate experience*: roughly, what we should now call sensation and perception, but from a subjective point of view. The task of the psychologist was to analyse these conscious processes into elements, to discover by what means the elements were connected, and to formulate the laws of connection. The method of psychology was that of introspection, which meant, not just thinking aloud, but making careful observations and reports on subjective experiences. This was a skilled task, for which training was necessary, just as any other scientist must be trained to make observations. A simple Wundtian demonstration would be to listen carefully to the regular beat of a metronome, and report on the way in which these beats are *experienced* as rhythmical. (Wundt: *An Introduction to Psychology*, 1912.) It follows from Wundt's definition that most of what one usually calls 'thinking' was not the province of psychology: later, Külpe and his colleagues rejected thus ruling (see *Thinking as a Private Experience*). Wundt's definitions seems odd to us today, because practically every introductory textbook on which we have been reared starts by insisting that psychology is the science of *behaviour*. Peter McKellar, in 1968, was perhaps the first author in modern times to specify a wider definition, building it into his title *Behaviour and Experience*. But notice that the textbook writers, following Watson, have been doing just the same sort of thing as Wundt: giving a definition by subject-matter. This is always a dangerous move in science, and generally results in those who insist on the definitions ending up in blind alleys. Meanwhile, progress is being made either by those who have reacted against the definition, or by those who have luckily never heard of it. We have occasion elsewhere to discuss the reactions of Watson, and of Külpe and his colleagues at Würzburg; and the partly independent line of Freud. Here, we need to consider a reaction that was concerned with the dynamics of thought.

Wundt's psychology was concerned with *content*—the discriminable 'bits' or elements of conscious experience. Coexistent with that approach was a psychology that dealt with acts. Wundt's contemporary Franz Brentano, not primarily a psychologist but a philosopher interested in perception, among other topics, argued that, for example, when one sees a colour, it is the act, the *seeing*, that is mental, and thus the concern of psychology. Brentano's ideas influenced, among others, Carl Stumpf, Otto Külpe, James Ward and William McDougall. Among Stumpf's students were Wolfgang Köhler and Kurt Koffka. These two, with Max Wertheimer, became the founders of Gestalt psychology. 'Gestalt' has sometimes been translated as 'a whole that is greater than the sum of its parts'. In contrast to Wundt, the Gestalt psychologists stressed that analysis of conscious experience into elements is less useful, because that is to destroy its essential nature. Experience is a matter of wholes, not parts. When you see a table, you see it as a piece of furniture, not a set of separate sensations of shape, colour, etc.; you hear a tune, not a succession of separate notes. These are the psychological realities, it was argued, and they should be what psychologists are concerned with. One of the great tenets of the school was that *organisms organize*—'the great tautology' of psychology, Boring calls it. All organisms have a built-in tendency to organize the input from the environment, this tendency becoming more effective as one moves up the phylogenetic scale. The organization was often thought of in terms of *fields* and *field theory*, so that the model for Gestalt accounts was physics. A 'perceptual field', for example, was thought to be like an 'electrical field' inasmuch as alteration to any part tends to produce a restructuring of the whole. Further, it was assumed that the environment is represented on the cortex in a way that was physically, or rather topographically, similar to what was 'out there'. This was the doctrine of physiological isomorphism. A simple example would be that an almost-closed circle, when perceived, would be represented in such a way that excitation could spread across the gap, resulting in perception (actually *mis*-perception) of a closed circle. Observation suggested that organization took certain forms. Organization was not a classifying of discrete events (like concept identification) but rather a restructuring according to certain general principles, the Laws of Form. Among these are the tendencies to see part of the environment standing out as a *figure* from the remainder (the *ground*); to prefer 'good', i.e. well-organized, closed, stable forms; for such forms to persist and recur. (For a concise summary, see Boring's *History of Experimental Psychology*; for a critique, see Hamlyn's *Psychology of Perception*). One result of this way of looking at things was that perception, learning and thinking become not so much separate processes, as different aspects of the basic process or organizing or structuring. A situation in which a goal cannot be reached immediately is perceived in one way; what is needful, following the Laws of Form, is for the situation to be restructured so that a route to the goal is seen. This is at once perception and problem-solving; and it is learning because the process does not reverse. Once you have 'seen' the solution you do not, in general, forget it.

The Behaviourist reaction against Wundt took the opposite road. Emerging at about the same time as Gestalt psychology, it saw the organism as a passive receiver of input, acting only in response to stimulation, and without built-in tendencies to organize. Behaviour could be accounted for by the building up of systems of most likely responses, according to which of these resulted in a satisfying state of affairs. However, the two schools shared another characteristic besides that of reaction: an interest in animal psychology. For Gestalt psychologists, mental processes can be studied conveniently in animals, not just for their own interest, but because it is assumed that the basic tendency to organize is common to at any rate the 'higher' species. But in men, such fundamental processes are obscured by experience, social factors, and other uncontrollable variables, whereas, says Köhler (1925): '... one may be allowed the expectation that in the intelligent performances of anthropoid apes we may see once more in their plastic state processes with which we have become so familiar that we can no longer immediately recognize their original form.' As a matter of fact the phrase 'phylogenetic scale' may lead the unwary to think and talk as if there were a sort of ladder, with men on the top rung. From an evolutionary point of view this is far from the case. Our nearest relatives the apes, far from representing as it were a step down, are rather a good many steps sideways. They are in no sense our ancestors, but rather very distant cousins, our respective families of hominidae and pongidae having diverged at an extremely remote period. (See Hodos and Campbell, 1969). Obviously animal studies can help us to understand man, but we must be aware of the size of the gap. Non-verbal organisms were of course ruled out of Wundtian psychology because they could not introspect. The Behaviourists were interested in animals partly because in them one could neatly and conveniently investigate the relationship between Stimulus and Response. It was partly, too, that Watson just wanted to study animals, and so had one more reason to turn against the psychology that rejected them.

Both these lines of interest in animals were anticipated. Thorndike, inspired by Lloyd Morgan's lectures in 1896 on *Habit and Instinct*, began to study chicks, kept at first in his bedroom until his landlady objected. He criticized the anecdotal nature of much that was currently written about animals. He began by interpreting animal behaviour in the conventional psychological terms of the day. An experimenter would try to imagine himself as the animal subject, and introspect his own mental processes. One can get some idea of what this is like by using Peterson's (1920) 'Mental maze':

$$B — X — T — R \ldots G$$
$$\diagdown \diagdown \diagdown$$
$$D \quad Q \quad P$$

The longer the series, the more difficult it is. The experimenter sees this, the subject does not. The experimenter tells the subject, 'Your starting point is B, your goal is G. Choose between X and D.' If he chooses X, he gets T and Q; if D, B and X; and so on. It is quite an enlightening thing to try out. Be that as it may, the unsatisfactoriness of this *empathic* approach was one of the reasons for the rejection of introspection. Thorndike turned to more objective techniques, the most famous of which involved the puzzle box from which various species, but particularly cats, could escape by some fortuitous movement, and so reach food. With successive trials the movement occurred more readily: Thorndike called it 'learning by trial and error with accidental success'. Cats who had learned in one box did better than chance in a similar box: Thorndike rejected the suggestion that they had formed any abstract idea of the solution, and explained this transfer of behaviour by generalization. Indeed he rejected the notion of an *idea* at all: what the cats learned, he held, was not an association between the stimulus of the box and the idea of the right behaviour, but between the stimulus and the response itself. Thus the experiments produced records of stimuli and responses, or trials, errors, and successes, the non-subjective nature of which naturally appealed to Watson, and which were the ancestors of the endless miles of Skinnerian cumulative records. (These came at last to replace the organism: Dr. J. R. Millenson once remarked to me: 'We are not studying a rat, we are studying *this*', indicating the rows of little red lines emerging from the kymograph.) Meanwhile, the Gestalt approach to animal problem solving was being foreshadowed by Hobhouse (1901). Dogs could obtain meat from a shelf by pulling a string; sometimes, by choosing between the correct, and a dummy or unattached, string. They had the opportunity to see a relationship between elements of the problem. The famous major study was of course the accidental result of Köhler's internment on Tenerife during the 1914–18 war. Objecting to Thorndike's procedure, in which, he argued, the subjects had no chance to behave intelligently, Köhler posed for his apes tasks which could be solved by a restructuring of the perceived situation. These tasks are well known and we shall not discuss them in detail here. In some, detours had to be adopted to reach food, in others boxes or sticks were

44

available to reach it. One feature that brings out the perceptual element is the importance of the original disposition of the problem elements. This is seen in Köhler's diagram of the routes followed by a hen and a dog (Figure 2.1).

It is not until the hen manoeuvres itself into a certain position that the solution appears. The dog's behaviour, that of the hen on starting its straight run, and that of a chimpanzee in using a stick to pull in a banana, or a box to climb on, were described as showing 'insight' or 'intelligence' (Köhler uses the same word, which is translated sometimes by one, sometimes the other). Now 'intelligence'

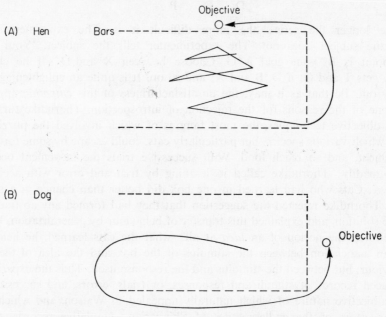

Figure 2.1. Köhler's simple detour problem (Reproduced from W. Köhler, *The Mentality of Apes* (1925). By permission of Humanities Press Inc., New York, and Routledge & Kegan Paul Ltd., London)

can, as we shall see when discussing *Intellectual Abilities*, be used just to describe the role or function, or type, of behaviour, as one can study intelligently or stupidly. But Köhler evidently means more than this, and the concept of *insight* has been something of a puzzle ever since. The behaviour which is the evidence for insight seems to be characterized by suddeness; smoothness; and novelty: while insight itself precedes the actual behaviour, and is, in fact, the sort of restructuring we have already described. The situation is made more complex by the psychoanalytic use of 'insight' to mean something like an awareness of hitherto unconscious mental processes; and by possible equation of either or both these uses to the subjective phenomenon often called the 'aha!' experience. Even without these complications, Köhler's account has been severely criticized. In the first place, as Osgood (1953) points out, the behavioural criteria are qualitative only. We are not told *how* sudden, e.g. how soon after presentation of the problem, the solution must be to count as evidence for insight. Chance (1960) points out that Köhler took no account of the inherited repertoire of behaviour, as it has been analysed by ethologists. His argument is that 'complex responses are . . . not based on perceptual organizations, but on innate constituents which are motor patterns'. On this view 'insight' would occur when an individual animal happened to possess the relevant patterns. A somewhat similar line is taken by Schiller (1952). On the other hand Birch (1945) emphasized the importance of past experience in accounting for 'insightful' behaviour. He raised chimpanzees under controlled conditions, and tested their ability to use a hoe to reach a piece of food. On the whole they were unsuccessful. They were then allowed to play with sticks for three days, and retested. They all solved the problem within twenty seconds. Birch concluded that past experience played a large part in 'insight', and that an interpretation of it in situational terms alone was inadequate. Köhler, of course, had not known the previous history of his subjects. Harlow (1949) believed that he had shown how insight might come about *through* practice, in his experiments on learning sets. His subjects learned slowly, or indeed failed to learn, successive problems, but eventually were able to produce virtually instant solutions. Something similar, Harlow thought, must have happened to Köhler's chimpanzees. Finally the point that insight precedes behaviour is not a criterion, but an inference: there is no way of telling for certain what passes in the chimpanzee's mind as he sits looking. The most we can say is that it *looks as if* the solution had dawned. Nevertheless Köhler's book *The Mentality of Apes* is still well worth reading, giving a view of animal behaviour that is now rather novel, and being full of infectious zeal to prove that apes *are* intelligent.

Besides, it is fair to say that the Gestalt psychologists have been less concerned with how the present situation may have arisen, than with what happens now it is here. An explanation of this in terms of cognitive restructuring was for a number of years likely to be less popular than one in terms of a repertoire of responses, practice, and so on: partly because it seemed, and perhaps was, less precise and less testable, and partly because internal, and especially 'mental' variables were out of favour. This is perhaps particularly relevant when we come to consider human subjects. Gestalt procedures and theory were applied to human problems with greater or less variation. Köhler himself included a few experiments with children for comparison with the animals. Here is one:

> 'A little girl of one year and three months, who had learned to walk alone a few weeks before, was brought into a blind alley, set up *ad hoc* (2 metres long, and 1½ wide), and, on the other side of the partition, some attractive object was put before her eyes; first she pushed towards the object,

i.e. against the partition, then looked round slowly, let her eyes run along the blind alley, suddenly laughed joyfully, and in one movement was off on a trot round the corner to the objective.'

This is very similar to the behaviour of an adult dog. It illustrates one of Köhler's defences of insight, virtually that the behaviour speaks for itself. He says: 'For one who has actually watched the experiments discussions like the above have something comic about them. To secure these facts against mis-interpretation seems almost pedantic.' But of course it is not the existence of the behavioural phenomena that is in question; it is the concept of insight as a possible explanation of it.

The best-known classical Gestalt study of human problem-solving is Max Wertheimer's *Productive Thinking*, published posthumously in 1945. This was intended to be the first of three books, the others to deal with 'broader aspects of the psychology of thinking', and with Gestalt logic respectively. In the event, Wertheimer was only able to present his studies of a sample of problem situations. He begins by distinguishing two main traditions of inquiry into thought processes. One is that of logic. Traditional logic, stemming from Aristotle, had regarded logic as an analysis of thought processes (we shall discuss this point again later); and this gave rise to psychological experimentation on such operations as abstraction, generalization, definition, drawing conclusions, etc. The second approach was the associationistic one. (We have called this the learning theory/S–R approach). This regards thinking as dependent on the acquisition, recalling and recombining of associative bonds. Both these Wertheimer regards as inadequate. Actually I think we must regard the biological approach of Piaget as another fundamentally different line (Wertheimer does not mention Piaget); and possibly also the structural theory of Guilford. The two views are inadequate because, whatever they contribute to certain aspects of thinking, they do not help us 'to distinguish between sensible thought and senseless combinations'. Thinking may be logically correct and yet without application—indeed the logical analysis of thought deliberately concentrates on *form*, even if the content is nonsensical. Associationism may lead to the solution of a problem by mechanical repetition of what has been learned, or by trial-and-error testing; but this is not *productive* thinking. In order to show what *is* productive thinking, Wertheimer discusses at length several different every-day, and deceptively simple, problems, some being problems in human relations; as well as the great discoveries of Galileo and Einstein. The most often quoted of these is the first in the book, and it is in some ways the best to illustrate Wertheimer's method. It is concerned with finding the area of a parallelogram. In one case, it is a question whether, having learned a rule for this, subjects can see what to do when the figure appears in an unusual orienta-tion. In another case, it is a question of whether children will prefer a simple, elegant formula to a clumsy, though correct, one. In another case, children and adults, who knew how to find the area of a rectangle, were asked to find that of a parallelogram. Throughout the book, Wertheimer is concerned with qualitative, not quantitative, responses. His report on this case is worth quoting almost in full.

'There are different types of reaction.

First type. No reaction at all.
Or someone says, "Whew! Mathematics!" and dismisses the problem with, "I don't like mathematics."
Some subjects simply wait politely for what is to come, or ask, "What else?"
Others say, "I don't know; that is something I have not learned." Or, "I learned that in school but I have completely forgotten it", and that is all. Some show indignation: "How do you expect me to be able to do that?" To which I reply, "Why not try it?"

Second type. Others search their memory intensively, some even frantically, to see if they can recall anything that might be of help. They search blindly for some scraps of knowledge that might apply.
Some ask, "Could I ask my older brother? He surely knows." Or: "Could I look for it in a geometry book?" Which is certainly one way of solving problems.

Third type. Some start making speeches. They talk around the problem, telling of analogous situations. Or they classify it in some way, apply general terms, perform some subsumptions, or engage in aimless trials.

Fourth type. But in a number of cases one can observe real thinking at work—in drawings, in remarks, in thinking out loud.
1. "Here is this figure—how can I get at the size of the area? I see no possibility. The area just in this form?"
2. "Something has to be done. I have to change something, change it in a way that would lead me to see the area clearly. Something is wrong."

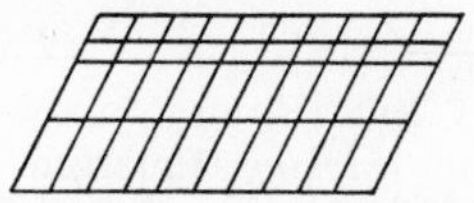

Figure 2.2(a). (From pp. 45–48 in *Productive Thinking*, Enlarged Edition, by Max Wertheimer. Copyright 1945, 1959 by Valentin Wertheimer. By permission of Harper and Row, Publishers, Inc.)

Figure 2.2(b). (From pp. 45–48 in *Productive Thinking*, Enlarged Edition, by Max Wertheimer. Copyright 1945, 1959 by Valentin Wertheimer. By permission of Harper and Row, Publishers, Inc.)

At this stage some children produce Figure 2.2(a). In such cases I add: "It would be nice to be able to compare the size of the area of the parallelogram with the area of the rectangle." The child is helpless, then starts anew.

There were other cases in which the child said: "I have to get rid of the trouble. This figure cannot be divided into little squares." (See Figure 2.2(b).)
3. Here one child said suddenly: "Could I have a folding ruler?" I fetched one. The child made a parallelogram of it, then turned it into a rectangle. (See Figure 2.2(c).)

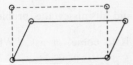

Figure 2.2(c). (From pp. 45–48 in *Productive Thinking*, Enlarged Edition, by Max Wertheimer. Copyright 1945, 1959 by Valentin Wertheimer. By permission of Harper and Row, Publishers, Inc.)

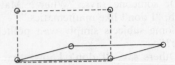

Figure 2.2(d). (From pp. 45–48 in *Productive Thinking*, Enlarged Edition, by Max Wertheimer. Copyright 1945, 1959 by Valentin Wertheimer. By permission of Harper and Row, Publishers, Inc.)

I enjoyed this. I asked: "Are you sure this is correct?" "Sure," he said. It was only after considerable difficulty that I succeeded in making him doubt his method—by using an appropriate drawing such as Figure 2.2(d). Here he said at once: "The rectangle is much bigger—it doesn't work . . ."
4. A child took a piece of paper and cut out two equal parallelograms. Then, looking happy, he put the two together in this way (as in Figure 2.2(e).)

Figure 2.2(e). (From pp. 45–48 in *Productive Thinking*, Enlarged Edition by Max Wertheimer, Copyright 1945, 1959 by Valentin Wertheimer. By permission of Harper and Row, Publishers, Inc.)

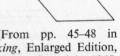

Figure 2.2(f). (From pp. 45–48 in *Productive Thinking*, Enlarged Edition, by Max Wertheimer. Copyright 1945, 1959 by Valentin Wertheimer. By permission of Harper and Row, Publishers, Inc.)

But he did not know how to proceed further.
This was in itself a fine happening. . . . I may remark that in a number of cases I myself gave the child two samples of the figure. The reactions I got were sometimes as shown in Figure 2.2(f).
Some indulged in several trials of this kind, even putting one figure above the other congruently or conversely. Such help seems to be effective only under certain conditions. Which ones?
But there were other cases in which the thinking went straight ahead. Some children reached the solution with little or no help in a genuine, sen-

sible, direct way. Sometimes, after strained concentration a face brightened at the critical moment. It is wonderful to observe the beautiful transformation from blindness to seeing the point!

First I shall report what happened with a $5\frac{1}{2}$-year-old child to whom I gave no help at all for the parallelogram problem, after she had been shown briefly how to get at the area of the rectangle, she said, "I certainly don't know how to do *that*." Then after a moment of silence: "This is *no good here*," pointing to the region at the left end; "and *no good here*", pointing to the region at the right (Figure 2·2(g).)

Figure 2.2(g). (From pp. 45–48 in *Productive Thinking*, Enlarged Edition, by Max Wertheimer. Copyright 1945, 1959 by Valentin Wertheimer. By permission of Harper and Row, Publishers, Inc.)

"It's troublesome, here and there." Hesitatingly she said: "I could make it right here... but..." Suddenly she cried out, "May I have a pair of scissors? What is bad there is just what is needed here. It fits." She took the scissors, cut the figure vertically, and placed the left end at the right.'

This example receives a lengthy analysis from Wertheimer. One important point he makes is that the Gestalt approach does not, as is sometimes thought, consist in ignoring the role of past experience: 'The crucial question is not *whether* past experience, but *what* kind of past experience plays a role—blind connections or structural grasp with resulting sensible transposing; also *how* material gains from past experience come in, whether by external recall or on the basis of structural requirements, of material functional fitness.' Another important point is that in making the transposition of one end to the other, the subject must herself distinguish the ends as units—they are not 'given'. A third point is that in the course of the transition, the ends remain stable (as does the rest of the figure). This is almost identical with what Piaget terms conservation. In general, the solution requires *structural reorganization*. By this is meant: 'reorganization as sensibly required by the structure of the situation ... the transition seems inadequately characterized by stating that it is a transition to a more familiar figure; the transition here is to a form in which the matter becomes structurally clear'. Now by the time Wertheimer wrote, the doctrine of physiological isomorphism had been discredited, and it is not obvious what status this reorganization has. It would appear to be a mental process, but one for which no particular physiological basis is proposed.

At the end of his book, Wertheimer sums up his ideas thus:

'When one grasps a problem situation, its structural features and requirements set up certain strains, stresses, tensions in the thinker. What happens in real thinking is that these strains and stresses are followed up, yield vectors in the direction of improvement of the situation, and change it accordingly. S_2 (i.e. the goal or solution) is a state of affairs that is held together by inner forces as a good structure in which there is harmony in the mutual requirements, and in which the parts are determined by the structure of the whole, as the whole is by the parts.'

Although this process is expressed in terms of structures, the theory is clearly a dynamic one. And if one asks *why* these forces should act thus to produce good structures, Wertheimer's answer is:

'When a picture is given here of the inner structural dynamics in the determination of processes, it does not mean that in this development man is merely passive. An attitude is implied on his part, a willingness to face problems straight, a readiness to follow them up courageously and sincerely, a desire for improvement, in contrast with arbitrary, wilful, or slavish attitudes. This, I think, is one of the great attributes that constitute the dignity of man.'

This is clearly an affirmation of faith (from one of psychology's many refugees from Nazism); and partly a statement of assumption of basic processes. Wertheimer's book might, perhaps, be said to mark the high water mark of Gestalt work on thinking.

1945, a good year for problem solving, saw the publication of an extensive monograph on the work of Karl Duncker, begun in the thirties, and influenced by Gestalt thinking. He posed practical, though in some cases imaginary, problems about which subjects were to think aloud. One was: 'given a human being with an inoperable stomach tumor, and rays which destroy organic tissue at sufficient intensity, by what procedure can one free him of the tumor by these rays and at the same time avoid destroying the healthy tissue which surrounds it?' And here is Duncker's summary of the protocol of one subject.

1. Send rays through the esophagus.
2. Desensitize the healthy tissues by means of a chemical injection.
3. Expose the tumor by operating.
4. One ought to decrease the intensity of the rays on their way; for example—would this work?—turn the rays on at full strength only after the tumor has been reached. (Experimenter: False analogy; no injection is in question.)
5. One should swallow something inorganic (which would not allow passage of the rays) to protect the healthy stomach walls. (E: It is not merely the stomach walls which are to be protected.)
6. Either the rays must enter the body or the tumor must come out. Perhaps one could alter the location of the tumor—but how? Through pressure? No.
7. Introduce a cannula. (E: what, in general, does one do when, with any

agent, one wishes to produce in a specific place an effect which he wishes to avoid on the way to that place?)

8. (Reply:) One neutralizes the effect on the way. But that is what I have been attempting all the time.
9. Move the tumor toward the exterior. (Compare 6.) (The E repeats the problem and emphasizes, '... which destroy *at sufficient intensity*'.)
10. The intensity ought to be variable.
11. Adaptation of the healthy tissues by previous weak application of the rays. (E: How can it be brought about that the rays destroy only the region of the tumor?)
12. (Reply:) I see no more than two possibilities: either to protect the body or to make the rays harmless. (E: How could one decrease the intensity of the rays en route? [Compare 4.])
13. (Reply:) Somehow divert ... diffuse rays ... disperse ... stop! Send a broad and weak bundle of rays through a lens in such a way that the tumor lies at the focal point and thus receives intensive radiation.

(Total duration about half an hour.)'

Duncker adds as a footnote: 'This solution is closely related to the best solution: crossing of several weak bundles of rays at the tumor.' This rather well-known quotation brings out several points in Duncker's method. There is the prompting and the fact that the subject does not actually reach the solution. And there is a doubt as to *why* this is the best solution. Obviously it may be, but subjects could have no way of knowing this. So his attempts must of necessity include many blind alleys—in this he is more like Thorndike's cats than Köhler's apes. Indeed Duncker presents the relationships between the offered solutions in a way which suggests both a maze and the computer-programmed paths to solution described by Newell, Shaw, and Simon (see *Models*) as indicated in Figure 2.3.

Duncker's analysis of his subjects thought processes emphasized the gradual emergence of solutions, involving a reformulation of the original problem.

'The final form of an individual solution is, in general, not reached by a single step from the original setting of the problem; on the contrary, the principle, the functional value of the solution, typically arises first, and the final form of the solution in question develops only as this principle becomes more and more concrete. In other words, the general or "essential" properties of a solution genetically precede the specific properties; the latter are developed out of the former.'

This matches up well with common experience, where one quite often feels that one knows the *sort* of thing that is required, without being able to say precisely what. Memory too often works this way, e.g. in the 'tip of the tongue phenomenon'—one cannot recall a name, but knows it is not Jones or Smith—they don't 'fit'. Doubtless this is just a special case of the generally-found superiority of recognition over recall. Duncker's problems, as exemplified by the 'tumor' problem above, do seem to be nearer to real life situations than some other experimental tasks. It is common to have to solve problems with only

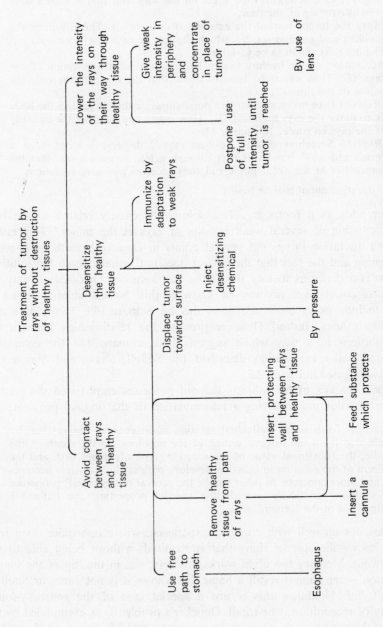

Figure 2.3. Duncker's representation of the solution process in the 'tumor' problem (From Duncker, 1945)

limited information and a background of more or less general knowledge, and with no absolute criteria for knowing which solution is best, even after the event. This does not necessarily make Duncker's procedure superior, of course. Perhaps its main merit was the simple but sensible expedient of asking subjects what they were thinking. One should note in passing that this was *not* the same as classical introspection, in which subjects have to stand back, as it were, and observe their own sensations.

Duncker's contemporary Norman Maier (e.g. 1930, 1931) used situations somewhat resembling his, although he was working in a somewhat more behaviouristic framework. He also asked somewhat similar questions, for example: '(a) does the solution develop from a nucleus, or does it appear as a completed whole? (b) what is the conscious experience of an individual just before the solution is found? (c) is the reasoner conscious of the different factors which aid in bringing about a solution?'

Maier used several problem situations, real ones and not imaginary like Duncker's tumour problem. In one of the best known, the subject was

> 'in a large room which contained many objects such as poles, ringstands, clamps, pliers, extension cords, tables and chairs. Two cords were hung from the ceiling, and were of such length that they reached the floor. One hung near a wall, the other from the center of the room. The subject was told: "Your problem is to tie the ends of those two strings together." He soon learned that if he held either cord in his hand he could not reach the other. He was then told that he could use or do anything he wished.'

Having found one solution, he was told to find another. There were four possible types of solution, as below, the last being the most difficult.

1. One cord anchored half-way between the two, e.g. by a chair.
2. One cord lengthened with the extension cord.
3. One cord pulled in with a pole.
4. A weight (pliers) tied to one cord and set swinging.

If a subject failed to find solution 4, he was given first one and then a second hint or 'help'.

Hint 1: E brushed past the central cord, setting it in motion.
Hint 2: S was handed the pliers and told 'With the aid of this and no other object there is another way of solving the problem.'

39.3 per cent of subjects found solution 4 without help; 37.7 per cent with help; 23 per cent not at all. At the end, subjects were asked for verbal reports. Maier summarized his results thus:

1. Usually the solution appeared suddenly and as a complete idea.
2. There was a marked tendency to repeat variations of previous solutions.
3. When suggestions or "helps" were necessary, the very "help" which

brought about the solution was not consciously experienced except in cases in which the solution appeared in steps.

4. The subjects' reports seemed to satisfy a "trial-and-error" theory...' (Maier, 1931)

However Maier went on to argue that this was not in fact adequate because it did not take account of the change in organization, the fact that the cord is seen as something which can move itself nearer the other. This was a new idea to the subject—shown by the fact that he did not think of it for himself. The fact that those subjects who utilized hints did not realize that they had showed that the hint could not have just added one more hypothesis to the subject's conscious reasoning processes. Then *some* were still unable to solve the problem even after the hint, so they could not *just* have been unconsciously trying out all possibilities on a trial-and-error basis. Therefore, Maier concluded (1931): 'mental trial-and-error can hardly be regarded as an explanation. What must be explained is how and why certain ideas appear in consciousness. After the idea is conscious the fundamental process is over. Association (in the usual sense) can explain why some ideas are recalled, but it cannot explain the appearance of other ideas, e.g. original ideas.' To this point we shall return when discussing creative thinking, and the computer simulation of thought.

Maier's work, like Duncker's, is attractive because it seems to match up to everyday experience. Maier's subjects seemed to respond in the same sort of way as Duncker's: it was as if they were saying 'What I need is something to set the string swinging—like a pendulum—a weight—aha, the pliers!' Viewed more analytically, one might say that what the subjects had to do was to abstract from the problem situation a general principle, even if this was not clearly formulated, from which a specific solution could be deduced. This is very similar to the abstract analogies deliberately used to aid in finding creative solutions in the method known as *synectics* (see *Creative Thinking*). It also might be said to exemplify the hypothetico-deductive method of scientific reasoning. Saugstad (1955, 1957) has argued against this view of Maier's results, and in favour of one that stresses the availability of functions. Saugstad and Raaheim (1960) say:

'In problem situations of such a concrete nature the solution is attained by the use of definite objects in definite ways and, in the attainment of the solution, the objects may be said to serve definite functions... The solution may be conceived of as the arrangement of a number of functions into some definite sequence.'

In one experiment, Saugstad had subjects list all possible uses for the objects later to be used in a Maier-type problem, and found that this significantly increased the probability of a solution. In the 1960 paper an experiment was reported in which subjects had, in order to solve a problem, to bend a nail and use it as a hook, and roll newspapers into tubes through which balls could pass. Before facing the problem situation, subjects were handed such bent nails and rolled newspapers, and asked to give examples of ways in which they might be used. Not surprisingly, subjects who received the demonstrations solved the problems more readily than those who did not. Thus, the authors conclude, '. . . a subject having available the necessary functions in the problem situation will solve the problem'. But this argument misses at least part of Maier's point. It is true that a weakness in Maier's argument is, that one cannot be sure in what sense the function (or idea) of a swinging rope is available to those subjects who have received the hint. But in trying to ensure that it is available, Saugstad is in danger of reducing the situation to absurdity. Presumably if given enough sufficiently detailed demonstrations, every subject could solve the problem. Indeed there would *be* no problem. The interesting result of Maier was that subjects who *used* the hint were not aware that they had received it. And given that a number of experiences are available to the subject, the question is, how are these recombined to reach a solution. Maier did not solve this problem, but he did pose it. Saugstad attempts to answer it, but in so doing changes the situation so that the problem disappears.

The other question that remains—the other side of the question, really—is why some subjects *failed* to solve the problem, even after hints. Duncker's answer to this was in terms of 'functional fixedness': subjects could not see, for example, that pliers could also be a weight. This is a special case of *set*, which has been investigated in a classic and still-continuing series of experiments by Luchins (e.g. 1942). (Luchins was one of Wertheimer's students.) This involves the well-known water-jar problems: given a set of containers of various capacities, the task is to obtain a specified amount of water in the smallest number of moves. *Set* may be defined as a tendency to respond in one particular way rather than in other possible ways. The particular variety of set in which Luchins has been interested, he calls *Einstellung*, a term introduced by the Würzburg psychologists (see *Thinking as a Private Experience*). Here, it is induced by posing a series of problems that can only be solved in one way, followed by one that can be solved either in that way or by an easier procedure. Luchins reports that the effect operates just as much with real jars of water as when the problems are on paper. My experience is that English students don't fall for it even on paper (I haven't ventured to try the real-life version). Set is of course not an explanation, but a phenomenon requiring explanation. Luchin's work does stress again, however, some of the dynamic aspects of thinking.

The experiments we have just discussed were taken by Scheerer (1963) as the starting point for some ingenious Gestalt-oriented investigations of his own. Many of these involved quite well-known puzzles. In one of these, the task is to connect nine dots, arranged in a square, with four straight lines, without lifting pencil from paper. Figure 2.4 shows the dots and solution.

Many people apparently find this difficult because they assume that one cannot extend the lines beyond the square, even though this is not a condition of the problem. It is necessary to start, as it were, from a different premise.

'This shift from one premise to a new one', says Scheerer, 'is what Gestalt psychologists call a "reformulation" or "recentering", of one's thoughts.' The observant reader will notice that perceptually, the right solution is an obviously less 'good' Gestalt than the wrong attempts. In other experiments, Scheerer used problems of the Duncker/Maier type. In one, a piece of string was necessary for solution, and subjects were unable to make use of the only available piece

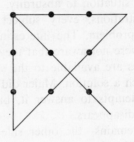

Figure 2.4. The nine dots problem

which was holding up a mirror or a calendar. Scheerer is insistent that subjects 'did not think they were forbidden to make use of it; they simply did not think to do so'. Still other experiments utilized the river crossing problem: eight soldiers have to cross a river, with the aid of two small boys and one boat which can carry at most two boys or one soldier. The solution to this is at the end of this chapter, so you can try it out. Scheerer's analysis of results is that 'insight' is necessary for solution, and that this involves, or even consists in, the 'recentering' we have already mentioned. It is impeded by fixation, of which some of the causes are these. First, starting with an incorrect premise. Second, a necessary element for solution (e.g. the string) may be 'embedded' in another context. Third, detours may be unacceptable as seeming to delay the achievement of the goal (cf. Köhler's hen and dog). This factor increases if motivation is high. The fourth factor is habituation, by which Scheerer seems to mean set in the Luchins sense. Scheerer concludes finally that: 'Fixation is overcome and insight attained by a sudden shift in the way the problem or the objects involved in it are viewed ... but precisely what brings it about is still unknown.' One must point out that there seems to be no particular reason to think that all problems resemble these.

The perceptual element in this approach, and the importance of what happens in the present, are found also in the 'neo-field' theory of problem solving proposed by Asher (1963). This takes just the opposite view to that proposed by learning theorists, since 'learning is a process of *forming* a concept within a cognitive system and problem solving is a process of *disrupting* established concepts ... in this sense, problem-solving is the inversive of learning'. Asher summarizes his theory thus:

> 'The neo-field theory attempts to conceptualize a cognitive sequence of events which occur in problem-solving activity. If these events occur, then there are implications for the optimal organization of the problem field for generating solutions. The model postulates that once concept formation is achieved within the individual's cognitive system, then any attempt to disrupt the established concept will be resisted by contradisruptive defenses. If these defenses are neutralized, which permits disruption of the existing concept, then tension will be produced as a function of the absence of closure. If the individual can sustain the tension, then a cognitive drive will be induced which has properties similar to biological drives. That is, there will be a change in sensory thresholds giving more sensitivity to cues related to the deprivation, and also there will be an increase in fantasy activity, the content of which is oriented to the deficit. The events in the cognitive sequence of selective perception and fantasy activity generate a series of alternate concepts to substitute for the one displaced, and these alternate concepts are the solutions, which have varying degrees of adequacy.'

This account, which seems to owe something to dynamic psychology as well as Gestalt, does attempt to deal with such phenomena as the difficulty of reaching new solutions, and the changes in interest and attention that often seem, subjectively to accompany problem-solving. But there is a possible objection, that the theory is hard to test. Fantasy, for example, while a most real phenomenon, is notoriously hard to pin down as an experimental variable. How is one to assess the strength of 'contradisruptive defenses'? Presumably if a concept is not changed, the defenses are too strong; if it is, they have been overcome. But this really tells us nothing: it is just a supposition. Roughly speaking, one feels that cognitive/dynamic/Gestalt approaches to cognition tend to be more subjectively plausible, and to deal with more important matters, while the learning theory/ S–R/association approaches are highly experimental, but less convincing and sometimes trivial.

LEARNING THEORY

However, it is to the learning theory approach that we now turn. Duncan (1959) reviewing some 100 references between 1946 and 1957, wrote:

> 'Problem-solving in human adults is a name for a diverse class of performance which differs, if it differs at all, only in degree from other classes of learning and performance, the degree of difference depending on the extent to which problem-solving demands relocation or integration of previously learned responses.'

3—T * *

He argued that the pressing need was for experimental determination of the variables affecting problem solution, and quoted evidence for the importance of the following:

1. Simple set—as in Luchins' studies.
2. Some 'complex sets'—as in the work of Duncker, Maier, and Saugstad.
3. Changes in relationships among the elements of a problem, as described by Wertheimer.
4. Level of problem difficulty, as for example in intelligence tests.
5. Aids toward solution, as given by Maier.
6. Certain characteristics of the subject, such as, rather obviously, age and reasoning ability.

This list of variables is obviously closely related to the definition of problem-solving already quoted. Duncan is taking 'problems' to be merely those situations on which experiments have been published under this heading. At the beginning of this chapter a wider definition was suggested, and a correspondingly wider list of variables will accordingly be at least mentioned.

Among the variables which Duncan might well have included are those concerned with past experience, as we have in fact already noticed. Schultz (1960) discussed the role of transfer in problem solving, arguing that in many experimental procedures, 'the situation's status as a *problem* was largely contingent upon the fact that the sequence of performances conformed to the paradigm for negative transfer.' In other words a situation becomes a problem when the subject has previously learned a response which is incompatible with that required for a solution. Schultz continues '... we have rarely attempted to study the conditions which are likely to produce positive transfer in these problem solving situations.' The obvious case where this has been done is the work on learning sets, but Schultz does not discuss this. In general though he is right; and this is still more the case if we move outside the laboratory and consider the role of individual experience. For the moment let us remain within it, to consider the way in which experience of a specific kind is made the cornerstone of a learning theory approach. Davis, in his 1966 paper, made this explicit. He distinguished three main theoretical approaches to problem solving: cognitive/dynamic, computer/mathematical, and learning theory. The last of these supposes that the organism possesses at any time a repertoire of responses, most of them having been built up or modified by a history of reinforcement; and that problem solution consists in the eliciting (and, normally, reinforcing) of a low dominance response. This basic assumption is variously used. A good example is the work of Kendler and Kendler (e.g. 1962). They quoted experimental evidence to show that separately learned habits can be combined to solve problems. Behaviour can be regarded as comprising sets of chained stimulus–response associations; and problem solution, as involving the association of response-produced cues from one behaviour chain to an overt response belonging to another. The

Kendlers' account is rather more sophisticated than this, however. They begin by discussing some of the methodological problems involved. The first concerns the status or place of problem solving (or, if you will, thinking) as a psychological process. The authors hold that it is not a basic process, but must be regarded as reflecting the interaction of what *are* basic processes, e.g. perception, motivation, and learning. This seems to be an assumption which might follow from a general behaviouristic orientation, but it is certainly not self-evident. 'Basic' presumably means that they are processes which we must accept as given, as a natural part of the organism, as requiring no further explanation at least at the psychological level. It is difficult to see why the manipulation of information— thinking—is less basic than its acquisition—learning. This of course raises the whole question of how behaviour is to be analysed, too large a one to discuss in detail here. The second issue concerns an appropriate experimental procedure: a choice must be made, say the Kendlers, between two main alternatives: a procedure that in some sense is, or simulates, a real-life situation; and a procedure designed to analyse and investigate basic processes. The latter tends to be characteristic of a behavioristic approach. In our previous discussion of this point we distinguished between the two varieties of the first alternative. For contrast, compare the approach of the Geneva (Piagetian) school, where the situations are much more realistic, even at the cost of varying them from one to another; but are still intended to uncover basic processes. (See *The Geneva School*.) The third issue is the choice of a pretheoretical model; that chosen by the Kendlers is a stimulus–response one. This means, not that 'we . . . *find* behavior atomized into individual S–R associations; we *represent* it as consisting of such.' The representation includes what are termed 'horizontal' and 'vertical' processes. Horizontal processes are the chained S–R associations of which behaviour is said to consist. Vertical processes refer to the fact that at any one time, behaviour consists of several ongoing behavioural chains, and that responses from one chain may be transferred to another.

The experimental situation on which the Kendlers mainly depend is the reversal shift one already described under the heading of *Concept Identification*. This therefore brings out the continuity of these situations and 'Problems', especially when regarded from a learning theory point of view. As already noted, students find reversal shifts easier, and rats find the opposite. The changeover seems to occur in children somewhere around the age of six. Several of the issues raised by this have already been discussed in the last chapter. In this case, the Kendlers' explanation was in terms of mediating processes, probably verbal; and it therefore became relevant to investigate the role of language. They are careful to stress that it is not necessary to equate a theoretical mediation process with any actually observed language. It would seem that they consider such processes to be hypothetical constructs of a particular type, namely one that states formal characteristics without specifying what psychological (still less physiological) form these may take. The Kendlers noticed that some young children would spontaneously verbalize the correct solution while at the same time making an incorrect choice (the opposite phenomenon to the one I noticed with adult subjects). This would be an example of vertical processes. In this case the processes are parallel, that is, they do not interact. Later, the child becomes able to integrate the two processes, and it is then that reversal shifts become easier, since a verbal one for the correct response becomes available. As the Kendlers point out, this phenomenon appears to be closely related to the function of language in regulating behaviour, as investigated by Luria (e.g. 1961). To this function we must return in discussing *Language and Thought*.

Probably the most thorough-going and hard-line S–R analysis of thinking so far presented has been that of Berlyne (1965). His book, *Structure and Direction in Thinking*, is a tour-de-force whose complex reasoning and mass of experimental evidence can only be suggested here. It was also one of the first major accounts of thinking to deal at all adequately with the work of the Russian and Genevan psychologists. For Berlyne, 'problem solving' is a special case of directed thinking. One essential feature of this is that 'responses are evoked by stimulus situations in which they would otherwise have been unlikely to occur'. This sets the scene for a learning theory analysis. Berlyne reviews the definitions of problem solving offered by a number of writers, and concludes: '... we can see a fair measure of agreement that a problem implies a condition of high drive which is not promptly relieved'. The fact that relief is not at once available could be expressed by saying that the problem is more or less difficult. Difficulty in turn Berlyne equates with conflict. Degree of conflict in any situation can be expressed by the formula $E \times U$ where E represents the total strength of competing responses, and U represents uncertainty regarding the subject's behaviour (that is, the inverse of the probability of predicting it). Conflict as such can take many forms, but in dealing with directed thinking we are particularly concerned with *conceptual conflict*. Conceptual conflict can be due to various causes, such as overloading of information-handling capacity; but 'most conceptual conflict by far must depend on learned antagonisms.' That is, there will be incompatibility between two (or more) symbolic responses (approximately equivalent to thoughts). Four variables will control the degree of conflict:

1. The number of competing responses.
2. How nearly equal in strength the competing responses are.
3. The total absolute strength of the competing responses.
4. The degree of incompatibility between competing responses.

There are many different types of conceptual conflict, according to Berlyne, which we shall not list here; rather let us move to some of the ways of reducing it by directed thinking. First of all, directed thinking 'has both information-rejecting and information-gathering aspects'. These aspects can operate in the following ways:

1. Disequalization. This is when the competing responses become less nearly equal. One way in which this can happen is when one or more responses is eliminated.
2. Swamping. A *new* response may be introduced, much stronger than any of the others.
3. Conciliation. Further information may show that apparently incompatible responses are actually not so.
4. Suppression. Total strength of competing responses can in certain circumstances be reduced 'by suppressing thoughts about conflict-ridden subject matter or avoiding stimuli that tend to evoke such thoughts'.

Competing responses are, following the assumptions of learning theory, those that have been most effectively reinforced. Berlyne's account is largely based on Hull's theory of learning in particular, and this was of course a very complex one. It postulated not just single responses, but 'behaviour chains' or sequences of stimuli and responses, which could moreover be organized in 'habit-family hierarchies'. These are really alternative routes between an initial situation and a goal. One route will normally be the most dominant at any one time, having been more effectively reinforced. Changes in dominance may occur in various ways, according to Hullian theory, including *Oscillation*, which is really a sort of let-out factor to account for random fluctuations in response strength.

To take one of Berlyne's examples, suppose a resident of Boston sets out to travel to New York. A number of alternatives are available: different modes of travel, or routes, represented by different behaviour chains. Normally he will choose that which has been most effectively reinforced. But he may, like a rat showing spontaneous alternation, choose another for apparently random reasons (he might just feel like a change). Or, external reasons may rule out some routes, such as having too little money to fly. This would be like blocking one alley of a maze. Then he takes the next most dominant route. But it may happen that he *can't decide* which route to take. Now there is a problem, in Berlyne's sense, and now directed thinking may come into play to reduce the conflict. This is done in the ways we have listed above, whose applications will be relatively obvious, e.g.

1. Disequalization. All flying is stopped by fog.
2. Swamping. A friend offers to take him by car for nothing.
3. Conciliation. He finds he can, say, go partway by bus, stop off, and continue by train.
4. Suppression. He refuses to consider the fact that he already has an overdraft.

Indeed, these applications are so obvious that one is forced to wonder just what it is that is being said. It may be that the simplified version we have had to present misses the fundamental value of the theory. On the other hand it may be that Berlyne's main contribution has been in amassing evidence about the ways in which conceptual conflict is reduced, this evidence being too detailed to present here. But while we have concentrated on some of these fairly specific aspects of Berlyne's account, it must be added that his model of thinking is of considerable theoretical sophistication. In addition to adopting a highly self-critical attitude, Berlyne discusses at great length the implications that Hullian and other S–R ideas have for the analysis of thinking in general. But perhaps the most remarkable feature of Berlyne's account is the highly plausible fashion in which ideas wholly outside the Behaviourist S–R tradition are introduced and discussed without bias in the context of his theory. This is particularly true of the Genevan psychologists led by Piaget. Here we have a group of workers whose traditional interests, attitudes, and methodology seem completely alien to those of a Behaviourist such as Berlyne. Yet notions such as operation and schema are discussed, without conceptual strain, in relation to the S–R conception of thinking proposed by Berlyne. We shall have occasion again to refer to *Structure and Direction in Thinking*, as must all serious students of the subject.

Forehand (1966) makes similar points about the two theoretical views so far discussed to those we have already mentioned. The Gestalt approach, he feels, with its 'unanalysed concepts of insight, fixation, and cognitive organization', is 'certainly too vague'. On the other hand the S–R approach, even with the addition of mediating little s and r, may be too simple. Here we should mention that Skinner, who is often classed as an S–R theorist, argues (e.g. Skinner, 1966) that the operant analysis of behaviour allows for a much more sophisticated account of thinking than does S–R learning theory, because it potentially allows us to specify under what environmental contingencies thinking (or problem-solving behaviour) occurs. The same sort of objections can be raised to this as have been made to Skinner's work on language. The first is that the specification of contingencies remains more of a pious hope than an actual achievement. And second, it has to be shown that such a specification would constitute an explanation; without going into the criteria for this, it would be reasonable to ask that it be shown that the contingencies constitute the necessary and sufficient conditions for thinking. On the other hand it would appear to be possible to increase the likelihood of appropriate behaviour by positive reinforcement. It is possible, as has been mentioned earlier, to view the development of learning sets in this light.

COMPUTER SIMULATION (See also *Models*)

The third body of work is the computer/mathematical one. This is not a theoretically distinct line; rather, it is a technique which has been applied to many psychological processes, including thinking. In that area, perhaps most work has been done on what can be called, by the general definition we have adopted, problem-solving. Essentially the technique is that of making models, and it is the subject of a separate chapter. In practice, there has often been an association between computer simulation of thought processes, and some form of stimulus–response theory. This is because the nature of computers is that they can conduct a small number of basic operations, and only these if they are exactly specified. These are things like adding, subtracting, or taking the larger of two items. Thus a computer program, in which highly complex manipulations are reduced to large numbers of small steps, is in principle rather like a learning theory in which behaviour is reduced to large numbers of S–R connections. Feigenbaum and Feldman (1963) for example, showed how complex thinking processes can be built up out of elementary symbol manipulation processes. Any material for computer processing must be quantifiable, and this is not always possible for dynamic theories of thinking.

Let us mention here one example to illustrate the approach. Simon and Barenfeld (1969) took as their problem situations some games, basing this on the extensive work of de Groot (*Thought and Choice in Chess*, 1965). He found that chess players extract a large amount of information in the first five or ten seconds of looking at a given state of play. Tichomirov and Poznyanskya (1966), and others, have been able to record eye movements during this period, with enough accuracy to determine the location of each fixation within one or two squares of the chess board. Simon and Barenfeld concentrated on this phase. They made two assumptions: (1) that information gathered is about relations between pieces—usually pairs—or between pieces and squares; (2) when attention is fixed on piece A, and a relation to piece B is noticed attention will next either return to A or move to B (i.e. not to some other piece). With these and some other minor assumptions they wrote a program that simulated quite well eye-movements actually recorded. Furthermore, one of the most striking phenomena in chess is the well-established fact that a grandmaster or a master can, after five seconds sight of the board, reproduce the positions almost without error. Weaker players cannot do this, and no one can do it with randomly-placed pieces. The master must be coding the situation in terms of a 'vocabulary' of familiar subpatterns, which enable him to reduce twenty or thirty pieces and positions to the well-known 'seven plus-or-minus two' *chunks* of information that can be held in immediate memory (Miller, 1956). Simon and Barenfeld report that the sequence of 'fixations and noticing acts' produced by their program, does include many of the configurations that would be familiar to a chess master, and which they would be likely to use for 'chunking'. Therefore, the mechanics built into the program suggest how the masters may perform their feats. This is a neat experiment, because it restricts itself to a small, precisely quantifiable part of a problem-solving process, and one, moreover, that is hardly amenable to introspection. It suggests applications to other situations, for example to other problems that have a clear perceptual element; and it suggests a way of improving skills like chess by explicit training in apprehension of the vocabulary or relationships. But a more general discussion of models must be postponed until later.

PSYCHOMETRICS

Psychologists who have been concerned to assess individual differences in intellectual abilities have often considered 'intelligence' to be largely a matter of solving problems. Problems of various kinds have generally formed part at least of intelligence tests. Butcher (1968) in his book *Human Intelligence* devotes a chapter to problem solving. But since we for our part have a chapter on intellectual abilities, we need not discuss these in detail here. The most relevant work would appear to be that of Guilford. The British line of investigation, running from Galton through to Burt, has tended to emphasize one general intellectual ability plus abilities specific to certain sorts of content—for example verbal, numerical, spatial. Guilford on the other hand, besides subsuming these abilities, has tried to give a picture of what is involved in certain sorts of activity, such as problem solving, creative thinking, etc. Guilford's account has the general title of 'structure of intellect', and Merrifield, Guilford, Christenson and Frick (1962) describe this model with particular reference to problem solving. The model is a three-dimensional one, which assumes that three main aspects must be measured if we are to have a full picture of intellectual functioning. Each of these aspects or dimensions has subdivisions (see *Intellectual Abilities* for a fuller account and diagram). These are as follows:

Operations: cognition; memory; divergent production; convergent production; evaluation.
Content: figural (form, size, texture); symbolic (e.g. letters, numerals); semantic (verbalized meanings).
Product: Units; classes; relations; systems; transformations; implications.

The permutations of these give the factors of which intellect is composed. Merrifield *et al.* constructed fifteen tests for the investigation of problem-solving. 'They present problems in which the solver's general task is to start with situation information and goal information and to bridge the gap between the two.' This of course is rather a narrow definition of problem-solving, resembling that of Bartlett. On the view we have advocated here, there must be many problems in which the goal is not known. However: the results of these tests, when factor-analysed, were accounted for in terms of four of the structure-of-intellect factors, viz. Cognition of semantic units; cognition of semantic implications; divergent production of semantic transformations; evaluation of semantic implications. (See the fuller account for the meaning of these.) 'There was no evidence of a unitary problem solving ability.' Presumably, still less would there be so if the range of problems were widened. But even if this analysis turns out to be correct, as Forehand (1966) points out, it tells us little about the conditions for or deter- minants of problem solving. On the other hand we should beware of dismissing too lightly an approach that may suffer from being unfashionable. A *structural* approach, as opposed to a functional or a dynamic one, is only now beginning to be respectable again, as we see from the recent interest in Piaget. As far as thinking is concerned, Guilford's approach has, as it were, slipped in through the back door of practical testing.

REASONING

A number of experimenters have set out to pose situations which would enable them to investigate (more-or-less) conscious reasoning processes. There is no sharp distinction between these experiments and those we have already discussed, except in so far as the latter generally started simply with a problem in order to see how it was tackled—possibly by reasoning, possibly not. The situations we now want to mention have often made use of logical propositions or relations. Then attempts are made to see what factors affects the ability to deal with these, apart from such individual differences as intelligence level or training in formal logic.

For example, Morgan and Morton (1944) gave their subjects logical proposi- tions in which the terms were either letters, or emotion-arousing words related to wartime interests. About a third of the responses seemed to be affected by this—i.e. a logically invalid conclusion might be accepted as true if it agreed with some strongly-held belief. Another phenomenon that has been discussed off and on for many years is the 'atmosphere effect'. Woodworth and Sells (1935) proposed the hypothesis that the global impression or atmosphere of the premises is an important factor in erroneous reasoning. 'An affirmative atmosphere in the premises makes it easy to accept an affirmative conclusion, etc.' Sells (1936) reported an experiment in which this was shown to be the case. Chapman and Chapman (1959) however, criticized his procedure, and reported contradictory results. This line of work has now been superseded by that of Wason and others (see below).

It might be thought that abstract formal logic is rarely used in real life (which is not to say it might not be more often used to advantage). Henle (1962) argues against this rather convincingly. She points out that while an older philosophical tradition regarded logic quite simply as the science of the laws of thought (the view criticized by Wertheimer, as we have seen); many more recent writers reject this. Cohen (1944) for example, writes: 'That the laws of logic are not the universal laws according to which we actually think is conclusively shown, not only by the most elementary observation or introspection, but by the very existence of fallacies.' Henle opposes this view, holding that fallacies are not necessarily due to *inability* to argue logically, but 'may be a function of the individual's understanding of the task or the materials presented to him'. Further, logical thinking is a necessity in the practical choices of everyday life, in communicating to others, reaching common decisions, and the like. Logical thinking is often involved in reaching a novel solution. Logic is 'a natural mode of functioning of the conscious mind'. With this, Wertheimer might well agree— his argument was that logic is not sufficient for productive thinking, not that it is not necessary. Freud too would probably agree—yet it may be partly due to the influence of psychoanalysis, with its emphasis on the irrational nature of unconscious thought, that logic has had a period of psychological unpopularity. We should note also Piaget's account of the logical structures which he holds underlie adult thought.

In a series of elegant and novel experiments, P. C. Wason has examined deductive reasoning, and particularly *the logical* relation of *implication*.

He has presented subjects (undergraduate students, therefore highly intelligent) with somewhat deceptively simple situations in which they have to prove the truth or falsity of a statement. For example: a subject is presented with four cards, bearing the symbols D, A, 3 and 8 respectively. He knows there is always a letter on one side of a card, and a number on the other. His task is to say which cards have to be turned over in order to find out whether the following sentence is true or false: 'if there is a consonant on one side of the card, then there is an even number on the other side'. Here it is convenient to use some simple terms of symbolic logic, viz.

$P = P$ is the case
$\overline{P} = $ not $P = P$ is not the case
$P \supset Q = $ If P, then Q. (This is the formal statement of the relationship of implication).

Sentences like the one just given are of the form: If P, then Q. From this it follows that the combination of events PQ is valid (if there is no consonant, P, there may still be an even number, Q); but the combination $P\overline{Q}$ is invalid.

The correct answer would be to turn over the consonant and the *odd* number. It turns out however that most subjects select the consonant and the *even* number, i.e. the ones mentioned in the rule. Very few subjects choose the odd number even though a consonant on the other side of an odd number ($\overline{Q}P$) will falsify the rule. The choice of the even number is perhaps understandable since although a vowel on the other side of it will not falsify the rule, a consonant will at least corroborate it. The failure to choose the odd number ($\overline{Q}$), however, seems to be very hard to eradicate, and most subjects will only admit it to be relevant (i.e. achieve insight) when actually faced with a consonant on the reverse of an odd number (Wason, 1969). Even if the experimental procedure is modified so that all the information is presented face upwards but with only one half exposed (to overcome the difficulty which some subjects experience in recognizing that 'the other side' of a card can be the one which is now face upwards), there is still no improvement in performance (Wason and Johnson-Laird, 1969).

Wason argues that these results raise a number of interesting questions about traditional views of cognition. The first concerns Piaget's theory of 'formal operations' which will be described more fully later (see *The Geneva School*). Briefly, Piaget holds that one aspect of intellectual development in adolescence is the capacity to handle hypothetical propositions about abstract situations. Wason's subjects should have been able to consider the *possible* combinations of values which could be present on the cards in front of them and make their selection accordingly. This of course is exactly what they do not do. It is not until they are faced with the perceptual evidence of P with $\bar{Q}$ that most subjects will select $\bar{Q}$. And encouraging subjects to think hypothetically about the various possible outcomes of turning the cards over is only successful in a limited number of cases. (Wason, 1969.) Wason argues that this is evidence for some form of 'cognitive regression'.

Secondly, it appears that some subjects, at least, are not able even to apply the Piagetian operation of *reversibility*, which is said to be achieved well before adolescence. For example, a subject can agree that $\bar{Q}$ on the other side of P falsifies the rule, while at the same time denying that P on the other side of $\bar{Q}$ does so. This is illustrated by the following protocol in which the rule is: 'Every card which has a red triangle on one side has a blue circle on the other side':

'E: Your task is to tell me which of the cards you need to turn over in order to find out whether the sentence in front of you is true or false.

S: A red triangle on one side ... although there were some in which both sides were red ... I don't know how many of them. At present we have two cards which could satisfy those conditions ... so you only have two cards to choose from: the red triangle and the blue circle.

E: What could be on the other side of the red triangle?

S: A red circle or a blue circle.

E: If there were a red circle on the other side, could you say anything about the truth or falsity of the sentence?

S: It would be untrue.

E: And if there were a blue circle, could you say anything about the truth or falsity of the sentence?

S: It would be true.

E: By the way, what was your choice of cards to turn over in order to find out whether the sentence in front of you is true or false?

S: The red triangle and the blue circle.

E: Are you quite happy about this choice?

S: Quite happy, as the other two do not agree with the statement made.

E: What could be on the other side of the red circle?

S: A red triangle or a blue triangle.

E: If there were a red triangle on the other side, could you say anything about the truth or falsity of the sentence in front of you?

S: The statement would be meaningless because it doesn't apply (sic).

E: In fact, it would be false.

S: It could be, but you are not doing it that way round. The statement would be untrue in any case, no matter what is on the other side (sic).

E: If there were a blue triangle on the other side, could you say anything about the truth or falsity of the sentence?

S: No.

E: Are you quite happy about needing to turn over just the red triangle and the blue circle in order to find out whether the sentence is true or false?

S: Yes.

E: Please turn over the red triangle and the blue circle and tell me whether the sentence is true or false.

S: The sentence is true.

E: I am now going to turn over the red circle, and I want you to tell me whether you still think the sentence is true.

S: Wait a minute. When it's put like that the sentence is not true. Either the sentence is true, or it is not true. You have just proved one thing and then you have proved the other. You've proved a theorem and then its corollary, so you don't know where you are. Don't ask me about the blue triangle because that would be meaningless.

E: Are you quite happy about needing to turn over just the red triangle and the blue circle in order to find out whether the sentence is true or false?

S: There is only one card which needs to be turned over to prove the statement exactly: the red triangle. Strictly speaking, you don't need the blue circle. You must find every card with a red triangle on it and turn it over, but there is only one.

E: But you just said when the red circle was turned over the sentence was false.

S: That is doing it the other way round.

E: The problem is very difficult. Very few people get it right. What we are interested in is why they don't get it right.

S: I am a member of Mensa. I wasn't going to tell you that until afterwards.'

I have a good deal of fellow-feeling for this subject, both as a member of Mensa (the society of allegedly high intelligence), and as one who was easily baffled by some of Wason's earlier problems. Wason comments: 'This subject had no difficulty in immediately mentioning the stimuli which could be on the other side of the cards—he did not prejudge the truth of the test sentence. What he evidently could not do was to admit the consequences of the falsifying contingency when the card was the "wrong way up".'

These results are fascinating, and open up a new approach to at any rate some types of problem solving. I am not sure though that the criticism of Piaget is entirely justified, since that theory, as I understand it, merely states that logical thinking is impossible *before* the necessary operations have developed. It does not suppose that logical thought is inevitable after that. Wason has been attacked, also, for the artificiality of his situations. N. E. Wetherick (1970), for example, argues that they are 'mere brain-twisters'.

SOME REMARKS ON PROBLEM-SOLVING

Of the various categories into which we have more-or-less arbitrarily divided our subject-matter, 'problem-solving' has perhaps the best claim to be considered synonymous with 'thinking' itself. But conversely it is possible to restrict the definition, and this at first sight offers more hope of bringing some order to the material. Davis (1966) with whose paper we started our discussion, makes a case for regarding all problem-solving as trial-and-error learning, in the sense that 'correct responses are selectively reinforced and incorrect responses are not reinforced'. Perhaps the most significant difference between problem solving and other forms of learning is that, in most problem-solving tasks, the response alternatives are not clearly defined for the subject. Therefore, from the problem stimuli presented, and instructions concerning the goal, the subject generates his own hierarchy of response alternatives, which he sequentially tests and rejects until the correct response, or correct combination of responses, is rewarded via solving the problem. But we can distinguish two types of problem, Davis argues, according to whether the trial-and-error is overt (Type O) or covert (Type C). In the latter, there are response alternatives whose functions are known. The problem is solved by covertly testing and rejecting these alternatives. Examples would be anagram problems; Luchins' water-jar problems; 'insight'-type problems. In Type O problems the outcomes of the response alternatives are *not* known to the subject, who must begin with covert trial-and-error to acquire the necessary stimulus–response outcome associations. This may be followed by covert testing. Examples would be classification, i.e. concept identification problems; and, presumably, Wason's reasoning problems. The main differences between the two types of problems, Davis says, can be summarized thus:

Type C	Type O
Outcomes known	Outcomes not known
Behaviour unobservable	Behaviour observable
Tasks usually concrete	Tasks usually abstract
Mentalistic concepts (set, insight)	Behaviouristic concepts (S–R associations)

One virtue of this analysis is that it does indicate some continuity between what has often seemed a very heterogeneous set of situations. On the other hand some may feel that it is really Type C problems that are legitimately called 'thinking', those of Type O being better classified as 'learning'. Another way of ordering the mass of material has been offered by Sir Frederic Bartlett (1958). Bartlett is concerned with thinking as a whole, not just 'problem-solving'; but his analysis, which will be mentioned again later, is certainly relevant here. Bartlett begins by arguing that we can regard thinking 'as an extension of evidence, in line with the evidence and in such a manner as to fill up gaps in the evidence'. Thinking is essentially a gap-filling activity, and there are three kinds of such processes.

> 'In the first the gap is filled by interpolation, in the second by extrapolation, and the third requires that the evidence given should be looked at from a special, and often from an unusual point of view, and that it should be recomposed and reinterpreted to achieve a desired issue.'

The last part of this is reminiscent of Gestalt writers; but Bartlett always took an independent line—and one which often enough has not received the attention it deserves. Here, his thesis is to draw a parallel between thinking and perceptual-motor skills. It is not just a similarity, however:

> 'When we say, as we now—I should claim—certainly can truly say, that thinking is an advanced form of skilled behaviour, what we mean is that it has grown out of earlier established forms of flexible adaptation to the environment and that the characteristics which it possesses and the conditions to which it submits can best be studied as they are related to those of its own earlier forms.'

This interesting line Bartlett develops through experimental studies, which we shall not, however, discuss here.

In everyday usage such phrases as 'I've got a problem' or 'He's a bit of a problem' indicate a wider range of situations than has been subjected to laboratory investigation. One who is good at solving problems would normally seem to be one with a large repertoire of responses and a high probability of making the right selection. The larger the repertoire, the larger the range of problems that can be dealt with. This may be a matter of training or experience. One point which Bartlett might have made in support of his thesis is the way in which some skills, at least, have been shown to continue improving, if slowly, for very long periods. (Crossman, 1959). This is plausible for some thinking activities such as artistic creativity and (possibly) statesmanship. One feels with elderly people that there is often a sense in which they are *wise*—or at least wiser than they were when young. In more traditional societies than ours, it would make sense to rely on their experience. But there is also the matter of choosing the right response, and this in real life is a vague criterion, as we rarely have a control condition. ('We were faced with the problem of Aunt Edna—we solved it by turning the spare room into a bed-sitter.') This suggests too the importance of emotional factors. Problems may be emotional in *content*. Indeed perhaps the majority of situations in which people are worried because they do not immediately know what to do are of this kind. Ability to solve such problems again often depends on having a greater repertoire of available responses. These may often be practical moves, which depend in many cases on education or money. And they may be social skills which have to be learnt. Lack of such a repertoire handicaps many 'problem families'. The other aspect of the relationship is that emotion may disrupt thought. Henle (1962) argued that motivational 'influences do not distort the reasoning process, as has frequently been stated or implied—indeed that they do not act at all on the reasoning process—but rather that they affect the materials with which thinking works'. Henle's next remarks are also very relevant.

> 'Although this is not the place for a detailed analysis, one or two specific effects of this kind may be suggested. (a) It may be that a strong attitude toward, or emotional involvement with, particular material is in part responsible for the difficulty which many unsophisticated subjects experience in distinguishing between drawing a conclusion that is logically valid and one that is believed to be correct. Over a wide range of practical situations these two tasks are not in conflict; and the distinction is thus not an easy one. There is evidence that attitudes and emotions may limit the ability to make distinctions (Henle, 1955). If this suggestion is correct, the more personally relevant the material employed, the more difficult it will be to accept the logical task. Such an effect might go a long way towards explaining the report of a number of writers that individuals are unable to reason logically about emotionally toned material. (b) An attitude can select from among the possibilities that the material presents, singling out, for example, one among several possible meanings.'

Another line of enquiry is suggested by Holsti (1965) who took as his material the diplomatic exchanges between the Great Powers just prior to the 1914 war. He held the evidence to show that as tension increased, misperception of the situation became more marked. In particular, both sides became convinced that they had no choice or freedom of action. At the same time the content of the exchanges became more stereotyped. This suggests that stress had the effect of decreasing the available range of responses. And this certainly seems to correspond to common experience. The more stressful the situation, the less able one is to think of alternative solutions. (Although no doubt the effect follows the well-known Yerkes–Dodson pattern, viz. that arousal and performance are related in a U-shaped curve.) The responses of neurosis, both experimental and spontaneous, are typically stereotyped; and perhaps one common factor in several types of therapy is that a decrease in anxiety allows alternative ways of behaving to become possible. Perhaps another is that an overlearned 'skill' of behaving, and indeed thinking, breaks down when attention is directed to it, so that alternative skills can then be acquired.

Lewis *et al.* (e.g. 1967), have shown the problematic nature of many situations can be reduced by the use of *algorithms*. An algorithm may be defined as an orderly sequence of instructions for solving a problem. 'Its great merit is that it reduces the problem-solving task to a series of comparatively simple

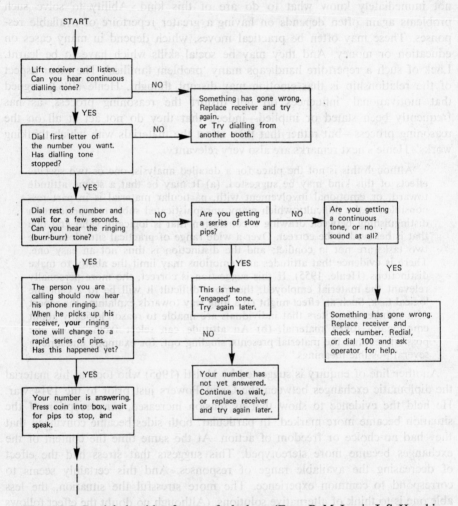

Figure 2.5. Partial algorithm for use of telephone (From B. M. Lewis, I. S. Horabin and C. P. Gane (1967). 'Flow charts, logical trees and algorithms for rules and regulations', *CAS Occasional Paper*, No. 2, H.M.S.O., London. Reproduced with the permission of the Controller of Her Majesty's Stationery Office)

operations.' These operations are usually choices between two alternatives. The algorithm can be set out diagrammatically, so that the subject is faced at each stage with two clear alternatives, and nothing more. He does not have to carry a host of conditions and forecasts in his head. (See Figure 2.5; and also *Models*.)

There would seem to be useful applications in instruction and in such puzzling situations as form-filling. Lewis *et al.* point out that 'being able to do something in the right way is often the best first step towards understanding'. Landa (1963) reported the successful use of algorithms to increase pupils' understanding of geometry. An algorithm is usually a device for getting someone to make the correct response; but it is also somewhat analogous to what a therapist does in getting a patient to face up to alternatives, and a sort of personality-insight program has actually been devised, and published as a paperback book. (Loewenstein and Gerhardi: *Meet Yourself as You Really Are*, 1942.)

FOCUS: NEGATIVE INFORMATION*

In these first chapters we have covered a great deal of ground, and it will have become obvious, as was pointed out earlier, that the lines dividing the experimental work considered under two separate headings are frequently blurred. The heading 'Reasoning', which we have used for one line of work, could well be said to apply to both chapters. It is one particular aspect of 'Reasoning' that we wish now to consider in some detail.

As we saw in Chapter 1, Bruner, Goodnow, and Austin (1956) noted that subjects found it difficult to deal with negative instances. In effect, they preferred to be told which attributes *were* involved in the concept rather than which were *not*. They could solve a problem more easily if they were told, by presentation of a positive instance, that red was an attribute of the concept; than if they learned from negative instances that black and green were not. Both Smoke (1933) and Hovland (1952) had observed similar difficulties in their subjects. Hovland found this even when the amount of information available from positive and negative instances was logically equivalent. A related phenomenon observed by Bruner *et al.* was the difficulty subjects experienced with instances providing *indirect* evidence that an attribute was irrelevant. For example, if both red and green appear in positive instances of a conjunctive concept, it can be inferred from this that colour is not a relevant attribute. Many subjects however preferred in addition to 'test' a black card in order to have direct evidence that none of the three colours was relevant.

This difficulty subjects have in handling negative information has provided

* A great deal of more recent relevant material has been published since this section was first written. For a discussion of it, the reader is referred to Wason and Johnson-Laird (1972).

the impetus for further research within the concept-identification experiment tradition. Freibergs and Tulving (1961) have shown that, *with practice*, subjects can solve problems consisting of negative instances in approximately the same time as they solve those with all positive instances. On the whole however no really clear-cut conclusions seem to have emerged about the 'negative information effect' from concept identification studies. On the other hand an inability to cope with negatives of various kinds has been found to occur in a variety of other experimental settings, and it is to some of these that we now turn.

We begin with the experiment of Wason (1960, 1966) mentioned in Chapter 1. Here subjects had to generate their own instances, and were told in each case whether or not they conformed to a rule. As we saw, Wason's subjects were unwilling to generate negative instances, i.e. instances which were negative as far as their own hypothesis was concerned; and it is only negative instances which can provide a conclusive test of the hypothesis. Two points can be made about this. The first is that subjects seemed to disregard the possibility that the positive instances they generated could conform to *more than one* rule. And secondly, it seems that subjects may regard negative instances as potentially less informative than positive ones, or even irrelevant altogether.

Wason's experimental studies of deductive reasoning mentioned earlier in this chapter throw further light on this latter point. Here, it will be remembered, subjects trying to prove or disprove a rule, rarely made the move that could falsify it. Given a statement such as: 'If there is a constant on one side of the card, then there is an even number on the other', they rarely chose to turn over a card with an *odd* number on it, even though if there turned out to be a consonant on the other side, the rule would be shown to be false. In symbolic logic terms, subjects fail to select 'not Q' ($\bar{O}$). One suggestion put forward by Wason to account for this very enduring error is that subjects *expect* the statement to be true because, generally, what people say *does* correspond to how things actually are. In Wason's terms they 'project truth'. This is borne out by many subjects' protocols. On the other hand, attempts to encourage the subject to 'project falsity' by asking him what letters (or numbers), if any, on the other sides of the cards would make the statement false, were to no avail (Wason, 1968). In another experiment, using a 'contradiction procedure', Wason, 1969, in the first instance encouraged subjects to imagine what values *could* appear on the other sides of the cards. If the subject still did not choose $\bar{Q}$, the card was turned over for him to see that P was on the other side of it (i.e. the rule was false). This procedure did in fact produce an increase in the number of times $\bar{Q}$ was chosen. It remains true, however, that in this experimental situation the subject does not spontaneously choose Q, and that one important contributory factor seems to be an initial projection of truth.

In the experiments we have just considered, the rules are all rather abstract, and it could be argued that this in itself is sufficient to confuse the subject and to prevent him showing spontaneous insight. Johnson-Laird and Wason (1970) have reported two experiments which examine the importance of the 'concreteness' of the task in determining the level of performance, one of which we have described earlier. In this, subjects had to prove that the rule 'If they are triangles then they are black' was either true or false, using boxes containing circular and triangular shapes. Whether the rule is to be proved true or false, the contents of the black box are irrelevant. The correct response is to examine all the contents of the white box; and insight can be said to occur when the black box is abandoned. All 28 subjects eventually did this, most of them fairly easily. Therefore this 'concrete' task seemed to be easier than the abstract ones. It raises the question whether insight into the logical relation of implication had been permanently gained. The Gestalt concept of insight implied that restructuring, once achieved, is not normally reversed. In this case, has the tendency to avoid the negative ($\bar{Q}$) been overcome? The second experiment reported by Johnson-Laird and Wason (1970) provides evidence that such is not the case. As the authors had concluded that the first experiment was too easy, they made the second considerably harder. The materials were cards each bearing four dots, which could be connected according to rules of varying degrees of complexity. The following instructions were given:

> 'I want you to imagine that I have taken some of these diagrams and put them in an envelope, sealed it, and then written a description of all the diagrams it contains.... Of course, I haven't put all the diagrams in the envelope and the description might also apply to some of the diagrams left outside the envelope.... Your task is to discover whether my description of the contents of the envelope is true or false. The way you will do this is by picking out, one at a time, those diagrams which you want information about. I will tell you whether each diagram you choose is inside or outside the envelope.'

The descriptions, or rules, whose truth or falsity had to be tested, were of three degrees of complexity, viz.

1. Doubly-quantified rules.
(a) Every dot is connected to some dot or other.
(b) No dot is connected to every dot.

2. Conjunction or disjunction of doubly-quantified rules.
(c) There is a dot which is connected to a dot but no dot is connected to every dot.
(d) There is a dot which is not connected to any dot or every dot is connected to every dot.

3. Triply-quantified rules.
(e) There is a dot connected to a dot to which another dot is connected.
(f) Every dot is connected to a dot to which another dot is connected.

The most difficult of these turned out to be (d). The crucial point about this procedure is, once again, that only negative instances are informative. The location of positive instances is unimportant since the description might also apply to some of the diagrams left outside. The subject must consider the alternative diagrams, decide which ones are positive and which negative instances of the description or rule, and inquire as to the location of the negative ones. Subjects were able to achieve the insight that only negative instances were important, only to lose it again when faced with a more difficult rule.

Johnson-Laird and Wason have this to say about these results:

> 'All the evidence from the previous experiments suggests that implication is a difficult concept to grasp fully, and perhaps when it is grasped, it is difficult to hold. When the subject is confused by too much noise, in the form of irrelevant complexity, he may well fall back on the more primitive "matching responses" . . . In Experiment II "matching responses" would of course result in selection of only positive instances. Implication critically involves the appreciation of negation, and negation is a second order, a more sophisticated concept than affirmation, in which a simple match exists between perceptual data and logical relation.'

A third set of experiments relevant to this issue relates to the role of linguistic processes in reasoning. If a subject is required to say whether a sentence like '29 is not an odd number' is true or false, an interesting interaction between the *meaning* and the *validity* of the sentence emerges. It takes less time to respond to true positives (29 is an odd number) and false negatives (29 is not an odd number) than to false positives (29 is an even number) and true negatives (29 is not an even number). Moreover, on the whole, negatives take longer than positives (Wason, 1961; but see Trabasso *et al.*, 1971). Similar results have been reported by Gough (1966) and Slobin (1966) who presented subjects with sentences which had to be judged true or false with respect to a picture. One of the most pertinent conclusions that can be drawn from these data is that not all negative statements cause the same amount of difficulty. How may this be explained?

Clark (1969) reviewing his own and other experimental work on reasoning, invokes the 'Principle of Congruence' to deal with these findings. This is one of three linguistic principles derived from Chomsky's (1965) theory of grammar. Clark points out that in order to answer questions about a sentence we must know more than its 'surface structure', i.e. its phonological structure. We must also know about the more abstract 'deep structure'. It is this that tells us about the relationships embodied in the sentence: for example, that in 'John watched the monkey' it was John who watched, the monkey who was watched, etc. The Principle of Congruence says that in answering a question the listener searches through his 'deep structure' memory for information which is congruent with, i.e. which matches, the information asked for. It may be necessary to translate or modify the question before this can be done. Take the number questions in the preceding paragraph. Presumably part of what is stored about '29' is '29 is an odd number'. Therefore questions which ask whether or not 29 is an odd number can be checked directly, in one operation; while questions which ask whether or not it is an *even* number require two operations, since no directly congruent information is stored. And the experimental results, as we have seen, show that the latter questions do take longer to answer. In passing we might note that some of the Gestalt-influenced writers such as Duncker had spoken of finding a solution which 'matched' what was required. Clark's views have a similarity to those of Wason, whose 'primitive matching' seems to resemble seeking 'congruence'.

Wason (1965) approaches the issue from a somewhat different point of view, based on consideration of the natural semantic functions of positives and negatives. For example, the natural function of a negative is to deny that something is the case. This is often done in order to correct a misapprehension; and it is interesting to notice that in some languages (such as French and German) special words exist to stress the fact that a negative is being used wrongly—'si' and 'doch' (29 ist nicht ungerade—doch!)

A similar line has been taken by Greene (1970) who proposed that although positive and negative may be logically equivalent, their functions are different. Like Wason she argues that the natural use of negatives is to signal a *change* of meaning: 'A negative implies something about a prior affirmative, while an affirmative implies nothing about its inverse.' It follows from this that the use of false negatives is 'natural', but that of true negatives is 'unnatural'. Negatives are concerned with *relationships* between statements, or between statements and a particular state of affairs. Positives re concerned with the state of affairs. Greene reports two experiments in which subjects had to say whether two sentences were the same or different in meaning: for example, '*x* exceeds *y*: *x* does not exceed *y*' (different); '*x* exceeds *y*: *y* does not exceed *x*' (same). Pairs in which the meaning changed were called 'natural', and those in which it did not were called 'unnatural'. It was predicted that response times to the natural pairs would be faster than to the unnatural; and this was borne out by the results.

This experiment illustrates nicely the interaction which exists in language between *syntax* (grammatical arrangement) and *semantics* (meaning). It shows that while holding syntactical structure constant one can reduce the difficulty a subject usually has in handling negatives, by varying the semantic function. Greene's 'reversal of meaning' hypothesis cannot, however, deal with the fact that true positives are easier than false positives (which of course it was not intended to do). Clark's theory, on the other hand, accommodates all four possible true-false positive-negative combinations by the one Principle of Congruence. But Clark might find it hard to handle the results of Greene's second experiment. She argued that the greater ease of 'natural' pairs might be that in these, the second sentence is a simple negative transformation of the first; whereas in 'unnatural' pairs more than this transformation has been carried out—*x* and *y* have been reversed in position. This argument makes no mention of the semantic factors which Greene says are crucial, but merely states that the subject has to do more 'processing'. To test this, pairs of sentences were used in which the semantic function of a pair was 'natural' but the transformational status was varied. Thus: (i) 'x equals y: x does not equal y' and (ii) 'x equals y: y does not equal x'. In both these pairs the meaning changes, but in (ii) the second sentence is a more complex derivation of the first. If transformational complexity is the important variable then reaction times should be longer to the second type of pair. This was not the case, so it would seem that semantic factors, not syntactical, are the important ones. On the other hand this conclusion does rest on a failure to reject the null hypothesis, and there also remains a doubt as to whether it would have been possible to decide from structural, non-semantic, features of the sentences used that they were the same or different.

We are left, then, at the present time, with a good deal of evidence as to the difficulty of negative information, but no conclusive explanation. It has often been pointed out that in learning, positive reinforcement has a different role to negative. A reward not only encourages you; it tells you you are correct. Punishment merely rules out one of possibly many wrong responses. Thus if one regards thinking as a sort of extension of learning, positive information would seem to be more relevant. We have quoted the view of Davis (1966) that problem solving is a matter of emitting the right response, which is then reinforced. A similar view might be taken if we regard thinking, with Bartlett, as a skill. In both learning and practising a perceptual-motor skill, it is more helpful to be told when we are doing something right. A good instructor tries to make clear exactly what one should be doing, and uses negatives only where they help to point this out. He avoids listing all the faults we *could* be making, as that will only give the pupil wrong ideas. And as we have already seen (Hovland, 1952), negative information is in any case less effective, even when logically equated with positive. We have seen that the Gestalt conception of thinking bears some resemblance to that of Bartlett; but it concentrates on the manipulation of information already supplied. In rather vague terms, the manipulation is aimed at matching up to something—either some kind of 'good' structure (Köhler, Wertheimer), or some form derived from the features of the problem (Duncker, Maier). Once again, negative information has little role to play. As we shall see later, Piaget's theory of the development of thinking includes the concept of information as a sort of 'food' by which mental processes grow. This information is basically knowledge about the way things are; the permanence of objects, the conservation of dimensions such as quantity. It is not until near the end of the developmental story (in Piaget's view, at adolescence) that the capacity develops to handle *hypothetical* situations, and with this, the ability to test hypotheses by seeking what would disprove them. So we return to negative information, and can argue that it presents difficulties because, as Wason suggests, it is essential only to a more specialized and high-level type of thinking, namely scientific thinking.

79

We have noted Popper's now well-accepted view that the scientific usefulness of a theory is determined by its falsifiability. Seeking negative information to falsify a view is thus a feature of a rather unusual and advanced sort of information-processing, or thinking, which is hard to acquire and to practice consistently.

FURTHER READING

Berlyne, D. E. (1965). *Structure and Direction in Thinking.* Wiley.
Chance, M. R. A. (1960). 'Köhler's chimpanzees—how did they perform?' *Man,* **60,** 130–135. Reprinted in Riopelle, A. J. (Ed.) (1967) *Animal Problem Solving.* Penguin.
Scheerer, M. (1963). Problem Solving. *Scient. Am.* **208,** 118–128. Reprinted in Riopelle, A. J. (Ed.) (1967) *Animal Problem Solving.* Penguin.
Wason, P. C. and Johnson-Laird, P. N. (1972). *The Psychology of Reasoning.* Batsford.
Johnson, D. M. (1972). *A Systematic Introduction to the Psychology of Thinking.* Harper and Row.

Solution to 'River-crossing Problem' (p. 56).

To begin with, Boy 1 takes the other across the river and leaves him there. He then takes the boat back to the soldiers, one of whom takes it, on his own, to the opposite side. Boy 2 brings it back to the side with the soldiers, picks up Boy 1 and they return to the opposite bank. Boy 1 remains while the other takes the boat back to the soldiers, as before, and the cycle continues.

3

Creative Thinking

BEGINNINGS

Stuart Golann (1963) reviewing the literature on creative thinking, distinguished three issues requiring elucidation: What is creativity? How does it occur? and under what conditions does it occur? As we shall see, final answers have not been found for any of these questions.

The psychological study of creativity may be said to have begun with Sir Francis Galton. Galton may be ranked with Darwin and Freud as one who has, in recent times, most fundamentally changed our way of looking at human behaviour and experience. As C. D. Darlington (1962) points out, it has taken nearly a century to appreciate this, and the applications of Galton's ideas are still virtually unlimited. His contributions to psychology were multitudinous: but the great central theme was the problem of individual differences. A case can be made for saying that this is the most fundamental problem of psychology. The subject matter which we study is manifestly diverse, it is composed of individuals. The problem is to say whether such subject-matter can yield general laws, and if so of what sort. There appear to be two main answers to this, one of them having three varieties. The first answer is that of G. W. Allport (e.g. 1942) that the importance of individuals lies precisely in their uniqueness, and that while we can discover lawfulness within the history of any one individual, we cannot generalize from that case to others. In later writings, Allport (1961) modified this extreme view to some extent. The inadequacy of such general laws as we have for understanding a given individual is real enough. But Allport's view is mistaken for two reasons. One is that it seems a counsel of despair; and the other is that, as Eysenck (1953) has pointed out, *understanding* an individual, in a personal or clinical sense, is really quite a different under-taking to *explaining* his behaviour in some scientific sense. If we reject Allport's line we are left with the possibility of general laws, of which I suggest there are three possible sorts. The first is the actuarial or sociological law, it is what insurance or marketing companies do. They cannot predict just *who* will die at such and such an age, or buy a particular product; but they can say, often very accurately, *how many* will do so. The objection to this is that it is precisely the *who* question that the psychologist wishes to answer. The second sort of general law may be called the 'common properties' law. It is assumed that there are basic mechanisms of mind or behaviour which can be studied in any convenient individual. This was the approach advocated explicitly by Wundt and particularly by his pupil E. B. Titchener; and less explicitly by the hosts of experimenters who have established facts about short-term memory, or spaced practice, or whatever, from a sample of available students. The point about this is not that it is wrong, but that it has to be shown to be right. It is the approach of both physics and zoology. But physicists are by the nature of their science essentially concerned with the common properties of matter, which are not affected by chance variations of any significance. And for zoologists these are only a slightly greater difficulty. Behaviour, on the other hand, is necessarily an individual matter, and the recent revival of interest in cultural studies has shown how even apparently basic mental operations may vary with environment and, perhaps, heredity. The third answer is to try to establish dimensions along which individuals can be placed. There are several difficulties here also. One is, of course, that the dimensions used may turn out to be nonsense—and Eysenck (1953) presents a sort of obituary list of now forgotten attempts. Another is that the dimensions we have are still too broad to characterize any individual completely. Nevertheless this may well be the most profitable line. Even now, if we know an individual's score on a standard test of intelligence, we know quite a useful fact about him. From this fact alone little can be predicted; but all scientific predictions are arguably matters of probability, and we can give an estimate of the likelihood that the person will be able to do some tasks well, and others badly or not at all.

It was the genius of Galton, to return to him, to see the problem and to show how the third sort of law might be arrived at. As has often been told, Galton was inspired to start his investigations by the work of his cousin Charles Darwin. *The Origin of Species* showed how differences between varieties of living things could have come about: Galton wondered about those between different races and individuals. Differences between races were apparent in an age which saw explorers, Galton himself among them, venture at last to the most remote areas. But as for individuals, the received view was that, apart from a few idiots and a few geniuses, all were equally endowed, and achievements were mainly the result of hard work—'Self-help' in the famous phrase of Samuel Smiles. Darwin himself thought this, and said so in a letter to Galton telling him what a revelation the latter's work had been to him. Galton started from the now familiar statistical concept of the 'normal' distribution. This was originally devised by mathematicians to deal with the distribution of errors in astronomical observations. Quetelet (1835) began to show that measurements of the human body tend to follow the same distribution. Galton argued that since psychological characteristics must be based on physiological ones, they too should be normally distributed. He then divided his distribution into sixteen grades, and worked out how many persons should fall in each. This was the starting point of the researches published as *Hereditary Genius* (1869). The next step was to obtain observations of the actual numbers of people of varying degrees of mental capacity. Galton concentrated on the upper end of the scale, and took his original data from the British membership of the *Dictionary of Men of Our Time* (1865) and from the obituaries of eminent persons in *The Times* for 1868. From theory and data Galton put his rank of 'eminent' at one in 4,000 of the population. Galton's definition of genius was that of Johnson's Dictionary, viz. mental powers or faculties; or a man endowed with superior faculties. In order to explain the presence or absence of such faculties, Galton collected large numbers of pedigrees of persons eminent in all sorts of fields—the law, the Church, mathematics, rowing, north-country wrestling. He found a tendency for an eminent person in any field to be related to other similar persons. From this he concluded that superiority was mainly inherited. This now seems to be wrong, and indeed Galton can be criticized for not realizing the differences that cultural, socioeconomic and educational factors must make. Galton's genetics, too, were not correct, though on the right lines: he was ignorant, together with the rest of the world, that Mendel had just solved this problem. On the credit side, Galton produced two statistical concepts of fundamental importance: regression to the mean, to account for the fact that the normal distribution remains stable over time; and correlation, which besides being the basis on which factor analysis, and so the whole modern theory of psychological dimensions, rests, allowed the notion of partial causation to enter science. Like all of Galton's works, *Hereditary Genius* is well worth reading, teeming with facts and speculations. One particularly fascinating attempt was to compare the relative abilities of different races. By counting the numbers who attained eminence, or moderate superiority, or competence, and the numbers who fell below average, Galton was able to conclude that the negro races were two of his sixteen grades below the English, while the Athenians of 530–430 B.C. were two grades above. 'This estimate, which may seem prodigious to some,' says Galton, 'is confirmed by the quick intelligence and high culture of the Athenian commonality, before whom literary works were recited and works of art exhibited, of a far more severe character than could possibly be appreciated by the average of our race, the calibre of whose intellect is easily gauged by a glance at the contents of a railway bookstall.' What he would make of the present provision, one can only wonder. From his conclusion that ability was mainly inherited, Galton went on to recommend the deliberate improvement of the nation's resources by encouraging, in practical ways, the well-endowed to marry each other, and discouraging the more impoverished. But the science of Eugenics has never made much headway, partly due to the questioning of Galton's hereditary explanation, partly for political and ethical reasons, and partly, no doubt, due to a loss of Victorian certainty about what characteristics are in fact desirable.

Galton himself provides a highly relevant case study of creative thinking, being not only entitled to the epithet 'genius', but also technically extremely inventive. Despite his own distinguished heredity, one might argue that he was rather a product of that particular English milieu in which opportunity and challenge were nicely balanced, and the distinction between amateur and professional obliterated. But we must leave this extraordinary man, and note that after him, investigations of creative thinking were comparatively sporadic until fairly recently. The revival of interest has been largely due to the technological needs of the great powers, which have directly and indirectly led to large amounts of research. This revival may be conveniently dated to J. P. Guilford's now famous Presidential Address to the American Psychological Association in 1950. He began: 'I discuss the subject of creativity with considerable hesitation, for it represents an area in which psychologists generally, whether angels or not, have feared to tread.' A search of the Psychological Abstracts for the twenty-three years of its existence revealed only 186 references to creativity. He does not refer to Galton. A bibliography published in 1965 by T. A. Razik listed 2,088 creativity items since 1950; and the flood shows no sign of diminishing. One is reminded of E. G. Boring's estimate that at the present rate of increase, the United States would quite soon possess more psychologists than people. When Guilford spoke, his own research had been in progress for less than a year, and his results will be discussed later. Much of the research in this area has been on possibly non-typical samples. Smith (1968) analysed a sample of 105 studies published between 1956 and 1965, and showed that 60 per cent were on American university students, and 80 per cent on highly circumscribed populations. Such restriction is of course true of much psychological research. It may be somewhat less critical for creativity, since there is, as we shall see, at least some evidence from elsewhere.

This formidable literature can perhaps usefully be divided into four main areas, though these will overlap substantially. The areas we suggest are: attempts to test or assess; analyses of the process; attempts to improve; and analyses of the conditions.

ASSESSMENT

An early set of tests of creative thinking was devised by Chassell (1916). It included some items like those of conventional intelligence tests, e.g. cat is to mouse as hawk is to ? Other items were directly concerned with inventiveness, e.g. invent a device for turning the pages of sheet music (it is not recorded whether any of those were successful—presumably not, at least commercially). And others were 'imaginative', e.g. imagine the effects of cutting along a Möbius strip (a strip of paper, etc., with one end turned through 180° and fastened to the other). Such tests, while ingenious, had the obvious disadvantages of being quite unstandardized. It is, perhaps, even easier to invent plausible-looking tests of creative thinking than of intelligence; but harder to make them valid and reliable. *Reliability* refers to the consistency of a test, the degree to which it will theoretically yield identical results under identical conditions. *Validity* is concerned with the extent to which we know what a test is assessing. This is a more useful way of putting it than, as is sometimes said, that a valid test is one that measures what it is supposed to measure. This is because that statement leads to the supposition that something corresponding to what we set out to measure must exist. This is by no means certain: in the present case, for example, Berlyne (1965) argues that there *is* no special category or process of creative thinking. Another issue which test-makers must face is, whether it is essential to base tests on some general theory, or whether it is sufficient to use any more or less *ad hoc* techniques, so long as they turn out to predict behaviour in some other relevant situation.

As far as creativity is concerned, the general theory view has been advocated most strongly, and indeed voluminously, by Guilford and his coworkers. As we have already briefly noted, Guilford's theory rejects the idea of one main cognitive ability with a number of subsidiary, specific, abilities. It is proposed instead that all intellectual activities can be considered as being organized along three dimensions: operations, content, and product. (See *Intellectual Abilities.*) Each dimension is subdivided, and this structure can be thought of as a cube composed of a number of smaller cubes. Each cube represents an intellectual factor or ability; and some six of these are closely related to creativity. One important general point which Guilford made on the basis of this analysis, was that conventional intelligence tests dealt with only one group of abilities. Specifically, they demanded 'convergent' thinking: all the test items were such that one answer only is correct, and all others, even possibly better ones, are wrong. The testee is given no credit for devising original answers. If creativity is to be measured, Guilford argued, tests must be made of divergent thinking: tests on which there is not just one correct answer, but to which several, perhaps unlimited, different answers may be made. Somewhat similar points had in fact been made by earlier writers. For example Selz (1913) used the terms reproductive and productive thinking to distinguish the cases where new ideas were produced from those where they were not. Bartlett (1958) says: '... it would seem that, when a thinker is working in an open, or relatively open, system, he inclines to prefer the evidence which releases the greater rather than the smaller number of possibilities'. These writers, however, were not concerned to devise tests. Divergent test items have become widely used in various contexts, and include, for example, asking for as many synonyms as possible for a stimulus word; as many uses as can be thought of for some common object such as a brick; as many objects as possible with some common property such as whiteness or hardness. Usually a time limit is imposed. This convergent–divergent dichotomy is perhaps one of those psychological concepts that have taken on a popular life of their own (like IQ, introversion, conditioning) and acquired in the process evaluative overtones, so that we rather feel we *ought* to think divergently. This is certainly not necessarily so. Moreover, Guilford's theory certainly does not include the concept of two sorts of people, creative and noncreative, who think divergently and convergently respectively. Guilford (1963) states:

> 'I formerly believed that the most conspicuously creative abilities are to be found in the general category of divergent thinking, with the exceptions of the factors of redefinition, which are in the convergent thinking category, and the factor of sensitivity to problems, which is in the evaluative category. I have suggested that, although these factors seem to represent ways in which creative thinkers are to be distinguished from other thinkers, many other intellectual abilities may play roles from time to time in the creative person's work. Among the other factors it now seems that the layer in the structure of intellect having to do with transformation should be given special consideration. This category includes such factors as visualization, redefinition, and judgment.'

Kettner, Guilford, and Christenson (1959) described the factors related to creative thinking as: ability to see problems; fluency of thinking; flexibility of thinking; originality: redefinition; elaboration. The apparent obviousness of this list is deceptive. These names are just the most plausible titles for factors resulting from factor analysis of subjects' performance on various tasks. But they also correspond to cells in the structure of intellect theory.

However, the existence of correlations between test items, even when predicted, does not prove the existence of a 'thing' intelligence, or originality. There is the further difficulty of discovering whether the factors relate to any behaviour that could be classified as creative. One attempt which Guilford (1963) has reported to investigate this, involved asking a group of thirty-five 'recognized creative scientists' (mostly with a physics or engineering background) to rate twenty-eight of the most likely factors derived from the structure of intellect model, for their importance in creative work. The subjects were given a non-technical definition of each with an example. The four rated highest were as follows:

1. *Technical name*: Divergent production of figural transformations.
Non-technical definition: To abandon conventional problem-solving methods that have become unworkable and to think of original solutions.
Example: Putting the eye in the point of the needle to make the sewing machine possible.

2. *Technical name*: Cognition of semantic transformations.
Non-technical definition: To see beyond the immediate and obvious.
Example: Recognizing that modifying the 'airplane' itself may be a better solution to the problem of landing high-speed jets than lengthening the runways.

3. *Technical name*: Cognition of semantic systems.
Non-technical definition: To comprehend the nature of the basic relationships inherent in a problem preparatory to solving it.

Example: Recognizing that sales may be increased by reducing the price of an object but that maintaining profits also requires reducing the unit production costs.

4. *Technical name*: Convergent production of symbolic transformations.
Non-technical definition: To recognize that the elements of a structure can be reorganized in such a way that they will have new functions.
Example: Seeing that an algebraic equation, having been factored in one way, may be factored in another way if the terms are rearranged.

Of these results one may say that, while interesting, they are quite likely to be misleading, due to the subjects misunderstanding either the factors, or themselves, or both. The first factor is practically a layman's definition of creativity in itself, and most scientists would doubtless like to think it characteristic of themselves. Technically, factors 1 and 2 are quite distinct; but for someone not familiar with the model, it is hard to see a difference between 'to think of original solutions' and 'to see beyond the immediate and obvious'. This is only one investigation, but it does illustrate the gap that often seems to occur between theory and reality. And even if the factors can be reliably tied to creative work, Guilford (1963) himself warns: 'To a very large extent certain intellectual abilities should determine what the scientist is *able* to do. His motivation, and his environmental opportunities, help to determine what he *will* do. This could well apply *a fortiori* to scientists' performance on tests. To these points we shall return later.

Let us look next at one of the most controversial of the studies stemming largely from the convergent–divergent suggestion. This is the well-known work of Getzels and Jackson (1962). They took as their subjects 449 adolescents from a mid-Western school in the United States, and gave them a standard intelligence test (Binet, WISC, or Henmon–Nelson), and five creativity measures:

(a) Word association: as many as possible to common words.
(b) Uses for things.
(c) Hidden shapes. Finding a geometric figure hidden in a more complex one.
(d) Fables. Subjects had to supply a moralistic, a humorous, and a sad ending for each of four fables.
(e) Problems. Subjects had to construct problems which could be solved with certain supplied information.

On the basis of these measures, two groups were selected:

Group 1. $N=26$. In top 20 per cent for creativity, but below top 20 per cent on IQ.
Group 2. $N=28$. In top 20 per cent for IQ, but below it for creativity.

These two groups were then compared in various respects. (1) The school achievement scores of the two groups were equally superior to those of the school population as a whole, which, be it noted, had a mean IQ of 132. (2) Teachers rated the high IQ group as more enjoyable to have in class. (3) There were no differences on need for achievement (nAch) between the two groups, or between them and the rest of the school. (4) Subjects ranked a number of personality characteristics for desirability. The only big difference concerned 'sense of humour' ranked last by the high IQ group, which seems hard to believe, but second by the high creatives. (5) This result leads on to more qualitative differences. The nAch stories (written about some of the ambiguous pictures used in the Thematic Apperception Test) were analysed for other themes besides achievement; and the creative subjects made greater use of stimulus-free themes, unexpected endings, humour, incongruities, and playfulness. We can quote one now well-known protocol.

> 'Here, for example, in response to the stimulus-picture perceived most often as a man sitting in an airplane reclining seat returning from a business trip or professional conference, are case-type stories given by a high IQ subject and a high-creative subject.
> *High IQ Subject.* Mr. Smith is on his way home from a successful business trip. He is very happy and he is thinking about his wonderful family and how happy he will be to see them again. He can picture it, about an hour from now, his plane landing at the airport and Mrs. Smith and their three children all there welcoming him home again.
> *High Creative Subject.* This man is flying back from Reno where he has just won a divorce from his wife. He couldn't stand to live with her anymore, he told the judge, because she wore so much cold cream on her face at night that her face would skid across the pillow and hit him in the head. He is now contemplating a new skid-proof face-cream.'

Other examples bring out a mocking attitude to conventional values—or perhaps, to the task. They seem convincing evidence: but of what? The 'creativity' measures are really *ad hoc* ones. All that can be said is, that two groups of subjects have been distinguished who differ in a number of respects, which form interesting syndromes but may or may not be related to creativity. That could only be established by follow-up studies. Getzels and Jackson concluded, among other things, that the present educational system fosters convergent as opposed to divergent thinking. But their study provides no real evidence for this, as we do not know what happens under other systems. Still less can one conclude from these data that the system inhibits creative thought. (In actual fact, one feels it may well do; but this study is not evidence for it.) We will take up the question of the relationship of creativity to education as a *Focus* topic.

Another controversy that Getzels and Jackson started, or at least helped to make prominent, is the relationship of creativity to intelligence. If you accept Guilford's theory, this is a pointless question to ask; and even if not, the creativity measures are not standardized in the same way as conventional intelligence tests, so a straight comparison does not necessarily tell us very much. Nevertheless a lot of studies of this kind have been made. Torrance in 1967 presented all the published correlation coefficients he could find, 178 of them. The median correlation was $+0.20$. As far as it goes, this value holds mainly for verbal tests of creativity. Nonverbal tests gave a median correlation of only $+0.06$. But it would be wrong to conclude from these figures that there is no relationship between intelligence and creativity. Rather, what seems likely is that a certain minimum level of intelligence is necessary, and after that it does not matter much. What the minimum level is, is not certain, but it may be quite low. This is the conclusion to which Barron (1969) comes, I think rightly.

Another issue raised by Getzels and Jackson was taken up by Wallach and Kogan (1965). They argued that the reported results might be confounded by the work being done in an atmosphere of school and tests. They stressed the playfulness that often seems necessary for creativity, and the interaction of emotional and motivational factors, such as anxiety and conflict, with emotional ones. Accordingly, studying primary school children, they had the teachers carry out the tests as part of normal lessons and games. Their measures of creativity were based on the assumption, deriving from a learning theory approach, that the essential feature is formation of associations. Test items included listing as many round things as possible, and specifying similarities between pairs of objects. Wallach and Kogan distinguished four types of children:

> *High creativity—low intelligence.* These children are in angry conflict with themselves and with their school environment and are beset by feelings of unworthiness and inadequacy. In a stress-free context, however, they can blossom forth cognitively.
>
> *Low creativity—high intelligence.* These children can be described as "addicted", to school achievement. Academic failure would be perceived by them as catastrophic, so that they must continually strive for academic excellence in order to avoid the possibility of pain.
>
> *Low creativity—low intelligence.* Basically bewildered, these children engage in various defensive maneuvers ranging from useful adaptations such as intensive social activity to regressions such as passivity or psychosomatic symptoms.
>
> *High creativity—high intelligence.* These children can exercise within themselves both control and freedom, both adultlike and childlike behaviour.'

One feels tempted to ask, Which of these, dear reader are you? Nevertheless the emphasis on factors other than merely cognitive, and on reactions to the situation, is, I think, right.

It characterizes also the work of Liam Hudson, which it is convenient to consider under the heading of "assessment" since that was its starting point, though it has wider implications. Hudson (1966) reported in *Contrary Imaginations* a five-year programme of research in which he tested each year about 150 fourth, fifth and sixth form (i.e. 14–18 years) public and grammar school boys in the U.K., who were thought to be potential University students. The University intake is about 15 per cent of the relevant age group in this country. These boys were given the AH5 test of general intelligence; tests of spatial reasoning, vocabulary, and general knowledge, and an interests questionnaire; and six tasks related to creativity. These were: a 'uses of objects' test; a 'meaning of words' test; a task in which they had to draw a picture suggested by the title 'Zebra Crossing'; a list of controversial statements on which they were invited to comment freely; a list of personal qualities to rate for desirability; and a short autobiography to write. Hudson's report has three main themes: an attack on conventional testing and oversophisticated statistics; the tests and their results, particularly in relation to the convergent-divergent issue; and a suggested explanation of creativity. The first seems somewhat wayward; the second interesting; the third also interesting, but dubious. Hudson complains, to begin with, of the triviality of much research, especially on testing, and the proliferation of vague or pretentious theories. These criticisms of psychology often have been, and still are, justified. Hudson is also right that 'the subtlest analysis in the world cannot make sense of poor primary data.' But the answer is not to throw away tests which do enable us to make better, though far from perfect, predictions. Still less is the answer to abandon statistics because: 'At present psychology is an exploratory science, and most of our statistical needs are simple.' On the contrary, our needs are much more complex than those of most other sciences, because we must necessarily deal with many variables. Indeed it is perhaps only with the advent of multivariate analysis that we begin to see how this may be done. This goes back to the basic issue over individual differences with which we began.

Hudson's actual investigations, giving as they do an insight into the thoughts and feelings of individual boys, are both ingenious and useful. But his results, like those of Getzels and Jackson, are derived from a highly selected sample: boys attending perhaps one of the most rigid forms of education to be found anywhere, and with a strong class bias. By way of conclusions, Hudson lists six generalizations about creativity that have been commonly held, and which he assesses in the light of general research, but particularly of his own. We shall paraphrase them, and his comments.

1. That conventional IQ tests are outdated. For the general population this is not so; but for very able people such tests become of little use. An IQ below 115 suggests lack of ability at science, but over 125 bears little relation to it. For arts, the figures are vaguer but probably lower: perhaps 100 and 115.

2. That we now have tests of creativity. Hudson holds, as I have already suggested, that this is not so. However IQ tests cannot be used in their place, in view of point 1.

3. That personal factors, not intellectual ones, are the most crucial in actual achievement. Hudson's data, as well as other findings which must be mentioned later, support this. We can compare Guilford's remarks already quoted. We want to know what factors cause a person to enter a given field, and, once in

it, to use his potentialities to the full. This theme Hudson takes up again in *Frames of Mind* (1968).

4. That divergers are potentially creative, convergers are not. This is an over-simplification. Convergent thinking is obviously likely to be important in some areas, and convergent thinkers are likely to be attracted to these—physics, mathematics, etc. Furthermore—it is rather a far cry fom divergence as measured by, say, the number of uses one can think of for a brick, to the ability to make a scientific or engineering discovery. What is required is not necessarily number of new ideas, but the *right* idea. Some creative people, at least, would seem to have few but good ideas.

5. That convergers are neurotic, divergers not. There seems to be little evidence here. And it is largely a matter of opinion, and custom, what is regarded as a good, and by implication normal, life.

6. That conventional education is hostile to creativity, but 'progressive' education is not. This is a complex issue: Hudson thinks that the evidence is insufficient, but that creativity probably is restricted by standard education.

Hudson's explanation of creativity, and some of his subsequent findings, will be discussed later.

We have suggested several times that there are no satisfactory tests of creative thinking. Such a statement can only be substantiated by proving a negative, involving reviewing all the many proposed testing techniques. Without doing this, one can say that a search of the literature reveals no test satisfying the usual criteria for well-established measures, and that a number of review articles reach the same conclusion.

Probably the most extensive range of tests is that developed by E. Paul Torrance, based initially on the structure of intellect model, at the University of Minnesota. Some of the main tests are these. (See e.g. Torrance, 1967).

> Incomplete figures: make a sketch incorporating some given lines.
> Circles: draw as many pictures as possible using a basic circle shape.
> Picture construction: draw a picture using a gummed coloured paper shape.
> Product improvement: think of improvements to a toy monkey or a dog.
> Unusual uses: think of uses for a common object.
> Ask and guess: give as many questions about, explanations for, and consequences of, a picture, as possible.
> Sounds and images: write down images and ideas brought to mind by recorded sounds.
> Impossibilities: list as many as possible.
> Consequences: imagine what would happen in various unlikely situations, such as if rain stood still in the air.
> Common problems: list problems that might arise in a common situation, such as taking a bath.

Goldman (1967) reviewing the Minnesota tests, reports some quite high reliability coefficients, both split-half (i.e. where half the test is compared with the other half) and temporal stability (two scores on the test with an interval between). Occasional coefficients of $+0.90$ are obtained, though there is wide variability. Validity is another matter, and Goldman reports no findings here that are at all convincing. One must agree with Vernon (1964):

> 'Just because a set of tests looks as though it involves creativity and gives lowish correlations with g, v, or k tests does not mean that it measures what we recognize as creativity in daily life, unless we can show that they actually differentiate between adults and children known on other grounds to be creative and noncreative, and that they are considerably more valid for this purpose than g or other tests.' (g is general intelligence, v verbal ability and k spatial ability.)

Similarly, Yamamoto (1965) reviewed a number of studies involving different techniques or criteria for validation. These included school or college achievement; ratings by supervisors; teachers nominations; peer nominations; work performance record; and psychiatric diagnosis (schizophrenics showed 'a marked impoverishment of imagination or creative thinking'). Yamamoto concluded that really satisfactory evidence was still lacking. And this, I think, is still true, partly due to some of the problems which will be discussed in the following sections.

ANALYSES OF PROCESS

The nature of the creative process is a question that has quite properly, and often very revealingly, attracted the attention of a very wide range of writers—biographers, historians, aestheticians, sociologists, inventors and so on, besides psychologists. There are perhaps four groups of approaches that are mainly 'psychological'. There are first those that do little more than state some apparent feature, such as 'seeing connections' or the like. It is perhaps not unfair to class Edward de Bono's (1967) 'lateral thinking' here. What we may term a *structural* approach has already been exemplified in the work of Guilford. Then we may group together a number of accounts as being mainly concerned with the *dynamics* of the process, i.e. supposing some kind of active force. And lastly the *associationistic* views deriving from S–R theories of learning. The accounts tend to be very diverse partly because there is no general agreement as to what is to count as creative. And here it is useful to consider the analysis made by Irving Taylor (1959) of 100 definitions of creativity.

He distinguished five levels of creative thinking, as follows. (1) The *expressive* level is a matter of 'independent expression where skills, originality, and the quality of the product are unimportant.' This is the level of free play. (2) The *productive* level is characterized by restriction and control of play, and by improvement in technique. Games, routine art and crafts, domestic skills such as cooking, could be productively creative. (3) At the *inventive* level there is flexibility in perceiving 'new and unusual relationships between previously separated parts'. It is the level of the new practical device or ingenious new method, art that is original rather than traditional or merely a copy. (4) *Innovative* creativity involves significantly modifying the basic foundations or principles underlying a whole field of art or science. Impressionism might be an example in painting, behaviourism in psychology. (5) *Emergentive* creativity is marked by the appearance of 'an entirely new principle or assumption . . . at a most fundamental and abstract level': relativity, for example.

These levels are obviously not hard and fast categories, but neither are they just points on a continuum. One would argue, I think, for qualitative differences between the child, the inventor, and the genius, and very probably quite different modes of thinking are involved. At the same time there may well often be an interaction between, say, fundamentally new thinking and a childlike playfulness, or a craftsmanlike skill. The analysis, while not offering explanations, does help to sort out some confusions. There is sometimes a tendency to think that artists, in particular, cannot be truly creative *unless* they are freely, independently expressive. On the other hand research has tended to centre, for economic and political reasons, on levels 3 and 4, and on science and technology. But the most difficult problems relate, perhaps, to the highest levels.

An early but influential analysis was offered by Graham Wallas (1926) who described four stages in creative thinking: preparation, incubation, illumination, verification. Several other writers have made somewhat similar analyses. Wallas's version received some support from the work of Catherine Patrick (1935, 1937) who asked professional poets and painters, and non-artists, to produce a picture or a poem to order. She was able to distinguish the four stages, though as interwoven processes rather than as a temporal sequence of events. One difficulty with this approach is that the first, the third and the fourth stages are really just names for what must take place—obviously one must think about the problem, have an idea, and check it out. The second stage, on the other hand, is an attempt to explain *how* the idea comes. Incubation, that is some sort of problem solving process going on outside of conscious awareness, is thus a supposed phenomenon for the existence of which evidence is required. Now it is true that it is common experience that solutions often appear after a rest period. But incubation is usually taken to mean more than this, namely that something has been happening *during* the rest period. Ghiselin (1952) gives accounts from several creative persons of the way in which their ideas have been formulated 'unconsciously'. Poincaré's mathematical solution while boarding a bus, and Kékulé's dream of the benzene ring, are well-known. Experimentally, however, incubation is hard to pin down. It might be that rest alone accounts for the effect, perhaps in some way allowing for dissipation of inhibition. Or it might be a case of massed versus spaced practice—it is common to find a problem cropping up in one's mind at odd moments. On the other hand incubation can hardly be considered as equivalent to having the mind distracted from the immediate task. Gall and Mendelsohn (1967), took subjects who had reached an impasse on problems drawn from Mednick's Remote Associate Test (see below), and gave them either distraction by a nonverbal task; or continued work on the problems; or free association to the elements of the problem. Continued work proved the most effective, a lesson to us all. This however illustrates the difficulty of such investigations, for anecdotal incubation is typically a long drawn out process. Uffa Fox, the well-known yacht designer, remarked that he often put unfinished plans away in his desk for six months or a year.

One implication of the idea that unconscious processes are somehow involved is that conditions thought to facilitate access to them should aid creativity. In particular large claims have been made for drugs of various sorts, by authors such as Huxley and Leary. Reference can be made to creative writers like Coleridge and De Quincey, both opium addicts. James Agate, the great critic, could only write on champagne. But such specialists are, perhaps, rare. The recent emphasis has been on 'psychedelic', hallucinogenic drugs of which lysergic acid diethylamide (LSD-25) is the best known and perhaps the most powerful. There is so far little reason to believe in their efficacy. Commenting on a file compiled by a Harvard research team, concerned with the effects of hallucinogens on creative abilities, Arthur Koestler (1968), who had himself tried the effects of LSD, concluded:

> '... not a single item contains anything of artistic merit or of theoretical value; and the drug-induced productions were all far beneath the writers' normal standards. ... While working on the material I was reminded of a story George Orwell once told me ... a friend of his while living in the Far East, smoked several pipes of opium every night, and every night a single phrase rang in his ear, which contained the whole secret of the universe; but in his euphoria he could not be bothered to write it down and by the morning it was gone. One night he managed to jot down the magic phrase after all, and in the morning he read: "The banana is big, but its skin is even bigger." '

The current wave of interest in drugs, many of which are themselves very ancient—for alcohol and marijuana, at least, have been used since prehistoric times—doubtless has highly complex causes. But I would suggest that it is relatively easy to confuse a subjective feeling of being highly creative with actual creative activity in the sense of producing new and viable artefacts or ideas. Then, too, there may be a sense in which some form of personality development, which may possibly be aided in some cases by drugs, can be considered creative. This will be particularly likely if it results in spiritual or philosophical utterances. Barron (1969) remarks that the popularity of mountain tops for purposes of spiritual revelation may be related to the toxic effects of oxygen shortage. Barron, however, makes the most positive assessment I have seen of the role of LSD in creative thinking. He quotes a number of studies as evidence for the often-quoted subjective effects, viz:

1. Intensification of aesthetic sensibility.
2. Unusual associational patterns are much more frequent.
3. Intuition in relation to other people is increased.
4. Higher purposes and the motivation to make one's life philosophically meaningful becomes very important.
5. A mystical experience of absolute freedom may occur.

Barron quotes a well-controlled study by McGlothlin, Cohen, and McGlothlin (1967) which did find a slight positive effect of LSD on performance of some of the Guilford tests of divergent thinking. More impressive evidence of creative activity is hard to come by while retaining experimental control. Harman *et al.* (1966) using highly trained engineers, architects, mathematicians, etc., claimed that a controlled administration of LSD aided in the solution of specific problems. On the other hand Zegans, Pollard, and Brown (1967; not quoted by Barron), reported a negative result, using an admittedly unselected group. One may suggest that the effects of any drug will be very strongly influenced by such factors as the subject's personality, training, and expectations.

Koestler (1964) while rejecting the drugs hypothesis, has presented his own theory of creativity which does involve unconscious processes. *The Act of Creation* is partly a vast and erudite compendium of accounts of creative activity from all sorts of sources. The theory does not consider 'the unconscious' as a sort of agency that does creative work for us; it is rather that certain processes are necessary for creation that are, as it were, unsuitable for conscious expression. These processes are of two sorts, catabolic and anabolic; or, they have two roles: 'first, to encourage a kind of promiscuous mixing of ideas, then to act as a matchmaker'. In everyday thinking we are bound by logical rules, by learned ways of doing things, set ways of expression. A sort of regression is necessary, such that 'the mind in labour is liberated from the tyranny of rigid, over-precise schemata; it is enabled to unlearn and acquire a new innocence of the eye, a greater fluidity of thought'. But then it is necessary for the right or productive combination of new ideas to emerge; and as to how this happens Koestler seems unclear. To be fair, I think no one has got very near to solving this central puzzle. The closest Koestler gets is to speak of mathematicians being guided by beauty rather than logic. This seems little more than another way of saying that creative people tend to guess right. It also follows from Koestler's analysis that skills and virtuosity impede creativity: they are 'at the opposite pole to creative originality'. I believe this is a misleading way to look at it, and prefer Kuhn's concept of an 'essential tension' between rules and change, which will be mentioned again later.

Koestler's account obviously owes a great deal to psychoanalysis, as must any theory that emphasizes unconscious processes. Freud's general notion about creative activity was, that it depended upon sublimation of instinctual energy; that is, diverting it from its natural outlet to productivity. The most detailed account of a case of this is his analysis of Leonardo da Vinci (Freud: *Leonardo*, 1910). He shows that Leonardo, as far as can be ascertained, led a sexual life markedly lacking in direct expression, and largely homosexual in orientation. This leads to an interpretation based on Leonardo's family circumstances, childhood fantasies, and artistic interests. As a general account of creativity, of course, it immediately raises two major problems: there are plenty of sexually inhibited people who are not in the least creative, and plenty of creative people who are if anything more active than average. Indeed Kris (1953) says:

> 'Psychoanalytic observation does not throw light on the puzzling question of natural gifts for art—either for certain skills, or for creative activity in general—and cannot directly contribute to an understanding of the level of performance. It only partly answers the question of why an individual turns to art as profession or preoccupation; ... But psychoanalysis can elucidate the functions which in an individual life art may fulfill.'

Nevertheless there do seem to be certain resemblances between some of the unconscious mental processes described by Freud, and those that appear often to be relevant to creativity. There is first of all the fact, stressed by Koestler, that great thinkers often report the inadequacy of what Freud termed the secondary processes—everyday, conscious, rational thought. The primary processes, on the other hand, as glimpsed for example in dreams, are non-logical, flexible, allusive, bizarre; thus they allow us to see things in a new light, or in new relationships to each other. Picasso made a bull's head from the saddle and handlebars of a bicycle. He said his hope was that someone on seeing this would say: 'Ah. I could make a bicycle out of that.' Surrealism, of course, was a whole school of art concentrating on dream-like images. Salvador Dali's paintings have the characteristics of hypnogogic imagery—bright, coloured, novel, etc. Scientists—such as Einstein, quoted by Koestler—also speak of some kind of intuition of how things must be reorganized, the reasons for which have to be worked out rationally afterwards. Kris (1953) presents several anecdotal accounts of inspiration, such as this one from A. E. Housman:

> 'Having drunk a pint of beer at luncheon—beer is a sedative to the brain and my afternoons are the least intellectual portions of my life—I would go out for a walk. As I went along, thinking of nothing in particular. there would flow into my mind with sudden and unaccountable emotion, sometimes a line or two of verse, sometimes a whole stanza at once, accompanied, not preceded by a vague notion of the poem as a whole. Then there would usually be a lull and perhaps the spring would bubble up again. I say bubble up because the source of the suggestion thus offered to the brain was an abyss.'

Kris extends his coverage to scientific creativity:

> 'Scientific thinking is ... never sharply separated from the realms of the unconscious, and the psychoanalysis of inventors and research workers shows

that there is an intimate connection between these higher mental functions and unconscious wishes and desires and their infantile roots.'

This seems to be about as far as a purely psychoanalytic interpretation has so far been able to take the matter.

Donald Schon (1963) stressed the role of *metaphor* as 'the source par excellence of new ideas'. Metaphor in turn depends upon unconscious processes.

> 'We appear to have several routes of access to unconscious material. One is fantasy, the little playlets in which we are chief actors, that come unbidden to mind. Another is free association, the train of symbolically related thoughts that come in response to a stimulus when we let thoughts come, without attempting to direct them. Projection is a form of restricted free association, in which every association is built around the stimulus projected upon, and is in effect a different way of looking at that thing.'

Metaphor is considered a projective process. Schon's ideas were one source of the technique of *synectics* developed by Gordon, with whom he worked in market research and advertising. Another source we may discuss here is that of *brainstorming*. This is probably the best-known method of trying to improve problem-solving. It assumes that the source of creative ideas is unconscious, and that access to this source is usually inhibited by conventional taboos on expressing 'uncensored' material. Brainstorming is a group technique in which the members enter into an agreement to withhold their censure from each others' ideas. It is argued that a potentially good idea may seem silly at first, so should not be prematurely dismissed; and further, that the ideas of each member of a group will stimulate the others, producing a better flow of associations than could be achieved alone. Such was, essentially, the process as described originally by Osborn (1957). It has become widely used, but in practice is often little more than an unstructured discussion, or an excuse for a senior person to sound off. Even when properly applied, however, it is not really clear how many new ideas are generated.

A fascinating attempt to get closer to this problem, and apply the results commercially, has been made by William J. J. Gordon (1961) under the name *Synectics* (see also Prince, 1968).

> 'The word *Synectics*, from the Greek, means the joining together of different and apparently irrelevant elements. Synectics theory applies to the integration of diverse individuals into a problem-stating problem-solving group. It is an operational theory for the conscious use of the preconscious psychological mechanisms present in man's creative activity.'

The method involves drawing together a number of (ideally) specialists in different fields, who work together in a very close group, sometimes living in one house, cooking and eating together, etc. In synectics sessions, a leader directs participants at each stage, doing his best to stimulate and motivate them. There are two basic parts to the process: 'Making the strange familiar' involves absorbing the details of the problem to be solved, which is usually a fairly well-defined one occurring in an actual business or industry. Here specialist knowledge is useful. Then the group tries to find new ways of looking at the problem, or 'making the familiar strange'. For this, analogical thinking is used, four sorts of analogies proving particularly useful. It seems that these are to be thought of as 'psychological tools' which are relatively easy to use, since we have all experienced them, but which in some sense replicate what normally goes on unconsciously. *Direct analogies* are just ways of finding something that resembles the problem situation in some respect; but it turns out that for technical problems biological comparisons are often most useful. 'This is because the language of biology lacks a mystifying terminology, and the organic aspect of biology brings out analogies which breathe life into problems that are stiff and rigidly quantitative.' For example: the problem was to devise a roof to be white in summer, and black in winter, so as to reflect and absorb heat respectively. Weasels, chameleons, and flounders all change colour—the last suggested a roof surface of black material in which white plastic balls would rise or sink. *Symbolic analogies* involve finding a key word or phrase which expresses the essence of the problem situation, and which is sufficiently general to suggest other ideas; e.g. 'dependable intermittency' for a ratchet. *Fantasy analogies* involve supposing an ideal situation in which the problem would be solved, even if known laws of nature have to be suspended. Gordon points out the resemblance of this to Freudian wish-fulfilment, the difference being that the latter is an unconscious mechanism. *Personal analogies* require participants to feel themselves into the situation, to imagine they are literally part of it. Gordon presents some protocol extracts when the problem was to devise a constant speed mechanism, with input varying from 400 to 4,000 rpm, and output constant at 400 rpm.

'A: Okay I'm in the damn box. I grab the in-shaft with one hand and grab the out-shaft with the other. I let the in-shaft slip when I think it's going too fast so that the out-shaft will stay constant.

B: But how do you know how fast the out-shaft is really going?

A: I read a watch and count.

C: How do you feel in there?

A: Well, my hands are getting ... too hot to hold I guess ... at least one hand, that is ... the one that's acting like a clutch ... slipping.

C: B, how about you hopping into the box.

B: I see myself in there but I can't do anything because I don't have anything to measure rpm or time ... I guess I'm in the same spot as A.

C: How about you, D?

D: ... I'm in the box and I am trying to be governor ... to be a feedback system ... built in ... Let's see. If I grab the out-shaft with my hands ... and let's say there's a plate on the in-shaft so that my feet can press against it. I put my feet way out on the periphery of the plate and ... what I really would like is for my feet to get smaller as the speed of the in-shaft increases because then the friction would be reduced and I would hold on to the out-shaft for dear life and its speed might remain constant... The faster the in-shaft went the smaller my feet would become so that the driving force would stay the same.

C: How could you get your feet smaller?

A: That's not the way to ask the question... better say, "How keep friction constant?"

E: If for some reason, some anti-Newtonian reason, your feet came closer together on the plate as the speed of the in-shaft increases then your leverage would be reduced... I mean that you might keep the resultant force in the out-shaft constant.

C: I kind of go for that "anti-Newtonian" thing... we're fighting centrifugal force here.

E: How about a non-Newtonian liquid?... a liquid which draws near to the center of rotation instead of being flung out?

B: You'd have an anti-gravity machine.

E: Fine.

A: The only thing that gets closer and closer to the axis of rotation is a string with a weight on the end... a string tied to a stick. You twirl the string and it wraps around the stick till it gets shorter and shorter... finally you don't have any string left.

E: How about a liquid made up of many strings... or even better an elastic fluid... Listen! Imagine a fluid that's made up of a billion rubber bands. The faster the axis of rotation goes the more the rubber bands wind up on the axis.

C: You'd have to have those rubber bands sticking and unsticking all the time... or breaking and unbreaking, wouldn't you?

E: Maybe... maybe... but it's not nuts...

B: You know what I like about this crazy way to think about this? It's got a built-in governor... that's the trouble with present mechanisms. They're hooligans with tachometers and rpm measurers... a womb hung round with barking dogs... this damn anti-Newtonian liquid would tell itself when to take it easy.'

This and other protocols illustrate what appear to be some important features of the technique. There is a marked playful element, but the play is directed and highly motivated. Participants are emotionally involved and competitive. There also seems to be an element of release, specifically from the disciplines in which participants have been trained. The whole procedure, which the leader imposing bizarre and tension-creating tasks, is reminiscent in some ways of Zen training; and intellectual and emotional 'insight' seem to come together. Take the well-known koan (or *hua ton*) exercise, in which a goose is supposed to have entered a glass bottle when small, and grown too big to exit. How to get the goose out without harming it, or breaking the bottle? When the student has struggled sufficiently with his problem, the master reveals the solution, viz.: the goose is out. Strictly speaking, to explain this destroys its meaning; but I take it that part of what the master intends to convey is that what is supposed to be the case can equally well be supposed to be otherwise. Similarly in creative problem-solving: we start with a number of 'givens'—facts of the problem, scientific laws—but it is necessary, or useful, to enter a state where these can be altered at will. Convergent thinking is abruptly replaced by divergent; or more dramatically, the rules are broken—they were, in any case, imaginary.

The importance of analogies for creative thinking, at any rate in science, is stressed by Bartlett (1958) in a more limited sense than that of Gordon. He says: '... an experimenter ... must be strongly influenced by two sorts of consideration: what instrumentation is available to him at the time, and what use he can make of the nearest analogous case to his own.' Bartlett presents several interesting case-studies, but confesses that he cannot really understand how a creative thinker decides what lines to pursue and what to abandon. He thinks it may be some kind of 'matching' process, so that the thinker has a 'preperception' that certain results will not 'fit'. This of course is closely similar to the role which Bartlett attributed to *schemata* in *Remembering* (1932); and it is reminiscent of Duncker's work on problems. C. A. Mace once pointed out that artists too must know when to stop, and that it is as if a sort of homeostasis were operating—adjustments continue to be made until some kind of balance is achieved. Wertheimer too, as we have seen, stressed the importance of working towards a 'good' and satisfying state of affairs. It seems that Wertheimer would not make a sharp distinction between the bright five year old, and Einstein or Gauss, whom he also quotes.

In this respect, curiously enough, the gestalt view resembles that of learning theory. Berlyne (1965) for example, begins by adopting the distinction made by Selz (1913) between reproductive thinking and productive thinking, referring respectively to 'the kind of thinking that simply reproduces previous experience and the kind that generates new mental content'. Then in terms of Berlyne's S–R analysis:

> 'Reproductive thinking is what happens when responses suitable for the solution chain are already high up in the hierarchies that confront the thinker at the choice-points through which he passes ... Productive thinking, on the other hand, occurs when the sought-after responses are low in their respective hierarchies and overshadowed by stronger but less adaptive competitors.'

It is thus not quite clear what Berlyne means by 'new' contents—he seems to equate it to 'less readily available'. However, on this basis he argues:

> 'Creative thinking often receives special treatment as a phenomenon apart, but this practice seems unjustified ... For one thing, the distinguishing marks of creative thinking, in so far as they depend on social evaluation, do not imply that it depends on unique psychological processes. Second, creative

thinking is productive thinking and must surely be investigated in conjunction with noncreative forms of productive thinking, which, in their turn, cannot be fully understood until we know more about reproductive thinking.'

This assumption may or may not be justified. Some attempts have been made to work the general idea out in more detail. Mednick (1962) defines the creative process as 'the forming of associative elements into new combinations which either meet specified requirements or are in some way useful'. To assess the ability to do this Mednick has devised a Remote Associates Test (RAT), in which subjects have to supply associative links between apparently unconnected stimuli, such as *mouse, blue, cottage*: the link would be *cheese*. Scores on the RAT are reported to correlate with such criteria as ratings by research supervisors, and flow of ideas taken as numbers of words produced in a set time from a small group of letters. Mednick has several hypotheses about the way associations are organized within the individual. Some stimulus words may have stronger associates than others; individuals who have specialized knowledge in some areas will tend to have strong systems of associations in those areas, making it difficult for them to produce new ideas. This would tie in with anecdotal evidence, and with the techniques of synectics. Massed practice should be more effective than spaced in producing new ideas, since one has to work through the set of strong and close associations, as it were, each time one tackles the problem. This agrees plausibly with the anecdotal and other reports of the intensity and duration of creative work, as stressed by Anne Roe (see later). It is not clear how far these hypotheses have been tested; they would seem particularly appropriate for examination by the computer techniques devised by Kiss (see *Models*) to map associative networks.

Computer simulation brings us to the last analysis of creative processes to be discussed here. Newell, Shaw, and Simon, in a series of papers, have described computer programs that have produced, for example, proofs of the theorems in Russell and Whitehead's *Principia Mathematica* (1935)—and in one case a more elegant one than did the original authors. As will be pointed out when these studies are dealt with in more detail, this is unconvincing, principally because there is no real reason to suppose that the steps taken by the computer resemble those of mathematicians, unless we already know the latter.

ATTEMPTS TO IMPROVE CREATIVITY

We shall discuss here attempts to increase creativity within a fairly short time-span, rather than by long-term educational policies, which will be considered separately as a special issue. One might say that the simplest analyses of the process lead to the simplest methods of improvement. Thus Maltzman (e.g. 1960) adopting an S–R framework, reports a series of experiments with the relatively limited aim of increasing the frequency of uncommon responses.

A list of free association stimulus words is presented a number of times, with instructions that the subject is to respond with a different word each time. 'Under these conditions the responses become more uncommon. When presented with new stimulus materials, subjects receiving such training are reliably more original than subjects receiving no training.' This latter point is particularly interesting; and while the procedure seems quite a long way from creative thinking as we more usually consider it, it does suggest that it may be relatively easy to increase at any rate the availability of ideas. Davis and Manske (1966) in a small experiment, found that subjects produced more and better ideas in a uses of objects test, when they were asked to imagine themselves in specific situations. Sydney Smith was sure that one could improve a sense of humour by practice, and his wit consisted largely in a flow of unusual associations.

Berlyne (1965) developing his general associationistic theory of thinking, suggests how submerged responses may be strengthened. The first way is by extinction of more dominant responses, and this, Berlyne argues, is what happens in 'implicit trial-and-error'. Alternatively the weaker responses may be reinforced. This is illustrated by Saugstad's procedure for improving performance on Maier's problems (see *Problem Solving*). Thirdly a supplementary stimulus can have the effect of raising a response to a higher position in the hierarchy. An example is Maier's hints or helps to his subjects, such as brushing against the string in the pendulum problem.

Increasing the flow of ideas is as we have seen one of the aims of brainstorming. Parnes (1962) argues that the essential feature is that of *deferring judgment*, at least while the 'storm' is on. It then becomes a question as to whether this is more effectively done by groups or individuals. The evidence is unclear. Parnes (1959) concludes that groups are slightly better, and Barron (1969) is quite sure that they are. But Bouchard (1969) and Bouchard and Hare (1970) conclude 'the group brainstorming, over a wide range of group sizes, inhibits rather than facilitates creative thinking, and pooled individual effort is a more productive procedure than group effort'. As Barron (1969) points out, much may depend on the type of problem. Still more may depend on the participants and the setting—especially in view of Hudson's results discussed below. The position is even more uncertain when it comes to synectics, since this is an expensive and private business process whose results are not necessarily available in statistical form. Synectics would appear, however, to be commercially successful. These group techniques have been particularly popular in the highly competitive atmosphere of American business and industry. Not only is this calculated to increase motivation, but one might speculate that the effect of being suddenly allowed and encouraged to let one's ideas flow might well be much greater than in, say, an English university, where such freedom is a traditional value.*

* Among Peter Ustinov's famous reminiscences of his schooldays is that in response to the question 'Name one Russian composer' he wrote 'Rimsky-Korsakov'. He adds: 'That was wrong. The correct answer was Tchaikovsky.'

Hudson's studies of English boys in a rather rigid educational framework are relevant here. Consider the protocols from two highly talented boys on a uses of objects test—object, a barrel.

'S1: Keeping wine in; playing football.

S2: For storing old clothes, shoes, tools, papers, etc. For pickling onions in. For growing a yew tree in. For inverting and sitting on. As a table. As firewood chopped up. As a drain or sump for rainwater. As a sand pit. At a party for games. For making cider or beer in. As a play-pen for a small child. As a rabbit hutch, inverted with a door out of the side. On top of a pole as a dove cote. Let into a wall as a night exit for a dog or cat. As the base for a large lamp. As a vase for golden rod or michaelmas daisies, as an ornament, especially if it is a small one. With holes cut in the top and sides, either for growing wallflowers and strawberries in, or for stacking pots, and kitchen utensils. As a proper garbage can or wastepaper basket. As a ladder to reach the top shelves of a high bookcase. As a casing for a home-made bomb. Sawn in half, as a doll's crib. As a drum. As a large bird's nest.'

It would be nice to see the association theory that would account for this. I do not say it would be impossible; it would be nice. These two boys could be called convergent and divergent. But this perhaps tells us little, as Hudson brought out by some ingenious experiments reported in *Frames of Mind* (1968). In one of these, boys were asked to respond to creativity tests in two roles: that of Higgins, a conventional, 'convergent' engineer, and McMice, a bohemian artist. The following, edited by Hudson, suggests the result.

'*Higgins* (Milk bottle): Holding milk, making bombs with, space capsule for a beetle.
(Car tyre): Swimming in, running at high speed towards a wall in.
(Jar of treacle): Oiling heavy bearings with so as to sabotage machinery, laying a trail for catching edible locusts in Australia.
(Elastic band): Using as a driving band for a small motor.

McMice (Milk bottle): Jamming penis in, storing baboon's testicles in for giving virility to important people, cutting throats with, symbol of Britain's middle and lower "solid" middle classes, throwing at Edward Heath in motorboat.
(One pound note): Sticking on Op-art mural depicting magnificence of Britain, her Commonwealth and Empire, for burning slowly in front of a British audience composed largely of grocers, wrapping round a severed thumb, and pinning it on.
(Car tyre): Playing quoit deck tennis with, putting baby in and leaving baby to grow up therein, until body can expand no further, try as it may.'

So bizarre were some of the responses obtained by Hudson that he found himself, I regret to say, unable to print them. Such results bring out the artificiality of the usual test procedures, and the importance of what may be called the demand characteristics of the situation. It looks as though we can all be McMice given the right conditions—or perhaps, secretly, we really are all McMice.

There is thus at least some evidence that the frequency of new ideas can be increased experimentally by various techniques. This has come to be a highly desired state of affairs. Edwards (1968) lists forty-three organizations in the United States offering training in creativity. Here it becomes almost impossible to separate specific increases in originality from general changes in personality, effectiveness in work situations, and so on. Some of these factors will be discussed in the next section. But perhaps the most vexing question is one we have not so far considered: what is to count as creative? If one could specify adequate criteria, one might be able to set up rules for satisfying them, and thus be able to increase creative thought. Some definitions of creativity mention the processes supposed to be involved, or often-found characteristics of creative persons. This is unsatisfactory, partly because we do not know with any certainty what these are; but mainly because these are the independent and intervening variables, or some of them, which are the subject of our investigation. Two sorts of criteria are usually suggested for the dependent variables, that is the products of creative thinking. Both the suggested criteria, however, have difficulties. The first is novelty. Clearly any creative product must be novel in some sense, even if only to the originator: equally clearly this is not sufficient, or the productions of a lunatic would have equal status with those of a genius. And how novel does it have to be? Most if not all achievements are developments of what has gone before. So some criterion such as usefulness, practicality, or acceptability is suggested also. But this is not always easy to define, especially in the artistic field. And how widely, or soon, must the product be acceptable? Even such popular 'standards' as Bizet's *Carmen* were rejected on their first appearance. At present, it seems that anything created by an 'artist' is by definition a work of art, even if the process is quite accidental. Neither are scientific achievements always recognized immediately. Only Sir Arthur Eddington, it is said, understood the special theory of relativity on publication. Many inventions were made 'before their time' and failed to make headway—for example Sir George Cayley's aeroplane. Then again, often the apparently unpractical idea is the best—the observation built into brainstorming. And in many cases the creative idea solves a *different* problem from what was intended. This can be the effect called serendipity—the art of finding something by accident while looking for something else. Probably the most famous recent case is Alexander Fleming's discovery of penicillin, but the effect is familiar to every habitual searcher of scientific journals. There may also be a more important effect in that a new problem is seen that was not thought of before. Hadamard (1945) quotes example of this in mathematics. One can argue, indeed, that insofar as what is creative has not been done before, it is impossible by definition to specify rules which would guarantee important new work. The production of works of art, at least, according to rules has generally proved a failure—for example the rigid insistence on the unities of time, space, and action in classical French drama tended to make it dry and lifeless as compared to, say, Shakespeare, or indeed Molière. It is still useful, of course, to have techniques that merely make creative work more likely. And the undoubted cases of 'inspiration' should not lead us to neglect the fact that a great deal of work in science, the arts as well, is a matter of sound competent plodding—Eddison's 99 per cent perspiration. In terms of Taylor's levels of creativity, this perhaps applies particularly to levels two, three, and four. It has been said that science provides a means for non-creative people to be creative. This is true of the arts as well, where there is a demand for the product. We should expect a normal distribution of talent and achievement, so that it is misleading to speak of 'creative' and 'noncreative' as two distinct classes. Again in Taylor's terms, most of the experimental attempts to increase creative responses have concentrated on level three, the inventive. It seems less likely that synectics or remote associates would ever lead to new movements or principles in arts or sciences. For clues as to what lies behind these, we must turn to some of the conditions, or at any rate accompaniments, of creativity.

CONDITIONS OF CREATIVITY

There are, first, qualities of the individual. We have already seen that conventionally measured intelligence is not enough. Further evidence could be quoted from Terman's classic *Genetic Studies of Genius*. The main study began in 1921, when intelligence testing was in full vogue as psychology's most powerful instrument. A sample of some 1,500 Californian children were selected on the basis of an IQ of 140 or above, and followed through their subsequent lives. One main point that emerged was that the highly intelligent tended to be superior all round—in physique, social skills, etc. And another was that while many of the children fulfilled their promise in later life, by no means all did so. And conversely only some reached really outstanding achievements. In another volume in the series, Catherine Cox (1926) calculated the IQ's of famous persons of the past from their reported childhood achievements. Her well-known results show only an erratic relationship between estimated intelligence and ultimate fame. But such estimates are likely to be unreliable, at the least.

It seems that creative and non- (or less-) creative persons tend to see themselves differently. Barron (1952) distinguished these two groups by means of the Barron-Welsh scale, a set of drawings rated by artists, who tend to prefer the more complex, asymmetrical figures. Subjects scoring low on the BW scale described themselves as contented, gentle, conservative, unaffected, patient, peaceable; those who scored high, as gloomy, loud, unstable, bitter, cool, dissatisfied, pessimistic, emotional, irritable, pleasure-seeking. Van Zelst and Kerr (1954) found that scientists considered productive rated themselves as more original, imaginative, curious, enthusiastic, impulsive; but less contented and conventional. These adjectives agree quite well with the more detailed productions of both Getzels and Jackson's, and Hudson's, subjects. Both these studies found a vein of sarcastic or flippant humour among the more highly creative, which seems to give them almost another dimension. Hudson interprets this as a defence, which can also appear as pedantry, or take other forms. He argues that some of the differences between 'convergers' and 'divergers' (both of whom may be high achievers, and indeed high creatives) can be understood in terms of different defence systems. 'The impulse for self-protection seems to have invaded so much of some boys' lives that their every move is coloured by it. They present less a Siegfried or Maginot line, more a countryside laced with trenches.' But one must again remember the social and educational background of Hudson's subjects. In another of his ingenious experiments, Hudson (1968) obtained descriptions of 'typical' scientists, arts men, and others from his English schoolboys, and showed how already at school they tended to identify with a mythical version of their own likely future type of activity.

There are also many studies which try to arrive at a picture of the creative individual's personality by various of the usual personality study methods, e.g. Frank Barron in a series of reports over the last twenty years. In one of these, for example, Barron (1969) studied 'highly regarded doctoral candidates in the sciences' intensively by tests and clinical interviews.

'... the more highly regarded young scientists are (1) of superior measured intelligence; (2) exceptionally independent in judgment and resistant to group-endorsed opinions; (3) marked by a strong need for order and for perceptual closure, combined with a resistance to premature closure and an interest in what may appear as disorder, contradiction, imbalance, or very complex balance where the ordering principle is not immediately apparent; (4) unusually appreciative of the intuitive and non-rational elements in their own nature; (5) distinguished by their profound commitment to the search for esthetic and philosophic meaning in all experience.'

Hudson (1966) thought four characteristics most significant: persistence; self-confidence; predatoriness; crisis-seeking. Taylor and Barron (1963) summarizing several very extensive studies by such authors as Roe, McClelland, Saunders, MacCurdy, Knapp, and Cattell, reached 'a highly consistent picture of the productive scientist'. Of course this does not necessarily fit the great or very highly original scientist, or the artist. But here are the thirteen traits 'found in study after study' (our italics).

'1. A high degree of *autonomy*, self-sufficiency, self-direction.
2. A preference for mental manipulations involving things rather than people: a somewhat *distant or detached attitude* in interpersonal relations, and a preference for intellectually challenging situations rather than socially challenging ones.
3. High *ego strength* and emotional stability.
4. A liking for *method, precision*, exactness.
5. A preference for such defence mechanisms as *repression* and isolation in dealing with affect and instinctual energies.
6. A high degree of *personal dominance* but a dislike of personally toned controversy.

7. A high degree of *control* of impulse, amounting almost to over-control: relatively little talkativeness, gregariousness, impulsiveness.
8. A liking for *abstract thinking*, with considerable tolerance of cognitive ambiguity.
9. Marked *independence of judgment*, rejection of group pressures toward conformity in thinking.
10. Superior general *intelligence*.
11. An early, very broad *interest in intellectual activities*.
12. A drive towards *comprehensiveness and elegance* in explanation.
13. A special interest in the kind of *"wagering"* which involves pitting oneself against uncertain circumstances in which one's own effort can be the deciding factor.'

These are hardly, perhaps, traits established on an objective basis, so much as a general description of one species or group of creative persons. Apparently no such well-established descriptions exist for other groups.

The listing of traits leads naturally on to attempts to show how the personality of a creative person may function, and particularly how it may do so in relation to society. Hudson has found his work showing more and more clearly the importance of these aspects of the matter. In *Frames of Mind* (1968) he says: 'Faced with such a diversity of possible causes—genetic, physiological, psychological, educational, familial, cultural—I feel the need for a centre of focus . . . increasingly, I see our sense of identity as exerting a controlling influence over the intellectual choices we make, and the mental abilities we are willing to reveal.' This approach, Hudson argues, has several advantages. It is more predictive than other lines: 'We make better sense of an individual's responses to his environment from the moment we discover what that environment and those responses signify to him.' It provides the experimenter with 'a central vantage point' from which to survey the evidence. It opens up important areas where psychometrics have so far failed to make much progress, such as the relationship between private and working life. And this approach, Hudson thinks, helps to unify the existing diversity of evidence. Hudson agrees with Erikson (1963) that a main psychological activity of adolescence is the formation of a sense of personal identity.

> 'And I would add—as a working hypothesis—that once fashioned, this sense of identity serves as a self-regulating device, controlling the amount of ourselves that we permit to show. More specifically, that it is the "fit" or congruence between our sense of identity and our perception of any particular context that limits what ability and what feelings we are able on that occasion to display. And more specifically still, that our perception of both self and context is framed in terms of a few basic dimensions—of which respect for authority, convergence/divergence and sexual identification (or dimensions closely allied to these) are three.'

This is, perhaps, not so very different from McDougall's (e.g. 1908) sentiment of self regard; and the difficulty with the concept is to tell what status it has. Is it both conscious and unconscious? Is it more than a summary of attitudes, or not?

Nevertheless Hudson is clearly pointing the way to a needed investigation of *why* people make the choices, especially the intellectual choices that they do.

MacKinnon (1960) studied a sample of 'highly effective individuals' by the sort of intensive methods developed by the U.S. Office of Strategic Services to select outstanding personnel to act as leaders of wartime resistance groups and the like. The essential feature of these methods is that subjects and staff are brought together to live for several days in a suitably isolated environment—for which reason the phrase 'country house technique' has sometimes been used. Most of MacKinnon's findings agree with those already summarized. But he does stress that the creative persons he dealt with—and it is not clear precisely who these were—were noticeably conventional and respectable rather than 'Bohemian'. Secondly he states:

> 'The truly creative individual has an image of himself as a responsible
> person and a sense of destiny about himself as a human being. This includes
> a degree of resoluteness and almost inevitably a measure of egotism. But
> over and above these, there is a belief in the foregone certainty of the worth
> and validity of one's creative efforts.'

It seems that we are dealing here with members of society who are accepted and approved; and it is apparent that, in the United States at least, there are groups of people, certainly including creative individuals, which function in some sense as outgroups, and which are, perhaps, necessary for the ingroups to define themselves by contrast. Negroes, 'hippies', 'beatniks', artists, revolutionaries, have all been to some extent cast in this role. I think one can hardly take part in, or even observe, protest demonstrations of the kind that have occurred in recent years without being struck by the way in which both sides take up and develop their expected roles. A useful analysis of this apparent structural dichotomy might well be made on the lines suggested by Levi-Strauss. Donald Schon (1963) has proposed the thesis that the roles of the artist and the revolutionary 'were formed on the projective model of the (originally mediaeval) romantic lover'. I am not sure that this supposed derivation of the role helps to explain it: but Schon certainly perceptively points out the following characteristics.

'1. In order to play his role, he must move away from society.
2. He defines himself in opposition to society.
3. He is fated to his role; he has no choice; he is swept along, often against his will.
4. He seeks a bliss, through love, beyond the ordinary happiness associated with society and conventional success and morality.
5. He is able to progress, to obey his destiny, only through suffering— which he must seek out if the external world does not provide it for him.
6. He pursues an ideal, which demands of him the strictest fidelity— often without the slightest hope of reward.
7. Sustained consummation—complete possession—is disastrous.

8. His proper and fitting end is death in the service of the ideal—accompanied by the reward of bliss beyond.'

(It has been said that Louis Armstrong would have been a greater musician had he died before he was thirty.)

Given that such roles play an important part, interacting with the sense of identity stressed by Hudson, there remains the question of what individual characteristics are most closely linked to actual achievement. Perhaps the most helpful clue lies in motivation, considered in a broad sense. I say this partly because of human adaptability. Given virtually any activity, if individuals are inspired to devote themselves to it, some will achieve more than they or anyone thought possible. Saint-Exupery tells of a pilot who crashed in impenetrable jungle in South America. On reaching civilization, against all odds, he remarked: 'I have done what no animal could do.' Within individual careers, one is constantly surprised by what can be done given the will, to use a psychologically old-fashioned term. I have known a boy whose low intelligence made him effectively unemployable, who knew by heart all the hundreds of London Transport bus routes. Anecdotes of great men often show turning points at which intense interest or ambition was aroused: for example Galton's reading of the *Origin of Species*; in the case of W. C. Fields, seeing the Byrne Brothers' juggling act at the age of nine. (Fields is said to have habitually practised juggling at night standing by his bed, into which he would fall when exhausted.) Anne Roe (1952) presented a now well-known intensive study of distinguished scientists. She stressed their dedication:

> 'Although a few of them have cut down somewhat on their hours of work as they have grown older, it is still the common pattern for them to work nights, Sundays, holidays, as they always have. Most of them are happiest when they are working—some only when they are working. In all these instances, other aspects—economic returns, social and professional status—are of secondary importance.'

The persistence and dedication of many artists, and indeed great achievers in every field, is a matter of biographical record. This is not to be taken as a matter of moral duty, though that may play a part in some cases. It is simply an often-found characteristic. Now I am not of course suggesting that hard work alone equals creativity. Nor am I dismissing the other characteristics reliably reported of creative persons; I am considering motivation rather as the clue to the role of those other characteristics, and their interaction with particular circumstances and opportunities. Nor, finally, do I imagine that to say creative people are highly motivated explains their behaviour. Rather, it is the motivation that has to be explained. Various attempts have been made to do so.

Some of these are in terms of individual development, some in terms of more general background and cultural factors, which we must discuss later. Hudson's explanation is 'an existential one'. Let us first point out that the four characteristics he considers crucial—persistence, self-confidence, predatoriness, crisis-seeking—can all be grouped under a broad motivational heading. The last aspect he thinks is the most vital one, and his view of it is this:

> 'In searching for crises, therefore, the intellectual plays a solitary game in which, in a sense, the integrity of his personality is at stake. He abandons himself, and finds, once the crisis has passed, that he has survived intact. This is not thrill-seeking for its own sake, but thrill-seeking of a kind which enables a man to stir the embers of a primitive desire: the longing to be engulfed totally by someone else. His difficulties (and our apprehension) arise both from the fear of abandoning his autonomy, and from the more specific horror that this impulse was originally incestuous. It was directed towards his mother.'

This line of thought seems rather more Freudian, or perhaps Kleinian, than existential. Melanie Klein (e.g. 1937) extending psychoanalysis to the study of very young children, brought out the importance of two basic and contradictory needs: for protection and support, and for independent development. Each has its accompanying danger, loss of identity and abandonment respectively. But if it is true that we all have these two tendencies, why do they make some of us creative, but not others? If the answer is that such unconscious motives are more powerful, or more accessible, in creative people, is it not odd that the latter present surface personalities, at least, as diverse as say Joseph Haydn, Samuel Johnson, T. E. Lawrence, and Albert Einstein?

Another view, also somewhat psychoanalytical in orientation, comes from D. C. McClelland (1961). He summarized studies of successful physical scientists in the United States, and listed a number of frequently found characteristics, such as a tendency to come from 'radical protestant' homes, without being religious themselves; to avoid personal relations and complex human emotions; to be interested in outdoor, 'masculine' pursuits, and in intellectual activities of an analytical kind. In one of his experiments, scientists and non-scientists were asked to rate a number of metaphors for nature: the scientists tended to like such phrases as 'a pillar of strength, and virility'; 'a perfect woman nobly planned'; 'the nurse, the guide, the guardian of my heart and soul'. They did not like 'the desolations of many generations'; 'a great cave that encompasses us and swallows us up like atoms'; or 'a Titan waiting terribly to break forth'. A significant number of successful scientists seemed to have had a period of relatively severe illness in childhood. McClelland's view is that Physical scientists tend to retreat from human contact, possibly due to failure to resolve early emotional conflicts as described by Freud, and to find both refuge and revenge in analysing, that is attacking, the inanimate world. McClelland thinks it may be possible to distinguish such personalities from those of, say, business entrepreneurs in terms of the family affection received by the latter, giving them an orientation to people rather than things.

This does at last suggest (as does McClelland's work on the need for achievement, to be discussed later) the possibility of isolating some of the relevant variables in an individual's background. Perhaps more has been done in this line with respect to the relatively simpler concept of intelligence (see *Intellectual Abilities* . There are many instances of eminent persons coming from home backgrounds that could be regarded as stimulating and challenging—the James's and the Sitwells, for example. But anecdote can show us every conceivable variety of background to future great achievement, ranging from aristocratic luxury (e.g. Bertrand Russell) to abject poverty (e.g. Charles Dickens). There are sons who complete their fathers' work and extend it, and those who reject everything their parents stand for. Oden (1968) following up Terman's original gifted group as they reached mid-life, compared the 100 most successful with the 100 least successful. 40 per cent of the most successful came from a professional background. 96·5 per cent of their parents had encouraged college attendance. Both figures were substantially less for the least successful group. Schaefer and Anastasi (1963) studied 400 American high school boys, who were divided into creative and control groups by teacher ratings and two creativity tests. The creative subjects tended to have academically superior backgrounds, parents who seemed interested in the boys' fields of study, and fathers whose favourite leisure occupation was reading. These findings are interesting and valuable, but so far it is clearly impossible to disentangle environmental and hereditary effects, to name only the main groups of variables. Freeman, Butcher and Christie (1968) reviewing the evidence, are doubtless right to conclude: 'The important variable however is the response of the child to these parental attitudes.' What I feel to be important, on a mainly intuitive basis, is a background which motivates by expectation, as it were. This would accommodate many different sorts of family background, and put the emphasis not so much on a materially rich environment, as on parental attitudes, not necessarily consciously held or deliberately expressed. The effect will be partly associated with social class, in societies where this is important. I think it is still true in this country that in some families it is simply assumed that children will take on certain sorts of role: higher education, management, leadership, or what have you. Public school education (British type) fosters this. In other families such roles are not thought of. I suppose the extreme case would be the traditional caste system of India. Another part of this effect is related to opportunity. An individual may well be able to cope in more 'advanced' circumstances simply by playing his part. One feels that there might not be so very much difference, in some respects, between managing, say, a comprehensive school, a brigade, or a government Department. And in times of emergency individuals do successfully make such switches. An odd example is the case of open tennis. Formerly a small body of professional players, such as Rosewall, Gonzales, Segura, seemed all approximately equal, and of a standard far above the amateurs. But when open tournaments began, it quickly appeared that this was illusory, and players like Gonzales, who had seemed quite the equal of the best, were beaten by fairly average amateurs. This raises all sorts of ancillary hypotheses about achievement and expectation—for example that apparent differences in difficulty may be largely in the eye of the beholder. Achieving societies sometimes try to make eminence seem attainable—the field-marshal's baton in every knapsack; any boy can become President. The late Colonel Wintle, a worthy addition to the long line of English eccentrics, claimed that those he commanded did not accept the impossible: 'Sergeant-major, I want three men: one to clean the latrines, one to write a sonnet, one to govern Siberia.' 'Yes, sir! First three men, one pace forward! You, latrines. You, sonnet. You, Siberia.' And very well they did it, so he said.

Some of the specifically educational attempts to increase creativity will be described later. At this point let us move from the individual to the cultural background in which he finds himself. Witkin (e.g. 1967) has argued for the importance of a field-dependence–field-independence in differentiating between cultures. This refers to the extent to which perceptual judgments are influenced by the environment, which in turn is held to be typical of general 'cognitive style'. (See our discussion of this in *Development and Culture*). The dimension is illustrated by the rod-and-frame test, one of the means used to measure it. Basically, the subject has to adjust a straight line to the vertical, against the background of a frame which can be tilted by the experimenter. Field dependent subjects are influenced by this; field independent persons retain their own 'knowledge' of the vertical and work from it. We have already noted that creative people tend to be independent and autonomous in their judgments, and Spotts and Mackler (1967) reported that field independence correlates with divergent thinking tests. Mac-Kinnon (1960) found that 'those who placed the rod most accurately were shown to be the more original, more complex, and more spontaneous subjects on several other tests'. Dawson (1967) in a study of two West African tribes, found the Temne more field-dependent than the Mende. The Temne place great stress on conformity to adult authority, are mother dominant and oriented to tradition. The Mende are less tradition-oriented, use deprivation rather than physical punishment to control children, and give the child responsibility at an early age. Unfortunately there is, as far as we know, no evidence that either tribe is more creative than the other. Freeman, Butcher and Christie (1968) think that 'the most appropriate conceptualization' of these and related results is to be found within the framework of conceptual systems theory (Harvey, Hunt and Schroder, 1961).

'The theory proposes that a person's concepts are ordered according to certain patterns of organization. It is assumed that one of the most important structural characteristics of this organization is its degree of abstractness or conceptual level. A person at a high level is more likely to explore situations and to be creative and adaptable when faced with a changing environment. In contrast the person at a low level manifests thinking which is stereotyped, overlearned and dominated by the rules of authority. According to the theory optimal environmental conditions which allow the highest levels to be reached are characterized by maximum information feedback and allow the person to learn from the feedback.'

Cross (1966) attempted to compare parental attitudes of these types with conceptual levels of 14-18 year-old boys, assessed by a sentence completion task. Cross concludes, perhaps rather grandly in view of the limited sampling of conceptual level:

'From a conceptual system view, a person in a training environment which is interdependent (i.e. non-authoritarian) obtains maximal feedback from his successes *and* his errors; therefore, he gains a realistic perspective, i.e. he acquires the appropriate dimensions needed to evaluate and respond to input from the environment. Parents who grant their child a great deal of autonomy allow him to learn about the environment on his own terms. By tolerating different points of view, they permit and encourage divergent thinking and diversity in the child so that he learns different patterns of dealing with the world.'

Freeman *et al.* like this idea, and contrast it with a horror story from Cropley (1967):

' "Tom had been raised from an early age by his mother alone. She was an energetic woman who dominated the boy at all times. She told him when he might play, when he must do homework, when he must read 'good' novels, and so on. She insisted that he must play chess with her at a given time each evening, insisted on a certain schedule for piano practice and ran his life completely. She administered severe corporal punishment for trivial offences, and was, overall, domineering, controlling, intrusive, and authoritarian." Tom was a brilliant student at school and university; he has made no contribution, either theoretical or practical to his profession.'

While Poor Tom might well join such historical characters of psychology as Anna O. and little Albert, one may suggest that numbers of eminent persons have had childhoods scarcely less unfortunate.

A broader approach is to look at cultures known to have been highly creative, and make some suggestions as to what characterizes them. Probably the most ambitious attempt to relate psychological and historical factors has been made by David McClelland (e.g. 1953). He started from the list of twenty 'psychogenic needs' worked out by Henry A. Murray (1938) and selected one of these, the need for achievement or nAch for short, for special study. McClelland measured this need by applying a standard scoring system to the responses made to four of the ambiguous pictures of the Thematic Apperception Test. He went on to argue that a measure of the need could be derived from documents such as children's readers, or literature in general, of a given period. Murray's brief definition of nAch was:

'To accomplish something difficult. To master, manipulate, or organize physical objects, human beings, or ideas. To do this as rapidly and independently as possible. To overcome obstacles and attain a high standard. To excel oneself. To rival and surpass others. To increase self-regard by the successful exercise of talent.'

McClelland seems to view the need slightly differently, essentially as a desire to be successful. He has shown that a high level of nAch in children's books tended to be followed, when that generation reached adulthood, by a rise in various indices of economic prosperity of a number of countries in the period 1925 to 1950. nAch, he held, was associated with a Protestant ideology, leading parents to stress self-reliance, self-denial, and other good economic virtues; the idea is derived, of course, from Max Weber and R. H. Tawney. Tawney showed, in *Religion and the Rise of Capitalism*, how closely linked were the beliefs of the reformed Church to material prosperity: wealth as a sign of grace, etc. Again, the level of nAch in classical Greece has been estimated from the surviving literature for the period 900 to 100 B.C., and related to economic development expressed by the growth of Greek trade, in turn shown by mapping the geographical distribution of the earthenware jars in which oil and wine, the most important commodities, were transported. This work, ingenious and plausible though it certainly is, is open to criticism. The first point is made by Roger Brown (1965) about some earlier studies, in the course of a masterly dissection of the whole issue: namely that both nAch and economic development may be the result of another factor or factors. A second point is that the concept of nAch is based on achievement in a particular culture, that of the United States of America in the twentieth century. A moment's reflection shows that in many other societies the goals of high achievement have been so different as to make the transfer of the concept dubious to say the least. A third, related, objection is, that if nAch *is* an explanation, it seems much too simple.

To see this, let us mention briefly some of the outstanding features of classical Greece. Galton is but one of an endless stream of writers to extol the Greek achievement: so many that the tale risks becoming tedious. But it is, in fact, perhaps the most extraordinary chapter of human history to date. We must realize that after settled and massive civilizations had already existed for thousands of years, some relatively small groups of semi-nomadic peoples moved into the islands and mainlands of the Aegean, and in a few hundred years produced a totally new social and political environment, in which were created —not just developed, but *invented*—philosophy, science, medicine, history. At the same time heights were reached in visual arts, literature, and statecraft which have, at least, never been excelled, though possibly equalled. We must remember too that our knowledge is in many respects fragmentary. Only a small proportion of the classical drama survives; metallic sculpture is largely missing, that in stone is broken and dispersed (and was often much different originally, being brightly painted); graphic art apart from vases, and music, are entirely lacking. The Greeks were, first, of very mixed genetic inheritance, often intermingling with diverse native populations. The essential core of Greek society was the city-state or *polis*. The well-known phrase 'man is a political animal' is not a description, but a biological definition: man is an animal, but distinguished by living in a particular form of organization. Greek city-states, of which there were eventually hundreds, varied widely in size and customs. But they had some characteristics more or less in common. They were small by modern standards: Miletus, which is the place at which scientific speculation first appeared in human history, had some 20–30,000 citizens. They were intensely conscious of their own identity, fiercely independent, and wildly quarrelsome. They were still semi-nomadic. Not only could an expedition always be gathered to found a new colony in unknown parts; but on occasion a whole community would abandon the physical embodiment of the state, as the Athenians did when under the threat of Persian invasion they took to the sea. There was a tremendous emphasis on individual achievement. It was the conscious ambition of talented men to excel others, to gain praise and honour. Yet at the same time it was felt that in certain essential respects all citizens were equal. In some cases this was taken so far that important offices of state were filled by lot. Another pair of contrasting features lay in the facts that while the great achievements of the period largely involved for the first time breaking through from belief to scientific hypotheses and evidence and from rule-of-thumb technology to scientific explanation; yet this was done in a context of devout religion and of traditional practices. Greek religion tended to emphasize this life rather than the next. It provided clearly and explicitly such functions as ritual celebration of the life of the community, on the one hand; and on the other periodic release from the restraints of civilized life. (For the latter, perhaps, the present-day pop festivals are partly a confused substitute.) From religious festivals emerged the classic drama, which not merely reached heights of poetry and music (the latter lost); but functioned as a communal expression of fundamental individual emotions—indeed as a sort of group therapy, if Freud's interpretation is correct. Religious, too, at least in origin, was the emphasis on bodily excellence, culminating in the various festival games, at once ritual and competitive. An unparalleled feature, as far as I know, was that athletes were naked. And finally let us mention that the Greek ideal would now be called an all-rounder: specialization, and above all specialization in any merely mechanical or technical pursuit, must inevitably restrict excellence of balanced development.

We have spent some time on this endlessly absorbing subject, not so much to provide an exhaustive explanation of Greek creativity, as to show how difficult it is to be exhaustive, and how virtually impossible to distinguish necessary and sufficient conditions. That being so, how much less likely is it that such conditions—which were in any case highly unstable—could ever be created deliberately.

Discussion of societies which have been markedly innovative should not lead us to ignore those that have produced great works, especially of art, in less dramatic and more traditional fashion. China before modern times, and mediaeval Europe, are cases in point. But if one considers periods when rapid changes, and possibly progress, have come about, one is struck by several features. Renaissance Europe is probably the next best example. There is an amazing outpouring of talent in every direction: philosophy, the arts, science and technology, trade and exploration, war and conquest. This tends to mean that the period is one of general disorder. Traditional methods, and ways of thinking, are disrupted and discarded. Yet these ways are essential to new achievements. Kuhn (1963) has described the 'essential tension' that must exist in a society, or in individuals, between tradition and iconoclasm. 'The scientist requires a thorough-going commitment to the tradition with which, if he is successful, he will break.' A relatively neglected part of this tradition, I think, has been technique. Creative work very often requires a great deal of work devoted to the perfection of technique. Indeed this is quite comonly what is found fascinating, so that it plays a motivating role. Visual artists, in particular, seem often obsessed with this into old age. Then, if technique is inadequate, creative achievement is unlikely; but if techniques present no problems, the essential tension is lacking. This possibly helps to account for the hideousness of most modern architecture, and the pointlessness of much contemporary art. When one can do everything, there is no need to do anything. Then, too, there is the interaction of technique, or skills, with personality. In Zen, perfection of technique—in say archery, flower-arrangement, or tea-making—has been made the vehicle and criterion of personality development. What are the effects of the intensive preoccupation with mastery characteristic of many geniuses? Finally we must note the importance of demand. Different societies require and reward different talents, and, as we remarked above, so adaptable are human beings that whatever the desired activity, some will excel at it. Demand increases the numbers of persons in any given field, and thus the chances of some being eminent. It makes the field a socially acceptable one to enter and devote oneself to. Motivation, and competition, are raised to high levels by large rewards. Thus the numerous courts of Germany, each employing musicians, provided the conditions for the Bach family, and for J. S. Bach. The Greeks rewarded dramatic gifts with prestige, the Elizabethans with popularity and wealth. The latter fact encouraged an active school of poets and playwrights, of whom Shakespeare is only the most eminent. The United States produces multitudes of able scientists, athletes, and popular musicians: currently, as far as one can tell, no Aristotle, Leonardo, or Einstein.

GENIUS

The comparison just made leads us to ask whether there is a separate category of achievement to be labelled 'genius'. Albert (1969) points out that little attempt has been made to review research on this topic since Terman (e.g. Terman and Chase, 1920). And in fact publication on genius seems to have diminished concomitantly with the increase in that on creativity. Since the vast bulk of the latter has been American, it is not implausible to link a lack of psychological interest with a deficiency in those conditions that produce genius. The term has often tended to carry qualitative or even mystical overtones that make it difficult to investigate. Galton entitled his book *Hereditary Genius*, but, as we have seen, dealt really with eminence, regarded as the extreme end of a normal distribution of talent. And this would probably be the most acceptable view today. A slightly different approach is offered by Merton (1961). He first presents evidence that it is the norm in science for a given advance to be made simultaneously, or nearly so, by several investigators at once. Some of these cases are well-known, but many more, Merton argues, are not so for various reasons: publication may be forestalled, or a scientist may be diverted into other activities, and so on. But this does not mean that some scientists are not deserving of the title genius. By examining the discoveries of very eminent persons such as Kelvin, Merton shows that, indeed, much of his work would have been done in any case if not by him —but by many different people. Kelvin's genius therefore lay not so much in uniqueness, as in frequency of being right; and this, Merton thinks, is typical. One is somewhat reminded of Shaw's notion of geniuses as rather like electric light bulbs, burning brighter with a greater amount of the Life Force.

But this does not hold very well for all cases, especially for those artists, like Flaubert or George Eliot, who work slowly and painfully. (When asked how he had spent the day, Flaubert is said to have replied: 'I spent the morning deciding to put in a comma. In the afternoon, I took it out again.') Some evidence for a separate category of the highest achievers comes from developmental studies. Lehman (1953) studied the age distribution of achievements in many different fields. In some of these, at least, there was a difference between notable achievements and really outstanding ones. Overall, the typical achievement distribution shows a rapid rise from late adolescence to the early thirties, followed by a steady decline into old age. Outstanding achievements appear earlier, reach a peak earlier, and die off more rapidly and completely. This evidence does not exactly square with that of Merton, but that may be due to differences in criteria. One other fact may be mentioned, and that is the virtual non-existence of women geniuses, although many women of course achieve eminence. Conversely, males are in general more at risk throughout life. There are more men than women at the bottom end of the intelligence scale as well as at the top. These differences may well be largely cultural, but it is not implausible to suppose a genetic factor also. Males, for example, are more prone to mental disorders such as schizophrenia whose causes seem to include an hereditary element.

The difficulty with this category of person as a subject for psychological study is that they are not readily available. Wertheimer (1945) reported a long series of conversations with Einstein. But apart from showing that relativity did not come by the operations of formal logic, the account is rather disappointing. Ghiselin (1952) has collected a number of autobiographical accounts, but the general upshot of these is that geniuses cannot tell us how they do it.

In popular imagination genius is 'next to madness'. This could have several interpretations. We have seen that unconscious mechanisms are thought by some to play a part in creative thinking. There is not only the question of a resemblance between the sort of analogical thinking found both in creativity and in dreams and schizophrenia; there is the possibility of involvement in unresolved emotional conflicts, if Hudson is correct. Openness to new ideas may include the bizarre or eccentric—Newton with his theories about the pyramids, or Freud with his belief in the Baconian authorship of Shakespeare's works. Then there is the role of some original thinkers as described by Schon—the extremes of 'romantic' behaviour could appear 'mad' to the more conventional. And indeed, as Laing (e.g. 1960) and others never tire of telling us, the whole concept of madness is largely determined by a given society itself. (See also *Thinking as a Private Experience*).

Genius at present seems something on which the psychologist can comment only. Perhaps such geniuses as chance to read this will be inspired to volunteer as much-needed subjects.

FOCUS: EDUCATION FOR CREATIVITY?

With the rapid increase in psychological interest in creativity, and the apparent relationship of the topic to national success, there have been many attempts in schools to 'improve creative thinking'. Parnes and Brunelle (1967) reviewing forty such attempts, concluded that students could be reliably taught to improve their sensitivity, fluency, flexibility, originality and elaboration. This raises the question first, of what is actually done, and secondly of whether it should be done at all. It may seem perverse to suggest that there is anything wrong with increasing a child's originality, but if this discussion starts arguments it will have been worth presenting.

We have already seen that Hudson agrees with Getzels and Jackson on the probably inhibiting effects of conventional schooling. But, as he points out, this is more a matter of belief than evidence. Much education, certainly in the academic 14–18-year-old range that Hudson studied, is highly formal and even rigid. But very successful and creative people certainly emerge from it, and the relationship of cause and effect is unresolved. Similarly in the United States, Torrance and Hansen (1965) reported that over 90 per cent of the questions asked by a sample of junior high school social studies teachers called only for the reproduction of textbook information. But it is not very clear how general this is. Moustakas (1966) for example, asserts that 'Facts, knowledge, intellectual gains are the important values...' in many classrooms, and illustrates it with Dickens' account of Mr. Gradgrind. But Margaret Mead (1962) points to the many excellent, inspiring teachers who also exist. Obviously both are right, at least within the accepted framework of education, which we must discuss later. So-called 'progressive' schools, of which A. S. Neill's Summerhill is probably the best-known in this country, are often contrasted with more conventional education. But we know of no evidence that they produce more creative adults. Freeman, Butcher, and Christie (1968) review a number of individual schools and teachers allowing greater or less self-expression, and conclude '. . . that under instructional methods which optimize their abilities creative children enjoy themselves to a greater extent.' This may well be a positive good, but it is not *necessarily* linked to future performance.

Now one of the many difficulties with experimental research in education is the extreme malleability of children. Beginning teachers may find this hard to believe, but experienced ones will not doubt that if Sir is pleased with rows of neat sums, that is what he will get, whereas if he prefers poems or puppets, his children will obligingly produce them, and very good ones, too. Hudson (1968) has shown that apparent 'convergers' can be just as fluent as divergers when the instructions are unambiguous. '("So *that's* what you want," they seem to be saying. "Why didn't you say so in the first place?"), (Hudson, 1968). And Robert Rosenthal, of course, has shown how teachers' expectations can influence even such ostensibly objective measures as standard IQ tests, without either children or teachers being aware of what was happening. Rosenthal and Jacobson (1966) told teachers that some of their children, actually a random sample, 'would show unusual intellectual gains during the year'. Eight months later the test scores of at any rate the first two grades were reported to be significantly higher.

Accordingly it is not surprising when success is reported in altering much more flexible behaviour. One such report, quite a substantial one, is presented by Richard Crutchfield (1965). Crutchfield's view is that, with the present rate of technological advance, it is impossible to predict what specific facts, or even skills, children need to acquire now for future use. Rather, 'What education today must . . . seek to do is to bring about the optimal development of the whole individual. He must be equipped with *generalized* intellectual and other skills, skills which will enable him to cope effectively with whatever the state of the world is as he will later encounter it . . . Central among these generalized skills is the capacity for creative thinking.' Furthermore, Crutchfield believes that most children's capacity for creative thought has hardly been tapped, and that almost every child can benefit from 'explicit training'. This training takes the form of auto-instructional materials in booklet form. There are sixteen booklets of about thirty pages each, and they embody the story of Jim and Lila, two schoolchildren who, aided by their kindly Uncle John, work their way through a series of problems, overcoming handicaps and becoming progressively more confident in tackling new situations and thinking creatively. Crutchfield's account needs to be quoted in full here.

'Each lesson is a complete problem-solving episode, containing all of the principle steps and processes inherent in creative problem solving. To begin with, Jim and Lila confront a mysterious occurrence, for example a puzzling theft and disappearance of money on a riverboat, or strange happenings in a deserted and reputedly haunted mansion. They are encouraged to generate many ideas and to check these possibilities against the facts. With new facts coming in, they revise their hypotheses. When these fail to solve the problem, Jim and Lila are led to reformulate the problem, to see it in a different way, and thus to generate new ideas. As further incidents occur, they are led closer and closer to a solution, until finally things fall into place, and they achieve the solution. The structure of the lessons is such that the alert reader is very likely to discover the solution for himself, a step ahead of Jim and Lila. This deliberately contrived "discovery experience" is thought to be an extremely important factor in the development and reinforcement of creative thinking skills and attitudes in the student. The lessons are constructed not only to give the reader repeated experiences in the solution of interesting problems, but also directly to instruct him in helpful strategies or heuristic procedures for creative problem-solving, by showing him how he can use them in the concrete problems. The procedures pertain to the formulation of the problem, the asking of relevant questions, the laying out of a plan of attack, the generation of many ideas, the search for uncommon ideas, the transformation of the problem in new ways, the evaluation of hypotheses, the sensitivity to odd and discrepant facts, and the openness to metaphorical and analogical hints leading to solutions. As we have said, the lessons are also intended to promote beneficial attitudes and motivations in the reader. Mainly, the aim is to build up the child's successful experience in coping with thought problems, thus reinforcing his interest in such activity and his self-confidence in the mastery of creative thinking skills. At the same time, we undertake to instil in him a variety of dispositions which favour the creative process—open-mindedness, suspension of premature criticality of ideas, readiness for the arousal of curiosity, intuitiveness, and the like. Above all, it is indispensable that the instructional materials actively interest and involve the reader . . . Jim and Lila—and hopefully the reader, too—thus come to discover that creative thinking is exciting, enjoyable, and personally significant.'

Crutchfield reported in 1965 two large-scale studies involving 267 fifth and sixth grade children given the experimental materials, and 214 controls. Pre- and post-test procedures included: measures of intelligence, personality, and cognitive style; inventories to assess the subject's attitudes about creative thought, and himself as a creative thinker; several of Torrance's tests of creativity; and a number of specially designed tests of creative problem-solving proficiency. (Among the latter was Duncker's good old x-ray problem.) On these problems, the trained children produced twice as many ideas as the controls, and their ideas were rated twice as good. They achieved three times as many solutions. The improvement generalized to other sorts of test, e.g. Torrance's Unusual Uses test and Toy Improvement test. Children at all levels of intelligence (presumably a normal distribution) surpassed the controls. Negro children, mainly from disadvantaged backgrounds, also improved, but only half as much as the whites. The effects, especially the problem-solving skill, still persisted six months later, as a follow-up study showed. On the other hand, no great change in attitudes was found, and least in subjects' self-confidence and self-evaluation as creative thinkers.

This shows, then, the sort of effect that can be, apparently quite easily, obtained with a wide range of children. There are difficulties. Does the effect transfer to real-life problems? Does it last? Is it confounded by some sort of 'Hawthorne' effect (i.e. roughly, that subjects will improve whatever you do to them)? Is it merely a sort of test sophistication? Such questions cannot yet be answered.

It would seem clear, even without considering Rosenthal's results, that if you want to influence children in school, you will do well to start with the teachers. And accordingly many experimenters have set themselves to change teachers' attitudes. Torrance (1965) summarizes studies showing how the behaviour of teachers can make differences in creative functioning. As he pertinently asks: 'How else can one explain why certain teachers produced so many students who made outstanding discoveries?' (The fact is documented by Peterson, 1946.) Torrance (1967) suggests a number of 'workshops' to aid teachers in developing the relevant skills. These include practising such techniques as: recognizing and acknowledging potentialities; being respectful of questions and ideas; asking provocative questions; recognizing and valuing originality; developing elaboration ability; unevaluated practice and experimentation; developing creative readers; predicting behaviour; and so on. Barron (1969) used some of Gordon's analogical *synectics* techniques with teachers and principals in Californian state schools, who attended a series of 'retreats' in an old country inn. Carefully chosen speakers set a tone of 'unconventionality' and 'positive-toned daring'. The audience was 'startled' by a 'new and imaginative approach' to marijuana and prostitution—namely to make them legal, though with social controls. Starting from such a base-line, it is perhaps not surprising that 'significant gains' were obtained on a variety of measures such as the Barron-Welsh Art Scale, and three of Guilford's divergent tests. The teachers later reported more empathy with the culturally-deprived children in their classes.

So, anyway, both teachers and children can have their scores on creativity tests increased. But we have earlier noticed the lack of evidence that these reliably relate to later achievement. With the despised three Rs, at least one was fairly sure they would come in useful sooner or later. It is important to remember, as Bruner (1966) points out, that the whole theory of modern education is, if not radically unsound as Lady Bracknell announced, at any rate very unusual. It is *formal*, conducted in special buildings by special people at set times; and it is universally compulsory. These characteristics, which came into full existence, in England at any rate, only a hundred years ago, are taken for granted. No one seems to think it odd that Article 26 of the Universal Declaration of Human Rights is the Right to compulsory education. A few writers such as Paul Goodman and John Holt now question this. A third still relatively unusual feature is that education is deliberate: scores of clerics, inspectors, government ministers, lecturers know exactly what and how children should be taught, and do not hesitate to impose their views on others as effectively as may be. But no one with more than a nodding acquaintance with education can avoid an overwhelming impression that much is mere fad and fashion. Children once were taught to draw still-lifes; now, for no better or worse reason, they are bizarrely taught child art—they are given big splotchy brushes and runny poster paints so that they must necessarily produce the big, splotchy, runny pictures that delight connoisseurs of the genre. Suddenly, primary school children, who can scarcely speak English, are taught French—by teachers who cannot speak it themselves.

Psychologists have been closely involved in such goings-on for at least seventy years. It is not entirely their fault. Often enough, some psychological procedure, finding, or theory has escaped from its inventors and run amok in the world at large. We must all have our repressions removed, or our IQ's tested, or our factors analysed. What should be the relationship of psychology to education? I would suggest, it is that of science to technology. By this I mean, that the task of psychologists, as scientists, is to establish, in R. S. Peters' phrase, what is the case and always will be the case. *Some* of what they establish will be useful to educators, whose task is a technological one in that it is essentially to bring about certain ends by whatever means are to hand (and, of course, are ethically acceptable). The decision as to ends is a third sort of question, a philosophical one. It does not follow that anything psychologists happen to be interested in can be lifted straight into the classroom. But psychology inevitably interacts with what is done there for several reasons. First there are the cases where it has actually been established, with reasonable certainty, how best to bring about a given end. Then psychologists, dealing with human beings as their subject matter, form opinions about what ought to be done, and because of their position are listened to. Then again, psychological findings, original or distorted, tend to modify views of ethics—punishment is less efficient, therefore it is also wrong. And then there are the fashions which education often eagerly takes over from psychology—testing, programmed learning, activity methods, holistic perception, etc., etc. Creativity is one more. We do not know what it is, how to test it, produce it, control it or predict it. These are excellent reasons for continuing research; they are less satisfactory for subjecting children to arbitrary training procedures, assessment, and value judgments.

POSTSCRIPT

We cannot leave the fascinating subject of creativity without one more anecdote: the incomparable Max's account of the origins of the theory of relativity, as told to him by the great scientist himself.

'One winter's evening, after a hard day's work, I was sitting by my fireside —for I have an open fire in the English fashion, not a stove: I like to sit watching the happy faces in the coals—when my eye lighted on the tongs

5—T * *

122

in the fender. Of course it had often lighted upon them before; but this time it carried to my brain a message which my brain could not understand. "Here," I mused, "are two perfectly parallel lines. And yet they meet at the extreme ends. How is that?" My friend Professor Schultz had promised to drop in and smoke a pipe with me that evening, and when he came I drew his attention to the phenomenon. He knelt down by the fender, pushed his spectacles up on his forehead, gazed closely, and muttered, "Gott im Himmel—ja!" I asked him—for he is a very ready man—if he had any explanation to offer. He rose from his knees and sat down on a chair heavily, burying his head in his hands. Suddenly he sprang to his feet, "Einstein," he said, "I believe that the iron-worker who made those bars must have heated them red-hot and then bent the ends towards each other." Dear old Schultz! Always so ready!—so shallow! I suppose I ought not to have laughed; but I did; and Schultz went out in some anger. It was dawn when I rose from the fireside. The fire had long ago burnt itself out, and I was stiff with cold. But my mind was all aglow with the basic principles of Relativismus.

"The world," I said quietly, "shall hear of this, Dr. Einstein".' (From Max Beerbohm, 1923)

FURTHER READING

Barron, F. (1969). *Creative Person and Creative Process*. Holt, Rinehart and Winston, Inc.
Hudson, L. (1968). *Frames of Mind*. Methuen.
Mooney, R., and Razik, T. A. (1967). *Explorations in Creativity*. Harper and Row.
Shouksmith, G. (1970). *Intelligence, Creativity and Cognitive Style*. Batsford.
Taylor, C. W., and Barron, F. (1963). *Scientific Creativity*. Wiley.
Vernon, P. E. (1970). *Creativity: Readings*. Methuen.
Wallach, M. A., and Kogan, N. (1965). *Modes of Thinking in Young Children*. Holt, Rinehart and Winston, Inc.

4

Intellectual Abilities

It might seem obvious at first sight that the analysis and measurement of intellectual abilities would be closely related to the study of thinking. Actually, as Butcher (1968) points out, there has tended to be a separate development of psychometric and experimental approaches. It is noteworthy that the word 'intelligence' does not even appear in the index of Berlyne's *Structure and Direction in Thinking*. We have already discussed some of the areas in which 'intelligence' and 'thinking' do overlap: the study of creativity has often taken a psychometric approach. Intelligence has always been held to be one component of creativity, though only one. But it is fairly clear that intelligence testing itself does little to explain creative thinking beyond suggesting minimum levels required. Conversely, tests of intelligence have often incorporated problems: but the interest of testers has often been merely in how many of a given set of problems were solved by subjects of a certain age. Piaget was unusual in being interested in the reasons for wrong answers; and this set him off on his vast experimental programme, as we shall see later. However, while Piaget has certainly presented by far the most comprehensive and theoretically ambitious account of intellectual development, he has had rather little to say about the structures underlying adult differences in problem-solving or other 'intelligent' behaviour. Piaget takes us to the stage of formal operations, which all normal persons reach, and which corresponds roughly to the baseline of adult intelligence as measured by tests. But what of the difference between, say, the man in the street, a good professional mathematician, and a Gauss or a Poincaré?

As we have already seen, the psychological study of individual differences in mental capacity takes its origin in large part from Galton. Gardner Murphy (1949: *An Historical Introduction to Modern Psychology*) stresses the importance of Galton's evolutionary inspiration: 'It cannot be emphasized too strongly that the central idea of nineteenth-century biology, and hence of all studies within the life-sciences, was the Darwinian conception of the transmutation of species.' At the same time, of course, classical experimental psychology adopted physics as a model. One of the vital distinctions between the two approaches, as Murphy points out, lies in their view of time; or put it another way, their view of processes as historical or non-historical. For the physical sciences, the processes that are the subject of enquiry remain the same at whatever period they occur. And 'period' here refers to a point in the history of the universe, or of a species, or of an individual. This assumption is found in the psychology that takes physical science as a model: the British Associationists; Wundt and Titchener; Pavlov and Watson; a modern stimulus-response theory (see *Problem-Solving*). As Murphy puts it:

> 'The evolutionary approach changed all this. It made it necessary to conceive that life processes might be going on today in a form essentially different from those which occurred before, because of a higher level of complexity reached; and it made it possible to think of unidirectional trends which are irreversible.'

Thus developmental problems, and problems of individual differences, could come to be seen, not as obstacles to the solution of psychological questions, but as themselves constituting the questions to be answered. It is interesting here to note Freud's partial synthesis of the two approaches. We can see how he reached towards an evolutionary view of the development of consciousness, and that he gave a developmental account of adult behaviour. But at the same time his concept of the mind remained that of a closed energy system, and the 'stages' are physical rather than biological in character, for they remain in being and are capable of reactivation. It was left for Piaget to attempt a thorough-going biological account of mental development.

The early detailed study of individual differences was largely the work of those inspired by Galton and especially of J. McKeen Cattell, who worked with Galton after having been Wundt's assistant. Thus he was interested in combining the two approaches, and brought individual differences into American psychology, where practical results were of importance. Testing soon turned out to be extremely useful for educational purposes, and then, more dramatically, for assessing recruits in the 1914–1918 war. At just the same time Watson was promising even more effective results by the use of conditioning. But since as we have just noticed he adopted the physicalist standpoint, psychometrics and behaviourist experimental psychology continued to develop apart. Perhaps the most ambitious attempt to integrate the assessment of intelligence with the rest of psychology, on the other hand, was made by Charles Spearman. Spearman, a professional soldier who turned to psychology in middle life, followed in the tradition of Pearson, Galton's pupil and biographer. Developing the technique of correlation, he published in 1904 his tremendously influential *two-factor* theory of intelligence. The idea was that any intellectual activity must have two sorts of ability underlying it: one specific to the activity (such as verbal or numerical ability); and one that is common to all such activities. This last was *general intelligence* or *g*. The idea seemed plausible; but where Spearman was so ambitious was in believing that he had analysed the nature of *g*, and that this analysis provided psychology at last 'with its prime requisite, a genuinely scientific foundation'. (Spearman, 1923.) This foundation consisted of laws or principles, which Spearman had had the good fortune to discover: and 'these principles (together with commentaries upon them) appear to furnish both the proper framework for all general textbooks and the guiding inspiration for all experimental labours.' The announcement of a philosopher's stone always makes us suspicious, and Spearman's *noegenetic* principles, as he termed them, are something of an anti-climax. The three most important are these:

1. Apprehension of experience. 'Any lived experience tends to evoke immediately a knowing of its direct attributes and its experiences.'
2. Eduction of relations. 'The presenting of any two or more characters tends to evoke immediately a knowing of relation between them.'
3. Eduction of correlates. 'The presenting of any character together with a relation tends to evoke immediately a knowing of the correlative character.' (Spearman, 1923).

These difficult-sounding principles are still enshrined in practically every test of general intelligence: in every question of the form 'A is to B as C is to ?'; in every item, in fact, in which you must see a relationship and/or find a correlate. The principles, like the two-factor theory, seem plausible, if not quite so world-shaking as Spearman thought them (he went on finally to claim: '. . . in the said principles must lie, therefore, an exhaustive determination of the entire cosmos, not only in so far as this can be truly known, but even to the extent that it can be thought of at all'). Apart from the persistence of Spearman-type items, the interest of the theory lies in the attempt to deal with intelligence both by a theoretical analysis and by experimental isolation of factors. We may contrast this approach with that of Binet. Introductory textbooks often place Binet at the head of the testing stream; but in some ways the tests were Binet's least theoretically interesting contribution to psychology. To discuss his other work would take us too far afield: let us mention here that Binet started from the practical necessity to distinguish those children who were 'unable to profit in an average measure, from the instruction given in the ordinary schools' (Binet and Simon, 1905). With this in mind, Binet defined intelligence thus: 'It seems to us that in intelligence there is a fundamental faculty, the alteration or the lack of which is of the utmost importance for practical life. This faculty is judgment, otherwise called good sense, practical sense, initiative, the faculty of adapting one's self to circumstances.' (Binet and Simon, 1905.) Binet's tests were accordingly of the following type:

Age 3
1. Points to eyes, nose and mouth
2. Repeats two digits
3. Enumerates objects in a picture
4. Gives family name
5. Repeats a sentence of six syllables.

Age 8
1. Compares two objects from memory
2. Counts from 20 to 0
3. Notes omissions from pictures
4. Gives day and date
5. Repeats five digits.

Age 15
1. Repeats seven digits
2. Finds three rhymes for a given word
3. Repeats a sentence of twenty-six syllables
4. Interprets pictures
5. Interprets given facts.

'The fundamental idea of this method,' as Binet and Simon pointed out, 'is the establishment of what we shall call a measuring scale of intelligence.' The great advance was to provide a practical tool, rather than a theoretical insight; and much scorn was poured on 'contemporary authors who have made a specialty of organizing new tests according to theoretical views, but who have made no effort to patiently try them out in the schools. Theirs is an amusing occupation, comparable to a person's making a colonizing expedition into Algeria, advancing always upon the map, without taking off his dressing gown.'

It is therefore perhaps not surprising that Binet's tests were taken to America (by Goddard, famous for his account of the unfortunate Kallikak family) and enjoyed immense success there, while being relatively neglected in France, where the view of intelligence to flourish has been the vast theoretical structure of Piaget.

WHAT *IS* INTELLIGENCE?

We have now introduced one of the main themes around which the analysis of intellectual abilities has tended to centre: the definition of intelligence. A common layman's question to psychologists is: How can you measure intelligence when you can't even agree on what it is? Apart from Spearman, with his intended scientific principles, and Binet with his practical necessities, many early writers tended to give 'definitions' of intelligence based mainly on their own hunches, such as 'the ability to solve problems', 'the ability to learn', etc. This was not only highly confusing, but somewhat unfortunate from a theoretical point of view. Not only were such definitions unsupported by evidence; they tended to suggest that 'intelligence' referred to something that actually existed in some sense, and hence could be measured if only we had the right means. Hence long and muddled arguments about whether tests were *really* measuring intelligence. This line of thought was severely criticized by Gilbert Ryle (1949).

In *The Concept of Mind* he attacked many conceptual mistakes, as he thought them, of psychologists. His main target was the dualistic nature of body and mind, deriving from Descartes, according to which there are two quite distinct entities, existing separately. Accordingly it is a puzzle to explain how they can interact, how one can influence the other. This Ryle held to be a pseudo-problem which, however, had bedevilled much of the theorizing about behaviour since Descartes' day.

The belief in two separate sorts of phenomenon also helps to explain why psychology as a whole developed as it did; and why so many psychologists have been passionately concerned to show what is, and what is not, properly the concern of their science. As Ryle puts it:

> 'When the word "psychology" was coined, two hundred years ago, it was supposed that the two-worlds legend was true. It was supposed, in consequence, that since Newtonian science explains (it was erroneously thought) everything that exists and occurs in the physical world, there could and should be just one other counterpart science explaining what exists and occurs in the postulated non-physical world. As Newtonian scientists studied the phenomena of the one field, so there ought to be scientists studying the phenomena of the other field. "Psychology" was supposed to be the title of the one empirical study of "mental phenomena".'

Of course many other sorts of people studied behaviour in various ways, for example historians, economists, and dramatists.

> 'But, according to the para-Newtonian programme, psychologists would study human beings in a completely different way. They would find and examine data inaccessible to teachers, detectives, biographers, or friends; data, too, which could not be represented on the stage or in the pages of novels. These other studies of man were restricted to the inspection of the mere tents and houses in which the real men dwelt. The psychological study of man would use the direct access to the residents themselves. Indeed, not until psychologists had found and turned the key, could the other students of human thought and behaviour hope to do more than batter vainly on locked doors. The visible deeds and the audible words of human beings were themselves exercises of the qualities of their characters or intellects, but only external symptoms or expressions of their real but privy exercises.'

Hence the use of introspection as the systematic method to get at mental processes, which were to be analysed on the model of physics or chemistry. Later, as we have seen, Watson took the other tack, and argued that psychologists must deal only with the material world, that is, behaviour. (See *Focus* on *Introspection*).

But, Ryle argues, the physical model is not an appropriate one, as psychologists, in 1949, were beginning to realize:

> 'The Newtonian system is no longer the sole paradigm of natural science. Man need not be degraded to a machine by being denied to be a ghost in a machine. He might, after all, be a sort of animal, namely, a higher

mammal. There has yet to be ventured the hazardous leap to the hypothesis that perhaps he is a man.'

Ryle's views are obviously of direct relevance to the study of thinking. As far as intelligence is concerned, Ryle's argument is that the dualist mistake led to the notion that the 'intelligence' of any action is defined by certain mental operations, which presumably precede the action. Applying this to some well-known experiments, Köhler's apes would be said to be intelligent if they first solved the problem by 'insight', and then carried it out; but not if they merely hit on the solution by accident. As Ryle puts it: '... the absurd assumption made by the intellectualist legend is this, that a performance of any sort inherits all its title to intelligence from some anterior internal operation of planning what to do'. It is absurd, not because such planning does not take place (although it may be impossible to be sure about it), but because the argument involves an infinite regression. If an action can only count as intelligent if it is preceded by an intelligent plan, the same must apply to the operation of planning; and so on *ad infinitum*. 'If, for any operation to be intelligently executed, a prior theoretical operation had first to be performed intelligently, it would be a logical impossibility for anyone ever to break into the circle.' Instead, it is the *manner* in which behaviour occurs that defines it as intelligent or otherwise. 'When I do something intelligently, i.e. thinking what I am doing, I am doing one thing and not two. My performance has a special procedure or manner, not special antecedents.' The characteristics of such procedures or manners will depend on the circumstances in which the action is carried out. Thus it follows that there is no way of listing in advance a set of actions which are always intelligent, or always stupid. Any activity—say writing an essay, or doing the washing—can be done intelligently or unintelligently. Nor can we define intelligence by the components of the activity, or by the mode in which it is carried out. It might be intelligent to write very slowly for a term essay, but stupid in an examination. Similarly it might be intelligent in the first case to allow the mind to wander freely, but less so in the second : convergent thinking would then be more desirable than divergent. (In discussing creative thinking, we have seen that psychology has suffered in the past from a tendency to believe that first one, and then the other, mode of thinking was 'really' intelligent, and by implication desirable.)

Thus in Ryle's view it is a fundamental mistake to suppose that 'intelligence' is an entity separate from the behaviour from which it is inferred. We can say that a student is working intelligently; and if we observe this consistently, we can say that he is intelligent. But it would be wrong to suppose that there is an operation, or some kind of force, 'intelligence', which lies behind or explains the behaviour. But how do we decide whether or not the student is working intelligently? Ryle's argument here is perhaps less clear—or less satisfactory for psychologists who are seeking cut-and-dried rules to apply. Let us look at the two main examples offered.

'In judging that someone's performance is or is not intelligent, we have, as has been said, in a certain manner to look beyond the performance itself. For there is no particular overt or inner performance which could not have been accidentally or 'mechanically' executed by an idiot, a sleepwalker, a man in panic, absence of mind or delirium or even, sometimes, by a parrot. But in looking beyond the performance itself, we are not trying to pry into some hidden counterpart performance enacted on the supposed secret stage of the agent's inner life. We are considering his abilities and propensities of which the performance was an actualization. Our inquiry is not into causes (and a fortiori not into occult causes) but into capacities, skills, habits, liabilities, and bents. We observe, for example, a soldier scoring a bull's eye. Was it luck or was it skill? If he has the skill, then he can get on or near the bull's eye again, even if the wind strengthens, the range alters, and the target moves.'

And so on. Ryle considers in more detail, as a paradigm case, what happens when a person argues intelligently. He makes four points. First, the person may be arguing to others, or silently to himself; that does not affect the intelligence or otherwise of his argument. Second, much of his argument will be new; part of being intelligent is being able to innovate. Third, part of it is being ready and able to deal with unexpected contingencies, even if they actually never arise. If an opponent did produce a new line, the intelligent arguer would be able to deal with it. And fourth, 'there is the cardinal feature that he reasons logically, that is, that he avoids fallacies and produces valid proofs and inferences, pertinent to the case he is making.'

It is hard to disagree with any of this; yet psychologists are probably left asking how it helps in the everyday business of testing and predicting. Of course this is unfair, since that was not the object of the analysis. But it may partly explain why psychologists have often continued to write as though Ryle's arguments did not exist. We have spent some time on them, partly because we believe they are of fundamental importance, and partly because no-one concerned with psychology as a whole, apart from intelligence, should be unaware of *The Concept of Mind*. Indeed all serious students should read it.

As Butcher (1968) however, points out, the word 'intelligence' remains useful so long as we are aware of its misleading properties. The matter is taken further in an article by Miles (1957) which is however largely concerned with what is meant by 'definition' rather than what is meant by 'intelligence'. Miles gives six senses in which 'definition' can be used, as follows.

1. 'Real essence' i.e. the question as to what intelligence 'really is'. This seems to suppose that because there is a word 'intelligence' there must also be a thing to which the word refers; but this is not so.

2. Lexical (i.e. dictionary, definitions and the appeal to ordinary usage: the argument that 'intelligence' must mean such-and-such, because that is how it is ordinarily understood. This, Miles argues, is really a request for a list of the things that count as intelligent. (Just as the question 'What is an ichthyologist?'

might mean what does he do? How is he distinguished from any other sort of biologist?) But there is no such list, as shown by Ryle. And even if there were, the psychologist is not bound to use the word intelligence in the same way as other people: if he wants 'intelligence' to mean 'scoring highly on tests', he is entitled to use it so, though he must be prepared for confusion.

3. Stipulative definition. This is in fact what we have just mentioned: an arbitrary definition fixed by the user, which is perfectly acceptable as long as we all know what is happening. ('When *I* use a word,' said Humpty Dumpty, 'it means what I want it to mean—neither more nor less.')

4. Description plus naming.

and

5. The search for a key. Both these are the stipulative definitions: but they bring out the point that the latter imply something important that groups the phenomena together, or underlies them. In other words a stipulative definition need not be entirely arbitrary. A psychologist might say, 'I shall apply the name *extravert* to people who score highly on certain tests, prefer bright lights and parties to sitting at home with a good book, are more prone to hysteria than to anxiety neurosis, etc. Further, their behaviour is related to differences in the nervous system, which I can demonstrate experimentally.' If someone replied: 'Well, *I* shall use the name for bandy-legged red-haired men living north of the Thames,' the first answer is that each is entitled to his own use. The next answer is that the first use makes more sense because it can be shown that those characteristics do go together in a theoretically important way, connected by an experimentally-demonstrable substrate.

6. Operational definition. This boils down to saying, 'How do you test whether a person is intelligent?' The psychologist's answer is, of course, 'By means of instruments devised for that purpose.' Intelligence is what the tests measure. (This too is a stipulative definition: we are saying that correct responses to test items are what we are going to count as intelligent.) This apparently circular definition is far from useless, since what we usually want tests for is to predict performance in some other situation. We establish empirically that those who score highly on tests also do well, say, at University. We can refer to this for short by the word 'intelligence', without going any further. Miles, indeed, concludes that this approach is 'fundamentally sound'. It may be sound, but it is rather unsatisfying. One reason for this is that circumstances could arise in which common sense would say that giving the *wrong* answers was the intelligent thing to do; for example if, being in the Army, one wished to avoid some onerous or dangerous promotion. This may seem trivial; but it is actually the problem that faces cross-cultural investigators of intelligence, as we shall see later. Secondly, however, surely as psychologists we want to know more about abilities than how to predict them on a purely *ad hoc* basis. We hope to reach some adequate theoretical analysis. And it is to some of the attempts to do so that we now turn.

EXPERIMENTAL INVESTIGATIONS

These attempts have centred round the method and results of factor analysis. Factor analysis is a development from the concept of correlation, by which Galton was able for the first time to express quantitatively a partial relationship between two variables. Factor analysis is in essence a series of correlations, between every pair of a set of variables. A group of variables that correlate highly with each other, but not with others, suggests the existence of some 'factor' underlying them. Suppose we set out to investigate athletic ability. We might measure a number of athletes on the usual track and field events. We might find that, perhaps, there were high correlations between distance races; sprint races and long jump; and throwing events such as shot, hammer and javelin. There might be lower, but still positive, correlations between these three groups. It would then become a matter for discussion whether we preferred to postulate a general athletic ability, with some specialized factors; or a whole series of roughly equal factors. This example illustrates some of the strengths and weaknesses of the factor analytic method. The main advantage is that it does permit a quantitative analysis in place of speculative musings. But there are several drawbacks. First, the scores to be analysed can only come from what is thought to be worth measuring. For intellectual abilities, this is usually tests of various kinds; in our example, there are many other possible measures of athletic ability, such as weight-lifting. Similarly for intelligence. It would be desirable to sample a wider range of behaviour, but clearly it is impossible to examine all of it. Secondly, the analysis does not yield psychological factors, but only statistical ones, i.e. consistencies between sets of scores. Knowing the items from which the scores come, it is plausible to name a factor 'verbal ability' or the like. But this is an interpretation of the analysis, and goes beyond it. Burt (1968) one of the main pioneers and champions of factor analysis, recognizes this danger well:

'Unfortunately most investigators appear content to name their group factors after the nature of the tests for which they have high loadings; and the nature of the tests is usually inferred from the names given to them and the purposes for which each was constructed. Earlier investigators, particularly in Britain, nearly always checked their inferences about the nature of their tests and their factors by picking out the individuals who obtained the highest scores for each and then asking for introspective descriptions of their mental processes when carrying out the tests. (This was sometimes supplemented by independent reports on their efficiency in relevant respects.) Unfortunately, with the advent of behaviouristic principles, introspection has fallen into disuse. It is, however, urgently to be hoped that it will once again be revived as an essential part of factorial and test research.'

Butcher (1968) however concludes:

'Factor analysis, with all its inherent drawbacks, and with all the additional hazards of misguided application and faulty drawing of conclusions (which it shares with most other techniques of any value), has been and is the only available method to show clearly what is common and what is specific in a complex set of performances.'

Unfortunately there is as yet no general agreement as to what has been clearly shown. The main issue is between those who, like Burt, argue for a general factor with various sorts of subsidiary factors; and at the other extreme those such as Guilford who prefer a relatively large number of specific factors. As far as reference to thinking goes, it seems the importance of the Burt view is in its treatment of the determinants of general intelligence, and particularly the relative roles of heredity and environment. The Guilford approach, on the other hand, gives an analysis of the operations involved in problem solving, creativity, etc., as we have already seen. These are not basic differences between the two, merely matters of emphasis.

Spearman (1904) in putting forward his two-factor theory, distinguished it from three other sorts of theory, which he termed the monarchic, oligarchic, and the anarchic. (The metaphor is politically unsound, but let that pass.) The monarchic view would be that there is just one sort of intellectual ability, which is manifested in every task. On the oligarchic view there are several factors of ability, each covering a number of tasks; on the anarchic view there are as many abilities as cognitive tasks. America, which has politically rejected both monarchy and anarchy, has psychologically favoured oligarchy. The pioneer was L. L. Thurstone, who on the basis of extensive analysis of a varied set of tests, concluded that the evidence justified the postulation of seven 'primary mental abilities'. These were as follows (Thurstone, 1938).

S — spatial ability
P — perceptual speed
N — numerical ability
M — memory
V — verbal meaning
W — verbal fluency
I or R — inductive reasoning.

Later studies showed that these factors are not all equally applicable to every age range. It is also important to note that they are themselves intercorrelated: in other words they have something in common. Thurstone in fact subsequently showed how one can obtain an estimate of general intelligence from scores on the tests designed to assess the 'primary abilities'. To some extent, therefore, the monarchic–oligarchic–anarchic question is one about the degree of generality we wish to have. And this may be partly a practical matter for purposes of selection, guidance, etc.

Thurstone's factors have probably been so far the most influential in determining how psychologists think about intelligence. Perhaps more interesting from a theoretical point of view, however, is the approach of J. P. Guilford and his coworkers. (Summarized by Guilford and Hoepfner, 1966.) Guilford's system, which we have already had occasion to mention, and which goes under the general title of the *structure of intellect*, begins with a theoretical analysis. He argues that any account of intellectual abilities must deal with three classes of variables: the activities or operations performed; the material or content on which operations are performed; and the product which is the result of operations. The operations, content, and products are as follows.

Operations: cognition; memory; divergent thinking; convergent thinking; evaluation.

Contents: figural (e.g. images); symbolic (letters, syllables, other conventional signs); semantic (meanings, concepts); behavioural (e.g. social perceptions and concepts).

Products: Units; classes; relations; systems; transformations.

The *operations* are fairly easy to understand, and we have already met the distinction between convergent and divergent thinking. Among the *contents*, the figural and symbolic somewhat resemble Bruner's ikonic and symbolic levels of thinking, to be discussed later. (See *Development and Culture*.) The introduction of behavioural contents would appear to be an important innovation. Guilford and Hoepfner (1966) say: 'information, essentially non-verbal, involved in human interactions, where awareness of the attitudes, needs, desires, moods, intentions, perceptions, thoughts, etc., of other people and ourselves is important.' What is meant by *products* is a little harder to understand, and it will be useful to quote Guilford's own definitions.

'The product may be a unit of information, which is defined as a relatively segregated or circumscribed portion of information, with a "thing" character. The product may be a class, which we define as an aggregate of units of information, grouped because of their common properties. A relation, a third kind of product, is defined as a connection between units of information, based upon variables that apply to them both. A system is defined as an organized or structured composite of units of information, having interacting or inter-relating parts. The concept of "group" in mathematics would be an example in the symbolic category, as a set would be an example of a class. A transformation is some kind of change of existing or known information; a reinterpretation. An implication is some kind of extrapolation of knowledge. In the area of cognition, this would include such things as expectation and knowledge and antecedents or consequents. In the area of productive thinking it would include drawing inferences or conclusions.' (Guilford, 1963)

These three dimensions can be shown diagrammatically (Figure 4.1). It is then clear that on this analysis, intellect consists of a number of separate factors

134

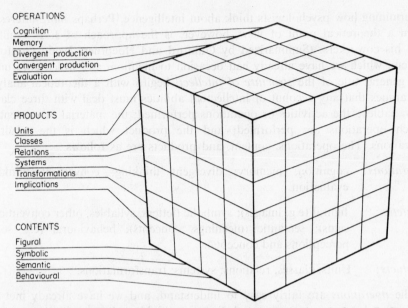

OPERATIONS
Cognition
Memory
Divergent production
Convergent production
Evaluation

PRODUCTS
Units
Classes
Relations
Systems
Transformations
Implications

CONTENTS
Figural
Symbolic
Semantic
Behavioural

Figure 4.1. Guilford's 'Structure of intellect' (Reproduced from J. P. Guilford, 'Intellectual resources and their values as seen by scientists,' in C. W. Taylor and F. Barron (Eds.), *Scientific Creativity: Its Recognition and Development* (1963), Wiley, New York)

or abilities, viz. 5 × 4 × 6 = 120. There is no general factor. Further, the analysis shows what factors *ought* to exist; their actual existence has to be shown empirically. Guilford and his associates present evidence for many but not all of the cells. Merrifield and others have shown which of the abilities would be expected to be involved in problem-solving and creativity, respectively (see relevant chapters). Apart from the general drawbacks of factor analysis, there would seem to be two main objections to the Guilford system. The first is that while the theoretical analysis seems quite plausible, its correctness is still a matter of proof. It is not something that can be proved correct by logic, or by evidence other than that from its own factor analytic studies. Merrifield (1966) makes this clear: 'One may question the choice of the three-category scheme—why not a two-category description, or one with four categories? Two categories seemed too few to account for the observed differences among factors and four categories seemed more than necessary.' The second objection is that such a detailed analysis has so far not proved to be very predictive. This is not an objection to its correctness, but only of its practical usefulness.

In contrast, the system favoured by Sir Cyril Burt might be termed a constitutional monarchy. Burt summarizes the approach thus:

'The measurement of any individual for any one of a given set of traits may be regarded as a function of four kinds of components: namely, those characteristic of (i) all the traits, (ii) some of the traits, (iii) the particular trait in question whenever it is measured, (iv) the particular trait in question as measured on this particular occasion'. (Burt, 1940)

Or in other words, general, group, specific, and error factors. These can also be seen diagrammatically as constituting a hierarchy, with general intelligence at the top and specific factors at the bottom. Such a diagram is presented by Vernon (1950) (Figure 4.2). In Butcher's opinion, 'The hierarchical theory has

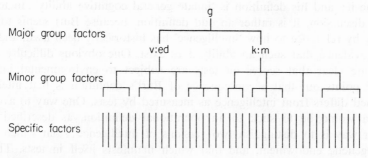

Figure 4.2. The hierarchical structure of abilities (Reproduced from P. E. Vernon, *The Structure of Human Abilities* (1950), Methuen by permission of Associated Book Publishers Ltd., London)

major advantages over almost all other models of human abilities.' He mentions two such advantages. The first is that: 'It accounts for the proliferation of apparently conflicting findings and the multiplicity of ability factors that have been described and labelled. Much of this apparent confusion has been caused by the comparison of factors operating at different levels in the hierarchy, and this in turn is largely due to the initial selection of tests and people.' And the second major advantage 'is that one is thus enabled to recognize that different kinds of factor, and the tests based on them, serve very different purposes in assessment and prediction. Other things being equal, measurement of a general factor will account for more variation in performance and provide prediction over a wider range of tasks than measurement of a major or minor group factor.' Burt also emphasizes that his analysis is consistent with the neuro-physiological evidence. He writes, 1949:

'My own view, based largely on Sherrington's anatomical and physiological studies of the brain and nervous system, was that the structure of the mind is essentially hierarchical. Mental processes and mental capacities appear to consist of systems within systems. According to their relative complexity, the various components seem assignable to one or other of four or five distinguishable levels. In the nervous system the simplest types of process are the innate reflexes, some of which enter into almost every form of mental activity: these, however, are essentially unconscious, and therefore do not concern us here. If we confine ourselves solely to so-called "cognitive" (or as I should prefer to say "directive") processes, the simplest forms of all consist either of elementary sensory impressions or of elementary motor reactions. These constitute the lowest mental level. The next includes the more complex processes of perception with equally complex reactions on the motor side. The third is the level of mechanical association—of memory and of habit. The fourth and highest level of all involves the apprehension and application of relations. "Intelligence", as the "integrative function of the mind", is involved at every level; and its manifestations therefore differ not only in degree, but also in their qualitative nature.'

Since Burt does include a factor of general intelligence, it is necessary for him to define it: and his definition is 'innate general cognitive ability'. In terms of Miles's discussion, it is rather an odd definition, because Burt seems to justify it partly by reference to how 'intelligence' has historically been used, and partly by the evidence that such an ability does exist. One obvious difficulty is, that it is quite clear that scores on tests are subject to environmental influence. Butcher points out that a consequence of Burt's definition is that intelligence as defined differs from intelligence as measured by tests. One way to avoid this dilemma would be to stick to an operational definition, as described above. Another way is to distinguish two versions of intelligence: that which is part of the genetic endowment, and that which manifests itself in tests. This was proposed by Hebb (1949) who called the versions A and B; and Cattell has a very similar concept in his Fluid and Crystallized Intelligence (e.g. Cattell, 1963).

'THE ORGANIZATION OF BEHAVIOR'

The views which Donald Hebb presented in *The Organization of Behavior* (1949) can now be seen as the germ of much current work. I do not mean that Vernon, for example, has carried out his cross-cultural investigations merely because of what Hebb said, but rather that we are now in a position to see how forward-looking was Hebb's widely-acclaimed book. As far as intelligence is concerned, there seem to be two important points. The first concerns the definition of intelligence; the second the relationship of heredity and environment. First, definitions. Like so many writers before and since, Hebb could not avoid this hornet's nest; and it is interesting to compare the views of the psychologist with those of Ryle, the philosopher, published in the same year. Hebb starts from the well-known animal experiments on 'insight' and hypothesis-testing. He points out that both 'insight' and 'hypothesis' had been defined as forms of behaviour, and argues that this will not do: they must be 'something postulated, hypothetical, *inferred* from behaviour.' This gives rise to a general criticism of the more extreme behaviourist viewpoint:

'Psychology has sometimes in the past been too free in postulating special processes to explain behavior. Now it is doing penance by going to another extreme, scientifically just as sinful. This current misconception of the scientific method makes any hypothetical entity somehow disreputable. Psychologists now seem to feel that it is risky indeed to depart from statements of fact; nothing should be mentioned that is not "operationally" demonstrable.'

But, then, what sort of a thing *is* intelligence, or insight (according to Hebb the terms are 'fully equivalent')? The 'real meaning' is 'that of a causal factor in behavior'. For Ryle, this was the starting point: we all know that we speak of intelligence as if it were a causal factor—but what does this mean? And we have seen what answer he gave. For Hebb the statement is almost a finishing point, though he takes one further step forward, thus: 'It may be suggested that if they are to be used, "intelligence" should refer to the enduring aptitude, the existence of a causal factor in problem-solving that may or may not lead to the solution of a particular problem; "insight" to refer to its operation in the particular instance.' By speaking of an 'aptitude' Hebb approaches closely to Ryle's view (he used the words 'capacities, skills, habits'). But Ryle also says: 'Our enquiry is not into causes'; while Hebb immediately proceeds: 'There is still a difference of opinion as to what this causal factor in behaviour is, and how it operates.' And from there he embarks on his attempt to reconcile intelligence with theories of learning, and with neurophysiology.

Here a fairly substantial quotation may be useful. The thesis runs throughout the whole book, but the gist is this. Hebb first gives a hypothetical account of the motor and neurophysiological events that might occur when a concept is acquired. The series of events is termed a 'phase sequence' (p. 133 of his book). Later (p. 164) he takes up the story again:

> 'It has already been seen how insight, as a sudden perception of new relationships, can result from the simultaneous activity of two conceptual cycles in adult learning (pp. 133–134). This need not be elaborated further; the new relationship is a change of the phase sequence, and each phase sequence has its distinctive motor facilitation, so the change would be evident in a discontinuity of behavior—the actual evidence from which the insight is inferred.
>
> Apart from the special case of a sudden solution following failure, insight is essentially the phase sequence itself, the autonomous central factor in behavior. It is that which makes behavior directed, instead of random; the mechanism that is both anticipatory, adjusting behavior to an obstacle *before* the obstacle is reached, and recurrent, so that the chimpanzee, trying to reach a banana, *remembers* the stick he saw a moment before, goes and gets it, and rakes in the fruit.
>
> Phylogenetic differences of insight are thus the differences in the complexity of phase sequence that is possible in the brain of a higher or lower species. The lack of insight in the earliest learning of primates becomes comprehensible, since the phase sequence must first be organized.
>
> Also comprehensible is the slowness with which insightful learning develops in these species, by the very mechanism that makes their ultimate level of behavior more insightful than any other. The larger association cortex of primates, both in absolute terms and in A/S ratio (p. 124)* means a slower establishment of sensory control, and so a longer time to set up the phase sequence and insight. At the same time, in a larger association

* This is the ratio: $\dfrac{\text{total association cortex}}{\text{total sensory cortex}}$

138

cortex, the number of assemblies of cells that can function as separate closed systems will be larger. This means that the higher animal at maturity will see any particular situation in a larger number of ways. The comparatively small sensory projection means also that the phase sequence can escape from complete sensory control more frequently, and for longer periods, so that the insightful behavior of higher species is less a response to the immediate environment and more an integration of serial stimulation from situations that cannot be surveyed as a whole.

Finally, all this explains how insight depends on experience and yet is not a simple, direct result of learning, or the operation of specific habits (Birch, 1945). The perception of new relationships discussed above is usually not delayed, but immediate; the animal put into a new situation will perceive its parts as familiar, and as related in a meaningful way (that is, by the mechanisms discussed on pp. 130–134). The behavior is then insightful as an organized set of responses to a new total situation. An organization that consists of a *new* temporal combination of elements which themselves were organized by experience obviously depends on learning, but is not learned. Heredity sets a limit to the amount of development of the phase sequence and determines the principles of development, but experience is necessary as well.'

Now the supposed neurophysiological mechanisms need not detain us long, for even as Hebb wrote it was becoming apparent that his model would not do. And as far as definitions go, it is most odd to say that insight *is* a phase sequence. As a good behaviourist, Hebb wants to avoid postulating mentalistic entities to explain behaviour, and instead postulates neurophysiological ones, which he then equates with the behaviour itself. The phase sequences, if they existed, would be mechanisms underlying behaviour; they could not constitute behaviour, whether intelligent or not; still less could they constitute intelligence, or insight—if there were such a thing, which on Ryle's analysis there is not. Twenty years later, Hebb gave an exactly comparable account of imagery, which will be quoted in due course (see *Imagery*). It is also interesting, incidentally, to compare the point about increasing freedom from sensory control with the theories of Piaget, whom Hebb, as was customary at that time, does not mention at all.

The virtue of Hebb's account lies rather, first in redirecting the attention of psychologists to central processes, and secondly in stressing the interaction of hereditary and environmental factors. So we come to the second main point for discussion. To begin with we have yet another sort of definition; but enough has been said on that topic.

'It appears that the word "intelligence" has *two* valuable meanings. One is (A) an *innate potential*, the capacity for development, a fully innate property that amounts to the possession of a good brain and a good neural metabolism. The second is (B) the functioning of a brain in which development has gone on, determining an *average level of performance or comprehension* by the partly grown or mature person. Neither, of course, is observed directly; but *intelligence B*, a hypothetical level of development in brain function, is a much more direct inference from behaviour than *intelligence A*, the original potential.'

HEREDITY AND ENVIRONMENT

Thus Hebb once again showed, as psychologists seem to have to show their colleagues at regular intervals, that we must deal with both inherited and acquired factors in explaining behaviour. Burt, in conformity with his definition of intelligence as 'innate general cognitive ability', has, while taking account of both, put the greater weight on inheritance. His arguments have been put in many publications, but nowhere more cogently than in a famous paper of 1955, 'The evidence for the concept of intelligence.' Summarizing Burt is rather like reducing Bernard Shaw to one of his own postcards; but the main points are these. He first traces the origins of the concept in four areas: the observational psychology of antiquity, of the Middle Ages, and of the faculty psychology of more modern times; the biological views of Herbert Spencer and Darwin, and later Piaget; the physiological research stemming from the work of Hughlings Jackson, and Charles Sherrington (stressing the integrative general functions of the brain); and the study of individual psychology starting with Galton. 'These converging lines of inquiry,' writes Burt, 'furnished strong presumptive evidence for a mental trait of fundamental importance defined by three verifiable attributes: first, it is a *general* quality; it enters into every form of mental activity; secondly, it is (in a broad sense of the word) an *intellectual* quality— that is, it characterizes the cognitive rather than the affective or conative aspects of conscious behaviour; thirdly, it is inherited or at least *innate*; differences in its strength or amount are due to differences in the individual's genetic constitution. We thus arrive at the concept of an *innate, general, cognitive ability.*' From these historic words Burt goes on to present the evidence.

There is first the fact that an extensive testing programme showed, 'almost without exception, *positive and significant correlations between every form of cognitive activity*'. Burt points out, as we have already noted, that later investigators such as Thurstone were also obliged to conclude from similar results, that we must think of a general factor. Statistically, such a factor was found, in Burt's studies and those of others, to account for about 50 per cent of the individual variability among school-children. The role of the general factor does gradually diminish with age, as specialized abilities develop. Second, there is the question of whether this factor is cognitive: it might, for example, be one of motivation. The variability might be accounted for by a general factor of, say, laziness. Burt's answer to these is likewise a correlational one. There is an old traditional division of human psychological activities into cognition, conation, and affect; roughly, thinking, willing, and feeling. Burt found that measurements in these three areas showed low, though positive, correlations. This agrees, of course, with the very well-known studies of Terman (1925) who found that his large sample of gifted Californian school-children tended to be above average in every respect. But as for factors, it appeared quite clear that the most closely grouped correlations were those between the cognitive activities. Another, separate, group, was an emotional one, which was not sharply separated from the conative or motivational group. Thirdly there is the question as to the innateness of the factor; and it is this that has roused more controversy, probably, than any other of the arguments about intelligence. Burt's treatment is correspondingly more complex than for the first two items, and merits a new paragraph.

He starts with Galton. Galton has been criticized (e.g. by Hunt, 1961) for not taking into account factors of social advantage: he showed, for example, that eminent fathers tended to have eminent sons at a rate far above the average for the population. Naturally, it is sometimes said, this may be due to the superior environment provided by the father, and not to inheritance as Galton claimed. But Burt points out that Galton was well aware of this objection, and sought to meet it in various ways: first by comparing men of good heredity, with those of mediocre, while holding social advantage constant; second, by noting cases in which children of distinguished parents were not in fact influenced by them; and third, by examining cases in which a gifted child emerged from an undistinguished background. Even though the parents were not gifted, since the family circumstances were not good, the ability must, somehow, be due to heredity. Burt agrees with Galton that these three sorts of case provide only a *prima facie*, not a conclusive argument. Today, we should probably be even more cautious, since we are perhaps more aware that we do not really know what constitutes an effectively stimulating environment for the individual case—though there are some suggestions, as we shall see later. Galton accordingly suggested, and in some cases carried out, other sorts of investigations such as the study of foster children. Most notably, he was the first to propose the use of twins in this problem. He distinguished three questions to be answered: is intelligence inherited or not? if so, how? and what are the relative roles of inheritance and circumstances? Burt now proceeds to deal with each of these. First the facts as to whether intelligence is inherited. And the first point, and a very important one, is that:

'With a few rare exceptions, like eye colour or serological differences in the blood, every observable characteristic that geneticists have so far studied has proved to be the product of the joint action of both heredity, and environment. There are no such things as hereditary characters; there are only hereditary tendencies.'

The obvious sources of evidence are, children brought up in very constant environments, such as orphanages; and children of very similar (effectively identical heredity, namely monozygotic twins. Both these sources support the hereditary proposition. The measured intelligence of institutionalized children resembles that of the parents more than that of such children in general. The data on twins are well known, and some figures will be quoted later. Secondly, there is the question of mode of inheritance. This genetic issue is not particularly relevant to our present discussion, and Burt's contribution here has been somewhat superseded by the recent great advances in this field. We turn therefore to the third question, the relative influence of heredity and environment. Burt's conclusions here are based on the statistical analysis of data from children of different degrees of relationship, particularly twins. The data are test results, 'adjusted' by reference to the children's teachers. On this basis Burt concludes that about 12 per cent of the total variance is due to non-genetic factors, and 88 per cent to genetic factors. This is the most questionable of Burt's findings.

With much of what Burt says we can agree. That there is a strong hereditary component in 'intelligence', whatever we mean by that, seems indisputable. A very convincing demonstration of this is offered in a well-known paper by Erlenmeyer-Kimling and Jarvik (1963). They collated the correlation coefficients from fifty-two studies of different degrees of familial relationships. (Figure 4.3.)

Category		0·00 0·10 0·20 0·30 0·40 0·50 0·60 0·70 0·80 0·90	Groups included
Unrelated persons	Reared apart		4
	Reared together		5
Fosterparent - child			3
Parent - child			12
Siblings	Reared apart		2
	Reared together		35
Twins Two-egg	Opposite sex		9
	Like sex		11
Twins One-egg	Reared apart		4
	Reared together		14

Figure 4.3. Correlation coefficients for intelligence test scores from 52 studies. Vertical lines represent median scores, while horizontal indicate the ranges, (From L. Erlenmeyer-Kimling and L. F. Jarvik, 'Genetics and intelligence: A review', *Science*, 1963, **142**, 1477–1479. Copyright 1963 by the American Association for the Advancement of Science)

There is a clear tendency for correlations to rise with nearness of relationship— but also with nearness of upbringing; and with wide variations in both cases. It is another matter, however, to claim, as Burt does, that we can attribute numerical values to the roles of heredity and environment. There are perhaps three lines of criticism, all of which Burt recognizes, but which in the opinion of some he does not entirely deal with. There are first statistical arguments, which are highly technical and into which we do not propose to enter. Then there are criticisms of twin studies as a technique. Vandenberg (1966) lists four of these. (a) The first point seems to be that while we can be sure that within one pair of identical twins the hereditary factors are identical, there is no ways of controlling the genetic variability between groups of twins. Twins are not all that numerous, and sampling may produce misleading results. Vandenberg's example is colour-blindness: if a group of twins happened to contain some colour-blind individuals, evidence would be found for a strong hereditary factor; whereas if no colour-blind individuals were included, no such factor would appear. Colour-blindness is obvious; but intellectual components are not. A related point, not made by Vandenberg, might be that there is known to be a 'twinning factor'. Some families tend to produce twins, and thus comparisons with the rest of the population may be confused. (b) When pairs of identical and non-identical twins are compared, it is assumed that the degree of environmental influence is held constant. This may not be so. Non-identical twins may be treated more differently than identical ones, for example, simply because they *are* less alike. (c) The twin method deals only with variance within the families, which is only part of the total variance; it is assumed that as between families, the role of the environment is approximately constant. (d) Early studies suffered from the unreliability of methods of classifying twins as identical or not. This is now less of a difficulty. Vandenberg seems to conclude that all of these criticisms can be more or less discounted, largely on the grounds that differences will average out if large enough samples are taken. This is possibly too optimistic a view, since the fact is that we really do not know what are the important environmental factors in intellectual development. This leads us to the third line of argument, which is that it seems to be becoming increasingly clear that what is important is the *interaction* between heredity and environment; so that to quantify these two factors does not really help very much in explaining the final result.

However we choose to regard the hereditary component of intelligence, little prospect exists of altering it, unless we wish to propose, as Galton, logically, did, some form of genetic engineering. He advocated Eugenics or selective breeding; now, the possibility of direct intervention in genetic transmission is in sight. But both of these seem ethically objectionable. Thus it is the environmental side that is in some ways of greatest interest; and recently much work has centred on the prospects of analysing precisely the way in which intellectual abilities arise in particular circumstances. We have already seen, when discussing creative thought, that there is no simple answer to this. Interest in the environmental side came to the fore in 1961 with the publication of J. McV. Hunt's *Intelligence and Experience*. In particular, Hunt set out to destroy the myths, as he held them to be, of fixed intelligence and unalterably (because genetically) predetermined development. As so often with effective polemics, Hunt was to some extent attacking a man of straw. We have already noted Hebb's views of 1949 (which Hunt quotes plentifully); and other psychologists, from Galton on, had always allowed that intelligence could change and develop with time. Hunt, to make his case, begins by stating: 'The view that intelligence is a capacity fixed once and for all by genetic inheritance has had wide currency,' and quotes 'most of the general textbooks written before World War II' in support, as well as Burt's famous definition. While Hunt perhaps overstated his case, it certainly was true that the dramatic success of testing in the twenties and thirties did help to produce a general assumption that the measured IQ was a pretty stable quantity. This assumption, incidentally, underlies the formation of *Mensa*, the international society whose qualification for membership is an IQ in the top two per cent of the population as a whole. The idea arose from a radio broadcast by Cyril Burt, in which he suggested that such a group would provide a useful research instrument, and that it might, perhaps, be consulted by Government on questions of national importance. The latter has not yet come to pass; a certain amount of useful research has emerged; and *Mensa* continues to recruit members on the basis, usually, of one test, which ensures their lifelong eligibility for membership.

Against this assumption Hunt ranged evidence from three sources: from studies of identical twins reared apart; from repeated testing of the same children in longitudinal studies; from studies of the effects of training. The first source is principally the work of Newman, Freeman, and Holzinger (1937) who collated data on 19 pairs of identical twins reared apart from an early age. The largest difference in IQ points was 24, though the average was only 8·2, which is not so very far from the average difference of 5·9 points for identical twins reared together. Taking the second line, a number of studies have tested individuals at intervals over a long period of time. These generally show a progressive decline in correlation with the original tests, and sometimes quite large changes. Honzik, Macfarlane, and Allen (1948) for example, found variations of from 6 to 16 years in 10 per cent of a sample of 222 children. There were even more numerous studies on which Hunt could draw to demonstrate the effects of schooling. But this method of investigation is among the hardest to control adequately: for example, it is very often the case that variations in schooling are due to circumstances over which the investigator has no control, such as the availability of schools in a given community. Rarely does an experimenter have the opportunity to arrange two properly matched samples, with a well-designed experimental procedure. On the whole, however, it is generally found that IQ scores go up when schooling is available. Some of the most convincing studies were those of R. A. Spitz (1945, 1946). He compared the development of babies in two institutions. In one the babies, though born of socially well-adjusted mothers, got very little attention or variation of stimulation; in the other the opposite was the case, and the children were those of delinquent girls in a penal institution. The investigation was done over the first year of life, during which the IQ scores of the second group remained fairly constant at around average, while the relatively neglected babies' scores dropped from average 131 to average 72.

From this evidence Hunt went on to discuss many other views of the relationship of intelligence and experience, with which we deal in appropriate places. He ended, however, on a notably optimistic note: '... it is no longer unreasonable to consider that it might be feasible to discover ways to govern the encounters that children have with their environments, especially during the early years of their development, to achieve a substantially faster rate of intellectual development and a substantially higher adult level of intellectual capacity.' Ten years later, do we agree? Ten years is a very short time in which to look for any dramatic advances. There are, rather, a few hints about the way in which the discoveries Hunt forecast might come.

One of the most talked-about, at least, of these, has been due to Robert Rosenthal and his coworkers. His essential finding is stated in a paper of 1966:

'Experiments have shown that in behavioral research employing human or animal subjects, the experimenter's expectancy can be a significant determinant of the subject's response.' (Rosenthal, 1964)

In the 1966 paper Rosenthal and Jacobson reported increases in children's test scores due apparently to teachers' expectations. A non-verbal intelligence test was given to all the children in an elementary school, comprising six grades (age levels), with three classes at each grade, respectively above average, average, and below average in school achievement. In each class an average of 20 per cent of the names were given to the class teacher, and was told that these children would show 'unusual intellectual gains' during the academic year. Eight months later, the children were retested with the same test. Over the school as a whole, the experimental subjects showed significantly ($p = 0.02$) greater gains in IQ scores than the rest. Nearly all of this difference was due to the first two grades (ages 6–8 years). The results for these two grades can be expressed as in Table 4.1 following.

Table 4.1—*Percentages of experimental and control subjects gaining 10, 20 or 30 IQ points (first and second grade children). Reprinted with permission of author and publisher from R. Rosenthal and L. Jacobson, 'Teachers' expectancies: determinants of pupils' IQ gains'. Psychological Reports (1966), 19, 115–118.*

IQ gain	Control Ss*	Experimental Ss**	x^2	p***
10 points	49	79	4·75	0·02
20 points	19	47	5·59	0·01
30 points	5	21	3·47	0·04

* N = 95   ** N = 19   *** p one-tailed

Now obviously nineteen children is not a large sample; and it is notable that half the control subjects gained IQ points, which may suggest that the test used is one of low reliability. Also, there is no question of an increase in ability, merely in test scores. Nevertheless the impressive fact remains that some children, at least, made large increases in test scores, that is, in *effective* ability, merely because they were expected to do so. As Rosenthal concludes:

> 'The most important question which remains is that which asks how a teacher's expectation becomes translated into behavior in such a way as to elicit the expected pupil behavior. Prior research on the unintentional communication of expectancies in experimentally more carefully controlled interactions suggests that this question will not be easily answered.'

These notable results also make one wonder, if teachers can have such an effect over eight months, what must be the total result of the cultural environment in which we find ourselves; and to this matter we now turn.

FAMILY AND CULTURE

The obvious starting point is the home. We have already mentioned some hypotheses as to how different home backgrounds may affect creative thinking —and how these are at present quite inconclusive. The present case is similar. In general, however, there is a conclusive relationship between 'poorness' of home and intellectual retardation. The extensive studies of Mia Kellmer Pringle in Britain, for example (*Deprivation and Education*, 1965), show that children in institutions are fairly consistently inferior on average to those in normal homes, as far as test performance goes. Language development in particular suffers. As Butcher (1968) mentions in summarizing this work, the deficit may well be reversible, and may indeed be partly due just to the lesser ability of such children to cope with stressful test situations. But total deprivation of home life does not help us to isolate the factors that are important. More evidence comes from Vernon (1965) who studied West Indian children in a variety of home and school situations. Here, he says,

> '... it is clear that the most important single factor in children's performance on g and verbal tests is the cultural level of the home, parental education and encouragement, reading facilities and probably the speech background ... Of the other factors in the home situation ... the most important seems to be the purposefulness and rationality of the family atmosphere.'

This is rather more specific; and we must return to Vernon's important cross-cultural studies later. But Freeberg and Payne (1967) reviewing the evidence on the role of parental influence, are probably right to conclude that at present, advice to a parent on how to improve his child's learning ability could only be 'little more than generalization to provide "maximum environmental enrichment" '.

There are just a few pointers in the direction of more specific factors. Bloom (1964) believes optimistically that it is already possible to 'specify some of the major characteristics of an environment which will positively or negatively

146

affect the development of general intelligence or school achievement'. Let us quote some examples. The first two are summarized by Freeberg and Payne.

'Bing (1963), used sixty mothers of fifth-grade children. All of these children had similar total IQ scores and were divided by sex into "high" and "low" verbal groups. This grouping was based upon the contrast of verbal scores with spatial and numerical scores. For example, a "high verbal" subject was one whose verbal scores were high in relation to his numerical and spatial scores. Data was obtained from questionnaires and from interviews with the mothers as well as from observations of an "interaction situation" during which the mothers engaged in various problem-solving activities with the child. Responses on the retrospective questionnaire and interview indicated that mothers of "high verbal" children provided more verbal stimulation in early childhood (highly significant for boys but not for girls). These mothers also remembered more of the child's early accomplishments (significant for boys but not for girls), were more critical of poor academic achievement, provided the child with more storybooks, and let him take more part in mealtime conversations... In the observational situation, mothers of children with high verbal ability generally provided more assistance voluntarily, provided it sooner when requested by the child, and pressured the child more for improvement.'

This sort of report is impressive until one tries to see how the variables can possibly be disentangled. *Which* of the mother's heterogeneous activities is or are vital? It is not even clear that it is the activity of mothers that results in higher verbal scores of the children. It might well be that children who innately have greater verbal gifts, elicit more activity from the mothers. (The opposite case of this arises with those who later become schizophrenic—it is never clear whether this is partly due to 'cold' mothers, or whether mothers tend to be 'cold' towards incipient schizophrenics.) Then again, the mothers *say* they remember more accomplishments; but this could be due to the mothers' own greater verbal (or other) ability, which the sons inherited. On the other hand if they do remember more, maybe highly verbal sons give them more to remember. Or, perhaps, these mothers are better at remembering, and their sons inherit this superior memory, which in turn helps them to learn language better. Or, yet further, it may be that both sons and mothers are responding to some other factor entirely, such as the father's personality, or the physical environment provided by him. To confuse the issue still more there are problems of data recording. Remembered happenings are notoriously unreliable, and there is no guarantee that the presence of observers does not radically alter the normal situation. All this is not to decry such investigations, which increasingly supply us with information; it is merely to point out the extreme complexity of the situation.

The second example (also considered by Freeberg and Payne) is provided by Wolf (1964). He attempted to relate parental influences to intelligence test performance of the child, using data obtained from 60 fifth-grade students and from interviews with their mothers.

'Those aspects of the home which were considered as most relevant
to the development of general intelligence were incorporated as items in an
interview schedule of 63 questions. The items were then used as a basis for
ratings on 13 scales designated as "Environmental Process Characteristics". . . .
The correlation of the total score (which was a summation of the 13 scale
scores) and the child's IQ score was striking $+0.69$. Of particular interest
for our purposes are the individual correlations with the intelligence test
score. The best relations were found for those scales dealing with the parents'
intellectual expectations for the child, the amount of information that the
mother had about the child's intellectual development, the opportunities
provided for enlarging the child's vocabulary, the extent to which the parents
created situations for learning in the home, and the extent of assistance given
in learning situations related to school and non-school activities.'

These results fit in with the general picture; and of course the same points
apply as to the previous study. In general, Freeberg and Payne conclude:

'Children of superior intellectual ability come from homes where parental
interest in their intellectual development is evidenced by pressures to succeed
and assistance in doing so, particularly in the development of the child's
verbal skills.'

Our third example takes a rather different line. Lyn Carlsmith (1964) examined
the effect of the absence of fathers from their families due to the Second World
War. College and high school students were the subjects, a total of 1,460 young
people who came from homes in every way normal, except that about one-third
of the fathers served overseas for varying lengths of time, while their families
remained behind. All the subjects were born between 1941 and 1945. The interesting results come from the boys, who constitute the majority of the sample.
Various measures of intellectual ability were taken, most importantly yielding
scores for verbal and mathematical aptitude. Carlsmith summarizes his results
thus:

'1. Early and long separation from the father results in relatively greater
ability in verbal areas than in mathematics.
2. No separation produces relatively greater ability in mathematics.
3. Late brief separation may produce an extreme elevation in mathematical ability (relatively to verbal ability).'

These results, from a careful and systematic study, which moreover has the
advantage of being based on a large-scale natural experiment, are impressive.
The fact that the evidence for the family conditions is retrospective is in this
case an advantage: a definite fact such as father's absence is much less liable
to distortion than sons' achievements as recalled by mothers; and there is no
possibility of subjects' development being affected by knowledge of the experiment, which is a difficulty in so many educational and developmental investigations. In general, boys do better on mathematical, and girls on verbal tests, and
it is plausible to suppose that this has something to do with sex-role identification. But, as Carlsmith points out, even if we accept this, a number of puzzling
questions remain. His discussion can usefully be quoted at length.

'While the findings reported here are provocative, they leave several questions unanswered. For example, is the principal effect of early separation from the father an acceleration of verbal ability or a depression of math ability? This question cannot be answered from the data presented here. However, the studies of problem-solving techniques used by children (e.g. Bieri, 1960; Milton, 1957; Seder, 1955) suggest that this may be an inappropriate question. More specifically, these studies suggest that math and verbal-aptitude scores may simply reflect two aspects of a single, more general characteristic: conceptual style or approach to problem-solving. In these studies, two styles of conceptualization are usually differentiated: an "analytic approach" which is characterized by clear discrimination between stimuli, a direct pursuit of solutions and a disregard for extraneous material; a "global approach" characterized by less clear discrimination of stimuli and a greater influence from extraneous material. The first approach is more typically used by boys, while the second is more typical of girls. It seems reasonable to assume that boys using the analytic approach to problem-solving would score relatively higher on math-aptitude than on verbal-aptitude tests; boys using the global approach would show relatively greater ability on verbal-comprehension tests. Thus the relative superiority of math or verbal aptitude is, in effect, a single measure of the boy's conceptual style or approach to problem-solving. It follows that any antecedent variable, such as presence or absence of the father, may directly influence conceptual approach (i.e. aptitude pattern), but only indirectly influence performance on a particular test.

A second query that is sometimes raised in response to the data reported here concerns the possible influence of anxiety on the math aptitude of father-absent boys. It is argued that the early experience of father absence produces high anxiety and that anxiety has a more debilitating effect on proficiency in mathematics than on verbal skills. Data in support of this argument are drawn largely from studies of emotionally disturbed individuals which indicate that some aspects of verbal ability are less vulnerable to stress and are therefore used as indicators of the "pre-morbid" level of intellectual functioning (e.g. Mayman, Schafer and Rapaport, 1951). Contrary to this position is a directly relevant study by Alpert (1957) which relates a number of anxiety scales with the math- and verbal-aptitude scores obtained on the College Board tests by a large sample of Stanford males. While most of the anxiety scales correlate negatively with both aptitude scores, the author states (p. 46) that "in *every* instance in which the data were significant, the correlations with mathematical aptitude were in the same direction as those with verbal aptitude, but in no instance were they of as large magnitude". Several of the correlations between anxiety and verbal aptitude are fairly high, but not one of the correlations with math aptitude reaches an acceptable level of significance. Since none of the father-absent students in this study can be considered severely emotionally disturbed, there is no reason to suspect that extreme stress or anxiety is responsible for the observed differences in their aptitude scores. If anxiety had any effect at all, the Alpert study indicates that verbal aptitude, rather than math aptitude, would be expected to show the greater decrement.

... A final puzzling question is why conceptual approach or pattern of aptitudes should be so clearly sex-typed in our culture. An adequate explanation of this recurrent finding is not available, but several studies suggest that the masculine analytical approach is acquired through close and harmonious association with the father. Seder (1955) found that boys who used the global approach to problems had fathers who spent little time with them or who were very passive with their sons. Bieri (1960) reports that boys who willingly accept authority and describe themselves as more similar to their mothers are poor performers on differentiation-analytic tasks. Levy (1943) reports the same findings for "maternally overprotected" boys. Finally, Witkin (1960) reports that boys who perform poorly on analytic problems perceive their fathers as dominating and tyrannical.

A study of male college students at Stanford University relates College Board aptitude scores with certain childhood experiences reported by the students (Maccoby and Rau, 1962). Boys who achieve a more feminine pattern of aptitudes (i.e. math aptitude relatively lower than verbal aptitude) than their peers report that in their childhood their fathers were away from home for one to five years; they almost never talked about personal problems with their fathers; they were often fearful of their fathers; and they were punished exclusively by their mothers.

All of these studies consistently point to a close, positive relationship between father and son as a prerequisite for development of a masculine conceptual approach. However, they still do not explain why the relationship exists or how this approach develops. Milton (1957), who reports a striking correlation between problem-solving skill and sex-role identification in both boys and girls, suggests simply that girls typically won't learn the necessary skills, since problem solving is inappropriate to the female sex-role. This reasoning suggests that a conceptual approach is developed fairly consciously and probably not until after the child enters school. The accumulated evidence on learning of sex-role identity suggests that this occurs quite early in childhood through a largely unconscious process of imitation or identification with one of the parents. Whether the conceptual approach develops later as a result of sex-role identity (as Milton suggests) or early along with sex-role identity (through a similar process of identification) cannot be ascertained from the information available ... At the present time, we can only say that aptitude patterns or conceptual approaches are related to both sex-role identity and to father-son relationships, and that absence of the father during certain early periods of the child's life has an important effect on later cognitive development.'

These considerations bring us to the larger question of cultural differences. In a later chapter (*Development and Culture*), we shall look at some of the cross-cultural evidence about thinking in general; here, we are interested in the relationship of culture and intelligence. This subject has been exhaustively reviewed by Philip Vernon (1969). As usual, Vernon's impeccable and scholarly account makes one wish one could simply quote it *in extenso*. Instead, let us pick out what seem to be the most relevant aspects in the present context. Following on from Hebb's notion of intelligence A and B, Vernon adds intelligence C. A is the genetic potential; B is 'the effective all-round cognitive abilities to comprehend, to grasp relations and reason, which develops through the interaction between the genetic potential and stimulations provided by the environment'. C is the results obtained on intelligence tests—really a sample of B (if the tests are good ones).

All these can clearly be affected by hereditary factors; B and C can be affected by environmental influences. The latter may be somewhat arbitrarily divided into deficiencies and differences. Thus there are factors that can handicap test performance, and those, more general, that reduce effective intellectual performance (intelligence B). But it may also be that different cultures lead to differences in intellectual functioning, which can hardly be described as deficiencies—though they will produce lower scores on tests standardized in another culture. This point Vernon somewhat discounts. In a paper of 1965, Vernon lists the main environmental handicaps to intellectual development, as follows:

1. Physiological and nutritional deficit.
2. Perceptual deprivation in pre-school years.
3. Repression of independence and constructive play.
4. Family insecurity and lack of playfulness.
5. Female dominance (this may favour verbal as compared to spatial abilities).
6. Defective education.
7. Linguistic handicaps.
8. Adult roles and adolescent aspirations (in minority cultures, children may be affected by gradual realization of their depressed status, lack of opportunities, etc.).

For each of these there is considerable evidence; and for the most part they seem, in any case, highly plausible. But the picture is far from being so (relatively) simple. In the first place most of the measures are intelligence C, i.e. test scores. Now there are very great difficulties in applying tests cross-culturally, even if we are sure that this is what we want to do. Frijda and Jahoda (1966) point out that it is virtually impossible to be certain of the cross-cultural equivalence of three aspects: verbal materials and instructions; the test materials (where non-verbal); and the test situation. The first two are rather obvious, though vital. The third is well illustrated by an account by Warburton (1951) of testing Gurkha recruits (quoted by Butcher, 1968).

'The most striking thing about the recruits was their lack of pep and slowness of movement. They just plodded solemnly along. The slow, deliberate manner in which they handled the apparatus made a striking contrast to the hurried scampering of the British troops. On the other hand, if they thought that speed was the main requirement of the test, as some of them did in the early stages of the experiment, they jumbled all the apparatus together, in a nonsensical way, and finished in record time... Morale was high. No one appeared to sulk because he was unable to answer all the questions. No one quarrelled with his neighbour. The general attitude was one of amiable cooperation. The recruits were not curious about being tested and had little insight into the reasons for the experiment... It was typical that, because most of the apparatus was made of wood the psychologist was known as the wood officer.'

Frijda and Jahoda, however, see these difficulties as only one aspect of the problems involved in cross-cultural studies. Among the others are these. The adequacy and comparability of descriptive categories: behaviour must be classified, and it is not clear that categories can be transferred—does it even make sense to speak of 'intelligence' in cultures other than that which has developed the concept? Functional equivalence of the phenomena under study: testing of course, *has* no equivalent in technologically simple societies. Adequacy, representativeness and comparability of samples: not only are basic facts of age, etc., sometimes hard to obtain, but the whole pattern of life may differ chronologically from one group to another. Problems of interpretation: these may still exist even if all the preceding questions are dealt with. Such difficulties may obtain even in studying different groups within one society: it is far from obvious that testing is perceived as the same activity even by, for example, grammar school and secondary modern children. On the other hand there is hardly such a thing now as a culture unaffected by Western European norms. In this sense, it can be argued that any differences are effectively deficiencies. This is more or less the line that Vernon takes:

'...it seems reasonable to regard the Puritan ethic of the western middle class as producing the greatest development of intelligence, in contrast both to western lower class and to the "less civilized" cultures... The evidence ...that Intelligence B is built up in response to environmental stimulation and is therefore affected in many ways by cultural differences does not mean that tests constructed in western cultures are always worthless elsewhere. Despite the valuation of different skills in different ethnic groups, all groups have increasing need for complex, symbolic thinking. Researches in Africa and other countries in fact show that adaptations of western tests possess promising validity in assessing educational aptitudes and work effectiveness, though this may be partly because they are measuring language skills required for advanced schooling in the former situation, or acculturation and cooperativeness with white employers in the latter.'

In general, departures from the 'favourable' environment of middle class western culture will produce deviation from 'normal' scores on tests. Let us illustrate this with some examples. Wiseman (1964) presented the results of a large-scale study of 14-year-old children (secondary modern) in Lancashire and Cheshire (Manchester, Salford, and Stockport). Scores on tests of intelligence, reading comprehension, and mechanical arithmetic were compared with several social variables indicating conditions in the area. Table 4.2 shows the results. The overall picture is fairly clear, but we must note that the brighter children of the area are not included (selective secondary schooling put them in grammar schools). This may account for the backwardness correlations being higher than those for brightness. 'Backwardness' in this study meant a standard score of -1.0 or below, 'brightness' one of $+1.0$ or above (calculated from the *whole* population). Notice also that it is *intelligence* rather than attainment that seems most closely related to environmental conditions. In a series of interesting studies,

152

Table 4.2—Product-moment correlations between attainment and social variables. (Reproduced from S. Wiseman, Education and Environment (1964), by permission of Manchester University Press, Manchester.)

Variable	Backwardness			Brightness		
	Intell.	Read.	Arith.	Intell.	Read.	Arith.
Mental deficiency	0·84	0·64	0·60	−0·55	−0·06	−0·22
Birthrate	0·69	0·37	0·53	−0·30	0·02	−0·28
Illegitimate children	0·66	0·48	0·72	−0·43	0·07	−0·15
T.B. rate	0·63	0·32	0·51	−0·16	0·16	−0·22
Neglected children	0·50	0·23	0·57	−0·23	−0·25	−0·21
J. index	0·37	0·35	0·12	−0·25	−0·16	−0·18
Death rate	0·36	0·15	−0·01	−0·08	0·14	−0·20
Persons per acre	0·33	0·37	0·51	−0·19	0·14	−0·22
Infantile mortality	0·25	0·16	0·14	−0·20	−0·17	−0·09
Infectious diseases	0·03	−0·21	0·08	0·00	−0·18	0·00
Average correlation	0·47	0·29	0·38	−0·24	−0·03	−0·18

Vernon (1969) studied boys of very diverse background in England, Scotland (the Hebrides), Jamaica, Uganda and Canada (Indians and Eskimos). Intelligence tests as such were not used, but tests of verbal and educational ability, induction, conceptual development (including some Piaget-inspired tasks), creativity, and perceptual and spatial ability. Consider the Hebridean children, half of them from Gaelic-speaking and half from English-speaking homes. Vernon writes:

'Apart from the linguistic differences both groups are of interest as growing up in a relatively isolated community, free from the rush of modern civilization. There are strong traditions of responsible and provident living, of rather rigid upbringing, and respect for formal education. The Gaelic-background group was handicapped in oral vocabulary, the sorting test and Piaget,* but did not differ significantly from the English-background boys in other respects. Both were superior to English norms in scholastic achievement and learning tests, though there was some restriction in originality. The test correlations were unusual in showing no distinction between g and verbal abilities. This does not seem to be due so much to linguistic heterogeneity as to a strong contrast between the more culturally stimulating and sophisticated homes vs. the more traditional and restricted.'

Venturing further afield, let us take one example: of a test which

'was very difficult both for Ugandans and Jamaicans—a speeded form board which required fitting a set of triangular pieces together to make a number of shapes. Explanations of this peculiar difficulty have been offered at many levels, one being simply that, unlike Western children, African children up to 6 years would scarcely ever see a picture book or play with blocks or bricks. But this would also be true of Eskimos, who score 92 and 95 on Kohs' and Picture Recognition. Segall, Campbell and Herskovits (1963) stress the effect of an "uncarpentered" environment on visual illusions.

* i.e. conceptual development.

Many Africans live in rounded houses, and see curved trees and hills, but little furniture or rectangles. However, the present writer's sample were mostly reared in town houses with rectangular rooms, windows and doors, and some furnishings. More plausible, perhaps, is the suggestion that most African babies are bound to and carried on their mothers' backs for the first year or two; hence not only is their vision restricted (largely to a rounded object), but they also obtain very little manipulative or kinaesthetic experience. To this the writer would add the inadequacies of psychomotor experience throughout childhood (cf. Biesheuvel, 1966) and the absence of interest in constructive play or of cultural pressures to practical achievements. Few homes would provide knives and forks, doorknobs, scissors, buttons, pencils, or toy objects to manipulate, and African parents seem more apt to frustrate than to encourage curiosity and exploratory activities or to reward the acquisition of skills. Thus to a remarkable extent pre-school children are content just to sit doing nothing, and they are notably passive and submissive when school attendance starts. This apparent apathy may also derive in part from poor health conditions and malnutrition–protein deficiency is widespread in Uganda.'

Thus the elucidation of particular environmental conditions and their relationship to particular intellectual differences is a matter for painstaking investigation, to which Vernon has already made a considerable contribution (among others, of course). Later, I find somewhat odd an almost missionary tone that creeps into Vernon's otherwise faultlessly objective treatment.

'We would naturally expect the education system to provide the chief mode of attack on the syndrome of negative factors in a backward culture or subculture. Schooling is given by fairly small numbers of the more intelligent members of the population, who should be open to new ideas and who can be trained to follow new methods and aims; and they influence the minds of a large proportion or even the whole of the population over the period when concepts, skills and values are being built up ... The greatest promise of quick advance lies in the field of language-teaching, that is the spread of effective methods of acquiring a language which is suitable as a medium for advanced education, communication and thinking among children whose mother-tongue is ineffective for these purposes. This applies equally to dialect-speaking Africans, to Jamaicans in Jamaica or Britain, and to lower working-class or deprived children in any western nation whose natural speech is of the 'public' type. However it is not sufficient to teach the second language as a subject, i.e. peripherally. Our own results have shown that current techniques, not only in Jamaica and Uganda but even in Canada, produce some competence in written English tests but fail to develop English as a central tool of comprehension and thought. But linguistic and psychological research, together with the experiments under way in American introductory schools, in Kenya and elsewhere, offer prospects of a considerable breakthrough.'

Some of the difficulties are then listed, and Vernon continues:

'And yet it is not impossible to plan and carry through radical changes—an outstanding example being supplied by Soviet Russia. There can be no doubt that over the past 50 years the average level of Intelligence B of the

Russian population has been raised tremendously. Ruthless techniques may indeed have been applied which other countries would be loath to adopt, and they have not always achieved their purpose. But to a large extent they have succeeded in transforming a country which was as economically weak, as educationally backward, and as culturally and linguistically heterogeneous as many underdeveloped nations of today.'

Substitute Christianity for intelligence, and this has a quite Victorian air. I yield to no one in my admiration of English as a language: but I seriously wonder whether education in the sense that seems to be meant is the wisest course for the human race. With the destruction of other cultures we may be losing an irreplaceable source of variation and stimulation, just as with the killing off of the other races, such as many of those in South America, we are losing for ever a pool of genetic heterogeneity. Most of the human race's great cultural achievements seem to have involved some mixing, even clashing, of races and cultures. And it may be suggested that the Greece of Pericles, and the England of Shakespeare, were a great deal nearer to the present underdeveloped countries than to Western urbanized society, both economically and educationally. The question of which type of society is superior—if indeed it makes sense to ask the question—is one that cannot be answered by science; it is essentially a question of values, on which each person must decide for himself. The related, and bitterly argued, question, of whether one race is innately inferior to another in its genetic endowment, is amenable to factual investigation, though the evidence is confused and unsatisfactory. It is an important question, and we shall treat it as a special issue.

FOCUS: IS ONE RACE INFERIOR TO ANOTHER?

In the preceding pages we have emphasized how, historically, the concept of intelligence has meant all things to all men. While writers such as Guilford stress the diversity of mental abilities which are subsumed under intelligence, there are others who argue forcibly for a general factor view. And of course there are those who regard intelligence as altogether a vacuous notion. Arthur Jensen, whose work we consider more fully in a moment, argues that we can measure intelligence more easily than we can define it (Jensen, 1969a). Given these alternative conceptions of intelligence the confidence many people place in the Intelligence Quotient is curious. Of course it is partly a matter of self-reinforcement—psychologists, envious of the exact measures possible in the pure sciences, tend to encourage each other in the view that all has not been in vain. At any rate the IQ is one of the few things which has earned psychologists something approaching scientific and professional respectability.

In some ways this is unfortunate, and some would say, unjustified. This is because, inevitably, intelligence tests have been administered on a progressively wider scale to an ever wider section of humanity. And despite the increasing sophistication of testing methods and the development of so called 'culture fair' tests, to a certain extent we have lost sight of some of the basic problems which accompany the measurement of intelligence. Do we know what we are measuring? And do we know whether what we are measuring is *appropriate* for the population we are studying? Recently many of these issues have crystallized into a sometimes vicious debate concerning racial differences in intelligence. Specifically, it seems generally agreed on the basis of many independent studies that the average IQ of the American Negro population is very much lower than that of the white population. Another far more ominous element running throughout the issue is the suggestion made in some circles that the basis of this (very reliable) difference may be genetic. We shall not try here to give comprehensive coverage of this very topical and current debate. Already two whole issues of *The Harvard Educational Review* and two moderately sized textbooks have been devoted to a detailed discussion of the whole problem. Instead we shall try to present the arguments, as we see them, as fairly as possible with as much of the experimental and other evidence as seems necessary. As far as possible we shall steer clear of the many statistical disputes which have inevitably arisen and we shall say virtually nothing about the science of genetics itself. It is hard not to sound patronizing but one plea at the outset. While it is sometimes difficult to adopt a dispassionate attitude in matters of this nature, it is essential to be reasonably informed about the facts and other circumstances surrounding the issues. Anyone proposing to enter the debate therefore, in anything more than general terms, should assimilate as much of the appropriate literature as possible.

Perhaps the most appropriate starting point is A. R. Jensen's recent article 'How much can we boost IQ and scholastic achievement?' (Jensen, 1969a).* It is this paper which has provided the impetus for much of the current argument, although of course more recently H. J. Eysenck has entered the arena with his highly controversial book *Race, Intelligence and Education*, 1971.

In his lengthy paper Jensen develops some often very complex arguments about racial differences in intellectual abilities. Given the enormous intricacies of the supportive arguments and material it might be useful at the outset to have a more general statement of Jensen's position. Jensen argues that there is strong evidence for the involvement of genetic factors in individual differences in IQ. The extent of this influence is debatable but numerous experimental studies seem to suggest that genetic factors may be as much as four times as important as the environment. On average the measured IQ of the American Negro is about 15 points (1 Standard Deviation) below that of the American White, and American Negroes are disproportionately represented in the lower socio-economic groups. In addition 'compensatory' educational programs, such as Head Start, for culturally deprived children (of whom a high proportion of

---

* All subsequent quotations are from this article unless otherwise stated.

course are Negroes) have been largely unsuccessful. It is possible therefore that genetic factors may be implicated in these racial differences and that our efforts might be perhaps more profitably directed toward providing a wider range of 'educational methods, programs and goals, and of occupational opportunities, just as wide as the range of human abilities'.

Now how does Jensen arrive at these controversial and somewhat startling conclusions? Take first of all the whole question of the hereditary basis of IQ. For Jensen the concept central to the resolution of the problem is *heritability*. This he says

'is a population statistic, describing the relative magnitude of the genetic component (or set of genetic components) in the population variance of the characteristic in question. It has no sensible meaning with reference to a measurement or characteristic in an individual.'

In other words, heritability (or *H*) is a statistical description of the variabilty of test scores in a given population. It tells us, more specifically, how far we can account for this variability in terms of the *genetic* variability of the individuals in the population. If the value of *H* is high, we infer that the variable in question (be it extraversion, divergent ability, memory span, IQ or whatever) is controlled to a large extent by genetic factors. If the value is low then we infer that genetics play a minor part and that any variability must be due to other influences. Many of Sir Cyril Burt's numerous kinship studies are concerned with arriving at an accurate estimate of *H*. Now the point to be emphasized here is the absolute reliance which Jensen places on the concept of heritability, kinship studies (especially Burt's) and the statistical analysis of variance model he selects. In fact his whole case depends upon an acceptance of these. And on the basis of the available data Jensen argues that there is overwhelming evidence for the decisive role of genetic factors in determining variability of IQ scores. 'The environment' is of relatively minor importance.

Later Jensen turns to 'the possible importance of genetic factors in racial behavioural differences': something which he says 'has been greatly ignored, almost to the point of being a tabooed subject, just as were the topics of venereal disease and birth control a generation or so ago'. He cites Shuey's (1966) review of the literature on Negro intelligence and points out, as mentioned previously that, in general American Negroes perform 'about 1 standard deviation (15 IQ points) below the average of the white population in IQ, and this finding is fairly uniform across the 81 different tests of intellectual ability used in the studies reviewed by Shuey'. And furthermore 'as a group, Negroes performed somewhat more poorly on those subjects which tap abstract abilities'.

A few lines later come his actual statements about race differences:

'. . . various lines of evidence . . . viewed altogether, make it a not unreasonable hypothesis that genetic factors are strongly implicated in the average Negro–White intelligence difference.'

Note, at this juncture, the fairly obvious point that we can accept that there is a strong genetic component in intelligence without necessarily accepting Jensen's conclusions about the possible genetic basis of racial differences in IQ.

Jensen gives extensive coverage to what he calls the failure of compensatory education—in fact he begins his paper with the provocative assertion that 'compensatory education has been tried and it apparently has failed'. Later he takes up the question once again, arguing that many 'enrichment' programs are defective on methodological grounds, particularly as regards the use of appropriate control procedures. He is dubious about some of the reported gains in IQ which he feels are probably spurious:

> 'I am inclined to doubt that IQ gains up to this amount in young disadvantaged children have much if anything to do with changes in ability. They are largely a result simply of getting a more accurate IQ by testing under more optimal conditions.... I would put very little confidence in a single test score, especially if it is the child's first test and more especially if the child is from a poor background and of a different race from the examiner.... I would urge that attempts to evaluate preschool enrichment programs measure the gains against initially valid scores. If there is not evidence that this precaution has been taken, and if there is no control group, one might as well subtract at least 5 points from the gain scores as having little or nothing to do with real intellectual growth.'

Although Jensen does accept that there *can* be improvements in measured intelligence he argues that there is still the question of 'what is really changed when we boost IQ?' And at this point he introduces another of the notions which has subsequently been bitterly disputed—compensatory programs may act in a selective fashion by accelerating the development of 'associative' (or rote) learning ability while having no effect on 'cognitive' (or conceptual) learning capacity. He adds

> 'The IQ gains reported in enrichment studies appear to be more in what Cattell calls "crystallized" in contrast to "fluid" intelligence.'

In one sense Jensen seems to be stressing the idea of *diversity* of intellectual ability—he quotes Gordon and Wilkerson (1966):

> 'It is not at all clear that the concept of compensatory education is the one which will most appropriately meet the problems of the disadvantaged. These children are *not* middle-class children, many of them never *will* be, and they can never be anything but second-rate as long as they are thought of as potentially middle-class children....'

Jensen himself claims '...we are finding that a unidimensional concept of intelligence is quite inadequate as a basis for understanding social class differences in ability.' And he envisages 'a continuum ranging from "simple" associative learning to complex cognitive or conceptual learning'. And then the crunch. 'I have hypothesized two genotypically distinct basic processes underlying this continuum, labelled Level I (associative ability) and Level II (conceptual ability).' Tests most closely related to Level I ability include digit memory, serial rote learning and paired-associate learning while 'concept learning and problem solving are good examples' of Level II abilities. Jensen develops the I-II distinction much more thoroughly, arguing that 'Level I ability is necessary but not sufficient for Level II. . . . Level I ability is distributed about the same in all social class groups, while Level II ability is distributed differently in lower and middle SES groups.' (SES—socio-economic scale.) And even more alarming is the proposition that ' . . . certain structures must also be available for Level II abilities to develop, and these are conceived of as being different from the neural structures underlying Level I'. So here in a slightly more formidable guise is Jensen's 'not unreasonable' genetic hypothesis. Jensen ends his paper with the following statement of his philosophy:

> 'If diversity of mental abilities, as of most other human characteristics, is a basic fact of nature, as the evidence indicates, and if the ideal of universal education is to be successfully pursued, it seems a reasonable conclusion that schools and society must provide a range and diversity of educational methods, programs, and goals, and of occupational opportunities, just as wide as the range of human abilities. Accordingly, the ideal of equality of educational opportunity should not be interpreted as uniformity of facilities, instructional techniques, and educational aims for all children. Diversity rather than uniformity of approaches and aims would seem to be the key to making education rewarding for children of different patterns of ability. The reality of individual differences thus need not mean educational rewards for some children and frustration and defeat for others.'

On the face of it these seem progressive, sympathetic and admirable sentiments, realistically argued and rationally expressed. Yet the article as a whole has unleashed a bitter outcry, recently further aggravated (and complicated?) by the publication of Professor Eysenck's book (Eysenck, 1971). We hope that what we have *outlined* as Jensen's position is a fair *summary* of the many complex arguments he developed in his original article. If not, then it is not for want of trying.

It is perhaps even harder to present, in summary, the essentials of the debate which has followed. However there do seem to be some clearly identifiable *themes* around which the bulk of discussion (?) has centred. It might help us to arrive at a more balanced assessment of the whole issue if we can extricate these from the general background of confusion.

First of all there is the question of the general presentation and interpretation of data. Martin Deutsch wastes no words in his reaction to Jensen's paper:

> 'I should like to make it clear at the outset, however, that in Jensen's article I found many erroneous statements, misinterpretations, and misunderstandings of the nature of intelligence, intelligence tests, genetic determination of traits, education in general, and compensatory education in particular.' (Deutsch, 1969)

And later after discussing some of these

'It is this kind of conflicting and contradictory reporting that makes it very difficult to take the Jensen article seriously in either scientific or logical terms.'

The points at issue here are often very subtle—it is worth noting however that a number of writers have lodged similar objections about the general presentation, discussion and interpretation of independently published data. There is the problem for example of the weighty Coleman Report (1966) which Jensen cites in support of his thesis. What he fails to mention according to Deutsch and others, is that this report has been 'massively criticized', particularly on methodological and statistical grounds. Then there are the many problems relating to the whole twin study methodology, which we have briefly considered earlier in the main chapter but which Jensen largely ignores. These have been well marshalled by a number of recent writers, including Mittler (1971) who, while concluding that twin research in psychology is on the whole justifiable, puts many of the problems in a nutshell.

'Even the most carefully conducted twin study can only yield findings which apply to a particular population studied at a given age and under given environmental circumstances. The same results need not necessarily be expected from a different twin population, especially if it is not developmentally comparable. A related problem concerns the legitimacy of deriving conclusions about the heritability of a characteristic in the general population from a study of twins, who as individuals are not representative of that population.'

This naturally raises the whole question of heritability estimates derived from kinship studies. As Hirsch (1968) points out:

'Only when we consider the number of possible genotypes and the number of potential environments that may influence trait expression do we begin to realize how narrowly limited is the range of applicability for any obtained heritability measure.'

And Deutsch again

'The estimates of heritability, upon which Jensen's entire argument depends, are only accurate if each possible genotypic child is placed randomly in each conceivable environment. To approximate such a study, researchers must at least include black children and a representative range of environments.' (Deutsch, 1969).

The second theme concerns Jensen's view of intelligence. It is clear that this has been a very important factor in the debate, and as one might expect, Jensen adopts a hard-headed operational approach.

'There is no point in arguing the question to which there is no answer, the question of what intelligence *really* is. The best we can do is to obtain measurements of certain kinds of behaviour and look at their relationships to other phenomena and see if these relationships make any kind of sense and order. It is from these orderly relationships that we can gain some understanding of the phenomena.'

Later he narrows his argument down:

> 'The term 'intelligence' should be reserved for the rather specific meaning I have assigned to it, namely, the general factor common to standard tests of intelligence. Any one verbal definition of this factor is really inadequate, but, if we must define it in so many words, it is best thought of as a capacity for abstract reasoning and problem solving.'

Eventually, of course, as we have seen, Jensen's arguments come repeatedly to rely on our acceptance of both the concept of IQ and the 'g' theory of intelligence. Not that there is anything inherently unacceptable about this, but as Deutsch points out:

> '... g represents only *one* theory of intelligence, among many others. It is by no means a universally accepted concept among psychologists and others who work in this area. Yet from Jensen's paper, the general reader would never know that there are competing theories, several of which are more widely accepted and based on more recent information and data....' (Deutsch, 1969)

Also it is hard not to sympathize with Hunt's sceptical comments:

> '... I must confess that I have long distrusted the statistical operations of correlational analysis and averaging once they leave me without at least an intuitive connection with behavioural and biological observables.' (Hunt, 1969)

It is worth noting in addition that nowhere in Jensen's article does one find a mention of Piaget. In short, Jensen's discussion of intelligence leaves us with only a truncated version of this much debated concept. Jensen does refer briefly to its long and intricate history (singling out, incidentally, Burt's recent, 1968, account as 'enlightening') and he does make the point, more than once, that '*intelligence* should not be regarded as completely synonymous with what I shall call *mental ability*, a term which refers to the totality of a person's mental capabilities'. But while it would be an oversimplification to regard the 'psychometric' and Piagetian 'open-ended' approaches to intelligence as mutually exclusive or opposites, Jensen's paper, long as it is, fails to emphasize that there are other views of 'intelligence' well established in the literature of psychology.

Our third theme concerns the role of the environment in intelligence—broadly *what* is the environment and how does it operate? Jensen has been harshly criticized for taking a naïve view of the part played by environmental influence in intellectual growth—in a sense of course this reflects the emphasis he places on the concept of heritability, twin study data, etc. Jensen's primary concern is to arrive at a statistical estimate of the contribution of 'the environment' to intelligence. This, as we have noted turns out to be around 20 per cent. In other words only about 20 per cent of the variability of test scores within a given population is due to nongenetic factors. But Jensen's analysis is more than a statistical one. He goes on to argue for a 'threshold' view of the environment. As he puts it:

'... it is doubtful that psychologists have found consistent evidence for any social environmental influences short of extreme environmental isolation which have a marked systematic effect on intelligence. This suggests that the influence of the quality of the environment on intellectual development is not a linear function. Below a certain threshold of environmental adequacy, deprivation can have a markedly depressing effect on intelligence. But above this threshold, environmental variations cause relatively small differences in intelligence.'

He then goes on to question the relevance of the 'sensory deprivation' experiments of, for instance, Skeels and Dye, who worked with orphanage children and the multitude of similar studies which are given considerable prominence by, for example, McV. Hunt (e.g. 1961).

'... typical culturally disadvantaged children', Jensen argues, 'are not reared in anything like the degree of sensory and motor deprivation that characterizes, say, the children of the Skeels study.'

They grow up, presumably, in conditions which are above the effective threshold for environmental deprivation. There is one more point to be made about Jensen's view of the environment (E):

'There has been a pronounced tendency to think of E as being wholly associated with individual's social and interpersonal environment, child rearing practices, and differences in educational and cultural opportunities afforded by socioeconomic status. . . . Certain physical and biological environmental factors may be at least as important as the social factors in determining individual differences in intelligence. If this is true, advances in medicine, nutrition, pre-natal care, and obstetrics may contribute as much or more to improving intelligence as will manipulation of the social environment.'

Now what are we to make of all this? Well we might overlook the confident assertion about what constitutes a slum environment—is it above or below the so-called threshold? But what about the 'one dimensional' view of the environment? L. J. Cronbach (1969) hits many of the relevant nails on the head:

'The phrase "improve the environment", born of the enthusiasm of the Social Darwinists, has misled environmentalists for two generations. Environments cannot be arrayed from good to bad, rich to poor. The highly stimulating environment that most of us think of as "rich" promotes optimal growth for some persons and may not be suitable for others. Environments can be varied along many dimensions. . . .'

Then again, while it is comparatively easy to single out some environmental influences, others are far more difficult to pinpoint, although their effects are no less real. Lyn Carlsmith (1964) for example, reports some significant findings based on studies carried out following World War II. There was a fairly clear cut relationship between 'father absence' during the war and verbal rather than mathematical ability. On the face of it mathematical skills would seem to be dependent, somehow, on the presence of a man around the house. Jensen does not mention the Carlsmith study and in fact dismisses the factor of 'father absence' as unimportant in the Negro/White IQ difference, referring again to the conclusions of the Coleman Report. There are also the so-called 'expectancy effects' to be taken into consideration; we have already mentioned the work of Rosenthal and his colleagues in this connection. And although it seems that methodologically this work is not wholly satisfactory, the notion that teachers' attitudes and beliefs can influence the performance of their pupils has a strong intuitive appeal. Individual differences in preferences for various subjects amongst school children often seem to have their origin in the teacher rather than the subject matter of the discipline itself. It is possible for a child to be put off a particular subject for good due to gentle sarcasm, ponderous irony or even more subtle negative attitudes he encounters on the part of his teacher during his early exposure to the subject. It is surely possible in these days of over-crowded classrooms that even the best of teachers will begin to respond not to individuals but to groups—the bright children, the quiet ones, the dull ones, the mischievous ones—the coloured ones? The point to be made is that patterns of social interaction and communication in the typical school are so intricate that we are not justified in assuming that all children automatically receive the same type of stimulation and instruction simply because they share the same teachers and curriculum. Again we may refer to Deutsch's paper:

> 'Jensen ... fails to acknowledge the role of the school environment, the complexities of the educational system, and of the interpersonal dysfunctioning that typically characterizes the relationship of the school administration to the teaching staff, the teaching staff to the children, and inversely, of the children to their teachers.' (Deutsch, 1969)

Much the same point is made more directly by Brazziel:

> '... until recently almost no psychometrists gave attention to the fact that white examiners in a black classroom are in many, many cases getting an invalid test performance. Their color, voice, manner, gestures turn many kids off and they refuse to try.' (Brazziel, 1969)

Complex though we have claimed the process of environmental interaction to be, we have noted already that Jensen's main concern is with the statistical weight of any such interactions. The magnitude of the heredity–environment interaction ($H \times E$), he argues, 'is a matter for empirical study, not philosophic debate', and can be reliably estimated from twin study data using the appropriate Analysis of Variance techniques. In fact Jensen concludes that the variation of IQ scores due to $H \times E$ is negligible:

> 'Those who call themselves "interactionists", with the conviction that they have thereby either solved or risen above the whole issue of the relative contributions of heredity and environment to individual differences in intelligence, are apparently unaware that the preponderance of evidence indicates that the interaction variance, ... is the smallest component of the total phenotypic variance of intelligence.'

Once again, Jensen mentions the work of Burt. And once again we have to accept a whole set of assumptions about kinship studies and statistical reliability. Richard Light and Paul Smith (1969) argue that Jensen's choice of Analysis of Variance model must be regarded with caution because it always produces the *lowest possible* estimate of IQ variance due to interaction. The authors are principally concerned with the small sample sizes of twin studies, the way in which these are indiscriminately combined by Jensen and the non-random differences which are present in the allocation of blacks and whites to different social environments. In short they claim that Jensen's parameter estimates, especially the estimates of the $H \times E$ interaction are unreliable. And they develop a rather complicated statistical 'social allocation' model which is designed to highlight how crucial this may be. The authors' own conclusions can be stated:

> 'We have shown how a small amount of interaction between genetic endowment and environment can easily explain how two races with identical genetic endowments can have large differences in mean IQ's. We have further argued that even assuming the twin studies data were of excellent quality, the data are not at all statistically inconsistent with the existence of something like a ·10 interaction component of variance, and that this magnitude of interaction could account for mean differences of more than one standard deviation in black–white IQ's without any genetic differences between races....' (Light and Smith, 1969)

Summing up Jensen's view of the environment, Martin Deutsch concludes:

> '...Jensen's main omission is the picture of a complex and multifaceted environment, with which individuals interact in highly complicated and differentiated ways. Once that concept is firmly fixed, it would seem impossible to hold a simplistic view of the respective roles of heredity and environment in influencing intelligence test performance.' (Deutsch, 1969)

A fourth theme relates to the status of 'compensatory' education and the notion of Level I and II abilities. As we have already mentioned, Jensen considers enrichment programmes such as Head Start to have failed because they are largely attempts to foster Level II ('cognitive') abilities which, it is suggested, depend on the presence of certain genetically determined neural structures for their development. Well first of all, *has* compensatory education failed? Unfortunately there is no straightforward answer to this question simply because there is no general agreement as to whether it has yet been properly tried. On the one hand we have the fairly tough line taken by Jensen who is in no doubt:

> 'We *have* learned from many of the programs evaluated by the US Commission on Civil Rights what kinds of measures have produced no signs of success, though they have been put to the test for from three to eight years. It is a half-truth to say that these programs have not had a fair trial.' (Jensen, 1969b).

According to McV. Hunt however, it is Jensen who is responsible for the half-truths:

'Compensatory education has not failed. Investigations of compensatory education have now shown that traditional playschool has little to offer the children of the poor, but programs which made an effort to inculcate cognitive skills, language skills, and number skills, whether they be taught directly or incorporated into games, show fair success.... All this in seven years sounds to me like substantial success.... Thus Jensen's opening statement is a half-truth, and a dangerous half-truth, placed out of context for dramatic effect.' (Hunt, 1969)

There are other writers who agree with Hunt. And probably as many who would side with Jensen. But while it would be pointless to follow this particular line any further, there is an important difference in attitude lying behind the controversy which it would perhaps be helpful to point out here. Hunt is afraid that Jensen's opening sentence about the failure of compensatory education '... is but a half-truth which can help to boost the forces of reaction which could halt support for research on how to foster psychological development....'" In other words the scientist should be aware of the wider implications which his views have and choose his words carefully. Jensen on the other hand seems to take a far more pragmatic view.

'In our present state of ignorance about how best to teach children who are spread over an enormously wide range of abilities and proclivities and diverse cultural backgrounds, we are hardly justified in launching nationwide compensatory programs of massive uniformity.' (Jensen, 1969b)

Although Jensen does go on to say that the expenditure involved might well be better spent on developing different types of programmes, it is clear from his writings as a whole that he may well be guided by an entirely different set of considerations to that of many other research scientists. This is not to say that Hunt's views are those of a liberal-minded waster while Jensen's are those of an uncompromising skinflint. It is rather that Jensen takes a somewhat narrow, uncomplicated view of the role of the scientist in society while Hunt sees his position in a much wider social context reflecting ultimately perhaps a more responsible attitude. We shall return to this question in a moment.

Although it seems we cannot decide whether or not compensatory education has failed, is there anything to be said about Jensen's Level I and II abilities? We remarked earlier how Jensen seems in one sense to be stressing the notion of diversity of intellectual abilities. Nobody presumably would want to find fault with this, but the broad categorization of mental abilities under two headings has come in for some fairly vigorous criticism. McV. Hunt for example, commented:

'... Professor Jensen's distinction between associative learning and cognitive learning is but a conceptual drop in the bucket.' (McV. Hunt, 1969)

On the other hand it is hard not to agree with Jensen's indignant rejoinder that although learning is a complex process, although the I–II distinction is a simplified way of describing it, psychology, like any other science has always tried to organize diverse phenomena into coherent groups. There is nothing new in this—nor is there anything particularly revolutionary about the I–II distinction itself. Psychology has often adopted similar dichotomies, perhaps the most reminiscent being the old distinction between 'trial and error' and 'insightful' learning.

What *is* significant about Jensen's dichotomy however is the disturbing implication that differential teaching will be required for blacks and whites. Deutsch has remarked:

> '... it would be doubtful that a child taught consistently by associative, rote techniques would be able to shift to a situation in which instruction was carried out by conceptual methods. This is a critical point for occupational and status advancement, inasmuch as the greater rewards in an advanced technological society go with the more conceptual work. To assume that rote-learning and conceptual-learning groups could be maintained without status attributions and implications as simply a part of "diversity rather than uniformity of approaches and aims"..., would imply a highly naïve view of the social milieu.' (Deutsch, 1969)

These sentiments are echoed by Cronbach (1969):

> 'Jensen seems to argue that the disadvantaged should be taught by rote methods. But the cut-and-dried answers that can be learned by rote are not the answers that one needs if he is to cope with a changing world and to live an appreciative and expressive life.'

Once again it is difficult to avoid the conclusion that Jensen takes a very short-sighted, superficial and unrealistic view of the world in which we live.

Running through the whole debate is the persistent leit-motif which we have already identified and which is the subject of our final theme. To what extent should the scientist be influenced by the social, moral, ethical and other issues which he feels are raised by research which he may be contemplating or carrying out? Although we have considered various aspects of the Jensen controversy in some detail, it is probably this issue more than any other which is the cause of many of the misunderstandings and heated exchanges of the whole debate.

The traditional image of the scientist as an objective totally rational being devoid of all feeling who works inexorably through a logical progression of neat experiments with ruthless efficiency has never been, and one hopes never will be, a realistic one. In fact these days it is becoming a truism to point this out. Rightly or wrongly he is tied up in a complex emotional fashion with his work about which he has certain expectations and fears. He also has perhaps an elaborate set of priorities about what problems deserve investigation and in what order, and what he regards as constituting an acceptable answer. Recently it has been argued that he also has a responsibility to the non-scientific community in the very general sense that he should be aware of his own place in society and in the more specific sense of being aware of the implications that his work has for humanity at large. What this means in terms of scientific policy is not always obvious but it is clear that some fairly difficult decisions will have to be made. What is more important is that the climate of opinion is beginning, in some circles, to swing away from the narrow traditional view of science as constituting simply (if that is the right word) the discovery, presentation and interpretation of facts towards a more complex conception of the scientist as being essentially as much a social animal as anybody else and as an individual whom we expect therefore to be controlled by the same moral and other considerations as the intelligent layman.

Let us explore some of these ideas in the context of the issue under discussion. First of all there is absolutely no doubt as to Jensen's position *vis à vis* the scientist's duty:

> 'I strongly disagree with those who believe in searching for the truth by scientific means only under certain circumstances and eschew this course in favour of ignorance under other circumstances, or who believe that the results of enquiry on some subjects cannot be entrusted to the public but should be kept the guarded possession of a guarded elite. Such attitudes, in my opinion, represent a danger to free enquiry and, consequently, in the long run, work to the disadvantage of society's general welfare. "No holds barred" is the best formula for scientific inquiry. One does not decree beforehand which phenomena cannot be studied or which questions cannot be answered.'

One should note in particular the last few lines of this quotation which are characteristic of the totally uncompromising attitude Jensen repeatedly adopts.

Jensen is as hard-headed where his hypothesis about racial differences in intelligence is concerned:

> 'The fact that a reasonable hypothesis has not been rigorously proved does not mean that it should be summarily dismissed.'

And later,

> 'My position is that reasonable hypotheses concerning socially and educationally relevant questions should be subjected to appropriate investigation and the findings be published and widely discussed by the scientific community and the general public as well.' (Jensen, 1969b)

It is this unrelenting pragmatism which has been criticized by many as outmoded and irresponsible. Not that there is always a clear line to be taken. Often we do not know even in the vaguest terms the consequences that a particular piece of research might have. The development of the internal combustion engine was basically a fine achievement and 'a good thing'—until everybody has a car. This is not to say that there are not circumstances where the publication of a piece of work could have clearly foreseeable detrimental effects but the decision is too complex for there to be one single rule which can be applied in every situation.

What Jensen fears most of all, perhaps, is any form of censorship. But social responsibility in science is not just a matter of sitting on hot bits of information until the climate is right for their release. Deutsch quotes a statement from the Society for the Psychological Study of Social Issues:

'When research has bearing on social issues and public policy, the scientist must examine the competing explanations for his findings and must exercise the greatest care in his interpretation. Only in this way can he minimize the possibility that others will overgeneralize or misunderstand the social implications of his work.' (Deutsch, 1969)

There is here an important issue which Jensen entirely ignores. We have already referred to the criticisms which have been made of the way in which Jensen's original paper was written, the presentation and interpretation of evidence etc. Perhaps this is the point: given the very dubious nature of the hypotheses in question perhaps the article should not have contained any reference to a genetic hypothesis at all. There are doubts as to the status of the concept of heritability, there are reservations about kinship studies, questions about statistics, etc. Jensen is as aware of these problems as anybody else. Yet there are, in the article, statements about the possible implication of genetic factors in racial differences in intelligence. Why? Much of the paper could have been written without any mention of the 'not unreasonable' genetic hypothesis. Why go any further than arguing that compensatory educational programmes should be streamlined for individuals and allow for individual differences in intellectual abilities? And furthermore why does Jensen think his genetic hypothesis *worthy* of investigation? There must be countless 'not unreasonable' hypotheses in this field which have as great a claim on a research worker's time and attention. Why single out this one?

There is also the question of the press, popular or otherwise. It might be argued that we cannot expect even scientists to be perfect and that when informed professional people write papers in learned journals read only by a small minority of informed professional people, certain things are taken for granted, e.g. presumably Jensen is aware that the '*g*' theory of intelligence is not the only one around and that kinship studies are not paragons of experimental design. To spell all this out would be both tedious and unnecessary. But again the issue is not so simple. Articles, like Jensen's, which touch on important social issues have a nasty habit of finding their way into the news media in an often adulterated and much oversimplified form. And perhaps more important, the rebuttals, the protracted debates about statistics, etc., rarely get reported. And we might argue that it is not enough to shrug one's shoulders and reply that we get the press we deserve. William Brazziel in his Letter from the South (1969) quotes a recent court case in which 'The defense ... quoted heavily from the theories of white intellectual supremacy as expounded by Arthur Jensen.'

One cannot fail to be impressed by an event such as this. And these arguments, taken as a whole, show how far-reaching the effects of a particular piece of

168

research can be, and they demonstrate the complexity of the problems which
accompany what we call scientific research.

In the parliamentary phrase, the debate continues.

FURTHER READING

Butcher, H. J. (1968). *Human Intelligence*. Methuen.
Eysenck, H. J. (1971). *Race, Intelligence and Education*. New Society/Temple Smith.
Harvard Educational Review (1969). Vol. 39, No. 1.
Richardson, K. *et. al.* (1972). *Race, Culture and Intelligence*. Penguin.
Vernon, P. E. (1969). *Intelligence and Cultural Environment*. Methuen.
Wiseman, S. (1967). *Intelligence and Ability*. Penguin.

5

The Geneva School

This is perhaps a better title than 'Piaget', because while the work we are to discuss is either that of Jean Piaget himself, or derives directly from him, a large number of co-workers have also been involved, and the whole corpus, still growing, really now assumes the aspect of a school, rather in the sense used by Woodworth in describing his 'Contemporary Schools' of 1931. 'For us,' Woodworth said, 'a "school" is a group of psychologists who put forward a certain system of ideas designed to point the way that all must follow if psychology is ever to be made a genuine, productive science of both theoretical and practical value.' Forty years later, we might think that something has been achieved. In general, the notion of 'schools' of Psychology has disappeared. Few are now bold enough to think they have found a way that all must follow. How far Piaget and his colleagues think so, and perhaps how far they are right, will appear in the sequel.

JEAN PIAGET

At the moment of writing, Piaget may well be the greatest living psychologist. Boring awarded to Carl Stumpf the title 'last of the giants'. He meant the last in his roll-call of experimental psychologists, strictly so defined. It would be rash to call any contemporary the last of a presumably continuing series—that of psychologists—but certainly Piaget does seem cast in the mould of Boring's heroes. Indeed in some quarters, particularly educational ones, he seems to have assumed almost archetypal characteristics; an impression enhanced by the appearance of introductory books and articles illustrated with photographs of a white-haired gentleman beaming benignly through his spectacles as he puffs a philosophic pipe.

This impression may be misleading. With the gradual popularization of Piaget's work among educationists, misconceptions about Piaget's work have proliferated. For a long time (say 1920 to 1960), two main mistakes were made. The first was that of the main body of hard-headed experimental psychologists, and consisted in simply ignoring Piaget, or at best dismissing him briefly as 'interesting'

(Osgood's work, 1953) but essentially anecdotal. Moreover his work was apparently based entirely on his own three children. One of the first to correct this mistake was J. McV. Hunt, who in *Intelligence and Experience* (1961) presented a two-chapter summary of Piaget's work to date. John Flavell followed this in 1963 with a whole-volume account which has deservedly become required reading; and since then introductory, critical, and experimental studies have grown from a trickle to a flood. One of the most illuminating is that of Furth: *Piaget and Knowledge* (1969). The present chapter is heavily indebted to all of these.

The second mistake has been made, and continues to be made, by educationists. It has too often been assumed that because Piaget has written about children's thinking, his work must have a direct and simple application to the classroom. Generations of trainee teachers have had children pouring liquids from tall thin beakers into short fat ones, or rolling out plasticine sausages under the impression (presumably) that they would thereby somehow become better teachers. Personally, I doubt it. Such demonstrations, while they may at least bring students into direct contact with a bit of childrens' thinking, have rather little to do either with teaching or with Piaget's immensely complex system. The system does have great implications for education, as Piaget is very well aware; but gross oversimplification is simply misleading. Again, we owe to H. G. Furth an important book which sets the matter straight: *Piaget for Teachers* (1970).

But both of these mistakes are being put right, and Piaget's return from the psychological wilderness he occupied for so long is to be welcomed. The isolation was due partly to Piaget's own background and personality, which have resulted in him taking throughout a highly independent line. Piaget was born in 1896 and set out to be a zoologist: a highly precocious one, publishing his first scientific work—a note on a partly-albino sparrow—at the age of ten. This biological orientation is the most important single clue to understanding Piaget. Becoming interested in psychological problems, he spent some time applying Cyril Burt's tests of children's reasoning to French subjects. Here he was fascinated, not so much by the techniques of measurement and standardization that had enthralled Galton and later the American testers, as by the processes by which children reached their answers. Perhaps especially, the wrong answers. Here we have another important clue. Burt's test embodied Spearman's noegenetic principles, which as we have seen he believed were the fundamental laws of thought. But how did they arise? In a sense Piaget's work might be seen as a detailed map of the country from whose borders Spearman had glimpsed some of the mountain peaks. In an autobiographical article, 1969, Piaget says:

> 'While I wanted to devote myself to biology, I had an equal interest in
> the problems of objective knowledge and in epistemology.' (Epistemology is:
> the theory or science of the method or grounds of knowledge, OED). 'My
> decision to study the development of the cognitive functions in the child

was related to my desire to satisfy the two interests in one activity. By considering development as a kind of mental embryogenesis, one could construct a biological theory of knowledge.... A synthesis of these various interests has only recently been completed in a volume published by Callimard entitled *Biologie et Connaissance* (1967). There is found a biological theory of knowledge which I had always envisioned.' (Piaget, 1969)

We can go further than this and say that what Piaget has produced is not just a new theory, but a new area of science. We can think in broad terms of all science originating in 'philosophy', a general pursuit of knowledge. As areas of interest become amenable to controlled experimental investigation, they tend to be distinguished as 'sciences', such as physics, chemistry, etc. Psychology can be seen as still in the process of budding off, with many problems still in an uncertain position. Free will is a question which might appear to be answerable by methods of science, but which possibly, for various reasons, will remain a problem for philosophy; a problem for argument rather than fact. The genesis of knowledge is in the opposite case. Until very recently, the question of how knowledge comes about is one to which only argument had been applied. One of the main issues was whether knowledge can be inborn, or whether all we know is acquired through experience. We have seen the former line taken by the philosophical predecessors of the Gestalt school, and the latter by the British empiricists whose heirs were the strictly environmentalist behaviourists. It has been the achievement of Piaget to bring this question out from the domain of argument and assumption, and into that of empirical investigation. In doing so he has produced a new psychological theory; as we have already stressed, a biological one.

PIAGET'S PSYCHOLOGY

Students often complain that they find Piaget difficult. For this there are several reasons, the most obvious being that he *is* difficult. This in turn seems to have two causes, one being the nature of the subject matter, and the other Piaget's treatment. It turns out that intellectual development is one of the more complex aspects of human behaviour, and its understanding involves, perhaps not surprisingly, many concepts, particularly logical ones, that are hard to grasp. The more esoteric reaches of learning theory are equally difficult (and possibly a good deal more boring), but these are usually left to graduate study and research. Then Piaget's presentation is not immediately comprehensible. We do not get, for the most part, the neat listing of procedure, results, discussion to which we are accustomed. (Actually such a format is, often enough, merely a conventional way of presenting what was really a much more confused sequence of events.) Instead each work tends to be a highly abstruse discussion of some aspect of the whole general theory, illustrated rather than proved by length protocols. A second main reason for difficulty probably lies in the biologica orientation. This has very deep roots indeed. I think it goes back to the victor won at the close of the mediaeval period over the ideas of Aristotle. Aristotl had been a biologist; and he had interpreted even inorganic phenomena in bio logical terms. His conception of motion, for example, involved the principl that everything in the universe had a natural place, which it tended to mov towards. Despite many attacks on this, it was left for Galileo to substitute th principle of inertia. In Aristotle's own terms, 'final causes', i.e. ends or goals wer now abandoned in favour of 'efficient causes', or agents as it were pushing t cause some phenomenon. What followed Galileo, of course, was the explosion o success of the physical sciences. Now as R. S. Peters (1953) has pointed out behaviour came late on the scene as a subject for science. When it did, in th nineteenth century, the dominant models for a respectable, explanatory, powerfu science were well established. Thus it is not very surprising that the Britis Associationists set out to create a mental chemistry, and their stimulus–respons heirs such as William Estes a 'new mental chemistry'. It is not surprising tha Freud produced a mental dynamics, Lorenz a mental hydraulics, and the Gesta school a mental physics. And it is not so surprising that today we still find i hard to accept that a biological model can be just as scientific as one whic seems to offer an explanation of man as a complicated machine.

A third cause of difficulty is that newcomers to Piaget's work concentrate on and get bogged down in, an aspect which, while vital, should come second i understanding: the question of stages. Piaget gives an account of the stages o intellectual development. It is a very complex account, and newcomers to i sometimes assume that their first task must be to grasp exactly what is said t take place at each successive age. But, as we have already suggested, Piaget ha not been primarily interested in a normative account, in establishing standard for each age range (As Gesell, 1948 for example, did). Rather his interest i first in explaining the sequence of events. This means that what the student need to concentrate on is understanding what sort of a process Piaget consider intellectual development to be, and how and why it proceeds as it does. Accord ingly in this presentation we are giving our first attention to these matters, an shall offer a chronological account later.

We have already stressed Piaget's biological orientation. This has a numbe of implications, several of which are brought out by Furth. One is that the uni of behaviour is different from that of a 'mechanical' type of theory. The earlie and stricter forms of behaviourism envisaged a set of Stimuli giving rise to a se of Responses, rather like coins producing cigarettes from a vending machine More sophisticated behaviourists like Hull tried to describe the internal mecha nisms of the machine. For Piaget, it is only meaningful to speak of behaviour a a two-way interaction between the organism and the environment.

'One cannot conceive of an organism unless it finds itself in some meaningful exchange with the environment. Likewise there is no biological
environment unless one postulates the presence of an organism that is
responsive to, hence adapted to the particular environment.' (Furth, 1969)

To make this clearer, consider a simpler organism than man, such as a tree.
The way in which trees in general, and any tree in particular, grow and develop,
can only be understood as a process of interaction between the organism and
the nutrient or harmful aspects of the environment. This leads us to a second
implication of the biological position, concerned with organization. Any living
organism manifests organization. (We have noted earlier that the Gestalt psychologists made much of this point.) Again, however, this is not just a matter
of separate parts each having a function in a total machine. It is essentially a
matter of a continuing process of adaptation. One point made by Furth brings out
the aspect of continuity: 'No organization has a zero point from which it can
definitely be said to begin.' If a car engine is constructed, there are at first
separate parts; then these are put together; and at that point the organized whole
starts its existence. But when does the organized existence of an oak-tree start?—
with the sapling? or the seedling? or the acorn? or the flower of the parent
tree? This helps to bring out the concept of stages of development, to which
we will return later. Here, let us stress that at each point of sampling the tree's
existence, regulatory mechanisms are present, tending to preserve the organism
in a balanced state. At the animal level, or the physiological level, we speak of
homeostasis. At the level of intellectual or cognitive functioning, mechanisms of
assimilation and *accommodation,* to be discussed in a moment, perform a similar
function.

This brings us to Piaget's general view of intellectual functioning. It is customary to say that Piaget has described the growth of intelligence. That is perfectly true, but we must notice that 'intelligence' has here a rather wider meaning
than any we discussed earlier.

'Intelligence is the totality of behavioural coordinations that characterize
behaviour at a certain stage. Taken in its most general sense and including
all preforms and forms of intelligence proper (wherever one places the
dividing line), intelligence is the behavioural analogue of a biological organ
which regulates the organism's behavioural exchange with the environment.
This interaction constitutes behaviour. All adaptive behaviour implies some
knowing in the form of at least minimal knowledge concerning the environment.' (Furth, 1969)

This is the sort of quotation where it is as well to take a deep breath and read
it again slowly: and also, to return to it later after further exploration. And we
shall now give two more of the same kind. Piaget's aims may be summarized,
according to Flavell, as: 'the theoretical and experimental investigation of the
qualitative development of intellectual structures.' Now for some of Piaget's
own words on intelligence. He defines it:

'... not by a static criterion, as in previous definitions, but by the direction that intelligence follows in its evolution, and then I would define intelligence as a form of equilibration, or forms of equilibration, toward which all cognitive functions lead.' Equilibration in turn is: 'not an exact and automatic balance, as it would be in Gestalt theory; I define equilibration principally as a compensation for an external disturbance'. (Piaget. 1962)

The 'static' criteria which Piaget rejects are of course exemplified by the definitions we have quoted under the heading of *Intellectual Abilities*. Spearman's noegenetic principles are typical, but later writers such as Guilford also concentrate on compiling a list of capacities, even though a much more complicated one. Somewhat confusingly, Guilford terms his system the *structure of intellect*. Actually it is Piaget who is much more concerned with structure; what Guilford has done is to detail a large number of *functions*. Piaget continues the passage just quoted:

'When there is an external disturbance, the subject succeeds in compensating for this by an activity. The maximum equilibration is thus the maximum of the activity, and not a state of rest. It is a mobile equilibration, and not an immobile one. So equilibration is defined as compensation; compensation is the annulling of a transformation by an inverse transformation. The compensation which intervenes in equilibration implies the fundamental idea of reversibility, and this reversibility is precisely what characterizes the operations of the intelligence. An operation is an internalized action, but it is also a reversible action. But an operation is never isolated; it is always subordinated to other operations; it is part of a more inclusive structure. Consequently, we define intelligence in term of operations, co-ordination of operations.'

What Piaget means by *operations, transformations*, and *reversibility*, should become clearer as we go on.

There are other approaches that have helped to shape Piaget's thinking. As we have noted, the problems on which he has concentrated, those of epistemology, have hitherto been part of philosophy. Furthermore, French psychology, apart from work in testing and occupational guidance, has traditionally been strongly philosophical in treatment. There has been a concentration on a detailed discussion of problems and concepts, rather than on experimental investigations. The educational aim has been understanding and clarity of thought, rather than establishment of facts. This may help to explain why Piaget's writings seem, to experimentally trained psychologists, to contain a disproportionate amount of theorizing. Then there is the use of logic and mathematics. These have been introduced by Piaget insofar as they seemed to him essential characteristics of thought processes. We should note that it is *not* a matter of constructing mathematical or logical models that 'fit the data' and consequently allow of prediction (as Restle, for example 1962, has done). Nor is it simply a matter of investigating the variables at work when people tackle logical problems (see *Problem Solving*). Rather, it is that Piaget believes his investigations show that the underlying structure of thought is itself essentially logical. This does not mean that people always think logically, as they manifestly do not. Nor does it mean that, except for the most sophisticated adults, people are aware of the logical qualities of their thinking. It means that the way people actually do think, that is to say, the intellectual aspect of their interaction with the environment, can only be understood by grasping the logical operations which underlie it. Thinking, for Piaget, has a logical ground-plan, just as Plato assumed the universe has a mathematical one. (Piaget is likewise in the Platonic tradition in assuming that all knowledge does not come through experience. But he follows Aristotle in being a biologist, and hence is able to give a new account of the genesis of knowledge, through the interaction of the organism with the environment).

Within psychology, we have noted Piaget's early interest in testing. For a time, at least, he was influenced by psychiatry and in particular by psychoanalysis. He worked at Bleuler's psychiatric clinic, and this may have provided the stimulus for his 'clinical' method of investigation. This has been used in many—though not by any means all—of the Geneva school studies. Essentially it involves setting the subject some task or question, or putting him in a situation; observing his response; and in the light of that, modifying the situation so as to elicit a further response; and so on. In the case of verbal subjects, the procedure is supplemented by (or may entirely consist of) question and answer. This method obviously departs from what many psychologists have been brought up to regard as holy writ, namely that procedure must not be varied between subjects. It does, on the other hand, resemble the technique of psychoanalysis. There are some points of resemblance, also, between the two theories. It is sometimes suggested that Freud's child is all emotion, and Piaget's all intellect. This of course is a distortion. We shall see that Freud had a great deal to say about thought processes; and Piaget's work includes much on moral development and motivation. But it is true that the theories have different emphases. They constitute by far and away the two most extensive accounts of human development, and a detailed comparison is a desideratum. Cobliner (1967) in a long but rather disappointing paper, seems mainly concerned to show that whatever it was, Freud said it first. He does, however, make the useful point that Piaget's interest in the development of cognitive autonomy parallels the psychoanalytic interest which has grown up in ego psychology. He also points out that Piaget himself has virtually ceased to draw any inspiration from psychoanalytic work during the last thirty or forty years. In fact, psychoanalysis is not so much a strong influence as an interesting parallel development. Since the two theories do deal with different aspects of behaviour, there is no particular reason to expect them to say the same things. Then again, there is a considerable time gap between them. Although Freud did not die until 1939, his theories were largely formulated in the scientific context of the previous century. Perhaps one of the most fundamental differences is that Freud assumed a physical model for the mind rather than a biological one. This helps to explain why 'structures' for him are stable and fixed. And it is why early stages of development can be reactivated later. For

Piaget, this is impossible: the sapling stage of a tree could not be reactivated when the tree is full-grown. Each stage is essentially a development from the preceding one, incorporating and superseding it.

ESSENTIAL FEATURES OF THE SYSTEM

We turn now to some of the basic characteristics of the Piagetian system. We begin with the matter we have just raised, that of stages. The various stages of cognitive development, and samples of behaviour held to be typical of them, are probably the most widely known aspect of Piaget's work. We should note several points about these stages. First, they are not just a convenient way of dividing up the data, as a historian might, for the purpose of writing a chronological account, devote chapters to successive centuries. Piaget's stages are conceived of as qualitatively different from each other, and the transition from one to the next constitutes a natural break in development. At the same time there is no abrupt point of change. Societies often formalize the changes that take place in human development, and act as if some clear break occurred on the twelfth, or eighteenth, or twenty-first, birthday. But we all know that this is a convention, and the person is not dramatically different from one moment to the next (except in so far as he now starts a new role). So it is, according to Piaget, with intellectual development. Second, the stages are invariant in order of appearance. This is of course a normal feature of biological stages. Adulthood could not precede adolescence, nor fruit come before flowers. But this point should not lead us to think that the theory must necessarily specify the chronological age at which each phase appears. Although Piaget does give ages, these are not fundamental to the theory. They are not norms, in other words. They are simply typical ages at which the various phenomena have been found in the population studied by the Geneva workers. In psychometric terms, the stages constitute only an ordinal scale. That is to say, the different items (or stages) can be reliably arranged in relationship to each other; but we cannot say with certainty what distance or period of time separates each from the next. If we could, we should have an interval scale. That is what constructors of conventional intelligence tests seek to produce. As Hunt (1961) points out, if true norms could be established for Piagetian operations, we should not only have a new intelligence test: we should have the possibility of the first developmental scale of intelligence with a real theoretical basis. We have seen previously that hitherto tests have been based either on *ad hoc* or common sense assumptions (e.g. Binet); or on an analysis of intelligence at one level, namely the adult level (e.g. Spearman, or Guilford). It appears that in fact some of Piaget's co-workers such as Inhelder and Vinh-Bang, do hope to produce such a scale. (See also Mehrabian and Williams, 1971.)

A third point about the stages is one we mentioned earlier. It concerns their hierarchical nature. Each later stage depends upon, and integrates within itself, the earlier stages. It is not the case that as more complex operations develop, the simpler ones are just laid aside or fall into disuse. They actually no longer exist in their original form because they are incorporated into the next stage of development. An analogy here is with the acquisition of a sensorimotor skill. In learning, say, to drive a car, one learns first steps such as putting the car in gear. Later this is incorporated into a coordinated sequence of moving off from a stationary position. In some ways the Piagetian view of intellectual development does in fact suggest a set of cognitive skills, and this is shown also by the fifth point about stages. The *fourth* point, however, is that each stage is an integrated whole, as stated by Piaget in the passage we have quoted. Here we see an influence from the Gestalt school. But again, it is not just a matter of the whole being greater than the sum of its parts. Rather, each piece of behaviour is consistent with, and contributes to, the rest. The fifth point, now, is that a stage is not a matter of passing through a door from one stage of operating to another: a 'stage' covers the preparation, development, and achievement of a set of operations. This is again suggestive of a skill, and particularly of the old 'plateaux' theory as formulated by Bryan and Harter (1899). According to this, in a skill such as that of telegraph operators, one first learned, say, the skill of associating single letters with particular keys, giving a period of slow improvement. This skill had to be thoroughly assimilated before the next stage, that of whole words, could be acquired. On this in turn a sentence stage was based. Thus the pattern of skill acquisition was a sequence of gradients alternating with plateaux. This veteran theory may possibly have influenced Piaget. More generally, the skills aspect is illustrated by Furth in explaining Piaget's concept of intelligence. He says:

> 'Lorenz suggests that no animal below man is capable of driving a nail straight into a piece of wood. Such an action is certainly not an ultimate test of intelligence and perhaps would not be suspected of having anything to do with intelligence until one realizes that it is not because of lack of strength, of inability to hold or swing a hammer, or lack of interest, that primates as well as young children cannot perform this task. What is lacking are rules of coordination that govern the strokes which compensate for each slight deviation from the vertical. Lower organisms do not have the capacity for this elementary degree of learned skill which can be called "control of an action pattern by continuous compensatory movements." Intelligence is found, thus, not in the activity as such, but in the rule which implicitly governs this activity.'

This may be compared with Ryle's view quoted in *Intellectual Abilities*. And we can notice again the concept of equilibration—compensating for each slight deviation from the vertical.

The last feature of the stages that we want to mention is known as *décalages*. There are two varieties of this feature. Horizontal décalage refers to the fact that development within a stage may be uneven. Conservation is a mental operation which develops at a certain stage, but not all its aspects necessarily appear together. Conservation of mass typically emerges about a year before conservation of weight. Vertical décalage refers to a formal similarity between stages. For example, a child can find his way about the house when quite young, it is as if he had a cognitive map in Tolman's sense. But not until much later can he actually draw such a map or indeed understand a plan of a house. To use again our analogy of a tree, the successive appearance of leaves and blossom, formally rather alike, might be seen as a vertical décalage.

Piaget's theoretical writings can in one sense be thought of as an attempt to systematize a vast collection of data. These data are observations of behaviour, including verbal behaviour, gathered by the so-called 'clinical' method which we have already described, and in later studies, especially on perception, by more conventional techniques. The data so collected form the *content* of the system. We must comment also on the aspects of *function* and *structure*, which are what the theory is about. Here once again Piaget's work stands in contrast to that of the dominant American-Behaviourist tradition, and more in line with the tradition of continental Europe. Wundt's psychology was a structural one, and Titchener carried his assumptions with him to the U.S.A. But they did not strike root. What flourished in that practical society was *functionalism*. The functionalist approach was partly inspired by William James, who presented a simplified version of the philosophical doctrine of pragmatism put forward by C. S. Peirce. It seemed that there were grounds for defining the truth as that which worked. While this may not be so (and indeed Peirce never said it), it was just the sort of notion to appeal to psychologists who wanted to have some practical influence on the world. And from functionalism there emerged J. B. Watson, with his claims that by the new techniques of conditioning he could take a baby and produce any desired sort of adult. Later still B. F. Skinner has shown how reliably rats can be brought to press levers, and pigeons to play ping-pong. In his novel *Walden Two* he tells how a whole community might be operantly conditioned to live in harmony—for its own good, of course (see also Skinner, 1972). It is function that seems to be the important aspect of behaviour. As we have seen, even the 'Structure of Intellect' is really a list of functions.

Now Piaget does have something to say about function. Function here implies certain fundamental modes of operation, which appear throughout the course of development and are essential to it. These are termed *functional invariants*. The first we have already met: it is *organization*. A tendency towards organization is characteristic of living and developing organisms. The second mode of operation is *adaptation*. This refers to the fact that an organism at any stage of its existence is the resultant of an interaction between the organism and the environment, which has gone on in the past and still continues. Adaptation occurs in two ways, or involves two processes, called assimilation and accommodation. *Assimilation* occurs whenever an organism utilizes something from the environment and incorporates it. Food is a good example. At a psychological level, new stimulus situations are commonly seen, or interpreted, in terms of what is already familiar. This is clearly seen in language, when new objects are given the name of familiar ones that resemble them. This happens with both children and adults. Another example would be racial (or other) stereotypes. If one has a stereotype of Frenchmen as passionate lovers, there will be a tendency to see any new Frenchman in this way. The mechanism of assimilation is even wider than this: it includes all the cases where we act in a new situation as in the past. Thus in a sense it is the counterpart in Piaget's theory to the phenomenon of transfer, with its various explanations such as stimulus generalization. The behaviourist, basically stimulus–response account of transfer is in terms of the properties of the stimulus, and their connections with various responses. Piaget's account is in terms of structures (which we shall come to soon) within the organism. This example helps to show how wide is the gap between the two approaches, since for the Piagetian theory it is clear that eating and transfer both manifest the same functional invariant. An S–R account sees these two phenomena as completely separate, examples of motivation and learning respectively. *Accommodation* is in a sense the complement. It operates as variations in the environment demand behaviour which modifies the internal structures. In terms of food once more, the acquisition of new tastes would represent this aspect of adaptation. Such adaptability is of course typical of higher organisms. Psychologically, the reorganization thought by Gestalt theorists to be typical of insightful problem-solving would be a special case of accommodation. The mechanism can also be compared to that of Freud's reality principle.

It is, however, *structure* that has been Piaget's over-riding concern. Structure refers to the inferred organizational properties of intellectual functioning. The structures in which Piaget is interested are not observed directly: they are postulated as in some sense underlying the behaviour that is observed. So once more we have a sharp contrast with strict behaviourism, this time in line with the dichotomy described by Anderson as running through the whole study of thinking, and which we mentioned when discussing *Concept Identification*. Watson, of course, went to the extreme of ruling out all inferred events within the organism. Later behaviourists such as Hull, as we have seen, were obliged to break this rule; and quite recently the Harvard psychologists led by Bruner have been able to adopt a more eclectic position. Piaget has stood throughout uncompromisingly at the other end of the scale. It is not just that we are obliged to speculate about internal events: it is that these events are at least part of what psychology ought to be about. It is the view taken, in different ways, by the Würzburg school, by Freud, and by the Gestalt psychologists.

Piaget himself claims that he is the first to present a synthesis of genesis and structure. By this he means that it is theoretically possible to suppose either that organisms are infinitely modifiable, or that they are permanently structured in a certain way. A simple evolutionary theory, for example, supposes that development of a species occurs through the purely chance variations of each generation.

Such a view, Piaget remarks, influenced the early associationists, and through them the S–R theorists. In the course of development of each individual, some connections are reinforced, according to the prevailing environmental contin gencies, and others not. In principle, there is no limit to this process. That i: why Watson was able to make his claim about producing any type of adult This, in Piaget's terms, is 'genesis without structures'. The opposite view i obviously 'structures without genesis' which is typified in biology by Weismann (1902); in philosophy by Husserl (1913); and in psychology by the Gestalt school Piaget considers that Koffka, for example, believed that: 'development is deter mined entirely by maturation, i.e. by a preformation which itself obeys Gestalt laws'.

Piaget now develops his own view. Genesis and structure are indissociable This has two aspects. First: 'Genesis emanates from a structure and culminate: in another structure.' Earlier, we gave the example of the oak-tree. Piaget gives : rather complicated example of logical structures, which we shall not describe here, leaving them to the chronological account to follow. But he concludes: 'Whenever one is dealing with a structure in the psychology of intelligence, it: genesis can be traced to other more elementary structures which do not con stitute absolute beginnings themselves but have a prior genesis in even more elementary structures, and so on *ad infinitum*. I say *ad infinitum*, but the psycho logist will stop at birth. He will stop at the sensorimotor level and at this level there is, of course, the whole biological problem because the neural structure: themselves have their genesis, and so it continues.' The second aspect is that: 'every structure has a genesis'. This of course is the converse of the first aspect.

> 'The clearest result of our research on the psychology of intelligence is that even the structures most necessary to the adult mind, such as the logico-mathematical structures, are not innate in the child; they are built up little by little.... There are no innate structures: every structure presupposes a construction. All these constructions originate from prior structures and revert, in the final analysis, as I said before, to the biological problem.' (Piaget, 1968)

The relationship between genesis and structure is further analysed in discuss ing the concept of equilibrium. This was mentioned earlier: now it will be helpfu to give a short account in Piaget's own words:

> 'In order to define equilibrium, I shall make use of three characteristics. First, equilibrium is noted for its stability. But let us note at the outset that stability does not signify immobility. As you know very well, there are in chemistry and physics mobile equilibria characterized by transformations in opposite directions that are compensated in a stable fashion. The concept of mobility thus does not contradict the concept of stability; equilibrium can be both mobile and stable. In the field of intelligence we have great need of this concept of mobile equilibrium. An operational system, for example, is a system of actions, a series of essentially mobile operations which never-theless can remain stable in the sense that, once constituted, the structure which determines them will not become modified.

Secondly, every system is subject to external intrusion which tends to modify it. We shall say that there is equilibrium when this external intrusion is compensated by the actions of the subject. The idea of compensation seems to me fundamental in the definition of psychological equilibrium.

Finally, the third point I should like to emphasize is that equilibrium, thus defined, is not something passive but, on the contrary, something essentially active; the greater the equilibrium, the more activity is required. It is very difficult to conserve equilibrium from the mental point of view. The moral equilibrium of a personality presupposes force of character in order to resist temptation, to conserve the values one holds, etc. Equilibrium is synonymous with activity. In the field of intelligence the same holds true. A structure is in equilibrium to the extent that an individual is sufficiently active to be able to counter all intrusion with external compensations. Moreover, the intrusion will ultimately be anticipated by thought. Potential intrusion can, at the same time, be anticipated and compensated, thanks to the inverse or reciprocal operations.

Thus defined, the concept of equilibrium seem to have particular value with respect to the synthesis of genesis and structure, inasmuch as the concept of equilibrium encompasses the concepts of compensation and of activity. If we consider a structure of intelligence, a logico-mathematical structure of whatever kind (a structure of pure logic, of class, classification, relation, etc., or a propositional operation), we first of course, find activity, since we are dealing with operations, but above all we find the fundamental characteristic of logico-mathematical structures, namely, reversibility. A logical transformation can, in effect, always be inversed by a transformation in the opposite direction or reciprocal transformation. Now it is obvious that this reversibility is very close to what earlier I called compensation in the field of equilibrium. Nonetheless, there are two distinct realities involved. When we are dealing with a psychological analysis we are always obliged to reconcile two systems: that of awareness and that of behaviour or psychophysiology. On the plane of awareness we have to do with implications, while on the behavioural or psychophysiological side we have to do with causal series.* I can say that the reversibility of operations, i.e. of logico-mathematical structures, is the property of the structures on the plane of implication, but in order to understand how genesis leads to these structures we must have recourse to causal language. It is here that the concept of equilibrium as I have defined it enters in as a system of progressive compensations. When the compensations are achieved, i.e. when equilibrium is attained, the structure is constituted in its reversible state.'

*David Elkind adds an editorial footnote to this:

'Perhaps what Piaget means here is that it makes little sense to talk about thoughts causing one another, since the connotation is that of physical or material things acting upon one another. To say that thoughts imply one another removes this ambiguity, since implication has logical and not physicalistic connotations.'

I hope this makes clearer the concepts of genesis, structure, and equilibration. As often with Piaget, it may pay to return later to the details after completing an overview of the whole. Meanwhile . . . let us proceed to another structural concept which must be mentioned, the scheme or schema. There is an obscurity in that both these words have been used to translate Piaget's *schème*. And in fact, as Furth points out, Piaget seems to mean two different things, rather confusingly sometimes using the same word for both. The concept of a schema has appeared in the writings of such rather diverse authors as Henry Head, F. C. Bartlett, and D. O. Hebb. It usually corresponds more or less to Drever's (1952) definition of 'a sort of mental framework'. Except that this suggests some sort of hardware, the definition does fairly well for Piaget. In *Mental Imagery in the Child* (1966), he spells out the distinction. A schema is 'a simplified model intended to facilitate presentation.' It seems that this is partly just a matter of showing that images are, like all other mental phenomena, organized. A scheme, on the other hand, is 'a generalization instrument enabling the subject to isolate and utilize the elements common to similar successive behaviors.' This again sounds like what we commonly speak of as transfer. And indeed this should be so, since these schemes are precisely the structures involved in assimilation and accommodation, as explained earlier. The schemes now so called, however, are what other writers have referred to as schemata. They are structures underlying particular aspects of experience and behaviour. Flavell speaks of: 'a cognitive structure which has reference to a class of similar action sequences, these sequences of necessity being strong, bonded totalities in which the constituent behavioural elements are tightly bonded' (Flavell, 1963). As development proceeds, the structures become more and more complex; and also, in a sense, more and more cognitive. The simplest sort of structure is a reflex. The child is born with this. As explained above, Piaget would say that while reflexes themselves have a history of development, to trace it further back is a task for the neurophysiologist, not the psychologist. But conversely, even a reflex has a cognitive aspect. As Flavell puts it:

> 'Piaget would certainly say that an infant who performs an organized sequence of grasping behaviors is in fact applying a grasping schema to reality, and that the behavior itself does constitute the schema. However, and the point is a rather subtle one, to say that a grasping sequence forms a schema is to imply more than the simple fact that the infant shows organized grasping behavior.' (It may be that this is where we move from *schema* to *scheme*). 'It implies that assimilatory functioning has generated a specific cognitive *structure*, an organized *disposition* to grasp objects on repeated occasions. It implies that there has been a change in overall cognitive organization such that a new behavioral totality has become part of the child's intellectual repertoire.'

It will have become clear that the concepts of scheme and schema are hard to define exactly. Their theoretical status is still less clear. But our next task is to try to trace the course of intellectual development according to Piaget. It is, briefly, as Hunt says, the story of the way in which the organism interacts with the environment, through functional invariants, to form ever more complex structures. To quote:

'In the course of this dual adaptive process of assimilation and accommodation, the ready-made reflexive schemata of the newborn infant become progressively transformed through differentiations and coordinations into the logical "organization" (or operations for information processing) of adult intelligence. This is the epigenesis of behaviour. As it proceeds, the child becomes capable of taking account of stimuli more and more remote from him in space and time, and also of resorting to more and more composite and indirect modes of solving problems. In this sense, "life is a continuous creation of increasingly complex forms and a progressive adaptation of these forms to the environment" (Piaget, 1936).' (Hunt, 1961)

It is this theme which we shall try to trace through from birth to adolescence, illustrating it by a handful of the thousands of observations that have been reported. Many of those for the early stages are from Piaget's reports on his own children, which are particularly vivid. The stages are divided into substages; and as development proceeds more and more aspects of intellectual activity are involved. We shall reduce both these aspects to a bare outline, in the hope of conveying the essence of the story.

THE STAGES OF DEVELOPMENT

Piaget distinguishes four principal stages of development, with approximate age ranges as follows.

Sensorimotor:	Birth to $1\frac{1}{2}$ or 2 years
Preoperational:	$1\frac{1}{2}$ or 2 to 7 or 8 years
Concrete operations:	7 or 8 to 11 or 12 years
Formal operations:	11 or 12 up to (and including) adolescence.

The Sensorimotor Stage

The child is born with some mechanisms, or schemes, ready to function. These are reflex actions such as sucking and grasping. They are at first passively released, as can be seen by anyone who places his finger on a baby's palm. The hand closes automatically. But almost at once a change starts: active behaviour begins, in that there is a *search* for the stimulus. McV. Hunt gives us this account of Piaget's son Laurent.

'The shift from passive response to active search shows most prominently in the sucking of Laurent. On the day after birth, he seized the nipple as soon as it touched his lips. By the third day, all he needed in order to begin groping actively with an open mouth for the nipple was to touch the smooth skin surrounding the nipple with his lips. On the other hand, when the nipple touched one cheek, he groped on the wrong side as well as on the correct side. By the twentieth day, although Laurent might attempt to suck the skin of the breast, he soon withdrew, began to cry, and then groped actively with his mouth for the nipple. By this time, he no longer made errors; a touch on the cheek immediately guided his groping toward the side touched, and he persisted in groping until he found the nipple and began swallowing.' (Hunt, 1961)

Here we see at once several of the characteristics we have mentioned. The innate or ready-made mechanisms are exercised. But this is essentially a process of interaction with the environment. The operation is that of sucking, released by a stimulus in or near the mouth. But by the process of accommodation, the scheme quickly becomes more adapted to reality; the response is released by the appropriate stimulus only. One might contrast this with the ethological concept of sign-stimuli: accommodation is precisely the process that is lacking in stickle-back development, so that any red round object continues to release mating behaviour. Again, we can notice that an S–R theorist would say, ah, what has happened is that only sucking on the nipple has produced milk, so that rein-forcement produces a more discriminant response. The compleat Piagetian might reply, that what is interesting is the internal mechanism by which this is brought about—and this is *accommodation*. Secondly, it is not just a question of stimuli and response, but of interaction. Following the sensory deprivation experiments first reported by Bexton, Heron and Scott (1954), we all now accept the necessity of environmental stimulation for a living organism to function. Piaget takes the matter further, referring to such stimulation as *aliment*—food. Just as food is necessary for bones and muscle—physical structures—to grow, so environmental stimulation is necessary for cognitive structures—schemes—to develop. And again, the work of Berlyne, Butler, Harlow, and others (see e.g. Fowler, 1965) has made all psychologists aware of the rather obvious fact that organisms *seek* stimulation. Again, Piaget stresses the use to which such stimulation is put: it is *assimilated*. It is not like a car needing petrol, but rather, as we have stressed, like a plant needing nutrients, out of which more complex structures are built.

Each scheme is to begin with independent of the others. There is no connec-tion, for the infant, between grasping something and sucking it. Gradually the schemes become coordinated, so that something heard becomes something to look at; something seen, an object to grasp; an object grasped, a thing to suck.

'At age two months and four days, Laurent by chance discovers his right index finger and looks at it briefly. At two months and eleven days, he inspects for a moment his right hand, perceived by chance. At two months fourteen days, he looks three times in succession at his left hand and chiefly at his raised index finger. At two months seventeen days, he follows the spontaneous movement of his hand for a moment, and then he examines it several times while it searches for his nose or rubs his eyes. At two months nineteen days (please note for subsequent reference), he smiles at the same hand after having contemplated it eleven times in succession. I then put his hand in a bandage; as soon as I detach it (half an hour later) it returns to the visual field and Laurent again smiles at it.' (Piaget, 1936)

This exemplifies the 'clinical' technique: observation, followed by alteration of the situation (the bandage) to see what will happen next, or to test a hypothesis. Notice also how selective the account is: Piaget presumably made many other observations during this period. He presents us with the set that seems to him to illustrate best the phenomenon he is concerned with. The fact that Laurent can now move his hand in order to see it (and conversely place it visually as an aid to moving it) implies that a higher-order coordinating mechanism has come into existence. The example also shows how far back Piaget traces development. Until he wrote, development did not seem to require such a fine analysis. Compare the discussion of genesis and structure above. There is here also an interesting comparison with psychoanalytic views on the development of object permanence. Melanie Klein in particular developed Freud's ideas as they applied to very young children. Her observations suggested that the breast is at first perceived as an object separate from the mother: it is just the food giving (or restricting) object. The child experiences an uncoordinated set or sequence of separate stimuli which only gradually sort themselves out into categories, so to speak. This might be compared to accounts of the distortions of perception experienced in schizophrenia or under hallucinogenic drugs. Some types of schizophrenic patient, at least, are typically disoriented in space and time. And it is in the coordination of operations that we see the origins of perception of space and time. Perception of space develops as the separate perceptions of bits of space come together like pieces of a jigsaw; and so with time.

> 'At five months and twenty-four days, Laurent makes no attempt to follow with his eye any of the objects I drop in front of him.... At six months three days, with Laurent lying down, I drop a box 5 cm. in diameter vertically and too fast for him to be able to follow the trajectory. His eyes search for it at once on the sofa on which he is lying.... At seven months twenty-nine days, Laurent searches the floor for everything I drop above him, as if he has in the least perceived the beginning of the movement of falling.' (Piaget, 1937)

It must be stressed yet again that the rapid summary given here simply has to ignore the enormous complexity and subtlety of Piaget's analysis. It is no more than a synopsis, with a few snatches of dialogue. So we go on. The coordination of objects in time and space leads to the ability to manipulate the environment. Lucienne, for example (Piaget's second child) learned how to swing the dolls hanging from the hood of her cot by shaking her legs. And from this, it becomes possible to differentiate between means and ends, as shown by this observation of the third child Jacqueline.

> 'At the age of eight months twenty days, Jacqueline tries to grasp the cigarette case which I present to her. I then slide it between the cross strings which attach her dolls to the hood. She tries to reach it directly. Not succeeding, she immediately looks at the strings which are not in her hands and of which she sees only the part in which the cigarette case is entangled. She looks in front of her, grasps the strings, pulls and shakes them. The

cigarette case falls and she grasps it. . . . Second experiment: same reactions
but without trying to grasp the object directly.' (Piaget, 1936)

Of course Piaget does not mean that Jacqueline consciously reasoned out this
problem: nevertheless a logical cognitive structure has developed as a result of
which she is able to respond appropriately. We are at a stage of ability which
recalls animal problem-solving. What characterizes the more advanced forms of
problem-solving indeed on our rather wide view of it what characterizes *thinking*, is the ability to manipulate the environment symbolically. That is, internally.
For this it is necessary that space, time, and causality become objective: the
world is not in a constant state of flux, the living organism is not a helpless
responder to every changing stimulus. Further developments which illustrate this
internal manipulation follow. Two sorts of behaviour which can be seen as
complementary demonstrate the functional invariants. Imitation and play are
characteristic of childhood. Imitation implies that a scheme is modified to match
some external model, i.e. accommodation. In play, on the other hand (at any rate
certain forms of play), an object stands for another. A clothespeg is a doll; indeed
a doll is a child. There is usually some resemblance between the two objects,
though it may be a remote one. Nevertheless play does not depend upon a mistake, but on letting one thing symbolize another. Both these traits are in turn
related to an interest in novelty in variation: what Piaget calls 'a discovery of
new means through active experimentation'. As mentioned above, this is characteristic of the child from the start: we now move on to a new phase, a more
deliberate, more cognitive phase. Piaget's description of Laurent at 14 months
using a stick to obtain a piece of bread is irresistibly reminiscent of Köhler's
account of Sultan obtaining a banana (see *Problem Solving*). But the Gestalt
theory supposed that Sultan's insight was the outcome of the innate structure of
the mind (and brain) such that his internal representation of the unsatisfactory
stimulus situation was modified to become 'good'. Piaget, on the other hand lays
his emphasis on the preceding experiences of playing separately with the stick and
other objects serving the function of a stick. On the other hand, neither is it a
question of these separate activities or 'habits' being reinforced and then put
together. Genesis and structure are both part of the same whole process.

The 'achievement phase' of the sensorimotor stage, then, is marked by the
internalization of sensorimotor schemes. The child's continuous interaction with
the environment results in: the beginnings of intelligence; the construction of
reality; symbolic imagery. New means to an end can be invented through mental
combination. The child is no longer restricted to a direct route to a goal, since
some representation of the environment exists for reference.

'At eighteen months and eight days, Jacqueline throws a ball under a
sofa. Instead of bending down at once and searching for it on the floor,
she looks at the place, realizes the ball must have crossed under the sofa,
and sets out to go behind it. There is a table at her right and the sofa is
backed up against the bed on the left; therefore she begins by turning her

back on the place where the ball disappeared, goes around the table, and finally arrives behind the sofa at the correct place. Thus she has closed the circle of displacements by an itinerary different from that of the object and has thereby elaborated a group through representation by the invisible displacement of a ball and of the detour to be made in order to find it.' (Piaget, 1937)

Compare this with the diagrams of the routes to a goal taken by a hen and a dog (*Problem Solving*). Similarly, imitation can be deferred: the model is stored for later reproduction. Jacqueline watched an infant throw a tantrum, which she had never seen before, and imitated it some twelve hours later. Symbolic play, appearing in developed form, illustrates the same theme: Jacqueline played 'going to sleep', with various objects that stood for her usual pillow. It is by this age ($1\frac{1}{2}$ to 2 years) that the first words appear. We have compared some of the behaviour to that of the apes studied by Köhler. Some attempts have been made to teach chimpanzees language, which we discuss elsewhere (*Language and Thought*). And although the comparison seems an apt one, it must not be stretched too far. In the early stages an oak tree and a tomato plant might look rather similar. Piaget gives another analogy:

'Sensorimotor intelligence acts like a slow-motion film, in which all the pictures are seen in succession but without fusion, and so without the continuous vision necessary for understanding the whole.' (Piaget, 1947)

The Preoperational Stage

This is sometimes called (as by Flavell) a substage. By this is meant that Piaget really distinguishes three main types of thinking: sensorimotor, concrete operations, and formal operations. Very roughly, in the first thinking involves responding to the more-or-less immediate environment. In the second, the environment can be manipulated internally, but not with complete freedom; thinking is still bound to the environment in ways we shall shortly describe. In the third stage, thinking becomes free from the environment, and can be purely abstract. But the middle period is marked by such far-reaching changes that it is convenient to think of it as two phases: a preparation phase and an achievement phase. Like every other stage, the preoperational one is marked by several interrelated features. As at every point in the Piagetian scheme of things we are to think not of static but of constantly developing mechanisms.

Whereas the sensorimotor child is essentially tied to overt acts, the preoperational child is capable of symbolic representation. For the sensorimotor child, thinking and behaviour are one, as it were. One aspect of this is that the infant is unable to distinguish between himself and his environment (a feature also stressed by psychoanalysts). In order to do so, and in order to represent the environment, the ability must develop to discriminate between what Piaget terms *signifiers* and *significates*. *Significates* are things represented by signifiers.

Signifiers are of two kinds: *signs* and *symbols*. *Signs* are used by general agreement and are arbitrary in the sense that there is no physical resemblance to the thing indicated. Nearly all words are of this kind (except for onomatopoeic words) and words are in fact the commonest signs. There are others, such as those used in mathematics. *Symbols* on the other hand are private to the individual, and usually do resemble what they stand for. Dream symbols and other kinds of imagery, and early linguistic sounds, are examples. However, although the discrimination between the representative, so to speak, and the thing represented is an essential feature of thought, it is not the possession of signifiers that results in representation. Rather, the ability to represent the environment develops first, and makes use of signifiers of various kinds. It is true that thinking cannot develop fully without the concomitant development of signifiers, especially language; but it is not true that no thought processes at all can develop without signifiers. Here Piaget cuts a couple of psychological Gordian knots: the imageless thought controversy, and the long debate over the relative primacy of language or thought. The latter will be dealt with in a separate chapter (*Language and Thought*).

In the stages of development we have discussed so far, then, there are representations, which are internalized actions, but these actions are still centred on the body itself. 'These representations do not allow the objective combinations that operations permit' (Piaget). It is the growth of these 'operations' that now concerns us. To illustrate what Piaget means here, he noted that children of four and five, who went by themselves to and from school, could not make a plan or model of their route using building blocks. One way of expressing this is to say that thought is egocentric. The child cannot, as it were, stand outside himself. He no longer confuses himself with the environment, yet neither can he see himself as one object in that environment. A boy A may understand that he has a brother B, yet deny that B has a brother. The relationship is one-way, and centred on himself. This is a feature which has been thought important in many aspects of human development. G. H. Mead, a pioneer social psychologist, spoke of the ability 'to take the role of the other'. In Piaget's view early speech is egocentric, in that the child does not adapt it to the needs of others. Another feature of preoperational thought is the tendency to respond as it were automatically to only one feature of a stimulus situation. The response is stimulus-bound. This is seen in the experiments on conservation which we shall illustrate shortly. These also, however, demonstrate what may be considered 'the most important single characteristic of preoperational thought' (Flavell); namely its irreversibility.

Reversibility is, conversely, one of the most fundamental features of fully developed thinking. At its simplest, the concept is that mature thinking can manipulate the environment freely. The objects of thought can be played with, as it were: a situation can be imagined, changed, restored to the original, without regard to the way things actually are. But reversibility also underlies many aspects of reasoning. Mathematics, for example, is only possible if the mind accepts that any operation of addition can be reversed exactly by subtraction: that $6+4=10$ is logically equivalent to $10-4=6$. It has been one of Piaget's most surprising findings that this basis for thinking only develops slowly during the course of childhood.

It can be seen that reversibility is also involved in the egocentric attitudes described above. It is best illustrated, however, by the experiments on conservation. Piaget considers the absence of conservation to be 'the most certain sign of the absence of operations.' Conservation is the principle that a measurement on some basic dimension such as weight, quantity, number, mass, etc. can only be altered by manipulation along that dimension; it is not affected by changes in any other variable. Given a pint of water, it can only be increased or decreased by actually adding or taking away water; not by dividing it into small quantities, pouring it into the bath, colouring it green, or whatever. This seems obvious to adult thought, but is not so to the preoperational child, who responds to appearances, whose thought is still bound to the stimulus situation. This phenomenon has produced perhaps the most famous series of Piagetian experiments. An account of one of these now follows.

'*Conservation of continuous quantities.* In one of the first kinds of experiment, one concerning the conservation of quantities of liquid, Piaget and Szeminska (1941) give the child-subject two beakers of equal dimensions (See A_1 and A_2 in Figure 5.1). They contain the same quantity of liquid as shown by the levels in the beakers. The liquid in A_2 is then poured into two smaller beakers of equal dimensions (B_1 and B_2). The child is then asked whether the quantity of liquid poured from A_2 into B_1 and B_2 is still equal to that in A_1. If the child answers yes, the liquid in B_1 is poured into two smaller containers (C_1 and C_2), and that in B_2 is poured into containers (C_3 and C_4), identical with C_1 and C_2. As the liquid is divided in this fashion, the problem concerning the conservation of its quantity is put to the child in form of a question as to the equality or nonequality with that in one of the original containers. Moreover, as a check on the child's answers, he is commonly asked to pour the liquid into a container of a shape differing from that of the original beaker. Again the problem is to see if he judges the quantity to remain the same or to be changed thereby.

Here is the record of the experiment with Clairette Blas, a four year old.

Blas (4:0) "Have you got a friend?—Yes, Odette.—Look, we're giving you, Clairette, a glass of orangeade (A_1, three-fourths full), and we're giving Odette a glass of lemonade (A_2, also three-fourths full). Has one of you more to drink than the other?—The same.—This is what Clairette does: she pours her drink into two other glasses (B_1 and B_2, which are thus half-full). Has Clairette the same amount as Odette?—Odette has more—Why?—Because we put less in (she pointed to the levels of B_1 and B_2, without taking into account the fact that there were two glasses).—(Odette's drink was then poured into B_3 and B_4). It's the same—And now (pouring Clairette's drink from B_1 and B_2 into L, a long thin tube which is almost full)?—I've got more.—Why?—We poured it into that glass (pointing to the level in L), and here (B_3 and B_4) we haven't.—But were they the same before?—Yes.—And now?—I've got more."

Clairette's orangeade was then poured back from L into B_1 and B_2:
"Look, Clairette has poured hers like Odette. So is all the lemonade (B_3 and

190

B_4) and all the orangeade (B_1 and B_2) the same?—It's the same (said with conviction).—Now Clairette does this (pouring B_1 into C_1 which is then full, while B_2 remains half-full). Have you got the same amount to drink?—'I've got more. —But where does the extra come from?—From in there (B_1).—What must we do so that Odette has the same?—We must take that little glass (pouring part of B_3 into C_2)—And is it the same now? Or has one of you got more?—Odette has more—Why? Because we poured it into that little glass (C_2).—But is there the same amount to drink, or has one got more than the other?—Odette has more to drink.—Why?—Because she has three glasses (B_3 almost empty, B_4 and C_2, while Clairette has C_1 full and B_2)." (Piaget and Szeminska, 1941, p. 6.)'

From Hunt (1961)

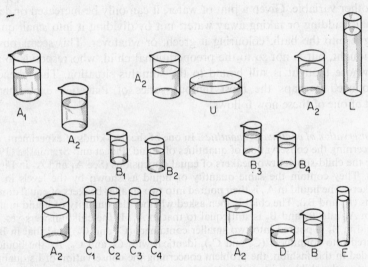

Figure 5.1. The containers used to investigate the conservation of continuous and discontinuous quantities. (Reproduced from B. Inhelder (1953), 'Criteria of the stages of mental development' in J. M. Tanner and B. Inhelder (Eds.), *Discussions on Child Development*, International Universities Press by permission of World Health Organization, Geneva)

Such a protocol speaks for itself. We notice here the questioning technique used in these experiments. A criticism sometimes made is that words are being put into the child's mouth, or that a desired answer is being elicited more subtly, perhaps without the experimenter being aware of it. There can be no absolute proof that this is not so. The possibility of uncontrolled variables still awaiting discovery always remains. The reader must decide for himself whether he is more impressed by this, or by the quality of the protocol and the number of similar reports. Another criticism (e.g. Green and Laxon, 1970) is that what Piaget has really shown is merely the development of language. This would presumably be applied to the example quoted by saying that Clairette simply does not understand the meaning of 'same' and 'more'. Again, the reader must decide, and of course not just on the basis of a single answer.

Concrete Operations Stage

What, then, is it that allows the child to develop 'reversible' thinking? What are the famous operations that are now achieved? Flavell puts it thus:

'It will be recalled ... that the term *action* is a very fundamental and generic one in Piaget's system. Cognition at all genetic levels is best characterized as the application of real actions by the subject, either in relation to something in the milieu or in relation to other subject actions. In the sensory-motor period these actions are externalized and observable for the most part: the child brings thumb to mouth, removes an obstacle to obtain a desired object, etc. As the child progresses through the post-infancy years, on the other hand, we know that his cognitive actions become more and more internalized, schematic, and mobile, and of course more and more divested of their concrete, substantial qualities. But most important of all, for present purposes, these now internal, now representational cognitive actions gradually cohere to form increasingly complex and tightly integrated *systems* of actions. These systems are equilibrated, organized affairs in the sense that one action may annul or otherwise compensate for another previously performed; two actions can combine to produce a third, and so on. That is to say, the system these actions form is truly a system, with definite structural properties; it is something quite other than a simple concatenation or colligation of juxtaposed terms. When cognitive actions achieve this special status, that is, when they are organized into close-knit totalities with definite, strong structure, they are called by Piaget cognitive *operations*.'

I hope that is quite clear. It now starts to get a bit more difficult. The operations can only be understood in terms of logico-mathematical structures which as it were represent the essential nature of thought. Logic is the mirror of thought: but it is a mirror which, like that in *Snow White*, reflects the truth, not just the appearance. It is not that thinking behaviour is conveniently summarized by logical formulae or mathematical equations. Nor is it that one system provides a model for the other. Rather, the logico-mathematical structures constitute the most general and abstract level of analysis of thought processes. To use a perhaps trivial example, the relationship is something like that between cooking and chemistry. A skilled cook need know nothing of chemistry; yet her ingredients can certainly be chemically analysed, and if the underlying chemical structure were lacking, there could be no cake.

Further, however, the abstract level of analysis has so to speak a life of its own. A chemist could devise new tastes to which there is no corresponding food. Similarly Piaget's logical analysis enables him to postulate structures to which no behaviour has as yet been shown to correspond.

The operations are representational acts which are 'an integral part of an organized network of related acts.' They include operations such as adding, subtracting, multiplying, dividing, setting terms into correspondences, classifying, ranking, etc. There are also infralogical operations which are concerned with position and distance relationships, and part-whole relationships, of real objects.

The main logical structures with which Piaget is concerned at this stage are what he calls *groupings* (groupements). There are nine of these: one minor preliminary grouping, and eight major ones. Of the eight, four show operations (rules) that can be done on classes, and four those that can be done on relations. The operations are the same in each case, and are set out in the preliminary grouping. We shall now describe the four rules.

First imagine that we wished to classify the subject matter of zoology. Consider the position of one variety, spaniels, in relation to the classes of domestic dogs, canines, mammals, and vertebrates. Let letters stand for the classes, thus

E = all vertebrates D^1 = all vertebrates other than mammals
D = all mammals C^1 = all other mammals
C = all canines B^1 = all other canines
B = all domestic dogs A^1 = all other domestic dogs
A = all spaniels

These classes can be borne in mind when considering the relationships. The relationships are expressed by the signs $+$, $-$, and $=$. These have a somewhat different meaning to the usual arithmetical one. $+$ means 'taken together with', $-$ means 'less', and $=$ means 'is equivalent to' or 'amounts to saying'. There are four relationships: Composition. Associativity, General Identity, and Reversibility.

1. *Composition.* The product which results from combining any element in the system with any other by means of the defined operation, is itself an element in the system.

An example is $(A + A^1 = B) + (B + B^1 = C) = (A + A^1 + B^1 = C)$

What does this mean? The letters stand for classes, as above. A group of letters in a bracket is therefore a statement. $(A + A^1 = B)$ means: the class 'all spaniels' (A), taken together with the class 'all other domestic dogs' (A^1), is equivalent to the class 'all domestic dogs' (B). Similarly with the second statement: all domestic dogs' are the same as 'all canines'. The other rules can be translated into words in the same way.

2. *Associativity.* The sum of a series of elements is independent of the way they are grouped. Examples:

$$(B - A^1 = A) + (C - B^1 = B) + (D - C^1 = C)$$
and $\qquad (B - A^1 = A) + [(C - B^1 = B) + (D - C^1 = C)]$
are both equal to
$$(D - C^1 - B^1 - A^1 = A)$$

This could be expressed lengthily as for Rule 1. But it is perhaps more helpful to say that it shows that any class can be defined by the relationships between the other classes. All the three lines of the example are different ways of expressing the relationships between classes A, B, C, and D (and A^1, B^1, C^1). It does not matter how the statements are arranged.

3. *General Identity.* There is one and only one element (the identity element) which, when added to any other element, leaves the latter unchanged. Piaget defines the identity element as the sum of two null classes or $(0+0=0)$

Example: $(C - B^1] =]B) + (0 + 0' = 0)] = (C - B^1 = B)$

4. *Reversibility.* For each element there is one element, called its inverse, such that when the two are combined, the result is the identity element.

Example: The inverse of $(A + A^1 = B)$ is $(-A - A^1 = -B)$
therefore $(A + A^1 = B) + (-A - A^1 = -B) = (0 + 0 = 0)$

Special Identities. In addition to the general identity element as in Rule 4, each element in a system such as the present one also functions as an identity element in certain circumstances, according to the rule: Every class (element) plays the role of identity element with respect to itself, and with respect to its supraordinate classes. Taking A together with A is equivalent to A. Adding A to B still gives B, because A is included in B.

Example: $(A + A^1 =]B)] + (A] + [A^1 = B)] = (A] + [A^1 =]B).$

This oversimplified outline (as it is, believe it or not) gives only the general idea of the whole set of logical structures described by Piaget, for some of which, as already mentioned, no behavioural counterparts have yet been demonstrated. The important points to understand are I think two. There is first the *point* of having such structures in the theory. I have tried to say what I think this is above: it is a question of the most abstract and general level of analysis of thought processes. The second point is to see how the logical operations do in fact underlie actual examples of children's thinking. It is less important, it seems to me, to try to understand immediately all the complexities of the logical system.

Consider the example of the lemonade. Clairette does not realize that the two small classes B_1 and B_2 *must* equal A_2, even though she has just seen them poured from it. Or, as one might say, *defined* as it, just as 'canines' $(B + B^1 = C)$. The appearance predominates over the logical arrangement of elements. This is because the logical operations have not yet developed. Or rather, they are still in the course of development. Thus a given child may fluctuate between the logical and the appearance response even in a single session. This is seen in an experiment on conservation of discontinuous quantities, using beads in place of lemonade.

'Von (5 years 10 months) put one pink bead into A_2 each time I put a blue one into E. "Who has the most?—*It's the same in both*—Why?—

We put them in together—And if we made two necklaces?—*Both the same* —Well, why is the level in there (E) higher than the level in the other (A₂)? —*Because here* (E) *is round and long, and there* (A₂) *it's round and bigger* (=wider) *and we put in the same amount.*—(The beads in A₂ were then poured into D which was then full.) Now what about this (E) and that (D)?—*They're the same*—Why?—*Because that one* (D) *is smaller* (=lower) *and this one* (E) *is longer*; [Reader, note!] it's bigger and so there's more. *it's bigger and so there's more.*—More what? (E and D were both full to the brim, so Von was therefore not distinguishing between the volume of the glasses in the quantity of the beads.)—*More beads. There are more beads in there* (E).—And if we made two necklaces?—*You* (E) *would have more; the blue necklace would be longer.*—And what about the pink one (D)?— *Shorter, because there are less beads."* ' (Piaget and Szeminska, 1941) (see Figure 5·1)

Thus the logically correct assessment of the situation corresponds to reality: there are in fact equal numbers of blue and pink beads. But appearances deceive. Philosophically, one sees here another link with Plato. Logically, we see that what is required is first, reversibility: the knowledge that if the beads were poured back again, they *would* be the same as before. Or perhaps more precisely, the ability to respond as if one had this knowledge. Secondly, what is involved is logical multiplication: the ability to manipulate the two dimensions of height and width at the same time. Von is deceived by the predominance of one of these. Perhaps this example helps to show, therefore, the relationship between the highly abstract logical rules, thinking, and behaviour.

We shall give one more example (from Hunt, 1961) which illustrates some other aspects. Children were presented with a box containing 20 wooden beads, of which two were white and the rest brown. This set of classes can be set out as in the zoological classification above.

B = all beads

A = all brown beads. A^1 = all other (i.e. white) beads

'The child was then asked whether the box contained *more wooden beads or more brown beads*. This question concerns the elementary form of the additive composition of classes: $A + A^1 = B$, and therefore $A = B - A^1$ and $A^1 = B - A$, and $A < B$. In order to make the problem interesting for the children, Piaget and Szeminska (1941, p. 164) asked them whether a necklace made with the brown beads would be longer, shorter or equal in length with a necklace made from the wooden beads. Furthermore, to be sure the children grasped the difference between A and B, before asking this question, they put two empty boxes beside the box of beads and asked the child-subject: "If we take out the brown beads and put them here (first empty box) will there be any beads left in this one (the full box)?" Children of all ages above four years regularly answered that the white beads would be left. The examiners also asked: "If we take out the wooden beads and put them there (in a second empty box) will there be any left in this one (the full box?" The children readily understood this question too, answering *no*. On the other hand, understanding these two questions did not imply a correct solution to the problem of the length of the necklaces.

At the early substage of the intuitive phase, children could not understand that there would be more wooden beads than brown beads. Although they agreed that all the beads were made of wood, the answer to the question "would there be more wooden beads or more brown beads?" was regularly answered: "More brown ones." Piaget attributes this confusion to the child's inability to think simultaneously of both the whole (wooden beads) and the parts (brown beads and white beads). As a result, the child cannot regard wooden beads as resulting from the addition of brown beads *and* white beads. Once his attention is focused upon the subordinate classes, he can grasp only the part–part relationship of the brown beads to the white beads; the part–whole relationship escapes him because his thought lacks reversibility.

At the more advanced substage of the intuitive phase, children discover that there are more wooden beads than brown beads by a kind of trial-and-error process. Thus Gale, age six years, at first answered the question "Which would make the longer necklace, the brown beads or the wooden beads?" by saying that the necklace of brown beads would be longer. When asked why, she answered: "Because there are more brown beads." When the question is then asked, "Are there more wooden beads than brown beads?" Gale answered, "More brown beads . . ." Then suddenly she says, "No, more wooden beads . . . no, they're the same." Apparently the part–whole relationship between brown beads and wooden beads is as yet too tenuous to predominate over Gale's focus on the part or subordinate classes of brown beads and white beads (Piaget and Szeminska, 1941). Tail, aged seven years and two months, also answers at first that there would be more brown beads than wooden ones. When asked whether the white beads are made of wood, he answers *yes* and similarly for the brown ones. When the examiner asks the leading question "Then there are more wooden beads or more brown ones?" Tail answers "More wooden ones, because there are two white ones as well (as the brown ones)." In spite of this answer, when Tail is asked which necklace would be longer, he answers that one made with brown beads would be longer, and only when the leading questions are repeated does he discover that the necklace made of wooden beads would be longer because of the two additional white ones (Piaget and Szeminska, 1941).

At the level of concrete operations, children answer immediately, spontaneously, and with strong confidence that the necklace made of wooden beads would be longer than the one made of brown beads "because there are more wooden beads than brown beads." Thus, at this operational level, the child's thought moves readily back and forth between the parts and the whole. He can simultaneously take into consideration both kinds of classes because, in the language of Piaget, his thought has been "decentred" and has become "reversible".' (Hunt, 1961)

Formal Operations

Thus we reach the second great milestone. What lies ahead? Well, as Flavell points out, the 'concrete operational' child, while now far ahead of the infant or ape level, is still restricted in his thought processes. Concrete operations are relatively still tied to the actual physical world that presents itself. Much of the effort of thinking goes into struggling to order the dimensions of the world that we have just seen to be so confusing. And this is done in the course of developing a whole set of concrete operational systems, which do not yet become integrated into a consistent whole.

'The most important general property of formal-operational thought, the one from which Piaget derives all others, concerns the *real* versus the *possible*.' So says Flavell. By this he means that the formal operational thinker is able to manipulate, not just representations of things that actually do exist; but all the things that might possibly exist. From this other characteristics follow. Hypothetico-deductive thinking becomes possible: the adolescent can reason that if a certain view of reality is true, then certain consequences follow, and these can be tested. Thinking can now be about propositions, rather than just facts. For this reason Piaget refers to formal operations as second-degree operations, or operations to the second power. And formal operational thinking tends to be systematic, rather than random or trial-and-error. We can illustrate these characteristics in a moment. First let us stress that besides a change in the nature of intellectual operations, there is throughout the course of development a progressive increase in *scope*. This can be seen as the final stage in the line of development described by Hunt: taking account of stimuli more and more remote in time and space. But the intellectual operations are also relevant to all behaviour in so far as it comes under cognitive control at all. Thus the adolescent becomes able to reason and speculate not only about purely intellectual problems, but about emotional ones, about human relationships, ethical questions, the future of mankind, etc. Adolescence is commonly marked by enthusiasm for speculation: practising and exercising, one might say, the formal operations just as the sensorimotor child explores his environment with fingers and mouth. (An example of vertical décalage.)

To explain the nature of formal operations, we shall first give an experimental example, with a commentary by Flavell. Then we shall try to set out the main logical structures described by Piaget; and finally give another experimental example, behind which the logical operations can be distinguished.

The first example concerns a sort of scientific investigation.

'In experiment 1, the child is given four similar flasks containing colorless, odorless liquids which are perceptually identical. We number them: (1) diluted sulphuric acid; (2) water; (3) oxygenated water; (4) thiosulphate; we add a bottle (with a dropper) which we will call g; it contains potassium iodide. It is known that oxygenated water oxidizes potassium iodide in an acid medium. Thus mixture $(1 \times 3 \times g)$ will yield a yellow color. The water is neutral, so that adding it will not change the color, whereas the thiosulphate (4) will bleach the mixture $(1 \times 3 \times g)$. The experimenter presents to the subject two glasses, one containing 1×3, the other containing 2. In front of the subject, he pours several drops of g in each of the two glasses and notes the different reactions. Then the subject is asked simply to reproduce the color, yellow, using flasks 1, 2, 3, 4, and g as he wishes.' (Inhelder and Piaget, 1955)

Now for two children's reactions to this problem.

'REN (7 : 1) tries $4 \times g$, then $2 \times g$, and $3 \times g$: *I think I did everything ..
I tried them all*—What else could you have done?—*I don't know.* We give him
the glasses again: he repeats $1 \times g$, etc.—You took each bottle separately. What
else could you have done?—*Take two bottles at the same time* (he tries $1 \times 4 \times g$,
then $2 \times 3 \times g$, thus failing to cross over between the two sets (of bottles) for
example 1×2, 1×3, 2×4, and 3×4).—When we suggest that he add
others, he puts $1 \times g$ in the glass already containing 2×3 which results in the
appearance of the color: Try to make the color again.—*Do I put in two or three?*
(he tries with $2 \times 4 \times g$, then adds 3, then tries it with $1 \times 4 \times 2 \times g$). *No, I
don't remember any more. etc.*'

'CHA (13 : 0): You have to try with all the bottles. I'll begin with the one at
the end (from 1 to 4 with g). It doesn't work any more. Maybe you have to mix
them. (He tries $1 \times 2 \times g$, then $1 \times 3 \times g$.) It turned yellow. But are there
other solutions? I'll try ($1 \times 4 \times g$; $2 \times 3 \times g$; $2 \times 4 \times g$; $3 \times 4 \times g$; with
the two preceding combinations this gives six two-by-two combinations
systematically). It doesn't work. It only works with $1 \times 3 \times g$. Yes, and what
about 2 and 4?—2 and 4 don't make any color together. They are negative.
Perhaps you could add 4 in $1 \times 3 \times g$ to see if it would cancel out the color (he
does this). Liquid 4 cancels it all. You'd have to see if 2 has the same influence
(he tries it).—No, so 2 and 4 are not alike, for 4 acts on 1×3 and 2 does not.—
What is there in 2 and 4?—in 4 certainly water. No, the opposite, in 2 certainly
water since it doesn't act on the liquids; that makes things clearer.—And if I
were to tell you that 4 is water?—If this liquid 4 is water, when you put it with
1×3 it wouldn't completely prevent the yellow from forming. It isn't water;
it's something harmful.'

On these two protocols Flavell gives the following illuminating commentary.

'Let us first examine the younger child's behavior. Notice that it is by
no means unsystematic and unorganized. He proceeds by making what is in
effect a one-many multiplicative correspondence ... between the perceptually
salient element g and the other four, yielding as product $(g \times 1) + (g \times 2) +
(g \times 3) + (g \times 4)$. This systematic structuring of the data, though it happens
to be inadequate to the solution of the problem is a definite cut above pre-
operational behavior on the scale of genetic maturity. It turns out that
preoperational children generally make a few random associations of elements
(without really knowing what these associations are capable of proving)
and intersperse this activity with phenomenalistic and other types of pre-
logical causal explanations.
But the differences between this behavior and that of the adolescent are
nonetheless striking for all its advances over that of the younger children.
REN is capable of forming only a few of the total number of possible
combinations.... CHA, on the other hand, seems disposed right from the
outside to think in terms of all possible combinations of elements (or at
least, what amounts to about the same thing, all the ones necessary to
arrive at a full determination of the causal structure). Moreover, he appears
to possess a systematic and orderly method for generating these combina-
tions: $(1 \times g) \times (2 \times g)$, etc., and then $(1 \times 2 \times g) + (1 \times 3 \times g)$ etc. His language
alone clearly attests to his hypothetico-deductive attitude towards his data:

there are a number of statements of the "if ... then" type (and none of this type of REN's protocol).

These statements are worth a closer look. Take for example CHA's assertion: "If this liquid 4 is water, when you put it with 1×3 it wouldn't completely prevent the yellow from forming. [Therefore] it isn't water [since it does in fact prevent the yellow from forming]; it's something harmful." It is clear that the content very much concerns the possible rather than the real, since the event *4-does-not-prevent-the-yellow-from-forming* is nowhere seen in reality. In general, Piaget finds that contrary-to-fact "what if" suppositions of this kind tend to be foreign to the thought of middle childhood. Further, the total assertion consists of more than simple statements about data (whether true statements or false). Of greater developmental significance is the fact that it comprises a statement *about* these statements, a proposition about propositions: namely, the assertion that one statement (liquid 4 is water) logically implies another (liquid 4 will not prevent the yellow from forming). As we said earlier, it is because adolescent cognition shows this implicative, propositions-about-propositions character that Piaget uses the expressions *interpropositional thought* and *second-degree operations* to describe it.

All the traits of formal thought we have described go to make it a very good instrument for scientific reasoning. As CHA's protocol shows, he is quite capable of achieving the correct solution of what is in all essential respects a genuine problem of scientific discovery. The hypothetical-deductive attitude, the combinatorial method, and the other attributes of formal thought provide him with the necessary tools for separating out the variables which might be causal, holding one factor constant in order to determine the causal action of another, and so on. He is not only able to imagine the various transformations which the data permit in order to try them out empirically; he is also capable of giving correct logical interpretation to the results of these empirical tests. If it eventuates, for instance, that the yellow color is produced by the combination $1 \times 3 \times g$ and no other, he is able to conclude that $1 \times 3 \times g$ is the necessary and sufficient cause e.g. $1 \times 2 \times 3 \times g$ also suffice to produce the color, but 2 is not necessary to the combination), and he then knows his problem is solved. This is clearly a good imitation of how the scientist goes about his business.' (Flavell 1963)

This version of scientific activity may be compared with that presented by Bruner, Goodnow and Austin (1956, see *Concept Identification*).

Now to describe the main logical structures of the formal operations period. These are termed *groups* and *lattices*. The *groupings* already described in the concrete operations phase are a sort of hybrid of these two, having some of the properties of each. For these structures, it is convenient to use some of the terms of symbolic logic.

Not (negation)	:	$^-$
And (conjunction)	:	$\cdot$
Or (disjunction—either or both):		$\vee$
If ... then (implication)	:	$\supset$

Statements are represented by letters, as p, q, r, s, etc. Thus we have various more complex statements, for example:

$p \quad = p$ is true (assertion)

$\bar{p} \quad = $ not p or p is false (negation)

$p.q \quad = p$ and q are both true (conjunction)

$p \vee q = $ either p is true, or q is true, or both are true (disjunction)

$\bar{p}.\bar{q} \quad = $ neither p nor q is true (conjoint negation)

$\bar{p} \vee \bar{q} = $ Either p is false, or q is false, or both are false (incompatibility).

We can now describe an example, based on one from Hunt, of a lattice. Suppose that the animals on a certain island can be either vertebrate (V) or invertebrate (I); and they are also either terrestrial (T) or aquatic (A). The lattice gives the logical possibilities for the existence of animal life on the island. Notice in working it out that what is involved is *possibilities*. We can take p to stand for the assertion of vertebrate animals ($p=$ there may be vertebrate animals). Then not p states the opposite ($\bar{p} = $ there may be invertebrate animals). Similarly q and $\bar{q}$ for terrestrial and aquatic. Another way of symbolising the situation is to take the first four simplest or base possibilities, and let a, b, c, d stand for these — a = vertebrate terrestrial, b = vertebrate aquatic, etc. Then the whole range of possibilities is:

1.	0	No animals at all	$(p.q) \vee (p.\bar{q}) \vee (\bar{p}.q) \vee (\bar{p}.\bar{q})$
2.	a	VT	$p.q$
3.	b	VA	$p.\bar{q}$
4.	c	IT	$\bar{p}.q$
5.	d	IA	$\bar{p}.\bar{q}$
6.	$a + b$	VT, IA	$(p.q) \vee (p.\bar{q})$
7.	$a + c$	VT, IT	$(p.q) \vee (\bar{p}.q)$
8.	$a + d$	VT, IA	$(p.q) \vee (\bar{p}.\bar{q})$
9.	$b + c$	VA, IT	$(p.\bar{q}) \vee (\bar{p}.q)$
10.	$b + d$	VA, IA	$(p.\bar{q}) \vee (\bar{p}.q)$
11.	$c + d$	IT, IA	$(\bar{p}.q) \vee (\bar{p}.q)$
12.	$a + b + c$	VT, VA, IT	$(p.q) \vee (p.\bar{q}) \vee (\bar{p}.q)$
13.	$a + b + d$	VT, VA, IA	$(p.q) \vee (p.\bar{q}) \vee (\bar{p}.q)$
14.	$a + c + d$	VT, IT, IA	$(p.q) \vee (\bar{p}.q) \vee (\bar{p}.\bar{q})$
15.	$b + c + d$	VA, IT, IA	$(p.\bar{q}) \vee (\bar{p}.q) \vee (\bar{p}.q)$
16.	$a + b + c + d$	VT, VA, IT, IA	$(p.q) \vee (p.\bar{q}) \vee (\bar{p}.q) \vee (\bar{p}.\bar{q})$

Now for a group. A group is a set of operations that can be performed on elements of a system. The elements can be propositions or statements, of the kind already described. The most important group is known as the INCR group. This comprises four transformations, viz.,

1. *Identity* (I). This changes nothing in the proposition.

E.g. I $(p \vee q) = p \vee q$

2. *Negation* (N). This changes everything in the proposition, i.e. assertions become negations, and conjunctions become disjunctions; and vice versa.

E.g. $N(p \lor q) = \bar{p}.\bar{q}$

3. *Reciprocal* (R). This permutes assertions and negations, but leaves conjunctions and disjunctions unchanged.

E.g. $R(p \lor q) = \bar{p} \lor \bar{q}$

4. *Correlative* (C). This permutes conjunctions and disjunctions, but leaves assertions and negations unchanged.

E.g. $C(p \lor q) = p.q$

It can be seen that these tranformations represent in the most abstract form ways in which the environment can be manipulated symbolically. To put it another way, they are operations of the most general kind that underlie reasoning of a scientific type. Many of Piaget's experiments are in fact on scientific problems, such as working out the relationship between weight and distance given a simple balance. We shall give one example. The subject has in front of him a roulette-like wheel which when spun always stops in one position. The subject has to work out why. On the wheel are a set of boxes which, unknown to the subject, contain either magnets or wax. It is the magnets, in fact, that control the position (see Figure 5.2).

Here is one protocol:

'GOU (14:11): *"Maybe it goes down and here it's heavier* (the weight might lower the plane, thus resulting in the needle's coming to rest at the lowest point) *or maybe there's a magnet* (he puts a notebook under the board to level it and sees that the result is the same).—What have you proved?—*That there is a magnet* (he weighs the boxes). *There are some that are heavier than others* (more or less heavy). *I think it's more likely to be the content* (in substance).—What do you have to do to prove that it isn't the weight?—(He removes the diamond boxes which are the heaviest). *Then I changed positions. If it stops at the same place again, the weight doesn't play any role. But I would rather remove the star boxes. We'll see whether it stops at the other boxes which are heavier* (experiment). *It's not the weight. It's not a rigorous proof, because it does not come to rest at the perpendicular* (to the diamond boxes). *The weight could only have an effect if it made it* (the plane) *tip. So I'll put two boxes, one on top of the other, and if it doesn't stop that means that the weight doesn't matter:* (negative experiment) *You see.*—And the color?—*No, you saw when the positions of the boxes were changed. The contents of the boxes have an effect, but it's especially when the boxes are close together; the boxes are only important when they are close* (he puts half of the boxes at a greater distance). *It's either the distance or the content. To see whether it is the content I'm going to do this.* (He moves the star boxes away and brings the other closer.) *It's more likely to be distance* (new trial). *Is seems to be confirmed, but I'm not quite sure. Unless it's the cardinal points* (he takes

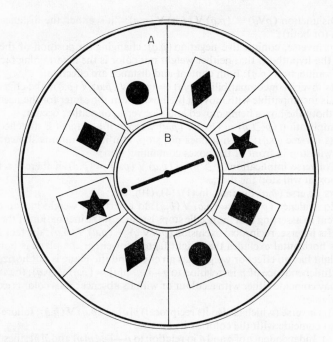

Figure 5.2. Apparatus used to study propositional disjunctions and exclusions. 'One pair of boxes (the starred ones) contains concealed magnets, whereas the other pairs contain only wax. The large board (A) is divided into sectors of different colours and equal surfaces, with opposite sectors matching in colour. A metal bar is attached to a non-metallic rotating disc (B); the disc always stops with the bar pointing to one pair of boxes. The boxes (which are matched pairs as to colour and design) can be moved to different sectors, but they are always placed with one of a pair opposite the other. The boxes are unequal in weight, and this provides another variable.' (From Figure 5 of *The Growth of Logical Thinking from Childhood to Adolescence: An Essay on the Construction of Formal Operational Structures*, by Barbel Inhelder and Jean Piaget, translated by Anne Parsons and Stanley Milgram, © 1958 by Basic Books Inc., Publishers, New York and by Routledge and Kegan Paul Ltd., London)

off the stars). *No, it's not that. The stars do have an affect. It must be the content. If it isn't a magnet, I don't see what it could be. You have to put iron on the metal boxes. If the magnet is there* (disc), *it will come* (to) *these boxes. If it is in the boxes* (stars) *there is iron under the disc* (he removes the star boxes). *I'm sure it's the boxes.*" (Inhelder and Piaget, 1955)

Correspondence between performance and theory. Inhelder and Piaget (1955) distinguish the following 16 binary propositional operations in GOU's protocol:

(1) Disjunction $(p \lor q) = (p.\bar{q}) \lor (\bar{p}.q) \lor (p.q)$: "it's either the distance or the content (or both);"

(2) Its inverse, conjunctive negation $(\bar{p}.q)$: changing the position of the boxes verifies the hypothesis that neither weight nor color is the determining factor;

(3) Conjunction $(p.q)$: both content and distance are effective;

(4) Its inverse, incompatibility $(p/q) = (p.\bar{q}) \lor (\bar{p}.q) \lor (\bar{p}.\bar{q})$; the effect of the magnet is incompatible with moving the boxes from the center for the needle may stop without the boxes being moved and vice versa, or neither occurs;

(5) Implication $(p \supset q) = (p.q) \lor (\bar{p}.q) \lor (\bar{p}.\bar{q})$: if a magnet is attached

(6) Its inverse $(p.\bar{q})$: when it does not stop, non-implication is shown; to the disc, it will stop in front of the boxes containing iron;

(7) Converse implication $(q \supset p) = (p.q) \lor (p.\bar{q}) = (\bar{p}.\bar{q})$: if there is a magnet in the box, it will stop the disc;

(8) Its inverse $(\bar{p}.q)$ operates in (1), (4), (10), etc.;

(9) Equivalence $(p = q) = (p.q) \lor (\bar{p}.\bar{q})$: to assert that weight has an effect is equivalent to asserting that the needle stops because of the inclination of the plane;

(10) Its inverse, reciprocal exclusion $(p \lor\lor q) = (p.\bar{q}) \lor (\bar{p}.q)$: the fact that the plane is horizontal excludes the weight factor, for either the plane is horizontal and weight has no effect or weight has an effect and the plane is not horizontal;

(11) Independence of p in relation to q—i.e., $p[q] = (p.q) \lor (p.\bar{q})$: the stopping point may coincide either with a colour or with its absence; thus color is excluded as a variable;

(12) Its inverse (which is also its reciprocal) $\bar{p}[q] = (\bar{p}.q) \lor (\bar{p}.\bar{q})$: failure to stop may also coincide with the color or its absence;

(13-14) Independence of q and $\bar{q}$ in relation to p—i.e., $q[p]$ and $\bar{q}[p]$; these operations are found in (15);

(15) Complete affirmation or tautology $(p*q) = (p.q) \lor (p.\bar{q}) \lor (\bar{p}.q) \lor (\bar{p}.\bar{q})$; all possible combinations, thus absence of particular links, for example between the box which contains the magnet and the colored sector on which it has been placed;

(16) Its inverse, complete negation or contradiction (0); to deny that weight has an effect and to reassert it would be a contradiction (Inhelder and Piaget, 1955, pp. 103-4).'

Even after giving a fairly substantial direct quotation, we want now to give another. In addition to his many scholarly writings, Piaget has given us a number of short summaries of his views as a whole, which are often helpful in conveying the essence of his ideas. One such is *Logic and Psychology* (1953) from which the following passage comes. It follows a rather fuller account of the logical structures we have just described.

'To give a complete account of these structures we would have to show that the 16 binary operations of two-valued propositional logic are present in the intuitive thought of adolescents aged 12 to 15. But it is unnecessary to give examples here, as we have already shown that adolescents do, in fact, use these 16 binary operations, as well as a certain number of ternary operations or operations of a higher rank.

Further, and this is extremely important, the subject can proceed from any one of these operations to any other. On the other hand, the child aged 7 to 11 when given an inductive problem in physics, as in the case of Mlle. Inhelder's problems, limits himself to the raw experimental data. He classifies, orders the data in series, sets up correspondences between them, etc., but does not isolate the factors involved or embark upon systematic experimentation. The adolescent, however, after several preliminary attempts tries to discover all possible combinations, so as to select the true and discard the false. In the course of this selective activity he intuitively constructs a combinatorial system. It is for this reason that he repeatedly passes from one propositional operation to another. The method of solution in each actual problem situation then consists in the selection of the true combination (or combinations) out of the whole set of possible combinations.

Propositional operations do not therefore appear in the adolescent's thought as unrelated discrete operations; they form a system or *structured whole*. What we have to discover is in what manner this structure is given for the subject.

As we have seen, the fact that the logic of propositions proceeds from the possible (i.e. theoretical) to the actual and consists in truth-selections leads to a very simple hypothesis as to the psychological meaning of the system of propositional operations; and consequently, as to the way in which the *structured wholes*, such as the lattice or the group INRC, which are a feature of these operations, appear in the child's mind.

If this hypothesis were not accepted, what other explanation could be given for these structures? By way of a first hypothesis they might be regarded as the cumulative product of past experience. But such an interpretation seems improbable since they are completely unconscious. The adolescent is not conscious of the system of propositional operations. He undoubtedly uses these operations, but he does this without enumerating them, or reflecting on them or their relationships, and he only faintly suspects that they form such a system. He is unaware of this, in the same way that in singing or whistling he is unaware of the laws of harmony. The view that such unconscious structures result from a summation of acquired experiences is thus quite unacceptable.

A second hypothesis would be to treat these structures as *a priori* forms of the mind; for such forms, if they exist, can remain unconscious and nevertheless still influence the development of thought. But if we really are concerned here with a priori forms why do they appear at so late a stage?

A third hypothesis might be to regard them as arising from the late maturation of certain neural connections (we know, for example, that it is possible to apply propositional operations to neural networks). But if the logical structured wholes exist as ready-made traces in the nervous system, they ought to appear in their entirety during thinking. This is simply not the case: only certain parts of such structures are actualized, the rest remain in the form of possible transformation.

We thus come to our fourth and last hypothesis, already touched upon, in which the lattice and the group INRC are regarded as structures belonging to the simple forms of equilibrium attained by thought activity. In the first place these structures appear psychologically in the form of a few concrete operations but what is more important they provide a field of possible transformations.

A state of equilibrium, it should be remembered, is one in which all the virtual transformations compatible with the relationships of the system compensate each other. From a psychological point of view, the logical structures correspond precisely to this model. On the one hand, these structures appear in the form of a set of virtual transformations, consisting of all the operations which it would be possible to carry out starting from a few actually performed operations. On the other, these structures are essentially reversible, that is to say, the virtual transformations which they permit are always self-compensatory as a consequence of inversions and reciprocities.

In this way, we can explain why the subject is affected by such structures, without being conscious of them. When starting from an actually performed propositional operation, or endeavouring to express the characters of a given situation by such an operation, he cannot proceed in any way he likes. He finds himself, as it were, in a field of force governed by the laws of equilibrium, carrying out transformations or operations determined not only by occurrences in the immediate past, but by the laws of the whole operational field of which these past occurrences form a part.'

So we return to the concept of equilibrium. This passage, which we can assume expresses succinctly Piaget's view of the essence of intellectual development, repays rereading. If you do this, try to compare the points made with what we have said in this chapter. Even on rereading, however, it is not entirely clear: the reasons for this are among those to be presented in a moment.

So we come to the flowering—or possibly the budding—of intelligence. Do not forget that in tracing the story, we have concentrated on the increasingly abstract analysis that is appropriate with greater complexity of behaviour. The enormously increased range of activities and interests that characterizes the adolescent as compared with the infant does, however, ultimately depend, in Piaget's view, on the growth of the intellectual structures.

GENERAL REMARKS ON THE PIAGETIAN THEORY

In previous chapters, we have several times had a relatively large amount of discussion as compared to the amount of experimental work. Since we have just had several thousand words on the work of one man, one might now expect a truly massive discussion. This will not be so. For one thing, in the next chapter will appear some of the independent tests, and extensions, of the Geneva theories. For another thing, a full objective assessment of Piaget's work is not yet possible. The work is still developing: Piaget cannot yet be assessed, as he must ultimately be, as an historical figure. Neither can the theory be assessed in the light of a large body of experiments by independent investigators. Such experiments, though now more numerous, are far from systematic. And for a third thing, this chapter has already gone on nearly long enough.

Nevertheless there are some points that can usefully be made about the work as it stands. One of these is raised by Bruner: why stop at formal operations? Is there not a difference between the adolescent who is unaware of the logical structure of his problem-solving, and the scientist who actually studies such operations? Here we see a resemblance perhaps, to the traditional theories of intelligence from which Piaget started out so long ago: intelligence test scores take sixteen as a base line. (Science fiction writers, and Bernard Shaw in *Back to Methuselah*, have imagined a stage even beyond the mature adult: after manipulating the environment symbolically, the next step is for the mind to manipuulate it directly.) Next, we might point out that vast though Piaget's work is, it is still incomplete as an account of intellectual development. Cultural variables must be taken into account. To use the tree analogy once more, Piaget has not given us an analysis of the organism's aliment, or nutrient; or of the environmental factors in growth. Something of this has been attempted by the Harvard school, as we shall see later.

Then there are factors that make Piaget's work difficult to assess. It is not easy to select particular parts of it for experimental test. This is partly because the whole theory hangs together, so that isolated parts are less meaningful out of context. It is also because Piaget has often not been particularly interested in the sort of data that *can* be tested. Such data might include age norms, for example. Partly because of this, Piagetian publications often lack the details necessary for replication: just how many subjects, of what characteristics and background, were tested by which procedure and with what results. Rather, the experiments often appear more as illustrations to the theory rather than proofs of it. And this in turn reinforces the impression gained by many (Flavell, for example), that it is the theory that has primacy, rather than facts. If the theory shows that logically certain structures should exist, then they must exist even if no behaviour has been found to correspond to them. This appears to defy the widely accepted scientific dictum of Occam's razor: that entities (here, intervening variables) should only be postulated if they are essential. This raises another major difficulty, which we have already discussed: the *status* of the intellectual structures. In what sense are they an explanation? Here perhaps the clue is again a biological one. Just as Ryle attacked the notion of 'intelligence' as a sort of force or engine inside, causing behaviour, so Piaget is not saying that there are two separate things: behaviour, and structures causing behaviour. In the same way, a tree is not leaves and bark caused by, say, the sap, or the cellular structure. It is the old question of what sort of explanation we are looking for. The biologist sets out, first at any rate, to give an account of the structure and development of the organism in which he is interested. Piaget has tried to do this for knowledge or, if you like, intellect.

A further point is that it may well turn out that Piaget's achievement in giving us such a description is secondary in importance to two other aspects. The description may prove in details to be inaccurate. The achievement lies in taking a fundamentally biological approach rather than that of the physical sciences. And perhaps even more general still is the achievement of bringing under scientific treatment a major area of enquiry which had hitherto remained within philosophy.

FOCUS: REVERSIBILITY

Those who, with praiseworthy determination, have reached this point in our discussion of the Geneva School will have appreciated the enormous complexities of Piagetian theory if nothing else. We have stressed that many of these are of a *conceptual* nature and that a temporary abandonment of concepts familiar to us may be necessary for a proper understanding of Piaget's system. We believe this to be true despite Berlyne's (1965) gallant attempt to 'translate' some of Piaget into acceptable Neo-behaviouristic terms, a venture which, incidentally, illustrates quite nicely the reductionist philosophy inherent in Behaviourism. More of Berlyne later. We propose now to select one of the concepts central to Piaget's theory, *reversibility*, and subject it to a fairly detailed conceptual and empirical analysis. We shall be particularly concerned with the part played by reversibility in the development of the concrete operations of thought in view of Piaget's claim that operational reversibility is basic to these, permitting, as it does, the eventual acquisition of the concepts of number, weight, and volume conservation.

In a very general sense we could conceive of reversibility as simply something like *flexibility* of thought, i.e. the individual capable of reversible thought is able to *manipulate* his internal environment. He can imagine *possible* ways of achieving certain goals or arriving at a certain state of affairs, rather like a chess player working out the implications of particular moves, before choosing between them. Reversibility therefore can lend movement and direction both of a temporal and spatial kind to his thought processes. One can see how images of various types might play an important part in this, and indeed some investigations have demonstrated individual differences in the capacity to manipulate (or 'reverse') e.g. a visual image in specified ways (see *Imagery*). The importance of reversibility therefore, considered as a general feature of thought, is not difficult to recognize.

'Reversibility' in Piaget's formal logical system however is altogether a very different matter, since it amounts to far more than the simple notion of flexibility of thought. Let us first of all collect together some of the important characteristics of reversibility. Sigel and Hooper (1968) have this to say:

> 'It should be emphasized, in this regard, that reversibility is a rather complex process in Piagetian theory. Two reversibility concepts have been defined by Piaget: *negation*, which applies only to classes, and *reciprocity*, which applies only to relations.'

Richmond (1970) makes this distinction more explicit:

> 'Reversibility with classes is achieved by performing an opposite action which will undo the first. Reversibility of relations is achieved by performing a second action which exactly compensates for the first condition without undoing it.'

Richmond refers to the first type as 'inversion' and to the second as 'reciprocity'.

Bruner *et al.* (1966) put the matter as follows:

> *'Inversion* is a simple "returning to the starting point" by "undoing" the operation that has just been performed.... The use of the operation of inversion is implied in the answer of the child who says, when asked to judge the relative amounts of clay in a ball and a sausage (made from a ball declared by the child a moment before to be the "same" as the other ball), "They are the same because you can make the sausage back into a ball again and they will be the same"...
>
> ... *Compensation* refers to the "logical multiplication of relations". Unlike the operation of inversion, there is no literal undoing or reversing of one's actions in the compensation operation. Rather, the operation of compensation depends on an understanding of the reciprocity of two relevant dimensions, for example, length L, and width W. Reciprocity refers to the fact that as L declines, W must increase in order to maintain a constant amount, K: i.e., $L \times W = K$.... Thus compensation would be implied in the answer of a child if he were to say, when asked to judge the relative amounts of clay in the ball and the sausage, "they are the same because the sausage is *longer*, but the ball is *fatter*".'

It might be as well here to sort out some points of terminology (note Bruner's use of the term 'compensation' rather than 'reciprocity'). We can do this with the aid of Figure 5.3 below.

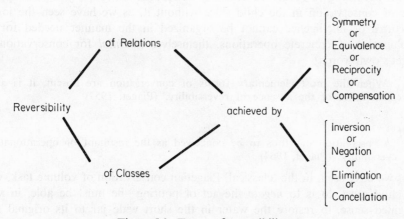

Figure 5.3. Forms of reversibility

The terms on the extreme right have all been used by a number of writers (including Piaget) to refer to the same operations and, as far as I can see can safely be regarded as alternative expressions, where indicated.

Let us now return to the main issue. The two forms of reversibility, inversion and reciprocity are closely related, logically and psychologically. Yet it is not until the stage of formal operations that they are integrated into a single stable system. In the words of Piaget himself:

'No groupments are present at the level of concrete operations to combine these two kinds of reversibility into a single system.'

And finally, to complete the picture we should also note the following extremely subtle (yet according to Piaget, crucial) distinction between 'renversabilité' and 'réversibilité'. Berlyne (1965), translating 'renversabilité' as revertibility and 'réversibilité' as reversibility, quotes Piaget's succinct exposition of the difference:

'We shall call "reversibility" the capacity to carry out one and the same action in both directions, with an awareness that it is a matter of one and the same action. . . .
'We shall say that an action is "revertible" or that there is an empirical return to the starting point when the subject comes back to the latter without an awareness of the identity of the action carried out in both directions.'
(Piaget, 1957)

This of course immediately alerts us to the whole problem of *criterion*. How do we *recognize* reversibility, and even more difficult, how do we distinguish operationally between reversibility and revertibility? Piaget (1968) has in fact claimed that at least one investigation reported to invalidate aspects of his theory, is itself invalid because of a failure to make this important distinction.

Now according to Piaget, reversibility of thought is necessary for the appearance of conservation in the child since without it, as we have seen the logical structures of intelligence cannot be organized in the manner needed for the development of concrete operations, themselves *essential* for conservation. In Piaget's own words:

'When the most elementary forms of conversation are absent, it is a consequence of the absence of reversibility.' (Piaget, 1957)

and:

'Conservation has thus to be conceived as the resultant of operational reversibility.' (Piaget, 1964)

As we have seen, in the 'classical' Piagetian conservation of volume task, what the child must do is to *negate* the act of pouring—he must be able, in some imagined sense, to restore the water in the short wide jar to its original state (inversion). Alternatively (or perhaps in addition) he must realize that although now the level of water in the shorter jar is lower than the level in the tall thin one, this is offset by a simultaneous increase in the width of the shorter jar (compensation).

Now this account of conservation has recently come under considerable attack from various quarters, particularly from Behaviouristic psychologists who wish to view the achievement of conservation as the end result of a period of learning, during which the individual comes to discriminate the various 'cues' or dimensions which are reliable indicators of quantity (i.e. 'relevant') from those which are not (i.e. 'irrelevant' e.g. height of liquid). Before looking at some of these accounts in more detail however, there are some other useful points which are worth considering and which are perhaps best dealt with first.

There seems little doubt for instance that there can be reversibility of thought without conservation, and conversely, conservation without reversibility. That is to say, many children apparently appreciate that for instance the liquid in the short fat beaker could be poured back into the tall thin one, and are able to predict more or less correctly the level it would reach while at the same time still failing to conserve (Acker, 1968; Berlyne, 1965; Bruner et al., 1966). Then, in addition, there are children who apparently do not spontaneously show recognition of reversibility but are able to conserve (Bruner et al., 1966; Lovell and Ogilvie, 1960; Wallach et al., 1967). But once again, the question is partly one of criterion. Piaget (1968) for instance has criticized the work of Bruner on the grounds that he 'does not distinguish reversibility, which is a logical and operational notion from an empirical return which is a physical notion . . .' (see the discussion of renversabilité and réversibilité above). And of course Piaget might well argue, in addition that cases of conservation without reversibility, resting as they do on negative evidence, are cases where there has been inadequate questioning of subjects, misclassification of responses, etc.

The question of the operational criteria for reversibility is worth pursuing a little further. The type of problem which arises is illustrated quite nicely by some recently reported experiments on conservation. Hooper (1969) investigated conservation in 6–8-year-olds, using small seeds rather than water as the 'quantitative invariant'. Only 4 per cent of conserving subjects gave a reversibility type of 'explanation', for their judgments, a figure which of course is very low and not at all encouraging from Piaget's point of view. On the other hand Hooper reports that references to the initial state of equality of the two amounts of seed were common. Now, what is reversibility! Could not a recognition of the initial equality of the two portions of seed be as valid a criterion of reversibility as a statement to the effect that 'you can pour the seed back'?

Likewise Wallach et al. (1967) distinguish between the 'equality before' and 'reversibility' type of explanations (a term which incidentally they, like Hooper, use to refer to what Piaget would call inversion or negation), and in fact very few of the subjects in their study justified conservation with a 'reversibility' (or, strictly speaking inversion) type of argument. The majority of subjects in one condition however, in which water was used, gave 'equality before' explanations, suggesting once again that the issue is partly semantic. It is worth noting also that a large number of subjects in this study justified conservation using a 'compensation' type of argument.

Finally, Lovell and Ogilvie (1960) reported results of a study of conservation of substance (bits of plasticine) in Junior School children (7–11 years). *A propos* reversibility they state quite emphatically:

> 'Our criterion is that the child gave evidence of his awareness of the equality of the balls at the beginning.'

In view of this obviously very *loose* criterion it is hardly surprising that the authors report a relatively high proportion of 'reversibility explanations' from children showing conservation, increasing from 57 per cent for the 8-year-olds to 78 per cent for the 11-year-olds.

Now of course these experiments are not conclusive proof that Piaget is right (or wrong) in his claim that reversibility is a necessary prerequisite for conservation. What they *do* quite clearly demonstrate however is that certain difficulties will inevitably arise when theoretical concepts are subjected to experimental analysis and that in the absence of explicit criteria the issues of importance are not going to be easily resolved.

Berlyne (1965) has an interesting anecdotal example of how, in some circumstances, reversibility, in the form of inversion, could lead to wholly *false* conclusions: imagine a child faced with two identical rubber bands, one of which is then stretched. If the child is asked to compare the *lengths* of these we would not expect him to say that they were the same, simply because the longer rubber band could be released and would then return to its original length. For him to reason in this way would be quite wrong. A similar argument applies to the liquid conservation task—the child would be quite wrong to say that, because the water could be poured back, the *heights* of the columns of liquid are therefore equal. Why then expect the child to say that the *quantities* are the same merely because he recognizes the possibility that the initial act of pouring could be reversed?

The same type of argument is put somewhat differently by Murray and Johnson:

> 'Logically reversibility is irrelevant because it does not provide evidence that the property of the object in question did not, in fact, change while it was in the transformed state, e.g. because a stretched rubber band can be returned to its original shorter length clearly does not mean that it was not longer when it was stretched, when reversibility is offered as a justification of conservation, strictly speaking the child is incorrect.' (Murray and Johnson, 1969)

Berlyne also dismisses the possibility that *compensation* could provide the basis for conservation:

> 'The sight of increased height together with decreased width cannot be what leads an older child or an adult to conclude that quantity is unchanged. It would indeed be fallacious to draw such a conclusion on this basis, since a simultaneous increase in height and decrease in width does not imply unchanged volume. A decrease in width has to be accompanied by just the right degree of increase in height if it is to be compensated, and normal

life experience does not enable us to recognize at a glance whether an increase in height is large enough or too large or too small to compensate a decrease in width."

And in a review article Green and Laxon (1970) make the following observations:

'It is curious that this red herring of Piaget's should have lain around so long when it is perfectly obvious that most adults find the task of measuring volume by eye well beyond their capacities. There is a whole packaging industry based upon this simple fact of life. Just as curious is the way in which Piaget, and every other investigator for that matter, has studiously overlooked the fact that for such judgements to be successful they would have to be three dimensional. If water is poured from a large diameter jar into one of half the diameter the water rises not to twice but four times the original height. Because the cross-section of a jar is a function of the square of its radius, the frontal area of the liquid (width by height) will vary considerably. Multiplication of relations under these conditions requires the child to equate not width by height but width squared by height. It is hardly surprising that he finds this task beyond his powers. . . .'

And in fact Beilin (1969) found that conserving children were not able consistently to identify the change in one dimension necessary to compensate for a change in the other.

If we accept for the moment then that reversibility has little to offer in the way of a possible basis for the development of conservation we might inquire why it is that a lot of children *do* often justify conservation judgments by giving a reversibility type of explanation, and why 'training' in reversibility can produce conservation in nonconserving children. (Wallach and Sprott, 1964; Wallach et al., 1967).

One possibility is that reversibility, or more loosely, a reference to the original state of equality of two jars of water provide a simple and straightforward demonstration of quantitative invariance, the appreciation of which *follows* rather than *precedes* the development itself. Something along these lines is suggested by Green and Laxon (1970).

'It may well be that, once a child has achieved true conservation, reversibility may be incorporated into his conceptual system not only as being consonant with conservation of quantity, but as a means of checking that in point of fact nothing has been added or taken away. . . .'

and later

'Multiplication of relations is not a means of attaining conservation, but a way of resolving the paradox posed by perceptual cues of extent after conservation has been achieved by learning to rely on numerative procedures and by grasping the identity concepts.'

We shall consider the significance of the last part of this sentence in a moment. The success of reversibility training on the other hand may lie in the fact that a recognition of the original state of equality enables the child more easily to appreciate that nothing has been added and nothing taken away, said by Smedslund (1962) to be essential for the acquisition of conservation. Or alternatively, reversibility training may be effective in the way suggested by Bruner *et al.* (1966), whose elegant experiments we now propose to consider in more detail, Bruner *et al.* dedicated their book *Studies in Cognitive Growth* to Piaget, 'friend and mentor' who, it is clear, did provide the impetus for much of the theoretical and experimental content of the book. We intend to cover the theoretical aspects of Bruner's work elsewhere and for the moment we shall restrict ourselves as far as possible to one or two of the experiments which are presented.

Bruner and Carey (Chapter 9) begin their attack on Piaget's concept of reversibility in the following way:

> 'On purely logical grounds, we believe he (Piaget) has missed the heart of conservation. Both inversion and compensation to be effective must rest upon an appreciation of the original equality of the quantities involved. A continued grasp of this initial equality is crucial to both inversion and compensation. Indeed, the inverse operation of "pouring back" is effective for achieving conservation only in so far as it is a path to the original equality of the two "standard" beakers. And compensation and inversion it can be even more forcefully argued, depend on the maintenance of some primitive identity in two "versions" of an event. Such identity can be illustrated by the case in which one uses, say, a single quantity of liquid, first contained in a standard beaker, then poured into another that is taller and thinner. The only "similarity" between the two is achieved through maintenance of their identity.'

Bruner then goes on to report an experiment conducted by P. Nair which explores the importance of identity in conservation of quantity. Five-year-old children played a sort of game with ducks, the idea being basically that the ducks were moved by the child around tanks ('lakes') of various shapes and sizes, the water travelling with the duck each time a move was made. After each move, two questions were asked:

(a) 'Is there just as much, more, or not as much water here [pointing to the new container] as here [pointing to the original one]?'

(b) 'Is this the same water as the duck had there [pointing back]?'

The order in which these questions were asked was reversed for half the subjects. And, in addition, all subjects were initially classified as either 'conservers' or 'nonconservers' on the 'classical' Piagetian liquid conservation task.

One somewhat disquieting result is quickly glossed over by Bruner—36 per cent of the original conservers fail to show conservation in this experiment! However, interesting as this is, we can accept Bruner's contention that these results 'are not the main findings.' There are probably two major results.

(i) The majority of original conservers (64 per cent) who again showed conservation, recognize the *identity* of the water as well as the equivalence of the quantities—but the converse is not true. There are many children (35 per cent of both conservers and nonconservers) who apparently agree to the identity of the water while denying the invariance of the quantity. And (not surprisingly) practically none recognized the quantitative equivalence without agreeing to the identity of the water. On the basis of these results Bruner suggests 'that a recognition of identity is a necessary but not a sufficient condition for the recognition of quantitative equivalence'.

(ii) Considered as a whole the 'lakes' experiment seems to incorporate a procedure conducive to conservation—almost 30 per cent of the original nonconservers now give conservation responses. Bruner claims that this is because it highlights the identity of the water, not only in having the *same* water transferred from tank to tank but also by actually asking a question about its identity.

Bruner therefore is arguing for a clear logical and psychological distinction between *identity* and *equivalence* conservation, recognition of the former being a necessary condition, and perhaps also providing a particularly favourable basis for the development of the latter. It is worth noting here that Elkind (1967) has taken a similar line in his contention that identity and equivalence are conceptually distinct.

Throughout the whole of *Studies in Cognitive Growth* Bruner develops his thesis of 'Instrumental Conceptualism' which we in fact cover much more fully later. One of the main features of this is the belief that very young children are apt to assess or 'understand' their environment in terms of its sensory or 'surface' characteristics. That is, the *colour* of things how they *feel* and so on will largely determine how a child reacts to them. In Bruner's terms it is the 'ikonic' features of stimuli which determine the response. Now in the classical Piagetian liquid conservation task the most noticeable ikonic feature is the height of the column of liquid in the jars, a feature to which the child readily attends and on which he bases his judgments of the quantity of water. In addition, Bruner argues, he fails to take into account the fact that the *width* of the jar has also altered since he tends to focus on only one perceptual aspect at a time (we might say that this is due to his relatively limited capacity for processing information). Thus he fails to conserve because he is 'perceptually seduced' by one of the ikonic characteristics of the display—the *height* of the liquid.

An older child is far less distracted by sensory features of the environment. According to Bruner he is much more likely to represent the conservation task in some kind of symbolic fashion, involving particularly a recognition of the identity of the water, and perhaps in addition an appreciation that nothing has been added or taken away. Thus he will not be 'seduced' by the misleading ikonic cue of the height of the liquid and therefore will be able to conserve.

This account of conservation receives additional support from an experiment designed to test the 'perceptual seduction' hypothesis, Bruner argues that if we can 'shield' the child from the ikonic features of the display and force him to

214

'code' the problem in symbolic terms, along the lines suggested above, we would expect a sharp increase in judgments of conservation. The experiment in question was rather complex and took the form of a 'training' procedure. Broadly it was an attempt to encourage the child to represent the conservation situation symbolically, e.g. the pouring of water (if any) took place behind a screen so the child never saw the height of the column of liquid. In another part, no screen was used and he was asked to predict the level of water *if* it were to be poured. (See Figures 5.4(a) and (b).)

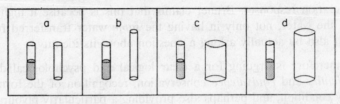

Figure 5.4(a). Pairs of beakers used in screening experiments. (Reproduced from J. S. Bruner, R. R. Olver and P. M. Greenfield *et al.*, *Studies in Cognitive Growth* (1966), Wiley, New York)

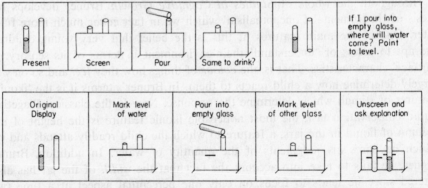

Figure 5.4(b). The screening procedures: The unmarked screening procedure (Part I) is at the upper left, the water-level guessing procedure (Part II) is at the upper right, and the screening-marking procedure (Part III) is across the bottom of the figure. (Reproduced from J. S. Bruner, R. R. Olver and P. M. Greenfield *et al.*, *Studies in Cognitive Growth* (1966), Wiley, New York)

The classical Piaget conservation task was administered both before ('pretest') and after ('posttest') this procedure. The results are shown in Figure 5.5 below.

There are two points which Bruner wishes to emphasize:

(i) 'Perceptual screening' produces posttest judgments of conservation in all but the 4-year-olds. And it can be inferred from the protocols that these are based largely on an identity argument.

(ii) Removal of the screen seems to produce a kind of 'regression' in almost all

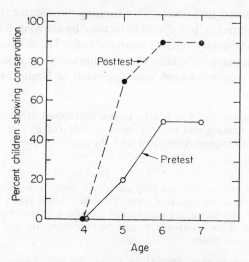

Figure 5.5. Percentage of children showing conservation before and after screening. (Reproduced from J. S. Bruner, R. R. Olver and P. M. Greenfield *et al.*, *Studies in Cognitive Growth* (1966), Wiley, New York)

4-year-olds who had shown conservation when it was present. But older children who had become conservers with perceptual screening maintained their judgments of conservation when it was removed.

It is as if the very young children, while potentially capable of conserving, are unable to resist the sight of the change in height of the water—they are 'perceptually seduced'. By virtue of the training procedure however the older children have apparently developed an appreciation of the *identity* of the two versions of liquid, and are able to overcome the tendency to base their judgments on ikonic features. Of reversibility Bruner has this to say:

'There are some puzzles here that turn up in the reasons children give. To be sure, reversibility and compensation are all represented in the reasons children give for conservation. . . .'

But as he goes on to argue,

'Reversibility and compensation could not by themselves be *producing* conservation, bringing it into being. They are too often encountered in instances in which the child has not achieved conservation. . . .'

Bruner's approach to the problem of conservation has a great deal to recommend it. It might prove useful as a sort of model or integrative paradigm for a diverse set of experimental data—at any rate there is no doubt that it has had a stimulating effect on research and theory in this field. Wallach *et al.* (1967) for instance have suggested that reversibility training may derive its success from the fact that it helps eliminate 'perceptual seduction' by showing that sensory features do not provide consistently reliable quantity cues. There have in addition been a number of attempts to combine the 'equilibration' approach of Piaget with the perhaps more straightforward 'cue' approach of Bruner. Halford (1970) for example argued that:

> 'The problem for the S is not to ignore perceptual criteria, which would amount to substituting one kind of inconsistency for another, but to render the perceptual judgements consistent with the cognitive ones.'

and later

> '... the child should adopt quantity cues, not because he sees height to be irrelevant, but because quantity cues yield the same result as height and breadth cues if the latter are considered jointly, and certain other requirements are met. Thus consistency can be achieved in the sense that all cues yield the same result.'

Then finally there is the attempt to place the development of conservation within the general framework of *attention*, which provides a useful link with the models of concept identification and discrimination learning which we considered earlier (*Concept Identification*).

On the other hand Bruner's work has not gone undisputed—we have already referred to some of Piaget's recent objections to Bruner's experiments. And at least two recent studies have failed to replicate the beneficial effect of 'perceptual screening'. One of these, it should be stressed, did not utilize exactly the same screening procedure as Bruner and Carey had used (Hooper, 1969). Strauss and Langer (1970) however were dissatisfied with certain design features of the original Bruner study and carried out a complete replication with certain modifications. We do not know for example for just how long the training procedure was effective—if only a transient effect, Piaget's objection of 'pseudoconservation' might apply (Piaget, 1968). Unfortunately the opportunity to determine this never arose because the screening procedure proved ineffective in producing conservation.

It is perhaps surprising that a lot more could be said about this topic in spite of the rather narrow and specialized nature of the research in question. But reversibility *is* an extremely important concept in Piaget's system, it does occupy a central theoretical position. It is only right therefore that it should continue to be subject to rigorous analysis.

217

FURTHER READING

Furth, H. G. (1968). *Piaget and Knowledge*. Prentice-Hall.
Hunt, J. McV. (1961). *Intelligence and Experience*. Ronald Press.
Phillips, J. C. (1969). *The Origins of the Intellect*. W. H. Freeman.
Piaget, J. (1967). *Six Psychological Studies*. University of London Press.
Piaget, J., and Inhelder, B. (1969). *The Psychology of the Child*. Basic Books.
Richmond, P. G. (1970). *An Introduction to Piaget*. Routledge and Kegan Paul.
Sigel, I. E., and Hooper, F. H. (1968). *Logical Thinking in Children*. Holt, Rinehart and Winston.

6
Development and Culture

An extra-terrestrial scientist, observing human behaviour from a high-altitude UFO, might suppose that a good deal of it was purely instinctive. He (or it) might notice that on sunny days large numbers of the species hurry towards the sea, in a way reminiscent of lemmings: some never reach it before the cooling temperature reverses the flow. More seriously, some actually die in the attempt. The behaviour would appear to be a fixed action pattern, controlled by simple stimuli. But this would be false. Again, several writers in recent years, of whom Desmond Morris is probably the most famous, have emphasized the animal-like characteristics of our race. Our view in this book is that this is, on the whole, unhelpful in understanding the more important parts of behaviour. By far the greater part of human activity is characterized by two things that differentiate man from other species on earth: cognition and culture. The gap between the problem-solving of even the brightest ape, and an average child, is great. Even greater is that between the social life of animals, and that of men. We know of no human society, however technologically primitive, that lacks highly complex rules.

Until very recently, we think, psychology has been neglectful of this. There has, of course, been the long battle between the environmentalists and the hereditarians, with first one side on top, then the other. At the time of writing, the popular line seems to be environment, with a determined counter-attack led by writers such as Jensen and Eysenck. Much of the environmentalist argument, however, has been based on learning theory and a relatively simple analysis of stimuli and responses. Further, it seems to us that an either/or debate is itself not a useful one. To move away from this has been one of the really fundamental contributions of Piaget.

In this chapter we take that work as a starting point; and go on to the role of the home and family, culture, the work of the Harvard school, and some of the anthropological approaches. Here we reach one of the frontiers of what is conventionally regarded as 'psychology'. Such frontiers are of course largely arbitrary, but some bounds must be set for practical reasons.

SOME PIAGETIAN RESEARCH

As has been pointed out in the preceding chapter, Piaget's theory rests upon an interaction between the organism and the environment. Piaget and his collaborators, however, have concentrated upon the organism and its internal structures, rather than on the essential external stimulation. A great amount of research more or less independent of the Geneva workers has now appeared, and in this perhaps three main themes appear. There are first of all attempts at replication, at checking the reported findings. Sometimes these use the original methods, sometimes other procedures designed, usually, to bring the investigation into line with conventionally accepted ways of experimenting. The danger here, of course, is that changing the method may alter or destroy the phenomenon: the baby may go with the bath-water. Secondly there are attempts to modify the order of development as described by Piaget. What difference does some change in the environment make? Are the stages really invariant in order, and can they be hastened or delayed? Thirdly there are cross-cultural studies: attempts to see whether Piaget's findings hold in other societies, and whether the theory can help us to understand such societies.

We shall look at some examples.

Braine (1959) reported an interesting series of experiments, one of the first to try to check some of Piaget's findings by a modified method. One of Braine's most important points was that Piaget's own methods might produce poorer results than the children were actually capable of. He quoted experiments with animals (e.g. Harlow, 1951) showing that under favourable conditions quite complex 'thinking' tasks can be mastered. Further, in Piaget's methods, a number of factors are confused: there is not only the basic factor of the child's intellectual ability, but also his interest in the particular task, his experience of the materials and techniques involved, and, most importantly, his grasp of language. Piaget's tasks, beyond the sensorimotor stage, are largely verbal, with both instructions and responses involving understanding and interpretation of words. Braine proposed to reduce these variables by adapting methods from the behaviouristic tradition, namely those of discrimination learning.

Braine took one particular inference for study: If A is greater than B, and B is greater than C, then A is greater than C. This involves a logical operation which is embodied in many intelligence test items; and the inference had been extensively studied (Piaget, 1953; Piaget et al., 1948).

In one typical Piagetian task a bead was moved along a wire, and the child asked to move another bead the same distance. The wires could be put in different relations to each other, e.g. one in advance of the other, or at an angle to it, or bent, in order to see whether the child had a general idea of 'the same distance'. In another task, the child had to build a tower of bricks the same height as one built by the experimenter. Measuring rods were available, which could serve as the middle term in the inference. Piaget's subjects were between four and eight years old. For such children, Braine argued, part of the difficulty of these tasks may lie, not so much in their reasoning ability as in their unfamiliarity with measuring instruments, or with what the experimenter means by 'as long as' or 'the same distance'.

Braine used a set of vertical rods of different lengths, under the base of which a candy reward could be placed. In some cases the task was made more difficult by adding Müller-Lyer type fins to the rods. The children were aged from 3:6 to 7:0. Their task was to choose the longer (or shorter) of two rods presented together. There were three phases to the experiment. In the first, the two rods were always clearly different in height. In the second, the difference was not clearly discriminable. But it was demonstrated by the experimenter, using a measuring stick of intermediate length. This stick had a projection at the top, which could pass over the shorter rod, but not over the longer, thus making the difference quite clear. In the third phase the child was asked to say which rod was the taller or shorter, as the experimenter measured them.

Braine concluded, from this and similar experiments, that the inference involved (if A is greater than B, and B than C, then A is greater than C) is available to children at least two years earlier than reported by Piaget. Similarly for some related reasoning operations. However, Braine found nothing to make him reject Piaget's theory of emergent levels of development. This is just one set of experiments. Sigel and Hooper (1968), reviewing these and many others, seem to think that these results are fairly typical. In other words, there is a good deal of support for Piaget's stage theory of development, though to check every aspect will require a truly gigantic research programme. Occasionally somewhat dramatic attacks are launched on 'Piagetian theory. A national newspaper headline in 1971 read 'Piaget Scuppered'. This referred to a series of experiments by P. E. Bryant (1971), which suggest that some of Piaget's procedures are at fault in that they tend to confuse the child by producing conflicting hypotheses. If this is eliminated, Bryant claims, children may show more advanced intellectual operations than Piaget's theory predicts. Similarly, disagreement is often reported with the age norms reported by Piaget. Probably Piaget himself, and many others, would not regard this as a damaging criticism. Indeed, as we mentioned earlier, Piagetian theory in a sense ought to predict differential effects of the environment. But we should also note that in controlling variables, Braine has altered the task. It may be that the phenomenon under study was then no longer that in which Piaget was interested. Braine himself touches on this point in bringing out an important theoretical difference between Piaget and the behaviourist tradition:

'For Piaget, intellectual processes are not hypothetical constructs, which require specification in terms of the experimental procedures by which they may be elicited, but realities which need only to be diagnosed through intuitive analysis of an S's behavior and language.'

It will be seen that part of Braine's procedure was a learning process. He was therefore in a sense modifying the child's behaviour. A more direct attempt to modify the development process has been made by Smedslund. He reported (1961) a series of experiments on training in the concept of conservation. (See also *The Geneva School: Reversibility*.) The series constitutes a short but systematic set of attempts to test alternative hypotheses. Smedslund begins by distinguishing four main possible interpretations of the data of cognitive development. *Nativism* implies that given the appropriate circumstances (roughly, absence of positively disruptive factors such as brain damage), the behaviour under discussion will simply appear. In this case, logically correct responses to conservation problems would appear, because the underlying structures were 'built-in' to the organism. *Learning theory* would assume that concepts (or more strictly perhaps appropriate behaviours) are acquired as a result of repeated reinforcement of responses; and that they can be extinguished by non-reinforcement. *Maturation theory* would suggest that the structures are not built-in, but develop as the nervous system matures, independently of specific experience. *Equilibration theory* is the Piagetian view: logical structures develop in the course of interaction between the organism and the environment, as has been explained. These distinctions are useful inasmuch as they do yield different predictions, which can be tested experimentally. But they are an oversimplification. There is, for example, an element of nativism in Piaget's theory, since the most elementary structures (reflexes) are built in, as well as the potentiality for change. Again, it is never easy to separate a maturational theory, which involves a 'normal' environment, from an interactionist theory which, in principle, specifies particular environmental factors. What *is* a normal environment? It may also be argued that these four theoretical approaches differ in their explanatory status. Maturation, in particular, is often regarded as merely descriptive.

But to proceed to the experiments. Pure nativist theory, Smedslund argues, can be dismissed. Young children just do not show conservation, for example, even when they are in possession of all the facts. Rather, they try to explain and confirm their perception-bound judgments. A plasticine ball is rolled into a sausage, which a child judges to be bigger: the child says, 'Yes, I can feel that the sausage is heavier,' etc. This experiment, in which plasticine is made into different shapes, is the classical one for investigating conservation of substance and weight. The experimenter can either leave the quantity unchanged, and ask for judgments, or alter the quantity without the subject's knowledge, and ask for explanations. Smedslund used the latter technique to test the various hypotheses.

For example: thirteen children, aged 5 to 7 years, were selected who already showed conservation in a pretest. A number of subjects who showed no conservation were given a training procedure involving weighing materials on a balance. Of these, eleven ended by giving only correct answers and explanations, and these were compared with the thirteen in the experiment proper.

In this, the materials were pairs of objects made of plasticine. There were two brown balls; two red bricks; and two green sausages. Sometimes only the first pair, or the first two pairs, were used. The child was given a pair of objects, and told that the two weighed the same. Then the shape of one was changed, and in doing so the experimenter took away a small piece of the plasticine. For example, one of the two brown balls would be changed into a sausage. The child was asked to say whether the two objects would now still weigh the same; or whether one would now weigh more, and if so which one. The two objects were then placed on the scales, and the child shown that the weights were different: the ball, of course weighed more. Finally, the child was asked to account for this difference. Thus three steps were involved: prediction, control, and explanation. The same procedure was used with the two bricks (one changed to a cake) and the sausages (one changed to a ball).

It will be seen that this procedure is designed to set up a cognitive conflict (rather like Festinger's cognitive dissonance) which the child has to resolve. Remember that these children had acquired the concept of conservation, either 'naturally' or through training. These were the results.

'None of the subjects who had acquired the principle during the experiment showed any resistance to extinction, whereas about half of the subjects who had acquired the concept in a "normal" way maintained it in the face of apparent non-conservation. The typical behaviour of those who did not resist was to show little surprise and to switch rapidly back to non-conservation with explanations referring to the perceptual appearance of the objects: "The ball weighs more, because it is rounder and fatter." "The brick will weigh more, because it is bigger," etc. The subjects who resisted said: "We must have taken a little away from that one" (the lighter object), "I think you have taken away some of the clay!" "We must have lost some clay on the floor," etc.'

Smedslund takes these results as evidence, though not conclusive, against a learning theory view. Similarly, it should follow that *absence* of reinforcement will not hinder acquisition of a concept, and this was found in the next study.

'The belief in conservation of substance did not seem to be acquired by observations of an empirical law, or by reinforcement from the experimenter, but as a solution of a conflict between the incompatible schemata of addition/subtraction and deformation, or some other kind of conflict.'

Other of Smedslund's studies fill out some of the variables which must be involved, though as he points out the situation is too complex to make this more than a start. Taking these and other studies, the evidence so far suggests that the main stages of thought described by Piaget are not amenable to substantial alteration by short-term reinforcement or lack of it. Long-term manipulation of important environmental variables, that is to say over a period of years, is very difficult to achieve experimentally. Harlen (1968), after a review of a substantial body of literature, suggests that:

'... the impact of experience can hasten the natural development of thought processes but not radically change the rate or order of their appearance. What need to be determined are the limits of the period during which the development of certain concepts can be assisted by training or experience and the type of treatment which is appropriate.'

Which is as much as to say that the whole question is wide open. Something more may be gained, however, from studies of different cultures. It does at present appear that in some of these at least, variations from the Piagetian account occur. Marion De Lemos (1969), for example, made a rather careful application of Piaget's tests of conservation of quantity, weight, volume, length, area, and number to two groups of Australian aboriginal children.

'Although traditionally a hunting and nomadic people, the majority of Aborigines today live on government settlements or missions, mainly in the northern and central areas of Australia. These settlements generally provide food, clothing, housing, and in some cases also employment. However, they are usually situated some distance from the centres of European population, and the influence of European contact has therefore been limited. Living conditions are generally poor, and material possessions few. The majority of adults are illiterate, and tribal customs and traditions have been retained to a greater or lesser degree, depending on the length of contact with the settlement. In some areas settlements have only recently been established, and in these cases the tribal life and customs would remain strong. Although schools have now been established on all missions and settlements, the standards and levels of achievement are not comparable with those in normal Australian schools.'

The results were in general clear. The main stages of development described by Piaget were apparent. The responses and explanations of the Aboriginal children were in some cases almost word-for-word translations of those given by Swiss children. But conservation developed much later in the Australian children; and in some cases appeared not to develop at all. There were also some discrepancies between these results and Piaget's theory: for example the invariant order of development for conservation of quantity and weight, postulated by Piaget and Inhelder (1962) was not confirmed. What, however, are the reasons for the slow or non-development of such a basic concept as conservation? De Lemos considers five possibilities. The Aboriginal children lack schooling: but other studies (e.g. Price-Williams, 1961) have found conservation in unschooled children. However it may be that while schooling itself is not vital, it does help to provide the relevant sorts of experience. Another obvious circumstance is lack of contact with a technological society. There is some evidence that in Western society, there is a relationship between conservation and residence in an industrial city (Peluffo, 1962). In passing, one wonders what took place in the highly cultured but preindustrial societies of the past. Then there is the question of the interaction of age with particular experiences. It may be, though there seems to be no firm evidence, that schooling, for example, must occur at some critical period to affect development. Language is another possible variable, though it should not be a major factor according to Piaget. Finally there are genetic differences. De Lemos did find some support for this. One of her groups was of almost pure Aboriginal descent; half the other group had superior, despite identical environmental conditions. (See *Intellectual Abilities* for related work.)

Some other aspects of Piaget's work have been examined cross-culturally. For example, Looft and Bartz (1969) included such studies in their review of animism. However, by far the greatest concentration has been on conservation, probably because this takes such a central place in Piaget's theory. He himself considers it to be 'a necessary condition for all rational activity' (Piaget, 1952). The achievement of conservation marks the transition from stimulus-bound to abstract thinking. But under what environmental conditions does it come about? Lita Furby (1971), in a closely reasoned paper, gives us the beginnings of the answer. To start with, the various reports are contradictory, especially about the effects of schooling. As already mentioned, De Lemos, for one, thought it probably not of prime importance. Greenfield (1966), however, in her detailed study of Wolof children in Senegal, concluded: 'It is always the schooling variable that makes qualitative differences in directions of growth.'

On the face of it, this seems unsatisfactory, for 'schooling' is surely compounded of a host of variables. Furby however concentrates on the conservation task, and points out that it involves three distinct steps or operations. As Elkind (1967) shows, the tasks used to examine conservation are conservation of equivalence tasks: they concern the invariance of the relation between two quantities in spite of a transformation performed on one of the elements of that relation. Such a task necessitates first, conservation of identity: the realization that a given quantity remains the same in spite of a transformation (such as pouring into a differently shaped container). Next logical reasoning: as in Smedslund's tasks, inferring the relationship of A to C from a knowledge of A to B and B to C. Third, perceptual flexibility: ability to judge correctly despite manifest differences in appearance. These operations, Furby argues, may be differently affected by experience. Further, the experiences themselves differ along at least two dimensions. There is first the amount of 'magical' thinking, as opposed to empirical reasoning, that is permitted, or encouraged, by the culture. A separate issue is the amount of physical interaction with the environment, which should encourage perceptual flexibility, and which may be lacking in Western urban environments. Furby quotes Goodnow and Bethon (1966):

'As one Chinese boy explained, a catty of rice may come in different shaped bags, but it is always a catty; he has carried them and he knows!'

This analysis enables Furby to make some coherent sense out of apparently contradictory results. She presents her theoretical framework as a table. (See Table 6.1).

Table 6.1—Summary of theoretical framework. (This table from 'A theoretical analysis of cross-cultural research in cognitive development: Piaget's conservation task', by Lita Furby is reprinted from Journal of Cross-Cultural Psychology, *Volume 2, No. 3 (September 1971), pp. 241–255 by permission of the publisher, Sage Publications, Inc.)*

Type of reasoning	Perceptual flexibility	
	High (manual environment)	Low (automated environment)
Empirical (Western culture)	No difficulty with conservation of identity or perceptual flexibility.	No difficulty with conservation of identity.
	Should perform better than any group.	Difficulty with perceptual flexibility.
		Should perform better with screen present (i.e. screening off confusing stimuli).
Magical (non-Western culture)	No difficulty with perceptual flexibility.	Difficulty with both conservation of identity and perceptual flexibility.
	Difficulty with conservation of identity.	Should show the poorest performance but schooling can help by teaching empirical reasoning.
	Schooling can help by replacing magical thinking with empirical reasoning.	

Furby herself notes two reservations about this analysis. One is that many of the data come from the work of Bruner and his colleagues (see below) which in some cases is lacking in precision, and also uses different criteria for conservation from those of Piaget. The other is that the theory now needs to be tested by investigations concentrating on the supposed variables. While these points are certainly true; and while the situation is probably even more complex: nevertheless Furby's analysis shows the way forward. We are forced to leave the validation of Piaget's theories with that favourite phrase of reviewers of research, 'further work is needed.'

HOME AND FAMILY

Formal schooling for all is a modern phenomenon of Western society. (Some may even think it ironical that Article 26 of the Universal Declaration of Human Rights is the right to compulsory education.) When introduced into a society which has hitherto been without it, it is likely to have dramatic effects on intellectual processes. This seems to be supported by the research (see also *Intellectual Abilities*). Another phenomenon of our culture is the small nuclear family. The role of this in emotional development has received much attention (e.g. Bowlby and Fry (1970). As regards intellectual development, the research is suggestive rather than conclusive. The work of Carlsmith (1964) has been quoted; and see also *Creative Thinking*, particularly the review by Freeman, Butcher and Christie (1968).

Dewing (1970), reviewing the literature, concludes:

> 'Parent variables of importance in the development of creative children appear to be: (1) an unpossessive relationship which encourages the child to be self-reliant and independent; (2) permissive child rearing methods, and (3) diverse and intellectual interests of parents.'

Precisely how these variables exert their effect, and how they interact with the individual and with the culture as a whole, is unclear. The problem is exemplified by a study of Albert (1971), who found that:

> 'Among persons designated as "eminent" or "historical geniuses" there appears to be a rate of parental loss* at least three times that of the average college population (gifted), with the ratio of father-loss to mother-loss being 2 to 1, and, occurring proportionately among Ss in the arts, the humanities, the sciences, and the military.
> This datum raises the following questions: (a) Does parent-loss or attenuation in the exceptionally gifted lead to an early maturity or to a pseudo-maturity, to psychological problems or to cognitive freeing? (b) How does it play a role in the recurrent finding that creative persons of all ages and both sexes tend to be less consistently sex typed than less creative Ss. i.e. creative males being more "feminine" in some behaviors than less creative males, and creative females being more "masculine" in some behaviors than less creative females. (c) Such a high rate of parental-loss raises questions regarding the role of extended family and the role of "interested others" (third parties, such as tutors) in the development of the gifted and of the creative individual.'

In many ways the most attractive approach to problems of cultural influence is to speculate grandly in broad generalities supported by interesting anecdotes. This does have its uses, and we do not abstain from it here. We believe, however, that it may turn out to be essential to have much more detailed studies of more controllable variables of narrower range. A few reports have recently begun to point the way. For example Hamilton (1971) reported evidence that conservation was less well attained by children whose mothers adopted a relatively 'rejecting' attitude towards them. Marjoribanks (1971) attempted to relate four mental abilities to eight 'environmental forces' present in the home. The abilities were verbal, number, spatial and reasoning. The forces were: press for achievement; press for activeness; press for intellectuality; press for independence; press for

---

* Loss of one parent by death before the child was ten.

English; press for ethlanguage (i.e. any language other than English used in the home); mother dominance, father dominance. These forces were defined behaviourally: e.g. 'father dominance' is defined as (or assessed on) (a) father's involvement in child's activities and (b) father's role in family decision making. The environmental variables were found to account for a large percentage of the variance in verbal and number ability and a moderate percentage of the variance in reasoning test scores. There was a less clear relationship in the case of spatial ability. This is thus a step towards analysing more closely the general effects of 'home'; but it will readily be seen that such a variable as 'father's involvement in child's activities' must be a composite of many factors: what sort of activities, how much, how often, at what ages, with what attitude and what response, etc. So for all the others in the list, which makes no pretence to be exhaustive.

A further consideration is that if intellectual development is partly controlled by environmental variables, as it manifestly is; and if these can be analysed exactly, as they may be: then the levels of thought achieved in our present culture may be surpassed. J. McV. Hunt (1961) went so far as to claim that '... it is unlikely that any person has ever achieved his full potential for intellectual development'. This is going well beyond the evidence, which so far shows at most that development can be *hastened*; there is no way of turning the average man into an Einstein, or an Einstein into a superman. But we simply do not understand the relationship between the technology of a society and its intellectual achievement. The human race has not always been as it is now; the most recent technological changes have not had time to show themselves biologically. Only in the last hundred years has it been common for large populations to read and write. There is some evidence that these skills could be attained much earlier than they are conventionally taught. Downing (e.g. 1967) and others have reported varying degrees of success for the Initial Teaching Alphabet. Moore (1961) has used electric typewriters with pre-school children to by-pass the motor skills required for writing by hand. The elementary sound-sight associations may also provide a way of by-passing the cognitive structures usually involved in literacy. (For a review of pre-school education, see Kohlberg, 1968.)

CULTURE

All human behaviour, to be fully understood, must be considered in its cultural context. This is above all true of thought processes. First of all the content of thinking is largely controlled by the culture. Indeed unless we take a Jungian or similar view, it is entirely so. Then the function of thinking is largely social. Anchorites think, of course; nevertheless the most usual functions of thought are concerned with interaction. And the structure of thought appears to be mainly a cultural matter.

Holtzman (1968) argues that psychology must seek to lose its ethnocentric character. Külpe, acting as subject in the Würzburg experiments, provided a subject population of one German professor. Subsequently, our common material has been provided by students and Western school children. This may be acceptable if there are indeed basic mechanisms which can be studied in any random sample: but that is an assumption, not a fundamental fact as it is in chemistry or physics.

The ethnocentrism of psychology is not entirely wilful. There are many practical and methodological difficulties. All research depends on money, and cultural studies are expensive. Some of the more basic problems are discussed by Frijda and Jahoda (1966) and by Whiting (1968), among others. They are important for the understanding of thought processes. Frijda and Jahoda list five main points. First is the question of the adequacy and comparability of descriptive category systems; a difficulty which can generally be overcome if investigators are aware of it. Then there is the functional equivalence of the phenomena. School, or church-going, may serve quite different functions in two societies. Third there is the comparability of investigation procedures, which has at least three aspects: verbal materials, instructions, and tasks; test materials; test situations. Mere translation of instructions does not suffice, and in some cases may be almost impossible, due to different categorization, and different connotations of words (see *Language and Thought*). Again, the whole idea of 'a test' is now very familiar to children in our society (indeed in my experience children in any experiment invariably refer to the task as a test); whereas it may be strange, and meaningless, to others. For example subjects may have a high regard for accuracy, but none for speed. The fourth point is the adequacy, representativeness and comparability of samples. Equivalent groups may be non-existent, unavailable, or just hard to identify: for example accurate age records may be lacking. Lastly there are problems of interpretation. Even if the aim is merely descriptive, false generalization is very easy, for example.

Partly for these reasons, the systematic study of the thought processes of the whole of the heterogeneous human race is only beginning. Ironically, it is beginning at a time when the differences between races seem about to disappear for ever. We have discussed some studies of conservation (others are available in Price-Williams, 1969). Cole, Gay, Glick and Sharp (1971) report a series of studies of the Kpelle people of Liberia. Their subtitle is: *An exploration in experimental anthropology*. This work is perhaps less interesting for its actual experimental findings than for its promoting of what amounts to a new attitude towards cross-cultural investigation; and, perhaps, a rapprochement of psychology and anthropology.

Cross-cultural studies raise another aspect of one of the basic issues of psychology, namely the problem of individual differences. One answer might be to study each group in isolation, for its own sake, just as an animal psychologist might be solely interested in the behaviour of the white rat. Assuming that our interest is in the human race as a whole, we must face the question, in what sense, if any, is there equivalence between different cultural groups. A subsidiary question concerns the ratio of genetic to environmental determining factors. One answer is to state optimistically that we are, after all, all members of the same race, with a more-or-less common inheritance, and that the similarities clearly outweigh the differences. To give one example, Hammond's (1968) studies of conflict resolution are based on this assumption. A second view is exemplified by Vernon (1969). We possess tests of intellectual functioning, known to be predictive of achievement in Western society, and therefore it makes sense to use them for this purpose, whatever the origin of the subjects (see *Intellectual Abilities*). A third view is that we have no reason to assume psychological equivalences between cultures, and must start afresh with each one. New tests and experimental techniques need to be developed, as they have been in Western society. A fourth view might be that it is possible to demonstrate equivalence at some level of analysis: possibly at a behavioural level, but possibly at some level of theory or model. This is a complex anthropological issue, which we must discuss a little more later.

The view of Cole *et al.*, seems to fall somewhere between three and four. They were impressed by the way in which their Kpelle subjects employed complex cognitive skills in social situations, while not necessarily able to do so in conventional 'experimental' situations. The skills involved may be closely related: for example, learning rules, making correct discriminations; but they find their application in everyday, familiar situations. The whole range of situations has yet to be studied systematically:

> '...we have no tools for distinguishing social and nonsocial problem-solving situations in an analytic fashion. In fact, almost all experimental situations are *nonsocial* in the sense that their successful solution requires manipulations of objects or words abstracted from context, rather than relations with people. Is it possible that were we to find the social analogues of with people. Is it possible that were we to find the social analogues of these experimental situations, our informants would experience less difficulty and even show themselves to be quite clever? It seems suggestive to us in this regard that among the Kpelle the adjective *clever* does not apply to such technological operations as rice farming, house building, and car repairing. A farmer may be considered lazy or hard-working, but the term clever is restricted to the social sphere. A related fact is that the same kinds of people who found it difficult to explain the principles of good house building found it easy to tell us how their children should be raised.'

Cole *et al.* present as their major conclusion the conviction that

> '...cultural differences in cognition reside more in the situations to which particular cognitive processes are applied than in the existence of a process in one cultural group and its absence in another.'

This approach is one which has recently been taken up by Bruner (with whom Cole has collaborated). Both quote with approval the work of Labov (1970). Labov has been concerned to show that the application of standardized tests to different racial groups, in the United States in particular, is misleading. It is *not* that the groups are potentially, perhaps genetically, equal, but some are handicapped by poor environments, lack of schooling, etc.: it is that lack of competence cannot be reliably inferred from inadequate performance. Those who score relatively low on tests may employ equivalent (or even the same) skills elsewhere. Cole and Bruner (1971) put it thus:

'The problem is to identify the range of capacities readily manifested in different groups and then to enquire whether the range is adequate to the individual's needs in various cultural settings.'

How this is to be done is another matter: it is the question faced by Galton when he began to seek an answer to the problem of individual differences. (See *Creative Thinking*.)

INSTRUMENTAL CONCEPTUALISM

The group of Harvard psychologists which has been led by J. S. Bruner, and with which Cole has become associated, has produced a theoretical and experimental account of cognitive development, strongly influenced by cultural research. The other major source, and perhaps the main inspiration, of this work has been Piaget; although in many respects Bruner departs from Piaget's ideas. Like Piaget, Bruner has been concerned with the nature of knowledge about the world. It is instructive to compare what follows with Bruner's work on classifying set out in *A Study of Thinking* (1956). In *Studies in Cognitive Growth* (1966), two central beliefs are stated.

'The first is that our knowledge of the world is based on a constructed model of reality, a model that can only partially and intermittently be tested against input.'

The nature of this model is partly controlled by heredity, in particular by the inherited structure of the nervous system. The second belief or assumption is that

'our models develop as a function of the uses to which they have been put first by the culture and then by any of its members who must bend knowledge to their own uses'.

Each of these notions must be examined in a little more detail. The first is clearly very similar to the ideas of Gregory (1970; see *Models*). Bruner holds that reality is modelled, or represented, internally. That is to say that when we think, the material of thought is a copy of, or symbol for, what really exists. Bruner does not seem to comment on the advantages and disadvantages of this, as Gregory does. Instead he wishes to distinguish three techniques for constructing the models, or three modes of representation. These are termed enactive, ikonic, and symbolic. *Enactive representation* refers to cases where an action seems to stand for an object to which it is related. Bruner quotes Piaget's observation of the latter's six-month-old daughter Lucienne, who at first grasped and released the cover of her cot, then continued the hand-grasping without touching the material. In other words there is a lack of distinction between perception and action; or as Piaget puts it, things are 'lived rather than thought'.

Bruner quotes several well-established lines of thought to show that organisms (primates, at least) can discriminate many features of the environment from birth. This work includes that of Hubel and Wiesel (1963); Kessen (1965); Bower (1965); Fantz (1965); and Held (1965). The work of Kessen in particular, on the way in which day-old human babies regard, say, a solid-coloured triangle, shows that they definitely scan the shape, locating corners and lines. Thus they not only discriminate, but carry out appropriate motor activity. This leads Bruner to see the origin of enactive representation 'in the reafference that serves to relate the requirements of action to the properties of the visual field'. This mode of representation is transcended by the next, but is never entirely abandoned. Bruner differs from Piaget in holding that an earlier mechanism can coexist with a later one; in fact in adult life all three are available. Exactly what this means is not entirely clear, but it may be that skills provide an example. In walking, for example, there must be a fairly continuous flow of information from the environment (mainly through the feet and eyes), otherwise coordinated movement breaks down. Thus there must be some internal representation of reality; this is precisely the 'model' described by Gregory. In the case of Lucienne, one might say that the continued hand-grasping was simply perseverative; but this does imply some 'trace' of the stimulus, which continues to elicit the response.

Ikonic representation is representation in terms of images. Bruner based this conception largely on the work of Clementina Kuhlman, which seemed to show that children tend to sort objects by reference to their surface characteristics rather than any more fundamental dimensions. As discussed at some length (see *Imagery*) the conceptual and explanatory status of imagery is far from clear. This is particularly so in the present case. It certainly seems unjustified to conclude that the presence of imagery necessarily entails a certain sort of classification; especially if the argument extends to adult life. Asked to classify a series of famous persons including, let us say, Hitler, Stalin, and Groucho Marx, I should be vividly aware of the fact that all possessed moustaches; but I should be unlikely to class them as similar in any more important respect. (Groucho's, of course, belonged to his maid.) Lest this be thought irrelevant, Bruner himself quotes Napoleon's alleged remark that men who think in images are not fit to command, and argues that an image-bound general could not recognize the truth of Clausewitz's dictum, that war is a continuation of peacetime policies. 'The two do not look enough alike.' But thinking in images does not seem to be the same as being image-bound; and I find it hard to form any image of a peace-time policy.

But while the existence of imagery in individuals does not of itself prove that they think in a certain way, it does seem plausible to suppose that children at a certain stage represent the environment in a 'concrete' way: a 'match by direct correspondence', as Bruner puts it. Most writers except Piaget seem to think that this mode of representation remains available at later ages. (See *Imagery*.) On some views, it may become dominant again.

Symbolic representation implies that the connection between representation and what is represented is arbitrary. The obvious and most important example is language: in all but a few cases, there is no resemblance between a word and that for which it stands (the exceptions are onomatopoeic words). Symbolic representation, according to Bruner, is found only in man. It

> 'becomes specialized in expression in various domains of the life of a human being: in language, in tool-using, in various atemporally organized and skilled forms of serial behaviour and in the organization of experience itself'.

Language is said to be the first of these to develop. This is a little odd, for subhuman primates can use tools. There is also far more evidence available about language than about the other forms of symbolic representation. Language can be used as an example to show the essential characteristics of any symbolic system. The first is the arbitrary nature of the association between word and thing (symbol reference). The second is that words refer to classes of things, governed by rules in such a way that new members can be added (categoriality). The third feature is grammaticalness; that is to say, approximately, that language obeys a set of rules as to which utterances are permissible, or better, as to which *sorts* of utterances are permissible; for one who has learned the language can generate new, correct utterances without being able to state the rules. This brings out the fourth feature, effective productivity. One aspect of this is that language can be used speculatively, to imagine situations that do not exist in reality. Fifth is a set of 'design features' such as the use of the vocal-auditory channel, the broadcast nature of speech, the discrete nature of words, etc. Presumably these are different for other forms of symbolic representation. It is less clear what is the application of the other characteristics to, for example, tool using. Indeed it is not quite easy to see tool using as a mode of representation. Tools do often act as mediation between a real and a desired situation (one recalls Köhler's sticks and Maier's pendulum). The relationship between a tool and the thing produced is not arbitrary; but a tool is applicable to a whole class of things. It might be argued that a hammer bears the same sort of relationship to 'things to be hammered' as 'dog' does to dogs. Tools have rules for their use (skills) in somewhat the way that language does. It also may be said that tools provide a way of manipulating the environment which is to some extent independent of immediate perceptual features. Therefore the cognitive aspects of tool using are more like language than they are like ikonic representation.

We must now pass to the way in which these representational systems are said to develop. As noted above, this is a function of the uses to which they have been put by the culture and by the individual. Representational systems have evolved over a long period (perhaps 500,000 years) as a result of man linking himself with 'new, external implementation systems'. Of these there are three general kinds: amplifiers of motor capacities, i.e. tools; amplifiers of sensory capacities, i.e. signal and communication systems; and amplifiers of ratiocinative (thinking) capacities, 'of infinite variety, ranging from language to myth and theory and explanation'. Each sort of implementation system demands, and produces, an internal counterpart. This *seems* to mean that man hit upon the use of the hammer, say, and then developed the capacity for effective hammering; he hit upon an explanation, and as a result developed the ability to explain. It is perhaps more comprehensible to think of the two things—amplifier and capacity—proceeding together with continuous feedback. As far as the individual is concerned, three factors control the development of his model of reality. First there is the supply of amplifiers which his culture happens to have in stock. Second is the particular life led by the individual, his unique set of experiences. Third is: 'the extent to which the individual is incited to explore the sources of the concordance among his three modes of knowing—action, image, and symbol.' This last factor is more likely to be important in technologically advanced societies. This is partly because in such societies the individual is forced to transfer his activities from one sphere to another. Specifically, he typically learns in one situation (school, college, etc.), and applies himself in another. This results in 'a requirement of developing correspondence between what we do, what we see, and what we say'.

This system, though far less extensive than that of Piaget, is in some ways perhaps even harder to understand. This is largely due to a failure to define precisely the meaning and status of the concepts used. The theory is supported by a number of experiments designed to show, for example, the ways in which children of different ages and different cultures classify objects. The general conclusion is that technologically advanced societies demand, largely through the medium of formal schooling, a fundamental cognitive change: the development of the symbolic mode of representation and the 'confrontation' by it of the more elementary modes. On the face of it, this seems a plausible notion, though it needs to be made experimentally testable. One obvious line of evidence which casts doubt on this, however, is the historical existence of cultures which technologically would now be termed unsophisticated, yet which manifestly were pre-eminent in 'symbolic representation'. (e.g. the classical cultures of Greece, India, China.) A related point is what is meant by 'technology'. There is a sense in which the everyday skills of most people in a pre-industrial society are more technologically advanced than those of our own time. Mrs. Beeton (or her cook) surely possessed more technical skills, at least, than a housewife who relies on packaged instant foods.

To illustrate this school's work, consider an investigation by Maccoby and Modiano (1966). They used a simple but neat procedure, based on one designed by Olver (1961). Each of nine cards bore one word: banana, peach, potato, meat, milk, water, air, germs, stones. For Mexican children, maranja (orange) was substituted for peach, frijol (beans) for potato, and lumbre (fire) for germs. The cards were presented to a child one at a time, and the child was asked to say in what way it was different from the preceding items, and in what way the items so far presented were all alike. The items, when presented, were left in front of the subject. Three groups of subjects were taken: North American, and Mexican from a rural village and Mexico City respectively. A range of ages was examined. The responses were classified in various ways; and the results led the authors to conclude as follows.

'A city child coming from an industrial society starts by dealing with objects in terms of their perceptible, concrete characteristics. He soon comes to consider them in the light of what he can do with them. In time, he is led to more abstract formulations as to how things are, how they are alike and how different. Some go so far that they lose the sense of the concreteness of things and become buried in a dry nominalism. They are like people who see a painting immediately in terms of its style, period and influences, but with no sense of its uniqueness.

Peasant children do not change that much. They are much more similar to their older brothers: they both look. The older one looks at things more closely and considers more concrete ways to use them. While the older peasant child can say how things are alike, he feels more at home with their differences, for that is where reality lies for him. He does not think in generalities. At his best he shows a rich interest in and relation to individual people, individual objects, or particular events. At his poorest he sees only the concrete and the particular and walls himself off from anything beyond immediate experience.

Essentially, such cognitive styles reflect the demands of a culture. The modern industrialized world demands abstractions by its very arrangements. its stimuli, its contrasts, its laws of justice and exchange. What is demanded of the peasant, on the other hand, is that he pay attention to his crops, the weather, and the particular people around him.

The culture is reflected in its institutions—school, family, or work group. The child in an urban school is more likely to learn to manipulate concepts, to use his knowledge beyond school. In an industrialized society, when a child learns what things are, he is taught what he can do with them and where they can be found. In a peasant village, schooling does not get you a better job or even necessarily make you a better farmer. Some boys who do best at school lack the money to continue their education. The urban child can both live at home and advance to higher schools.

The villager tends to be more concrete and more authoritarian in moral outlook. His values are traditional and conservative, and economic scarcity reinforces moral realism. Traditional authoritarianism is rooted in work relations and in the family, where children are taught to obey without question. Unlike the urban world, the small village offers no alternatives to the influence of the family. Even those games by which an industrial society teaches reciprocity and abstract rules of justice are not played within the village (Maccoby, Modiano and Lander, 1964). Observers have noted that many a villager who migrates to the city feels freer when liberated from the restraints of village life (Lewis, 1959).

If the peasant child is not dulled by village life, he will experience the uniqueness of events, objects, and people. But as the city child grows older, he may end by exchanging a spontaneous, less alienated relationship to the world for a more sophisticated outlook which concentrates on using, exchanging, or catalogue. What industrialized, urban man gains in an increased ability to formulate, to reason, and to code the ever more numerous bits of complex information he acquires, he may lose in a decreased sensitivity to people and events.'

This passage gives a plausible account of the general outlook of the Harvard school. It is, of course, based only partly on experiment, and on small samples under particular conditions. The approach does, however, seem to open the way to a more exact, and more universal, account of thinking in its social context. This work is on the borderland of psychology and anthropology; and into the latter we now make a brief foray.

SOME ANTHROPOLOGICAL APPROACHES

Like psychologists, anthropologists have always been concerned with the problem of individual differences. Indeed Cole *et al.* (1971) remark: 'Anthropology developed as the study of human diversity.' They also point out that this has been closely related to cognitive activity in particular. Cultures, on the face of it, are manifestly different. Does this, or does it not, imply fundamental differences in thought? Again like Psychology, Anthropology has been subject to numerous changes of viewpoint in its short history. For a time, partly under the influence of evolutionary theory, it was widely held that the human race as a whole was developing towards some 'higher' state, and that existing societies constituted stages in this process. Western society, naturally, was the most advanced stage. Further, on the basis of the doctrine that ontogeny recapitulates phylogeny, it seemed that 'primitive' societies could be considered equivalent to European children.

It was in this tradition that Lucien Levy-Bruhl published his account of *How Natives Think* (1910). This was based on published reports rather than first-hand observation. Levy-Bruhl believed that the thought of 'primitive' peoples was essentially pre-logical, as he termed it. It was characterized by a fusion of emotional and intellectual elements; and by the famous *participation mystique*— roughly, an inability to distinguish clearly the self from the environment. This was thought to be manifested in the existence, for example, of sympathetic magical practices. The existence of witch-doctors, for example, whose function is to cure maladies supposedly brought on by witches, would be evidence for 'primitive' mental processes. There is, of course, a clear resemblance to some of Freud's ideas (see *Thinking as a Private Experience*).

This approach has for some time been out of favour. It was first strongly attacked by Franz Boas. In *The Mind of Primitive Man* (1911) he argued that many of the reports on which a theoretical writer like Levy-Bruhl relied were inaccurate, due to observers, steeped in their own culture, being unable to understand another. More fundamentally, Boas denied that differences in thought processes could be inferred from differences in social customs. Instead, he asserted: 'the functions of the human mind are common to the whole of humanity'. This, according to Cole et al., is now generally accepted by most anthropologists. Following Boas, a group of anthropologists arose in America, of whom the best-known are probably Margaret Mead and Ruth Benedict. These were not primarily concerned with thought processes, but with personality. I mention them here because they constitute the best-known link to date between the two disciplines, being quoted in numerous introductory textbooks of Psychology. The approach may be seen as paralleling functionalism, but with a strong Gestalt influence in the emphasis on the way the total cultural context produces a 'modal' or typical personality.

Despite early misinterpretations, there still remain the differences in beliefs and practices to be accounted for. Horton (1967) attempts to subsume both Western and African beliefs, for example, under the heading of explanatory theories. All people, he argues, try to make sense of their world. They seek some unity underlying the diversity of phenomena. (Compare Bruner's earlier work on concept identification.) They look for causal explanations that go beyond common sense; at least when common sense fails, for example in providing a cure (or explanation) for illness. In one case the explanation may be the existence of an ill-wisher; in the other, the presence of germs or viruses. (This account of Horton's work is based on the summary by Cole et al.) This is plausible insofar as it is not easy to distinguish the Western housewife's belief in the virtues of disinfectant, from the African's faith in an amulet. There is, however, a difference in the type of reasoning from which the beliefs derive, or so I would argue. An interesting speculation, but one that would lead us too far afield, concerns the belief systems of those who perpetuate faith. For example, those people who, in mediaeval times, supplied the numerous portions of the True Cross. We know that the prescriptions of medical personnel are heavily influenced by the advertising campaigns of drug companies.

However, the most serious and extensive attempt to deal with the thought of non-Western peoples, at any rate in recent times, lies in the work of Claude Lévi-Strauss and his followers. This goes under the heading of structuralism. This makes us think at once of Piaget; and in fact Piaget himself has grouped together his own work, that of Lévi-Strauss, and related work in mathematics and linguistics (Structuralism, 1971). There are some possibly superficial resemblances besides the more important ones. Both bodies of work are in a European, specifically French, tradition. Both are accused of being excessively difficult, and of building a vast weight of theory on insufficient, or uncontrolled, evidence. And the structuralist approach, as has been pointed out (see The Geneva School), has or long been out of fashion as compared to the practical functionalism of most of American psychology.

The system of Lévi-Strauss is a complex one, and becoming more so with successive publications. Perhaps the most general point for psychologists is the necessity to understand other cultures in their own terms. This does not mean that each individual culture has its own norms of behaviour, which are 'right' in that context (the implication of some of the cultural studies of, for example, Margaret Mead and Ruth Benedict). Rather, it means that Lévi-Strauss distinguishes two modes of thinking, characteristic of Western technological society, and non-technological cultures respectively. These are equally viable and, Lévi-Strauss would argue, equally logical. Whereas Western logic is abstract, however, the alternative logic is concrete. We shall illustrate this in a moment.

First, we must bring out another tenet of the system. Anthropologists are concerned to explain cultural practices. These include customs, rituals, beliefs, myths. They are expressed *par excellence* in language, but comprise virtually all the behaviour of individuals, in all societies. A 'custom' is not a peculiar tattooing of some remote tribe: it is simply a regularity of behaviour like shaving or not shaving, eating at dawn or noon, etc. Now, what are cultural practices *for*? Take such a universal practice as cooking. It is perfectly possible to live on raw food: yet in every society of which we have any record, food is cooked, often very elaborately. Animals, on the other hand, do not do this. Now Lévi-Strauss does not start with the observed culinary peculiarities of different societies and seek to explain them: rather he starts with what may be a more fundamental question, namely how it is that men can distinguish themselves from nature, of which they nevertheless remain a part, and on which they depend for subsistence. His answer is that what distinguishes man is culture. And cultural practices are chosen and perpetuated because they are fitted to symbolize the distinction. Thus cooking is a universal, basic symbol which all men use to distinguish themselves from the rest of nature. This is one fundamental symbol, and Lévi-Strauss entitles one of his books *The Raw and the Cooked*. But it is only one; and furthermore each such symbol can be, and is, systematically elaborated in enormous detail.

It will be seen that what is symbolized, according to Lévi-Strauss, is a *relationship*. This, it is argued, makes sense of the puzzling features of many customs, myths, and so on. When a culture pays particular attention to some such feature, it is not the thing in itself that is symbolically important, but its position in relation to something else. To elaborate the raw: cooked relationship; the same sort of relationship holds, for example, in respect of society, religion, and sound. Thus we get a set of equations:

FOOD	raw (changes to) cooked: fresh (changes to) putrid
SOCIETY	culture : nature
RELIGION	profane : sacred
SOUND	silence : noise

What is being said is that profane is to sacred as silence is to noise. (It is fairly plausible to assert that, until recent times, loud noises like church bells or bull-roarers had religious or ritual connotations.) To psychologists, this at once suggests the logical noegenetic laws of Spearman (see *Intellectual Abilities*). The difference is that Spearman conceived of the principles as operating on abstract concepts. In Lévi-Strauss's system, they would be expressed concretely. Another obvious comparison is of course with Piaget: and it is tempting to equate at once this concrete reasoning with concrete operations. I think this would be wrong, since what I understand Lévi-Strauss to be saying is that the two systems exist side by side; one does not have developmental or evaluative priority over the other. Historically, however, it seems that abstract 'scientific' thought appeared later on the scene. It is tempting to suggest that Piaget and Lévi-Strauss *ought* to be saying the same thing, even if they are not.

Yet a further connection is with Freud, by whom Lévi-Strauss has been influenced to some extent. The Freudian unconscious thinks concretely, expressing itself in images (see *Thinking as a Private Experience*). In individual development, the ego struggles to establish itself as a distinct entity; and it does so largely by means of language. But the ego, of course, is precisely that part of the personality that is capable of abstract thought. The two writers can be connected, but not equated. However, the comparison with both Freud and Piaget does bring out another feature. What, scientifically speaking, is the student of human behaviour—psychologist or anthropologist—trying to do? Is he simply recording data? Is he going further and recording regularities in the data (such as schedules of reinforcement and their outcomes, or kinship system)? Or is he to try to formulate some abstractions which are more general than the particular phenomena? We have seen that Piaget postulates complex logical structures which are said to underlie the behaviour of individuals. Other sorts of structure were described by Freud. These structures can on the one hand be seen as universals, that is, common to all human beings; and on the other, they can be seen as models, with many of the implications of that word. Lévi-Strauss himself is quite explicit about this. If the social or behavioural scientist, or more particularly the anthropologist, is concerned with social structures, then:

'The term "social structure" has nothing to do with empirical reality but with models which are built up after it . . . a structure consists of a model meeting with several requirements.

First, the structure exhibits the characteristics of a system. It is made up of several elements, none of which can undergo a change without effecting changes in all the other elements.

Second, for any given model there should be a possibility of ordering a series of transformations resulting in a group of models of the same type.

Third, the above properties make it possible to predict how the model will react if one or more of its elements are submitted to certain modifications.

Finally, the model should be so constituted as to make immediately intelligible all the observed facts.' (Lévi-Strauss, 1963)

There are obvious similarities to Piagetian and Gestalt theory; and Lévi-Strauss himself draws the analogy with psychoanalysis, which '. . . discovered the means to set up models in a new field, that of the psychological life of the patient considered as a whole'. The psychoanalytic model is discussed elsewhere, as are the implications of models as a scientific enterprise. The system of Lévi-Strauss can be criticized both on anthropological and scientific grounds (see, for example, Leach, 1970). For psychologists, it does provide a new perspective on thought processes. Here again there is an analogy with Freud. Just as before Freud psychology was centred on conscious experience; so until recently it has been centred on Western man. The behaviour of other cultures was often seen as a variation on, or a failure to attain, Western cultural norms. (This point is elaborated in *Intellectual Abilities*.) But Psychology must surely deal with all behaviour. The work of Lévi-Strauss attempts to unify the diverse phenomena in one way; and in so doing shows us the whole range of phenomena in a new light.

THOUGHT REFORM

Thought reform is the euphemistic term applied to the most extreme and deliberate form of social and cultural pressure on thought processes. All cultures, as we have seen, shape the way that individuals think, to a greater or less extent. In most cases, this is unplanned. Some cultures facilitate creative thought, others inhibit it (see *Creative Thinking*). Some tend to develop particular forms of intellectual activity (see above, and *Intellectual Abilities*). In some societies, such as that of Hitler's Germany, particular activities are suppressed. In others, such as Stalin's Russia, ostensible changes in thought are produced by violent means, to produce 'confessions' for political purposes. There are also, however, deliberate attempts to produce genuine and lasting changes. Psychotherapy does this. Missionary religions have for many centuries brought about dramatic effects on individuals. The most systematic programme of thought change so far known is that of contemporary China.

This programme has been reported by Lifton (1961). It seems that the programme embodied, in advanced form, probably all the techniques used at other times and places. It was applied both to Chinese citizens and to foreigners. There is little evidence that it was based on reported psychological findings, though it is difficult to see how any such could have made it any more effective. Three issues seem to be important here: what is done? how effective is it? what implications does it have? Very brief answers will be offered.

According to Lifton, the most basic feature is control of human communication: 'milieu control'. The entire social environment in which the individual finds himself is directed to one end. Within this, physical deprivations are used, first to lessen resistance; second to reduce the person to a child-like dependence; third as negative reinforcement to shape behaviour. In later stages, psychological pressures are mainly used. These include confusion; induction of shame and guilt; confession; successive increase of demands; persistent exhortation and 'help'; restriction of concepts through language manipulation. The effects of some of these are known from other studies (e.g. on frustration–regression, discrimination learning, psychotherapy, religious conversion, concentration camps). The procedures, in many cases, are quite effective. Individuals do seem to be genuinely 'converted'. They think differently. It is not just a case of now preferring a different mode of life or set of political opinions. Rather, it is that thought now proceeds upon a different set of assumptions. And these assumptions are themselves rigid and resistant to change. Thought is both directed and restricted. It seems likely that the changes tend to be permanent so long as milieu control is maintained, but are reversible (at considerable emotional cost) if the individual removes to a more open and flexible cultural environment.

It is sometimes said that the processes of socialization, education, and psychotherapy are equivalent to indoctrination. I disagree. There is a danger that they can become so: but there is a logical, and psychological, distinction between the individual who is more in control of his own behaviour and he who is less so; between one who can change his actions when reason or reality demand, and one whose responses are unalterable to certain stimuli. The latter is further from being human. Autonomy, as a prime human characteristic, is supported by what we know of evolution and of individual psychological development.

FOCUS: COGNITIVE STYLE

There have been many attempts in Psychology to account for individual differences in intellectual functioning. In some circles these differences have been ignored, while in others they are regarded as the *raison d'être* of Psychology itself. In this section we take a look at the increasingly popular concept of *cognitive style*, its relationship to individual differences, and its possible application to cultural variations in intellectual abilities.

For some, 'cognitive style' is a concept which has strong psychoanalytic connotations, some unfortunate connections with Rorschach science and which is usually associated with a cranky and long-winded literature. In recent years however it has become more 'respectable' thanks to the pioneering work of H. A. Witkin on 'field dependence' which we discussed briefly in *Creative Thinking*. (A good, if limited, historical account of the topic is to be found in Shouksmith's *Intelligence, Creativity and Cognitive Style, 1970*.) In the most general sense, cognitive style refers to individual characteristic modes of responding to the environment which are manifested in a wide variety of different situations. A very trivial example would be the way in which the optimist is reputed to describe his glass as half *full* while the pessimist sees it as half *empty*. The latter's generally more jaundiced view of the world leads him to interpret the identical state of affairs differently. Cognitive styles are often said to be trans-situational. That is to say, they are reflected across the whole spectrum of behaviour, although their origins may be very humble. Thus the pessimist is not only gloomy about how much is in his glass, but is also suitably depressing about the weather tomorrow, the chances of England winning the next Test Match, and whether his car will break down when he is on holiday.

According to Witkin and others, cognitive style does more than describe aspects of personality. 'They are known', he says, 'to be manifestations, in the cognitive sphere, of still broader dimensions of personal functioning. . . .' (Witkin, 1967). Thus cognitive styles link what we conventionally call 'personality' with 'cognition' Cognitive style is an attractive concept for psychologists interested in thinking because it caters for two features of thought which have traditionally preoccupied them—control and direction. The question of how ideas follow one another was one of the main issues for Associationism and later received considerable attention from the Würzburg group in their work on 'Einstellung' and 'determining tendencies' (see *Thinking as a Private Experience*). Cognitive style, by definition, possesses these selective, controlling and directional functions. The concept is also appealing in a less academic sense. We all know of people who habitually seem to get hold of the wrong end of the stick, we speak of somebody's 'whole approach' being wrong and we are often struck by great individual differences in style of work—how X cannot understand anything unless he can write it down or has grasped the main points first, how Y can only work in short frantic bursts of effort, and Z comprehends things best through the use of concrete analogies, etc. These are all subtle matters of individual preference which may well reflect some fairly basic underlying differences in cognitive style. The problem which arises of course is how to identify and measure them experimentally so as to give them more than anecdotal significance and usefulness.

The best-known attempts to do so are probably those of Witkin and his colleagues (Witkin *et al.*, 1954, 1962). Witkin's earliest investigations involved the use of the rod and frame test. Here, subjects are required to adjust a straight line (rod) to the vertical in conditions where there are few, if any, visual cues apart from the tilted square frame which surrounds the rod. The experiment can be carried out in a completely darkened room with a luminous rod and frame or simply by having the subject look into a suitably designed box, rather like a tachistoscope. Now according to Witkin people vary in the extent to which their judgments of verticality are influenced by the surrounding frame. Those who 'use' its orientation to set the rod are said to be field dependent in contrast to the field independent who adjust the rod regardless of the position of the frame, presumably by reference to postural cues. Witkin envisages the field dependence–independence distinction as a dimension rather than a matter of psychological types. Also the rod and frame test is not the only way field dependence can be measured. It may also be measured satisfactorily with the embedded figures test in which the subject must locate a specified geometric figure deliberately hidden within a larger complex design, and the body adjustment test which requires the subject to adjust the position of his own body to the upright whilst seated in a tilted room. (One can imagine that field dependent subjects would find a session in the 'Haunted Room' particularly distressing. This is a rather unnerving device, found at some fairgrounds, in which you sit in an apparently normal room on a long bench. The room suddenly begins to rotate slowly about a central pole bolted to the bench, giving rise to the impression that you are about to fall out and crack your head on the ceiling. A most disturbing experience.) According to Witkin the results of these three tests correlate very highly with each other, and longitudinal studies (i.e. repeated measures taken over a period of time) suggest that degree of field dependence is a stable feature of an individual's cognitive apparatus.

Witkin's next step was to extend the range of behaviour in which field dependence was thought to operate by showing that it is related to performance on tests of problem solving and the Wechsler Intelligence Scale. More specifically, field dependent subjects

> 'do less well at solving problems which require isolating essential elements from the context in which they are presented and using them in different contexts, as, for example, the tasks employed by Duncker in his studies of functional fixity.' (Witkin, 1965)

And to quote again,

> 'Field dependence measures relate very highly to scores on a triumvirate of Wechsler intelligence scale subtests (Block Design, Object Assembly and Picture Completion) which tap the same kind of analytical ability as do the tests of field dependence.' (Witkin, 1967)

To handle these findings Witkin proposed to substitute the dimension of field dependence with the notion of a 'global-articulated' cognitive style. In his own words,

> '...at one extreme there is a consistent tendency for experience to be global and diffuse—the organization of the field as a whole dictates the manner in which its parts are experienced. At the other extreme there is a tendency for experience to be delineated and structured—parts of a field are experienced as discrete and the field as a whole organized. To these opposite poles of the cognitive style we may apply the labels "global" and "articulated". (Witkin, 1965)

Having provided some sort of empirical basis for the 'global-articulated' style, Witkin has sought to investigate its origins which he claims may lie in the nature of the mother–child interaction (see also *Intellectual Abilities*) and generally to explore its usefulness as a cognitive variable. Many workers, including Witkin, have also attempted to relate articulation to various forms of pathology, especially schizophrenia of which the paranoid variety is generally associated with a highly articulated style. Rather fittingly, perhaps, alcoholics tend to be markedly field dependent (Karp *et al.*, 1965).

A formidable body of evidence, and in particular normative data on field articulation has accumulated during the past fifteen years or so. But doubts about the whole status of such cognitive styles still remain. Why is this? Well, there are probably a number of reasons not the least of which involves the question of definition. What does 'cognitive style' really mean? Vernon (1971) questions the assumption that the term refers to anything which is not covered by 'factor', arguing that work on styles has caused 'more confusion than clarification.' Then there are the general methodological problems relating to what one is measuring with, for example, a field dependence test. What validity does such a test have? This raises the very complex question of the meaning of correlations. We know that 'field dependence' correlates with certain specific subtests of the WAIS. Does this imply a 'spatial ability', an expression Vernon might prefer, or is one justified in inferring an underlying cognitive style? The answer in part depends on whether one believes there is anything to be gained from talking of such and such a 'cognitive style' rather than 'ability X'. Witkin presumably thinks there is and in fact tries to tie in the notion of articulation with the concept of 'psychological differentiation' which is a fundamental property of all psychological systems, to give it a more formal theoretical framework. And as we have seen Witkin further tries to link 'differentiation' to socialization influences in infancy, in particular the part played by the mother–child interaction in this process. But this is unconvincing in view of the practical impossibility of sorting out who is doing what, and to whom (see *Intellectual Abilities*).

The use of Witkin's rod and frame test in cross-cultural studies will be discussed later. For the moment let us keep in mind the difficulties surrounding research on cognitive style and turn to the work of those at the Menninger Clinic who have provided a more strongly theoretical account.

George Klein (1970) has given us perhaps the most up to date statement of the work and theory of this group in a collection of difficult but stimulating essays, *Perception, Motives and Personality*. This title in fact aptly sums up the general theoretical orientation and scope of enquiry of the whole Menninger programme. Although overlapping to some extent with the work of Witkin, Klein draws more heavily on the psychoanalytic traditions of Freud and Hartmann as well as the 'transactionalist' psychology of J. J. Gibson. His work as a whole is a curious mixture of the formally experimental, the theoretically unorthodox, the psychologically speculative and the frankly often tedious aspects of Rorschach 'science'.

Klein is probably most well known for his early experiments on 'perceptual attitudes', in particular the notion of 'leveling' and 'sharpening'. Klein and Holzman (1950) and Holzman and Klein (1954) presented subjects with a series of fourteen squares shown one at a time and asked for judgments of absolute size. After the first five (in fact the smallest five) had been shown a number of times, the smallest was removed, without subjects knowledge, and replaced with another square (number 6 in the series) larger than any of the previous five. Thus the average size of the stimuli as a whole was now that much larger. Judgments of size for each square were again obtained and the substitution procedure was continued until all fourteen squares had been presented. The results showed that when accuracy of size judgments is considered as a function of when they were made during the experiment some surprising individual differences emerge. Some subjects make highly accurate judgments throughout, allowing appropriately for the gradual changes in size. Others however disregard these changes and continue to judge size as if the original five small squares were still present, estimating for example a square of 13 inches as being only four. The authors refer to the former tendency as 'sharpening' and to the latter as 'leveling'.

According to Klein (1970) differences in 'leveling-sharpening' are a consequence of perceptual attitudes which reflect an individual's 'cognitive controls' and ultimately his cognitive styles. Let us sort out a few points of terminology here. 'Cognitive controls' are stable modes of cognitive functioning which are manifested in a variety of situations and which are intimately bound up with the whole structure of personality. Thus the general adaptive strategies employed by the 'sharpener' are said to be different from those of the 'leveler'. Cognitive style is regarded by Klein (1970) as

'... an arrangement of cognitive attitudes, constituting another structural level of personality.'

By this he seems to mean that cognitive styles derive from the interaction of the attitudes and controls with the world. For instance, as he puts it,

'... the leveling attitude produces an oversimplified world. The leveler adjusts to this internalized representation of the world, and the manner of doing so becomes itself an aspect of his cognitive *style*.'

Thus, in general terms

'Style refers to a level of organization in which such secondary developments from a person's various cognitive attitudes coexist in a balanced arrangement.'

Klein's use of 'style' then is rather more specialized than, for example, Witkin's. But it carries much the same connotations of control, direction, selectivity, etc. Tests of the applicability and usefulness of the various styles identified by the Menninger group, however, have been less satisfactory. True there is the work which relates different types of Rorschach response to varying cognitive styles and to the whole balance and structure of personality. And there is the suggestion that reactions to sensory isolation, for example, may vary according to cognitive style. But the contribution of the Menninger work has been principally in the field of psychoanalytic theory where it has reminded us how complex is the inter-action between motivation and 'the cognitive processes'. While cognition is undoubtedly subject to the pressures and modes of adaptation required by the internal structure of the individual, as Klein argues quite forcibly it is an over-simplification to regard motivation as having a distorting influence in perception, making it non-veridical (i.e. non-true to reality). To quote, 'Effective perception does not mean uniform perception among people; similarly, individual differences in perception do not necessarily imply "distorting" mechanisms.' And again, 'Different cognitive attitudes can, however, be equally effective and can lead to varying equally "veridical" experiences.' If cognitive style provides us with some-thing along the lines of Freud's 'protective shield against stimuli' (Freud, 1920), then the implication is that the effect will be to soften the blow rather than eliminating it altogether.

But the same criticisms that were levelled at Witkin *et al.* apply equally to the work of the Menninger Clinic. Although perhaps theoretically more elegant there are still the same questions about test validity, inferences made from cor-relations, as well as the special problems surrounding projective techniques. One major difficulty however concerns the way in which an operationally defined variable such as leveling-sharpening is related to the internal structure of the individual. In what sense does 'the avoidance and minimizing of distinctions and nuances in the perceptual sphere . . . have a parallel in an avoidance pattern in everyday behaviour' as proposed by Klein (1970)? What kind of evidence would be required to substantiate this claim? Regrettably, considerably more than is actually provided, which amounts to therapists' ratings of their subjects distinc-tive qualities', identified as self-inward' for levelers and 'self-outward' for sharpeners The discussion of this question, out of context, is perhaps a little unfair, but it does reinforce Vernon's argument that work on cognitive styles may have led to 'more confusion than clarification'. And to quote his final thought on the matter,

> 'Less ambitious studies, which were designed to show the scope, limitations and stability of some particular cognitive variables, might be more worth-while.' (Vernon, 1971)

That there are those who think otherwise is demonstrated by the considerably *more* ambitious attempts to relate cognitive style to cultural and racial differences in cognitive function. Some of these are discussed by Witkin (1967), including Dawson's (1963; 1967) studies of field dependence in two West African com-munities which we mentioned earlier (see *Creative Thinking*). In line with Witkin's thesis that differences in field dependence stem from varying child-rearing practices, one of Dawson's hypotheses was that field dependence in men would be associated with a high degree of strict control by the mother during infancy. As predicted, performance on the embedded figures did correlate with ratings made by the subjects themselves of the maternal strictness they had experienced as infants. And, as we have seen, Dawson's comparison of the Mende and the Temne tribal groups in Sierra Leone suggested that the more 'liberal' childhood environment found among the Mende was associated with less field dependence. The problem with these studies of course is that once again we are dealing with correlations. Perhaps field dependent subjects' memory of their mother's discipline is more vivid or simply distorted. Or perhaps child-rearing practices are not the only source of variation in the Temne and Mende ways of life. This is not to say that such studies are worthless but that, fairly obviously, that they are difficult to interpret.

Witkin (1967) also cites Berry's (1966a; 1966b) investigations of field dependence in Eskimo and Temne subjects. Eskimo children, rather like the Mende, grow up in an environment in which independence, freedom and the cultivation of individual skills is encouraged, and punishment rarely used. Berry's expectation that this would be correlated with field independence was borne out by the results of the embedded figures test. Interestingly, Berry also found some evidence that the Eskimo subjects were less influenced than the Temne by group endorsed opinion using an Asch-type paradigm in which subjects were required to judge the lengths of various lines in the face of a (fabricated) contradictory standard said to have been provided by an authoritative group.

In a paper entitled 'Cognitive Style among the Kpelle of Liberia?' Glick (1968) discusses some of the investigations which were eventually to appear in *The Cultural Context of Learning and Thinking*. His case is that

'... cognitive style is as much a cultural as an individual phenomenon. It is quite possible for all people to adopt similar styles of thinking but the conditions for eliciting these styles of thinking may vary with the individual or the culture.'

As one example of what he means by this, Glick cites an experiment concerned with the question of whether object classification is determined by the linguistic categories of the Kpelle language:

'... we presented our subjects with 20 objects which fall linguistically into four categories, five objects per category. These were types of foods, types of implement, types of food containers, and types of clothing. We presented these objects in haphazard array and asked the subjects to "put the ones together which go together." Contrary to the linguistic hypothesis our 20 objects were sorted into 10 categories. For example, a knife and an orange were put together because a knife cuts the orange. Our subjects were willing to give detailed justifications for this basis of sorting but were unwilling to change the sorts even when pressed. They often answered us that a wise man could only do such and such. In total exasperation, we finally said, "How would a fool do it?" The result was a set of nice linguistically ordered categories—four of them with five items each.'

Glick's argument is that, compared with the average American subject, Kpelle subjects adopt an entirely different approach to problems of this type. As he remarks, 'The Kpelle subject, faced with an array of familiar items functions at first as a pragmatist, his questions are "how do these things relate in my experiences?" ' (Glick, 1969). But it is not true that Kpelle subjects reason functionally where the typical Western subject would 'categorize'. The behaviour which actually occurs depends on the cultural context provided. Now is this a matter of 'cognitive style'? Technically, this depends, amongst other things, on the *generality* and *pervasiveness* of the 'pragmatic approach' in behaviour and whether there is any real sense in which it varies between individuals and cultures. We have no evidence on these points of course, and there is certainly no sense in which cognitive style can be said to have been measured in the same way as e.g. field dependence has. But it is nevertheless an interesting hypothesis, and somewhat reminiscent of the suggestion made by Vernon (1969) that African pre-school children tend to develop a 'passive' attitude towards the world, partly because curiosity, practical achievement are apparently not encouraged. Could we perhaps here also think in terms of an 'active–passive' cognitive style which varies between cultures?

At present answers to questions like these are bound to be inconclusive. The crosscultural study is becoming ever more popular, and the possibility of cultural differences in cognitive style does at least serve to remind us of the difficulties of interpreting such investigations, and for that matter alerts us to the whole question of what is meant by a 'culture-free' test. Interest in the role of cognitive styles in individual differences is growing but certainly many problems remain about its definition, conceptual status and measurement. If these can be overcome, and the concept provided with a sound empirical basis then there is no reason why cognitive styles should not play an important part in the psychology of individual and cultural differences in cognition.

FURTHER READING

Bruner, J. S. *et al.* (1966). *Studies in Cognitive Growth*. Wiley.
Cole, M. *et al.* (1971). *The Cultural Context of Learning and Thinking*. Methuen.
Klein, G. S. (1970). *Perception, Motives and Personality*. Alfred A. Knopf.
Lévi-Strauss, C. (1963). *Structural Anthropology*. Basic Books.
Price-Williams, D. R. (Ed.) (1969). *Cross-cultural Studies*. Penguin Books.
Sigel, I. E., and Hooper, F. H. (1968). *Logical Thinking in Children*. Rinehart and Winston.
Horton, R., and Finnegan, R. (1973). *Modes of Thinking*. Faber and Faber.

7

Language and Thought

Our aim here is to discuss the relationship between language and thinking. We do not propose to present a full account of language as a psychological phenomenon, important though that is; and still less shall we attempt to cover the independent science of linguistics. (For a discussion of these aspects the reader is referred to J. M. Greene's *Psycholinguistics*, 1972.)

A HUMAN PHENOMENON

A question that has constantly recurred in psychology is, can animals think? It is a question that has found its way into both scientific articles and examination papers, and is a never-failing source of interest to animal lovers. 'Every time I put on my hat and coat to go out,' says a proud budgerigar owner on the radio, 'he says "Goodbye". That shows he can think, doesn't it?' Similarly with language—'He understands every word I say.' At one level, the question is simply one of knowing what you mean by 'think' or 'understand'. At another level, however, something may be learned about these processes by examining the capacities of non-human species. Several attempts have been made to teach animals to speak. It is generally agreed that the speech of imitative birds such as mynahs, parrots, jackdaws and budgerigars, is not meaningful. Attention has therefore been given to the higher primates. Two well-known reports are those by Hayes (1951); and Kellogg and Kellogg (1933). Viki, the ape reared by the Hayes family, succeeded in learning a few simple speech sounds, such as 'cup'. 'Cup' however, for Viki, seemed to have a rather undifferentiated meaning, and to stand not only for the container but for 'drink' or even a general state of need. Further than this Viki could never go. Thus it seemed that it was at the point of acquisition of language that man parted company with his nearest cousins.

However, one of the difficulties with such experiments is that apes do not possess the same physical apparatus for speech as humans. Indeed, many other systems have been utilized for communication among various species. (For an account of signal systems among primates, see for example Ploog and Melnechuk,

1969.) It is not necessarily the case that humans acquired a flexible speech apparatus by good fortune, and so were able to develop language. Reynolds (1968) argues just the opposite:

'Human peculiarities of the auditory system, vocal tract, and motor system are better explained as the result of feedback from an evolving linguistic code than as necessary prerequisites for language.'

This view may be compared with that of Bruner, to be mentioned later.

A new approach was taken by Premack (1970). He succeeded in teaching a chimpanzee, Sarah, 120 words. The 'words' were plastic symbols, which Sarah had to place on a board in order to obtain a reward. The first stage was naming: Sarah had to select the symbol for 'apple' to get a piece of apple. By similar names, verbs, common nouns for foods, colours and miscellaneous objects, and an assortment of adjectives and relation-words such as 'on'. Using sentences of these words, Sarah could be instructed to carry out quite complex actions, such as: *put the apple in the red dish and the apple and the banana in the green dish.* Sarah could construct sentences such as: *Mary give fig Sarah.* The question arises is, of course, what is the chimpanzee now doing? Premack's argument is this:

'When does a piece of plastic become a word? We answer: when it is used as a word. For example, we consider a bit of blue plastic to be the name for apple because 1. it is the symbol used when Sarah requests apple, and 2. it is the answer Sarah gives to "what is the name of apple?" We can add that the plastic becomes a word when the properties ascribed to it are not those of the plastic, but those of the object it names.

We could see whether this condition was true for Sarah by use of matching-to-sample procedures. We gave her the apple and a pair of descriptive alternatives, and she had to tell us which of these was more like the apple. We began with four sets: red vs. green, round vs. square, square with stem vs. plain square, and plain circle vs. square with stem. Sarah gave consistent answers that tended to agree with those you and I would give.

Then we repeated the procedure exactly, but we replaced the real apple with the name for apple, a piece of blue plastic. Sarah assigned to the plastic the same properties that she had just ascribed to the apple: it was round, not square; red not green, and so on. This is evidence that the chimp thinks of the word not as its literal form (blue plastic) but as the thing it represents (red apple).'

A rather similar experiment is reported by Gardner and Gardner (1969), who were less interested specifically in the question of whether or not animals can learn to use a language. They were more concerned to find out whether an animal, in their case the chimpanzee, Washoe, could learn to communicate effectively with humans using 'American Sign Language', a system based on hand gestures developed originally for the deaf. Their results indicated that, like Sarah, Washoe was able to combine signs, etc., implying the operation of an elementary grammar. But generally Sarah's linguistic capabilities seem to exceed

9—T * *

by far those of Washoe, particularly if one accepts the more recent claims by Premack and Premack (1972) that Sarah can handle both negative and conditional statements.

This raises several interesting points. One is the question of the criteria by which to assess similarity to human behaviour, a matter to which we shall return in discussing computer simulation (see *Models*). Another is the relationship between the word and the thing for which it stands. It appears from Premack's report that Sarah responded to the plastic symbol as if it were the apple itself (at least in some respects; presumably she did not try to eat it). Now this is a rather low level of word use, typical, according to Piaget, of young children. The situation is, however, obscure: we must suppose that Sarah did not 'think' that the symbol was red, not green. It might appear that what Sarah had learned was a rather complex set of discriminated responses, rather than language in the full human sense. What are the characteristics of the latter? Lyons (1970) picks out two as being of particular importance. The first is *duality of structure*. Every known language can be analysed at two levels. The primary level is into meaningful units (usually, though not always, words). The secondary level is that of sounds (or phonemes, as the sound units are technically called). Sarah's 120-word language analyses into plastic symbols at the primary level, and into attributes such as shape and colour at the secondary level. The second characteristic is that languages are *creative*. That is to say that much of a language as spoken or written consists of sentences that have probably never been produced before, and certainly have never been heard or read by the person who now utters them. From Premack's account one cannot conclude that Sarah had this capacity. This characteristic seems to be unique to human language. (Of course Sarah's language was a humanly-devised one.)

A further point that arises is the possible relationship between Sarah's acquisition of a symbol system and her 'thinking'. One is reminded of a possibly apocryphal story of B. F. Skinner. It is said that after describing how pigeons can be operantly conditioned to play ping-pong, and the like, he was asked whether he had known that pigeons were so clever before he began his experiments. Another member of the audience reportedly said, that they *weren't* so clever before he began his experiments. Which comes first? Jenkins (1969) states:

> 'The major positions on the relations of thought and language can be characterized (or perhaps caricatured) in a series of brief answers to the multiple-choice question: "What is the relation between thought and language?"
>
> 1. *Thought is dependent on language.*
> 2. *Thought is language.*
> 3. *Language is dependent on thought.*
>
> The fourth answer might be fittingly cast in the devilish mode of the fourth alternative that one uses when he has run out of good responses:
>
> 4. *None of the above.* Or perhaps, *All of the above.*'

This introduces a review article at the end of which Jenkins concludes that the final answer is the correct one. The question will be a useful one to keep in mind in what follows. But we shall not try to order the material in the same way.

EXPERIMENTAL APPROACHES

Instead, we shall look first at some of the relevant experimental work, and then at some of the developmental and cultural factors. Rather early in the study of thought processes it was noticed that these were often accompanied by bodily changes or movements. Alexander Bain perhaps the first of the British Associationists to be mainly a psychologist rather than mainly a philosopher, wrote of a 'twittering of the organs'—delightful phrase. The Würzburg psychologists, finding that they could not account for thought by the introspection of immediate experience, stressed the motor concomitants of thought—knitting of the brows and other tensions of voluntary muscles. Titchener and his colleagues at Cornell, attacking the concept of imageless thought, held that the phenomenon was really the consciousness of kinaesthetic sensations. Humphrey (1951) observes:

> 'To have demonstrated the ubiquitousness of these vestigial motor responses during the thinking activity is the great positive contribution of the Cornell critics. Whatever the Cornell group did or did not accomplish, it did at least show the very close relation between abstract thinking and muscular response.'

It was left to Watson to substitute the concomitants for the thing itself. In *Behaviorism* (1920) he wrote: 'The behaviorist advances the view that *what the psychologists have hitherto called thought is in short nothing but talking to ourselves.*' This he extended first by stressing that whispered speech does not depend on the larynx alone but upon 'muscular responses of the cheek, tongue, throat and chest'. As Feigl puts it, 'Watson made up his windpipe that he had no mind.' Secondly Watson argued that *other* physiological changes may come to represent speech; in fact: 'any and every bodily response may become a word substitute'. As we have noted elsewhere, Watson was led by his desire to make Psychology an objective science to reject what could not be observed, both phenomena and concepts. Thus he sought to show not only that thought is accompanied by bodily movements, but that it actually *is* such movements. Such a crude reductionism probably no psychologist would now accept. Even experimentally, however, the theory will not do. One difficulty here lies in trying to prove a negative. If thought is found without movements of the speech muscles, the sub-vocalists can always argue for a failure of design or apparatus to be sensitive enough. But it is reasonable to expect that if there *are* incipient movements in verbal thought, they should resemble those of overt speech.

Thorson (1925) in a careful experiment, found that movements of the tongue were

> 'not universal in internal speech or verbal thought. When they do occur they correspond to movements in overt speech of the same words in only 4·4 per cent of these cases. Repetition of the same verbal thought is accompanied by repetition of similar tongue movements in only 10 per cent of the cases where movement occurs.'

Thorson concluded:

> 'there is no correspondence between movements of the tongue and verbal formulations in thought. This leaves only the hypothesis that the activities are intraneural, and do not necessarily involve complete motor expression at each stage of the process.'

It is true that Watson rejected the Thorson argument, making the 'failure to prove a negative' move (apparently Thorson had omitted to use the most appropriate instrument, a string galvanometer, whatever that was). Watson himself relies on two observations. First, that children talk even when they are alone, and seem to use this to plan their behaviour. Second, that deaf-mutes who used manual signs instead of words, tended to make the same movements while thinking. It seems hardly worthwhile to demolish such arguments neither of which, of course, proves anything whatever.

So much, then, for the motor theory in its extreme form. The view that thought is identical with language in some form is more sophisticated and has a long history. The nineteenth-century linguist Max Müller, heading a paragraph *Language and Thought Inseparable*, argued:

> 'We do not complain that we cannot move without our legs. Why then should it be thought humiliating that we cannot think without words? ... not only to a considerable extent but always and altogether we think by means of names.'

The first answer to this is that we can move without legs; not so well, but it can be done. So, as we shall try to demonstrate, with language. A second answer, however, is that it depends what you mean by thinking. If you use the word in a rather general way, as we do in this book, to mean more or less 'information processing', then of course the argument becomes pointless, for clearly some of this is done by animals and humans who do not possess language. On the other hand one could restrict the use of 'thinking' to those reasoning processes that involve words: when the issue would again be resolved. Humphrey (1951) put the question in the form:

> '... are the most complex psychological activities of which the human being is capable fundamentally speech activities, in the sense that they may be described as verbal formulations without remainder?'

In an erudite and elegant discussion, he presents five lines of argument to show that this is not the case. The first is the evidence for imageless thought (see *Thinking as a Private Experience*). The determining tendencies were clearly a part of thought, yet could not be put into words. Secondly, language itself must of its nature involve activities normally classified as thought, namely those of understanding. Words can be said with or without meaning or reference (e.g. by a human and a parrot). Conversely language can vary completely, while meaning is at least approximately the same—*pain* refers to more or less the same thing as *bread*. So 'language as utterance' certainly cannot be equated with thought. The third argument is from clinical observation of aphasic patients. Sir Henry Head (1926) showed for example that while patients lacking speech were handicapped in some thought activities, they were not so in others, such as playing draughts or dominoes. Fourth, Humphrey quotes experiments on concept learning, for example those by Heidbreder (1947). These showed, as is well known, that subjects can often respond correctly without necessarily being able to state the rule. (See *Concept Identification*) Similarly animal experiments on discrimination and generalization show something like conceptual thinking. Lastly there are arguments showing that language is only an instrument for expressing thought: it may be illogical or jumbled when the thought is perfectly clear. (This sort of argument would surely be supported by any creative writer.) Humphrey's arguments are likewise supported by M. Vernon (1967) who collated the results of thirty-three independently published studies in which level of verbal language was systematically manipulated, while thought processes were measured as the dependent variable. He concluded:

'...there is no relationship between level of language development and measures of thought processes in experiments where other relevant factors are either controlled or randomized.'

That the situation is fairly complex is suggested by a review, by McGuigan (1970) of covert oral behaviour during the silent performance of various tasks. Recording techniques have of course improved since the days of Watson and Thorson: EMG (muscle potentials) are now used. McGuigan's general conclusion is that covert oral behaviour increases during language tasks but not during non-language tasks. He adds:

'...covert oral behaviour during the silent performance of language tasks serves a language function; mediational theories, built on overt behaviour, help to suggest more precisely that the covert oral response facilitates the reception of external language stimuli and the internal processing of that information. Physiological considerations indicate complex and rapid feedback loops between speech regions of the brain and the speech musculature. These loops may function in the process of internal communications.'

Much of the most interesting work on the relationship between language and thought has arisen from approaches to the development of children. One of the most influential of these came from the Russian Lev Vygotsky, who died in 1934 at the early age of thirty-eight. His book *Thought and Language* (1962) is still full of interest. One of Vygotsky's several starting points was the early work of Piaget on the development of speech. Piaget had argued that much of the speech of young children is *egocentric*: it does not perform the normal adult function of conveying ideas to others. This, in Piaget's view, was because the nature of thought, in its early stages, is itself egocentric (see *The Geneva School*). As thought processes develop, so speech loses its egocentric character. We shall give some examples later. Vygotsky however felt both that Piaget's observations were not correct, and that the abandonment of egocentricity was not the end of the story. One must account for the existence in adult life of both *external* speech—normally directed towards others; and *inner* speech—normally directed towards oneself. Vygotsky set out to test three of Piaget's observations in particular. First that egocentric speech occurs in the presence of other children engaged in the same activity, but not when the child is alone: it is a 'collective monologue.' Second that the child thinks his egocentric speech is understood by others (when often it is not). Third, that egocentric speech is like 'external speech' in that it is not inaudible or whispered. Vygotsky reported three series of experiments designed to test these observations. In the first, a child who showed egocentric speech in the presence of others would be put in a group of deaf-mute or foreign language children. Egocentric speech dropped to little or nothing. Vygotsky argued that this was due to loss of the illusion of being understood. In the second series, the child was put by himself or with a group of strangers, thus removing the possibility of a collective monologue. Again egocentric speech decreased, though it did not disappear. In the third series loud music or other noise prevented the child from hearing his own speech or that of others, with the same result. Vygotsky concluded that he had disproved Piaget's view, and found convincing support for his own. Vygotsky's view was essentially that egocentric speech develops out of social speech: that was why it diminished when social conditions were reduced. These demonstrations seem perhaps less convincing to us than they did to Vygotsky. Such unusual conditions would surely be expected to affect speech in many ways. One cannot be certain that it was the absence of the illusion of being understood, for example, that was the crucial factor. Such an absence, in any case, seems a remarkably elusive phenomenon to demonstrate. However, Vygotsky went on to suggest that from egocentric speech there develops inner speech. This latter he regarded as 'to a large extent thinking in pure meanings'. Again: 'Its main distinguishing trait is its peculiar syntax. Compared with external speech, inner speech appears disconnected and incomplete.' A related characteristic is abbreviation. Vygotsky lists three *semantic peculiarities* of inner speech. The 'first and most basic' is the predominance of sense over meaning. By *meaning*, Vygotsky seems to imply the objective reference of a word; or, perhaps, the dictionary definition. The *sense* of a word, on the other hand:

> 'is the sum of all the psychological events aroused in our consciousness by the word. It is a dynamic, fluid, complex whole, which has several zones

of unequal stability. Meaning is only one of the zones of sense, the most stable and precise zone. A word acquires its sense from the context in which it appears; in different contexts, it changes its sense. Meaning remains stable throughout the changes of sense.'

The other two characteristics are perhaps harder to understand. One is that in inner speech new words can be formed by combining or merging others. The other is that the senses of different words can 'flow into one another'. All these features remind us of the parallel processing described by Neisser (see *Imagery* and *Models*). It would be rash to equate the two, however. Vygotsky actually postulated three 'planes': external speech, inner speech, and thought itself. He says:

'Inner speech is not the interior aspect of external speech—it is a function in itself. It still remains speech, i.e. thought connected with words. But while in external speech thought is embodied in words, in inner speech words die as they bring forth thought. Inner speech is to a large extent thinking in pure meanings. It is a dynamic, shifting, unstable thing, fluttering between word and thought, the two more or less stable, more or less firmly delineated components of verbal thought.'

Vygotsky's theory was essentially a developmental one. He saw thought and speech as two related but separate lines: 'They may straighten out and run side by side, even merge for a time, but they always diverge again.' The point at which they meet is about two years of age, and is marked by 'two unmistakable objective symptoms: (1) the child's sudden active curiosity about words, his questions about every new thing, "what is this?" and (2) the resulting rapid, saccadic increases in his vocabulary.' The child has realized that things have names. We might compare this with the end of the sensorimotor period as described by Piaget, when it becomes possible to deal with internal representations of the world.

The development of both speech and thinking show, according to Vygotsky, four stages. We will quote his own account.

'The first is the primitive or natural stage, corresponding to pre-intellectual speech and preverbal thought, when these operations appear in their original form, as they were involved at the primitive level of behaviour. Next comes the stage which we might call "naïve psychology", by analogy with the physical properties of his own body and of the objects around him, and the application of this experience to the use of tools: the first exercise of the child's budding practical intelligence. The phase is very clearly defined in the speech development of the child. It is manifested by the correct use of grammatical forms and structures before the child has understood the logical operations for which they stand. The child may operate with subordinate clauses, with words like *because, if, when*, and *but*, long before he really grasps causal, conditional, or temporal relations. ... With the gradual accumulation of naïve psychological experience, the child enters a third stage, distinguished by external signs, external operations that are used as aids in the solution of internal problems. That is the stage when the child counts on his fingers, resorts to mnemonic aids and so on. In speech development it is characterized by egocentric speech. The fourth stage we call the "ingrowth" stage. The external operation turns inward and undergoes profound change in the process. The child begins to count in his head, to use "logical memory", that is, to operate with inherent relationships and inner signs.'

In speech development, this is the final stage of inner, soundless speech. Another way of expressing the situation, according to Vygotsky, is this:

'Schematically, we may imagine thought and speech as two intersecting circles. In their overlapping parts, thought and speech coincide to produce what is called verbal thought. Verbal thought, however, does not by any means include all forms of thought or all forms of speech. There is a vast area of thought that has no direct relation to speech. The thinking manifested in the use of tools belongs in this area, as does practical intellect in general.'

With this it is interesting to compare Bruner's concept of *enactive* representation. It seems likely that Vygotsky's ideas would have developed further had he lived: possibly in the direction taken by his student A. R. Luria. The latter's work departs substantially, however, from the views we have just discussed. Luria has been influenced by Pavlov's notion of language as the *second signal* system. The first system, common to both men and animals, is that of conditioned reflex mechanisms. Language gives man a control system that can be independent of immediate stimulation from the environment. Obvious comparisons are with the accounts of how such autonomy becomes possible in Piagetian and Freudian theory. Luria stresses the directive function of speech, and has exemplified it in a well-known series of experiments, simple but neat. Some of these, rather like Piagetian observations, involve noting the child's reaction to commands. For example a child of 14–16 months has two toys in front of him, a rabbit and a hen. He obeys the instruction 'Give me the rabbit'; but when this is changed to 'Give me the hen' he is unable to alter his behaviour. The verbal instruction can initiate behaviour, but cannot fully control it. At 1:6 to 1:10 a child sees a penny placed under one of two objects, a cup and a box. He carries out the instruction 'Give me the penny' if required to do so at once; but if a delay is inserted between instruction and response the verbal control fails (Luria, 1969). One may compare the behaviour of animals in delayed reaction tests. In some other series of experiments, children have to squeeze a rubber bulb in response to a presented light or shape. Luria's results seem to show that instructions gradually enable the child to carry out more complex behaviour sequences; the child comes to *instruct himself*, making use of the commands he hears, at first aloud, then silently. Luria feels this is typical of normal development.

'The newborn child starts its life in conditions of immediate social contact with the adults. The mother gives the child certain orders and repeatedly speaks to it. She shows an object, pointing to it and saying "That's a doll", and the child turns its eyes towards the object; she gives the command "Give me the doll", and the child tries to do it. The child's conscious attitude is originally divided between two persons: it starts with the mother's command and ends with the child's movement. But during the subsequent period of the child's development the structure of this action begins to change; the child starts using its own language; by saying "A doll!" it singles out the object named, turns its eyes to the doll and tries to grasp it. The child's own speech begins to serve as a command, and the function, formerly divided between two persons, becomes now a new form of an inner self-regulated psychological process.'

Very similar views are put forward by Sokolov (1972).

Luria is of course aware that language has other functions besides the regulation of behaviour, viz. those of direct reference, of conceptual thinking, and of communication. But these are of less interest in the present context. Luria points to advantages which the 'second signalling system' gives man. New systems of connections can be learned quickly and relatively permanently. Such systems can be brought to bear in new situations (see *Problem Solving*). Verbal connections usually do not require constant reinforcement. They are flexible and can be easily altered when necessary. Some investigators (e.g. Jarvis, 1963) report experimental results contrary to those of Luria: but Beiswenger (1968) who obtained corroborative results, suggests a failure to replicate Luria's conditions. A more serious criticism, perhaps, is raised by Jenkins (1969) who feels that the concept of a 'second signal system' is so wide as to have little meaning. It is invoked to account for all the differences between animals and men. At the same time it is not clear exactly how it works: how it relates, for example, to the complexities of language itself.

As we noticed, one of Vygotsky's starting points was the early work of Piaget. Piaget felt that it was possible to distinguish two sorts of utterance in the speech of young children: socialised and egocentric. Roughly, the difference lay in the extent to which the child's speech functioned effectively as communication to another person. Piaget's notion of egocentric speech can be illustrated by the following example (quoted by Flavell). A story is told to a child, who is asked to tell it in turn. This is the original:

'Once upon a time, there was a lady who was called Niobe, and who had 12 sons and 12 daughters. She met a fairy who had only one son and no daughter. Then the lady laughed at the fairy because the fairy only had one boy. Then the fairy was very angry and fastened the lady to a rock. The lady cried for ten years. In the end she turned into a rock, and her tears made a stream which still runs today.'

Now for one child's version, with Piaget's commentary in brackets:

'Gio (8 years old) tells the story in the role of the explainer: "Once upon a time there was a lady who had twelve boys and twelve girls, and then a fairy a boy and a girl. And then, Niobe wanted to have some more sons (than the fairy. Gio means by this that Niobe competed with the fairy, as was told in the text. But it will be seen how elliptical is this way of expressing it.) Then she (who?) was angry. She (who?) fastened her (whom?) to a stone. He (who?) turned into a rock, and then his tears (whose?) made a stream which is still running today." ' (Piaget, 1926)

Piaget's interpretation is that the child fails to distinguish between his own position as teller of the tale, and that of the other child as listener. Thus he fails to provide the necessary information to convey the story. He speaks rather as though he were commenting on some action which both could see. (Rather as children like having done when looking at pictures with an adult.)

Since making these observations, Piaget has explored the relationship of language and thought in some complexity. He has not really been primarily interested in language as such, but in language as an expression, or tool, of thought. Egocentrism, for example, is not a failing of linguistic competence: it is a stage of the development of thought which necessarily gives rise to utterances of a certain type. Conversely, the Piagetian account of mental development shows the origin of logical operations in the early years of life, before language is available. Then in the concrete operations period the child works with a developing logical structure of thought, although his language is still often egocentric. Not until the logical operations are established can language be expected to reflect this. However, part of this process, as we have seen, is the development of means of representing the environment. Language is the most abstract and flexible of these, and thus it is an essential part of full intellectual functioning. But we must remember that the logical operations which Piaget holds to underlie thought are not expressed consciously even by children at the formal operations stage. The operations: 'go beyond language in the sense that the operational propositional structures constitute rather complex systems that are not inscribed as systems in the language even though the elaboration of the structures needs the support of verbal behaviour'. We should, however, says Piaget: 'envisage the influence of language as being less the transmission of ready-made structures than a kind of education of thinking and of reasoning due to the conditions of communication and precorrection of errors'. (Piaget, 1926) Furth, to illustrate the Piagetian view, quotes from Sinclair (1967):

'The possession of certain expressions does not structure operations nor does their absence impede their formation; the expressions are acquired and their use becomes functional according to a process similar to the mode of structuring of the operations themselves, namely through an interplay of decentrations and coordinations. The contribution of language must be sought for on another level. Language can direct attention to the pertinent factors of a problem, just as it can control perceptual activities, as Luria and his collaborators have shown. In this way, language can prepare an operation but is neither sufficient nor necessary to the formation of concrete operations.'

Sinclair was specifically concerned with the development of conservation, but this view holds throughout intellectual development.

The other developmental theorist we should mention is of course Bruner, whose work derives from both the Vygotsky-Luria line and more especially from Piaget. He postulates three mechanisms for representing the environment, which develop successively in the child: the enactive, ikonic, and symbolic modes. Cognitive growth depends upon the 'amplifiers' present in a culture. These are ways of increasing man's motor, sensory, and ratiocinative capacities. The last named range 'from language to myth and theory and explanation'. Bruner's argument is that man has developed 'by linking himself with new, external implementation systems.' Further, 'Any implement system to be effective must produce an appropriate internal counterpart, an appropriate skill necessary . . . for organizing our thoughts in a way that matches them to the requirements of implement systems.' Language is one such system: as such, it is one expression of symbolic representation. Presumably, though this is not very clear, symbolic representation is the 'appropriate internal counterpart' of language. Bruner says:

> '. . . symbolic activity stems from some primitive or proto-symbolic system that is species-specific to man. This system becomes specialized in expression in various domains of the life of a human being: in language, in tool-using, in various atemporally organized and skilled forms of serial behaviour, and in the organization of behaviour itself. We have suggested some minimum properties of such a symbolic system: categoriality, hierarchy, predication, causation, and modification.' (Bruner *et al.*, 1966).

We shall not discuss these properties here. Like Piaget, Bruner sees language as developing somewhat independently of 'thought'. Language becomes available to the child before it can be fully put to use: syntax develops more rapidly than semantics. That is to say that a child's language embodies complex abstract rules earlier than does his thinking.

> 'One is thus led to believe that, in order for the child to use language as an instrument of thought, he must first bring the world of experience under the control of principles of organization that are in some degree isomorphic with the structural principles of syntax.'

And this, for Bruner, is where the role of culture is all-important.

> 'Without special training in the symbolic representation of experience, the child grows to adulthood still depending in large measure on the enactive and ikonic modes of representing and organizing the world, no matter what language he speaks.'

(Bruner's theory of cognitive development is discussed in full in *Development and Culture*).

CULTURAL RELATIVISM

This matter of training we must leave for the moment. Bruner's theory raises another long-standing issue in the relationship of language and thought: the linguistic relativity view, sometimes expressed as the *Whorfian hypothesis*. Benjamin Lee Whorf, an expert on American Indian languages, was impressed by their differences, both from each other and especially from English, and felt that these had much to do with how the world was seen.

> 'The background linguistic system (in other words, the grammar) of each language is not merely a reproducing instrument for voicing ideas but rather is itself the shaper of ideas, the program and guide for the individual's mental activity, for his analysis of impressions, for his synthesis of his mental stock in trade. Formulation of ideas is not an independent process, strictly rational in the old sense, but is part of a particular grammar and differs, from slightly to greatly, as between different languages. The categories and types that we isolate from the world of phenomena we do not find there because they stare every observer in the face; on the contrary, the world is presented in a kaleidoscopic flux of impressions which has to be organized by our minds. We cut nature up, organize it into concepts, and ascribe significances as we do, largely because we are parties to an agreement to organize it in this way—an agreement that holds through our speech community and is codified in the patterns of our language. The agreement is, of course, an implicit and unstated one, BUT ITS TERMS ARE ABSOLUTELY OBLIGATORY; we cannot talk at all except by subscribing to the organization and classification of data which the agreement decrees.' (*Language, Thought, and Reality*, 1956.)

Now this, as it stands, is simply an assertion. Or rather, it is several assertions. One is that the world presents a 'flux of impressions which has to be organized by our minds.' We have met this view in Bruner's work on concepts, and we shall see elsewhere how he has developed it into the notion of a 'constructed' model of reality'. The view in its extreme form seems to me implausible. For one thing, the world does come organized into discrete units like trees, houses, and people. It is true that children have to learn names for these, and to learn which objects go together. But it seems most unlikely that the youngest child would take a tree for a man. The work of Gibson and Walk, Fantz and others (see *Imagery*) suggests the early possession of perceptions which are more than mere reception of sense data. A similar argument applies to animals lacking speech. However, it is probably more reasonable to think of the process not so much as an either–or issue, but in somewhat Piagetian terms as one in which there is always some structure, from which more complex structures evolve through interaction with the environment. Another point, however, is that there is a difference between saying that we have to *learn* what categories exist, and saying that there are no categories to learn. It may well be true that at early stages of development, both ontogenetic and phylogenetic, organisms respond to discrete stimuli, or classes of stimuli (a 'kaleidoscopic flux'): but that does not mean that there is no real set of categories into which these stimuli resolve themselves. Indeed one might argue that cognitive development involves precisely this higher-order perception of reality. A second assertion of the Whorfian hypothesis is that it is largely language that gives us the *means* of ordering the environment. And a third, implicit, assertion is that languages (which manifestly possess different vocabularies and grammars) cause us to order the environment in differing ways. Now the second assertion seems in one sense incontrovertible: obviously language is used, by all who possess it, to talk about the world. It is another matter to suggest, however, that we could not *think* about the world without language. Piaget, as we have seen, denies this: and his view seems more acceptable, for reasons which will appear. The third assertion is the linguistic relativity hypothesis proper. It has been an attractive hypothesis: it seems to have the same sort of attraction as Freudian defence mechanisms once had—'You're only saying that because. . .'. The collection of cultural curiosities is fascinating, particularly when they appear to be explanatory. Let us quote some of the well-known examples. There are first of all cases where one language has a wider or more detailed vocabularly for some set of phenomena than another. English is an example, having a vocabulary derived (mainly) from both Germanic and Romance sources: English frequently has two words where French, for instance, has only one—*fatherly* and *paternal*. In general, this multiple vocabulary is used to convey distinctions of meaning, often subtle ones. It has been remarked that if Shakespeare had thought that 'Making the green one red' meant the same as 'The multitudinous seas incarnadine,' he would not have written the one line directly after the other. More striking, perhaps, are the Eskimo words for three varieties of snow, or the Hanunoo (Philippine Islands) ninety-two words for different varieties of rice (Brown, 1965). Then there are cases where one language classifies a set of phenomena differently from another. A good example here is the colour spectrum, as shown by Figure 7.1 below, from Brown (1965).

These differences are fascinating, and it is easy to imagine that they imply a difference in perception and thinking. It is more difficult to obtain any very convincing proof. Roger Brown (1965) says:

> 'A Hanunoo boy, if he is going to name correctly ninety-two kinds of rice, must be able to conceive of the ninety-two, and a Bassa boy, if he is to use *hui* and *ziza* correctly, must think of purple plus blue plus green as similar but distinct from orange plus red.'

But this is unconvincing. It is not clear what Brown means by 'conceive of' (or Whorf for that matter, who also uses the expression); all the Hanunoo boy has to do is discriminate the varieties. It is true he may have to learn to notice the discriminatory features. Then again, it is not very surprising if purple, blue and green are thought of as similar: they *are* similar. It would indeed be odd if blue and orange were grouped together as distinct from purple, yellow, and red. Brown and Lenneberg (1954); and Lenneberg and Roberts (1956) sought support

English

purple	blue	green	yellow	orange	red

Shona

cips uka	citema	cicena	cips uka

Bossa

hui	ziza

Figure 7.1. Lexical mappings of the colour spectrum in three languages (Reprinted with permission of Macmillan Publishing Co., Inc., from *Social Psychology* by Roger Brown. Copyright 1965 by the Free Press)

for the linguistic relativity hypothesis by comparing English and Zuni (an American Indian language). They found a correlation between ease of naming colours and ease of remembering the same colour. (See also Lantz and Stefflre, 1964.) But it is usual to find that memory is aided by attaching labels to the stimuli; this does not necessarily mean that the latter are thought about, or even perceived, differently. (This question might be resolved if we knew whether or not subjects *did* label the colours verbally to themselves). Of course even if that could be shown, it would still be a question as to whether the language caused the thought, or vice versa: for where did the Eskimo get his words for snow? Even without a close analysis of the Piagetian type, common sense suggests a two-way interaction.

A rather more sophisticated account is presented by Greenfield, Reich and Olver (1966; See Bruner *et al.*, *Studies in Cognitive Growth*). This was part of an extensive programme in which children from widely differing cultures were compared: Mexican, Eskimo, Wolof (Senegal), and North American white (Massachusetts). In some of these experiments, children were asked to say how different objects were alike or different: that is, to classify them. A child would be shown two everyday objects or pictures, and asked how they were alike; then how a third was different from the pair; then how all three were alike; and so on, up to eight objects. Other procedures included asking the child to pick out a pair that was most alike. The children differed not only in respect of their languages, but in each culture, some of the children had had formal, that is more or less Westernized, schooling, others not. Interest centres on the choice of attributes for classification, the possible causative role of language. One can see this as a development of the work of Bruner, Goodnow, and Austin (1956; see *Concept Identification*). Greenfield *et al.* distinguish three ways in which language might affect classification. There is first the question of vocabulary, or lexical richness. Wolof and French, for example, differ in the availability of colour terms. Classification by colour is a relatively unsophisticated choice of attribute: a more sophisticated one is classification by function. Despite the superiority of

French in colour terms, however, colour matching was found more often among the children who spoke only Wolof. However, the latter did make rather more mistakes in colour matching, presumably because the language supplies a less precise tool for making discriminations. The second possible role for language concerns lexical *structure*, particularly the availability of superordinate words. Wolof contains no general word for 'colour', for instance. This, Greenfield *et al.* conclude, is most important: for classification essentially involves superordinate words, which are necessary to conceive of hierarchies. Clearly 'colour' is a more general concept than 'yellow'. The possession of the general word enables the child to extend his range of classification: to see that yellow and green are simply examples of one 'domain' of classification, namely colour; and that therefore other domains, such as function, are possible. The third point concerns grammatical structure or syntax Greenfield *et al.* distinguish three grammatical forms used in responding to the classifying task, viz. (1) pointing; (2) labelling (or naming); (3) complete sentence. The last is the most sophisticated. Knowledge of the second language (French) is clearly associated with the more sophisticated grammatical forms; but this association is not simple, being confounded by the effects of schooling. It is argued that 'the school is acting on grouping operations through the training embodied in the written language'.

In fact, the general conclusions of Greenfield *et al.* are not in terms of one language versus another. Rather, there is a difference in mode of thinking between 'modern urban and traditional rural' cultural backgrounds. This difference 'is most compactly described as a difference between abstractness and concreteness'. The difference appears to be most striking when children have or have not been to school. 'Schooling appears to be the single most powerful factor we have found in the stimulation of abstraction.' Greenfield *et al.* reject the Whorfian hypothesis in any simple form. Language is important: but different cultural contents demand different uses of language, and it is this that is important. The point is expressed thus:

> 'We believe that the difference between the city child and the rural child derives from a differential exposure to problem solving and communication in situations that are not supported by context—as is the case with, for example, most reading and writing, the use of monetary exchange, and schooling. . . . Where there is difference is in how language is used and what opportunities are provided for different uses. Here again, school is important. For it is the school children who have the greater opportunity to practice language in contexts that do not carry the meaning for them automatically, who are forced thereby to use sentences to the full. They are the ones who, moreover, are led by the nature of school lessons to translate their experience and actions into words and sentences that will satisfy a teacher—and thereby learn to reorganize experience and action to conform to the requirements of language.'

These conclusions should be compared with these of P. E. Vernon, discussed under *Intellectual Abilities;* and with the work of Basil Bernstein, to be mentioned shortly. In general, the linguistic relativity hypothesis cannot be supported in any simple or extreme form. This is not to deny that differences between languages *could* have some effect on the way we think. George Orwell, in *1984* envisaged a language, Newspeak, specifically designed and imposed by an omnipotent dictatorship with the function of restricting thought. H. D. F. Kitto, is only one of many writers to suggest that the revolutionary power and scope of Greek thought of the classical period was closely related to the peculiar qualities of the Greek language. The current view of known languages, however, emphasizes their similarities rather than their differences. This view is associated with the 'structural' approach in linguistics and particularly with the name of Noam Chomsky. We do not propose to go into linguistic questions, but shall quote one authority.

'Linguistics provides no support for those who believe that there is a fundamental difference between "civilized" and "primitive" languages. The vocabulary of a language will, of course, reflect the characteristic pursuits and interests of the society which uses it. One of the major world languages, like English, French or Russian, will have a large number of words relating to modern science and technology which will have no equivalent in the language of some "underdeveloped" people. Conversely, however, there will be many words in the language of let us say, some remote and backward tribe in New Guinea or South America which cannot be translated satisfactorily into English, French or Russian, because they are words which refer to objects, flora, fauna or customs unfamiliar in Western culture. The vocabulary of one language cannot be described as richer or poorer than the vocabulary of some other language in any absolute sense; every language has a sufficiently rich vocabulary for the expression of all the distinctions that are important in the society using it. We cannot therefore say, from this point of view, that one language is more "primitive" or more "advanced" than another. The point is even clearer with respect to the grammatical structure of languages. Differences there are between any particular "primitive" language and any particular "civilized" language. But these are no greater on the average than the differences between any random pair of "primitive" languages and any random pair of "civilized" languages. So-called "primitive" languages are no less systematic, and are neither structurally simpler nor structurally more complex, than are the languages spoken by more "civilized" peoples. This is an important point. All human societies of which we have knowledge speak languages of roughly equal complexity; and the differences of grammatical structure that we do find between languages throughout the world are such that they cannot be correlated with the cultural development of the people speaking them . . .' (Lyons, J., *Chomsky*, Fontana, 1970)

To be fair to Whorf, he did not suppose that some languages were inferior to others. Granted, however, that all languages are in important senses roughly equivalent, many cases can still arise in which language experience varies substantially as between individuals even within a given culture: and to some of these we now turn.

LANGUAGE DEPRIVATION

It is not quite easy to know where to place the work of Basil Bernstein. A long series of papers from 1958 on represents variations on a theme. But the theme itself seems gradually to have changed. Bernstein was originally impressed by the availability of different 'languages' in different social classes. His first formulation was in terms of a 'public' language, available to all classes, contrasted with a 'formal' language, available only to the more favoured socioeconomic classes. The characteristics of the public language included the following:

Short, grammatically simple, often unfinished sentences, a poor syntactical construction with a verbal form stressing the active voice. Simple and repetitive use of conjunctions (so, then, and, because). Frequent use of short commands and questions. Rigid and limited use of adjectives and verbs. Infrequent use of impersonal pronouns as subjects (one, it). Statements formulated as implicit questions which set up a sympathetic circularity, e.g. 'Just fancy?' 'It's only natural isn't it?' A statement of fact is often used as both a reason and a conclusion or more accurately, the reason and conclusion are confounded to produce a categoric statement, e.g. 'Do as I tell you,' 'Hold on tight,' 'You're not going out,' 'Lay off that.' Individual selection from a group of idiomatic phrases will frequently be found. Symbolism is of a low order of generality. The individual qualification is implicit in the sentence structure, therefore it is a language of implicit meaning.

The characteristics of a formal language can be inferred as more or less the opposite of these. In more recent writings, the terms *restricted* and *elaborated* codes are used. But the concept has become more intricate. Bernstein states, for example:

'...restricted codes have their basis in condensed symbols, whereas elaborated codes have their basis in articulated symbols...restricted codes draw upon metaphor whereas elaborated codes draw upon rationality.' (Bernstein, 1971)

Another statement is this:

'...the forms of an elaborated code give access to *universalistic* orders of meaning in the sense that the principles and operations controlling object and person relationships are made explicit through the use of language, whereas restricted codes give access to *particularistic* orders of meaning in which the principles and operations controlling object and person relationships are rendered implicit through the use of language...we can say that elaborated codes give access to universalistic orders of meaning, which are less context bound, that is, tied to a particular context.' (Bernstein and Henderson, 1969)

Bernstein quotes in several places the following illustration.

'Consider, for example, the two following stories which Peter Hawkins, of the Sociological Research Unit, constructed as a result of his analysis of the speech of middle-class and working-class five-year-old children. The children were given a series of four pictures which told a story, and were then invited to tell the story. The first picture showed some boys playing football; in the second the ball goes through the window of a house; the third shows a man making a threatening gesture; in the fourth the children are moving away. Here are the two stories:

> Three boys are playing football and one boy kicks the ball and it goes through the window   the ball breaks the window   and the boys are looking at it and a man comes and shouts at them   because they've broken the window   so they run away and then that lady looks out of her window   and she tells the boys off   (13 nouns, 6 pronouns).

> They're playing football   and he kicks it and it goes through there   it breaks the window and they're looking at it and he comes out   and shouts at them because they've broken it   so they run away   and then she looks out and tells them off (2 nouns, 14 pronouns).

With the first story, the middle-class one, the reader does not have to have the four pictures which were used as the basis for the story, whereas in the case of the second story the reader would require the initial pictures in order to make sense of the story. The first story is free of the context which generated it, whereas the second story is much more closely tied to its context. As a result the meanings of the second story are implicit.' (Bernstein and Henderson, 1969)

The impression we gain is so far indistinguishable from that of Piaget's egocentric speech, which has moreover the support of very numerous verbatim, rather than constructed examples. It is, however, worthwhile to pursue Bernstein's ideas a little further.

> 'It is not that the working-class children do not have, in their passive vocabulary, the vocabulary used by the middle-class children. Nor is it the case that the children differ in their tacit understanding of the linguistic rule system. Rather what we have here are differences in language arising out of a specific context. The first child takes very little for granted, whereas the second child takes a great deal for granted. Thus for the first child the task was seen as a context in which his meanings were required to be made explicit, whereas the task for the second child was not seen as a task which required such explication of meaning. It would not be difficult to imagine a context where the child would produce speech rather like the second.' (Bernstein and Henderson, 1969)

Here again we meet a familiar theme. We may compare Hudson's experiments in which apparent 'convergers' produced divergent responses in certain contexts; the reported rise in IQ scores of children expected to improve (Rosenthal); the testing of intelligence in cultures where the task seems meaningless (Vernon); and even, perhaps, the better intelligence scores obtained by elderly people when highly motivated (reported in Bromley, D. G.: *The Psychology of*

Ageing, 1966). In most of these cases, however, we are asked to accept experimental results rather than simply 'imagine' a different context.

Bernstein then goes on to discuss the particular contexts involved, arguing (of course) that lower-class homes demand the less abstract code.

> 'Mothers in the middle class—and it is important to add not all—relative to the working class (and again it is important to add not all by any means), place greater emphasis upon the use of language in socializing the child into the moral order, in disciplining the child, in the communication and recognition of feeling. Here again we can say that the child here is oriented towards universalistic meanings which transcend a given context, whereas the second child is oriented towards particularistic meanings which are closely tied to a given context and so do not transcend it.' (Bernstein and Henderson, 1969)

This quotation illustrates what I feel to be the main puzzle in Bernstein's work as it stands at present. Nowhere does it seem to be made clear just what is the relationship of language-to-socialization-to-thought. Since Bernstein repeatedly stresses that it is merely the *use* of language, not its availability, that is different, it is not clear how thinking is affected. If what Bernstein is saying is that different contexts demand (and produce) variations in behaviour, then language as such becomes unimportant: it is simply what verbal communications in one context are of one type, and in another of another. Indeed, it is commonly noted that students from working-class backgrounds quickly adopt the appropriate forms when they move into the University context. Bernstein himself suggests that 'symbolic orders other than language' might be considered in the same way. I thus feel that, interesting and suggestive as it is, Bernstein's work helps little to resolve the language–thought issue.

Labov (1970), presents a criticism of many of the reports apparently showing deficit of different sorts, including language, in differing cultural contexts. His main argument is that the actual investigations have not been culture-fair. They have been such that the subject from an economically deprived, or technologically undeveloped, background, is likely, through unfamiliarity, or fear, or other factors to be handicapped. Conversely, Labov argues, situations *can* be found in which such subjects can be perfectly competent. Cole and Bruner (1971) discussing this, feel that Labov goes too far. Their main point, however, is surely acceptable:

> 'The problem is to identify the range of capacities manifested in different groups and then to inquire whether the range is adequate to the individual's needs in various cultural settings. From this point of view, cultural deprivation represents a special case of cultural difference that arises when an individual is faced with demands to perform in a manner inconsistent with his past (cultural) experience. In the present social context of the United States, the greater power of the middle class has rendered differences into deficits because middle-class behavior is the yardstick of success.'

We may gain more information from looking at cases of actual deprivation of language experience. The few examples of 'feral' children (literally brought up by, or like, wild animals) would be logically appropriate; but the reports are highly uncontrolled, and it is never clear what abilities such children might have possessed in more normal circumstances. (For a review of such cases see Malson, 1972). A much better sample is provided by deaf children. Deafness has sometimes been referred to as 'intellectual starvation.' Deafness, when present from an early age, prevents a child having experience of spoken language, and normally prevents (or has in the past prevented) the child, in consequence, from acquiring verbal language until considerably later than other children, if at all. The traditional 'deaf-and-dumb' person was usually a language-deprived person, dumbness as a physical deficit being extremely rare. The effects of deafness on various sorts of intellectual test score have been the subject of much investigation. Hans G. Furth (1964) summarized the available results. He selected those studies which had used 'non-verbal' tests; though in practice, of course, this distinction is a loose one. They covered the following categories:

1. Conceptual (abstract): concept attainment; concept transfer
2. Conceptual (concrete): sorting; knowledge of classes; Piaget-type tasks; 'practical intelligence'
3. Memory
4. Visual perception.

The results of over forty studies were in nearly every case conflicting. On some intellectual tasks deaf persons were equal to hearing norms, on others they were inferior. The existence of the first set argues that in many respects the cognitive development of deaf persons is not impeded. Where the deaf did less well, a number of points need to be considered. It is harder to establish good rapport and communication when testing deaf children, for obvious reasons. A deaf population may include a greater proportion of psychologically or mentally abnormal or brain-damaged individuals than normal. Deaf children tend to be isolated and neglected; they receive less social reinforcement and may be less motivated than those who can hear (and speak fluently). Furth therefore concludes:

'(a) Language does not influence intellectual development in any direct, general, or decisive way. (b) The influence of language may be indirect or specific and may accelerate intellectual development, by providing the opportunity for additional experience through giving information and exchange of ideas and by furnishing ready symbols (words) and linguistic habits in specific situations.'

In a later review, Furth (1971) comes to even more equivocal conclusions.

One specific situation in which some children find themselves is that of being a twin. Twins have provided a natural experimental situation in which many psychological variables have been investigated, and these include language.

Twins, whether identical or not, if brought up together tend to spend more time in their own company and less in that of adults or other children, and there is evidence that this often is accompanied by retardation in language. The most famous study is that of Luria and Yudovich (1959). They examined in great detail a pair of five-year-old twins, Yura and Liosha G. They were uniovular twins, the last children of a large family, the family as a whole having a history of late speech development.

'The twins did not speak at all up to the age of two years; at the age of two and a half they had only learned to say "mama" and "papa"; at four years their speech consisted only in a small number of barely differentiated sounds which they used in play and communication. At this stage their mother was unable to note any stable words applied to any object or action. At the age of five the twins' speech consisted of a small number of customary words (often very distorted) and a few "autonomous" words and sounds; the words of common speech were used mainly in communication with adults and mostly in the form of replies to questions. In communication with each other the twins' speech consisted of sounds and separate words, inextricably connected with direct actions and accompanied by lively gesticulation. Their speech activity as a whole was very small and often during half an hour of play they pronounced only a few words and sounds. Usually this 'autonomous' speech was inhibited or ceased on the appearance of an adult and only when the observer was not noticed was it possible to hear during their play such sounds as "aga", "ni", "utsa", "en", "a", "bul-bul" etc. On an equal footing with these was repetition of their own names "Liosia" (Liosha) and "Liulia" (Yura). Sometimes general sounds were heard imitating the words of "autonomous" speech; "pi-pi" for chicken, "kua" for frog, etc. A small stock of normal words comprised names of domestic objects, parts of the body, a few animals and birds and elementary actions. The twins' speech was phonetically impaired, many sounds were not pronounced at all, many that should have been voiced were pronounced as softened.'

In terms of Luria's analysis of the role of speech, this meant of course that the twins had not acquired the 'sound signal system', and consequently were unable to advance intellectually.

'To this primitive speech, interlocked with action, there corresponded a peculiar, insufficiently differentiated, structure of consciousness; as has been shown, the twins were unable to detach the word from action, to master orienting, planning activity, to formulate the aims of activity with the aid of speech and so to subordinate their further activity to this verbal formulation. Therefore, even at the age of five to five and a half years our twins could not master skills nor organize complex play of a kind proper to children of this age, and were unable to engage in productive, meaningful activity. Their intellectual operations thus remained very limited; even such operations as elementary classifications were beyond them.'

At this point the twins were separated. Shortly afterwards, the more retarded of the two (Yura) was given a special programme of speech training. The speech

270

of both rapidly improved, that of Yura doing so faster. This was accompanied by intellectual development of the kind hitherto lacking. This report is chiefly of interest for the detailed account of the twins actual speech, their play activity and other behaviour. As an experiment, as Mittler (1971) points out, it is rather unfortunate that two variables, namely separation and training, were both introduced, since it is not clear which contributed most to the improvement. As evidence for the Russian view of the relationship of language to thought, the report is illustrative rather than conclusive. It may well be that the language deficit was accompanied by cognitive peculiarities, and that these disappeared together. But correlation, while suggestive of causality, does not prove it. Both effects may have been the result of lack of social contact or some other factor. This is one of the commonest difficulties in psychology. (Compare the reported effects of family conditions on intelligence, and McClelland's cultural theory of achievement motivation: see *Creative Thinking*). As we have seen, we owe to Francis Galton the notion of correlation. The importance of this major innovation lies not only in allowing us to consider *partial* causation; but in enabling us to report the extent to which two (or more) phenomena tend to go together, without necessarily making an inference of causality at all. Thus a more objective consideration becomes possible.

Herriot (1970) tells us despairingly: 'it must be stated that the present condition of the field of language and thinking is utterly confused.' Possibly it is not quite so bad. Returning to the questions posed by Jenkins, his conclusion is that all three answers are correct, viz. thought is dependent on language; thought is language; language is dependent on thought. This is really little more than a form of words, for as we must stress again, it depends on what you mean. It is not just that the two words refer, in common usage, to different phenomena. It is difficult to think of any acceptable sense in which language and thought could be considered synonymous. It is rather that it seems more useful to use the words to refer to different *sorts* of things. We use thought here to mean roughly 'information processing', and language to mean a particular system of communication. That being so, it will appear rather obvious that the latter will interact with some aspects, though not all, of the former. Some of the ways in which this can happen have been discussed. Neither our discussion, nor the published work available, is anything like exhaustive. But further, more detailed studies of interaction may well prove more fruitful than attempts to answer the questions posed by Jenkins.

THE MAGICAL POWER OF WORDS

Let us indulge, before leaving the question of language and thought, in collecting a few speculations about one aspect of words. As is well known, words often play an important part in magical rituals. Knowing the correct word often has magical significance. It was the custom of Aleister Crowley—or his duty, as he preferred to put it—to obtain at each equinox a Word which should foretell the character of the ensuing six months. His own personal Word, the essence of the doctrine he believed it his mission to proclaim, was *Thelema*—will. In some systems of magic (or 'Magick', if we stay with Crowley for a moment) significance is attached to obtaining the real name of a person. To do so is equivalent to gaining power over them. This theme is familiar to us from folk-lore. The wide-spread story of Tom Tit Tot, in which control is gained over a strange or supernatural being by learning his unusual name, is an example. The story may be better recognized by some under its German variant of Rumpelstiltskin. Indeed the word 'spell' itself originally meant 'word'. The gospel is God's word, partly at least the word with which in the beginning order was created out of chaos. The somewhat mystical notion of the magical power of words for which J. G. Frazer was largely responsible has been criticized by modern anthropologists. S. J. Tambiah (1968) for example, has this to say.

'... it is possible to argue that all ritual, whatever the idiom, is addressed to the human participants and uses a technique which attempts to re-structure and integrate the minds and emotions of the actors. The technique combines verbal and non-verbal behaviour and exploits their special properties. Language is an artificial construct and its strength is that its form owes nothing to external reality: it thus enjoys the power to invoke images and comparisons, refer to time past and future and relate events which cannot be represented in action. Non-verbal action on the other hand excels in what words cannot easily do—it can codify analogically by imitating real events, reproduce technical acts and express multiple implications simultaneously. Words excel in expressive enlargement, physical actions in realistic presentation.'

Tambiah seems almost to be classing together what several psychologists have been at pains to separate, namely visual or imagery representation and verbal or symbolic representation; contrasting the two with representation by action (enactive, in Bruner's phrase). Language as such, Tambiah is arguing, is not especially suited to magical ritual any more than to any other area which requires this mode of representation. This, however, does not entirely match up, as we have noted, with traditional lore or the customs of practising magicians. It is true that specific words have seemed to some people and in some contexts, at least, to have magical significance. Why should this be so? We can readily speculate that such an experience has its roots in infancy. Whatever the relationship of language to thought, it would seem clearly to be linked to awareness. Awareness and consciousness, refer to rather ill-defined phenomena. Eriksen (1960) more or less equates awareness with verbalization. This seems implausible. For one thing, it does not seem sensible to deny awareness to deaf persons lacking language. For another, the arguments of Piaget and Bruner, to the effect that language is only one variety (though the most flexible and powerful) of symbolic representation, seem convincing. For a third, verbalization seems a more discreet phenomenon than awareness. Awareness would seem to be a matter of a threshold, arbitrarily defined as a point on a continuum. Nevertheless, for a child, language does provide, it may be argued, one of the most important ways of becoming aware of himself, and of distinguishing between himself and different aspects of the environment. This usually occurs at an age (about two years) when the child is too young to give any accurate report of the experience. We might compare, however, the dramatic account of Helen Keller. The passage is famous, but bears repetition for its human quality apart from any scientific value.

> 'She (her teacher) brought me my hat and I knew I was going out into the warm sunshine. This thought, if a wordless sensation may be called a thought, made me hop and skip with pleasure.
>
> We walked down the path to the well house, attracted by the fragrance of the honeysuckle with which it is covered. Someone was drawing water and my teacher placed my hand under the spout. As the cool stream gushed over my hand she spelled into the other the word *water*, first slowly, then rapidly. I stood still, my whole attention fixed upon the motion of her fingers. Suddenly I felt a misty consciousness as of something forgotten ... and somehow the mystery of language was revealed to me. I knew then that w-a-t-e-r meant the wonderful cool something that was flowing over my hand. That living word awakened my soul, and gave it light, hope, joy, set it free! There were barriers still, it is true, but barriers that in time could be swept away.
>
> I left the well house eager to learn. Everything had a name, and each name gave birth to a new thought. As we returned to the house every object which I touched seemed to quiver with life. That was because I saw everything with the strange new sight that had come to me.' (Helen Keller, *The Story of My Life*. Doubleday, New York, 1936)

Now this is of course the account of one individual, and a most remarkable one at that. Her handicap itself makes her untypical. But it is not absurd to suppose something of the same experience happening to every child. There is, besides, a more mundane aspect. Learning the names of things does actually give the child some power over them: he can ask for what he wants. The long infancy of humans increases the importance of dealing with the environment symbolically. To a child it may indeed seem almost magical when a word brings about specific satisfaction. Take pain. The experience is perhaps common of waking up with a vague general distress which, as consciousness returns, focuses itself down to a specific toothache (say). One may formulate this in words: the relatively helpless child certainly needs words to convey the source of the pain. We might incidentally note that one of Aleister Crowley's precepts was to the effect that one shall make no distinction between any one thing and any other thing. Mystics commonly stress some state of 'oneness' as their goal, a state which, besides, defies precise verbal formulation. One may suggest that such experiences are in some respects analogous to those of the preverbal child.

The theories of developmental psychologists, as we have seen, do stress the importance of the emergence of speech. 'In the beginning was the deed,' Freud concluded at the end of *Totem and Taboo* (1919) (see also Peller, 1966). Piaget with the sensorimotor period might be said to have taken Freud's words as his text. Bruner makes enactive representation the first mode to emerge. The experiments of Luria illustrate the early dominance of action, controlled by the first signal system. Eventually in all these cases, language becomes the means, or a vital component of the means, whereby the environment can be handled abstractly, and the organism thereby becomes free of stimulus control. Obviously one does not want to suggest that these different writers are actually saying exactly the same things. We need to consider too, the stimulus–response approach as exemplified, for instance, by the work of the Kendlers (see *Concept Identification*). One of the differences that emerge is that some writers seem to conceive of two stages or aspects, others of three. And of course even where the number of categories is the same, we cannot assume that these are necessarily equivalent. We can suggest possibilities, however, by a table of examples. In this table, 'sensory' is preferred to 'visual' or to Bruner's 'ikonic', or to 'imagery'. The visual mode just happens to be the sense most dramatically developed in human beings. Imagery as a subjective phenomenon is regarded as the conscious awareness of 'sensory' representation. People with little or no subjective imagery will, it is assumed, still possess this means of processing information. *Ikonic* suggests vision and is used by other writers in different senses. Somewhat similarly, and following Piaget and Bruner, language is regarded as one case (though the most important) of symbolic representation. The following pattern emerges in Table 7.1 below.

The relative neatness of such arrangements is deceptive. It would, for example, be a mistake to equate consciousness, secondary processes, and language. At

Table 7.1—*A comparison of the stages of development envisaged by various theorists*

	Motor	Sensory (imagery)	Symbolic (language)
Luria	First signal system		Second signal system
Freud	Primary processes		Secondary processes
Bruner	Enactive	Ikonic	Symbolic
Piaget	Sensorimotor thought		
		Concrete operations	
			Formal operations
Tambiah	Action	?	Language
S–R approach, Kendlers	Lack of verbal mediation		Verbal mediation
Neisser	Multiple processing		Sequential processing
Vigotsky		Inner speech?	External speech

least, however, language would seem to be closely involved with the thought processes that impress us as distinctly human. Language thus tends to mark the boundary between non-human and human: and for this reason has gathered round itself a magical aura. It is worth noting that language is, after all, the medium of psychotherapy. In psychoanalysis this is made explicit: the basic technique is, of course, for the patient to say whatever comes to his mind. The importance of this is not merely that it is a way of allowing free expression to supposedly repressed thoughts and feelings: it is that the act of verbalizing, of making conscious of bringing under the control of the second signal system, is itself therapeutic. Indeed it is itself the 'cure'. We are well aware that psychoanalysis is often criticized as unproved and indeed untestable. For many centuries, however, it has been held that confession is good for the soul. I recall a conversation with Professor Joseph Wolpe on the latter's technique of progressive desensitization through imagination. Asked what was the difference between this and psychoanalysis, he replied that he supposed that the analysand 'learned the jargon'. Actually, of course, interpretations are usually offered in non-technical language; but maybe the learning of any language is the significant point.

FOCUS: VERBAL MEDIATION

When a cockney says that he has just done six months *bird*, the initiated will know that he has been in prison for six months, that he has 'done time'. The connection is one of the many examples of rhyming slang which demonstrate very crudely what is meant by verbal mediation. Bird, bird-lime, lime–time: thus *bird = time*. The link word providing the clue, as it were, to the association, is omitted although it must have played an essential role in its original development.

Mediation is an old construct in experimental Psychology—Hull (1930) is said to have been the first to make use of it when he referred to certain types of response as 'pure stimulus acts', viz. responses which have mainly a stimulus function in that they trigger off other responses which may themselves have the same function. In trying to recall a tune or poem, for example, it is a common experience to be able to do so successfully only by reciting the whole thing from the very beginning. Each line, each verse etc., serves as a cue for the next. In classical behaviour theory of course, mediating responses ('r's') are any events which link The Stimulus to The Response, themselves overt phenomena and, by implication, the important things in life. There is no doubt that the construct of mediation falls squarely in the Behaviourist camp. And as Garrett and Fodor (1968) have argued, '... there is a commitment on the part of mediation theorists to the canons of general S–R theory.'

Mediating responses are often said to be verbal, hence our topic for discussion —verbal mediation. It must be pointed out first that 'verbal mediation' means much more than the implicit and deliberate use of language in thinking. While we shall discuss these more general aspects, in fact mechanisms of verbal mediation in Behaviour theory are more narrowly defined and have been developed usually in the context of particular experimental paradigms as the investigation of Russell and Storms (1955) demonstrates. They reasoned that since for instance 'sailor' is a very common associate of 'soldier', and 'navy' of 'sailor', any response (in their experiment the nonsense syllable 'ZUG') which is associated with 'soldier' will become linked with 'sailor' and thus subsequently with 'navy' (soldier–sailor–navy). In their study, one group of subjects learned two lists of paired associate items. List 1 contained items such as ZUG-soldier while List 2 consisted of specially selected pairs such as ZUG-navy. And there was a significant difference between this experimental group as regards the learning of the second list, and a control group who did not learn the first list. The implication, therefore, is that learning ZUG-soldier facilitated the learning of ZUG-navy by producing the association 'sailor', which acted as a mediator between 'soldier' and 'navy'. The word 'sailor' itself of course was never mentioned and is usually taken to have occurred implicitly in response to the word 'soldier'. Note also that 'navy' is not commonly associated with 'soldier' according to the Russell and Jenkins (1954) word association norms.

This experiment exemplifies only one of the many mediational paradigms which have been explored over the years in numerous studies of verbal learning. We will take one more example, this time one which might be said to illustrate rather more dramatically the operation of verbal mediating processes. Glucksberg and King (1967) report the results of a study of 'mediated repression' in which subjects had first of all to learn the list of paired associate items (A–B) as set out below in Table 7.2.

Table 7.2—Material used by Glucksberg and King (1967). (From S. Glucksberg and L. J. King, 'Motivated forgetting mediated by implicit verbal chaining: a laboratory analog of repression,' Science, 1967, **158***, 517–519. Copyright 1967 by the American Association for the Advancement of Science.)*

A	B	A	D
CEF	stem	CEF	smell
DAX	memory	DAX	brain
YOV	soldier	YOV	navy
VUX	trouble	VUX	good
WUB	wish	WUB	need
GEX	justice	GEX	war
JID	thief	JID	take
ZIL	ocean	ZIL	drink
LAJ	command	LAJ	disorder
MYV	fruit	MYV	tree

List A–D was then presented and the subject was told that some of the response terms would be accompanied by an electric shock and that he was to anticipate which ones by operating a key in front of him. There were three such 'critical' pairs. It is important to note that the shock was always given even when the subject anticipated correctly. After reaching criterion the A items were again presented and the subject was required to recall the appropriate B items. The results showed that 29 per cent of these were forgotten in cases where A term had been associated with a 'critical' D item, compared with only about 7 per cent of the B terms associated with a neutral A item. Again the inference is that implicit associative processes are involved—the A item 'justice' might elicit 'peace' which itself is an associate of 'war', the D item. (In fact all the pairs of words were selected on this basis.) Working on the assumption that since 'war' is associated with shock it will elicit a conditioned fear response if the word is thought about or occurs again, then since the word 'justice' itself will be capable of eliciting 'war' via the mediation of 'peace', thinking about 'justice' is, by implication, aversive and the word will tend to be repressed.

It must be stressed however that this is really only a hypothesis—while these experiments do demonstrate the need for mediating processes, it is by no means clear exactly what these are nor how and when they occur. As Peter Herriot (1970) points out in his book *An Introduction to the Psychology of Language*, 'an experimental technique does not constitute an explanation.' And Herriot goes on to argue that there are good reasons for doubting the traditional associationist explanations of, for example, the Russell and Storms experiment. To begin with they make the unsatisfactory assumption that people have represented within them a response hierarchy associated with individual words which is aroused when particular words are presented. Thus the learning of ZUG-soldier is thought to generalize to ZUG-navy. Moreover the degree of facilitation does not seem to depend, as it should do, on the position or 'associative strength' of the mediator—or at least there have been no reports that it does. For another thing it is not clear where the effect occurs. The *chaining* theory which we have been considering assumes that mediation occurs during the test phase, that is, during the learning of ZUG-navy in the Russell and Storms experiment. But there is evidence that associations of the soldier–sailor variety are unidirectional—generalization will only occur from the stimulus word to the associate but not *vice versa*. So although 'navy' is a common response to 'sailor' the reverse is not necessarily true, the implication being that mediation occurs in the Russell and Storms paradigm not during the test phase but during the initial training phase—ZUG-soldier.

In similar vein Herriot dismisses Bousfield's (1961) account of semantic generalization. If an unconditioned response such as eyeblink is conditioned to a particular word (which thereby becomes the conditioned stimulus) generalization of the response occurs to words similar in meaning, but not sound. Bousfield's explanation was a mediational one in which it was assumed that any word presented to the subject is repeated implicitly (one might say 'rehearsed') and thus serves as the stimulus to its own associative hierarchy. In consequence all the members of this are also conditioned. Generalization of the conditioned response to other words would also occur if they share associates which are in the hierarchy of the training word. For example, a conditioned response to 'right' will generalize to 'wrong' and also to 'sin' because 'wrong' is a member of the associative hierarchy of 'sin'. A further objection to Bousfield's theory lies in the proposition that all the associates to a particular word are activated whenever that word is presented. This, Herriot argues, probably depends very much on the particular situation and its requirements—to use a vogue phrase, 'the demand characteristics of the experiment.'

One generally associates the concept of mediation with the knotty problem of *meaning*. Although our interests do not lie in this direction it is worth quoting briefly from the final paragraph of Herriot's abrasive chapter on this topic. He writes:

> 'The approach of behaviourists to "meaning" has developed astonishingly in recent years.... However, there has been little effort to show how non-linguistic cues are related to these processes. The writer believes that the connection of non-linguistic cues with language behaviour is of vital importance.' (Herriot, 1970)

These are sentiments we would echo. It is not our intention to underestimate the role of linguistic processes in thinking nor to minimize their importance generally but simply to consider them from the point of view that there are other modes of information processing. Commenting on recent trends in memory research Craik (1971) remarked:

> 'The present tendency seems to be away from mechanistic models... towards a flexible system with a large part played by such *optional* control processes as attention, rehearsal and strategies.' [italics mine.]

This is the view, *mutatis mutandis*, of 'thinking' which we wish to develop. Whatever 'mediation' amounts to it is clear that more than linguistic processes will be involved.

However, we turn now to J. Adams' book *Human Memory (1967)*. Here Adams proposes that an important mechanism in verbal learning is what he calls 'Natural Language Mediation.' Perhaps Adams declares his bias unintentionally in some remarks he makes about PA (paired associate) learning:

> '...a subject will very often *mediate*, or impose implicit verbal response chains between the stimulus and the response.'

Thus in Adams' view, apparently, mediation is by definition, verbal. At any rate the emphasis throughout the book as a whole is on the role played by such mediators in verbal learning, particularly the PA variety. To quote Adams again:

'... suppose the subject was given the pair CAT–RAT to learn. Through his mediational mechanisms he may impose the association that CAT sounds like RAT, that CAT and RAT have two letters in common, or that the CAT is an animal that likes to eat a RAT. When CAT is prevented as a stimulus in a retention test, the mediator and RAT are run off as an integrated response sequence, with the mediator covert and RAT overt.'

Adams is constantly at pains to stress the individual uniqueness and idiosyncratic nature of such associations. In fact it is clear that he wishes to separate completely natural language mediators (NLMs) from the kind of verbal processes we were concerned with earlier. In his own words:

'To identify them as self-imposed mediators from the natural language keeps them separate from mediators which are trained in the laboratory....'

It is clear also that he regards his own approach more productive than the traditional verbal mediation experiment:

'... Montague and Kiess have shown that paradigms of the AB–BC–AC sort vastly oversimplify the mediational behaviour that is actually operating. Over half of their subjects imposed NLMs on the pairs and used them as a supplement or a substitute for the mediators being trained.'

It comes as no surprise that subjects don't always do what they're supposed to do!

However let us consider one important experiment which illustrates Adams' approach to the question of natural language mediation. Adams and Montague (1967) investigated PA learning using the AB–AC–AB paradigm (that is, a design which is generally supposed to demonstrate the *retroactive interference* effect which learning a list of PA items, AC, has upon the retention of a previously learned list, AB). They classified the type of mediation used by subjects on the basis of questionnaire responses. The results are interesting even if they do confirm the obvious—most subjects employed some kind of NLM in learning the word pairs, as opposed to simply learning them rote fashion. The four categories of mediator were as follows in Table 7.3.

Table 7.3—Types of Natural Language Mediation. (*From* Human Memory *by J. A. Adams. Copyright 1967 by McGraw-Hill. Used with permission of McGraw-Hill Book Company.*)

Mediator category	Word pair	A typical mediator
Sentence association	Inshore–victor	I thought of troops landing on a shore
Word association	Retail–wealthy	Money
Sound association	Retail–fatal	The two words sound alike
Letter association	Portly–unearned	P–U

Sentence association was by far the most popular mnemonic device, followed by word, sound and then letter association. In fact rote learning was more frequent than the use of all the other three methods put together. Accuracy of recall is also related to whether or not NLMs are used. 80 per cent of A–B pairs which were originally associated by NLMs were correctly recalled compared with about 60 per cent of rote learned.

Unfortunately Adams' work as a whole contains biases which are, frankly, unacceptable. For instance, reporting a similar study by Montague, Adams and Kiess (1966) he says, 'If there was no NLM reported in acquisition the item was categorized "Rote".' So in effect 'Rote' becomes a sort of dustbin category, one which is defined in terms of the absence of NLM characteristics! By definition non-linguistic mnemonics are ignored and are scored as 'Rote'. Perhaps this is why the reported percentage of rote learned pairs *is* as high as it is—the category is cluttered up with a hotch potch of images, Bewusstseinslagen (See *Thinking as a Private Experience*) and other mnemonic paraphernalia, which do not count as NLMs and which Adams consistently overlooks. There is no point in labouring the issue, but surely to consign the rich diversity of nonverbal strategies and coding devices used in verbal learning to the category 'rote learning' is both misleading and shortsighted.

Although Adams gives us an impoverished account of what goes on in human memory, he is by no means alone in his devotion to mechanisms of verbal/linguistic coding in remembering. The majority of recent work on, for example, short-term memory also lays great emphasis on these operations and some theorists seem to regard them almost as essential for the permanent storage of information. This state of affairs has, of course, been much bemoaned of late by Allan Paivio and his colleagues who have sought to demonstrate the importance of nonverbal mediators in verbal learning, in particular imagery (see *Imagery*). In doing so they have certainly gone a long way towards providing an answer to what Paivio calls 'the classical behaviouristic argument', namely that '. . . imagery is subjective and inferential, words are objective and manageable.' (Paivio, 1969) Perhaps the extreme version of this view is to be found in Watson's proposition that what is unverbalized is, effectively, unconscious. (Watson, 1928)

In some of his perhaps less controversial writings Jensen (1968; 1971) has also concerned himself with the question of verbal mediation in learning and in intellectual development in general. His 1971 paper contains a review of the literature on verbal mediation research in the context of cognitive development. He writes:

'Behaviour theories of mediation based on the acquisition of verbal mediators through S-R associations, on the other hand, offer both a means of explaining mental development and of influencing its course through environmental intervention. Hence the attraction of this approach for those who wish to change behaviour, and particularly for those who seek to improve the intellectual capabilities of disadvantaged children.'

He then discusses the various lines of evidence which show the importance of 'verbalization' in studies of learning, problem solving, etc., and concludes that the only data inconsistent with his view came from studies carried out with deaf children who seem eventually to 'catch up' despite initial intellectual retardation. There are echoes of the 'race-intelligence' debate at this point:

> 'Such findings may lead one to wonder if the cognitive deficit of the disadvantaged can be adequately explained in terms of inadequate verbal stimulation. Verbal stimulation is increased in the school situation and yet the majority of disadvantaged children do not maintain gains in verbal intelligence which permit them to reach the same asymptote as the average level of the general population.' (Jensen, 1971)

Jensen attaches particular importance to 'spontaneous verbalization' which he seems to regard as a reliable guide to intellectual capacity. To quote:

> '... successful performance on intelligence tests, *especially* so-called nonverbal tests, requires spontaneous verbalization on the part of the subject. The subject who does not verbalize spontaneously is even more severely handicapped in a nonverbal test such as Raven's Progressive Matrices than on a predominantly verbal intelligence test such as the Stanford-Binet, which explicitly calls for verbal responses from the subject.' (Jensen, 1968)

In fact spontaneous verbalization is not found in mentally retarded children, and Jensen suggests that it might be generally less likely to occur in children from deprived backgrounds. It is interesting to note that semantic generalization does not occur in the mentally retarded either. (Razran, 1961)

On the whole Jensen's views on verbal learning are similar to Adams'. Both writers stress the importance of sentence type associations in learning—though Jensen restricts this to PA learning, having found *no* facilitation of serial learning with such mediators. And both seem to imply that subjects in verbal learning experiments use either a verbal mediation strategy or nothing at all (or at best some indeterminate form of rote learning). And neither of them shows that verbal/linguistic codes are *necessary* conditions for 'higher order' information processing.

We have deliberately adopted a wide definition of thinking in this section in order to include a great variety of work in verbal learning. (Verbal learning research incidentally is one of the areas selected by Bourne *et al.* in their recent book as an 'example' of thinking: Bourne, Ekstrand and Dominowski, 1971.) But what of the role of verbal processes in the more 'traditional' senses in which 'thinking' is used, such as concept identification and problem solving? There is little to add here to the argument already presented in the discussion of the relative merits of attentional as opposed to mediational models of discrimination learning (see *Concept Identification*). It will be remembered that Kendler and Kendler for example, have consistently maintained that very young children find nonreversal shifts simpler than reversal shifts in discrimination learning because they have not developed the appropriate verbal mediating responses. How far this interpretation is actually required by the reported facts has of course been a matter for much debate. (Incidentally it might be added to what we have already said that André, 1969, has reported that hearing children find reversal shifts no easier to execute than deaf children of comparable ages.) But it must be emphasized, if only to salve our own conscience, that the academic status of the mediational approach to concept learning is still something of a battlefront. There are regular 'official' dispatches (Kendler and Kendler, 1969), news and rumours of war (Keehn, 1969), and the occasional clash or open skirmish (see for example Goulet, 1971, and Kendler and Kendler, 1971), not to say direct frontal assaults (Mackintosh, 1965). In one of the most recent of these 'confrontations' we have seen L. R. Goulet blazing away at the combined forces of H.H. and T.S. in the *Psychological Bulletin*:

'... mediational and nonmediational mechanisms may operate jointly in determining shift performance.' (Goulet, 1971)

The Kendlers however mounted a swift counterattack (not a single page separates the two articles):

'Certainly our interpretation, which obviously needs additional refinement, is not only possible theory that can be proposed. Nor does our emphasis on mediated symbolic responses deny that other processes may be involved; we have only suggested that representational responses are the most important ones, . . .' (Kendler and Kendler, 1971)

And to date, the final shot, perhaps the unkindest cut of all, belongs to them:

'Attending to individual trees can prevent one from seeing the forest.' (Kendler and Kendler, 1971).

As the Kendlers themselves put it, definitely the last word.

When we consider the wider category of problem solving experiments there does not seem to be the same degree of dissent about the importance of verbal processes in such situations. Certainly, from a subjective point of view, being able actually to formulate a problem verbally often seems to go a long way toward solving it. This is reminiscent of Duncker's suggestion that finding a solution to a problem really amounts to restating it in different terms. There are two further points to be made about this. Because of the structure of language, a problem formulated verbally is *sequentially* organized. This means not only can it be understood by others but also that it is in a linear form more suitable for the decision-making processes and action sequences which will, ultimately, be involved. On the other hand, as we have seen, the whole emphasis of Gestalt accounts of the problem solving process is on the perceptual not verbal elements involved. And although part of what is required in *Synectics* involves the operation of verbal processes (see *Creative Thinking*), much is of a nonverbal nature. Finally Rankin's (1963) work seems to suggest that language can either inhibit or facilitate performance in certain problem situations. He presented subjects with a set of black shapes which could be fitted together like a jigsaw to form a single composite vertical column. One group was taught a different animal name for each one (the shapes vaguely resemble the animals in question) while a second group were simply asked to learn as much about the figures as they could without using names. Both groups were trained to the same criterion of recognition, the implication being that the first group used a verbal code while the second group stored the information in a sort of image form. All subjects were then required firstly to do the jigsaw problem in their heads (i.e. say how the various shapes should be fitted together to form the simple figure), and secondly to recall correctly the positions of the shapes in a serial learning task. The results showed quite definitely that subjects who had learned the shapes without names did better than those who had learnt them with, but worse on the test of serial learning. (This reminds one of the suggestion considered in Chapter Eight, that there are *two* alternative systems for information processing.)

What then of the role of verbal and nonverbal mediation in cognitive processes? We would stress again the wider view of thinking as involving the use of optional strategies, coding devices and other operations. Perhaps anyway the emphasis on associative processes is misleading. It is not at this level that language is a useful tool of thought but, as Bruner for example has suggested, because of its structural and other properties, it enables experience to be coded in a way which is suitable for dealing with particular types of information. That subjects behave in certain situations in such a way as to suggest the operation of particular verbal response hierarchies is beyond doubt. But it is a long haul from this to saying that language is necessary for thinking or that verbal mediation is essential for the development of certain cognitive skills or other intellectual abilities.

FURTHER READING

Britton, J. (1969). *Language and Learning*. Penguin.
Bruner, J. S. *et al.* (1966). *Studies in Cognitive Growth*. Wiley.
Herriot, P. (1970). *An Introduction to the Psychology of Language*. Methuen.
Voss, J. F. (1969). *Approaches to Thought*. Merrill.
Whorf, B. L. (1956). *Language, Thought and Reality*, M.I.T. Press.

8

Imagery

SUBJECTIVE EXPERIENCES

Imagery is a topic that many people find fascinating. For strong imagers, their experiences seem an indissoluble, and a very personal, part of their mental life. For those who have no, or only weak, images, there is the puzzle of what it can be that the others are experiencing. Within psychology, imagery as a topic for investigation has been in favour, out of favour, and now in once more: but we shall come to that later. Let us first list some of the main phenomena to which the name 'image' has been attached.

Imagery can exist in any modality, but by far the greatest attention has been paid to visual imagery. Presumably this is due to the primacy of sight in man. Dogs, perhaps, have strong olfactory images. McKellar (1965) found that of a sample of 500 subjects, 83 per cent reported visual imagery to be of the greatest use to them in thinking and remembering; 26 per cent named auditory imagery; none any other type. (It is not clear why these percentages do not add up to 100). This contrasts with the fact that 97 per cent reported possessing visual imagery, and 92 per cent auditory, while over half had a range of imagery which included movement, touch, taste, smell and pain. As far as common experience goes, an 'image' generally refers to some representation of an experience that normally results from sensory stimulation. That it is a difficult phenomenon to pin down exactly is suggested by the circumlocutions of ordinary speech: we speak of 'seeing in the mind's eye', or say 'I seem to hear his voice'. There is not an exact correlation with sensory input, for images of objects equally well known can be vague or clear; and they can be bound to what is known to be the case, or flexible. Richardson (1969, 1971) has suggested that the two main dimensions along which visual imagery will turn out to be measurable are vividness and controllability.

The best-known phenomena of imagery, mainly visual, are these. There are first of all ordinary walking images. A fairly strong visual imager myself, I do not recall seeing a comment on the way in which imagery as it were surrounds one: on the fact that as I sit at my desk, I am always more or less aware of a visual impression of what lies in the room behind me, and of the rooms behind that, the road outside, and indeed of all parts of the world that I know or can imagine. It is virtually impossible to comprehend a state of mind in which this was not so. And it is correspondingly easy to see why images seemed such essential elements of mind, and thus immediate targets for investigation, to the early psychologists. Especially, of course the psychologists of content. As we have seen, Wundt believed the task of psychology to be the analysis of immediate sensory experience. Imagery is the next step: an experience like sensation, but without the sensory stimuli being present. Thus when Külpe and his Würzburg psychologists set out to bring thought into the laboratory, it was images that they tried to study. But their method of systematic experimental introspection failed to solve the problems of thought—though it did reveal the existence of thought processes (the determining tendencies) *not* accompanied by images. This, plus the contemporary rise of Behaviourism, led to the concept and study of imagery falling into disrepute.

Dream images are discussed under the heading of *Thinking as a Private Experience*. Two curious categories of image closely related to sleep, however, are hypnagogic and hypnopompic images. These are the, usually visual, experience which many people have at the point of going to sleep or waking up respectively. McKellar (1957) found such imagery in at least three-quarters of a sample of 182 subjects. As with dreams, these images seem to be rather little under the subject's control. They are often brightly coloured, 'technicoloured' (unlike the majority of dreams); and they are often very unusual, seeming to resemble nothing the subject has ever seen before. They can also be perseverative. Hypnagogic images seem to have a close connection with sleep, in that they reliably herald it. Personally, I find further that I can sometimes apparently induce sleep by conjuring up an image of a hypnagogic type. Such might, perhaps, be the origin of 'counting sheep'. As it would be interesting to know whether the Reverend Dodgson was feeling sleepy on the hot summer afternoon on which he first described that typically hypnagogic image of a large White Rabbit taking a watch out of its waistcoat pocket. Collard (1953) however, reported a similar type of imagery with subjects who merely relaxed. In my experience hypnagogic imagery contrasts with the equally autonomous flow of often unrelated and 'original' words and phrases that accompany failure to sleep—a phenomenon of which James Thurber gave us a detailed account (The Tyranny of Trivia, in *Lantern and Lances*, 1963).

Some people experience imagery which shares some of these characteristics but in addition appears to be projected—it is seen 'out there', rather than in the head. According to McKellar (1957) some crystal ball gazers do this. They do actually seem to see pictures in the ball (or, presumably, in other suitable media such as pools of water, the traditional resource of fictional characters including She, and The Mummy as enacted by Boris Karloff). The better established case however, is eidetic imagery. The subject, after examining a picture or object for a few moments, sees a clear representation of it on some neutral ground. Galton

ound that 18 out of 172 schoolboys reported 'projecting' images outside themselves. The phenomenon has given rise to a long controversy, with very conflicting reports as to its reality and possible determinants. Intensively studied by
E. R. Jaensch between 1920 and 1930, interest in it has recently been revived
with the well-controlled studies of Haber and Haber, (1964); Leask, Haber, and
Haber (1969); and Stromeyer and Psotka (1970). We consider it at the end of this
chapter as a *Focus* topic.

One of the more individualistic forms of imagery reported by Galton goes by
the general name of association imagery. The characteristic of this is that some
abstract quality or concept is represented concretely. Days of the week may be
linked with colours, so that Monday, for example, is not just metaphorically
termed black, but is represented in the subject's mind by an actual impression of
blackness. More incomprehensible to the non-possessor are the various diagram
forms noted by Galton (and sometimes called Galtonian forms). He found 5 per
cent of his subjects reported the forms; McKellar gives 8 per cent. Subjects represent such abstract notions as the calendar, or parts of it; numbers; historical
time; and so on to themselves in diagrammatic form. For example the year may
be seen as a circular shape, with the seasons marked on it. The week might be
a circle, oval, rectangle, straight or crooked line, etc. Some forms are regular in
shape, others bizzare, and subjects are sometimes reduced to strange gestures to
convey some three-dimensional image. Odd as they are, such forms often seem
essential to their possessors, who are surprised to learn of their uniqueness.
Galton quoted one case of an exceptional calculator who apparently depended
upon a number form. But this does not always seem to be true of such calcu-
lators (e.g. Hunter, 1962). McKellar thinks that so-called 'photographic memory'
may be a related phenomenon. I think this unlikely. In my experience, one can
tell nothing from a diagram form (of which both the present writers have rather
good sets) that one did not consciously know without it. For example, if asked
the date of Queen Victoria's accession, I immediately see it on that steeply rising
bit between 1830 and 1840; but only because I have actually learned that it was
in fact, 1837. Cutts and Moseley (1969) likewise seem to think that photographic
memory, which as they point out is a very inexact phrase, has relatively little
to do with imagery. It is interesting, but probably fruitless, to speculate upon
the origin of the particular forms due, perhaps to some forgotten childhood
perception, or misperception.

Related to association imagery is synaesthesia. This is imagery which is, as
it were, cross-modal. As Vernon (1937) puts it: 'a stimulus presented in one
sense mode seems to call up imagery of another mode as readily as that of its
own.' McKellar (1957) reported this in 21 per cent of his subjects. The effect
must be distinguished from synaesthetic description. We are accustomed to
speak, by analogy, of a smooth or hot sound, a loud colour, etc. ('The pale
yellow smell of broken glass', I heard once.) In synaesthesia music actually
elicits visual imagery, or the like. This would be visual-auditory synaesthesia,

which is by far the commonest: but most of the other possible combinations do seem to occur, if rarely. It is, perhaps, difficult to see immediately that this 'crossing of the wires' effect should have any theoretical significance.

Hallucinations are cases of apparently perceiving, as if it were really there, something which is not present. In passing, we should distinguish hallucinations from illusions, which are misperceptions of something that really is there, and from delusions, which are false beliefs. Some other forms of imagery, e.g. eidetic, can resemble hallucinations in vividness and clarity; but the defining characteristic of an hallucination is that the subject believes the object to be present, and acts as if it were. Partly for this reason it is hard to be sure of the frequency of hallucinations in the normal population. William James (1905) claimed that 10 per cent had a vivid hallucination at some time in their lives. McKellar (1957) quotes a figure of fourteen out of seventy-two student subjects. Hallucinations can be induced hypnotically, which suggests that they might be common given appropriate circumstances. Dreams share in a sense the quality of apparent reality, at least while they last. Technologically unsophisticated peoples sometimes take dreams as real; and one occasionally does have an apparent memory which turns out to have been a dream.

'Body-image' is a term which refers, sometimes perhaps in a rather confused way, to our knowledge of where our bodies are. One knows, without having to look, whereabouts one's limbs are at any moment, and how far they will reach. It is not just a case of feedback from other senses, such as touch, or muscle movements. This is shown by two related phenomena. One is 'phantom limb'. Persons who have lost a limb often, for some time afterwards, experience it in some sense as still there, make allowances for its supposed position, etc. The second fact is that the body image can be extended to cover inanimate objects. One who is used to wearing a hat makes an allowance for it when entering a low doorway. A car driver comes to know exactly (if he's lucky) what space his vehicle will fit into. Dynamic psychologists relate the concept of body image to that of self-identity. Clothes and motor cars, of course, have both been said to be in some sense extensions of the self. One of W. C. Field's most characteristic jokes involved misplacing his hat on to his cane instead of his head: thus a temporary loss of identity. For psychotherapists, 'image' sometimes means just a visual image, and enters into some versions of behaviour therapy. Another use seems more akin to 'idea' or 'concept'. For example Biddle (1969) speaks of reversing 'threatening and frightening mental images so that the patient can picture objects as manageable.' At the same time this use seems to approach the sort of 'image' involved in archetypes (see *Thinking as a Private Experience*). Image in that sense is as it were the subjective experience aspect of a sort of schema or mental framework. (See also Shapiro, 1970)

The term 'after-images' is, according to Drever (1952) erroneously used for after-sensations.' An after-sensation, in turn, is: 'the continuance of the process in the sense receptor, after the external stimulus has ceased, giving rise to further ense experience; the phenomena are very apparent in the case of vision.' They an be either positive or negative. Richardson (1969) reviews evidence suggesting that central stimulation alone might be sufficient to produce an after-image or rather an *apparent* after-image); but the argument is unconvincing. Richardson also quotes James Ward (1883) to the effect that the after-image is 'the primary memory image.' That is to say, it represents the first stage of information storage, a sort of short-term memory store. Under experimental conditions, an after-image is a retinal effect that persists for a few seconds after stimulation has ceased. This is a special case of the phenomenon that changes in the retina are not coterminous with stimulation. In ordinary perception, the transmission of information about the world to the brain takes a period of time, though a very short one. Any events that occur after the actual stimulation has ended can be called memory events. However, the after-image seems very remote from what is usually meant by 'imagery', and will not form part of our present discussion.

These then are, briefly, the main types of subjective experience to which the term 'image' has been applied. They do not by any means exhaust the uses of the word in Psychology. It is often used more generally to mean something like representation.' For example Miller, Galanter, and Pribram (1960) define the image as: 'All the organized, accumulated knowledge that the organism has about itself and the world.' 'Imagery' occupies a central place in the general theory of cognitive development proposed by Bruner *et al.* under the title of *instrumental conceptualism.* Its precise status is here hard to define, but seems certainly other than a pseudo-sensory experience. It is with imagery in a narrower sense that we are mainly concerned here, though larger issues will be also relevant to the discussion.

Limiting ourselves for the moment to subjective experiences, there appear to be four main issues. There is the problem of methods of investigation; there is that of classification, or the isolation of dimensions along which imagery could be measured; there is the question of the function of imagery, if any; and there is the matter of the theoretical status of imagery. It is to the last that the work of Miller *et al.*, Bruner *et al.*, Neisser, and other cognitive theorists is particularly relevant.

STUDYING IMAGERY

All methods of studying imagery depend upon introspection, in the sense that the subject must report upon an experience which is private (as, of course, are all experiences). Some of the general problems of introspection we shall discuss in dealing with *Thinking as a Private Experience.* The early history of introspection is told by Boring (1953). (See also Natsoulas, 1970.) Its fall into disrepute as a method was closely related to the simultaneous fall of imagery as a field for investigation. That story has been presented by Holt (1964) incidentally giving us the classification of types of imagery which he had learned from Boring, who had it from Titchener who in turn, Holt thinks, derived it from Fechner. *The return of the ostracized* was the title of Holt's paper. In carping mood, one sometimes feels that *The rediscovery of the obvious* could be the title of this and several other papers in Psychology. In this particular case, Holt argues that the return was due to increased interest in a number of related phenomena, which drew attention to the subjective contents of mind. Military demands led to research into the behaviour and experiences of pilots and astronauts, and the conditions affecting vigilance tasks such as radar operating. Politics have produced first-hand accounts of 'thought-reformed' prisoners. For little-understood cultural reasons, interest increased in hallucinogenic drugs, and possible cases of hallucination such as flying saucers. Experimental research advanced in such fields as sensory deprivation; likewise in brain physiology including E.E.G. studies, lobotomy (after which some patients lost their powers of imagery), the auras and hallucinations associated with epilepsy, direct stimulation of the brain, and photic stimulation. A 'new' psychology of thinking began to appear, partly due to increased recognition of such grand old men as Werner and above all Piaget. It may well be that much of this work began by being respectably behaviouristic only to lead rather quickly to the postulation of subjective variables. The desire for respectability seems still to persist. Hebb (1968, 1969), for example, has published two articles in which he takes the extremely odd view that reports of imagery are not introspective. He seems to think that in a case of phantom limb, for instance, the neural pathways that were activated by the real limb, are reactivated; and that therefore, by a step which is hard to follow, the subject's report of sensation is not introspective.

Various attempts have been made to overcome, or compensate for, the subjective element in the study of imagery. A good summary of many of these is given by Woodworth and Schlosberg in their *Experimental Psychology* (several editions from 1938 on), where incidentally imagery finds its place in the chapter on Memory. These attempts followed on the early investigations of Fechner (1860) and Galton (1880, 1883). Fechner was the first to point out the range of individual differences in imagery. Some of his subjects, asked to call up an image of some particular object, were able to do so successfully, while others could attain only a fleeting, unstable impression. Galton's investigations are more famous, and it is indeed *de rigueur* to recall the questionnaire he despatched to his friends and acquaintances, requesting them to imagine a familiar scene, their breakfast table as they sat down to it that morning. (What splendidly Victorian images that conjures up.) Then they had to report how the image compared with the original: whether the objects were well-defined, the brightness equal to that of the original scene, the colours distinct and natural. Responses ranged from those who reported virtually no difference between the image and the reality, to those so totally without imagery that they thought it a mere fiction, 'the mind's eye' being a phrase of poetic license with no reality in experience.

Galton's questionnaire was expanded by Betts (1909) to cover all the sense modalities. The 'comparison with reality' technique has been revived recently by Sheehan (1966, 1967) using Betts' questionnaire.

There appear to be about five other sorts of method of investigation that have been tried at one time or another. One confusing factor has been that many of the early investigations were aimed at discovering whether people could be divided into 'types' on the basis of which sensory modality of imagery was predominant. Subjects were said to be visual types, auditory types, or kinaesthetic types. Other types were said to be rare, though Emile Zola was reported as an olfactory type. This line of thought has fallen into disuse, partly no doubt due to the general loss of interest in imagery, but mainly because the alleged types were both hard to establish certainly, and apparently unrelated to any other meaningful variables. Another factor, mentioned by Neisser (1968) is the separation that developed between testing and experimental work in psychology. We noted this in discussing *Intellectual Abilities*: and it was not realized for some years that tests of spatial ability might have something to do with imagery.

Now to some methods. One of the early ones was to analyse production of the subject: either free associations, or a piece of published writing. The numbers of visual, auditory or other responses or descriptions were taken as evidence for the subject being of that 'type'. Taken alone, such data tell us little about what sort of imagery is actually used, or how it appears to the subject. There is some evidence, however, that certain authors do depend upon visual imagery. McKellar (1957) quotes the children's author Enid Blyton as writing down descriptions of scenes presented to her imagination (and apparently highly autonomous). P. G. Wodehouse writes of his novels in stage terms, almost as if he sees characters making entrances and exits (*Performing Flea*, 1953). The almost cinematic imagination of Thomas Hardy is pointed out by John Wain (introduction to *The Dynasts*, Macmillan Paperback edition, 1965).

A second approach was to get subjects to learn material presented either to eye or ear. Ease of learning was taken as the criterion of a visual or auditory 'type'.

A third related technique is distraction. A subject could be asked to learn something presented either visually or auditorily, with either visual or auditory distraction. 'Visual types' would be handicapped when subjected to visual distraction. A variation of this has been used by Kuhlman (1960). She found that children with much visual imagery (as assessed by spatial relations tests, see below) were poorer at concept learning tasks. The verbal labels and the visual images seemed in some way to conflict. This result is related by Bruner (1966) not to imagery types but to stages of cognitive development.

The fourth approach has had the greatest attention paid to it. Essentially it consists in getting the subject to carry out some task which it is supposed he cannot do, or cannot do so well, without using imagery. Mostly, visual imagery is involved. An early version of this (e.g. Binet, 1894) involved letters or numerals arranged in a square. These the subject had to learn in rows, but reproduce in columns. It was supposed that good visualizers would have no trouble in doing this. But they did. Müller (1917) found, according to Woodworth, that 'his most competent visual learner recited the digits forward in 8 seconds, but required 24 seconds to recite them downwards, and 59 seconds to recite them in oblique lines'. A similar technique required subjects to spell words backwards. Again, even highly visual subjects found this difficult, indeed Fernald, (1912) found no one who could do it at all. Modern versions of the approach are quoted with approval by Neisser (1970). For example, Brooks (1967, 1968)

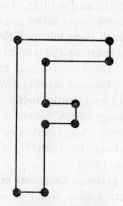

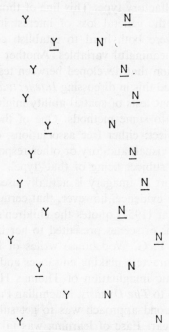

Figure 8.1(a). (Reproduced from L. R. Brooks (1968), 'Spatial and verbal components of the act of recall', *Canad. J. Psychol.*, **22**, 349–368 by permission of the Canadian Psychological Association and the University of Toronto Press)

Figure 8.1(b). Sheet used in the 'pointing' conditions. (The underlined letters are actually those which would be pointed to in categorizing the sentence, 'a bird in the hand is not in the bush'—see below). Reproduced from L. R. Brooks (1968), 'Spatial and verbal components of the act of recall', *Canad. J. Psychol.*, **22**, 349–368 by permission of the Canadian Psychological Association and the University of Toronto Press showed the subjects an outline figure, such as a block letter F, with dots marking all its corners. (Figure 8.1(a)) Each dot can be classed as a 'top/bottom point', i.e. it is on the top or bottom of the figure; or not. The subject then has to imagine the figure, and go round it mentally, saying 'yes' for each top/bottom point and 'no' for the others. Brooks' aim was to compare this with a procedure whereby the subject had to respond by pointing to yeses and noes that appeared in staggered positions on a sheet of paper. (Figure 8.1(b)). This method was slower, presumably because the visual search of a real object (the sheet of paper) interfered with the search of an image. (This therefore resembles also the earlier 'distraction' method). Brooks also used auditory stimuli. Given a sentence, subjects had to classify each word as a noun or not. In this case pointing was quicker than speaking. (Figure 8.1(b)). Neisser quotes a personal communication from Hochberg, who suggested, as a sort of simple demonstration of the role of imagery, trying to recall the number of windows in some familiar building. Neisser argues that one must do this by counting mental windows— 'image-based counting', he calls it—but that it can be done 'even without vivid, compelling or lifelike imagery.' He concludes that 'the information . . . was stored only in visual form' This is a little difficult to follow, since the absence of 'vivid, compelling or lifelike' imagery would seem potentially equivalent to the absence of imagery at all. It seems that Neisser distinguishes between 'imagery' and 'visual storage'. A further difficulty, however, in all these variations on the 'imagery task' approach is that some *other* criterion of imagery is required. Even if the tasks can be carried out, it does not follow that they are in fact accompanied by imagery (in the sense of subjective experience). And even if they are, it is a further question as to whether imagery is essential to them.

The same point applies to the psychometric approach. A number of tests of intellectual ability include items designed to assess spatial ability, which it seems plausible to suggest is related to imagery. One of the first to argue for this was El Koussy (1935) who factor analysed scores on a number of spatial tasks given to boys aged 11 to 13. Such tasks involve, for example, drawing the mirror image of a presented diagram; selecting a pattern that represents a given diagram when rotated in a specified way; deciding what sort of solid would be made when a flat shape is folded in a specified way. El Koussy found evidence for a factor of spatial perception, the k factor, which he said 'receives a ready explanation in terms of visual imagery'. His subjects reported using imagery during the tests. Guilford, too, finds a place for factors concerned with visual and auditory remembering in his three-dimensional *structure of intellect* model. Some sort of imagery-related factor receives support from the work of Barratt (1953) who, analysing the results of twelve spatial tasks, found three principal factors: spatial manipulation, reasoning, and shape recognition. The subjects were asked to report on imagery arising spontaneously while they worked at the tests, and Barratt argues that: 'the general conclusion, yet tentative, is that facility in imagery is important in spatial manipulation, is less important in shape recognition tasks, and is unimportant in spatial analytic reasoning'. Of course the presence of imagery does not prove its importance, and Chowdhury and Vernon (1964) found 'slight confirmation only of the supposed relevance of visual imagery to spatial ability' in a direct attempt to examine the relationship of imagery to abilities.

The most original, and perhaps the most fruitful, recent approach to investigating imagery is due to Allan Paivio and his associates. Paivio (1969) summarizes a long series of experiments (to which others have since been added). As far as method is concerned, the innovation consisted in establishing *imagery values* for words, on the analogy of association values. Subjects were asked to rank each of a list of 925 nouns from 1 to 7. A word was ranked high if it aroused a mental picture, or sound, or other sensory experience, very quickly and easily. The words were also rated for concreteness and meaningfulness. In a related experiment, Lindauer (1969) found high imagery values for tactual and gustatory words. Visual and olfactory words were intermediate, and auditory words were low in imagery. Paivio, Yuille, and Madigan (1968) reported *concreteness, imagery,* and *meaningfulness* values for 925 nouns. While not as well established as association values, which themselves are not indefinitely reliable (for example, the marketing of new detergents can suddenly give association value to syllables) this work does provide replicable criteria. Walker (1970) repeating Paivio *et al.*'s method, reported a correlation of 0·944 with their findings. The three values probably overlap, for meaningfulness and imagery correlated 0·72, and concreteness and imagery 0·83. Both these are obviously likely to occur. Once such values are established, experiments can be done in which they are systematically varied.

Attempts to assess body-image have largely been based on projective tests (e.g. Fisher and Cleveland, 1968). Maloney, Ball, and Edgar (1969) used the technique of having subjects point to parts of their own body which the experimenter indicated by a diagram. Body image was 'operationally defined as the ability to indicate either eye or ear cross-laterally or unilaterally and the ability to indicate points on the front and back of the body'. (Reported in Maloney and Payne, 1969.)

It is clear, then, that if we consider that in dealing with imagery we are necessarily dealing with subjective experience, it follows that our investigations must depend upon introspection. Introspection itself covers several varieties of procedure. Bakan (1954) for example, makes the point that has often been argued, that it is actually retrospection that is involved: it is actually impossible to report on mental events as they happen (rather as 'simultaneous translation' is not literally simultaneous). Bakan recommends that the psychoanalytic version of introsepction should be employed in experimental work. Whatever the merits of this, the issue remains one of the acceptability of reports of private experiences. Perhaps the most useful approach is to regard these in the same way as we do other self-reports, such as responses to personality questionnaires. We know that if a person responds 'yes' to the question 'do you enjoy lively parties?' he *may* be lying. Or he may attach quite a different meaning to 'enjoy', or to 'lively parties', from that of another person. We try to overcome these difficulties in various ways. We try to ensure that the questions are understood in much the same way by most people. We look out for any factors which might lead our subject to lie, or be confused; and in their absence assume that he will not. We do not depend on just one question. Fundamentally, however, what is done is to correlate responses on the questionnaire with some other behaviour; to which, preferably, it is theoretically related. There seems no reason why the same approach cannot be taken with imagery. (We owe this point to Dr. E. Valentine.) It might be objected that we could actually check a person's party-going behaviour, note whether he was smiling and laughing when the decibels rose above a certain level, or when social interaction reached some criterion. But this would not do: the most we could say, strictly speaking, is that our subject acted as people do when they say they are enjoying themselves. We are justified in assuming that he too is enjoying himself, unless there is any particular reason to doubt it. So with imagery. But conversely, it will not do to suppose that we can avoid subjectivity. Unless 'imagery' is used as another term for representation,' or 'mediating process', or the like, its investigation must ultimately rest on reports of private experience. (See *Thinking as a Private Experience* for a fuller discussion.)

CLASSIFICATION

It will be apparent from what we have said so far that the word 'image' has been applied rather vaguely to a wide range of phenomena. Most of these do have something in common; but the question that arises is, whether the separate phenomena can be sorted out in any useful way. The classification given by Holt, and the very similar one by McKellar (1957) are really just lists. Both use more-or-less the grouping we have given in the preceding section. Classical experimental textbooks (e.g. Valentine, 1939) restrict themselves to listing the modalities in which imagery can occur.

The first attempt in recent times to bring the whole field together is due to Richardson (1969). He first offers a definition:

'Mental imagery refers to (1) all those quasi-sensory or quasi-perceptual experiences of which (2) we are self-consciously aware, and which (3) exist for us in the absence of those stimulus conditions that are known to produce their genuine sensory or perceptual counterparts, and which (4) may be expected to have different consequences from their sensory or perceptual counterparts.'

As Richardson points out, the first two criteria are subjective, the second two are objective. He is surely right to consider both. His definition leads him to distinguish four classes of imagery. These are: after-imagery; eidetic imagery; memory imagery; imagination imagery. The first two categories are already familiar to us. By 'memory imagery' Richardson means:

> 'the common and relatively familar imagery of everyday life. It may accompany the recall of events from the past, the ongoing thought processes of the present or the anticipatory actions and events of the future.'

It is distinguished from after-imagery and eidetic imagery by being (1) more amenable to voluntary control and (2) less likely to be mistaken for a real perception. Under 'imagination imagery' Richardson groups: hypnagogic imagery; perceptual isolation imagery; hallucinogenic drug imagery; photic stimulation; pulse current imagery; sleep deprivation imagery; meditation imagery. As he points out, this group is distinguished from the other three not so much by its own characteristics as by its antecedent conditions. However, there are two other criteria: one, used by Perky (1910) is that 'imagination images' are defined as images of objects, etc., never actually seen by the subject. This seems a difficult criterion to apply exactly. Richardson prefers to say that:

> 'Imagination images tend to be novel, substantial, vividly coloured, when in the visual mode, and involve "concentrated and quasi-hypnotic attention with inhibition of association".'(The quotation is from Perky.)

Dreams would presumably come in this group, although this is not clear, and so apparently would all hallucinations, not just those known to be induced by specific conditions. The body-image is not mentioned. Images as involved in psychotherapy are classed under 'memory imagery'. Now this classification does at least give us some main groups rather than just a list of phenomena; but as Richardson himself points out, it is not the last word. The distinction between 'memory' and 'imagination' imagery in particular is hard to sustain. Take the case of reading a novel set in a familiar place: one may well have a mental picture representing a real scene but with an imaginary person in it. Again, a dream or hallucination might be of something real in every detail. Indeed the less an image resembled anything real, presumably, the less likely one is to believe it to be real, which is the distinguishing mark of hallucination.

Richardson accordingly pays attention to the possibility of dimensions along which imagery might be measured; and he suggests (1969, 1971) two: *vividness* and *controllability*. The first is that which had already struck Galton, and which Betts set out to investigate systematically. It seems at the present time difficult to assess the importance of this dimension. As far as spatial manipulation tasks go, at least, the vivid visual imager seems to do well, while the weak imager may or may not do well (Sheehan, 1966). Neisser (1970) thinks that the issue over vividness or 'reality' of images may be unimportant. Again, his argument depends upon distinguishing between behaviour and experience. Imagery, he says:

'... can be useful in both problem solving and memory where spatial arrangement is involved, or when the subject can reformulate his problem in visual terms. People differ in their ability to carry out detailed constructions of this sort; that is what the spatial-relations tests measure.... However, people also differ in the reality status that they assign to their images, in whether they really see anything while they are imaging. These individual differences are *not* necessarily related to performance.'

Now it is not clear whether Neisser is suggesting here the possibility that subjects might in some sense have the same experience, but describe it differently (assign it a different reality status); or whether he means what has usually been meant, that images actually do vary in their closeness to reality. If the latter, then he must be saying that subjects can be imaging, and that imagery can be useful, even when they do not 'really *see* anything'. In that case an 'image' seems to be a supposed process, inferred from a subject's behaviour on a spatial task and the fact that this is a 'visual' task. To tease it out still further, there is the possibility that Neisser means that there is always *some* experience when a person is 'imaging', even if infinitely far from vividness or reality. This difference between people, which seems in common experience as well as experiment to be a fact, remains a puzzle.

The other dimension, also intriguing, is that of controllability. Dreams are typically hard to control, especially nightmares. Many people have been annoyed by the film of the book, because 'that's not at all how I imagined it'—and having formed the image one cannot alter it. Rosemary Gordon (1949) set out to investigate this more systematically. She asked her subjects to imagine a car standing in front of a garden gate, and then to say if they could mentally alter its colour, see it lying on its back, running up a steep hill, and perform other feats. Gordon found that some subjects had the image completely under their control, while for others it was the image that was to a greater or less extent autonomous. Among Gordon's hypotheses had been the suggestion that autonomous imagery might be related to 'stereotypes', the moulds into which we often tend to fit members of a class. The term was suggested by the American columnist Walter Lippman in connection with racial prejudice (stereotype itself is a term in printing). Thus a Frenchman or a German tends to be perceived as fitting into a pattern of a supposedly typical Frenchman, etc. This in turn Gordon related to intolerance of ambiguity, as demonstrated for example by the series of line drawings (used by Frenkel-Brunswik, 1948) in which a dog gradually changes into a cat. Gordon did in fact find that all these traits tended to go together. This is an interesting lead, but attempts to follow it up by Costello (1956, 1957) and by Richardson (1962) and to relate autonomy of imagery to psychiatric disorders and to introversion–extraversion do not seem to have been very conclusive. Incidentally Richardson treats this whole issue under the heading of memory imagery, but surely to think of a yellow car and make it turn pink is imagination, if anything is.

Another approach to the question of dimensions has been to revive the old issue of imagery types. Principally, the argument is over visual versus verbal imagery. There is some difficulty in deciding just what is meant by verbal imagery. Richardson (1969) says:

> 'Verbal imagery ... may contain a variety of visual auditory and kinaes-
> thetic images, and in the case of the last, sensations. It is relatively rare to
> see words as though they are written on a blackboard, or on a kind of
> endless band of tickertape ... The more common forms of verbal imagery
> involve combinations of auditory and kinaesthetic imagery, and it is for
> these that the term "inner speech" has been traditionally employed.'

Assuming that the kinaesthetic aspects refer to some representation of movements of the vocal apparatus, and ignoring the reference to visual aspects, one
might conclude that verbal imagery is another name for subvocal speech; and
this is perhaps the simplest definition to work with, though it is not necessarily
the one that would be universally accepted. A series of experimenters have tried
to establish to what extent subjects depend upon visual or verbal imagery. For
example Golla, Hutton, and Grey Walter (1943) claimed that groups of subjects
could be distinguished in whom either verbal or visual imagery predominated.
There were also mixed groups. They reported that imagery mode was related to
certain characteristics of the E.E.G. Three groups or types were distinguished,
on the basis of the amplitude of the alpha rhythm. In type M, the alpha
amplitude was less than 10 microvolts with eyes closed; and there was little
change when the eyes were opened *or* when mental work was undertaken with
eyes closed. This type was said to correspond with the habitual visualizer. In
type P, an alpha amplitude of between 10 and 50 microvolts was characteristic
of all three conditions—eyes closed, eyes open, mental work. This type was held
to be the habitual verbalizer. Type R was said to be characterized by mixed
imagery, and in this a normal alpha amplitude of 10 to 50 microvolts with eyes
closed disappeared or was reduced when the eyes were opened. This work
therefore suggests a connection between visual imagery and alpha suppression.
A series of subsequent studies, e.g. Short (1953); Short and Walter (1954);
Barratt (1956); Slatter (e.g. 1960); have failed to establish this conclusively.
There is some evidence, e.g. Golla and Antonovitch (1929); Short (1953); that
verbal–auditory imagery is associated with less regular breathing patterns than
is visual imagery. There is also a series of studies, starting with Galton (1883)
relying simply on subject reports, to suggest the predominance of one mode or
the other. The possible importance of this must be discussed later.

We must first consider a different approach to classification, that of Piaget.
Having been for some time interested in imagery as an aspect of cognitive
development Piaget has now (Piaget and Inhelder, 1966; 1971 English translation) presented his findings in a long and difficult book. He begins by saying
that the relationship of imagery to the stages of development is not immediately

obvious, and that the first step must therefore be a classification. Piaget immediately breaks away from the sort of approach we have met so far.

'Images may be classified in terms of their content (i.e. they are visual, auditory, etc.), or according to their structure. This second viewpoint is the only all-inclusive one, and the only one which will concern us here.'

The classification, however, is a complex one. The first point is clear:

'A basic division into two large groups emerges if images are distinguished as *reproductive images* (R), which evoke objects or events already known, and *anticipatory images* (A), which, by figural imagination, represent events . . . that have previously not been perceived.'

At first sight, this is rather like Richardson's division into memory and imagination imagery. But Piaget at once points out that things are not so simple. One can never be sure just what a subject has actually perceived in the past; and more important, even the forming of an image of a well-known object may well involve a sort of anticipation. I take it that Piaget here implies that the formation of an image is a kind of construction, so that there is in a sense a foreknowledge of what the image will be; but also that the image itself is only a particular representation of the object, so that though the *object* is familiar, the image is new.

Both reproductive and anticipatory images are accordingly subdivided. Anticipation is of two kinds: *executional* and *evocational*. Executional anticipation is when the object is known, and the representation has to be anticipated; evocational is when the object is not known. Part of what Piaget is getting at here is that an 'image' is only one *sort* of representation of an object that is possible. This comes out more clearly in the subdivision of reproductive images. The latter are classified according to two aspects: their *content*; and their *degree of internalization*. Three sorts of content are distinguished:

'*static* reproductive images (RS), where such images refer to a motionless object or configuration (e.g. the image of a straight line); *kinetic* reproductive images (RK), where they evoke a movement figurally (e.g. the reproduction of two motions of the same constant speed crossing one another); and finally reproductive images of *transformations* (RT) where they represent in a figural manner transformations already known to the subject (e.g. the transformation of an arc into a straight line, when the subject has already verified this in his own perceptual experience with a piece of wire whose form is modified gradually).'

We now come to the matter of *internalization*, which as we might expect is most important for Piaget. Here his starting point is the consideration of how we can know what sort of an image a person actually has. He suggests that there are just four possible procedures: a verbal description by the subject; a drawing by the subject; a choice by the subject from a range of drawings put before him; and reproduction by gesture. Since he has worked with children, Piaget has used mainly the last three. Now the image is a representation, or as Piaget calls it, an imitation, of some object. The gesture, and the drawing, are also representations of the object. The image is an *internalized* representation; the gesture and drawing are *external* representations. But they are not only representations of the object: they also stand, in the experimental situation, for the (internal) image. There is a difference between a drawing and a gesture here: the drawing is, according to Piaget, more complex than the mental image; the gesture is simpler. These two sorts of reproductive image, gesture and drawing, can be termed RG and RD respectively; R alone standing for the reproductive mental image. The next point is that the degree of internalization depends upon two factors. The first is whether the reproductive behaviour is more or less immediate or deferred; the second is 'the internalization of the movements which this presupposes'. What these two points seem to come to is that a mental image (R) must necessarily be internal, by definition; a graphic reproduction (RQ), while itself external, involves internalization ('since drawing consists in externalizing a previously internalized mental image'); a gesture (RG) *may* be external, or may also involve internalization. To make this a little clearer, compare it with the classical behaviouristic experiments on imitation in animals (e.g. Warden and Jackson, 1935). It will be recalled that deferred imitation has often been taken as evidence of 'thinking' in the rat. Another case of non-internalized imitation or gesture would presumably be the empathic movements often made by spectators of athletic events. Immediate imitation Piaget signifies by I; deferred by II.

A further complication arises in that a mental image 'is defined as the evocation of a model without direct perception of it.' But in making a drawing from an object in front of one, some mental representation must exist, for it is the

Table 8.1—Classification of images according to Piaget and Inhelder (1971). (From Chapter 6, of Mental Imagery in the Child: A Study of the Development of Imaginal Representation, *by Jean Piaget and Barbel Inhelder, in collaboration with M. Bovet, A. Etienne, F. Frank, E. Schmid, S. Taponier, and T. Vinh Bang,* © *1971 by Routledge and Kegan Paul Ltd. Published in the United States by Basic Books Inc., Publishers, New York.)*

IMAGES	IMMEDIATE (I = fore-images) or deferred (II)	BEARING ON PRODUCT (P) or on MODIFICATION (M)
A. Reproductive (R):		
static (RS)	RS I or RS II	
kinetic (RK)	RK I or RK II	RKP or RKM
transformation (RT)	RT I or RT II	RTP or RTM
B. Anticipation (A):		
kinetic (AK)		AKP or AKM
transformation (AT)		ATP or ATM

latter that we try to set down on the paper (producing the RD that stands for R). This internal event Piaget calls a *fore-image*.

Finally we must turn to anticipatory images again. We might expect these too to divide into static, kinetic, and transformation images. But anticipatory images, according to Piaget, can never be static, since the act of anticipating itself involves change. But transformation images, whether anticipatory (AT) or reproductive (RT), are of two types: those that bear only on the result or product (P) of the transformation (giving ATP or RTP); and those that bear on the process of modification itself (giving ATM or RTM). This distinction seems to mean that, for example, if one imagines a straight line that changes into a curved one, one may or may not visualize the process of the change.

These multifarious distinctions finally yield the table shown above (Table 8.1). Each of the images thus classified may be either gestural (invitation); mental; or graphic. Thus according to Piaget there are forty-two varieties of imagery to be considered. We have presented the classification at some length not only because it is by far the most ambitious and detailed attack on the problem to date, but because it reveals a good deal about the Piagetian way of thinking. As far as Piaget and Inhelder themselves are concerned, they consider that:

'A preliminary classification such as that drawn up in Chapter One may be expected to have two uses. In the first place it provides a programme of experiments, and in the second place it helps us to come to terms with the problem of structure.'

THE FUNCTION OF IMAGERY

'The question has often been raised, and will continue to be raised for some time yet, as to whether the possession of vivid manipulable imagery in any particular modality has any special value to the thinker who possesses it.' (Richardson, 1969)

Now the puzzle about the function of imagery, apart from the elusive quality of the phenomenon, has seemed to me on the basis of first introspections, that one can do nothing with the aid of imagery that one might not do without it. Then it seems clear that there are certainly thought processes unaccompanied by imagery, as the Würzburg psychologists showed. And there would seem to be at least some individuals who possess minimal or no imagery. Imagery thus seems not essential for thought. But this may only be to say that there are wide individual differences, as in a psychological phenomenon we should expect. Imagery may play an essential role in some varieties of thinking, and/or in some people, and/or at some stages of development. It may be the case that there are individual differences not only in *ability to think visually* (e.g. spatial ability) and in *vividness*; but also in *awareness* of visual thinking. This seems less likely to be true of verbal thinking (or verbal imagery, or inner speech), since there is a close relationship between language and awareness. At present we have a number of suggestions along these lines, rather than firm answers.

There are first of all individual reports. McKellar (1968) for example, studied nineteen police officers, all of whom had both visual and auditory imagery, and fourteen of whom considered it essential in their work. He quotes one as saying: 'A police officer has a great advantage if he can imagine what someone looks like from a written description, or if he can form a picture in his mind from a plan or a sketch.' McKellar refers also to a study by Owens (1963) who reported that students of anatomy who were poor at visual thinking found the subject difficult. This brings us back to the question of intellectual capacities, such as spatial ability, which we have already discussed. A few studies, cited by Richardson, suggest further lines for investigation, such as the possible role of imagery in problem solving.

Both Berlyne and Neisser stress the perceptual aspects of images. Berlyne (1965) says:

> 'When we speak of sensory images, we mean central symbolic processes that are relatively near to the stimulus end of the chain' (i.e. the stimulus-response chain of thought).

He quotes the classic experiment of Perky (1910). She showed that subjects could confuse images with actual perceptions. Subjects were required to imagine pictures of specified objects on a blank screen. Sometimes faint pictures were projected on to a blank screen, and these influenced the subjects' descriptions of what they thought they were only imagining. Berlyne seems to look on imagery as simply a form of storage of information. He asks how one could know 'whether a human being is using sensory images as distinct from other kinds of symbolic responses, for example, sub-vocal words.' His test is this. Suppose someone, a spy for example, is to be questioned about a possibly assumed identity. An imposter will have learned the facts, mainly verbally, but one who has actually lived through experiences will have this information mainly in the form of memory imagery. The answers of the imposter will tend to be rigid and stereotyped, and lacking in detail. Such a test, Berlyne says, could never be foolproof.

> 'So we can see that there is no way of drawing a hard and fast dividing line between images and other symbolic responses. Nor is there much point in trying to do so. All possible gradations in informational closeness to the significate evidently exist among symbolic responses. We can do no more than classify symbolic responses as more or less "imaginal".'

(It seems unlikely that this would meet with the approval of an expert. In *A Scandal in Bohemia* Holmes remarks to Watson:

> 'You see, but you do not observe. The distinction is clear. For example, you have frequently seen the steps which lead up from the hall to this room.
> Frequently.
> How often?

Well, some hundreds of times.
Then how many are there?
How many? I don't know.
Quite so! You have not observed. And yet you have seen. That is just
my point. Now, I know that there are seventeen steps, because I have both
seen and observed.')

Neisser (1970) points out the similarities and common factors between imagery
and perception. As we have seen, he is inclined to discount the importance of
vividness. He readily admits, however, that this view seems contradicted by the
experiments of Sheehan (1966, 1967). Sheehan found that subjects with vivid
imagery, as assessed by questionnaire, recalled visual designs better than those
whose imagery was less vivid. In an attempt to resolve the question, Sheehan
and Neisser (1969) tried to assess vividness of imagery both as a general characteristic of subjects, *and* while the subjects were actually carrying out experimental
tasks. These were of two sorts: one involved memorizing patterns made by the
subjects from coloured shapes, and in the other, simple designs were presented
in such a way that the subject did not expect a recall test. Thus both deliberate
and incidental learning were examined. In general, no evidence was found that
those with initially high imagery ratings performed better. What did emerge was,
that ratings of imagery during recall tended to fluctuate: one experimenter, for
example, obtained higher ratings than the other. Imagery appeared to be more
important in the incidental learning task. Neisser concludes that the whole
question remains unsettled. He finally summarizes his position (at the time of
writing, 1970) thus:

'Imagery can be thought of as the activity of the visual organizing process
in the absence of relevant stimuli, under the control of stored information.
It is useful in both remembering and problem-solving, because it represents
spatial information effectively. All of us employ imagery to some extent,
but there are individual differences in this skill that can be measured by
tests of spatial-relations ability. The vividness, the reality-status of an image
is not well correlated with its usefulness or accuracy. The psychic reality of
images is like the subjective reality of deep-trance hypnotic experiences: it is
genuine for the person himself, but it does not endow him with any special
capacities. In other words, images can be dramatic as subjective phenomena,
and can be valuable cognitive tools, but these two dimensions are not the
same. He that speaks loudest does not always have the most to say.'

By far the most extensive recent programme to investigate the role of imagery
in learning has been due to Allan Paivio and his associates. Paivio (1970) reviewing the historical background of the concept of imagery, focuses on the
approach in which 'imagery is operationally defined in terms of stimulus meaning'. This has been done by establishing imagery ratings for words, as already
mentioned. One of the starting points for such experiments was the mnemonic
device which has been current for many hundreds of years, which involves first
learning a sequence of images, and then, given any material to learn, visualizing
each item (vividly, as is usually urged) in conjunction with one of the basic

series of images. A well-known version of this begins 'one is a bun, two is a shoe. . . .' Item one is then vizualized in a large bun, or covered with buns, etc. Paivio (1969) summarizes the series of experiments up to that time. Let us quote one example. This was

'a study which directly tested the effect of the imagery instructions and the concreteness of the mnemonic rhyme in the one-bun technique. The subjects (Ss) were presented one study and test trial with each of two 10-item lists of concrete nouns. The conditions for the first list excluded prior mnemonic instructions, and were identical for all subjects. The items were presented auditorily at a 4-second rate, the to-be-recalled nouns being preceded by the numerals 1–10. On the test trial, the numerals alone were read in random order and S attempted to recall the corresponding items. The second list was preceded by mnemonic instructions, with or without reference to the use of imagery, and training on either a concrete or an abstract rhyme. The concrete rhyme consisted of the familiar one-bun, two-shoe device, in which the "peg" words are concrete and relatively high in *I* (imagery). The abstract rhyme included peg words such as fun, true, free, bore, etc., all of which have lower *I* values than do the corresponding concrete pegs. The Ss given the imagery set were instructed to use mental images along with the rhyme in order to recall the items. The Ss not given the imagery instructions were instructed to recall the list by saying to themselves the rhyming words along with the to-be-remembered items, for example one-bun-pencil. Following the instructions, all Ss learned the appropriate rhyme, after which they were presented one study-test trial with the second list of nouns.

The results were quite unequivocal. Significant main effects obtained for control versus imagery instructions were completely qualified by a highly significant interaction of the two variables, presented in Figure 8.2. It can be seen that recall was comparable for all groups on the first mnemonic list, and that recall increased dramatically on the second list for Ss given the imagery set regardless of whether the mnemonic rhyme was concrete or abstract. The mnemonic instructions without imagery had no beneficial effect—in fact recall tended to be lower under the mnemonic than under the control condition.

The unexpected outcome was that concreteness showed no effects approaching significance.'

The results of this series of elegant and well-thought-out experiments allow Paivio to conclude:

'. . . that imagery-concreteness is the most potent stimulus attribute yet identified among meaningful items, while *m* (meaningfulness) and other relevant attributes are relatively ineffective; that both processes (i.e. non-verbal imagery, and symbolic processes) can be effectively manipulated by mediation instructions, but imagery is a "preferred" mediator when at least one member of the pair is relatively concrete; and that the two mechanisms are differentially effective in sequential and non-sequential memory tasks. The findings substantiate the explanatory and heuristic value of the imagery concept.' (The work of Paivio and his colleagues has now been published in a comprehensive and somewhat formidable text, *Imagery and Verbal Processes*, 1971.)

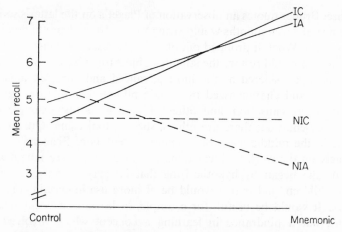

Figure 8.2. Effects of imagery instructions and concreteness of memory pegs in a mnemonic system. (A. Pavio (1968), 'Effects of imagery instructions and concreteness of memory pegs in a mnemonic system', *Proc. 76th Ann. Conv. A.P.A.*, **3**, 77–78. Copyright 1968 by the American Psychological Association, and reproduced by permission)

Recently much attention has been paid to the role of imagery in children's learning. Reese (1970) introduces a symposium on this topic to which Paivio, Rohwer, and Palermo are among the contributors. A theoretically more ambitious treatment had already been presented by Bruner, Olver, and Greenfield (1966). Bruner's theory of instrumental conceptualism has been considered also elsewhere: (see *Development and Culture*). Here we should note the central place in it occupied by imagery. Like Piaget, whose influence he acknowledges, Bruner has been concerned with the way in which the environment comes to be represented. He distinguishes three types of modes of representation: enactive, ikonic, and symbolic. They develop in that order, but the earlier modes do not disappear. As Bruner (1966) puts it:

'At first the child's world is known to him principally by the habitual actions he uses for coping with it. In time there is added a technique of representation through imagery that is relatively free of action. Gradually there is added a new and powerful method of translating action and image into language, providing still a third system of representation ... Each places a powerful impress on the mental life of human beings at different ages, and their interplay persists as one of the major features of adult intellectual life.'

In a sense *enactive* representation is hardly representation at all, for it is not clear that an action can stand for anything other than itself. (But compare Piaget's gestural imitation.) It is rather, so to speak, the base from which representation develops. It is marked by lack of the ability to distinguish between percept and response. Bruner quotes an observation of Piaget's on the latter's son Laurent, who at the age of seven months would swing to-and-fro a cigarette box which was presented to him. When it dropped out of sight, he resumed swinging his hand, as though the action would restore the stimulus object (or substitute for it). *Symbolic representation* is considered as the most advanced and complex mode, species-specific to man and characterized by certain minimum properties such as hierarchy, predication, causation, and others. Language is one example of such a system of representation; there are others, such as tool using. Our interest here, however, is in the middle stage of *ikonic* representation. Bruner here bases his theory largely on the work of Clementina Kuhlman (1960; see Kuhlman Hollenberg, 1970). She began by hypothesizing that imagery is the major vehicle of thinking in children, and that it would be of more use in certain cognitive tasks than others. It would be useful, for example, in learning a vocabulary of concrete nouns, but a hindrance in learning a concept which involved grouping together a number of perceptually diverse objects. Kuhlman selected two groups of American primary school children, one scoring high on a test of imagery, the other low. The two groups did, indeed, perform differently on the two types of task. In line with the notion that imagery represents an earlier mode of thinking, there was a positive correlation between use of imagery and school achievement in the first two grades of primary school. Thereafter, it dropped to zero. (Of course this could be due to the earlier stages of school work being more image-oriented, as it were.) Kuhlman further argued from her results that the poorer performance of high imagery children on conceptual tasks was due not to failure to generalize, but to a wrong choice of attributes, namely the use of surface features. Bruner concludes from this work and that of others such as Werner (1948) that:

'The concentration upon surface properties of the environment and the conversion of these properties through imagery seem to constitute a stage of growth that bridges the gap between the rigid serial representation or earlier enactive representation and the language-saturated phase of later childhood.'

It may be remarked in passing that while Bruner quotes a case of severe brain damage to illustrate enactive thinking, he does not suggest the analogy which might be drawn between ikonic thought and other cases of 'primitive' thinking. Among these would be schizophrenic thought; (see *Thinking as a Private Experience*) unconscious thought in the Freudian (and/or Jungian) sense; and, perhaps, magical thinking. In these cases we do find some tendency to group stimuli by surface characteristics, so that one thing can stand for another that resembles it only superficially. Bruner's work also leads us back to Galton, for it was his scientists and abstract thinkers who most conspicuously lacked imagery. I am not aware that this lead has ever been thoroughly followed up. (For example, at the secondary or tertiary education level.) Bruner's work has always been stimulating and it is particularly interesting to note his change of attitude in the ten years separating *A Study of Thinking* (1956) and *Studies in Cognitive Growth* (1966). The first was essentially a set of behaviouristic experiments, to account for the results of which it was necessary to postulate intervening cognitive variables, rather as Tolman had done. The other, as the title suggests, is essentially cognitively oriented, with a subjective and nativistic bias derived from the European tradition exemplified by Piaget, and influenced by the notion of human beings as living, developing organisms dependent upon the environment for psychological nutrient (Piaget's *aliment*). This is part of the current Zeitgeist. The reaction against an extreme viewpoint does tend, however, to produce some weaknesses of its own. In Piaget's work there sometimes appears to be a proliferation of theory at the expense of fact. In Bruner's, the status of the cognitive variables sometimes seems unclear. Anderson (1965) points this out in respect of the strategies of 1956: but the same point can be made about imagery. It may be my failure to understand, but I am not sure just what Bruner means by imagery. Is it any type, or only some? If some, how is imagery classified? If ordinary visual imagery is meant, is vividness or reality-quality important for ikonic thought? Or is 'imagery' more of a model—when children respond to surface characteristics it is *as if* they say saw the objects in their mind's eye? Does 'image' refer to the sort of inferred representational process of which Berlyne writes? Or is it merely a conjunction of two interesting facts: children tend to have imagery, and they tend to respond to perceptual properties of stimuli?

We must move on again to Piaget and his forty-two varieties. The classification outlines the programme of experiments which Piaget and Inhelder report (1966). Essentially, these consist in presenting children with tasks which can only be carried out if specific representational process—images—are present. The data are percentages of the large numbers of children examined at different ages who did or did not succeed. The tasks are for the most part extremely simple. For example two cardboard rectangles are presented, one directly above the other, and the child is asked to reproduce, or select, the pair that results if one rectangle is moved slightly to one side. From a long series of such experiments conclusions are drawn which we will summarize. The presentation does seem, however, to illustrate a frequent criticism of Piaget's work, that it is not always easy to see just how the theory relates to the facts, and in particular whether it is the only theory that is compatible with them. It is not really possible to pursue this point without embarking on a book as long as Piaget and Inhelder's own. We must try to summarize the outcome.

There are eight main headings. The first concerns the original classification. This is held to be largely supported by the findings, though with some modifications. Second, there is the question of the evolution of images. It is 'of a kind intermediate between that of the perceptions and that of the intelligence'. Piaget specifically denies 'the commonly held conception of the mental image as conservation or retention of past-perceived configurations and events'. That would, presumably, be the conception of a writer such as Berlyne. An alternative hypothesis would be that images simply reflect the total development of intellect as established by Piaget. Instead, only two stages are described: the first begins with the appearance of the image, probably at the same time as the emergence of symbolic functions, i.e. about $1\frac{1}{2}$ to 2 years; the second begins at 7 to 8 with the appearance of anticipatory images. These stages, of course, correspond to the pre-operational and operational stages of thought, and in line with this, images in these periods are static and mobile respectively. The third matter concerns the general characteristics of the image. Here a definition is offered:

> 'The visual image is a figural evocation of objects, relations, and even classes, etc. It converts them into a concrete and simili-sensible form, though at the same time it possesses a high degree of schematization (one can have an unlimited number of perceptions of an object, but only a few images of it.)'

Imagery as a mode of thought seems to have two drawbacks, in Piaget's view: it must always retain an element of the concrete, and thus cannot be the mode for purely abstract thought. Similarly it can never be wholly mobile. This *seems* to mean that, in Gordon's or Richardson's terms, it is never wholly controllable. Imagery in children has further general characteristics, which are related to the first two. 'Pseudo-conservation' arises from a mistaken clinging to particular characteristics of an object to the neglect of more fundamental ones. This seems akin to Kuhlman's 'surface characteristics' tendency. Secondly because the image is not entirely mobile, it cannot deal with continuities. This point is not perfectly clear: Piaget seems to think it characteristic of all imagery.

> 'Try, for instance, imagining a cyclist's leg movement. One can visualize slight displacements as a foot goes down, round, and up again. But one thinks one has got the continuity only to realize that one has prolonged the image in thought, and that one is no longer actually "seeing" the whole in motion.'

Piaget next deals with the relationship of imagery to perception and imitation. These three are what are termed 'figurative mechanisms'. That is to say, they are the ways we have of forming a representation of the environment, as opposed to the operative mechanisms, which are ways of manipulating it. In contrast to the work quoted by Neisser, Piaget's experiments show important differences between perception and imagery. He concludes that imagery cannot arise from perception; rather, it is the result of internalized imitation. This is related to the distinction between *scheme* (schème) and *schema* (schéma).

> 'If we use the term "scheme" to designate a generalization instrument enabling the subject to isolate and utilize the elements common to similar successive behaviours, then there are perceptual schemes, sensori-motor schemes, operational schemes, and so on. And in this sense there also exist imaginal schemes enabling the subject to construct analogous images in comparable situations. But if we use the term "schema" to designate a simplified model intended to facilitate presentation (such as a topographical

schema, etc.), then there can be no perceptual "schemata", since the "schema" serves only for figuration and evocation. Imaginal figuration, on the other hand, is "schematized" precisely in the "schema" sense, though at the same time it may involve "schemes".'

The next two headings deal with the relationships between images and pre-operational thought respectively. This is a complex matter. We have already seen that the development of imagery is in some ways parallel to that of thought. The image corresponding to preoperational thought is static, just as that stage of thought is irreversible. In general, Piaget and Inhelder conclude:

'... the laws of the image account for the existence of or at least reinforce certain aspects of pre-operational thought Reciprocally, pre-operational thought explains certain characteristics of the image.'

In the operational stage likewise, the image becomes less static as thought becomes more flexible. Again there is an interaction or 'collaboration', complicated by the limitations of imagery as a representation of the environment—it is only an approximate copy, for example.

'The image is not actually an element of thought, but like language, and, at least in spatial spheres, with more evident success than language, it does serve as a symbolic instrument signifying the content of cognitive significations.'

It is thus necessary to consider in what sense the image is symbolic. This is part of a more general question, namely the role of what Piaget terms the 'semiotic' function. This includes:

'arbitrary and social "signs", motivated "symbols" (resemblance between symbolizer and symbolized), individual "symbols" (symbolic play, dream, etc.) and social symbols.'

This semiotic function is important, for without it:

'thought could not be formulated, and consequently could not be expressed intelligibly either to others or to oneself (internal language, etc.).'

Language alone cannot fulfil this role. In the first place, it is too abstract, too impersonal: it can express, for example, numbers, but not the personal number-forms by which individuals may represent them. Secondly, images are needed to store experience of the environment. This seems to be the same point as that of Berlyne in his 'spy' example. Several complex arguments are presented to show that images can in fact be regarded as symbols. This leads to the final main point, the epistemological significance of the image. Briefly, this is that it fits into the general Piagetian theory of knowledge as assimilation. Here as elsewhere Piaget rejects the notion that knowledge can be simply a copy of reality.

The whole body of results and theory is finally summarized thus:

'All in all, what has been shown by our study of images, considered as the highest forms of the figurative instruments, is this. In the first place, the representation of a perceived or perceptible datum does not constitute a cognition, and it does not become a cognition until it is based on an operational comprehension of the transformations accounting for the datum. But, in the second place, we have also seen that once the functional interaction of the figurative and operative functions is assured, the image's symbolic role is by no means as negligible as the extreme reaction to classical associationism might have suggested. The image ensures finer analysis of "states", and even aids figural anticipation of "transformations", in spite of the irreducibly static character of such a figuration. This makes the image an indispensable auxiliary in the functioning of the very dynamism of thought—but only as long as it remains consistently subordinate to such operational dynamism, which it cannot replace, and which it can only express symbolically with degrees of distortion or fidelity according to circumstances.'

After that rather long exposition, which is however justified by the extent of Piaget's enquiries, there remain two areas in which imagery must be mentioned as having a function. The role of the body-image is clear, since it is the representation of knowledge without which we could not move about the world. However, there appears to be relatively little firm experimental evidence available. The body image is reported to become less clear in schizophrenia. Darby (1970) reports a not very successful attempt to remedy this by making patients more aware of their own bodies. Body image seems subject to distortion by some psychogenic drugs (e.g. psilocybin; Fisher, 1969). (As was Alice's after eating the mushroom.) Possible disturbance of body image during adolescence are discussed by Laufer (1968) from a psychoanalytic viewpoint. Meisels and Guardo (1969) relate the concept to the development of personal space schemata. The function of imagery in psychotherapy is uncertain. Behaviour therapists seem to think that an image of a situation can be used as a half-way house to the real thing. A similar use has been attempted in psychotherapy. For example Brown (1969) reports:

'When a patient revealed an object or situation that made him feel tense or nervous, he was told to put his ideas and feelings about the object or situation into a mental image—an imagined situation, a fantasy, a caricature, a cartoon, or a representation in animal form.'

Where what is involved is the 'image' of a parent, or whatever, presumably a subjectively experienced image is not necessarily involved, but rather a set of attitudes.

THE STATUS OF IMAGERY*

The work of Bruner et al., and that of Piaget and Inhelder, brings us again to consider the more general use of the term 'image' by cognitive theorists. The main concern of Miller, Galanter, and Pribram (1960) was to show how actions come under the control of mediating strategies, or in their terms the relationship

* We are very grateful to George Butterworth for his contribution to the following discussion.

between PLANS and the image. Behaviour is considered as under the control of PLANS, or hierarchies of feedback loops known as TOTE units (Test Operate Test Exit). These utilize information from the environment and feedback from ongoing behaviour, in such a way as to make the behaviour conform to an expected outcome. This outcome is encoded in the *image*, which as we noted earlier is the organism's knowledge about itself and the world. 'Image' is thus a representation, but the term is extended to be all-embracing. Miller *et al.* maintain that much adult behaviour is verbally mediated (possibly through 'verbal imagery'); but their general use of the term implies that under most circumstances the 'image' in planning behaviour is not available to self-conscious awareness.

The notion of an image in this sense has been popular for some time now, especially with certain groups of physiological psychologists and neurophysiologists working within the framework of Russian 'Pavlovian' experimental psychology (whose work Pribram often refers to in more recent elaborations of the ideas contained in *Plans and the Structure of Behaviour*). Sokolov (1960) for instance suggested that the physiological basis of habituation (the gradual disappearance of the response made to any stimulus which is constantly repeated) was a 'Neuronal model'—a kind of neurophysiological record of the relevant features of the stimulus in question. So long as feedback from this 'image' shows that there has been no change in the stimulus, Sokolov argued the organism will habituate. Whenever a discrepancy occurs, however between the model and the stimulus the 'orienting reflex' reappears—the organism alerts and attends to the stimulus. (Direct physiological evidence for the operation of this kind of mechanism in a slightly different behavioural context is provided by for example Anokhin, 1969).

Neisser (1963, 1967) has made much of a distinction between two different modes of information processing: parallel and sequential. (See *Models*). The concept is derived from two alternative ways of programming computers for pattern recognition tasks. Neisser suggests that conscious awareness is a sequential process—a 'train of thought'—but that unconsciously information is also processed in parallel. He further relates parallel processes to unconscious though as described by Freud, and to creative thinking. The theory does not seem altogether satisfactory, for reasons discussed elsewhere. But it could be argued that as far as perception and visual imagery are concerned—and we have seen that Neisser considers these closely related—parallel processes offer the possibility of the integration and simultaneous representation of the sequential elements of input such as the scanning movements of the eyes. These two sorts of process are likewise very reminiscent of the differences between language and imagery pointed out by Piaget and Inhelder.

Luria (1966) also postulates a dichotomy of information processing systems in the human cerebral cortex, on the evidence of the behaviour of individuals with circumscribed brain lesions. He found two major categories of effect:

(1) The disruption of spatial and logico-grammatical relationships resulting from lesions in the parieto-temporo-occipital zone (the region of simultaneous syntheses).

(2) The disruption of the performance of skilled movements, including eye movements, and disturbance of the 'regulatory role of speech' when lesions were in the frontal, pre-frontal, temporal and central areas (the regions of successive syntheses). This may be compared with Miller *et al.*'s notion of an 'image' as a simultaneous representation, and a PLAN as a sequential control operation.

We should also notice that Paivo and Csapo (1969) argued that visual imagery is subserved by, or rather functions as, a parallel processing system, whereas the verbal symbolic system is specialized for sequential processing. Accordingly, they hypothesized:

> 'that performance in nonsequential memory tasks would ... vary directly with the availability of both memory codes, but the verbal code alone would be crucial in sequential memory.'

In support of this, they carried out the following experiment.

> 'The availability of imagery was manipulated by the use of abstract words, concrete words, and easily labelled pictures as stimuli. The availability of the verbal code, in the case of pictures, was varied by presenting the stimuli at rates presumably above and below implicit labelling threshold. Immediate memory span and serial learning constituted the sequential tasks; free recall and recognition memory, the nonsequential tasks. Consistent with predictions (1) memory for pictures was significantly inferior to words only in the sequential memory tasks, and then only at the fast rate; (2) both pictures and concrete words exceeded the abstract words in serial learning at the slow rate; and (3) pictures were significantly superior to abstract words at the slow rate in both nonsequential tasks, with concrete words intermediate in each case.'

'Imagery', therefore, is used in a variety of ways, some more general, some more specific. The most general use is as the whole body of knowledge an organism has. Then there seem to be some more restricted uses, implying certain areas of knowledge, such as the body-image, or the 'image' of the parents as used in psychotherapy. Then there is imagery as a possible part of thought processes, as discussed by Piaget and Inhelder. Here imagery divides itself into two, as it were, one half being imagery as more usually understood, the other being verbal imagery, which seems to be equated with inner speech. In these cases the question arises as to whether the image can be regarded simply as a copy of the environment. Piaget denies this. Views such as those of Neisser, stressing the closeness of imagery and perception, come nearer to the 'copy' thesis. Berlyne's version is perhaps nearer still. An image in all these senses is a representation; but usually some awareness of the representation is also implied. If we accept the close relationship between parallel and sequential processes on the one hand, and visual and verbal imagery on the other, then consciousness would not seem to be an absolute requirement. And as Piaget and Inhelder argue, we can speak of an image even when the object it represents is present to the senses. Thus of Richardson's four criteria for mental imagery, viz. quasi-perceptual, awareness, absence of sensation, and having different consequences from those of real stimuli, I should be inclined to accept only the last.

The rejection of imagery by a strictly behaviourist approach would seem to have been based on two arguments methodological and conceptual. Imagery, it might be argued, is a subjective experience which can only be reached by introspection, and this is unacceptable since it does not conform to the general scientific principle that observation should be public and objectively verifiable. Further, imagery must be ruled out of the realm of psychology since science should not postulate processes of which objective knowledge is impossible, and which seem to offend the principle of parsimony. Apologists for imagery need to consider answers to those objections. The methodological argument refers to conscious experience; and the first answer is that even a strict behaviourism readmitted experiences as 'verbal reports'. A second answer is that it still makes sense to speak of 'imagery' even without conscious experience, meaning certain events in a sequence leading from Stimulus to Response (this seems to be Berlyne's approach). But there is nothing special about imagery here: and even if we do not need introspection for this purpose, it is foolish to pretend that *no* subjective experiences exist; and these can only be reached in one way. This way is discussed in the *Focus* of the chapter, *Thinking as a Private Experience*. Thus a better answer seems to be a fairly commonsense one, that it is in general unwise to reject any source of data, while remaining aware of any peculiar difficulties. And a better one still might be, that we prefer to have as many checks on our observations as may be, and that this applies to imagery in just the same way as it does to bar-pressing. One version of this is to regard introspections in the same light as questionnaire responses: useful in so far as they correlate with known behaviour. Another approach is to seek techniques for objectifying the variables involved, as Paivio has done with his imagery norms for words.

The consideration of imagery as conscious experience raises the conceptual issue. Awareness is held to be a criterion of imagery by Richardson. In that case, imagery would at least be directly observable by one person. If we do not want to make conscious experience an absolute criterion (and that is the view we favour here), then direct observation becomes impossible. Probably no one, however, would now insist that psychology should not deal with un-observable concepts, or postulated intervening variables. This is essential even in the physical sciences: what else is gravity, for example? But it is less clear just what is the theoretical status of the concept in different writers. Berlyne, for example, seems to mean that an 'image' is an inference drawn from behaviour. But are we to regard imagery simply as a convenient way of summarizing data? MacCorquodale and Meehl (1948) in a classic paper, distinguished between intervening variables and hypothetical constructs. The first can be regarded as a sort of shorthand way of expressing some value of a known dimension; or rather, the relationship between an independent and a dependent variable. For example, take hunger. It would be possible to restrict one's use of the word 'hungry' to mean something like 'deprived of food for n hours', or 'a food-deprived rat presses a bar when that results in obtaining pellets'. Hypothetical constructs, on the other hand, constitute some postulated, unobserved, process.

Similarly, 'processing an image' might be restricted to 'responding to surface characteristics'. Most theorists would want to say more than this. Hypothetical constructs, however, are of at least two kinds. In one case, some actual process is supposed, but nothing is said about what constitutes it. Broadbent's (1958) filter is an example. To speak of a 'filter' is equivalent to saying 'stimuli are selected', or 'a filtering process takes place'. We need not necessarily say anything about how or where this occurs. Hypothetical constructs in psychology are often of this kind. On the other hand we may try to say more; as for example Hebb (1949) did with his cell assemblies, or the Gestalt psychologists with their physiological isomorphism. When such neurophysiological speculations are made, they tend often to be quickly disproved by physiologists, as happened in both these cases. The mental structures of Piaget would seem to be somewhere between these two extreme types. A 'scheme', for example, is an 'instrument'; it is presumably not just a re-description of a way of behaving. And it would certainly be a mistake to think that no psychological construct can be real, or even worth bothering with, unless we can show what is its physiological substrate. The real criterion is, how useful and how testable are the hypotheses that can be derived from it.

FOCUS: EIDETIC MEMORY

We turn our attention now to a particular type of image which is currently being intensively studied in a number of psychological laboratories around the world—the eidetic image. What is eidetic imagery, and how does it differ from other types of image? What is its function? These are, broadly, the questions we intend to consider in this section. We shall not attempt to review in detail the history of the topic. The early literature is not large and has been extensively documented elsewhere (see, for example, Jaensch, 1930). And Leask *et al.* (1969) and Richardson (1969) cover the very few investigations which have been reported since this time. Suffice it to say that the term *eidetic*, meaning that which is seen, was used first by Jaensch to refer to the particularly vivid form of image described more precisely by Richardson as:

> '... a form of percept-like imagery differing from after-imagery by persisting longer and not requiring a fixed gaze for its formation. It can occur in relation to a complex stimulus pattern and its vivid details are described in the present tense while being seen projected on some external surface.

The colouring of this image is always positive and even the after-image to a small homogeneous colour patch is typically positive for the eidetic individual.' (Richardson, 1969)

Haber and Haber (1964) have developed a standard controlled technique for studying eidetic imagery in children, some details of which can be given. Briefly, in their experiments the subject was seated at a table with an easel, on which were presented various stimuli—pictures, etc. Normal conditions of illumination prevailed and a tape recorder was used to record the exchanges which took place. The following instructions were given to all subjects.

'Now, I am going to show you some pictures... I do not want you to stare in one place, but to move your eyes around so that you can be sure you can see all of the details. When I take the picture away, I want you to continue to look hard at the easel where the picture was, and tell me what you can still see after I take it away. After I take it away, you also can move your eyes all over where it was on the easel. And be sure, while the picture is on the easel that you move your eyes around it to see all of the parts.'

Other relevant details were:

'all four pictures were presented for 30 sec. each. E watched closely to be sure the pictures were scanned and not fixated. The first picture was of a family scene, black pictures pasted on a grey board to form a silhouette. The second, constructed in the same way, was of an Indian hunting, with a deer, other animals, and some birds.... The third, in full colour, showed an Indian fishing in a canoe with many fish in the water. The fourth, also in colour, from *Alice in Wonderland*, depicted Alice standing at the base of a large tree staring up at the Cheshire cat....'

After each picture was removed the experimenter tried to elicit as much information as possible about what the subject could now see on the easel, prompting whenever necessary. A careful check on eye movements was also kept. We shall consider the results of the Haber studies in more detail later.

On Richardson's definition it is clear we are dealing with a type of imagery of a very special sort, which as we shall see, is found in only a very small proportion of individuals. This does not mean of course that it is not potentially informative. The study of unusual or atypical psychological conditions can often be very instructive—see, for example, the recent work on disorders of memory, perception and language found in cases of mental illness and brain damage (e.g. Shallice and Warrington, 1970; Teuber and Milner, 1968); the unique opportunities provided by cataract removal in the blind for testing theories of perception (e.g. Gregory and Wallace, 1963); or, for that matter, psychology's long-lasting love affair with the geometric and other visual illusions. As Weiskrantz (1968) argues, whenever psychological processes are disturbed in an unusual fashion we are entitled to make inferences about the underlying mechanisms—what they might be, how they interact and so on—in an effort to gain more insight

11—T * •

314

into the processes in question. Whatever status we accord the eidetic image, it is clear that similar arguments apply.

One recent particularly striking case of what appears to be eidetic imagery is reported by Luria (1968). In a beautiful little book, *The Mind of a Mnemonist*, Luria gives us a detailed account of the mind and abilities of one man, Shereshevskii (S.), whom he had known for over thirty years. According to Luria, this man lived in an image-laden, almost fairy-tale world. Every sensation, every experience gave rise to a rich complex of vivid mental images. His powers of retention were, to all intents and purposes, limitless. He was able, for instance, to reproduce without error list upon list of items which had been presented to him 15 or 16 years previously. And not surprisingly he became a well-known stage mnemonist. S.'s problem in fact was not in remembering things but in *forgetting* them, an exercise which he claims required special techniques. Further investigation showed that in learning a series of words, S. might imagine a street and locate the images aroused by the words at various points—in doorways, on fences etc. Recall involved a search process *par excellence*—S. would simply take a mental walk along the route in question and pick out the appropriate images. Sometimes he made mistakes but it seems that these were essentially perceptual rather than failures of memory. S.'s own account of this is convincing enough:

> 'I put the image of the *pencil* near a fence... the one down the street, you know. But what happened was that the image fused with that of the fence and I walked right on past without noticing it. The same thing happened with the word *egg*. I had put it up against a white wall and it blended in with the background. How could I possibly spot a white egg up against a white wall? Now take the word *blimp*. That's something gray, so it blended in with the gray of the pavement... *Banner*, of course, means the Red Banner [of course!]. But, you know, the building which houses the Moscow City Soviet of Workers' Deputies is also red, and since I'd put the banner close to one of the walls of the building I just walked in without seeing it... Then there's the word *putamen*. I don't know what this word means, but it's such a dark word that I couldn't see it... and, besides, the street lamp was quite a distance away....'

S. apparently was also synaesthetic; that is to say, imagery aroused by a particular word or event was often in more than one modality. In S.'s own words:

> '... I recognize a word not only by the images it evokes but by a whole complex of feelings that image arouses. It's hard to express... it's not a matter of vision or hearing but some over-all sense I get. Usually I experience a word's taste and weight, I don't have to make an effort to remember it—the word seems to recall itself. But it's difficult to describe. What I sense is something oily slipping through my hand... or I'm aware of a slight tickling in my left hand caused by a mass of tiny, lightweight points. When that happens I simply remember, without having to make the attempt....'

S. also claimed people's voices change noticeably many times a day and is alleged to have told Vigotsky that he had 'a crumbly yellow voice'.

As far as his intellectual abilities were concerned, S. claimed to be at an advantage with certain types of problem. An account of these would necessitate lengthy explanation but it is clear that S.'s unique capacities did enable him to handle some problems with remarkable ease and with others he shows a highly idiosyncratic mode of approach, quite different from the strategies the 'normal' thinker would employ. S. did experience great difficulty however in handling homonyms, synonyms, metaphors and a whole range of abstract concepts. Apparently not even the most complex forms of synaesthetic imagery enabled him to cope with the latter. There is a limit, we might say, to what can be achieved through ikonic representation.

Fascinating though these findings are, Luria argues (p. 62) that S.'s memory should *not* be thought of as eidetic. Synaesthesia for instance, is not a typical characteristic of eidetic memory. Moreover Shereshevskii 'had far greater mobility with his images in that they could be made to serve his purposes'. So we are back with the problem of criteria. There is no point in quarrelling with Luria's interpretation here—synaesthesia certainly must complicate the picture, but an accurate assessment of S.'s abilities really requires a clear set of criteria for eidetic imagery. To these we now turn.

There are two questions to be considered. Firstly, what *kind* of image is the eidetic image? What are the *correlates* of eidetic imagery? Second, what evidence is there for the remarkable claims sometimes made about the ability of those possessing eidetic imagery to retain information? Can we be sure that the increased capacity, such as it is, is due to the special qualities of eidetic imagery rather than simply to the possession of a 'good memory'?

With regard to the first question, we must deal at the outset with the possibility that the eidetic image is just a particularly durable form of after-image. Richardson (1969) specifically mentions this in his definition, and Leask, Haber and Haber (1969) in a detailed and highly informative review of their own and other studies of eidetic imagery in children, are satisfied that it can be ruled out. Three of the criteria for eidetic imagery which they discuss are relevant—the duration of the image should be substantial, especially larger than is likely from after-images of comparable stimuli; the subject must be able to move his eyes over the stimulus during the inspection period; he must also be able to move his eyes over his image. The last two points are particularly important if after-imagery is to be ruled out. We can accept therefore that unusual physiological, basically retinal, processes are not responsible for eidetic imagery. But what else can we say about it? Well there is the question of its incidence. At one time it was thought to be a fairly common phenomenon, especially in children (Jaensch's estimate is about 60 per cent) but the meticulous studies of the Habers suggest the much lower figure of 8 per cent. However a higher percentage is reported by Siipola and Hayden (1965) in a study of 34 mentally retarded children. They found 9 of their subjects to be eidetic, and 8 of these were said to have brain damage. The implication of brain pathology reminds one of the work of Penfield (see, for instance, Penfield, 1966) who reported the results of a series of investigations with patients having temporal lobe epilepsy. Such patients often complain of rather disturbing visual disorders, sometimes hallucinatory, and of course suffer from epileptic seizures. If these cannot be satisfactorily controlled with drugs there is no alternative but to resort to surgery —temporal lobectomy. Penfield (a neurosurgeon) took the opportunity, at operation, of observing the effects of stimulating the temporal lobes of his patients with electrodes. Apparently some of them reported sensory experiences of the kind which would normally occur in the presence of an external stimulus—flashing lights, noises, etc. With others it was as if the memory traces of previous events had been revived—the patients reported experiencing vivid detailed images and sensations which flowed by as if a film were being shown. Naturally one would be cautious in making too much of these data but it is interesting that Penfield mentions 8 per cent as being the number of subjects exhibiting this behaviour. This of course is exactly the percentage of children classified by Haber and Haber as eidetic. Taking into account also the findings of Siipola and Hayden, could there be a link here? Could eidetic ability be due to some disturbance of information processing resulting from brain damage, possibly very slight? To put it crudely, when parts of the brain (especially the temporal lobes) are knocked about, is this one of the more unusual consequences? Of course this is pure speculation—there is no evidence for instance that all eidetic individuals are brain-damaged (although Leask et al., 1969, do report a significantly greater incidence of eye problems, possibly of central origin, in one of their eidetic samples). But it remains an interesting possibility.

Apart from the possible implication of brain pathology, there seems little else we can say about those classified as eidetic, as individuals. In Leask et al.'s own words:

> '... eidetic children seem to be randomly distributed in all variables examined. While only a small number of possibly relevant variables have been explored, these include some of the more obvious ones. It should be added that all of the Es who worked with these children felt the same way: except for their imagery and its properties these children all seemed to be among those typically found in any elementary school.'

On the other hand there is more we can say about the special qualities of the eidetic image itself. Most of the subjects studied by Leask et al. apparently were able to terminate their eidetic images by blinking, but it is not clear how this works. In addition there is the possibility that an eidetic image may be restricted to the eye initially exposed to the stimulus—obviously the question is difficult to resolve since testing for laterality involves closing one eye, which of course is tantamount to blinking. There are also individual differences in the ability to control eidetic images, that is, to 'move' them from one surface to another. And very few children are able to develop 3-D eidetic images of 3-D objects. Finally, if eidetic images are allowed to disappear spontaneously, all children (in the Haber studies) report an identical pattern of fading by parts.

There is very strong evidence, then, that eidetic ability does involve imagery, and imagery of a very special kind—it is a *perceptual* phenomenon. And unless we are to claim that a very small percentage of children is capable of systematically duping experimental psychologists in an identical fashion we must conclude that we are dealing here with a most unusual ability indeed.

Our second question concerns the extent to which eidetic imagery makes possible the retention of large amounts of information—the term 'photographic memory' comes to mind here. Is the eidetic image like a photograph? Can information literally be read from it as has been reported by some? Leask *et al.* make the simple but important point that the duration of eidetic imagery must not be confused with the information content of it—the availability of the 'trace', or whatever, for abnormally long periods is quite a separate matter from the amount or type of information it contains.

Under standard conditions of testing it would appear that 'normal' eidetic subjects recall details of the stimuli presented with only marginally increased accuracy. (Leask *et al.*, 1969.) In fact it seems that these subjects distinguish between their eidetic ability and more conventional memory processes. They do not form images of stimuli which they label or describe while examining them. As Leask *et al.* remark, 'Imagery and memory seem opposites, not confounded'. Further explanation of the relationship between memory capacities and eidetic imagery proved enlightening. Eidetic subjects were able to develop images of printed verbal material but the quality of these was generally poorer than those formed from pictures. And there are some interesting scanning and position effects in the subjects' recall. In general both clarity of image and accuracy of recall of ten letter nonsense sequences were related to recency of scanning. If the subject was required to report the letters in the opposite order from which they were originally scanned (from right to left when the items have been scanned from left to right), he was, on average, more accurate than when his order of report was the same as the direction of scanning. Moreover his 'serial position curve' does not show the traditional primacy effect generally found in verbal learning experiments. Finally, it seems that the very attempt to assess the memory potential of an eidetic image is doomed to failure since most eidetic subjects are, in fact, incapable of developing images of very complex stimuli, especially if they contain verbal material. Leask *et al.* designed a 'rogues' gallery' composed of black and white drawings of twenty-five different 'rogues' each having his number below and his name above. It was their intention to compare their subjects' recall of this information from an eidetic image with recall from ordinary memory. But, as the authors comment,

'Only four of the Ss developed eidetic images of the gallery, and these images were so incomplete that the children were unable to report much. There is the possibility that the 3-sec exposure for each rogue was not long enough to permit an eidetic image to develop. However, many of the children felt that they would never develop an eidetic image of it even with extremely long exposures, since there was too much information to take in. Although the gallery is a meaningful stimulus, it is not cohesive in that it is a composite of 25 separate pictures that do not necessarily fit together. Apparently such a non-cohesive, yet saturated, stimulus is too difficult and disrupts the eidetic process.'

And summarizing their work on this whole question,

'In summary, the exceptional memory claimed for eidetic children fails to be substantiated. If it is accepted that such children have an image they are describing, that image contains a large amount of information—far greater than an after image is likely to have—but no more than a response from memory has. We have not been able to undertake quantitative descriptions of the image content as compared to memory content—we do not know if the same or different information is present in an image as compared to a memory of a picture.'

A recent single case study reported in *Nature* however, does complicate the issue. The authors of this paper, Stromeyer and Psotka (1970) describe in detail the results of their research with a 23-year-old female teacher possessing a quite remarkable eidetic ability. The technique used was similar to one used with some eidetic subjects by the Habers (Leask *et al.*, 1969). Two stimuli which are designed to form a composite third when one is superimposed on the other, are presented successively to the subject. In the case of the Stromeyer and Psotka study the stimuli were random dot stereograms—patterns of, for example, tiny white dots on a black background. In normal circumstances one of these is presented to each eye simultaneously in a stereoscope, a device which enables the two to be combined perceptually. The patterns for the left and right eye are identical apart from a particular area, often symmetrical or in the shape of a letter, which is shifted a few dots sideways in one of the patterns relative to the other. When viewed stereoscopically the effect is of the critical figure or letter standing out in depth, even though each pattern appears 'random' when viewed alone. In Stromeyer and Psotka's experiments the stereograms were presented successively, and it is worth pointing out that normal subjects cannot detect the target figure when the interval separating the two patterns exceeds about 150 ms. (Eriksen and Collins, 1967). Stromeyer and Psotka's eidetic subject however was able to do this virtually without effort even when the interstimulus interval was as great as three days and the dots very small indeed. Inspired guesswork was effectively ruled out by conducting 'double blind' experiments in which the experimenter does not even know what the figures are and thus cannot influence the subject.

As the authors note, these experiments seem incredible. It seems that this subject possesses a highly unusual form of eidetic imagery, more like in fact the classical 'photographic memory'. But what is being studied here is not, strictly, *recall*—although this subject is able to carry round an accurate representation of a random pattern of dots for three days it is not clear in what sense this information is *available* to her. It is a pity that the authors do not provide any comparable details of their subject's memory for conventional verbal and pictorial stimuli, such as, for example the 'rogues' gallery'. Would her performance substantiate Leask *et al.*'s claim that in the eidetic subject 'imagery and memory seem opposites, not confounded'? In other words even if an eidetic image is a perfect photograph, is it necessarily looked upon as a form of *memory*? For that matter could eidetic imagery ever provide a useful basis for efficient remembering—the whole point about memory is that it is *organized*, often conceptually. Might retrieval of information be a rather clumsy process, like searching for the relevant page of a book or the beginning of a particular passage of music on a gramophone record?

This brings us to our final question which concerns the function of the eidetic image. On the basis of what we have argued in the preceding paragraphs we can, I think, reject to begin with the idea that eidetic imagery is a specialized medium for storing information in memory. There are however clues in what we have already said in the main section of this chapter about 'ordinary' imagery processes. It will be remembered that Paivio, Haber and Neisser, among others, have all put forward the suggestion, in their different ways, that information processing can take place in two alternative modes or systems. Paivio, for instance, suggested that visual imagery functions primarily as a parallel processing system while verbal symbolic processing is essentially sequential. J. S. Bruner of course has proposed a similar distinction between ikonic and symbolic modes of representation, the former (representation through imagery) gradually decreasing in importance as the latter (representation through symbols, especially language) eventually becomes the dominant mode, at least in children brought up in a Western culture. This last point is of particular relevance here since Bruner's studies suggest that some non-Western cultures do not contain the 'amplifiers' which foster the development of the symbolic mode, with the result that the individuals in such cultures remain at the ikonic level of functioning. Might it be, then, that eidetic imagery is a relic, as it were, of this ikonic mode? This would explain the relative rarity of eidetic imagery in adults (and perhaps the accuracy and persistence of it when it *is* present) compared with children. But is eidetic imagery more common among primitive peoples? Well, broadly the answer is, yes. Doob (1965) using the standard Haber and Haber procedure claimed that 20 per cent of his Kamba subjects (Central Kenya) were definitely eidetic. Feldman (1968) studied eidetic imagery in Ghana. In one sample of 39 children, 69 per cent were found to be eidetic while 48 per cent of a sample of 83 illiterate adults were classified as eidetic. Levak (1969) studied two groups of Bororo subjects (Brazil) one of which was relatively civilized or acculturated in comparison with the other. The ages of the subjects in the two groups were uncertain but seem roughly comparable. Seven out of thirty-nine unacculturated subjects showed a degree of eidetic ability while none of the other group ($N = 33$) were found to have it. On the other hand, Doob (1966) describing eidetic imagery as a 'cross cultural will-o'-the-wisp', found a slight *positive* relationship between the incidence of eidetic imagery and acculturation in groups of subjects in Tanzania. And there are other negative results which we could, but will not bother to quote. Doob incidentally reminds us of some of the unique problems which accompany cross-cultural work:

> 'Almost always at least half a dozen spectators stood round to watch and listen; infants, crowing chickens, placid dogs, and sometimes cattle also intruded. The general atmosphere, in short, was jolly, cordial, and incredibly noisy; . . .' (Doob, 1965)

These, of course, are not the only problems. Feldman points out that the phrase 'picture in the head' used as a translation of eidetic imagery can be misleading, since it is commonly used, at least in Ghana, to mean 'having a clear memory'. And Levak's subjects were apparently highly suspicious of the experiment, some suspecting witchcraft. And then there are the many questions relating to the suggestibility of subjects, their susceptibility to 'set', desire to please etc., infrequently considered and difficult to control. Some form of the 'composite stimuli' procedure mentioned previously could profitably be used in crosscultural work.

Eidetic imagery then remains much of a mystery. It clearly exists in a small number of individuals as a form of imagery separate from conventional memory processes. Whether it is more than a curiosity, however, is a matter for debate and further research.

FURTHER READING

Haber, R. N. (1969). *'Eidetic Imagery'*, Scient. Am., **220**, 136–144 (Reprint 522).
Horowitz, M. J. (1970). *Image Formation and Cognition.* Appleton–Century–Crofts.
McKellar, P. (1968). *Experience and Behaviour.* Penguin Books.
Paivio, A. (1971). *Imagery and Verbal Processes.* Holt, Rinehart and Winston.
Piaget, J., and Inhelder, D. (1966). *Mental Imagery in the Child.* Routledge and Kegan Paul.
Richardson, A. (1969). *Mental Imagery.* Routledge and Kegan Paul.

9

Models

THE USE OF MODELS

The making of *models* as an aid to scientific understanding has a long and distinguished history. The first scientific model is said to have been made by Anaximander (?611–?547 B.C.). It was a map. One of the things that the legendary Greek philosophers did when they invented science was to make a representation of the known facts that was true in some important respect. A map, to be of use, must represent correctly in at least one respect. For example, a map would be of some use if it showed in which direction towns lay from each other, even if the distances were wrong. In Hereford Cathedral you may see the famous Hereford *Mappa Mundi*, a mediaeval representation of the world which shows Jerusalem at the centre, in accordance with its theological importance, and which is adorned with mythical creatures such as sciopods. The *Mappa Mundi* may have helped the devout to find Heaven, but it would not have been much use to pilgrims seeking the Holy Land.

Often we think of a model as a small and perhaps incomplete version of some 'real' thing: a model train, for example. Some model builders, wishing to bring out the value of what they are doing, break away entirely from this view. Ross Ashby (1962) argues that:

> 'All machines (systems) that resemble another machine (system) in some
> well-defined way stand in the same fundamental "model" relationship to it.'

One of the points he wants to bring out is that two models of the same thing may themselves be completely unalike. A jelly and a set of electrical circuits could both be models of the brain, it just depends which aspects we are interested in. But Ashby's view leads to absurdities, for it would be odd to say that the solar system is a model of any orrery (a working representation of the sun and planets, named after the eighteenth century astronomer Lord Orrery).

Chapanis (1961) has a somewhat more restricted version:

> 'Scientific or engineering models are representations, or likenesses, of cer-
> tain aspects of complex events, structures, or systems, made by using
> symbols or objects, which in some way resemble the thing being modelled.'

To be useful, the resemblance must of course be significant in some sense; but the question of the usefulness of models we must leave for the moment. Chapanis' definition enables us to bring out some other points. One is that, in general, a model is in some respects at least *simpler* than the original. If it were equally complex, it would be strange to call it a model. It follows from this that certain features only are selected for imitation. A decision has to be made before starting. If, later, conclusions are drawn from the model, they are likely to be affected by the choice that was originally made. With many everyday models, this is obvious. If designers of a new aeroplane make a mock-up to show the shape of the fuselage, it would not be expected to fly, and conclusions could not be drawn about the engine, or about the seating arrangements. Or indeed a model aeroplane *may* fly, but be driven by a rubber band. It would be false to conclude from the model that that is how the real thing is powered. If this example seems ridiculous, it serves to show that if computers, for example, solve problems, they are not necessarily 'thinking': or more precisely, they are not necessarily doing whatever it is that humans do when they solve problems.

Thring has devised robots which can do some human-like activities (rather slowly and laboriously) such as walk up stairs and sweep the floor. They are not very interesting to psychologists, since their mode of operation is quite different from that of human beings.

Similar arguments apply to the various automata of which people were fond in the eighteenth and nineteenth centuries, and which could dance or play the organ. At one end of this scale, it might not be impossible in the future—indeed theoretically it must be possible—to construct an imitation human being by constructing and assembling a replica of each part. Grey Walter (1953) has however pointed out the practical problems in producing even a brain, to consist of 10,000,000,000 imitation neurons at say sixpence each. (Since he wrote the sixpence has unfortunately disappeared as a unit of currency.) Frankenstein's creation I would not regard as a model, as it was made up from parts of actual human bodies.

Resisting the temptation to wander off in pursuit of zombies and golems, and returning to Chapanis, let us note that he refers to 'representations . . . of events, structures, or systems'. *Representation* is a rather general word. It could certainly include physical objects; but it could also include pictures or diagrams, and abstract expressions such as mathematical equations. It seems at present that the most useful sorts of model for understanding thought processes are those using computers: and it is these with which we shall largely be concerned. The reasons for this will, we hope, appear. But one superficially plausible reason can be disposed of. The machinery of some computers bears a resemblance to the machinery of the brain. Computers are basically of two types: analog and digital. In *analog* computers the elements of computation are represented by continuous variables. A slide rule is an example—numbers are represented by length. *Digital* computers operate on discrete elements. In hand calculating machines these are the usual decimal numbers. In high speed computers, they are on–off elements, simply because these are technically easier to manipulate. A computer contains a large number of such elements, and a brain contains a large number of neurons, which can be seen as operating in a somewhat similar way. However, the importance of this is obscure. In the first place the number of elements in the (human) brain is vastly greater than in the computer. Next the intricacies of the connection of the elements in the brain are far from being fully understood. There is, for example, the fact that when parts of the brain are destroyed, the rest of it can, at least to some extent, adapt so as to minimize the effects of the damage. There is the fact of the *two* hemispheres, complementing each other in ways not yet entirely clear. Thirdly, it is by no means certain what are the implications of possessing a particular *sort* of physical representation of symbolic processes. (I have in mind here the sort of case that McLuhan has tried to sustain, arguing for instance that particular representational systems are necessarily linked to particular thought processes.) This leads to a more specific point, which is brought out by Gregory (1970). He is concerned with the perceptual part of the nervous system, and argues that this, at least, cannot operate in a series of discrete steps. Perception must operate continuously; it must be a system that responds directly to changes in input; but it does not require the power of precise analysis that a discrete system gives. Gregory points out that the distinction between analog and digital computing systems misses the most important distinction.

> 'The point is that both "analogue" and "digital" systems represent things by their internal states. The essential difference between them is not in *how* they represent things but rather in *what* they represent. The distinction is between representing events *directly* by the states of the system, and representing *symbolic accounts* of real (or hypothetical) events. Real events always occur in a continuum, but symbolic systems are always discontinuous.'

Now clearly (as Gregory goes on to say) there certainly are important mental activities, such as logic and mathematics, which are symbolic and discontinuous. But the point is that there is only one type of nervous system. This has to accommodate both continuous representation (perception), and discontinuous (logic). The partial resemblance between the nervous system and one species of computer is thus unlikely to be of theoretical importance. Digital computers, in particular, have been used to simulate all sorts of mental processes, including both perception and reasoning. But the success or otherwise of these attempts does not depend on a physical resemblance between brain and machine.

Gregory's paper (and of course many others) is concerned with the way the environment is represented internally, and the extent to which this can be considered as a 'model' of what is real. This sense of 'model', to which we shall return, is an important one for the study of thinking. For the moment, let us pursue some of the more general issues. There are two related issues in particular: the explanatory status of models, and the relationship of a model to a theory;

324

and the usefulness and drawbacks of models. (Gregory's ideas of course were influenced by Kenneth Craik, e.g. 1943.)

R. B. Braithwaite (1962) argues that the word 'model' has been used in three ways in the social sciences. The first is as a synonym for a 'theory' (which may be formally stated to a greater or less extent). The second way is as a simulation of something, which might be a theory or any other system. The third way is as a sort of explication of a theory: expressing an unfamiliar theory in terms of one already familiar.* Braithwaite defines a *scientific theory* as: '. . . a deductive system consisting of certain *initial hypotheses* at the summit and empirically testable generalizations at the base.' Understanding a theoretical concept essentially involves demonstrating its role in a scientific theory. Analogies (models) outside the theory are not necessary for understanding. Models are linked to theories, however, in each of Braithwaite's three senses. First, some theorists, particularly in the behavioural and social sciences, have used the term 'model', according to Braithwaite, when they should more correctly have used 'theory'. They do this because the theory they are presenting seems rather a slight one, undeserving of the title 'theory'; or because they are stating some aspects of the theory in an unusually explicit way; or because the theory is supposed to hold only approximately. Braithwaite suggests, rather charmingly, that in all these cases:

'It would be better to call it a *theoruncula* or (affectionately) a *theorita*, using a Latin or Spanish diminutive, than to call it a model.'

Moving next to Braithwaite's *third* sense of model, he argues that although a model is logically unnecessary for the understanding of a theory, it can be of practical help in so doing, simply because it reduces the necessity of handling unfamiliar concepts. It is the *second* sense that is of most interest, however, for this raises the question as to what a model can do that a theory cannot, if anything. Braithwaite first defines this sense by saying that: '. . . a model for a theory T is another theory M which corresponds to the theory T in respect of deductive structure.' This is a rather strict definition, implying that the theory and the model are equivalent in every important respect. This being so, it is not surprising that Braithwaite goes on to argue that models can often add little to theories. Indeed they can *only* contribute usefully, he holds, when they add new hypotheses to the theory, which either relate together the theoretical concepts of the theory, or contain new theoretical concepts. In these cases, however, while the model may suggest an addition to the original theory, it cannot prove that this is, indeed, the way in which the theory ought to be extended. A model, in fact, provides an analogy only. This is the word used by Chapanis. It also relates to the well known distinction made by Boring (1953) between a theory, which is an 'as', and a model which is an 'as if'. By this is meant that a theory strives towards an accurate statement of reality. A model can provide some suggestions

---

* This interpretation of Braithwaite's views was suggested by Dr. Vernon Gregg.

as to what this might be. Sometimes this may be simply a matter of grouping phenomena together in a convenient and plausible way. It is suggested that this may be how much of psychoanalytic theory is best considered. This would come under Braithwaite's first sense of model, namely as a tentative theory.

It is probably this sort of case that makes models sometimes appear, to their constructors and others, to constitute explanations. The question of what is to count as explanation is a complex one, and is particularly intractable in the behavioural and social sciences. A rather simple sense of 'explanation' is 'that which satisfies an enquirer'. One way to do this is often merely to name the phenomenon, preferably with a long and scientific sounding name. Many a patient is reassured by having his discomfort classified as 'neuralgia' (which merely means 'nerve pain'). Psychoanalysis has often scored heavily here, and when the classification is backed up by an exciting and plausible story about infantile sexuality, sibling rivalry, and Oedipus complexes, the 'explanation' has often been widely accepted in the virtual absence of any evidence at all. (This is not to say that no such evidence exists.) A rather more sophisticated version of explanation consists in specifying the necessary and sufficient conditions for any phenomenon. This is what, in principle, the strict Behaviourists such as Watson and Skinner have tried to do: with notable lack of success, as many would argue, except for trivial cases. A third sort of explanation consists of a general principle with logically deducible consequences. This is what I take Braithwaite to mean by a 'theory'. In both these latter cases, as we have seen, a model, of itself, does not necessarily add anything. It is the theory that constitutes the explanation, not the model.

Thus far we have tended to disparage models. It can also be argued however that they have, at least potentially, a number of important advantages. This is especially true of working models; and of these, it is more true of computer simulation models. Several of these advantages are brought out by Ross Ashby (1962). The first is vividness: a physical model or simulation brings home to the onlooker (student, other research worker, etc.), what is meant, more clearly than a description could. Of course this could also be misleading. A second useful application is as *archive*: successive versions of a model, each incorporating new items of knowledge about the brain, or whatever it may be, constitute in themselves a record of the research. It is helpful to researchers to be able to look back on the history of their work, to consider what turned out to be fruitful or otherwise. This may seem a trivial point, but my experience of research is that, whether from excitement or laziness, one frequently fails to record the reasoning behind one's experiments, and later wonders why one did them. Ashby's third and most important use is for deduction and exploration. This means in the first place, testing. Does the model actually work? If not, the assumptions on which it is based may be false. In that case, the theory needs to be reassessed. Secondly, it means looking to see what consequences follow when the model is put to work. For example, one could in theory make a working model of Watsonian man, composed of sets of reflexes; or Hullian man, filled with interacting intervening variables. Would such models work? If they did, how like men would they be? Could one make a Watsonian child and then (as Watson claimed) produce any given type of adult? Merely to ask the questions points up at once the possible inadequacies of these theories. A third aspect of the exploratory function is that the model may turn out to have unexpected properties, which might give us new ideas about the system being simulated.

Some further points can be made.* Models may clarify the ideas of their constructor. This is particularly true of computer simulations, because computers are so literal-minded. To make a program that works, one is forced to reduce one's ideas to a series of very small steps, each following from the one before according to very rigid logical rules. This may be a useful discipline. Second, models may introduce one to new concepts which turn out to have much wider applications. An example is feedback, a concept well known in simple mechanical control systems such as the governor on an old-fashioned gramophone; but seen by Norbert Wiener to apply to control systems in general, from guided missiles to human individuals and societies. For a time feedback seemed to have an almost magical explanatory power, in so many phenomena was it seen. This points to some of the traps or dead ends into which model building can also lead. The modelling may become an end in itself. This seems to happen particularly with the construction of elegant computer programs. Now there is no good scientific reason why a lifetime should not be spent in this (or any other) activity. And there is no way of being certain that the most abstract research will not ultimately turn out to be of great practical use. But from a shorter term point of view, programming may be regarded as a means to an end, not an end in itself. This relates to the second drawback, that the delight of successful modelling may give the impression, to the modeller (or modellist, as Braithwaite calls him), and to others, that more has been achieved than is actually the case. Models may, as we have noted, be only analogous, not homologous. That is to say, they may be only superficially similar, not alike in any fundamental respect. They may get the same results as the real thing, but by completely different means. Thus they would tell us nothing about how the real thing works, or even be misleading. This is really the same point that we have discussed above in using the expression 'as if'. An 'as if' by itself is not enough; we need some evidence that it is the *right* 'as if'. For perhaps we should point out, finally, that models are most often made precisely in situations where we do not have all the facts. This is certainly true in the simulation of thought processes. The model suggests what the facts *may* be.

There is one other issue that needs to be discussed before we turn to some examples. It is the question as to how we can tell, given a model that works, that it is a correct representation of the thing simulated, at least as regards the aspects in which we are interested. The best known way is called Turing's Test. The

* The next four points originate from Professor B. M. Foss.

mathematician Alan Turing (1950) was concerned with the problem of whether a machine could be said to think. He imagined a game in which a man, a woman, and an interrogator were in separate rooms, communicating by teleprinter. The object of the interrogator is to discover which is the man and which the woman. Her object is to deceive him. In such a situation, Turing argued, a correct identification could well be impossible. Then imagine the woman replaced by a machine: if it is still impossible to tell the difference, then the machine could be said to think. This seems to me not to be so, but to confuse the evidence for thinking with thinking itself. But this of course depends on what you *mean* by thinking.

Notice that this argument does not say that the interrogator *could* not tell the difference between the man and the machine: it only says *if* . . . (like Alice). And *if* the difference could not be told, then it would certainly be *as if* the machine were thinking. Perhaps it is not unfair to regard Turing's test as a circular argument, for it seems to say that if you can't tell the difference—then you can't tell the difference. But to say that one cannot tell the difference between two things, is not to say that the two things are the same. It *suggests* that they are the same, but does not prove it. To say what *would* prove identity would require a very long philosophical detour. Perhaps sharing a reluctance to make this, some investigators have instead adopted the normal psychological procedure of applying statistics. The responses of man and machine to a particular situation can be recorded, and a test used to see whether there is any significant difference. If there is, the machine can be modified until the difference becomes non-significant. A slightly more sophisticated version of this is to do it during the course of an experiment, so that the machine (computer program) is continuously monitored, and modified to match the known responses of human subjects (Feldman, 1962).

These approaches, however, do not overcome the main difficulty, which is that while we *may* be able to show that there are no differences in observable behaviour, what we are really interested in is *unobservable*. As we noted, this raises the question—one which continually recurs—as to what we *mean* by 'thinking'. Bourne, Ekstrand, and Dominowski (1971) present a textbook of *The Psychology of Thinking* in which they explicitly take the position that thinking is a form of behaviour. For them, therefore, models must present no problem, for if the machine makes the same sort of responses as do humans when we say they are thinking: then it too is thinking. This view seems unsatisfactory, for reasons which will be discussed in the final chapter.

After these considerations, let us look at some examples of attempts to simulate aspects of behaviour using computers; particularly, behaviour related to thinking.

COMPUTER SIMULATIONS

The numerous simulations available in the literature do not fall into any systematic pattern. Some investigators have thought it best to confine themselves to very limited aspects of behaviour, in the hope of reducing the variables involved; others have felt it more meaningful to tackle more complex aspects. We do not propose to summarize reports as a whole, but shall give a variety of examples.

1. Perception of the Problem Space

Dr. P. C. Wason who, in addition to his other talents (see *Problem Solving*) is a master at postal chess, discusses (1972) the psychology of chess. He points to the fact that computers have not yet been programmed to play chess at above a good club standard. The numerical complexity of chess is of course great. Wason tells us that the first four moves alone can occur in 197,299 different ways, leading to 72,000 possible positions. An estimate of the approximate number of different possible games is 25×10^{115}. We may therefore be duly impressed by the abilities of those who surpass the computer in dealing with so complex a situation. Yet chess is relatively very simple. There are only thirty-two pieces and sixty-four squares, and all the pieces have their moves constrained. How much more complex must thinking about the real world be; and thus how much less likely that computers will be able to replicate what the human brain does. (See also our *Focus* topic).

Wason quotes some interesting experiments by de Groot. Complex game positions were displayed for five seconds, and subjects were then asked to set out what they had seen on a board. Masters were able to place over 90 per cent of the pieces correctly; weaker players only about 40 per cent. No such difference was found when the display was of pieces placed randomly. Thus what the master possesses is not a better memory for detailed placements but, presumably, a better stock of situations, from which he is able to reconstruct what he has seen. Just how this is done is not clear. Chess masters are not able to tell us by introspection how they can select moves that will lead on to success. If they were, of course, chess would hold no more interest than noughts and crosses. This situation, of first perception of a chess board, is an interesting one as representing a relatively controlled problem, and one that might lend itself to computer simulation.

Simon and Barenfeld (1969) concerned themselves with the eye movements of subjects choosing a move. Such eye movements had been recorded by Tichomirov and Poznyanskaya (1966) and others (de Groot, 1966; Winikoff, 1967). While this can be done with fair accuracy, it is not possible to record precisely which single square is being fixated at any given moment. In any case, it is likely that any fixation tells the subject something about not just one square, but also about several neighbouring ones. Simon and Barenfeld conclude that:

> 'The eye-movement records . . . show rather consistently that the fixations of subjects move from one square of the board to another at a maximum rate of about four fixations per second. It appears that at each point of fixation the subject is acquiring information about the location of pieces at or near the point of fixation, together with information about pieces in peripheral vision (within, e.g. 7° of arc) that bear a significant chess relation ("attack", "defend", "block", "shield") to the piece at the fixation point.'

Baylor (1965) and Baylor and Simon (1966) had previously devised a computer program that searched for checkmating combinations. This included subroutines for finding specific states of affairs, such as the direction between two squares, whether a specified piece was under attack, and so on. Simon and Barenfeld modified this program to make a new one, called PERCEIVER, which simulated the eye movements of human subjects. (The tendency to give programs names imparts to them a ghostly personality which may be misleading.) PERCEIVER, in addition to rules about noticing relationships between pieces, incorporated two assumptions: (1) that the information being gathered is about relations between pieces, or pieces and squares; (2) that when fixation is on piece A, and a relation to piece B is noticed, fixation will either move to B or return to A. With these (and some minor) assumptions, PERCEIVER replicated fairly well the eye movements recorded from an actual subject. One interesting discrepancy was that while the program had been constructed to fixate only occupied squares, six of the human subject's fixations were on unoccupied squares. It is interesting because the reason for the behaviour is unknown. Biological phenomena seem always to involve what appears to be a random element. It will be recalled, for example, that Hull was obliged to postulate an 'O' or oscillation factor towards the output end of his chain of intervening variables. Harlow developed error factor theory in an attempt to reduce to order the unsystematic learning of his monkeys. It was, also, the wrong responses of children to intelligence test questions that aroused Piaget's interest.

Still, PERCEIVER's performance was quite a good simulation. Simon and Barenfeld go on to seek an explanation of the performance of both program and human. They point to the well-established limit of 'seven plus-or-minus two' *chunks* of information that can normally be held in short-term memory. 'Chunks' in this case must be configurations of pieces which are well known to masters but less so to beginners. In any board in the course of play, including the actual situation used in this experiment, a number of such configurations must necessarily appear. And the recorded eye movements do show that the subject could be extracting information about them (as of course could PERCEIVER, since it simulates the eye movements).

Now this is an interesting start to an analysis of this particular problem solving situation. It suggests that one of the important things that happens in

learning to deal with complex situations is, that attention becomes more
systematic. Relevant cues are noticed more, and sooner; less relevant ones do not
obtrude. And the situation is reduced to order by means of acquiring a
vocabulary of recognizable situations, with known, or likely, consequences (and
causes). From a practical point of view, this in turn suggests that in order to help
people to deal with complex situations, we should supply them with an appropriate vocabulary. And this, indeed, is what is commonly done in teaching high
level intellectual skills such as diagnosis (in medicine, social work, engineering,
history or whatever). The teacher tells the pupil: 'This is a typical case of . . .
Notice the following features . . . When you see this, it usually means that such
and such has happened . . .' This process could perhaps, by closer analysis, be
improved. This acquisition of a vocabulary has a negative aspect also. We have
met it, under the labels of functional fixedness and set, in the classic experiments
of Maier and Luchins (see *Problem Solving*). Classification of a stimulus situation
in a certain way often permits a swift and appropriate response to be made:
but it may also, in novel circumstances, impede the production of new or creative
behaviour.

Theoretically, this brings us back to Gregory's distinction between continuous
and discontinuous processes; and to the matter of internal models. The configurations stored by the master chess player can be conceived of as models of the
environment, brought into play when they seem to be appropriate. Gregory
(1970) discusses the control of skilled behaviour. This control, he argues, is not
direct, except in the case of reflexes, but by way of 'internal neural models of
reality'. It is obvious that in many situations, separate responses cannot be made
to each change in the stimulus array. An example is typing. One begins by
learning to press a particular key at the sight of a particular letter. As the skill is
learned, a pattern of responses is made to a stimulus configuration—a word, or
later a phrase. The typist has acquired a vocabulary or repertoire of models.
Looked at from another angle, it would appear to be impossible for an organism
to respond to every stimulus. There are just too many: and a lot of them are
irrelevant. Living organisms cannot operate inductively, at least we have no
knowledge of one that can (I suppose God could). The redundancy of the world
must be reduced, or if one likes utilized. A few cues call up the appropriate
behaviour. When this appears to be innate and species-specific, we call it
instinctive; when it is learned, we call it a skill.

This mode of operation has both advantages and disadvantages. Among the
advantages are these, according to Gregory. It is economical in the sense that a
high level of performance can be maintained with a limited rate of information
transmission. As noted above, only key features of a stimulus situation need be
identified. Then the model is predictive. In a given situation we know what to
do next. Thirdly behaviour can continue in the temporary absence of input (e.g.
blinking or sneezing while driving). Behaviour can likewise continue when the
input changes in kind. And behaviour can transfer to situations similar to the

one for which the model was developed. (I take Gregory's point here to be that one model could embody features common to two or more situations which differ in other respects.) But there are also disadvantages. It may be that, although a new situation resembles a previous one sufficiently to call up the first model, it actually differs from it in important respects, so that the resulting behaviour is in fact inappropriate. Internal models tend to be resistant to change: if the environment is changing rapidly, inappropriate behaviour may likewise be elicited. (See also the *Focus* section.)

As we noticed when discussing *Problem Solving*, F. C. Bartlett (1958) put forward a concept of thinking as a skill. Considering the work mentioned above, it can be said that at least part of the processes involved in solving problems appear to be controlled in a way analogous to that of skills. But the postulation of internal 'models' cannot be the whole story as far as thinking is concerned. To begin with, we must distinguish between the way a stickleback responds to a stimulus configuration of the type 'red belly'; and the way in which a doctor responds to the configuration 'red spots on face and torso, high temperature'. One is innate, the other learned. More important, one is fixed, the other (we trust) modifiable. Most people would find it odd to speak of the stickleback 'thinking', but natural to speak of the doctor doing so. It might be said from this point of view that a characteristic of 'thinking' is adaptation: and that, as we have seen, is one of the basic functional invariants described by Piaget (see *The Geneva School*). And we have seen how adaptation is said to take place through the dual processes of assimilation and accommodation. The development of thinking, according to Piagetian theory, is in the direction of an increasingly abstract and general representation of the environment, and away from control by immediate stimuli (consider the famous conservation experiments, for example). But at the same time it seems plausible to suppose that the internal models must also become more accurate representations of the world as it really is. (As we pointed out in discussing Bruner's work on *Concept Indentification,* the argument as to whether there is a reality that can be known may in the last resort be a philosophical one. I take the view that it is, at any rate, better to assume that this is so: partly because this seems to fit in better with biological evidence; and partly because not to do so seems to leave science as a completely pointless enterprise.)

This discussion all stems from the experiment of Simon and Barenfeld, which as we have said made a useful start in analysing the perceptual aspects of a problem situation. The weakness of the approach, so it seems to us, is one that we find common to a great many studies using computer simulation. We find it hard to see what has been gained by the use of the computer. It is interesting to record the eye movements of human subjects, for this tells us something about what information they are processing. It is interesting to apply to this the knowledge we have of short-term memory. Some general rules can then be extracted from the data, and a computer programmed in accordance with them. Not very surprisingly, it produces an approximate copy of the human performance. So what?

2 Heuristics.

Apter (1970) points out that a basic difference in approach to the computer simulation of thought processes lies in the distinction between *algorithms* and *heuristics. Algorithms* were introduced when discussing *Problem Solving.* An algorithm is a set of rules which, if followed exactly, must lead to the desired result. The rules often are cast in the form of a series of YES–NO decisions; and they can often, for ease of use, be laid out in diagrammatic form. They are particularly helpful when one wishes to reduce the complexity of a situation for some practical purpose. For example one could have an algorithm to simplify use of a telephone system, or filling in an income tax form. In a sense, these are special cases of the algorithmic approach. What an algorithm essentially consists of, is the set of all possible choices in a given situation. One path through this set of choices (or possibly more than one) will lead to the desired result or solution; the others will not. The constructor of the algorithm for practical use so arranges things that if the user correctly makes his series of simple choices, dead ends are avoided. But in these cases the constructor, if not the user, knows in advance what outcomes are desirable. From the *user's* point of view, the situation is a problem situation. He is like a rat in a maze: however the algorithm-maker has kindly supplied instructions at each choice-point, so that he need never make a wrong turn, even though he does not know where he is going to end up.

But situations are 'really' problems when no god-like algorithm maker has prepared the ground. Take an example. In the early days of the 1939–1945 war, a German invasion was expected in England. To avoid aiding the enemy, all the direction signs on roads were removed. (It was suggested that it might be even more confusing to reverse them, but this I believe was not done, possibly as not quite playing the game.) However, this made things difficult for English travellers also. Now what was such a traveller to do? There were three possible courses of action. He could choose a road at random. He could systematically explore each road in turn until he reached his destination. Or he could make as rational a choice as possible, in the light of whatever general information was available: direction of the sun, lie of the land, etc. Now the first of these is obviously trial-and-error behaviour, like that of Thorndike's cats, or a rat in a maze (except that, if the choice were lucky, one-trial learning would probably occur). The second method is algorithmic: systematic trial-and-error. (This is called an *exhaustive* algorithm.) The third method involves heuristics. Heuristics are rules which make a solution more likely, but do not guarantee it.

It will be seen that the first two methods, on average, will be enormously time consuming. We have mentioned the very great number of possible pathways in even such a constrained situation as chess. It is quite clear that chess players do not, in fact, adopt trial-and-error or algorithmic methods. And it seems highly plausible to suppose that this is not how human beings solve problems in general, except for some very limited cases (for example one might search the drawers of a filing cabinet systematically for a missing document—but only after the filing system had failed to locate it). Indeed it is doubtful whether mammals, at least, rely on trial-and-error unless forced to do so. This of course was the burden of the Gestalt psychologists' complaint against the early Behaviourists. But their alternative explanation in terms of 'insight' was rather too vague to be really useful. Can the computer simulation of heuristic methods help us here?

The development of heuristics has been one of the main themes of the work of Newell, Simon and Shaw. This began in 1956 with the development of a computer program called the Logic Theorist, the first to embody heuristics. This approach was extended in a program called the General Problem Solver (GPS). GPS is intended to be a simulation of human problem solving, and as such an embodiment of a theory of such behaviour; and also an extension of the range of artificial intelligence. It is the first of these two aspects that interests us here. GPS, as the name implies, is meant to be applicable to a wide range of problems, though in practice it has been used mainly on tasks in logic and mathematics. Essentially, it operates by defining a problem as the difference between some situation or position, and some other, desired, situation. A 'problem' exists if there is no clear and immediate transition from one to the other. The method of solution is to find sub-goals or intermediate states which are closer to the desired state than was the original one; and which can be reached. The program thus deals with three kinds of symbols, which represent:

1. *Objects* in the task situation, characterizing
   (a) the present situation
   (b) the desired situation
and (c) possible intermediate situations.
2. *Differences* between pairs of objects.
3. *Operators* which can act on, and change, objects to which they are applied. (Apter, 1970).

When the problems are those of mathematics or symbolic logic, the rules governing the changes that can be made are clear and strict, and built into the situation. Decisions are necessary, however, as to which differences shall be tackled, and what operations shall be applied. These are made by an executive program, which embodies a number of general strategies. Some sorts of differences are more difficult to reduce than others. Thus if a line of action proves to result in differences which are becoming harder to reduce, that line of action is abandoned. Another strategy consists in imposing a limit on the number of steps that can be taken in pursuing any one line of action. It is assumed that if that (arbitrary) limit is passed, the line of action is, so to speak, leading away from the final goal rather than towards it. Another strategy is that, in choosing which of a set of differences to tackle first, the most difficult is selected. It is assumed that this will lead to easier ones.

These strategies are heuristics. They are intended to make a solution more likely, though not certain. And they are thought to be employed by humans, whether consciously or not, in problem solving. There are obvious resemblances to some of the classical reports of Köhler, Duncker, and others, as well as to some anecdotal accounts. Take the well-known two-string problem of Maier. There is an initial, situation, 'strings apart'; there is a desired situation, 'strings tied together'. A subgoal might be said to be 'one string-near to the other'. What operations can be performed on a string to bring this about? Make string rigid . . . have bird fly with it . . . set it swinging like a pendulum . . . Here a new sub-goal emerges: now how to achieve that? Duncker's diagram of the possible solutions explored in the 'tumour' problem will also be recalled. (See *Problem Solving*.)

Simon and Newell (1971), and Newell and Simon (1972) reviewing the work of the past dozen years or so, conclude that their simulations yield more than such general resemblances. That they provide, in fact, a theory of human problem solving. They are at pains to make clear what they mean by this:

> 'What questions should a theory of problem solving answer? First, it should predict the performance of a problem solver handling specified tasks. It should explain how human problem solving takes place: what processes are used, and what mechanisms perform these processes. It should predict the incidental phenomena that accompany problem solving, and the relation of these to the problem-solving process... It should show how changes in the antecedent conditions—both changes "inside" the problem solver and changes in the task confronting him—alter problem-solving behavior. It should explain how specific and general problem-solving skills are learned, and what it is that the problem solver "has" when he has learned them.' (1958)

A tall order: yet it is still only part of the whole picture. As Simon and Newell go on to say:

> 'This view of explanation places its central emphasis on process—on how particular human behaviors come about, on the mechanisms that enable them.'

Thus the approach is essentially a functionalist one, as befits its American origin. But it is far from clear that the work has achieved even that which is claimed for it. It is further stated that:

> 'Programs like Logic Theorist are explanations of human problem-solving behavior only to the extent that the processes they use to discover solutions are the same as the human processes.' (1971)

This seems distinctly odd. It is quite hard to see how identity can be the same as explanation. Two trains on the same route may reach Edinburgh from London by the same 'process'—same engine action, sequence of starts and stops, etc. But in what sense is one train an *explanation* of the other? Certainly, neither is a 'model' of the other in any of Braithwaite's senses. (Each of them is in Ross Ashby's sense; but this we rejected.) Presumably what is meant is one of two things. (1) That if a computer program reaches the same solutions as human subjects, then the methods it uses may turn out to be those actually used by humans. (2) That if the human processes are known, a program can be written to embody them. (This might be a way of testing them to see if they work; but it could not very well be a way of testing them to see if they work for humans. Or it might be a way of making the human processes more understandable— Braithwaite's Type 3 model. It seems doubtful that this is meant by Simon and Newell, however, for they specifically warn that the information-processing language used for the theory is harder to understand than that of ordinary language.) In any case, this hardly seems an explanation, since by definition the human processes must first be understood, before they can be simulated.

Now what does the theory look like? Simon and Newell state:

> 'The shape of the theory can be captured by four propositions:
> 1. A few, and only a few, gross characteristics of the human information-processing system are invariant over task and problem solver.
> 2. These characteristics are sufficient to determine that a task environment is represented (in the information-processing system) as a problem space, and that problem solving takes place in a problem space.
> 3. The structure of the task environment determines the possible structures of the problem space.
> 4   The structure of the problem space determines the possible programs that can be used for problem solving.' (Newell and Simon, 1972)

The details that fill out these main points are along the same lines as those of GPS discussed earlier. It is worth quoting, however, the summary given by Simon and Newell after their fuller account.

> 'That, in sum, is what human heuristic search in a problem space amounts to. A serial information processor with limited short-term memory uses the information extractable from the structure of the space to evaluate the nodes it reaches and the operators that might be applied at those nodes. Most often, the evaluation involves finding differences between characteristics of the current node and those of the desired node (the goal). The evaluations are used to select a node and an operator for the next step of the search. Operators are usually applied to the current node, but if progress is not being made, the solver may return to a prior node that has been retained in memory—the limits of the choice of prior node being set mostly by short-term memory limits. Those properties have been shown to account for most of the human problem-solving behaviors that have been observed in the three task environments that have been studied intensively: chess playing, discovering proofs in logic, and cryptarithmetic; and programs have been written to implement problem-solving systems with these same properties.' (Simon and Newell, 1971)

(Cryptarithmetic problems are those in which the task is, for example, to substitute digits for letters in an equation like DONALD + GERALD = ROBERT.)

Now this may well be a true description of the way in which humans go about these rather specialized sorts of problem. It may well be true of a much wider range of situations. And it certainly does have an advantage, as Simon and Newell claim, in diminishing some of the mystery of thinking. A concept like 'limited short-term memory' is a clear and definite one, thanks to the large amount of controlled experimentation in this area. Ray (1967) believes that:

'The Logic Theorist makes at least two general contributions to the psychology of thinking: it shows that the complex processes of problem solving can be compounded out of elementary processes, and shows that such elementary processes can solve difficult problems, thus taking away the "mystery" component of people's attitudes towards problem solving.'

Some comments may be made. It seems somewhat arbitrary what is to be regarded as an 'elementary' process. Clearly the heuristics of GPS are a very different matter from the 'elementary' processes such as reflexes, of which early Behaviourists believed all behaviour to be compounded. Then one might remark that the opposite of mystery is not simplicity, but knowledge. It is true that the somewhat mysterious concept of insight appeared partly as a reaction to the over-simplification of trial-and-error learning. But 'stamping-in', the postulated internal process in the latter sort of learning, is no more certain, and no more explanatory a concept, than those of 'restructuring', 'closure', and the rest of the Gestalt-theory processes. The information-processing approach does pin down some aspects rather more closely. What is more difficult to see, is that this is a result of the use of computers. Rather, it seems the result of the increasingly detailed knowledge coming from experiments on human subjects; or even of common sense.

Take, for example, the problem already mentioned:

Given $O = 5$

$$
\begin{array}{r}
\text{DONALD} \\
+ \ \text{GERALD} \\
\hline
\text{ROBERT.}
\end{array}
$$

Simon and Newell point out that:

'There are $9! = 362,880$ ways of assigning nine digits to nine letters. A serial processor able to make and test five assignments per minute would require a month to solve the problem; many humans do it in 10 minutes or less.' (Not including the present writers, however.)

But humans do not do it this way: they begin by arguing that $D + D$ must equal 10, therefore $T = 0$, with one to carry. They reason it out by steps which can be reliably traced by means of noting what they write down, what they say, and if necessary what they look at. If GPS can do the same, fine; but what have we gained?

3. Intelligence

Addicts of television space opera will be familiar with the situation that occurs when a leading character announces: 'We'll put the problem to the computer'; sometimes going so far as to add, '... and abide by its decision'. Can machines be more intelligent than we are?

The expression 'artificial intelligence' is sometimes used almost as a synonym for the computer simulation of thought processes. And all the examples we have given so far could be regarded as involving aspects of intelligence. Here let us look at one or two more specialized questions. They really centre on the main question of what it would mean for a machine to show 'intelligent' behaviour.

Michie (1970) asks us to consider one intellectual activity of a young child: categorizing the world, learning language and complex conceptual systems. No computing system yet devised, he says, can compete with this. Indeed none could, with any degree of generality, attempt items from the Stanford-Binet IQ tests; for example this one for $2\frac{1}{2}$-year-olds. with a brick, a button, a dog, a box and a pair of scissors laid in order on the table, the child is told (a) 'give me the dog'; (b) 'put the button in the box'; and (c) 'put the scissors beside the brick'. Of course a machine could be programmed to do each of these; but the essence of the task as an IQ test is that the child has not been 'programmed' for each specific task.

On the other hand Green (1964) argues that computers could well be so programmed as to achieve high scores on intelligence tests. And this could be said (see *Intellectual Abilities*) to be a reasonable criterion of intelligence. Green begins by arguing for a factorial view of intelligence, as composed of 'several clearly distinguishable, possibly correlated abilities'. Precisely what these are is less certain, but there would be general agreement that the list must include the following: verbal comprehension, fluency, perception, psychomotor coordination, number, memory, and reasoning. He then lists evidence to show that computers can be made to display all these general abilities. For example, Green, Wolf, Chomsky, and Laughery (1961) tried to show that computers could be given a form of verbal comprehension. They programmed a computer to answer questions of fact about a set of baseball scores for the year 1959. The program was designed to answer questions phrased in standard English such as 'where did the Yankees play on July 7th?', and 'how often did the Red Sox win at home?' This was achieved by the use of two routines—a linguistic routine which decides on the meaning of the key words in the sentence and arrives eventually at a specification list; and a processing routine which searches through the available stored data, attempting to identify a path which matches all the terms on the

338

list. Once this has been achieved, the missing piece of information can be identified.

Similar examples are given for the other abilities.

Another view of results in intelligence test questions of the form 'A is to B as C is to: D1, D2, D3, D4?' Evans (1968) presents a program to solve such items in geometric form. One example is shown in Figure 9.1.

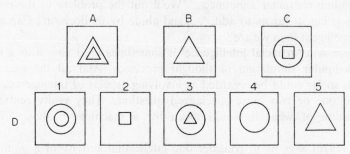

Figure 9.1. An example of the geometric analogy problems used by Evans (1968) (Reproduced from T. G. Evans, 'A program for the solution of a class of geometric-analogy intelligence-test questions' in M. Minsky (Ed.), *Semantic Information Processing* (1968) by permission of the M.I.T. Press, Cambridge, Mass.)

The solution process is analysed into four steps:

'(1) A and B are compared and the actions necessary to transform A into B listed, e.g. in the geometric problem shown, the circle around the top triangle is removed and this same shape is put around the bottom triangle.

(2) Similarities between C and A are listed, e.g. in the same problem the top shape is enclosed in another shape.

(3) In each of the Ds, features are listed that may relate the figure to C in the same way in which B is related to A.

(4) The D selected as the answer is the D which most closely matches in its relations to C the way in which B is related to A.' (Taken from Apter, 1970)

The actual program has to break down each of these main steps further into simple actions. As with other examples, this may well tell us something about the nature of such problems and how they are solved. The attempt to get machines to do this, however, also throws the tests into a new light. For suppose a computer scored 100 per cent on a standard test: should we call it a genius? And if not, why not?

One answer that has been offered is that a machine could only be called intelligent if it could learn; if it could adapt to new situations. Gelernter and Rochester (1958) describe a program to solve problems in geometry. Like GPS, it uses heuristics. Thus it is able to make 'best guesses'; these can be tested by another part of the program. Gelernter seems to say that the 'geometer' program shows intelligent behaviour, in that it tackles problems in a way similar to that of human beings. It does not learn however. It could be adapted to do so; and this would be easier than designing a machine of 'general intelligence'. By this presumably is meant one able to tackle the whole range of human problems. Gelernter argues further that the geometer is intelligent in that its behaviour is not predictable. It '... has on several occasions produced a proof that was a complete surprise to its programmers'. Now this may well make it useful; but one would hardly call a roulette wheel intelligent, notoriously unpredictable though it be.

Reader (1968, 1969) holds on the contrary that learning is essential for an intelligent machine. He quotes the example of Newell, Shaw, and Simon's (1958) chess-playing program. This could pass Turing's test of impersonating a human being at first, but could not continue to do so. For that, it must adapt or learn. Learning involves two essential activities: storing past information; and recognizing new situations as similar to (or different from) old ones. Both these can be done by machines, provided some criterion of similarity is specified. Reader outlines a possible machine (program) to incorporate the activities. He mentions two possible criticisms: one is that if all events are to be remembered, the burden will rapidly become impossibly large; the other is that the criterion of similarity, specified in advance, is inflexible. The first criticism is merely a practical (though important) one. It is true that the brain does not, as far as we know, store all information received. But we are not aiming here to stimulate human behaviour, but to create an intelligent machine. Presumably there is some sense in which we might be said to be more intelligent if we had more information available to us. The second criticism is more pointed. A machine could be provided with a range of criteria for similarity; but then it must also have a higher-order rule for choosing between criteria. The rule might be concerned with 'success'—but who or what is to define success? Perhaps ultimately the only objective criterion is survival—a biological criterion.

By Reader's definition, 'success' would be equivalent to 'continuing to pass Turing's test indefinitely'. I do not consider the test to be satisfactory, as already mentioned. However, Turing (1948) in a long paper which is still full of interest, made several other points about intelligent machines. He first lists possible objections. Some are emotional, such as the apparent infringement of the dignity of man as the only intelligent species. Some are practical, such as the relatively restricted machines that had been available (up to about 1940). The most pertinent is that machines can only show the behaviour they are programmed for. Turing argues:

> 'The view that intelligence in machinery is merely a reflection of that of its creator is rather similar to the view that the credit for the discoveries of a pupil should be given to his teacher. In such a case the teacher would be pleased with the success of his methods of education, but would not claim

the results themselves unless he had actually communicated them to his pupil. He would certainly have envisaged in very broad outline the sort of thing his pupil might do, but would not be expected to foresee any sort of detail. It is already possible to produce machines where this sort of situation arises in a small degree. One can produce "paper machines" for playing chess. Playing against such a machine gives a definite feeling that one is pitting one's wits against something alive.' (Turing, 1948)

After describing the capacities and potentialities of various categories of machine, Turing picks up the theme of education again. An intelligent adult is the result of twenty years education—not just formal schooling, but the whole cultural environment, involving the acquisition of rules and techniques—and also of standard, for what is to be called 'intelligent'. Machines, to be intelligent, will have to be educated; and this means interaction with other intelligent beings. This seems to me to be true. But it is only true because we do not know how education (in both 'school' and general senses) works. We can, I think, accept that if we made machines with the sorts of capacities of infant humans, and if we then gave them a human upbringing, they would turn out to be intelligent in a human sense. What we do not know, however, is precisely how the capacities work genetically and physiologically, and precisely how they interact with the environment. Some of the advances in understanding the latter issue are discussed elsewhere; as is the complex question of what is to count as intelligent behaviour.

4. Creative behaviour

An equally complex question concerns creative behaviour. Newell, Shaw and Simon (1962) gave four criteria, one or more of which must be satisfied if thinking is to be called creative.

'1. The product of the thinking has novelty and value (either for the thinker or for his culture).
2. The thinking is unconventional, in the sense that it requires modification or rejection of previously accepted ideas.
3. The thinking requires high motivation and persistence, taking place either over a considerable span of time (continuously or intermittently) or at high intensity.
4. The problem as initially posed was vague and ill-defined, so that part of the task was to formulate the problem itself.'

It may be suggested that of these, only 1 gives criteria (see *Creative Thinking*). 2 is a version of novelty, while 3 and 4 are frequent characteristics of creative thought, not criteria for it. Newell *et al.* consider, however, that the Logic Theorist was being creative when finding proofs for the theorems in Chapter 2 of *Principia Mathematica*, by Whitehead and Russell (1925–1927). It did so about three times out of four; and in one case, it is claimed, found a more elegant proof than did the original authors.

'Of course the Logic Theorist will not receive much acclaim for its discoveries, since these have been anticipated, but subjectively if not culturally, its product is novel and original... If we wish to object seriously to calling the Logic Theorist creative, we must rest our case on the way it gets the problems it tackles, and not on its activity in tackling them. Perhaps the program is a mathematical hack, since it relies on Whitehead and Russell to provide it with significant problems, and then merely finds the answer to these; perhaps the real creativity lies in the problem selection. This certainly is the point of the fourth characteristic we listed for creativity. But we have already indicated that the Theorist has some powers of problem selection. In working backwards from the goal of proving one theorem, it can conjecture new theorems—or supposed theorems—and set up the sub-goal of proving these. Historically, albeit on a much broader scale, this is exactly the process whereby Whitehead and Russell generated the theorems that they then undertook to prove. For the task they originally set themselves was to take the basic postulates of arithmetic (as set forth by Peano and his students) and to derive these *as theorems* from the axioms of logic. The theorems of Chapter 2 of *Principia* were generated, as nearly as we can determine the history of the matter, in the same way that sub-problems are generated by the Logic Theorist—as sub-problems whose solution would lead to the solution of the problem originally posed.

'We do not wish to exaggerate the extent to which the Logic Theorist is capable of matching the higher flights of the human mind. We wish only to indicate that the boundary between its problem-solving activities and activities that are important examples of human creativity is not simple or obvious.'

Now apart from the fun of it, there seem to be two good reasons for making creative computers. One is to find out how creative thinking comes about. This has already been discussed at length. The other is to get some creative work done, Newell, Shaw and Simon had previously predicted:

'... within ten years a computer will discover and prove an important mathematical theorem, and compose music that is regarded as aesthetically significant'.

As far as we are aware neither of these has yet occurred (1972). There has, of course, been much interest in computer art. Hiller (1956, 1960); Hiller and Isaacson (1959); and Hiller and Baker (1962), among others, have described the applications of computers to music. The last-named give an account of music produced by ILLIAC, a computer at the University of Illinois. Samples of classical music of specific historical periods were analysed statistically for various dimensions such as harmony. The probabilities of given harmonies being related to (dependent on) preceding harmonies were calculated. This may be seen as analogous to the production of statistical approximations to English. It was hypothesized

'... that harmonic progressions form larger harmonic structures which, in turn, may form still larger harmonic structures. These larger harmonic structures eventually become a series of modulations from key to key, forming the key structure, and certain of the keys form the structure of the composition in the largest sense, the tonal structure. If such is true, tonal structure would in the largest sense be an ever-broadening form of the simplest harmonic progressions.'

In this way ILLIAC has composed samples of music. Hiller and Baker suggested that, if it proved possible to go on to construct actual musical compositions, involving syntheses of the smaller units so far produced, then three types of validation of the method could be made. One would be to ask qualified musicians to 'discuss the synthesized music in terms of stylistic integrity, structural cohesiveness, and general musicial interest.' Mueller (1967) reports:

'The results of their work is not particularly imaginative, and it has a certain looseness of form which is rather characteristic of the student's work.'

The second would involve having the computer analyse the probabilities of its own music, and compare these with the probabilities originally fed into it. The third would be to have the computer analyse a sample of a human composer's music, and construct a sequel, which could be compared with what the composer had written. This last emphasizes that this work has not been intended to produce original musical works of merit, but to help in understanding the way in which music is composed by humans. It does, at least, seem to add something to our knowledge of the structure of music. Mueller remarks:

'The computer does not help at all in the problem of finding truly creative and perceptual significances in music as a communicative function, but it does seem to have the potential for speeding up the process of finding them.' Ibid. p. 274.

There have also been a number of well publicized attempts to have computers produce original works of art. The love poems of a computer belonging to the University of Manchester are well known. The Institute of Contemporary Arts in London, among others, has had demonstrations of visual art by computer. In some of these, a human stimulus in one modality such as sound, was transformed into another. I sang (as I call it) a few lines of *Johnson's Motor-car*, and patterns emerged on a screen. Whether these were superior to the singing I cannot say. In other of the demonstrations, and generally in computer art, the essence of the matter is to provide the machine with a stock of elements, and have it produce combinations of these, either quite randomly or according to certain constraints.

The assumption behind this has been criticized by Schon (1963). He argues that it is essentially an offshoot from the Associationist tradition of treating mental activity as though it were a sort of chemistry or physics, analysable into elements which combine according to certain rules. This he thinks is unsatisfactory, and especially as applied to creative thinking, for a number of reasons. One is the evidence, from Gestalt theory, that new ideas are not simply recombinations of old ones. Another is that the notion of simple elements, particularly as applied to ideas, is philosophically unsatsfactory. What is a 'simple' idea? Any concept must involve complex assumptions about the world. (Compare this with work on *Concept Identification*). And thirdly, creative work is not just a question of getting a set of novel ideas (however arrived at) and then selecting the best. What has to be explained is how the selection is made. And more particularly, how new criteria for selection emerge; and how this process interacts with the emergence of new material. Schon's own theory about this is discussed in *Creative Thinking*. And, as was suggested there, it may perhaps be that part of the attractiveness of computer art is the vogue for spontaneity and randomness in creative work. This is seen in the rise of action painting, the popularity of children's art, even painting by chimpanzees. Campbell (1972) has invented a device to transmute brain waves (i.e. the electrical activity of the brain) into music. This presumably eliminates the need for musical training or technique. I suppose the next step must be to retranslate the composer's music into the brain waves of the audience, making performers unnecessary too.

5. Storage processes

Our last examples will be concerned with the way information is stored, this forming the materials of thought. This approach can be compared with that of the classical 'Content' psychologists and the Würzburg school: see *Thinking as a Private Experience*.

G. R. Kiss (1967, etc.) has presented a series of reports concerned with the way words (or more strictly, representations of words) are stored. The models he has worked on have naturally undergone development, but the main features can be picked out. Kiss quotes experimental evidence which suggests several important points. One phenomenon is that of mediated transfer of learning: the facilitating effect on learning a word (as, say, a paired associate to a nonsense syllable) of having previously learned another word similar in meaning. Another feature is semantic generalization: a response conditioned to a word will generalize to another word of related meaning. Then there is the clustering effect found by Bousfield, Cohen and Whitmarsh (1958) among others. They presented subjects with lists of words, groups of which were taxonomically related, i.e. they could be classed together as names of animals or whatever. The words were presented randomly, but in free recall subjects tended to produce them in related classes. Evidence from word association experiments shows that the likelihood of a word appearing as a response correlates highly with its frequency in general usage. Such evidence led Kiss (1967) to a number of postulates about the way information is stored by humans. Here are the first two.

'1. Human beings have two qualitatively different resources for information processing: (a) serial (a central processor), (b) parallel (a network of interconnected elements)'. (In later writings this is referred to simply as a 'word store'.)

344

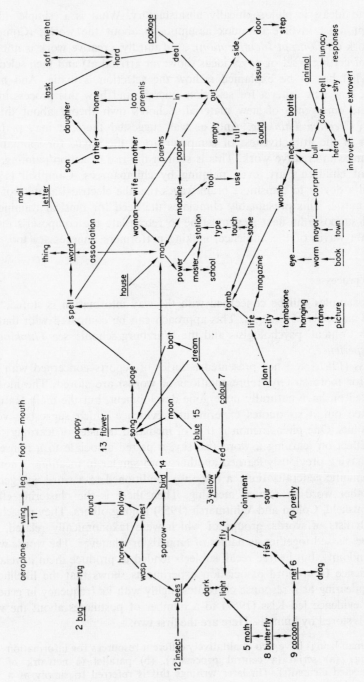

Figure 9.2. An associative word network. (Reproduced from G. R. Kiss, 'Networks as models of word storage' in N. L. Collins and D. Michie (Eds.), *Machine Intelligence (1)* (1967), Oliver and Boyd by permission of Edinburgh University Press).

'2. The serial and parallel processors interact. The serial processor can create, eliminate, and activate the elements of the network. It can "read" the current status of these elements, and it can create or eliminate the links between them. The central processor can gain access to information stored or associated with these elements.'

A series of further postulates sets out the ways in which it is supposed that words are stored, linked to each other, and retrieved. An aspect that is of particular interest is that it is possible to produce maps or networks of the way in which words are stored. This can be done by taking the associations to a stimulus word, then using those responses as stimuli, and so on. Figure 9.2 shows an example.

The 'strength' of the links between words can be taken from the frequency of occurrence of a response, or its probability estimated from its relative frequency, in a group (Figure 9.2 is based on responses of fifty subjects). Kiss (1969) reports two kinds of test of this model. One is to use the data from a small sample of subjects to predict the word association norms of a larger sample. The second is to attempt to predict the word association response probabilities to stimuli consisting of several words, from a knowledge of small-sample norms for the component words. Both sorts of test yield encouraging results.

Allan Collins and M. Ross Quillian have recently been developing a model of semantic memory, the Teachable Language Comprehender (TLC), which, they say, 'is a program capable of being taught to "comprehend" English text' (Quillian, 1969). It does so by relating written text to a large semantic network containing factual statements about the world (Figure 9.3 below shows part of such a network). The main points to note about the organization of this network are that 'word concepts' (located at *nodes*) are linked to one another in a hierarchical fashion—animal is a superset of bird which in turn is a superset of canary—and that properties are stored along with the word concept, rather like a dictionary. The model also favours generalizations, i.e. the fact that a canary can fly may be confirmed by ascertaining that a canary is a bird and that birds can fly. Exceptions to such generalization are stored as properties of the appropriate words, e.g. along with 'ostrich' is stored the fact that it cannot fly.

According to Collins and Quillian (1969a), a comprehension amounts to finding 'a path through the semantic network that interrelates the words of a sentence in a manner permitted by the sentence's syntax.' For example, comprehending 'a canary has skin' involves finding the path canary-bird-animal-skin. Having done this the relationship between the 'nodes' must be evaluated in the light of the relationships expressed within the sentence itself. The path connecting 'canary' to 'fish' for example would not permit the inference that a 'canary is a fish' but only that 'a canary is related to a fish'.

This is necessarily a very much oversimplified account of how TLC works but it will suffice for the present. It is not our intention, indeed it is outside our

12—T • •

346

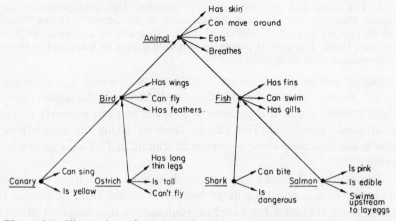

Figure 9.3. Illustration of the hypothetical memory structure for a 3-level hierarchy. (Reproduced from A. M. Collins and M. R. Quillian (1969), 'Retrieval time from semantic memory', *J.V.L.V.B.*, **8**, 240–247 by permission of Academic Press, Inc., New York)

competence, to judge how successful the program has proved to be in comprehending English text. More to the point is, how does it stand up as a psychological model of human memory? The basic procedure which Collins and Quillian have used to test their model involves a true–false reaction time technique. Subjects are required to evaluate a variety of sentences by pressing one button when it is true and another when it is false. Now if reaction time is related systematically to the time required to tread the appropriate path through the semantic maze, the model makes certain predictions about how different types of sentence should affect performance. It should, for example, take *less* time to confirm the sentence 'a canary can sing' compared with 'a canary can fly' since the property 'can sing' is stored at the node 'canary' whereas to retrieve the property 'can fly' requires a move from 'canary' to 'bird', where this information is stored. Similarly it should take even longer to judge the sentence 'a canary has skin' because the property 'has skin' is stored at the 'animal' node, requiring a move from canary to bird to animal. The model makes similar predictions about superset statements. 'A canary is a bird' should take less time than 'a canary is an animal', etc.

An experiment of this kind is reported by Collins and Quillian (1969b), and, with one exception which need not concern us here, results directly in line with prediction were obtained. A problem of conspicuous proportions however arises with *false* sentences—a canary is blue, a canary is a fish, etc. There seemed to be no way of accounting for the results in these cases, suggesting that differing individual strategies may be an important source of variation. In conclusion Collins and Quillian remark, not unsurprisingly, 'the process by which a person decides that a statement is false does not seem to be very simple'.

In all it is obvious that the model has problems, although it is still in its infancy. It works well with true sentences, but fails miserably with false ones. Furthermore, so far tests of the model have been limited to the use of simple sentences embodying simple relationships—'is', 'has', 'can', etc. Is this the appropriate way of testing the generality of the model? What effect do negative statements have? How is the imagery value of the words related to performance? All these questions can be regarded of course as 'matters for further research' to use the conventional phrase. But the issue perhaps runs deeper than the question of 'how well does the model fit the facts'. In short, is this the best way to go about things? Should one begin, as Collins and Quillian do, with an elaborate logical framework and proceed stepwise to build up an armoury of experimental data consistent with it? It can be argued that the starting point should be an empirically based structure which provides the basis for further experiments. In the present context one thinks of the work of Kiss who began with free association data, or Wickens (e.g. 1970) who uses a 'release from proactive inhibition' technique to uncover the basic dimensions of stimulus coding. This is not to deny the value of the very stimulating work of Collins and Quillian, but the difficulties they are apparently experiencing with their model does raise an important conceptual issue which faces many research workers.

With the networks just described, we come near to the maps with which our discussion of models began. We have at least some definite steps towards mapping a part of the mind that has hitherto seemed inaccessible. Like all maps and models, these are partial and hypothetical, and embody theoretical assumptions (basically, those of a sophisticated associationism) which may or may not be the most productive.

IS THERE INTELLIGENT LIFE ON EARTH?

—Yes, but I'm only visiting. So an amateur of graffiti reports.

The simulation of human behaviour raises questions about its nature. This is perhaps the most useful general result of the work. Hunt (1971) asks the question: 'What kind of computer is man?' His answer is in terms of a particular set of principles (called by the general title of Distributed Memory) which could 'guide the construction of a simulation'. They derive from the known experimental facts about human behaviour. Michie (1970) thinks that the time is almost ripe for the development of an 'integrated cognitive system' which could bring computer programs to a human level of performance. For one might reply to Hunt's question: 'What kind of man is the computer?' The current answer would have to be, not a very good one: as we shall see in our *Focus* discussion.

There seems no reason in principle why this should remain the case. Farrell (1970) in a long and rather difficult paper, discusses some of the steps that would have to be taken if a 'conscious device' were to be designed. By this he means one which would pass a Turing-like test: '. . . a device whose reactivity is such that, when we examine it to discover whether it can see, hear, and feel things, etc., we find that we cannot tell the difference between it and a human being'. His general line of argument seems to be that there is no reason to suppose that capacities could not be progressively added to a machine, until the point is reached at which the behaviour is indistinguishable from that of a human. There is an analogy between this and the growth of a child. A young child certainly cannot do all the things that are characteristic of adult intelligence (cf. Piaget). And we have no difficulty in distinguishing infantile from adult behaviour. But neither do we find it odd that the one develops into the other. It is true that we do not know *all* the processes involved: but there does not seem to be any reason in principle why we should not.

Such an attempt would not necessarily use computers, of course. Models can be useful in the absence of any definite representation of them, as Farrell points out (e.g. the work of Broadbent, the Treismans, and others on information-processing models). It raises the question of what a model is: with sufficient physiological knowledge, we could presumably actually perform the experiment of Frankenstein, using living cells as building blocks. If the result were brought up in a human environment, it would have to be human, I think; but would it be a model? At that stage of knowledge, it might not matter.

However constructed, could the 'model' surpass the human? The theme has fascinated science fiction writers. GPS excelled Russell and Whitehead at one proof; Rohm's Universal Robots wished to take over the world. J. McV. Hunt (1961) envisaged a substantial rise in the general level of intelligence as a result of better control of the environment. Aimé Michel, a writer on unidentified flying objects and other speculative topics, has argued ingeniously and wittily against the assumption that the present level of achievement is final. There is no reason to suppose that evolution has now ceased. The results of interaction between living things and technology are only beginning to be understood (see *Development and Culture*). Michel also presses home the point that if substantial developments in intellectual capacity were to take place (or if we were to encounter super-beings from elsewhere) it is likely that we should not be able to understand them. It seems unlikely that models devised by humans could surpass their makers in fundamental respects. But that is the sort of prediction that has the air of negative truth value. It may well belong to the same family as the inconceivability of a round earth, and the impossibility of space flight announced by the Astronomer Royal a short time before the launch of Sputnik I.

Do computers think? It depends what you mean. If by 'thinking' you mean, say, producing solutions to problems, computers can think. Borko (1962) quotes a problem from MacCullum and Smith (1951):

> It is known that salesmen always tell the truth and engineers always tell lies. G and E are salesmen. G states that D is an engineer. A declares that

B affirms that C asserts that D says that E insists that F denies that G is
a salesman. If S is an engineer, how many engineers are there?

Borko remarks: 'The logic machine can solve this problem. Can you?'

If by 'thinking' you mean all the activities which in humans we call by that
name, the answer is no. It might be asked whether the word 'thinking' has any
meaning outside of some reference group. But what is the group to be? Do
animals think? Children think, by common agreement: but when do they *start*
to think? Piaget has shown that the question is pointless. If we eventually meet
beings from elsewhere in space, will they 'think'? Will they do so 'better' or
'worse' than us?

FOCUS: WHAT SORT OF MAN IS THE COMPUTER?*

Work on behaviour simulation has been concerned exclusively with 'processing', i.e. the means by which a required output is obtained from a specified input.
In modelling human cognition, therefore, the researcher has a fixed aim—the
production of grammatically correct language, the solution to a problem, the
identification of patterns, etc. By providing suitable input he tries to test his
model of intervening stages of processes by determining whether the required
output occurs. In these terms computer simulation amounts to a Stimulus–
Response affair. A Stimulus is given, a Response elicited and the focus of interest
lies in what takes place between the two events.

In this section we concern ourselves with the adequacy of this approach, the
assumptions that lie behind it and, in particular, with the model of human
information processing which it tacitly endorses. For while it may be true that
some aspects of human cognition involve acting upon given inputs so as to
produce a 'suitable' output, there are many instances of activity where there is
neither a clearly defined stimulus initiating action nor a response terminating it.
This is clearly demonstrated by the extended deliberations of the creative process.
So to view all cognition as being primarily of a Stimulus–Response nature is
really to have an essentially mechanistic and deterministic model in mind—a
model, that is, in which it is the input that initiates and, to a large extent controls,
action, and human behaviour is dictated by external forces. Now a computer does
not *seek* activity—it stores programs until such time as they are required by the
input. On the other hand one of the most influential ideas to emerge in recent
years is that man is largely intrinsically motivated; he finds inactivity uncomfortable, he likes to manipulate the environment rather than be manipulated by
it, and he has attentional preferences. This would seem to mean that if our aim
is to simulate, and thereby gain more insight into, human behaviour, we should
begin with the human rather than his behaviour. Computer simulations which

* We are particularly grateful to Esme Burton who provided many of the ideas to
be found in this section, and wrote the original draft.

have employed 'mechanistic' programs may well produce outputs that correlate perfectly with the outputs from human subjects. But as we have seen already, whether this means that this is how people actually 'work' is really a psychological question and one to which we shall return in a moment. What concerns us at present however is the assumption that input–output correlation can be regarded as at all representative of the processes occurring in the *thinker*. It may be convenient for the researcher to accept it as such but in recent years there has been a tendency to conceive of cognitive behaviour as a matter of internal experience rather than mere response production. That is to say, what is important about behaviour is not so much what actually occurs but the effect that this has on the *behaver*, how it changes him and his model of the world. After all, in the final analysis we are not trying to simulate the output itself—this could be done presumably with a program which bore no relationship to the known facts about human information processing—but to test the operations involved in producing the output which are specified in the model, by way of the program.

Gregory (1970) expresses this point of view in a paper we have referred to already entitled 'On how little information controls so much behaviour', in which he proposes that in human behaviour 'the input' is merely a trigger for activity but does not determine its nature, and that the choice of action is based largely on prediction rather than perception. That is, the 'thinker' directs his behaviour towards an 'imagined' state of affairs in the creation of which sensory information (input) plays a very small part compared with motivational processes, memory for past events, and the prediction of possible future ones. (See also *Imagery*.) Now the crucial point which arises is that if Gregory is correct, and any cognitive activity is so complex as to involve many aspects of human behaviour, it will be impossible to simulate any single activity without, in the final analysis, producing a complete human simulation. That we are a long way from doing this is beyond dispute. To simulate a game of chess requires multiple prediction and a mass of interconnected feedback loops—and still no computer (with the exception of perhaps HAL in Kubrick's 2001) can beat a chess master. Chess at least has rules, identifiable strategies and precedents that can be incorporated into a program. But what of human problem solving, often unpredictable, irrational or creative, how much more complex would a simulation of this have to be?

There is another problem, one of definition. To simulate the solving of a problem is not necessarily to simulate human problem solving as there is no complete agreement on what this refers to. Perhaps for this reason the role of the 'thinker' in cognitive functioning has been more extensively investigated with regard to perceptual processes where there is on the whole a greater degree of unanimity about the meanings of the various terms used. But the issues preoccupying workers in this field are much the same as those which have emerged generally in this discussion. For example, one of the essential features of perception is that the perceiver should be able to catagorize events consistently, to classify. Yet as Mackay (1967) points out in a paper on pattern recognition, a sieve can be said to classify, to sort input according to size—but a sieve alone does not constitute an adequate model of *perception*. After elaborating on this he too concludes that:

> '... the mere appearance of internal configurations which match or correspond 1 for 1 to features of the environment though it may be a necessary feature of any model of perception, does not *ipso facto* guarantee that perceiving is going on in these models, nor that what is going on is in any sense an adequate model of what goes on in people's nervous systems when they perceive. In other words we must take into account ... the correlate of *action* and the planning of action and the part played by the percept in the planning of action.'

This takes us back to the point made a moment ago that the important thing about behaviour is how it changes the behaver.

The complexity of cognitive processes suggested by these arguments does not automatically rule out all attempts at simulation, but the implications that such ideas have for the structures and content of simulation programs does mean that they will have to be far more intricate, flexible and, paradoxically more *in*determinate than those which have appeared so far. If, that is, we are to incorporate the philosophy of the 'active' approach into our attempts to simulate human cognition. There are undoubtedly those however who regard the 'passive' approach as adequate and claim that satisfactory models *can* be developed without reference to notions of dynamism, planning and prediction, etc. It is this dispute in fact which forms the background of the rest of this section. The terms 'active' and 'passive' really provide the key to this as many of the arguments are concerned with the relative merits of 'active' as opposed to "passive" models of information processing. It is hoped that these will emerge more clearly from the discussion which follows.

The Gestalt psychologists were perhaps the first to suggest an 'active' and dynamic theory of perception, one which, as we have seen, they also applied to problem solving (see *Problem Solving*). Emphasis is placed in their account on the prevailing internal perceptual conditions with their attendant 'stresses and strains' rather than on how past experience controls behaviour. Another important feature of the Gestalt account is that it is not the characteristics of the *stimulus* which determine the percept but the internal activity of the observer, said to involve electrochemical events in the cortex. The pattern of neural firing in the visual cortex corresponds to the pattern of firing at the retina (i.e. the relationship is *isomorphic*) and the cortical firing sets up 'field forces' which interact with and operate upon the pattern received so as to produce the percept. Much the same principles apply to thought processes—in fact in Köhler's account of problem solving, 'insight' is inextricably bound up with the perceptual situation.

Historically the Gestalt theory may be compared to advantage with the one proposed by Hebb in 1949, which typifies the deterministic 'passive' approach. It might almost be said that Hebb sees perception as a reflexive process. In his account experience modifies the structure of the visual cortex leading to the development of 'cell assemblies', i.e. groups of neurons which will tend to fire together, and to induce firing in each other. Perception thus follows a predetermined path: the stimulus is scanned (this being the only 'active' feature of the whole process, and one which Hebb anyway claims is reflexive) and the various features, which are extracted by successive fixation, cause their corresponding cell assemblies to fire. These in turn produce firing in cell assemblies in the neighbouring 'association' areas which are linked with others in a 'phase sequence' or 'thought'. So given the existing stimulus and past experience there seems to be no way for the percept to other than what it turns out to be.

Hebb's theory suggests the passage of a river to the sea (cf. Thorndike). With succeeding years an ever-deeping gorge is formed making it more likely that the water will follow that particular path and no other. In other words it is a mindless, inevitable and non-conscious process. The Gestalt theorists on the other hand, and more especially present-day 'active' theorists, have the river saying, or rather gurgling, to itself, 'Now last time I sent water down *this* way, and it seemed an easy, quick path; I know there are other paths, but let's try this one again.' (So next time you come across a river which can't make up its mind, don't rush it, it needs time to think about these things.)

Of course the incorporation of 'consciousness' into a model works rather better with humans than rivers but is still regarded as unnecessary, unparsimonious in some quarters. As an example we may cite Morton and Broadbent's (1967) article entitled 'Passive versus Active Recognition Models, or Is Your Homunculus Really Necessary?' Their argument is that to believe in a homonculus who monitors incoming stimulation, saying, 'Now let me see, what could this be,' merely complicates the issue and transfers the problem of recognition from brain to—well, what? What is a homonculus, or for that matter, what is consciousness? Morton and Broadbent favour a theory based on the notion of a 'logogen'. All perceivable units (e.g. phonemes, words etc.) have logogens. Information relevant to recognition is coded in terms of 'cues' and fed to these and increases the level of 'activation' within some of them When the activation in any logogen exceeds a critical level, it 'fires' and the appropriate word or whatever is recognized. The information which is fed in can come from any relevant sensory source. In addition, the critical or threshold level of a logogen is varied according to contextual probabilities under the supervision of the 'Ideogen System', which consists of higher order units which accumulate the statistical properties of language (or whatever the input is) including, for example, transitional probabilities between words. In these terms perception becomes a signal detection problem and needs no 'homunculus' to explain it. But what about such factors as motivation and other variables we have associated with the 'active' model? Morton and Broadbent have this to say:

'Connections between Ideogens and [still] higher-order nodes can be re-garded as concerned with predicting and understanding, and at such levels we have no objection to an active network. . . .'

But are we not merely arguing about a definition of perception? 'Predicting and understanding' surely is an essential feature of what is meant by the term perception. Mackay's sieve could classify and produce an output; but it still did not *perceive* because, for one thing, it did not understand what it was doing.

Neisser (1967) in fact makes prediction an essential part of perception. Since his ideas about information processing have become synonymous with what we have called the 'active' approach and since we have more than once referred vaguely to 'Neisser's theory' elsewhere, it would seem worthwhile to examine his views in more detail. Neisser uses the expression 'analysis-by-synthesis' to describe the predictive nature of perception. This term was used by Halle and Stevens (1962; Stevens and Halle, 1967) in a model of speech recognition which Neisser appears to have adopted in its entirety and applied to visual pattern recognition. The basis of Halle and Stevens model is that recognition is not a matter of examining the input to see (or hear) what it *is*, but involves predicting what the input could or is likely to be, and then matching this to the input (the basis of matching is not certain). The prediction, construction or *synthesis* of possible input is achieved by the existing mechanisms for speech *production*, the impulses from which are directed away from the articulatory mechanism during speech *recognition*, and instead 'an equivalent auditory pattern' is derived which can be compared with the input pattern. Thus the perception of speech proceeds not by 'analysis-by-examination' of input but by 'analysis-by-synthesis'.

Neisser's version of this model applies of course to visual perception, but although containing modifications it does retain the essential features. He argues that perception is an active process not only in terms of *how* we recognize but also in *what* we recognize; that we are not normally confronted with discrete objects but with a stream of input out of which the units or objects of recogni-tion have to be isolated; and that what is treated as a unit of perception will be determined usually by the perceiver—he can identify, for example, individual letters or whole words or even phrases as single units, depending on what he sees as appropriate in the circumstances. As Neisser puts it:

'Neither the object of analysis nor the nature of the analysis is inevitable, and both may vary in different observers and at different times.'

The first stage in perception for Neisser is the 'pre-attentive process' which segments the total field into suitable units for perception which are then pro-cessed serially. Because it deals with the entire input at once, i.e. because it is 'wholistic', the pre-attentive stage can accommodate 'the whole is more than the sum of its parts' phenomenon. That is to say, it can determine which aspects of the input should be the parts, by reference to the whole, something which creates difficulties for a passive, analytical model in which the identification of the whole can only follow the analysis of the parts.

'Focal attention' directs the processing towards one segregated object which is then analysed via 'figural synthesis', the 'analysis-by-sythesis' of Halle and Stevens. Neisser uses Hebb's (1949) example of the palaeontologist to illustrate this process—the palaeontologist is given a few fossil remains and uses his know-ledge of anatomy and so on to reconstruct what the dinosaur, or whatever, probably looked like. In similar vein Gregory (1970) uses the example of medical diagnosis: a few symptoms are sufficient to indicate past, present and future to the doctor. The origins of the 'fossil remains' used in the process of perception, however, are unspecified. In fact apart from the suggestion that Hebb may have some enlightening skeletons in his cupboards, the issue is glossed over indecently quickly. Halle and Stevens did allow for some preliminary analysis of auditory input, perhaps in terms of a form of spectrum analysis. Presumably similar processes occur in visual perception, some of them automatic as suggested by, for instance Hubel and Wiesel (e.g. 1962; see also Hubel, 1963), others perhaps more flexible and under the control of context, external cues and instructions about *which* 'fossil remains' should influence the process of analysis-by-synthesis. And, from the remains, a visual image is constructed according to what the object probably is: it is this construction which is perceived, *not* the input itself.

There are of course difficulties with this formulation, perhaps the major problem being one of veridical perception. If we only *imagine* what things look like, how can we ever know whether we are right; how can there be such a great consensus of opinion as to how things look? Presumably there is some kind of checking process (as found in the Halle and Stevens model) for matching the 'construct' to the input. But if all that is seen of the input is 'a few fossil remains' how can the complete construct be checked? Continuous cross check-ing and feedback from the context, the outcome, etc., provides an answer in the case of certain types of input such as passages of prose. However the human perceiver is perfectly capable of identifying single letters or forms in the absence of context and with negligible error. Furthermore, the palaeontologist has rules to guide him in his 'construction'. But what are the rules of perception, and how do they develop? The answer cannot be that they come from previous experience because this itself must require the rules as well. Learning from experience anyway would be a laborious process because in the final analysis one can never know *where* one went wrong but only that one had made a mistake. Since perceptual experience consists exclusively of the experience of internal construc-tions, perceptual errors in this kind of model really only provide a signal that a different construction is required. And the possibility that such rules are genetically (i.e. via evolution) provided is surely very difficult to entertain seriously in view of the enormous complexity of perceptual processes.

These difficulties aside however there are good reasons for investing one's psychological shirt in the active information processing approach advocated by

Neisser and those who support him. For one thing he eliminates the artificial barrier between, for example, perception and thought. 'Thought' becomes merely a matter of perception where the 'fossil remains' are internally rather than externally provided (although both play a part). 'Imagination' and hallucination can be considered in the same way. 'Cognitive styles' (see *Development and Culture*) and schemata can be described in terms of characteristic modes of constructing, creativity as an unusual change in construction. This is not to say of course that one is explaining such phenomena but to discuss psychological processes in these terms does represent a useful way of interpreting a large number of apparently unconnected phenomena. And for another thing, the active view of cognitive functioning has definite advantages generally in dealing with human information processing. Let us consider some of these.

Firstly, as Neisser himself points out, the rate of transmission of information through the human nervous system is low—too low to permit reading speeds which even an average reader can achieve, if each word or phrase had to be examined and analysed. There must be, therefore, a considerable amount of guesswork and prediction involved, straight 'analysis' only playing a small part in comprehension. This of course is reinforced by the fact that readers often understand the meaning or gist of a sentence while practically oblivious of its exact lexical content.

Secondly, to repeat a point we have already made, perception frequently continues when sensation has ceased. This is necessary for many human activities—driving, reading when turning the page, piano playing. Again these observations pose problems for a passive analytical model of information processing.

Thirdly, since only very little external stimulation is needed for perception, active models allow perception to occur when the 'signal to noise' ratio is low—for example when one is faced with the 'cocktail party' situation.

And finally, the basis of cognition is never really sensory information. A chair, for example, can be ugly, uncomfortable and 'in the way', properties which are all only indirectly related to sensory experience. As Gregory (1970) argues, 'objects have all manner of vitally important properties which are seldom sensed, so current sensory information cannot be adequate for dealing with objects'.

Active processing models do of course have their disadvantages. As we have seen, they learn slowly from experience, they are prone to error and often may be seriously disturbed by such 'incorrect constructions'. (One is reminded here of Guthrie's claim that Tolman's 'cognitive' theory of maze learning in rats leaves an animal 'buried in thought'). On the other hand, such 'disadvantages' are strikingly characteristic of much of human cognitive activity! In conclusion, however, the active approach, where the *perceiver* controls the nature of what is perceived, and how it is perceived, seems to be the most promising. But it has been argued here that if simulation of such processes is to be successful, programs of considerably greater complexity will be required

356

than have apparently been attempted so far. This is not to say they will be impossible to write but simply that if computer simulation is to become more than a sterile technological exercise dealing with trivial aspects of human behaviour, the directing and controlling functions of the individual and his perception of the world will have to be incorporated into future programs, perhaps at the expense of the technical intricacies which appear to be the *sine qua non* at present.

FURTHER READING

Apter, M. J. (1970). *The Computer Simulation of Behaviour.* Hutchinson.
Borko, H. (Ed.) (1962). *Computer Applications in the Behavioural Sciences.* Prentice-Hall.
Feigenbaum, E. A., and Feldman, J. (Eds.) (1963). *Computers and Thought.* McGraw-Hill.
Minsky, M. (Ed.) (1968). *Semantic Information Processing.* M.I.T. Press.
Wathen-Dunn, W. (Ed.) (1967). *Models for the Perception of Speech and Visual Form.* M.I.T. Press.
Welford, A. T. and Houssiadas, L. (Eds.) (1970). *Contemporary Problems in Perception.* Taylor and Francis.

POSTSCRIPT

This little offering comes from Hilbert Schenk Jr.

ME
I think that I shall never see
A calculator made like me.
A me that likes Martinis dry
And on the rocks, a little rye.
A me that looks at girls and such,
But mostly girls, and very much.
A me that wears an overcoat
And likes a risky anecdote.
A me that taps a foot and grins
Whenever Dixieland begins.
They make computers for a fee,
But only moms can make a me.

10

Thinking as a Private Experience

Thought processes can be investigated by studying observable behaviour; by attempting to simulate them, especially by the use of computers; by looking at the cultural context of thought; and in other ways. As we have tried to show, during the ascendancy of behaviourism the importance of private experience was discounted. Currently this aspect is reinstated, with a particular emphasis on imagery. Here we discuss some of the systematic attempts to investigate private experience, and the method on which these essentially depend, that of introspection.

Conscious experience, of course, was the classical subject-matter that Psychology inherited from philosophy. Curiously enough, however, when psychologists began to investigate conscious experiences more systematically, they also began to find a great many more sorts of mental events than they had expected; and some of these were quite surprising. Perhaps the first systematic explorer was, appropriately enough, Francis Galton (1879).

THE SYSTEMATIC INVESTIGATION OF CONSCIOUSNESS

Galton, as we have seen, does not fit neatly into a philosophical, clinical, or even experimental tradition. An innovation of his however turned out to be highly relevant to the two last-named. This was the systematic analysis of associations to a given stimulus. It seems that Galton's interest was aroused by the ancient question of free-will, which he hoped to test by introspection of his own mental processes: '... whenever I caught myself in an act of what seemed to be Free Will... I checked myself and tried hard to recollect what had happened before, made rapid notes and then wrote a full account of the case'. He found the cases without apparent causation to be very few. We should probably argue now that this is a matter that cannot be settled empirically; but Galton, with his restless curiosity, went on to try to discover just how ideas arose in sequences. That they did so of course was the common assumption of associationism: Galton was the first, apparently, to observe and experiment systematically on the process. He began with the famous stroll down Pall Mall in London. Paying

358

momentary attention to each successive object that caught his eye, he mentally noted the thoughts that arose in connection with it; and then passed on to the next. So superior is Galton's own account to any précis that it must be quoted.

'I never allowed my mind to ramble. The number of objects viewed was, I think, about 300, for I have subsequently repeated the same walk under similar conditions and endeavouring to estimate their number, with that result. It was impossible for me to recall in other than the vaguest way the numerous ideas that had passed through my mind; but of this, at least, I was sure, that samples of my whole life had passed before me, that many bygone incidents, which I never suspected to have formed part of my stock of thoughts, had been glanced at as objects too familiar to awaken the attention. I saw at once that the brain was vastly more active than I had previously believed it to be, and I was perfectly amazed at the unexpected width of the field of its everyday operations. After an interval of some days, during which I kept my mind from dwelling on my first experiences, in order that it might retain as much freshness as possible for a second experiment, I repeated the walk, and was struck just as much as before by the variety of the ideas that presented themselves, and the number of events to which they referred, about which I had never consciously occupied myself of late years. But my admiration at the activity of the mind was seriously diminished by another observation which I then made, namely that there had been a very great deal of repetition of thought. The actors on my mental stage were indeed very numerous, but by no means so numerous as I had imagined. They now seemed to be something like the actors in theatres where large processions are represented, who march off one side of the stage, and, going round by the back, come on again at the other. I accordingly cast about for means of laying hold of these fleeting thoughts, and, submitting them to statistical analysis, to find out more about their tendency to repetition and other matters.'

In the last sentence particularly we have the essential Galton. The method he devised was to present himself with a series of 75 words and note down the first two ideas that occurred, timing his response by a chronograph. This he repeated, using the same list, four times at intervals of about a month. And 'a most repugnant and laborious work' he found it. Galton found he had produced a total of 505 ideas; but only 289 were different. 23 per cent of the words had produced the same idea on each occasion. Estimating as well as he could the period of his life at which the associations had originated, Galton found that those occurring most frequently tended to be older established. With some difficulty, he worked out a classification of the ideas. They fell into three main groups:

'First there is the imagined sound of words, as in verbal quotations or names of persons. This was frequently a mere parrot-like memory which acted instantaneously and in a meaningless way, just as a machine might act. In the next group there was every other kind of sense-imagery; the chime of imagined bells, the shiver of remembered cold, the scent of some particular locality, and much more frequently than all the rest put together visual imagery. The last of the three groups contains what I will venture, for want of a better name, to call "Histrionic" representations. It includes those cases where I either act a part in imagination, or see in imagination a part acted, or, most commonly by far, where I am both spectator and all the actors at once, in an imaginary theatre. Thus I feel a nascent sense of some muscular action while I simultaneously witness a puppet of my brain—a part of myself—perform that action, and I assume a mental attitude appropriate to the occasion.'

Allowing for the difficulty of devising such a classification for the first time, it is interesting to compare this with Bruner's three modes of representation: symbolic, ikonic and enactive (see *Development and Culture*).

Of experiments such as these, Galton remarked: 'They lay bare the foundations of a man's thoughts with curious distinctness, and exhibit his mental anatomy with more vividness and truth than he would probably care to publish to the world.' Hence, perhaps, some of Galton's repugnance—Freud was soon to experience even greater difficulties. Galton did not explore this phenomenon, which might have made him, and not Freud, the great discoverer. Instead his interest was restricted to the genesis of ideas and the role of consciousness.

'The more I have examined the workings of my own mind, whether in the walk along Pall Mall, or in the seventy five words, or in any other of the numerous ways I have attempted but do not here describe, the less respect I feel for the part played by consciousness. I begin with others to doubt its use altogether as a helpful supervisor, and to think that my best brain work is wholly independent of it. The unconscious operations of the mind frequently far transcend the conscious ones in intellectual importance ... Consciousness seems to do little more than attest the fact that the various organs of the brain do not work with perfect ease or co-operation. Its position appears to be that of a helpless spectator of but a minute fraction of a huge amount of automatic brain work.'

In this we have perhaps one of the many tributaries eventually leading to the Behaviouristic river in spate.

Curiously enough Galton's words just quoted could almost have been written by Wundt, whom we have already met in connection with problem solving and the Gestalt movement. His main concern was the analyses of immediate experience: as Boring puts it, the analysis of conscious processes into elements, the determination of the manner of connection of these elements, and the determination of their laws of connection. Much of the early history of Psychology was influenced by reactions against this would-be Napoleon, as James called him. But among Wundt's multifarious interests was also the role of unconscious thought in creative synthesis:

'Our mind is so fortunately equipped, that it brings us the most important bases for our thoughts without our having the least knowledge of this work of elaboration. Only the results of it become conscious. This unconscious mind is for us like an unknown being who creates and produces for us, and finally throws the ripe fruits in our lap.' (1862)

It is interesting to note the anonymous 'other' character of the unconscious which Freud expressed by use of the word 'Id'. (And a later dynamic psychologist George Groddeck, published *The Book of the It*.)

It was from Wundt's main activity, however, that there developed the work of the Würzburg school, (Würzburg is a German University town) to which we now turn. The Würzburg school began with Oswald Külpe. He started, under the influence of Wundt by holding that thought was not amenable to experiment—at least, no such experiments were available in the literature. Külpe, Boring tells us, determined to remedy this deficiency, just as Ebbinghaus (1885) had recently done for memory.

> 'Thought seems to be a course of association; if it is, then the introspective method ought to yield a description of thought.' (Boring)

George Humphrey (1951) has explained how:

> 'The classical theory of association came to its climax in the middle of the nineteenth century as a hypothesis claiming (a) to account for the way in which mental events followed each other, and (b) to explain the whole of mental life.'

It seemed obvious that the contents of the mind must consist of representations of the environment; (though there was of course a disagreement between those who thought some of the contents were inborn—the nativists—and those who followed John Locke in holding that the mind at birth was a blank slate to be filled in from experience. This controversy still continues. Either way, it was assumed that the external world presents itself to us through the senses, and then apparently the sensations are stored, in the form of images, or representations of the sensations. James Ward, a contemporary British psychologist, referred to the theory as 'presentationism'.) Thinking consisted in the manipulation of these units of thought, which can also be considered as ideas. Various principles of association were proposed to account for the ways in which the ideas were ordered, the most generally accepted being that of contiguity. If two ideas occurred together at any time, then in future the occurrence of one would tend to *reinstate* the other. As James Mill (1829) put it: 'Our ideas spring up or exist in the order in which the sensations existed of which they are the copies.' Long before the experimentalists at Würzburg got to work, the inadequacies of a simple associationism had been shown by argument, e.g. by Bradley in 1883. But Würzburg provided experimental evidence for two major features of thought which had before been ignored. One was a different sort of content, and one was a new sort of mechanism.

We must start by explaining the Würzburg method. It was based on introspection; and as already noted, this was a different matter from just talking aloud. It was not the free association of Freud nor the 'thinking aloud' of Duncker. It was a technique requiring skill and experience, in which the subject had to report objectively what he observed passing through his mind, as an astronomer might tell what he saw through his telescope. Robert S. Woodworth (e.g. 1938 etc.)

always referred to Subjects as Observers. In those days psychology students were not commanded or cajoled to act as subjects, rather it was the professor who took this role, and Külpe himself was the subject in many of the experiments. To make the method clear, consider the 'stimulus error'. A subject is presented with two points on his hand, which are brought closer together. At a certain distance he *feels* one; but he knows there are two. It is the sensation of one that the skilled introspectionist must report. If not, argued E. B. Titchener, he is doing physics, not psychology. Such introspections the Würzburg psychologists supplemented with questions from the experimenter, rather in the manner of Piaget—Humphrey criticizes them, unnecessarily I think, for varying the questions from one experiment to the next. And they also used apparatus—card changers to present stimuli, and timing devices such as the elegant Hipp chronoscopes— some of which, I am told are still in use in German universities. The whole series of experiments is voluminous, and we must pick out here the highlights.

Mayer and Orth (1901), asked their subjects to give a response to a stimulus word, and to report everything that went on in consciousness before the response was spoken. They tried to classify the reports into perceptions, images, and acts of will. But this was not adequate: 'The subjects frequently reported that they experienced certain events of consciousness which they could quite clearly designate neither as definite images nor yet as volitions.' These events Mayer and Orth termed *Bewusstseinslagen*, or states of awareness. They were undoubted mental contents that did not fit into the accepted framework. Next Marbe (1901), investigated judgment, asking his subjects to say which of two weights was heavier, to fixate the lightest of three greys, etc., and to tell what relevant contents passed through their minds. They could not. How do you know which of two weights is heavier? You just know. It was not that there were no images, ideas, or sensations to report, but that none of these were essentially related to the judging. There were no 'psychological conditions of the judgment'. Again it was a question of *Bewusstseinslagen*. Orth (1903), developed the concept so as to include James's fringes of consciousness. and much of what Wundt had called feelings. Next, H. J. Watt (1904) a Scotsman working in Germany, adopted the method of getting his subjects to give partially constrained associations to stimulus words; they were told, for example, to give the name of the class of things to which the word belonged (given 'dahlia' they should respond, for instance, 'flower'); or to name another of the same class; and so on. Watt tried to examine the thought processes by the method of fractionation. The introspective task was divided into four parts: the preparatory period; the appearance of the stimulus word; the search for the reaction word; the production of the reaction word. Subjects were asked to report their experiences during just one of these. Watt was particularly interested in the search period, since that was where the thinking seemed to be done, as it were. But as before, it appeared that in some cases the experiences 'could only be described in conceptual terms and not analytically according to the content'. This was the *Bewusstseinlage* once more. Watt therefore turned his attention to the effect of the task, or *aufgabe*. Assuming that the subject has a stock of associations on which to draw, what determines his choice of the appropriate one? Obviously it is the task set by the experimenter. But while the subject is clearly aware of this when it is announced to him, and may remind himself of it at intervals, he may *not* be aware of it at the moment of the search. Rather, it seemed that the task created an *einstellung* or set, such that the proper response just ran off, on presentation of the stimulus word, without the subject being conscious of how he found it. Therefore, Boring says (1957) interest has ever since centred on the *aufgabe*. And indeed we have already met the task, and the *einstellung* it creates, in the work of Luchins (see *Problem Solving*). But things move rapidly in psychology; and Boring is no longer correct, for current work on the neural dictionary, for example, is precisely on the search period. George Kiss's computer simulation studies (see *Models*) give us some idea of just how a stimulus word leads to a particular response. And Collins and Quillian (1969a,b) have made a start on examining how information is stored hierarchically, by measuring reaction time latencies to various 'simple' questions such as 'Is a cat a bird?' So in a sense Watt was right after all. This illustrates some of the virtues and limitations of the classical introspective method: the events of consciousness are of the greatest importance, and the introspectionists gave us an acute analysis of them. By no means all the mental events in which we are interested can be reached by this technique—but some can be reached by no other.

A further detailed analysis was given by Ach (1905). He used various sorts of reaction time experiments, simple and complex. Again subjects were often unable to specify exactly their experiences in the period between stimulus and response, beyond what Ach termed *Bewusstheit* or awareness. He regarded this as the 'presence of an impalpably given knowing'. It is not clear whether he considered this as a different sort of content of the mind or as an act. Humphrey (1951) summarizes Ach's complicated account thus:

'Normally, during the fore-period, when there has not been too much practice, the following complex-content is, for example, present simultaneously, as an awareness. (1) The coming stimulus (a white card), with a spatial determination, in so far as the subject knows that the uniquely determined change will take place at the point of fixation. (2) The subject is aware that thereafter must follow an unequivocally determined change on his side; that is to say, the reaction. (3) In addition there is a relation present between (1) and (2); there is awareness that the reaction must follow as soon as the stimulus appears. (4) There is a temporal component, in so far as the knowing is given, that the stimulus will appear within a certain known time. The subject knows, for example, that the stimulus will not come in a half-second, and will come within a minute. In addition to this immediately given content, "there are also the accompanying phenomena of sensory attention, such as sensations of tension in the upper part of the body, and in the optical sense organ as well as the visual perception (in our experiments with the closure plate of the card changer). At times some of the above-mentioned constituent parts of the awareness-complex come up in the form of images, particularly at the beginning of the fore-period or during the first experiments on any day. Individual capabilities play a large role here. But, nevertheless, there are an extraordinarily large number of experiments, in which, apart from the above-mentioned accompanying phenomena, the whole waiting content appears only as 'knowing', and this presence of a knowing-content we designate as an awareness." '

What a far cry such an account seems from our every-day laboratory experiments today; but notice that the procedure of a simple reaction-time has changed little, and a difference of fashion or interest should not be taken as necessarily one of importance. Ach also tried to take further the matter of *how* the task carries over to influence the response. His answer was in terms of *determining tendencies*. It is not very easy to see what these add to the already known facts: but it seems that the task, or particular aspects of it, were thought of as somehow pointing the mind in the right direction, as it were. Just how this occurs, was not known. Indeed it seems Ach was not very interested in the actual nature of the determining tendency; and thirty years later (1935) suggested that no answer was yet possible. From our present point of view, the important matter is that the tendencies were said to operate outside of consciousness.

'Thus the qualitative determination of the determined presentation is here without doubt to be referred to influences which function in the unconscious, understanding by the unconscious simply that which is not conscious. These acts, which work in the unconscious, proceed from the meaning of the aim-presentation, are directed towards the coming object-presentation, and which bring with them a spontaneous appearance of the determined presentation, we designate determining tendencies.' (Ach, 1905)

Interestingly enough, Ach quotes the case of post-hypnotic suggestion as evidence for the determining tendencies, and as we shall see this was an important source of Freud's ideas also. But notice the limited definition of the unconscious as 'simply that which is not conscious' in Ach's account.

Further experiments were reported by Messer (1906) and Bühler (1907–8). These did not change the two important results we have already noted: that there were contents of the mind not analysable by conscious introspection, and that there were dynamics of thinking proceeding outside consciousness. Messer pointed to the way in which the task gradually disappears from consciousness, yet continues to function. This is suggestive of Bartlett's view of thinking as a high-level skill. Bühler set out to examine thinking directly by posing to able exponents of it, including Külpe, such intentionally difficult problems as:—Does monism really mean the negation of personality? and the smaller the woman's foot, the larger the bill for the shoes? (We have not been able to find the solutions to these.) Attempting to analyse the experiences that preceded answering, Bühler was clear that:

364

'The most important bits of experience are ... something which before all shows no sensory quality, no sensory intensity. Something of which we may rightly predicate degree of clearness, degree of certainty, a vividness by means of which it arouses our psychic interest: which, however, in its content is quite differently determined from everything that is ultimately reducible to sensations; something for which it would be nonsense to try to determine whether it possessed a greater or less intensity, or even into what sensory qualities it could be resolved.'

These entities are what the subjects, using Ach's term, have designated as awarenesses, or sometimes as knowing, or simply as 'the consciousness that', but most frequently and correctly as 'thoughts'. Thinking, after all, consists of thoughts. In 1909 Külpe moved to Bonn, and the name Würzburg retreated into the wings of the psychological stage, which was now ready for psychoanalysis and unconscious thinking proper; for Gestalt psychology and the dynamics of thinking; for behaviourism and the rejection of thinking, at least as a central directive process. Now that we are again interested in the problems that occupied the Würzburgers, it is useful to look at their methods and their successes and failures.

FREUD

It is still not unusual to date the concept of the unconscious from Freud. Actually, a long history preceded his work, as has been shown by L. L. Whyte (1960); Joan Wynne Reeves (1965); and E. G. Boring (1957). We shall try to see what was new—indeed revolutionary—in Freud's contribution to the psychology of thinking.

Thirty years or more after his death, Freud remains puzzling, stimulating, and controversial. The extent of his work, and subsequent elaborations by other psychoanalysts, make it extremely difficult to summarize. Then again, Freud's ideas changed and developed through his life. This is because he was, as R. S. Peters (1951) put it: 'ostensibly a technologist'. That is to say he was concerned first of all with finding practical means to cure patients; only secondarily did he formulate theories to account for what he observed. But those theories became ever more all-embracing, so that chapters on Freud find their way into books on learning, social behaviour, child development and thinking as well as personality and pathology. Another difficulty is that while Freud certainly had important things to say on a vast range of psychological topics, it is often necessary to disentangle them from his concern with other matters. So it is with thinking; and we will start with a somewhat impressionistic account of Freud's general ideas. As is well known Freud's early evidence came from his work with Josef Breuer, in which psychoneurotic patients were treated by the hypnotic methods Freud had learned in France. Under treatment patients seemed to recall forgotten memories of traumatic experiences, following which the presenting symptoms were relieved. Breuer's explanation was in terms of 'hypnoid' states, arising, for example, during periods of exceptional stress. Freud thought the story was more complex, and pushed on alone. His next move was to investigate the sex lives of his patients. He later said: 'This experiment cost me, it is true, my popularity as a doctor, but it brought me convictions which today, almost thirty years later, have lost none of their force.' At this time, neurologists (as Freud was) dealt with what he himself referred to as a 'confused jumble of clinical pictures'. From this jumble, Freud was able to distinguish a group of patients, with various symptoms, but who also all had sexual problems, and who were helped by the hypnotic 'talking-through' technique. Freud now became aware of another factor that had helped to frighten Breuer off: the patient tended to develop a passionate, if ambivalent, attitude towards the doctor. This was subsequently named transference. Now Freud gave up hypnosis, which seemed to make the transference more difficult to handle, and the relief of symptoms more temporary. Freud's account must be quoted.

'One of my most acquiescent patients, with whom hypnotism had enabled me to bring about the most marvellous results, and whom I was engaged in relieving of her suffering by tracing back her attacks of pain to their origins, as she woke up on one occasion, threw her arms round my neck. The unexpected entrance of a servant relieved us from a painful discussion, but from that time onwards there was a tacit understanding between us that the hypnotic treatment should be discontinued.' (Freud, 1935)

Thinking back to watching Bernheim at work, who maintained that memories apparently lost after hypnosis could be recovered, Freud now set out to make the unconscious, conscious. But this was not so easy. Something seemed to *prevent* certain thoughts reaching consciousness; and so Freud was led to one of his major innovations, the postulation of a force of repression. 'It was a novelty, and nothing like it had ever before been recognized in mental life. It was obviously a primary mechanism of defence, comparable to an attempt at flight.' So the nature of the therapy changed: 'Its aim was no longer to "abreact" an affect which had got on to the wrong lines but to uncover repressions and replace them by acts of judgment.' And from there a new view of the mind emerged: 'Psychoanalysis regarded everything mental as being in the first instance unconscious; the further quality of "consciousness" might also be present, or again it might be absent.' (1935). Even bearing in mind all the precursors that Whyte and Reeves have summarized, we have here one of the fundamentally reorienting concepts of science. Human consciousness had seemed the standard against which mental events were to be compared: now it takes its place as a quality emerging at a particular stage of development (individual or evolutionary); rather as the Copernican revolution made our world no longer the centre of the universe.

Ernest Jones take the matter rather further by suggesting that perhaps even more important was Freud's description of two sorts of mental processes, which correspond very approximately to conscious and unconscious. These were named primary and secondary. Secondary processes are those seen in 'normal', rational, logical thinking. They are secondary in that they develop later than, and out of, the primary processes. These are seen in dreams and mental disorders. Freud's view of the contents of the mind we must shortly discuss further. Here let us say that the unconscious contents are partly innate, and partly acquired in the course of development. A child is born with instinctual tendencies which demand gratification. These are closely related to survival: they are needs for food, warmth, handling and affection. By virtue of the fact that another person is involved, since the human infant is virtually helpless for a long period, instant gratification is impossible. Primary process thinking reaches out towards gratification by substituting an image for the real thing. But at the same time tension is created by the frustrating person, who thus becomes the object of ambivalent emotions: desire and anger. Later these emotions are also directed towards the person perceived as responsible for the mother's frustrating behaviour, that is normally the father. And since in primary process thinking the thought is confused with the real thing, it is to the child as if he were really attacking his parents, and they in revenge attacking him. By the nature of human infancy, relationships with other people are present from the start. Freud called the drives (a better translation of *trieb*, Freud's word, than *instinct*) and feelings involved in these relationships, sexual. By this he meant that they are centred on the parts of the body associated with sexual arousal; that the fantasies aroused are specifically sexual—it is sexual contact that the child desires with his mother, and castration that he fears from his father; and that the attitudes formed now are the basis of adult sexuality later. But they are also the basis of all emotional relationships, and the intense and irrational feelings of childhood are always ready to be revived. This is seen at its clearest in the analytic relationship, and as we have mentioned is then called transference. Now these intense and ambivalent emotions arouse anxiety, which is relieved by rejection of the associated ideas from consciousness by the process of repression. Some of the instinctual contents of the mind are, according to the theory, repressed from the start, and never normally reach consciousness. Thus it is no longer a matter of ideas which just happen not to be the focus of attention, as in Galton's account, or which have somehow slipped below a threshold. Repression is an active and continuous process throughout life. Unconscious material can only become conscious if repression is overcome or evaded. This happens spontaneously in some dreams and psychoses; in disguised form in neurotic symptoms; and is brought about deliberately by psychoanalysis. Modern analysts in the direct line of descent, as it were, concentrate on analysing transference. Everything the patient says or does is taken to be the outcome of the emotional attitudes laid down in childhood, and now directed towards the analyst. The desirable outcome of the process is for the patient to be aware of, and so in command of, these attitudes, or as Freud put it, 'where Id was, there shall Ego be'.

Now in his conception of the contents of the mind, Freud was strongly influenced by the prevailing theories, such as what Ward called presentationism (as noted above). Joan Reeves (1965) has made this explicit:

'Freud ... took for granted a form of representative perception. The organism is not directly aware of what goes on outside it but only of that which is the product of its own receptor organs discharging. He fused this with a largely associationistic account of the contents both of the resultant experience and of that experience which arises from internal deficit and desire. That which the organism lives through primarily is, in effect, the *representative* product of externally-induced change and the *immediate* product of internal stimulation. But the elements of such experience, externally or internally originating, are sensations, images, ideas, affects, states of tension, feelings of relief or satisfaction all very loosely defined.'

Reeves stresses the close connection, in Freud's concept of the primary processes, between wishing and thinking: 'At this level the processes are inseparable and both are forms of action.' She distinguishes five senses in which Freud uses 'wish'. The last of these is particularly important for us here:

'Here we return to the notions involved in Freud's *Project for a Scientific Psychology* (1895) and which he carried over into *The Interpretation of Dreams*. In brief, he reinvokes the "constancy principle" (i.e. maintenance of equilibrium as an aim of the nervous system); takes somatic needs as basic; supposes that some object (say milk) succeeds in removing an initial state of unbalance (hunger). He then argues that the mnemic image of that which satisfied (i.e. milk) remains associated henceforth with a memory trace of the excitation produced by the need. Hence, when the need is next aroused, there is an attempt to "re-cathect" the image and re-evoke the original perception, i.e. "re-establish the situation of the original satisfaction." "An impulse of this kind," writes Freud, "is what we call a wish." And, he adds, "nothing prevents us from assuming that there was a primitive state of the psychical apparatus in which wishing ended in hallucinating." "The bitter experience of life" (e.g. of hallucinated milk not satisfying hunger) "must have changed the primitive thought activity into a more expedient secondary one".'

In passing, lest this seem too fanciful, is it so very unlike the rather common assumption that a promise is somehow a partial payment? Freud's notion was that a mental event could be experienced as equivalent to a behavioural one: such 'omnipotence of thought' was the basis of the subjective power of an infant's fantasies. Persisting in adult life, it is the basis of, for example, sympathetic magic, in which to wish harm to another is actually to bring it about.

Let us now mention some of the evidence on which Freud drew for his belief in unconscious mental processes. Of this his work on dreams is the most relevant to our concerns, but first more briefly some other aspects. A difficulty here is that it is often very unclear in Freud's writings what is to be taken as evidence, and what as explanation. First, posthypnotic suggestion. It has very often been shown that a subject can be instructed, while under hypnosis, to carry out some action later at a given signal, but not to remember consciously that he has been so instructed. Such an action might be, say, to fetch and open an umbrella. Later, on the signal, he does so. His apparent surprise and, sometimes, his creation of a false reason or rationalization for his behaviour, argue for the operation of some mental process actively kept out of consciousness. In this case, a rationalization might be that the subject of conversation had been hypnosis and similar magical and superstitious beliefs, and the subject wished to demonstrate his rejection of these by carrying out an action often held to be unlucky, namely opening an umbrella indoors. Neurotic symptoms clearly suggested similar processes, particularly in so far as they were relieved, as already noted, when apparently forgotten traumata were brought to light. Later in *The Psychopathology of Everyday Life* (1914), Freud applied the same sort of analysis to parapraxes, the everyday mistakes of behaviour and speech that have come to be called Freudian slips. He tried to show, by exploring the associations to each one, that the particular mistake is never mere chance, but is always related to some anxiety-provoking stimulus, often in quite complex ways. This makes examples too long to quote, but we should repeat the point that what arouses anxiety is ultimately the repressed material from early childhood. It is not simply a question of forgetting the annoying incidents of everyday life, it is rather that annoyance and forgetting are caused by stimuli that in some way repeat or are linked to the original traumata. Much the same applies to Freud's theory of humour. This is a topic of which psychologists have so far signally failed to give any good account. All the general theories merely state some categorical redescription, such as that all humour is really surprise. Freud did at least attempt an explanation, this being basically that jokes allow a partial and disguised expression to anxiety-related material. While he works this out plausibly in the case of many jokes, there seem to be at least two sorts that make a difficulty for the theory. Firstly there are many overtly sexual jokes—why are these not repressed? Then there are those where it seems most implausible to postulate repressed meaning, such as the short-lived race of elephant jokes (Why do elephants paint the soles of their feet yellow? So that they can float undetected upside down in custard. Etc.) On the other hand some humour that has been popular since Freud wrote is very reminiscent of some of the features of primary process thinking. Allen Eyles (1966), writing as a film critic, not a psychologist, has brought out very clearly the extraordinary play with confusion of identity that runs through all of the Marx Brothers' work. (For example Harpo's Punch and Judy scene in *Animal Crackers*. The supreme example is of course the *Duck Soup* scene in which both Harpo and Chico are disguised as Groucho, and we get the apotheosis of the old 'mirror' gag.) Also very apparent are the disregard of the ordinary laws of time and space ('You pay him enough, he could sail yesterday'); and sudden switches of meaning, puns being only one example, in which attention is distracted by just one aspect ('I'd horsewhip you if I had a horse'). Indeed Harpo is practically a running commentary on

Freudian theory and the id in particular. Lacking language, he seems to think in images and action. He often has an insatiable appetite and sometimes magical powers, the wish being the same as the deed. Nothing seems to stand between him and instant gratification of impulse; his feelings, too, are never hidden. Resisting the temptation to run on for several thousand words about this, (see *The Fool* by Enid Welsford, 1935, for an account of Harpo's predecessors), we can see humour as one source of evidence for Freud's theory. I think myself a full account of the phenomena must bring in some as yet unknown mental mechanisms, so as to include both timing and meaning as well as repressed anxiety.

But it was above all, of course, from the analysis of dreams—'the *via regia* to a knowledge of the unconscious elements in our psychic life'—that Freud derived his treatment; and of *The Interpretation of Dreams* he justifiably remarked, 'insight such as this falls to one's lot but once in a lifetime.' In dreams the conscious mind is inactive, and yet there is clearly mental activity. Freud held that dreams express unconscious emotions and desires, usually, but not always, in disguised form. The expression comes about because the mechanism of repression is to some extent released in sleep. The disguise comes about because the real contents of the unconscious would be so alarming as to awaken the sleeper, as does indeed occasionally happen. It follows that dreams have a manifest and latent content, and the latter can be inferred if we are familiar with the operation of the 'dream-work' which disguises it. As Freud put it in 1935

> 'There is no difficulty in discovering the general function of dreaming. It serves the purpose of warding off, by a kind of soothing action, external or internal stimuli which would tend to arouse the sleeper, and thus of securing sleep against interruption. External stimuli are warded off by being given a new interpretation and by being woven into some harmless situation; internal stimuli, caused by the pressure of instincts, are given free play by the sleeper and allowed to find satisfaction in the formation of dreams, so long as the latent dream-thoughts submit to the control of the censorship. But if they threaten to break free and the meaning of the dream becomes too plain, the sleeper cuts short the dream and awakens in terror. (Dreams of this class are known as *anxiety-dreams*.) A similar failure in the function of dreaming occurs if an external stimulus too strong to be warded off. (This is the class of *arousal-dreams*.) I have given the name of *dream-work* to the process which, with the co-operation of the censorship, converts the latent thoughts into the manifest content of the dreams.'

In *The Interpretation of Dreams* Freud described four main processes of the dream-work: condensation, displacement, 'making representable', and 'secondary revision'. Joan Reeves, among others, has pointed out here Freud's debt to associationism.

> 'The root processes of *condensation* appear to be (a) linking, (b) fusion, (c) complex interrelation on the basis of temporal contiguity, similarity, spatial contiguity and opposition—or all of these at once. In fact we en-

counter here the same root relations that underpinned our old friends the laws of association... Freud appears to give formal priority to contiguity in time and it is this line of thinking that suggests fundamental similarities between the Freudian and Pavlovian accounts of thought development. "Our perceptions", writes Freud, "are linked with one another in memory—first and foremost according to simultaneity of occurrence. We speak of this fact as "association?"'

But there is more to condensation than merely linking. It is not just that one idea tends to recall another with which it has become associated by contiguity, similarity, or whatever. It is that the two ideas are as it were collapsed into one, or become equivalent. It is in this way that many of the symbols of dreams come about: the process is extremely complex, so that a single image can often stand for, or express, numerous linked ideas. Here, similarity is perhaps the most important factor. This may be a chance resemblance, when a person, for example, with some characteristic such as red hair stands for another with the same feature. Or it may be more fundamental, so that objects or even situations with essentially the same structure stand for each other: any long, moving, or penetrating object, such as a snake, sword, umbrella, etc., is a penis, any containing, tube-like object a vagina. Here we are reminded of the ethological concept of sign-stimuli, though this may be an equivalence with which Freud himself would not have agreed. 'Free association' is a way of unravelling these links between ideas. It is really, in some respects, another way of investigating what we now call the search process, the process that Watt gave up in despair, and Kiss, and Collins and Quillian have latterly tackled with new methods. *Displacement* refers to the fact that emotion attached to one object or person can be transferred, in the dream, to another, usually resembling it in some way. Freud thought of the mind as a kind of closed energy system, with some kind of psychic force that, as it were, 'charged' certain ideas and not others, so that they became important in the individual's mind. Here there is a clear debt to Herbart; and again, a look forward to the ethological concept of 'displacement reactions'. *'Making representable'* refers to the process whereby the underlying dream thoughts, that is the latent content of the dream, are put into the form that is used by dreams; that is to say, imagery. Now it seems that Freud considered the underlying dream thoughts to be characterized in some sense by logical relations; and it is these that have to be translated by the dream-work for purposes of expression, and then translated back again by the analyst for purposes of interpretation. In view of the concept of primary processes as being illogical, this notion seems, as Reeves points out, to be a puzzle. It is also fraught with ambiguity. For example: it is said that the logical relation of negation may be expressed directly or indirectly. That is to say, an image can stand either for itself or for its opposite; if the dream shows the dreamer, say, being affectionate to his parents, this can mean either that he really does love them, or that he hates them. As has often been pointed out, such assertions become virtually impossible to test. Causal relations,

Freud states, are represented either by the relative lengths of parts of a dream, the shorter introductory part representing the cause of the remainder; or by a dream image changing into another, the first being the cause, the second the effect. As Reeves remarks, Freud was here concerned with a fundamental question about the nature of thought, which we must discuss again in a moment. The fourth main process of the dreamwork, *'making representable'* is a further stage of work on the material already translated into dream form. It seems designed to make the dream rather more connected and rational; it is analogous to what Bartlett (1932) termed 'effort after meaning'. This referred to the process employed by his subjects in trying to reconstruct a full story from remembered fragments.

There are some other aspects of the dream-work which we shall omit here. The more important question is, given that we now know how the form of the dream is brought about, what is the material that is thus translated? How are we to conceive of the latent content, the dream thoughts? From Freud's account in *The Interpretation of Dreams* it is extremely hard to be sure. Joan Reeves advances two important arguments on this question. Her first line is to stress that 'the dream-thoughts are rational and can be known'. This is exemplified by the following well-known quotation from Freud:

> 'We have introduced a new class of psychical material between the manifest content of dreams and the conclusions of our inquiry: namely, their *latent* content or (as we say) the "dream-thoughts", arrived at by means of our procedure. It is from these dream-thoughts and not from the dream's manifest content that we disentangle its meaning. . . .
>
> The dream-thoughts and the dream-content are presented to us like two versions of the same subject-matter in two different languages. Or, more properly, the dream-content seems like a transcript of the dream-thoughts into another mode of expression, whose characters and syntactic laws it is our business to discover by comparing the original and the translation. The dream-thoughts are immediately comprehensible as soon as we have learnt them. The dream-content, on the other hand, is expressed as it were in a pictographic script, the characters of which have to be transposed individually into the language of the dream-thoughts. . . .' (*The Interpretation of Dreams*, 1938).

Now in view of what we have said about the characteristics of unconscious thinking, this is odd. As Reeves puts it:

> 'Freud often stressed the unknowable nature of unconscious thought processes and their difference from conscious ones. He contrived, the while, to stress both the "rationality" of latent dream-thoughts and the irrationality of unconscious processes of which, as we have suggested, dream thoughts are sometimes treated as one class.'

Reeves suggests various solutions to this paradox. It may be, for example, that dream-thoughts are to be considered *understandable*, rather than rational. Or it might be (though this is unlikely) that Freud was only talking about the preconscious.

'A third alternative is to surmise that Freud tacitly assumed all unconscious thoughts, however bizarre, to be theoretically capable of logical formation.'

And further, that this is normally a gradual process, though Freud does not say this explicitly. From here Reeves goes on to her second argument, that if this is so, it implies an important advance on Freud's part. He clearly started with a concept of thought as 'contents' of the mind in the associationist tradition, which were as it were 'scanned' by consciousness. Freud does, in fact, define the role of consciousness as 'that of a sense-organ for the perception of psychic qualities'. Reeves' argument is that Freud moved from such an 'inspectionist' view of thinking towards a detailed dynamic analysis. Here I find Reeves herself not very clear, but what she intends may be apparent from the Freud quotation which she presents as supporting her argument:

'The ideas which are derived from the greatest depth and which form the nucleus of the pathogenic organization are also those which are acknowledged as memories by the patient with the greatest difficulty. Even when everything is finished and the patients have been overborne by the force of logic and by the therapeutic effect accompanying the emergence of precisely these ideas—when, I say, the patients themselves accept the fact that they thought this or that, they often add: "But I can't *remember* having thought it." It is easy to come to terms with them by telling them the thoughts were *unconscious*. But how is this state of affairs to be fitted into our own psychological views? Are we to disregard this withholding of recognition on the part of the patients, when, now that the work is finished, there is no longer any motive for their doing so, Or are we to suppose that we are really dealing with thoughts which never came about, which merely had a possibility of existing, so that the treatment would consist in the accomplishment of a psychical act which did not take place at the time? It is clearly impossible to say anything about this—that is, about the state which the pathogenic material was in before analysis—until we have arrived at a thorough clarification of our basic psychological view, especially on the nature of consciousness.'

This rather important quotation comes from the *Studies in Hysteria*, written jointly with Breuer. When he came to write *The Interpretation of Dreams* Freud was ready to extend his concept of unconscious ideas; and my understanding of what he wrote is somewhat different from that of Reeves. Some unconscious contents are to be thought of as originating in 'normal' thinking: 'the dream serves as a substitute for a number of thoughts derived from our daily life, and which fit together with perfect logic'. Thus a dream may express, sometimes openly, but more often in disguised form, something of which we are, or have been, perfectly well aware when awake, such as a desire to leave home, drive a car or what not. But dreams also express material that is not so accessible. And Freud, in fact, held that this feature was essential for dream-formation:

'In general ... I am of the opinion that unfulfilled wishes of the day are insufficient to produce a dream in adults. I will readily admit that the wish-impulses originating in consciousness contribute to the instigation of dreams, but they probably do no more. The dream would not occur if the pre-conscious wish were not reinforced from another source. That source is the unconscious. I believe that the conscious wish becomes effective in exciting a dream only when it succeeds in arousing a similar wish which reinforces it.'

He continues a little later, rather dramatically:

'These ever-active and, as it were, immortal wishes of our unconscious recall the legendary Titans who, from time immemorial, have been buried under the mountains which were once hurled upon them by the victorious gods, and even now quiver from time to time at the convulsions of their mighty limbs. These wishes, existing in repression, are themselves of infantile origin.'

But the precise nature of the wishes, that is, the nature of unconscious processes, is what is not clear, as we have noted. Perhaps we are to think of a sort of *schema,* a kind of framework or structure:

'It is quite true that the unconscious wishes are always active. They represent paths which are always practicable, whenever a quantum of excita-tion makes use of them. It is indeed an outstanding peculiarity of the un-conscious processes that they are indestructible. Nothing can be brought to an end in the unconscious; nothing is past and forgotten. This is im-pressed upon us emphatically in the study of the neuroses and especially of hysteria. The unconscious path of thought which leads to the discharge through an attack is forthwith passable again when there is a sufficient accumulation of excitation. The mortification suffered thirty years ago operates, after having gained access to the unconscious sources of affect, during all these thirty years as though it were a recent experience.'

This view may be the origin of the popular belief that 'nothing is ever forgotten'. It makes clear that a sense of time is not characteristic of the 'basic' thought of the unconscious (compare the loss of time sense common in schizophrenia). It brings out an important aspect of Freud's theory, that emotional mental structures once created remain in some sense in existence: this contrasts sharply with Piaget's account of cognitive structures, where each successive stage subsumes and transforms the previous one (see *The Geneva School*). And it shows, perhaps, that we should think of the unconscious pro-cesses as akin to attitudes or, as we put it above, *schemata*.

We have had several quotations from Freud, but here is another rather long one which seems to summarize his general view of thought processes:

'Why is it that the unconscious can furnish in sleep nothing more than the motive power for a wish-fulfilment? The answer to this question must elucidate the psychic nature of the state of wishing: and it will be given with the aid of the notion of the psychic apparatus.

We do not doubt that this apparatus, too, has only arrived at its present perfection by a long process of evolution. Let us attempt to restore it as it existed in an earlier stage of capacity. From postulates to be confirmed in other ways we know that at first the apparatus strove to keep itself as free from stimulation as possible, and therefore, in its early structure adopted the arrangement of a reflex apparatus, which enabled it promptly to discharge by the motor paths any sensory excitation reaching it from without. (Compare Piaget's sensori-motor stage.) But this simple function was disturbed by the exigencies of life, to which the apparatus owes the impetus toward further development. The exigencies of life first confronted it in the form of the great physical needs. The excitation aroused by the inner need seeks an outlet in motility, which we may describe as "internal change" or expression of the emotions". The hungry child cries or struggles helplessly. But its situation remains unchanged; for the excitation proceeding from the inner need has not the character of a momentary impact, but of a continuing pressure. A change can occur only if, in some way (in the case of the child by external assistance) there is an experience of satisfaction, which puts an end to the external excitation. An essential constituent of this experience is the appearance of a certain percept (of food in our example), the memory-image of which is henceforth associated with the memory-trace of the excitation arising from the need. Thanks to the established connection, there results, at the next occurrence of this need, a psychic impulse which seeks to revive the memory-image of the former percept, and to re-evoke the percept itself; that is, it actually seeks to re-establish the situation of the first satisfaction. Such an impulse is what we call a wish; the re-appearance of the perception constitutes the wish-fulfilment, and the full cathexis of the perception by the excitation springing from the need, constitutes the shortest path to the wish-fulfilment. We may assume a primitive state of the psychic apparatus in which this path is actually followed, i.e. in which the wish ends in hallucination. This first psychic activity therefore aims at an identity of perception: that is, at a repetition of that perception which is connected with the satisfaction of the need.'

So what is involved is a sort of matching process. Freud now goes on to show how thinking develops.

'This primitive mental activity must have been modified by bitter practical experience into a secondary and more appropriate activity. The establishment of identity of perception by the short regressive path within the apparatus does not produce the same result in another respect as follows upon cathexis of the same perception coming from without. The satisfaction does not occur, and the need continues. In order to make the internal cathexis equivalent to the external one, the former would have to be continuously sustained, just as actually happens in the hallucinatory psychoses and in hunger-phantasies, which exhaust their performance in *maintaining their hold* on the object desired. In order to attain to more appropriate use of the psychic energy, it becomes necessary to suspend the full regression, so that it does not proceed beyond the memory-image, and thence can seek other paths, leading ultimately to the production of the desired identity from the side of the outer world. (In other words: the introduction of a "test of reality" is recognized as necessary.) This inhibition, as well as the subsequent deflection of the excitation, becomes the task of a second system, which controls voluntary motility for purposes remembered in advance. But all this complicated mental activity, which works its way from the memory-image to the production of identity of perception via the outer world, merely represents *a round-*

about way to wish-fulfilment made necessary by experience. Thinking is indeed nothing but a substitute for the hallucinatory wish; and if the dream is called a wish-fulfilment this becomes something self-evident, since nothing but a wish can impel our psychic apparatus to activity. The dream, which fulfils its wishes by following the short regressive path, has thereby simply preserved for us a specimen of the primary method of operation of the psychic apparatus, which has been abandoned as inappropriate. What once prevailed in the waking state, when our psychic life was still young and inefficient, seems to have been banished into our nocturnal life; just as we still find in the nursery those discarded primitive weapons of adult humanity, the bow and arrow. Dreaming is a fragment of the superseded psychic life of the child. In the psychoses those modes of operation of the psychic apparatus which are normally suppressed in the waking state reassert themselves, and thereupon betray their inability to satisfy our demands in the outer world.' (Freud, 1938.)

I suppose a greater volume of criticism has been levelled at Freud than at any other psychological writer. We shall not here go into the general criticisms of Freudian theory which have been ably marshalled by, for example, H. J. Eysenck. In general, they are under two headings: that the theory, or parts of it, are so formulated as to be untestable: and that where the theory is testable, the evidence is either contradictory or lacking. I would make only a few points. The first is that one effect of Freud's admitted greatness is, perhaps, a tendency to assess his work as though it had just appeared, instead of more than seventy years ago. Freud must be assessed as are the other historical figures of psychology. Even when this is done, it is still not easy to be clear as to Freud's importance. Thomson (1968) says for example that Freud's 'influence has never been extensive in psychology' yet at the same time psychoanalysis 'has a central place in the psychology of the twentieth century'. Surely those statements are just the opposite of the truth. Psychoanalysis occupies a peripheral place with regard to psychology, in respect both of its subject matter and its exponents, but its influence is hard to overestimate: can there be a single psychologist, not to say educated person, today who is uninfluenced by Freud? It is true that we also want to know what in Freud's theory is actually of use to us today. We believe it is fair to say that the theory can still provide insights and stimulation even for hard-headed experimentalists (at random, let workers on attention, arousal, and search processes re-read Freud). In the study of thinking, Freud's work remains by far the most massive and detailed, as well as original account we have of unconscious processes. In general attitude to the phenomena, Freud can still re-orient our consideration, and in a way which is now far less unusable than when a strict Behaviourism held sway. On the other hand one of the greatest weaknesses of the theory, perhaps, is its relationship to the data (which of course are themselves subjective in the highest degree). Despite Freud's denials, the theory in general does impress one as more of an attempt to make sense of some remarkable observations than a well-tested account of how things really are. Of course it is no bad thing to make sense out of phenomena; but it is fundamental to scientific thinking to realize that a plausible story is not necessarily an explanation. It may be a theory, which we continue to hold so long as it remains undisproved. Or it may be more in the nature of a model. And this is perhaps the best way to regard Freudian theory. We observe that a patient develops intense emotions about his analyst, and subsequently shows greater or less change in personality: and we can at least say that it is as if he were re-living childhood experiences. Similar things happen outside analysis; many people have experiences which are irresistibly suggestive of a return to childhood. Of course for a psychologist 'regression' is the natural interpretation, but a different culture would probably provide another way in which to make sense of the phenomena.

JUNG

The continuators, as one might call them, of Freudian theory have for the most part been less interested in the unconscious as a concept than in other aspects. The exception is Jung. Here too I disagree with Thomson, who accords Jung an equal place with Freud, apparently mainly on the basis of his admittedly great erudition, which however is neither a necessary nor a sufficient condition of scientific merit. As is well-known, Jung extended the concept of the unconscious to include inherited material common to all members of the human race—the collective or racial unconscious. But it is a good deal more difficult even than it is with Freud to be clear about the nature of this material. Jung's *Psychology of the Unconscious* (subtitled *A contribution to the evolution of thought*) begins with a chapter 'Concerning the two kinds of thinking'. One is *directed thinking.*

> 'If we scrutinize our thinking more closely still and follow out an intensive train of thought—the solution of a difficult problem, for instance—we suddenly notice that we are *thinking in words*, that in very intensive thinking we begin talking to ourselves, or that we occasionally write down the problem or make a drawing of it, so as to be absolutely clear... Any very intensive train of thought works itself out more or less in verbal form— if, that is to say, one wants to express it, or teach it, or convince someone of it. It is evidently directed *outwards*, to the outside world. To that extent, directed or logical thinking is reality-thinking, a thinking that is adapted to reality, by means of which we imitate the successiveness of real things, so the images inside our mind follow one another in the same strictly causal sequence as the events taking place outside it.'

Jung's account here seems to combine several concepts. This type of thinking seems to be a matter of the outside world represented in images, in a 'presentationist' kind of way. But at the same time thinking is carried on in language, as Jung stresses again later, regarding language as 'originally and essentially nothing but a system of signs or symbols, which denote real occurrences, or their echo in the human soul'. And language, and so directed thought, are social in origin and purpose:

> 'The material with which we think is *language* and *verbal concepts*—
> something which from time immemorial has been directed outwards and
> used as a bridge, and which has but a single purpose, namely that of com-
> munication. So long as we think directedly, we think *for* others and speak
> *to* others.'

This would seem to agree with Freud's idea of reality thinking as operating on the environment and, perhaps, with Luria and Yudovich's (1959) studies of the private language of twins. Jung now adds another feature to his description:

> 'We also call this "thinking with directed attention". It has in addition
> the peculiarity of causing fatigue, and is for that reason brought into
> play for short periods only. The whole laborious achievement of our
> lives is adaptation to reality, part of which consists in directed thinking.
> In biological terms it is simply a process of psychic assimilation that
> leaves behind a corresponding state of exhaustion, like any other vital
> achievement.'

Apart from one's common experience that concentrated thinking is tiring, it is not really clear why this should be so. Neither is it clear what is meant by 'psychic assimilation'. Eating is not particularly tiring. We seem to see here the ghosts of Herbart's ideas, charged with greater or less energy. But Jung was in fact thinking in more mystical terms, expanding the concept of libido, Freud's term for sexual energy, to a sort of impersonal life force. The second sort of thinking is *dream or phantasy thinking*. This is defined partly by exclusion, although we are given some more explicit points.

> '...this sort of thinking does not tire us,...it leads away from reality
> into fantasies of the past or future. At this point thinking in verbal form
> ceases, image piles on image, feeling on feeling, and there is an ever-
> increasing tendency to shuffle things about and arrange them not as they
> are in reality but as one would like them to be. Naturally enough, the
> stuff of this thinking which shies away from reality can only be the past
> with its thousand-and-one memory images. Common speech calls this kind
> of thinking "dreaming".'

Here there seems to be a marked difference from Freud's view. As we have seen, Freud's idea was that dreams were a disguised form of expression of unconscious wishes; Jung seems to take dreams as a particular example of non-directed thinking. Let us illustrate this again:

> 'We have, therefore, two kinds of thinking: directed thinking, and dream
> or fantasy-thinking. The former operates with speech elements for the
> purpose of communication, and is difficult and exhausting; the latter is
> effortless, working as it were spontaneously, with the contents ready to hand
> and guided by unconscious motives. The one produces innovations and
> adaptation, copies reality, and tries to act upon it; the other turns away

13—T * *

from reality, sets free subjective tendencies, and, as regards adaptation, is unproductive.'

Next Jung goes into one of his many cultural excursions, in this case designed to show that directed thinking is a very recent and localized phenomenon; that it is not typical of non-technological, 'primitive' cultures, or even of the high cultures of antiquity. Thinking in those contexts was in terms of myths and symbols. And this thinking is equated with that of dreams, of everyday fantasy, e.g. daydreaming, and of children. From this excursion Jung returns thus:

'The question of where the mind's aptitude for symbolical expression comes from brings us to the distinction between the two kinds of thinking —the directed and adapted on the one hand, and the subjective, which is actuated by inner motives, on the other. The latter form, if not constantly corrected by adapted thinking, is bound to produce an overwhelmingly subjective and distorted picture of the world. This state of mind has been described in the first place as infantile and autoerotic, or, with Bleuler, as "autistic", which clearly expresses the view that the subjective picture, judged from the standpoint of adaptation, is inferior to that of directed thinking.'

Apart from Thomson, most historians of psychology tend to dismiss Jung as a mystic. He is certainly very clearly in the German philosophical–religious tradition, and much of his writing is obscure in the extreme. The concepts are vaguely expressed and are hard to disentangle from the vast and repetitious mass of literary, cultural, clinical, and anecdotal material, all of it highly selective. We cannot here attempt an assessment of this extraordinary output. I would suggest, however, two ways in which Jung may turn out to be of importance. There is first the fact that he is still really the only psychologist even to attempt to grapple with a vast mass of phenomena which have been, and continue to be, of the greatest importance to human beings, and which are certainly the concern of our science. Jung is perfectly correct to assert that the whole thought processes of many cultures take place within a framework of mythical and magical belief. Other phenomena with which he deals such as the paintings of schizophrenics, witchcraft and alchemy, reports of flying saucers, are real enough, and call for an explanation. What is more, the explanation must, I think, be at least partly a cognitive one. Numbers of people, not insane, do believe in flying saucers, or other matters, in the absence of what non-believers regard as adequate evidence. Psychology has to explain, not just the fact that people can hold strange beliefs; but why they hold these *particular* beliefs. Why some beliefs catch on, and not others. Or take the post-Jungian phenomenon of Beatlemania (of course there have been many similar cases). Talk of 'mass hysteria' merely describes, it does not explain the amazing scenes that occurred. When we consider those large numbers of girls tearing the clothes off their idols, or going to extraordinary lengths to make love to them or even to those who knew them, we seem transported to an archaic world of frenzied maenads and incarnate gods. Of such phenomena Jung has at least not been afraid. And in his specific approach lies the second point I want to make. An important feature of the Jungian racial unconscious is the concept of archetype. Archetypes Jung refers to as 'the primordial images common to humanity'; or 'dominants of the collective unconscious'. They 'are the deepest, most ancient, and most universal thoughts of humanity. They are as much feelings as thoughts, and have indeed an individual independent existence'. With this concept it becomes clear that Jung is in the Platonist tradition, and on the side of innate ideas rather than the 'blank slate' of the empiricists. But he gives what seems to me a psychological rather than a mystical explanation of the archetypes:

> 'I have often been asked where the archetypes of primordial images come from. It seems to me that their origin can only be explained by assuming them to be deposits of the constantly repeated experiences of humanity.' (*Two Essays on Analytical Psychology*, 1928.)

Jung goes on to give an example.

> 'One of the commonest and at the same time most impressive experiences is the apparent movement of the sun every day. We certainly cannot discover anything of the kind in the unconscious, so far as the known physical process is concerned. What we do find, on the other hand, is the myth of the sun-hero in all its countless variations. It is this myth. and not the physical process, that forms the sun archetype. The same can be said of the phases of the moon. The archetype is a kind of readiness to produce over and over again the same or similar mythical ideas. Hence it seems as though what is impressed on the unconscious were exclusively the subjective fantasy-ideas aroused by the physical process. We may therefore assume that the archetypes are recurrent impressions made by subjective reactions. Naturally this assumption only pushes the problem further back without solving it. There is nothing to prevent us from assuming that certain archetypes exist even in animals, that they are grounded in the peculiarities of the living organism itself and are therefore direct expressions of life whose nature cannot be further explained.'

With this we approach remarkably closely to the ethological concept of instinct, with its emphasis on innate releasing mechanisms. We might also note the view of sexual behaviour in man, now well known through the work of Kinsey, and of Beach, which stresses response to a range of stimulus situations of approximately similar characteristics. (Compare Freud's description of the child as a 'polymorphous pervert'.) It is hardly surprising if this extends to other sorts of situation. Nor is it surprising if there is an important cognitive component: that is just what we should expect with human beings. Another important comparison is with the 'internal models' postulated by Gregory (1970) and others, as controlling skilled behaviour, both innate and learned. (See *Models*.) 'Charismatic' is a much over-used word. But there are some persons who seem to exert an influence out of all proportion to what might be rationally expected. Hitler is a good example, because his ideas in retrospect seem so absurd, and his personal life and even appearance so peculiar; and yet there is no doubt at all about his ability to inspire intense personal devotion, and to arouse great emotion in crowds. It was as though he had a key which fitted the same mechanism in many minds; a super-releaser of aggression.

SOME EXPERIMENTAL WORK ON DREAMS

Recently a great deal of knowledge has accrued about the frequency and amount of dreaming. This work stems from the now famous observations by Aserinsky and Kleitman (1953) of eye-movements during sleep. As is well-known, it was found that sleep could be categorized according to the appearance or non-appearance of rapid eye movements (REMs) and in respect of particular EEG patterns. Further it was found that subjects tended to report dreaming when awakened during REM periods, but not when awakened at other times. It seemed that for the first time an objective record of dream activity was possible. The first finding was that dreaming occurred far more frequently and regularly than had been generally thought, occupying some 20 per cent of total sleep time in adults, in every night's sleep. A second finding was that there seemed to be a 'need to dream', for subjects who were prevented from dreaming for several nights, by being woken at the start of REM periods, tended to have more such periods than usual when left undisturbed. Unfortunately neither of these findings is as simple as was first thought. The association between dreaming and REMs is far from clear. Berger, (1967) concludes:

'Not only is it impossible at present to correlate dreaming wholly with a single state of sleep, but also one cannot invariably relate fine muscular or autonomic activity with dreaming during a particular sleep state ... It would seem that a skein of mental activity is continuously woven during sleep such that it waxes and wanes in intensity of imagery, emotional tone, and relation to present reality or past experience. Although the most vivid mental activity appears to be most frequently associated with the physiologically identified REM state of sleep, it is not invariably associated with it.'

This uncertainty is illustrated by an experiment of Antrobus (1963) who found that

'women who are persistent nonrecallers of dreams actually showed more eye movements during sleep than did frequent recallers. The nonrecallers spent less time in Stage 1, REM associated sleep, than did the recallers, but in that time their eye movements, and also small muscle movements, were significantly greater.'

This account comes from Singer (1966) who also reports some interesting experiments by Antrobus, Antrobus and Singer (1964) and Singer and Antrobus (1965) which are relevant here. They recorded EEG and REM from waking subjects in various conditions. In the first experiment subjects were asked, during periods of either continuous REM or no REM, to describe what had been passing through their minds. These reports were subsequently assessed by independent judges. Subjects were also asked to engage in visual imagery for short periods. The results were clear:

> 'The reports of content were judged as more "daydreamlike" by the raters when interruptions came after criterion period of no eye movement. More active, objective thought was characterized by greater eye movement. *Internal* visual imagery was associated with minimal eye movement while reported attention to external detail occurred in association with greater ocular motility.'

In a further experiment, subjects were asked to 'engage in a daydream of the fulfillment of a secret wish, one you haven't told people'—and later to attempt to suppress this thought. Relatively little eye movement was recorded during the wish fulfillment phase, but a great deal during the suppression phase. This Singer suggests may be analogous to the Freudian account of dream formation.

On the question of a 'need to dream', it is hard to see how a conclusive answer is possible. Webb (e.g. 1970) and others have pointed out that all that has been shown is a need for a certain type or level of sleep. This, as we have seen, tends to be accompanied by dreaming. Even if we had an absolutely reliable index of dreaming, it would probably be impossible to be absolutely certain about a need to dream, unless we also have a final answer to the body-mind problem. However, while the picture is somewhat complex, and philosophically uncertain, we certainly know a good deal more about dreaming than we did. Kales, Kales, Po and Klein (1966) collated a number of studies to give a general picture of the occurrence of dreaming. (Table 10.1).

These figures, if taken as reliable indices of dreaming, are puzzling. What are premature infants dreaming *about*? Can we relate the slight falling off at 5–13 years to a latency period? There seems no clear pattern among other species either, with rats showing as much activity as monkeys. Of course we always knew cats were up to something, not just lying there—no doubt some archetypal image from their Egyptian days of glory occupies them. Thus far, we can say that the experimental results support the notion that a good deal of mental activity occurs outside of consciousness: we are not here concerned with the phenomena of sleep as such, but only with evidence about unconscious thought. The fact that we do now have an indicator of dreaming, however, has led to attempts to manipulate dreams, and this sheds some light on how they might work. For example: Berger (1963) first obtained from his subjects a short personal history. From this in each case the names of past and present girl or boy friends were selected, and the significance of these for the subjects was assessed by recording GSR data when the names were spoken. The names were then recorded, and played over to the subjects while they slept, specifically a few minutes after the start of REM periods. A subject would be woken 20 seconds after the recording stopped, and asked to recount any dream that could be

Table 10.1—Age and REM sleep in humans. (Reproduced with permission from A. Kales, J. D. Kales, J. Po and J. Klein (1966), 'A review of recent sleep and dream studies,' Bull. Los Angeles Neurological Society, 31, 136–151.)

Age	REM as percentage of total sleep	REM sleep as percentage of 24 hours
Premature infant	60–84	40–56
Neonate 1–15 days	49–58	33–39
Infant under 2 years	30–40	17–22
2– 5 years	20–30	10–14
5–13 years	15–20	6–8
18–30 years	20–25	7–8
30–50 years	18–25	5–7
68–87 years	20–22	4–5

Table (contd.) REM sleep in various species

Species	REM sleep as percentage of total sleep	Notes
Man (young adult)	20–25	REM = 7·8% of 24 hours.
Monkey	11–20	In neonate REM % rises till 7th day.
Cat	20–30	REM = 16% of 24 hours.
Sheep	2–3	REM decreases sharply with ruminations.
Rabbit	1–3	
Rat	15–20	
Opossum	22–34	Great variation in REM %.
Hen, pigeon, chick	0·5	Very brief REM periods.
Reptile	None	

recalled. The dream protocols were later matched by an independent judge against the names used. The matching was correct in a significant number of cases. Some of these do rather strongly suggest features of the Freudian dream-work. The following examples are from Oswald (1966) who collaborated with Berger:

'The man stimulated with the name Jenny, the name of a previous girl-friend whom he had described as a red head, dreamt of opening a safe with a jemmy. "The only thing that was in colour was the jemmy . . . a sort of red . . . it seemed to stand out." After the name Sheila had been played, another man reported that he had dreamed he had left behind his book at the University, his copy of Schiller, the German poet and philosopher. A girl during whose dream Robert had been played, described a dream in which she looked at a film of a rabbit, which looked "distorted". In these instances we can see the operation of rhyming, assonant, or "clang" associations. The sound of the word determined the sense of the dream . . . We can detect another element in red-headed Jenny eliciting a red-handled jemmy, and Robert the "distorted" rabbit. It is as if, quietly ruminating on the stimulus, the mind has tracked off into considerations of the stimulus features and characteristics, how "Robert" was not quite the right name for a rabbit, how it was somehow distorted. We see these side tracking associations put into concrete form: the red handle of the jemmy. The same process is seen in the case of another man to whom Gillian was played. This was the name of an ex-girl-friend. Half-way through a long dream report he described the entry of an old woman who 'came from Chile.' She was a Chilean (Gillian), an old woman (ex-girl-friend). In the dream she ran about on wet rocky ground with bare feet. Which might have made her feel chilly!'

While fascinating, such results show only that stimuli presented below the threshold required to disturb sleep, can be incorporated into dreams in distorted form. Some of the distortions are like those mentioned by Freud, e.g. condensation, displacement, but it seems that so far relatively little has been added to clarify how these mechanisms may work, whether they are universal, etc. Several attempts have been made to exercise greater control over dreams by using hypnosis. There are two ways of doing this: by instructing the subject to dream during hypnosis, and by giving him a post-hypnotic suggestion to dream later when normally asleep. Again, some success has been reported in that dreams do seem to occur in both situations incorporating stimuli, either directly or in disguised form. But Hilgard (1965) reviewing the literature, found the evidence inconclusive:

'Most of the studies done by those under the influence of psychoanalytic theory found much in common between the hypnotic dream and the night dream. Thus the disguise of the true meaning of the dream within the hypnotic situation can be inferred from the statements of Farber and Fisher (1943); Fisher (1953); Mazer (1961); Nachmansohn 1925); Newman and others (1960); Roffenstein (1924); Rubenstein and others (1957). However, the problem of disguise turns out not to be so straightforward when subjected to experimental study. Thus Tart, (1964) found little or no evidence of disguise in his post hypnotically suggested dreams. Sweetland and Quay (1952) found the amount of disguise unrelated to the emotional impact of the substance of the dream; Moss (1961) also, using the semantic differential method to measure degree of disguise, found no relation to the emotion-arousing nature of the dream suggestion.'

This is not very encouraging: and it begins to seem as though the more we know, the less we understand. Tart (1969) distinguishes four types of mental activity during sleep. The first two are agreed by many experimentalists. The first, associated with a 'stage 1' EEG pattern,

'has the characteristics we usually associate with dreaming: vivid visual imagery, being located at some distant place, interacting with other characters, intense emotions, lack of recognition that one is actually lying in bed asleep, etc. The mental activity in the other stages of sleep (viz., 2, 3, or 4 EEG) is thought-like and has little or no visual imagery. Typical reports being on the order of "I was wondering what to buy at the store tomorrow."

Further, non-stage 1 mental activity seems less likely to be recalled by most subjects.'

A third, rare, type of dream has been called the 'lucid' dream.

'This has the unusual characteristic that the dreamer "wakes" from an ordinary dream in that he feels he is suddenly in possession of his normal waking consciousness and knows that he is actually lying in bed asleep: but, the dream world he is in remains perfectly real. What stage of sleep this lucid dream might be associated with is unknown.'

Tart compares the experience, which he has himself had three times, to some of the results of yoga training. His fourth type is the 'high dream' which is akin to the effects of LSD-25: intensification of perception, distortion of body image, etc.; but the dreamer recognizes during the dream that he is in an altered state of consciousness. The relationship between any dreams and 'psychedelic' chemicals is still not clear, though Torda (1968) and others, have reported that LSD decreases the latency of incidence of both REM and dreams. Foulkes (1964) has pointed out that the difference between Tart's first two types of activity, at least, was recognized by Freud, who distinguished between dreams and 'night phantasies', the latter being the more everyday sort of thinking associated with nonREM periods. Foulkes thinks the recent work on dreams tends to support Freud's 'position that dream-work processes distort these day-residues into sometimes barely recognizable components of bizarre dream episodes'. But it does not follow that the cause of dreams is as Freud suggested. Rather, Foulkes thinks, 'it seems as if the dream allows the dreamer, eventually rather than immediately to express himself in a rather profound way; it is not that the dream, by posing a basic challenge at the outset, forces him to do this'. As we have seen, Freud's view was not that the dream posed a challenge, but rather the unconscious wish of which the dream was a disguised expression. But it could still be true that dreaming is merely a sort of accidentally disordered thinking which incidentally allows expression to important material. The experimental recording of REM activity does show even more clearly than Freud himself could have realized, that the dreams dealt with by the analyst are only a very small sample of the whole. From the point of view of psychoanalytic theory as a whole, this does not matter, since what is being analysed is the patient's verbal and other behaviour within the analytic situation. It just so happens that dreams reported then are particularly revealing. Experiments have so far taken us little farther forward.

All the same, it would be nice to know what dreams are for, if anything. Christopher Evans (1966) has an analogy between dreaming and the process of 'clearing' computers (also Newman and Evans, 1965). We dream, he suggests, in order to run through the material acquired during the day. But it is difficult to see this as more than a possibly misleading analogy. It is true that some studies have shown a relationship between dreams and particular conditions of the subject. Van de Castle (1968) and Van de Castle and Kinder (1968) studied the effects of menstruation and pregnancy. In the latter case, as compared to controls:

'... pregnant women's dreams revealed a greater percentage of architectural references. Pregnancy-related concerns such as doctor's appointments, dietary restrictions, physical clumsiness, and reduced locomotion are represented. Themes of being physically and sexually unattractive are quite common along with feelings that their husbands find other women more appealing. Dependency-independency conflicts, particularly in relationship to their own mothers are also present. Most striking during the last trimester is the great frequency of dreams dealing with the unborn child which generally occur in a context of anxiety. The baby is often described as deformed, of unusual size, or possessing such skills as the ability to walk or talk at birth.'

With such dreams, characteristic of legends, we seem to be touching on a Jungian analysis.

C. S. Hall (1953, Hall and Van de Castle, 1966) analysed large numbers (some 10,000) of reported dreams in respect of their content. These were of course highly selected; and on the other hand the approach attracted criticism from psychoanalysts because Hall was concerned only with the manifest content. But as Van de Castle pointed out in defence, 'a dream is a manifest experience'—and therefore a legitimate subject for psychological study. Hall's results are in two parts: details of the subject-matter, colour, and other content characteristics of dreams; and a suggested function for dreams. The question of the content of dreams must be taken into account in any full explanation of unconscious thought, but at present all we can really do is note the observations. Thus it appears that the manifest content is overwhelmingly concerned with everyday experiences. Settings, characters, actions, are all drawn from everyday life. Some sex differences emerged: men dream twice as often about males as they do about females, while women dream equally about both; women dream in colour more often than do men. Such reports are so far just additional facts seeking an explanation. The emotional content of the dreams was marked predominantly by apprehension, anger, frustration and sadness. Hall's explanation of dreams, on the basis of an analysis of numbers of individual specimens, is a relatively simple one: 'The function of dreaming ... is to reveal what is in a person's mind.' The importance of dreams lies in gaining self-knowledge. This sort of view, of course, is remarkably hard to test. First one cannot be sure that self-knowledge is gained—how is it to be defined or measured? Second one does not know that it is the dream analysis that is important. It may be that any period of self-examination would yield similar results—whether these be merely subjective impressions or something more. I once systematically recorded all my dreams over a period, and while I think I gained some self-knowledge at that time it is just as likely to have been due to other experiences. Thirdly, even if it is possible to acquire knowledge in this way, that is far from conclusive evidence as to the function of dreams.

And there for the moment the matter stands. It seems one of those cases, not uncommon in psychology, where what appears to be a major breakthrough is left as it were in mid-air.

SCHIZOPHRENIC THOUGHT

In some ways the most private experiences of all are those of madness. 'Madness' is not a word that is in technical use: thoughts can become disordered for a number of reasons, such as brain damage or drugs. The thought disorders to which most attention has been paid, however, are those of schizophrenia. This itself refers to a whole group of disorders, affecting much more than thought processes. Stone (1968) for example, reviewing classical and modern textbook descriptions, a statistical survey, and case studies, found that: '... the evidence demonstrates no typical premorbid history, no standard time of onset, and no characteristic pattern of symptoms or thought disorder'. Rosenbaum (1968) agrees in speaking of 'a heterogeneous group of disorders'.

However there are some features that are rather frequently reported. As with many forms of mental illness, the symptoms are now often reduced or masked, and the progress arrested, by the use of modern drugs. The classical picture is given by, for example, Henderson and Gillespie's *Textbook of Psychiatry* (1927, 1st edition). They write of: 'a slow steady deterioration of the whole personality', characterized by progressive withdrawal from the environment and loss of contact with other people. Accompanying this, or rather forming part of the total syndrome, are loss of identity and disorientation—the patient loses the ability to know who, where, and when he is; disorders of emotion—there may be disharmony of mood and thought, so that laughter and tears occur inappropriately; disorders of perception such as hallucinations; and disorders of thought. There is usually an immediate impression of failure to communicate: either because the patient says nothing, or because what he says does not make sense. Language seems to be used in a different way, so that one thought does not follow from the previous one. Sometimes new words (neologisms) appear, which have no meaning for the listener. If one listens inattentively, a flow of long words may give an impression of profundity. Figure 10.1 gives a sample of writing by an incipient schizophrenic. At first sight a mere jumble, there are odd points that connect with reality, for example 'psw' may refer to some psychiatric social worker with whom there has been contact.

Some writers such as McKellar (1957) have described the various sorts of associations supposed to operate, such as similar sounds (clang associations) or oddities of meaning, somewhat like puns (knight's move thinking). McKellar also argues that one of the most important features is a loss of the ability to staff   6000

   3 × 2,000

$\left(\frac{6}{2}\right)$ incl psw teach

princ   3000

~~psw   teach~~   ~~1000~~

building rent   4000

  50,000 × $\frac{8}{100}$

expenses

   heat light
   cleaner secret (1 day pw)

~~shop~~
                                    _____
                                         13000

fee   400 pa

$\frac{1300}{400}$ = 30 students

Figure 10.1. Schizophrenic writing—a note
sent to one of the authors

think abstractly. He wished to draw analogies between schizophrenic thought and that produced by the 'psychotomimetic' drugs such as LSD, and indeed 'unconscious' thought generally. An inability to think abstractly was reported by Hanfmann and Kasanin (1942), using a conceptual task in which subjects had to sort blocks of various sizes and colours. Payne (1960), however, summarized the existing evidence as showing that schizophrenics are not concrete in thought. New concepts may be difficult for some, and schizophrenics may tend to form unusual concepts, especially under stressful conditions (such as being examined). Further, they may be overinclusive in thinking. This can be regarded as the failure of a filter mechanism which normally excludes irrelevant stimuli. Over-inclusion is stressed also by Craig (1971) and Hawks and Marshall (1971); and it does seem compatible with the psychoanalytic theory of schizophrenia (e.g. Arieti, 1955). Another view is that it is the disorganization of personality that is the primary factor, and that thought is disrupted when personal or emotional material obtrudes. Cameron (1938), quotes the case of a patient who, in a classi-fictation task, refused to put white and yellow blocks together because there were no Chinese persons working together with whites at the hospital. Bannister and Salmon (1966), and Bannister (1971), argued that the thought and language of schizophrenics is more disturbed when dealing with people than with objects.

388

Theories about the nature and causes of schizophrenia are many. Attempts to find a specific chemical factor have so far met with little success. There is good evidence, however, for an hereditary element. The well-known studies of Kallmann (1946, 1950) suggest a substantial genetic factor in schizophrenia. The existence of the hereditary element is also supported by the recent work of Mednick (1971).

At the psychological level, there are three approaches that should be mentioned briefly, which derive respectively from learning theory, psychoanalysis, and existentialism. The term 'schizophrenia' was coined by Bleuler (1911), who was trying to bring some order into the little-understood group of illnesses. He thought, working within a framework of associationistic psychology, that the primary disorder was a disturbance or splitting of associations; in other words the breakdown of normal thought processes. Secondary symptoms then ensued, including the use of fragments of ideas, false conclusions, displacements, symbolizations, condensations, aimless erratic thinking. This approach has been criticized as descriptive rather than explanatory, and Bleuler himself admitted: '... we do not know what the schizophrenic process actually is.' Stone (1968) concludes that there is no evidence for a distinction between essential and accessory symptoms (It may well be that this concept of 'splitting' has contributed to the popular identification of schizophrenia with 'split personality' which should refer, if to anything, to the rare cases of multiple personality.) An associationistic approach has been taken in recent times by Storms and Broen (1966), Panek (1968), and Broen (1969). This depends upon a Stimulus–Response account of thinking, which can be compared with that of Berlyne (see *Problem Solving*).

The psychoanalytic view is essentially that schizophrenia involves regression to a very early stage. This view is well expressed in *Chronic Schizophrenia* by Freeman, Cameron, and McGhie (1958). Besides a detailed theoretical discussion, this contains much acute observation, and reports of apparently successful treatment. Since the schizophrenic suffers from a loss of an adequately functioning ego, treatment involves rebuilding this by gradually developing the patient's confidence in himself as an autonomous person (it is in many ways the opposite of brain-washing). Reports of dramatic cures are rather frequent with psychological disorders, and schizophrenia as we have seen comprises a varied group. Nevertheless it does seem plausible to suggest that some forms, or possibly some symptoms, derive from the way the patient is treated, at first in the home and later in an institution. This is the line taken by the existentially-inspired writers, of whom the best known is R. D. Laing (e.g. 1960). The essence of this seems to be that schizophrenia is not to be thought of as a disease like measles, which the patient 'has'; but as an understandable and appropriate adjustment of personality to certain sorts of situation. In particular, an individual may react with bizarre behaviour, or complete withdrawal, to emotional and conflict-ridden family relationships. This behaviour is classified in our society as 'mad', and treated in a certain way; thus he enters a cycle of cause and effect from which escape is difficult. He becomes a non-person, the object of arbitrary procedures and treatment. Here Laing is undoubtedly right: such procedures are ethically objectionable, and unlikely to be effective therapeutically. It is another matter, however, to argue from the fact that certain treatments are unwise, to the notion that there is no illness to be treated. To take just one point: it cannot be just our particular society that is at fault. Kidson and Jones (1968) for example, reported among Australian aborigines an incidence of both organic and functional psychoses comparable to that of both organic and functional psychoses comparable to that of western societies, but a low rate of neuroses, psychosomatic illnesses, and suicide.

A still further step is taken when it is suggested that schizophrenic episodes may actually be beneficial, an experience from which a more developed, more aware personality may emerge. This is related to the somewhat similar experiences reported as a result of hallucinogenic drugs (e.g. Huxley, 1968) or religious and mystical practices such as fasting or meditation. For this there seems little evidence. We can readily disrupt our thought processes in all manner of ways; but it seems inherently implausible that this should have any adaptive value.

FOCUS: INTROSPECTION

For many years introspection was that which psychologists must not practise: of all temptations to be unscientific, this was the most sinful. Some behaviourists still maintain a hard line. Hebb (1968), for example, denies that introspection is involved in reporting imagery: such reports are merely verbal behaviour. 'My verbal response is no more dependent on introspection than a dog's yelp when his tail is trod on.' Well, we cannot of course ask the dog; but we can ask Hebb; and our argument is that there is no reason why we should not.

For Hebb, and for other behaviourists, speech is objectively observable; and from it we can *infer* something about internal processes. Boring (1953) said that this meant that introspection was being allowed to carry on its business under a new name. This, I think, is not so: we can distinguish between the statements of introspections, and introspection as a method. The statements can, if we wish, always be treated as behaviour. In the same way as we record 'the subject pressed the lever', we can record 'the subject said that ... he felt happy, cold, etc.' Such records must, of course, be subject to the usual checks used for all experimental data and in particular must yield acceptable levels of significance. It may also be argued that records of this type need a special sort of check, analogous to that used for personality questionnaire responses. Essentially this is, not to take response at its face value, but to establish empirically its relationship to some other variable. This might be an aspect of the stimulus conditions, and/or other behaviour. Some examples are given by Woodworth (1938). If this can be done then, it may be argued, statements of introspections can be considered acceptable in the same sense as other widely accepted sorts of psychological data. (See also *Imagery*.)

But is there, in fact, no difference between Hebb saying 'Ouch' and a dog yelping? The real issue must lie in whether there is another class of data, distinguished by being accessible only by a particular method, that of introspection. This question has a number of aspects. Philosophically, it is a version of the body-mind problem. Historically in the behavioural sciences, there has been the change from regarding consciousness as a reservoir of experience, to be investigated directly; to regarding it as a construct, inferred from other observations (Boring, 1953). As we noted, that is Hebb's view. But there are also more strictly psychological aspects.

The first of these is that 'the method of introspection' covers several different though related methods. McKellar (1962) offers a classification of these. He makes six sorts of distinctions:

'... we may first contrast the systematic methods of "classical introspection" with those of a relatively unsystematic kind. Secondly, the use of trained introspectionists differs from the work of the Gestalt psychologists and others who sought, by introspection, to study the phenomena of naïve human experience. Thirdly, introspections may be classified by the circumstances in which they are obtained: the laboratory, the clinic, the analytic situation, and daily life. Fourthly, some introspection is carried out mainly for communication to the experimenter, while in other cases it is carried out partly or largely to extend the investigator's own empathic understanding. Fifthly, introspection under normal circumstances may be contrasted with the use of the method in special, experimentally produced circumstances: those produced by drugs, sensory deprivation, hypnosis, etc. Sixthly, we may contrast introspections made or elicited by trained psychologists from those made or elicited by others.'

This is the only classification of introspective methods we have come across in the recent literature. Clearly, McKellar's distinctions do exist, though perhaps they are not all of equal theoretical importance. For example, introspections when the subject is or is not under the influence of a drug would not appear to be different *methods*, though the *results* will very likely be different in the two cases—as would the results of any observation. Considering the range of activities that have been referred to as 'introspection", three groups seem to be distinguishable, in terms of what it is that the subject is to do. There are, first, cases of self-observation. The individual reports on his own experience: he aims to observe. The individual reports on his own experience: he aims to observe his own mental events, in the same way as an astronomer observes stars or a behaviourist observes responses. Second there are self-reports: by this we mean cases where the person tells of his experiences, but without trying to be objective —as for example experiences under unusual conditions. Third there are cases of thinking aloud: the technique used for example in Duncker's (1945) well-known experiments on problem-solving. These distinctions are not absolutely clear cut, but they do, I think, refer to three different activities. Wundt distinguished between introspection and self-perception (Boring, 1953). By the latter I take it he meant what we have called self-reports. For introspection proper, trained observers were required. The distinctions are confused by several factors. Firstly, all the activities can in principle be more or less systematic. That is to say that the experimenter (who may also be the observer) can exercise a greater or less degree of selection. This feature however has in practice been an issue mainly in the first case. Watt (1904; quoted by Humphrey, 1951) developed the method of fractionation in an attempt to get at thought processes by systematic self observation. Secondly, the activities have in use sometimes been confounded. A good example here is psychoanalysis. The only point about the analytic use of introspection that is clear is that it comes at the extreme end of the non-selective range, since the prime rule for the patient is to hold nothing back. Now there is a sense in which psychoanalysis could be said to use what we have called thinking aloud: the patient simply says out loud what is passing through his head. He does not have to observe himself: that is the analyst's job. In this respect psychoanalysis takes on a curiously behaviouristic air, for the analyst deals with what is objectively observable: the patient's behaviour and speech. (A patient might make a remark, and add: 'I meant . . .';—and the analyst might reply: 'Let us look, not at what you meant, but at what you said.') Since the rule is to hold nothing back, however, the patient will inevitably also engage in self observation. And since the aim of analysis is to give the patient more control over his own behaviour, he will, if the analysis is successful, become more objective about what he says (and does). He moves, in a sense, from being subject to being experimenter. The analyst *also* makes inferences about the patient's internal experiences; and the patient learns to do this too. A third confusing factor, though of less importance here, is that it is difficult to be sure that introspection is not always in fact retrospection (Bakan, 1954).

It will be seen that the data resulting from all three methods can, if desired, be treated as verbal behaviour, in the way we have already discussed. A further step can be taken, and mental events inferred from this behaviour. The first method, however, that of introspection proper, is distinguished in that its essential aim is to make direct observations of a particular class: observations of events not otherwise accessible. The distinction between these and other events is expressed by Bakan (1954) as that between experience, and that of which the experience is. It is brought out by the example of the stimulus error. The phrase was coined by Titchener (Boring, 1957) to refer to the 'error' of an observer in lapsing from the psychological viewpoint, in reporting on phenomena, to some other viewpoint. The psychologist should report on what he experiences. It is for the physicist, or some other scientist, to report on the external stimuli that bring about the experience. Boring instances a two-point threshold: the Titchenerian psychologist's task was to report when he experienced the two points as one, regardless of the fact that he knew there were two.

This brings out another aspect: the question of trustworthiness. As Boring (1953) points out, in classical psychophysics controls are not used; the control lies in the training of the subject. Psychophysical experiments can be course be done with animals using methods of discrimination training. Titchener ruled animals (and children and clinical patients) out of psychology because they could not be trained to observe their mental events, and to distinguish between these and physical events.

Thus it seems important to know whether there is a unique method; and if so, whether this should be used by psychologists, either among other methods or as Titchener demanded exclusively. Classical German psychology, as established by Wundt, defined psychology as the science of experience: immediate experience, not inner experience, because there is no valid distinction between inner and outer experience. As Boring (1957) puts it: 'The data of experience are merely themselves; a perception does not have to be perceived in order to be a perception; it has only to occur.' This is interesting in view of Hebb's objection to introspection, quoted earlier. However, it follows from this definition that the method of psychology is that of self-observation. For Wundt, 'having an experience is the same as observing it' (Boring, 1957). Boring speaks with great authority, yet a glance at the simplest form of Wundtian experiment casts doubt upon this. Wundt (1912) himself gives, for example, as an introductory and basic experiment, listening to a metronome and observing the way in which we perceive the beats falling into a rhythmic pattern. The attempt to be more systematic led the followers of Wundt, notably Külpe and Titchener, to emphasize the training necessary for such self-observation.

A number of departures from, and reactions against, these views, took place in psychology. They include Gestalt psychology and psychoanalysis. The most extreme, as far as method is concerned, was Behaviourism. It was upon this point that Watson took his stand. As he wrote in 1920:

> 'Behaviourism, as I tried to develop it in my lectures in Columbia in 1912 and in my earliest writings, was an attempt to do one thing—to apply to the experimental study of man the same kind of procedure and the same language of description that many research men had found useful for so many years in the study of animals lower than man.'

Watson seems to have had several reasons for this view. One was his interest in the study of animal behaviour itself. Another appears to have been an intense dislike of any suggestion of mysticism, such as he felt was involved in the study of consciousness. The only point of theoretical interest, however, is that of objectivity. Watson (1930) equates behaviourism with objective psychology, and introspective psychology, with subjectivity. He does not, however, present any arguments in support of this.

Thus Watson agreed with the classical psychologists in insisting on a particular method, necessitated by a particular subject matter. Some attempts have been made, on the other hand, to resolve the opposition. Thus Boring (1953) argues:

'Operational logic, in my opinion, now fuses this single dichotomy because it shows that human consciousness is an inferred construct, a concept as inferential as any of the other psychologists realities, and that literally immediate observation, the introspection that cannot lie, does not exist. All observation is a process that takes some time and is subject to error in the course of its occurrence.'

But the dichotomy is not fused here, for if consciousness is inferred, it presumably cannot be observed directly: thus Boring comes down on the side of the physicist and not the (Titchenerian) psychologist. It is, beside, not satisfactory to reject a method merely because it can lie. Infallibility of method does not exist in science.

A more sophisticated attempt is due to Burt (1962). He argues that the early objection to introspection, that two observers would disagree, was merely the result of failing to realize the importance of individual differences. The behaviourist insistence that data be public is unhelpful, because certainty in science is unobtainable. This objection, argues Burt, rests on the distinction between what is 'public' and what is 'private'. Thus it is said that language is inadequate to convey the experience of one person to another. But, in general, we do understand what is meant. Then it is said that only one person can observe the events of consciousness. But strictly speaking this applies to every first-hand observation. The behaviourist attempt to make introspections respectable by treating them as verbal reports merely misdirects our attention, for it is precisely the subject's experience, not his verbal behaviour, in which we are interested. Burt next argues that the model of the physical sciences adopted by Watson was a crude and over-simplified one, which would not be accepted now. It is not clear, however what in Burt's view would be accepted; nor whether he thinks this, presumably more sophisticated, model appropriate for psychology. Finally Burt attacks the newer behaviourists' argument from the principle of parsimony. A system much as that of Hull, Burt claims, is far from parsimonious. And parsimony can only be achieved, in any case, when a science has reached a highly developed stage. Here again Burt's arguments are open to objection. Given that behaviourism is not parsimonious, it could still be more so than introspection. And by what criterion are we to tell if a science is highly developed, other than its degree of parsimony? If the principle of parsimony is accepted, then it is for each side to show that it is more parsimonious than the other. Burt concludes that introspection should be among the methods of psychology, though it should certainly not be the only one.

'Introspection is necessary, not only because it brings new questions to the fore, but also because it alone can supply much of the observational data needed to answer them . . . . We need to know what intervenes between the stimulus and the subsequent response; and here, so I have argued, intropection yields the most important clues.'

Burt's argument, then, seems to be that introspection as a method is not unique, but that the data it yields cannot be obtained in any other way. This implies a contradiction. Burt rests his case, first of all, on the notion of the probabilistic nature of science, arguing that no scientist in any field would insist on absolute certainty before accepting a datum. But, as he goes on to say, the crux lies in the distinction between what is 'public' and what is 'private'. Burt seems here to wish to deny any such distinction:

> 'Strictly speaking, *every* first-hand observation is necessarily "private". Whether certain observations are treated as "public" turns not on their specific or intrinsic nature, but merely on the context.'

I think Burt's argument is open to objection; but in practice, the objections may not matter much. First of all, it may well be that whether observations are *treated* as public depends on the context; but that does not answer the question whether they *are* public. Now, in what sense is every first-hand observation 'private'? This seems true in the sense that each individual experience is unique. Firstly each individual is unique, by virtue of different make-up, different history, etc. But even if an exact facsimile of an individual were produced, there must logically be two experiences, since to qualify as individuals the beings must at least be distinct in time and place. The experiences might be identical in content, but there would be no way of proving this with absolute certainty. But it does not follow that because there are always two experiences, there are always two things of which the experience is. The question as to whether there is a reality independent of observers has of course a long philosophical history. We have argued already that science, if it is to operate at all, must assume that this is so. But we could, in fact, rest the argument at the point of saying that there is a distinction between events which we may suppose to exist independently, and those of which we cannot suppose this. The first are 'public', the second 'private'. In the second class we put experiences; in the first, stimuli and responses. In practice, the distinction is often not very important. On the 'private' side, the difficulties of communicating experience have been exaggerated, as Burt points out. On the 'public' side, exact replications are rather infrequent.

R. S. Peters (1953) pointed out that both Titchener and Watson were part of the 'observationalist' tradition of science. Titchener held that we directly observe experience; Watson, that all we can observe is behaviour. Later behaviourists such as Hebb say, that we infer our knowledge of private events from the behaviour we see. In the case of adult human beings, this behaviour is usually verbal; but in the case of non-verbal beings, it may be, for example, discrimination learning. This, however, raises the question of what it is that we infer. To say that a child, an animal, or another adult has 'an image' seems a curiously artificial statement, unless we have from our own experience some notion of what sort of a thing an image might be. It seems odd, in other words, to suppose that 'image' has exactly the same sort of intervening variable status as, say, 'filter'.

A forceful movement, represented by writers such as Lacan, denies the whole possibility of applying to human beings principles of objective observation that derive from the physical sciences. (See, for example, Caws, 1968.) But this argument would lead us too far afield. Within the observationalist tradition, Peters criticized the insistence on method which was characteristic of both Titchener and Watson. Science is not such that there is any one method that guarantees success. Nor, indeed, are there methods that must be utterly proscribed. Rather, there are criteria for assessing any method as more or less useful. To put it another way, scientific 'method' is a much broader concept than the 'methods' of introspection or behavioural analysis. These are better regarded as techniques, being two of those in the scientist's repertoire. As Peters puts it: 'All that is required for an inquiry to be a theoretical science is that conscious attempts should be made to overthrow hypotheses'. There seems no reason, in practice, why introspections cannot be used for this purpose, even though they be held to be logically distinct from other sorts of observation. If introspection conflicts with itself or with other data, this is no different from any conflict of results.

It might be argued that it is simply a matter of what we are interested in. Presumably both Titchener and Watson were happy for the other to pursue his own path, but each insisted that 'you must not call it psychology'. But to define a science either by its subject-matter, or by its techniques, seems unhelpful. There is no way of saying in advance what will turn out to be relevant or useful. Rather, science as a whole is the enterprise of establishing statements which correspond with reality, and any one science is simply a group of loosely related enquiries, put together for convenience or because of demonstrable connections. Psychologists, we believe, are people who are interested in the behaviour and experience of men and animals. Like every scientist, the psychologist says with Molière 'je prends mon bien où je le trouve'. Introspection gives us information about experience. It yields some data otherwise inaccessible. It may besides bring to light facts that might otherwise be overlooked, or stimulate us to ask new questions. Like any technique, it has peculiar difficulties, especially when used in odd circumstances. These, however, are the natural hazards of science. The battle that began over sixty years ago, and which some are apparently still fighting, might now be amicably concluded.

FURTHER READING

Burt, C. (1968). 'Brain and consciousness.' *Brit. J. Psychol.*, **59**, 55–69.
Humphrey, G. (1951). *Thinking*. Methuen.
McKellar, P. (1962). 'The method of introspection'. In Scher, J. (Ed.) *Theories of the Mind*. Free Press of Glencoe, New York.
Reeves, J. W. (1965). *Thinking about Thinking*. Secker and Warburg.

Bibliography

Ach, N. (1905). *Über die Willenstätigkeit und das Denken.* Stechert, Gottingen.

Ach, N. (1935). *Analyse des Willens.* Berlin and Wien.

Acker, N. (1968). *Conservation and Coordination of Relations in Piaget's Liquid Quantity Problem.* Predoctoral Thesis, Institute of Child Development, University of Minnesota.

Adams, J. A. (1967). *Human Memory.* McGraw-Hill, New York.

Adams, J. A., and Montague, W. E. (1967). 'Retroactive inhibition and natural language mediation.' *J.V.L.V.B*, **6**, 528–35.

Albert, R. S. (1969). 'Genius: Present day status of the concept and its implications for the study of creativity and giftedness.' *Amer. Psychologist*, **24**, 743–53.

Albert, R. S. (1971). 'Cognitive development and parental loss among the gifted, the exceptionally gifted, and the creative.' *Psychol. Rep.*, **29**, 19–26.

Allport, G. W. (1942). *The Use of Personal Documentation in Psychological Research.* Social Science Research Council.

Allport, G. W. (1961). *Pattern and Growth in Personality.* Holt, Rinehart and Winston Inc., New York.

Alpert, R. (1957). *Anxiety in Academic Achievement Situations: Its Measurement and Relation to Aptitude.* Unpublished Ph.D. Thesis, Stanford University.

Anderson, R. C. (1965). In Anderson, R. C. and Ausubel, D. P. (Eds.), *Readings in the Psychology of Cognition.* Holt, Rinehart and Winston Inc, New York.

André, J. (1969). 'Reversal-shift behaviour and verbalization in two age groups of hearing and deaf children.' *J. Exp. Child Psychol.*, **7**, 407–18.

Anokhin, P. K. (1969). 'Cybernetics and the integrative activity of the brain.' In Cole, M. and Maltzman, I. (Eds.), *A Handbook of Contemporary Soviet Psychology.* Basic Books, New York.

Antrobus, J. S. (1963). *Patterns of dreaming and dream recall.* Unpublished Doctoral Dissertation, Columbia University.

Antrobus, J. S., Antrobus, J. S., and Singer, J. L. (1964). 'Eye movements accompanying daydreaming, visual imagery, and thought suppression.' *J. Abn. Soc. Psychol.*, **69**, 244–52.

Apter, M. J. (1970). *The Computer Simulation of Behaviour.* Hutchinson, London.

Archer, E. J. (1964). 'On verbalizations and concepts.' In A. W. Melton (Ed.), *Categories of Human Learning.* Academic Press, New York.

Arieti, S. (1955). *Interpretation of Schizophrenia.* Brunner, New York.

Aserinsky, E., and Kleitman, N. (1953). 'Regularly occurring periods of eye motility, and concomitant phenomena, during sleep.' *Science*, **118**, 273–74.

Ashby, W. R. (1962). 'Simulation of a brain.' In Borko, H. (Ed.), *Computer Applications in the Behavioural Sciences.* Prentice-Hall, Englewood Cliffs, N.J.

Asher, J. J. (1963). 'Towards a neo-field theory of problem solving.' *J. Gen. Psychol.*, **68**, 3–8.

Ausubel, D. P. (1963). 'Cognitive structure and the facilitation of meaningful verbal learning.' *J. Teach. Educ.*, **14**, 217–21.

Bakan, D. (1954). 'A reconsideration of the problem of introspection.' *Psychol. Bull.*, **51**, 105–18.

Bannister, D. (1971). 'Schizophrenia: Carnival mirror of coherence.' *Psychology Today*, **4**, 66–9, 84.

Bannister, D., and Salmon, P. (1966). 'Schizophrenic thought disorder: specific or diffuse?' *Brit. J. Med. Psychol.*, **39**, 215–19.

Barratt, P. E. (1953). 'Imagery and thinking.' *Aust. J. Psychol.*, **5**, 154–64.

Barratt, P. E. (1956). 'Use of the EEG in the study of imagery.' *Brit. J. Psychol.*, **47**, 101–14.

Barron, F. (1969). *Creative Person and Creative Process*. Holt, Rinehart and Winston Inc., New York.

Barron, F., and Welsh, G. S. (1952). 'Artistic perception as a possible factor in personality style: its measurement by a figure preference test.' *J. Psychol.*, **33**, 199–203.

Bartlett, F. C. (1932). *Remembering: A Study in Experimental and Social Psychology*. Macmillan, New York. Cambridge University Press.

Bartlett, F. C. (1958). *Thinking: An Experimental and Social Study*. Allen and Unwin, London.

Bartlett, F. C. (1961). 'Recent developments in the psychology of thinking.' In *Recent Trends in Psychology*, Orient Longmans, India.

Baylor, G. W. (1965). 'Report on a mating combinations program.' *SDC Paper No. SP-2150, System Development Corporation*, Santa Monica, California (cited by Simon, H. A. and Barenfeld, M. 1969).

Baylor, G. W., and Simon, H. A. (1966). 'A chess mating combinations program.' *AFIPS Conference Proceedings, 1966, Spring Joint Computer Conference*. Spartan Books, Washington, D.C.

Beach, F. A. (1965). *Sex and Behaviour*. Wiley, New York.

Beerbohm, M. (1923). 'A note on the Einstein Theory.' From *Mainly on the Air*, 1946, Heinemann, 1962.

Beilin, H. (1969). 'Stimulus and cognitive transformation in conservation.' In Elkind, D. and Flavell, J. H. (Eds.), *Studies in Cognitive Development*, O.U.P., New York.

Beiswenger, H. (1968). 'Luria's model of the verbal control of behaviour.' *Merrill-Palmer Quarterly*, **14**, 267–84.

Berger, R. J. (1963). 'Experimental modification of dream content by meaningful verbal stimuli.' *Brit. J. Psychiat.*, **109**, 722–40.

Berger, R. J. (1967). 'When is a dream is a dream is a dream.' In Clemente, C. D. (Ed.), *Physiological Correlates of Dreaming. Exp. Neurol.*, Suppl. 4, 15–28.

Berlyne, D. E. (1960). *Conflict, Arousal and Curiosity*. McGraw-Hill, New York.

Berlyne, D. E. (1965). *Structure and Direction in Thinking*. Wiley, New York.

Bernstein, B. (1971). *Class, Codes and Control*. Vol. I. *Theoretical Studies towards a Sociology of Language*. Routledge and Kegan Paul, London.

Bernstein, B., and Henderson, D. (1969). 'Social Class differences in the relevance of language to socialization.' *Sociology*, **3**, 1.

Berry, J. W. (1966a). *Cultural determinants of perception*. Unpubl. Ph.D. Thesis, University of Edinburgh.

Berry, J. W. (1966b). 'Temne and Eskimo perceptual skills'. *Int. J. Psychol.* **1**, 207–29.

398

Betts, G. H. (1909). *The Distribution and Functions of Mental Imagery*. Teachers College, Columbia Univ.

Bexton, W. H., Heron, W., and Scott, T. H. (1954). 'Effects of increased variation in the sensory environment.' *Canad. J. Psychol.*, **8**, 70–6.

Biddle, W. E. (1969). 'Image therapy.' *Amer. J. Psychiat.*, **126**, 408–12.

Bieri, J. (1960). 'Parental identification, acceptance of authority, and within-sex differences in cognitive behaviour.' *J. Abn. Soc. Psychol.*, **60**, 76–9.

Binet, A. (1894). *Psychologie des grands calculateurs et joueurs d'échec*. Hachette, Paris.

Binet, A. and Simon, Th. (1905). 'Méthodes nouvelles pour le diagnostic du niveau intellectuel des anormaux.' *Année Psychologique*, **11**, 191–244.

Birch, H. G. (1945). 'The relation of previous experience to insightful problem solving.' *J. Comp. Psychol.*, **38**, 367–83.

Bleuler, E. (1911). *Dementia Praecox or the Group of Schizophrenias*. Internat. Univ. Press, New York. (English Translation 1950).

Bloom, B. S. (1964). *Stability and Change in Human Characteristics*. Wiley, New York.

Boas, F. (1911). *The Mind of Primitive Man*. Free Press, New York.

Bolton, N. (1972). *The Psychology of Thinking*. Methuen, London.

Borko, H. (1962). 'Do computers think?' in Borko, H. (Ed.), *Computer Applications in the Behavioural Sciences*. Prentice-Hall, Englewood Cliffs, N.J.

Boring, E. G. (1953). 'A history of introspection.' *Psychol. Bull.*, **50**, 169–89.

Boring, E. G. (1957). *A History of Experimental Psychology*, 2nd Edn., Appleton-Century-Crofts, New York.

Bouchard, T. J., Jr. (1969). 'Personality, problem-solving procedure and performance in small groups.' *J. Appl. Psychol.*, **53**, 1–29.

Bouchard, T. J., Jr., and Hare, M. (1970). 'Size, performance and potential in brainstorming groups.' *J. Appl. Psychol.*, **54**, 51–5.

Bourne, L. E. (1966). *Human Conceptual Behaviour*. Allyn and Bacon, Boston.

Bourne, L. E., and Restle, F. (1959). 'Mathematical theory of concept identification.' *Psychol. Rev.*, **66**, 278–96.

Bourne, L. E., Ekstrand, B. R., and Dominowski, R. L. (1971). *The Psychology of Thinking*. Prentice-Hall, Englewood Cliffs, N.J.

Bousfield, W. A. (1961). 'The problem of meaning in verbal learning.' In Cofer, C. N. and Musgrave, B. S. (Eds.), *Verbal Learning and Verbal Behaviour*, McGraw-Hill, New York.

Bousfield, W. A., Cohen, B. H., and Whitmarsh, G. A. (1958). 'Associative clustering in the recall of words of different taxonomic frequencies of occurrence.' *Psychol. Rep.*, **4**, 39–44.

Bower, T. G. R. (1965). 'Perception in infancy.' Paper presented at Center for Cognitive Studies Colloquium, Harvard University.

Bowlby, J., and Fry, M. (1970). *Child Care and the Growth of Love*. Penguin Books, Harmondsworth.

Bradley, F. H. (1883). *Principles of Logic*. Oxford University Press, London.

Braine, M. D. S. (1959). 'The ontogeny of certain logical operations: Piaget's formulation examined by nonverbal methods.' *Psychol. Monogr.*, **73** (Whole No. 475).

Braithwaite, R. B. (1962). 'Models in the empirical sciences.' In Nagel, E., Suppes, P. and Tarski, A. (Eds.), *Logic, Methodology and Philosophy of Science*. Proc. of the 1960 Internat. Congress.

Brazziel, W. F. (1969). 'A letter from the South.' *Harvard Educ. Review*, **39**, 200–8.

Brentano, F. (1874). *Psychologie vom empirischen Standpunkt. Vol. I.* Duncker and Humblot, Leipzig.

Breuer J., and Freud, S. (1895). *Studies on Hysteria.* Strachey, J. (Ed.). Hogarth, London (1955).

Britton, J. (1969). *Language and Learning.* Allen Lane The Penguin Press, London.

Broadbent, D. E. (1958). *Perception and Communication.* Pergamon Press, Oxford.

Broen, W. E. (1966). 'Response disorganization and breadth of observation in schizophrenia.' *Psychol. Rev.,* **73,** 579–85.

Bromley, D. G. (1966). *The Psychology of Ageing.* Penguin, London.

Brooks, L. R. (1967). 'The suppression of visualization by reading.' *Q. J. Exp. Psychol.,* **19,** 289–99.

Brooks, L. R. (1968). 'Spatial and verbal components of the act of recall.' *Canad. J. Psychol.,* **22,** 349–68.

Brown, B. M. (1969). 'The use of induced imagery in psychotherapy.' *Psychotherapy: Theory, Research and Practice,* **5,** 120–1.

Brown, R. (1965). *Social Psychology.* Free Press, New York.

Brown, R., and Lenneberg, E. H. (1954). 'A study in language and cognition.' *J. Abn. Soc. Psychol.,* **49,** 454–62.

Bruner, J. S. (1966). *Toward a Theory of Instruction.* The Belknap Press of Harvard Univ. Press.

Bruner, J. S., Goodnow, J. J., and Austin, G. A. (1956). *A Study of Thinking.* Wiley, New York.

Bruner, J. S., Olver, R. R., and Greenfield, P. M. *et al.* (1966). *Studies in Cognitive Growth.* Wiley, New York.

Bryan, W. L., and Harter, N. (1899). 'Studies in the telegraphic language: the acquisition of a hierarchy of habits.' *Psychol. Rev.,* **6,** 345–75.

Bryant, P. E. (1971). 'Cognitive development.' In *Brit. Med. Bull., Cognitive Psychology,* **27,** 200–5.

Bühler, K. (1907). 'Tatsachen und Probleme zu einer Psychologie der Denkvorgänge.' *Arch. ges. Psychol.,* **9,** 297–365.

Bühler, K. (1908). 1. 'Über Gedankenzusammenhänge.' 2. Über Gedankenerrinerungen.' *Arch. ges. Psychol.,* **12,** 1–92.

Burt, C. (1940). *The Factors of the Mind.* Univ. of London Press, London.

Burt, C. (1949). 'The structure of the mind: a review of the results of factor analysis.' *Brit. J. Educ. Psychol.,* **19,** 100–14, 176–99.

Burt, C. (1955). 'The evidence for the concept of intelligence.' *Brit. J. Educ. Psychol.,* **25,** 158–77.

Burt, C. (1962). 'Brain and consciousness.' *Brit. J. Psychol.,* **59,** 55–69.

Burt, C. (1968). 'An illustration of factor analysis.' In Butcher, H. J., *Human Intelligence: its Nature and Assessment.* Methuen, London.

Burt, C. (1968). 'Mental capacity and its critics.' *Bull. Brit. Psychol. Soc.,* **21,** 11–18.

Butcher, H. J. (1968). *Human Intelligence: its Nature and Assessment.* Methuen, London.

Cameron, N. (1938). 'Reasoning, regression and communication in schizophrenics.' *Psychol. Monogr.,* **50,** 1–33.

Campbell, H. J. (1972). Radio Three Broadcast.

Carlsmith, L. (1964). 'Effect of early father absence on scholastic attitude.' *Harvard Educ. Rev.,* **34,** 3–21.

Cattell, R. B. (1963). 'Theory of fluid and crystallized intelligence: a critical experiment.' *J. Educ. Psychol.,* **54,** 1–22.

400

Caws, P. (1968). 'What is structuralism?' *Partisan Review*, **35**, 75–91. In Lévi-Strauss, C. *The Anthropologist as Hero*. (Edited Hayes, E. N. and Hayes, T.) M.I.T. Press, Cambridge, Mass.

Chance, M. R. A. (1960). 'Köhler's chimpanzees—how did they perform?' *Man*, **60**, 130–5.

Chapanis, A. (1961). 'Men, machines and models.' *Amer. Psychologist*, **16**, 113–31.

Chapman, L. J., and Chapman, J. P. (1959). 'Atmosphere effects reexamined.' *J. Exp. Psychol.*, **58**, 220–6.

Chassell, L. M. (1916). 'Tests for originality.' *J. Educ.*, **4**, 317–28.

Chomsky, N. (1965). *Aspects of the Theory of Syntax*. M.I.T. Press, Cambridge, Mass., 1965.

Chowdhury, K. R., and Vernon, P. E. (1964). 'An experimental study of imagery and its relation to abilities and interests.' *Brit. J. Psychol.*, **55**, 355–64.

Clark, H. H. (1969). 'Linguistic processes in deductive reasoning.' *Psychol. Rev.*, **76**, 387–404.

Cobliner, W. G. (1967). 'Psychoanalysis and the Geneva School of genetic psychology —parallels and counterparts.' *Int. J. Psychiat.*, **3**, 82–129.

Cohen, M. R. (1944). *A Preface to Logic*. Holt, Rinehart and Winston, Inc., New York.

Cole, M., and Bruner, J. S. (1971). 'Cultural differences and inferences about psychological processes.' *Amer. Psychologist*, **26**, 867–76.

Cole. M., Gay, J., Glick, J. A., and Sharp, D. W. (1971). *The Cultural Context of Learning and Thinking. An Exploration in Experimental Anthropology*. Methuen, London.

Coleman, J. S., *et al.* (1966). *Equality of Educational Opportunity*. U.S. Dept. of Health, Education and Welfare.

Collard, H. J. (1953). 'Hypnagogic visions.' *Light*, **73**, 4301.

Collins, A. M., and Quillian, M. R. (1969a). 'Experiments on semantic memory and language comprehension.' In Gregg, L. W. (Ed.), *Cognition in learning and memory*. Wiley, New York.

Collins, A. M., and Quillian, M. R. (1969b). 'Retrieval time from semantic memory.' *J.V.L.V.B.*, **8**, 240–7.

Costello, C. G. (1956). 'The effects of prefrontal leucotomy upon visual imagery and the ability to perform complex operations.' *J. Ment. Sci.*, **102**, 507–16.

Costello, C. G. (1957). 'The control of visual imagery in mental disorder.' *J. Ment. Sci.*, **103**, 840–9.

Cox, C. M. (1926); 'The early mental traits of three hundred geniuses.' In *Genetic Studies of Genius* Vol. 2. Terman, L. M. (Ed.), Stanford, Calif.: Stanford Univ. Press.

Craig, R. J. (1971). 'Overinclusive thinking and schizophrenia.' *J. Pers. Assessment*. **35**, 208–23.

Craik, F. I. M. (1971). 'Primary memory.' In *Brit. Med. Bull. 'Cognitive Psychology'*, **27**, 232–6.

Craik, K. J. W. (1943). *The Nature of Explanation*. Cambridge Univ. Press, London.

Cronbach, L. J. (1969). 'Heredity, environment and educational policy.' *Harvard Educ. Review*, **39**, 190–9.

Cropley, A. J. (1967). *Creativity Education Today*. Longmans, Green and Co., London.

Cross. H. J. (1966). 'The relation of parental training conditions to conceptual level in adolescent boys.' *J. Pers.*, **34**, 348–65.

Crossman, E. R. F. W. (1959). 'A theory of the acquisition of speed-skill.' *Ergonomics*, **2**, 153–66.

Crowley, A. (1970). *The Confessions of Aleister Crowley*. Hill and Wang.

Crutchfield, R. (1965). *New Approaches to Individualizing Instruction.* Educational Testing Service, Princetown, N.J.

Cutts, N. E., and Moseley, N. (1969). 'Notes on photographic memory.' *J. Psychol.*, **71**, 3–15.

Darlington, C. D. (1962). In Introduction to Galton, F. *Hereditary Genius.* Fontana, London.

Darwin, C. (1859). *The Origin of Species.* Murray, London.

Davis, G. A., and Manske, M. E. (1966). 'An instructional method for increasing originality.' *Psychon. Sci.*, **6**, 73–4.

Dawson, J. L. M. (1963). *Psychological Effects of Social Change in a West African Community.* Unpublished Ph.D. Thesis, Univ. of Oxford.

Davis, G. H. (1966). 'Current status of research and theory in human problem solving.' *Psychol. Bull.*, **66**, 36–54.

Dawson, J. L. M. (1967). 'Cultural and physiological influences upon spatial-perceptual processes in West Africa.' Parts I and II. *Int. J. Psychol.*, **2**, 115–28 and 171–85.

De Bono, E. (1967). *The Use of Lateral Thinking.* Jonathan Cape, London.

De Groot, A. D. (1965). *Thought and Choice in Chess.* Mouton, The Hague.

De Groot, A. D. (1966). 'Perception and memory versus thought: some old ideas and recent findings.' In Kleinmuntz, B. (Ed.), *Problem Solving*, Wiley, New York.

De Lemos, M. M. (1969). 'The development of conservation in aboriginal children.' *Internat. J. Psychol.*, **4**, 244–69.

Deutsch, M. (1969). 'Happenings on the way back to the forum: social science, IQ, and race differences revisited.' *Harvard Educ. Review*, **39**, 523–57.

Dewing, K. (1970). 'Family influences on creativity: a review and discussion.' *J. Special, Educ.*, **4**, 399–404.

Dienes, Z. P., and Jeeves, M. A. (1965). *Thinking in Structures.* Hutchinson Educational, London.

Doob, L. W. (1965). 'Exploring eidetic imagery among the Kamba of Central Kenya.' *J. Soc. Psychol.*, **67**, 3–22.

Doob, L. W. (1966). 'Eidetic imagery: a cross-cultural will-o'-the-wisp?' *J. Psychol.*, **63**, 13–34.

Downing, J. (1967). *Evaluating the Initial Teaching Alphabet.* Cassell, London.

Doyle, A. Conan. (1929). *A Scandal in Bohemia.* In *Complete Stories of Sherlock Holmes*, Murray, London.

Drever, J. (1952). *A Dictionary of Psychology.* Penguin Books, London.

Duncker, K. (1945). 'On problem solving.' *Psychol. Monogr.*, **58**, No. 5 (Whole No. 270).

Duncan, C. P. (1959). 'Recent research on human problem solving.' *Psychol. Bull.*, **56**, 397–429.

Edwards, M. O. (1968). 'A survey of problem-solving courses.' *J. Creat. Behav.*, **2**, 33–51.

Eimas, P. D. (1967). 'Optimal shift behaviour in children as a function of over-training, irrelevant stimuli and age.' *J. Exp. Child Psychol.*, **5**, 332–40.

Eimas, P. D. (1969). 'Attentional processes in optional shift behaviour.' *J. Comp. Physiol. Psychol.*, **69**, 166–9.

El Koussy, A. A. H. (1935). 'The visual perception of space.' *Brit. J. Psychol. Monogr. Suppl.*, No. 20.

Elkind, D. (1967). 'Piaget's conservation problems.' *Child Devel.*, **38**, 15–27.

Eriksen, C. W. (1960). 'Discrimination and learning without awareness: a methodological survey and evaluation.' *Psychol. Rev.*, **67**, 279–300.

402

Eriksen, C. W., and Collins, J. F. (1967). 'Some temporal characteristics of visual pattern recognition.' *J. Exp. Psy.*, **74**, 476–84.

Erikson, E. H. (2nd Edn.) (1963). *Childhood and Society*. N.Y.: W. W. Norton and Co.

Erlenmeyer-Kimling, L., and Jarvik, L. F. (1963). 'Genetics and intelligence: a review.' *Science*, **142**, 1477–9.

Estes, W. K. (1964). 'Probability Learning.' In A. W. Melton (Ed.), *Categories of Human Learning*. Academic Press, New York.

Evans, C. (1966). 'The stuff of dreams.' *The Listener*, December 8th.

Evans, T. G. (1968). 'A program for the solution of a class of geometric-analogy intelligence-test questions.' In Minsky, M. (Ed.), *Semantic Information Processing*. M.I.T. Press, Camb., Mass.

Eyles, A. (1966). *The Marx Brothers: Their World of Comedy*. Zwemmer, London.

Eysenck, H. J. (1953). *The Structure of Human Personality*. Methuen, London. 2nd Edn. 1960. Reprinted 1965.

Eysenck, H. J. (1953). *Uses and Abuses of Psychology*. Penguin Books, Harmondsworth.

Eysenck, H. J. (1971). *Race, Intelligence and Education*. Temple Smith/New Society, London.

Fantz, R. L. (1965). 'Ontogeny of perception.' In Schrier, A. M., Harlow, H. F. and Stollnitz, F. (Eds.), *Behaviour of Nonhuman Primates*. Academic Press, New York.

Farber, L. H., and Fisher, C. (1943). 'An experimental approach to dream psychology through the use of hypnosis.' *Psychoanal. Quart.*, **12**, 202–15.

Farrell, B. A. (1970). 'On the design of a conscious device.' *Mind*, **79**, 321–46.

Fechner, G. T. (1860). *Elemente der Psychophysik*. Breitkopf and Hartel, Leipzig.

Feigenbaum, E. A., and Feldman, J. (Eds.) (1963). *Computers and Thought*. McGraw-Hill, New York.

Feigl, H. Cited by Jenkins, J. J. (1969).

Feldman, J. (1962). *Computer simulation of cognitive processes*. In Borko, H. (Ed.), *Computer Applications in the Behavioural Sciences*. Prentice-Hall, Englewood Cliffs, N.J.

Feldman, M. (1968). 'Eidetic imagery in Ghana: a crosscultural will-o'-the-wisp?' *J. Psychol.*, **69**, 259–69.

Fernald, M. R. (1912). 'The diagnosis of mental imagery.' *Psy. Monogr. No 58*.

Fisher, C. (1953). 'Studies on the nature of suggestion: I. Experimental induction of dreams by direct suggestion.' *J. Amer. Psychoanal. Assoc'n.*, **1**, 222–55.

Fisher, R. (1969). 'Out on a (phantom) limb. Variations on a theme: Stability of body image and the golden section.' *Perspectives in Biology and Medicine*, **12**, 259–73.

Fisher, S., and Cleveland, J. E. (1968). *Body Image and Personality*. Dover Press, New York (Revised).

Flavell, J. H. (1963). *The Developmental Psychology of Jean Piaget*. Van Nostrand, New York.

Forehand, G. A. (1966). 'Constructs and strategies for problem-solving research.' In Kleinmuntz, B. (Ed.) *Problem Solving: Research, Method and Theory*. Wiley, New York.

Foulkes, D. (1964). 'Theories of dream formation and recent studies of dream consciousness.' *Psychol. Bull.*, **62**, 236–47.

Fowler, H. (1965). *Curiosity and Exploratory Behaviour*. Macmillan, New York.

Freibergs, V., and Tulving, E. (1961). 'The effect of practice of utilization of information from positive and negative instances in concept identification.' *Canad. J. Psychol.*, **15**, 101–6.

Freeberg, N. E., and Payne, D. T. (1967). 'Parental influences on cognitive development in early childhood: a review.' *Child Dev.*, **38**, 65–87.

Freeman, J., Butcher, H. J., and Christie, T. (1968). *Creativity: A Selective Review of Research.* Soc. Res. into Higher Educ. Ltd., London.

Freeman, T., Cameron, J. L., and McGhie, A. (1958). *Chronic Schizophrenia.* Tavistock, London.

Frenkel-Brunswick, E. (1948). 'Tolerance toward ambiguity as a personality variable.' *Amer. Psychologist*, **3**, 268.

Freud, S. (1895). 'Project for a scientific psychology.' In Bonaparte, M., Freud, A. and Kris, E. *The Origins of Psychoanalysis, Letters to Wilhelm Fliess, Drafts and Notes.* Imago, London. (1954).

Freud, S. (1910). *Leonardo da Vinci: A Study in Psychosexuality.* Random House Inc., New York, 1947.

Freud, S. (1914). *The Psychopathology of Everyday Life.* Benn, London. English translation 1960.

Freud, S. (1919). *Totem and Taboo.* Routledge and Kegan Paul, Ltd., London.

Freud, S. (1935). *An Autobiographical Study.* Int. Psychoanal. Library/Hogarth.

Freud, S. (1938). *The Interpretation of Dreams.* Allen and Unwin, London (revised edition).

Frijda, N., and Jahoda, G. (1966). 'On the scope and methods of cross-cultural research.' *Int. J. Psychol.*, **1**, 110–27.

Furby, L. (1971). 'A theoretical analysis of cross-cultural research in cognitive development: Piaget's conservation task.' *J. Cross-Cult. Psychol.*, **2**, 241–55.

Furth, H. G. (1964). 'Research with the deaf: implications for language and cognition.' *Psychol. Bull.*, **62**, 145–64.

Furth, H. G. (1969). *Piaget and Knowledge: Theoretical Foundations.* Prentice-Hall, Englewood Cliffs, N.J.

Furth, H. G. (1970). *Piaget for Teachers.* Prentice-Hall, Englewood Cliffs, N.J.

Furth, H. G. (1971). 'Linguistic deficiency and thinking: research with deaf subjects 1964–1969.' *Psychol. Bull.*, **76**, 58–72.

Gall, M., and Mendelsohn, G. A. (1967). 'Effects of facilitating techniques and subject-experimenter interaction on creative problem solving.' *J. Pers. Soc. Psychol.*, **5**, 211–16.

Galton, F. (1869). *Hereditary Genius.* Macmillan, London.

Galton, F. (1879). 'Psychometric experiments.' *Brain*, **2**, 148–62.

Galton, F. (1893). *Inquiries into Human Faculty and its Development.* Macmillan, London.

Gardner, R. A., and Gardner, B. T. (1969). 'Teaching sign language to a chimpanzee.' *Science*, **165**, 664–72.

Garrett, M., and Fodor, J. (1968). 'Psychological theories and linguistic constructs.' In Dixon, T. R. and Horton, D. (Eds.), *Verbal Behavior and General Behavior Theory.* Prentice-Hall, Englewood Cliffs, N.J.

Gelernter, H. L., and Rochester, N. (1958). 'Intelligent behaviour in problem-solving machines.' *IBM Journ.*, **2**, 336–45 (October).

Gesell, A. (1948). *Studies in Child Development.* Harper, New York.

Getzels, J. W., and Jackson, P. W. (1962). *Creativity and Intelligence: Explorations with Gifted Students.* Wiley, New York and London.

Ghiselin, B. (1952). *The Creative Process.* Univ. Calif. Press, Berkeley.

Glick, J. (1968). 'Cognitive style among the Kpelle of Liberia.' Paper presented at *Symposium on Cross-Cultural Studies* held by the American Educational Research Association in Chicago.

Glick, J. (1969). 'Culture and cognition: some theoretical and methodological concerns.' Paper presented at the *American Anthropological Association Meetings*, New Orleans, November 21, 1969.

Glucksberg, S., and King, L. J. (1967). 'Motivated forgetting mediated by implicit verbal chaining: a laboratory analog of repression.' *Science*, **158**, 517–19.

Golann, S. E. (1963). *Psychological Study of Creativity. Psychol. Bull.*, **60**, 548–65.

Goldman, R. J. (1964). 'The Minnesota tests of creative thinking.' *Educ. Res.*, **7**, 3–14.

Golla, F. L., and Antonovitch, S. (1929). 'The relation of muscular and the patellar reflex to mental work.' *J. Ment. Sci.*, **75**, 234–41.

Golla, F. L., Hutton, E. L., and Walter, W. G. (1943). 'The objective study of mental imagery: physiological concomitants.' *J. Ment. Sci.*, **89**, 216–23.

Gombrich, E. H. (1960). *Art and Illusion*. Phaidon Press, London.

Goodman, P. (1960). *Growing up absurd*. Gollancz, London.

Goodnow, J. J., and Bethon, G. (1966). 'Piaget's tasks: the effects of schooling and intelligence.' *Child Devel.*, **37**, 573–82.

Gordon, E. W., and Wilkerson, D. A. (1966). *Compensatory Education for the Disadvantaged*. College Entrance Examination Board, New York.

Gordon, R. (1949). 'An investigation into some of the factors that favour the formation of stereotyped images.' *Brit. J. Psychol.*, **39**, 156–67.

Gordon, W. J. J. (1961). *Synectics: The Development of Creative Capacity*. Harper and Row, New York.

Goss, A. E. (1964). 'Verbal mediation.' *Psychol. Record.*, **14**, 363–72.

Gough, P. B. (1966). 'The verification of sentences: the effect of delay of evidence and sentence length.' *J.V.L.V.B.*, **5**, 492–6.

Goulet, L. R. (1971). 'Basic issues in reversal shift behaviour: a reply to Kendler.' *Psychol. Bull.*, **75**, 286–9.

Green, B. F. (1964). 'Intelligence and computer simulation.' *Transactions of N.Y. Acad. Sci.*, **27**, 55–63.

Green, B. F. (Jr.), Wolf, A. K., Chomsky, C., and Laughery, K. (1961). 'Baseball: an automatic question answerer.' *AFIPS Conf. Proc.*, **19**, 219–224. (Cited by) Green, B. F., 1964, 'Intelligence and computer simulation.' *Trans. N.Y. Acad. Sci.*, **27**, 35–63.

Green, R. T., and Laxon, V. J. (1970). 'The conservation of number, mother, water and a fried egg chez l'enfant.' *Acta Psychologica*, **32**, 1–30.

Greene, J. M. (1970). 'Syntactic form and semantic function.' *Q.J. Exp. Psychol.*, **22**, 14–27.

Greene, J. M. (1972). *Psycholinguistics*. Penguin Books, Harmondsworth.

Greenfield, P. M. (1966). 'On culture and conservation.' In Bruner, J. S. *et al.*, *Studies in Cognitive Growth*. Wiley, New York.

Gregory, R. L. (1970). 'On how little information controls so much behaviour.' *Ergonomics*, **13**, 25–35.

Gregory, R. L., and Wallace, J. G. (1963). 'Recovery from early blindness: a case study.' *Exp. Psy. Soc. Monogr. No. 2*, Cambridge.

Grey Walter, W. (1953). *The Living Brain*. Duckworth. Penguin Books, 1961.

Groddeck, G. W. (1969). *The Book of the It* (translated from the German). Vision Press.

Guilford, J. P. (1950). 'Creativity.' *Amer. Psychologist*, **5**, 444–54.

Guilford, J. P. (1963). 'Intellectual resources and their values as seen by scientists.' In Taylor, C. W. and Barron, F. (Eds.), *Scientific Creativity: its Recognition and Development*. Wiley, New York.

Guilford, J. P., and Hoepfner, R. (1966). 'Structure of intellect factors and their tests 1966.' *Rep. Psychol. Lab., Univ. S. California, No. 36*. Los Angeles.

Guilford, J. P., Merrifield, P. R., Christensen, P. R., and Frick, J. W. (1960). 'A factor analytic study of problem solving.' *Rep. Psychol. Lab., Univ. S. California, No. 22.* Los Angeles.

Guthrie, E. R. (1952). *The Psychology of Learning.* Harper and Row, New York, 1st Edn. 1945.

Haber, R. N., and Haber, R. B. (1964). 'Eidetic imagery: I. Frequency.' *Percept. Motor Skills,* **19,** 131–8.

Hadamard, J. (1945). *An Essay on the Psychology of Invention in the Mathematical Field.* Princeton University Press.

Halford, G. S. (1970). 'A theory of the acquisition of conservation.' *Psychol. Rev.,* **77,** 302–16.

Hall, C. S. (1953). *The Meaning of Dreams.* Harper and Row, New York.

Hall, C. S., and Van de Castle, R. L. (1966). *The Content Analysis of Dreams.* Appleton, New York.

Halle, M., and Stevens, K. N. (1962). 'Speech recognition: a model and a program for research.' *IRE Trans. PGIT,* IT-8, 155–9.

Hamilton, V. (1971). 'Effect of maternal attitude on development of logical operations.' *Percept. Motor Skills,* **33,** 63–9.

Hamlyn, D. W. (1969). *The Psychology of Perception* (first published 1957). Routledge, and Kegan Paul, London.

Hammond, K. R., *et al.* (1968). 'Comparison of cognitive conflict between persons in Western Europe and the United States.' *Internat. J. Psychol.,* **3,** 1–12.

Hanfmann, E., and Kasanin, J. S. (1942). 'Conceptual thinking and schizophrenia.' *Nerv. Ment. Dis. Monogr.,* No. 67.

Harlen, W. (1968). 'The development of scientific concepts in young children.' *Educ. Res.,* **11,** 4–13.

Harlow, H. F. (1949). 'The formation of learning sets.' *Psychol. Rev.,* **56,** 51–65.

Harman, W. W., McKim, R. H., Mogar, R. E., Fadiman, J., and Stolaroff, M. J. (1966). 'Psychedelic agents in creative problem solving: a pilot study.' *Psychol. Rep.,* **19,** 211–27.

Harvey, O. J., Hunt, D. E., and Schroder, H. M. (1961). *Conceptual Systems and Personality Organization.* Wiley, New York.

Hawks, D. V., and Marshall, W. L. (1971). 'A parsimonious theory of overinclusive thinking and retardation in schizophrenia.' *Brit. J. Med. Psychol.,* **44,** 75–83.

Hayes, C. (1951). *The Ape in our House.* Harper and Row, New York.

Head, H. (1926). *Aphasia and Kindred Disorders of Speech* (2 volumes). Cambridge Univ. Press.

Hebb, D. O. (1949). *The Organization of Behavior.* Wiley, New York.

Hebb, D. O. (1968). 'Concerning imagery.' *Psychol. Rev.,* **75,** 466–77.

Hebb, D. O. (1969). 'The mind's eye.' *Psychology Today,* **2,** 54–7, 67–8.

Heidbreder, E. (1946a). 'The attainment of concepts. I. Terminology and methodology.' *J. Gen. Psychol.,* **35,** 173–89.

Heidbreder, E. (1946b). 'The attainment of concepts. II. The problem.' *J. Gen. Psychol.,* **35,** 191–223.

Held, R. (1965). 'Plasticity in sensory-motor systems.' *Scient. Amer.,* **213,** 84–94.

Henderson, D. K., and Gillespie, R. D. (1927). *Textbook of Psychiatry.* Oxford Univ. Press, London.

Henle, M. (1955). 'Some effects of motivational processes on cognition.' *Psychol. Rev.,* **62,** 423–32.

Henle, M. (1962). 'On the relation between logic and thinking.' *Psychol. Rev.,* **69,** 366–78.

Herriot, P. (1970). *An Introduction to the Psychology of Language.* Methuen, London.

Hilgard, E. R. (1965). *Hypnotic Susceptibility.* Harcourt Brace Jovanovich, New York.

Hiller, L. A. (1956). 'Computer music.' *Scient. Amer.,* **201**, 6.

Hiller, L. A., and Baker, R. (1962). 'Computer music.' In Borko, H. (Ed.), *Computer Applications in the Behavioural Sciences.* Prentice-Hall, New Jersey.

Hiller, L. A., and Isaacson, L. M. (1959). *Experimental Music.* McGraw-Hill, New York.

Hirsch, J. (1968). 'Behaviour-genetic analysis and the study of man.' In Mead, M. *et al.* (Eds.), *Science and the Concept of Race,* Columbia Univ. Press, New York.

Hobhouse, L. T. (1901). *Mind in Evolution.* Macmillan, London.

Hodos, W., and Campbell, C. B. G. (1969). 'Scala Naturae: why there is no theory in comparative psychology.' *Psychol. Rev.,* **76**, 337–50.

Holsti, O. R. (1965). 'East-West Conflict and Sino-Soviet relations.' *J. Appl. Behav. Sci.,* **1**, 115–30.

Holt, R. R. (1964). 'Imagery: the return of the ostracized.' *Amer. Psychologist,* **19**, 254–64.

Holtzman, W. H. (1968). 'Cross-cultural studies in Psychology.' *Int. J. Psychol.,* **3**, 83–91.

Holzman, P. S., and Klein, G. S. (1954). 'Cognitive system-principles of leveling and sharpening: individual differences in assimilation effects in visual time error.' *J. Psychol.,* **37**, 105–22.

Honzik, M. P., MacFarlane, J. W., and Allen, L. (1948). 'The stability of mental test performance between 2 and 18 years.' *J. Exp. Educ.,* **4**, 309–24.

Hooper, F. H. (1969). 'Piaget's conservation tasks: the logical and developmental priority of identity conservation.' *Child Dev.,* **8**, 234–49.

Horowitz, M. J. (1970). *Image Formation and Cognition.* Appleton-Century-Crofts, New York.

Horton, R. (1967). 'African traditional thought and Western science. Part I: From tradition to science.' *Africa,* **37**, 50–71. 'Part II: The closed and open predicaments.' *Africa,* **37**, 155–87.

Hovland, C. I. (1952). 'A "communication analysis" of concept learning.' *Psychol. Rev.,* **59**, 461–72.

Hubel, D. H. (1963). 'The visual cortex of the brain.' *Scient. Amer.,* **209**, 54–62 (Nov.).

Hubel, D. H., and Wiesel, T. N. (1962). 'Receptive fields, binocular interaction and functional architecture in the cat's visual cortex.' *J. Physiol.,* **160**, 106–54.

Hubel, D. H., and Wiesel, T. N. (1963). 'Receptive fields of cells in striate cortex of very young, visually inexperienced kittens.' *J. Neurophysiol.,* **26**, 994–1002.

Hudson, L. (1966). *Contrary Imaginations.* Methuen, London. Also Penguin, Harmondsworth. (1968).

Hudson, L. (1968). *Frames of Mind: Ability, Perception and Self-perception in the Arts and Sciences.* Methuen, London.

Hull, C. L. (1920). 'Quantitative aspects of the evolution of concepts.' *Psychol. Monogr.,* **28**, No. 1 (Whole No. 123).

Hull, C. L. (1930). 'Knowledge and purpose as habit mechanisms.' *Psychol. Rev.,* **37**, 511–25.

Humphrey, G. (1951). *Thinking: an Introduction to its Experimental Psychology.* Methuen, London.

Hunt, E. B. (1962). *Concept Learning: an Information Processing Problem.* Wiley, New York.

Hunt, E. B. (1971). 'What kind of computer is man?' *Cognitive Psychology,* **2**, 57–98.

Hunt, J. McV. (1961). *Intelligence and Experience*. Ronald Press, New York.

Hunt, J. McV. (1969). 'Discussion: how much can we boost IQ and scholastic achievement.' *Harvard Educ. Review*, **39**, 125–52.

Hunter, I. M. L. (1962). 'An exceptional talent for calculative thinking.' *Brit. J. Psychol.*, **53**, 243–58.

Huxley, A. (1968). *Doors of Perception and Heaven and Hell*. Chatto and Windus, London.

Inhelder, B. (1953). 'Criteria of the stages of mental development.' In Tanner, J. M. and Inhelder, B. (Eds.), *Discussions on Child Development*. Internat. Univ. Press, New York.

Inhelder, B., and Piaget, J. (1955). *The Growth of Logical Thinking from Childhood to Adolescence: an Essay on the Construction of Formal Operational Structures*. Trans. Parsons, A. and Milgram, S. Basic Books, New York, 1958.

Jaensch, E. R. (1930). *Eidetic Imagery and Typological Methods of Investigation*. Harcourt, Brace, New York.

James, W. (1905). *Text Book of Psychology*. Macmillan, New York.

Jarvis, P. E. (1963). 'Verbal control of sensory-motor performance: a test of Luria's hypothesis.' *Human Development*. (Quoted as in press by Beiswenger, 1968).

Jenkins, J. J. (1969). 'Language and thought.' In Voss, J. F. (Ed.), *Approaches to Thought*. Merrill, Ohio.

Jensen, A. R. (1968). 'Social class and verbal learning.' In Deutsch, M., Katz, I. and Jensen, A. R. (Eds.), *Social Class, Race and Psychological Development*. Holt, Rinehart and Winston, New York.

Jensen, A. R. (1969a). 'How much can we boost IQ and scholastic achievement?' *Harvard Educ. Review*, **39**, 1–123.

Jensen, A. R. (1969b). 'Reducing the heredity-environment uncertainty.' *Harvard Educ. Review*, **39**, 209–43.

Jensen, A. R. (1971). 'The role of verbal mediation in mental development.' *J. Gen. Psychol.*, **118**, 39–70.

Johnson, D. M. (1972). *A Systematic Introduction to the Psychology of Thinking*. Harper and Row, New York.

Johnson-Laird, P. N., and Wason, P. C. (1970). 'A theoretical analysis of insight into a reasoning task.' *Cogn. Psychol.*, **1**, 134–48.

Johnson-Laird, P. N., and Wason, P. C. (1970). 'Insight into a logical relation.' *Q. J. Exp. Psychol.*, **22**, 49–61.

Jones, E. (1953). *The Life and Work of Sigmund Freud*. Basic Books, New York.

Jung. C. G. (1916). *The Psychology of the Unconscious*. Kegan Paul, London.

Jung, C. G. (1928). *Two Essays in Analytical Psychology*. Routledge and Kegan Paul, London. Bailliere, Tindall and Cox, London.

Kales, A., Kales, J. D., Po, J., and Klein, J. (1966). 'A review of recent sleep and dream studies.' *Bull. Los Angeles Neurological Society*, **31**, 136–51.

Karp, S. A., Witkin, H. A. and Goodenough, D. R. (1965). 'Alcoholism and psychological differentiation: the effect of alcohol on field dependence.' *J. Abn. Psychol.*, **70**, 262–5.

Keehn, J. D. (1969). 'Consciousness, discrimination and the stimulus control of behaviour.' In Gilbert, R. M., and Sutherland, N. S. *Animal Discrimination Learning*. Academic Press, London.

Keller, H. (1936). *The Story of my Life*. Doubleday, New York.

Kellogg, W. N., and Kellogg, L. A. (1933). *The Ape and the Child*. McGraw-Hill, New York.

Kendler, H. H. (1964). 'The concept of the concept.' In A. W. Melton (Ed.), *Categories of Human Learning*. Academic Press, New York.

Kendler, H. H., and Kendler, T. S. (1962). 'Vertical and horizontal processes in problem solving.' *Psychol. Rev.*, **69**, 1–16.

Kendler, H. H., and Kendler, T. S. (1969). 'Reversal-shift behaviour: some basic issues.' *Psychol. Bull.*, **72**, 229–32.

Kendler, H. H., and Kendler, T. S. (1971). 'Definitely, our last word.' *Psychol. Bull.*, **75**, 290–3.

Kendler, H. H., Kendler, T. S., and Marken, R. S. (1970). 'Stimulus control and memory loss in reversal shift behaviour of college students.' *J. Exp. Psychol.*, **83**, 84–8.

Kessen, W. (1965). 'Looking at looking in the human newborn.' Paper presented at *Center for Cognitive Studies Colloquium,* Harvard University.

Kettner, N. W., Guilford, J. P., and Christensen, P. R. (1959). 'A factor-analytic study across the domains of reasoning, creativity and evaluation.' *Psychol. Monogr.*, **73**, 479.

Kidson, M. A., and Jones, I. H. (1968). 'Psychiatric disorders among aborigines of the Australian Western desert.' *Arch. Gen. Psychiat.*, **19**, 413–17.

Kiss, G. R. (1967). 'Networks as models of word storage.' In Collins, N. L. and Michie, D. (Eds.), *Machine Intelligence* (1). Oliver and Boyd, Edinburgh and London.

Kiss, G. R. (1969). 'Steps towards a model of word selection.' In Michie, D. and Meltzer, B. (Eds.), *Machine Intelligence* (4). Edinburgh University Press.

Kitto, H. D. F. (1953). *The Greeks.* Penguin Books, Harmondsworth.

Klahr, D., and Wallace, J. G. (1970). 'The development of serial completion strategies: an information processing analysis.' *Brit. J. Psychol.*, **61**, 243–57.

Klein, G. S. (1970). *Perception, Motives and Personality.* Alfred A. Knopf, New York.

Klein, G. S., and Holzman, P. S. (1950). 'The "schematizing process": perceptual attitudes and personality qualities in sensitivity to change.' *Amer. Psychologist*, **5**, 312.

Klein, M. (1937). *Psycho-Analysis of Children.* Hogarth Press, London.

Koestler, A. (1964). *The Act of Creation.* Hutchinson, London.

Koestler, A. (1968). *Drinkers of Infinity.* Hutchinson, London.

Kohlberg, L. (1968). 'Early education: a cognitive-developmental view.' *Child Dev.*, **39**, 1013–62.

Köhler, W. (1925). *The Mentality of Apes.* Harcourt, Brace, New York.

Krechevsky, I. (1932). ' "Hypothesis" versus "chance" in the pre-solution period in sensory discrimination learning.' *Univ. Calif. Publ. Psychol.*, **6**, 27–44.

Kris, E. (1952). *Psychoanalytic Interpretations in Art.* Int. Univ. Press, New York.

Kuhlman, C. (1960). *Visual Imagery in Children.* Unpublished doctoral dissertation, Harvard University.

Kuhlman Hollenberg, C. (1970). 'Functions of visual imagery in the learning and concept formation of children.' *Child Dev.*, **41**, 1003–15.

Kuhn, T. S. (1962). *The Structure of Scientific Revolutions.* Chicago Univ. Press.

Kuhn, T. S. (1963). 'The essential tension: tradition and innovation in scientific research.' In Taylor, C. W. and Barron, F. (Eds.), *Scientific Creativity: its Recognition and Development.* Wiley, New York.

Labov, W. (1970). 'The logic of non-standard English.' In Williams, F. (Ed.), *Language and Poetry.* Markham, Chicago.

Laing, R. D. (1960). *The Divided Self: a Study of Sanity and Madness.* Tavistock Publications, London.

Landa, L. N. (1963). 'Opyt primeneniya matematicheskoi logiko i teorii informatsii k nekotorym problemam obychenvya.' *Voprosy Psikhologii*, **8**, 19–40.

Lantz, D., and Steffire, V. (1964). 'Language and cognition revisited.' *J. Abn. Soc. Psychol.*, **69**, 472–81.

Lashley, K. S. (1938). 'The mechanism of vision: XV. Preliminary studies of the rat's capacity for detail vision.' *J. Gen. Psychol.*, **18**, 123–93.

Laufer, M. (1968). 'The body image, the function of masturbation, and adolescence: problems of ownership of the body.' *Psychoanalytic Study of the Child*, **23**, 114–37.

Leach, E. R. (1970). *Lévi-Strauss*. Fontana, London.

Leask, J., Haber, R. N., and Haber, R. B. (1969). 'Eidetic imagery in children: II. Longitudinal and experimental results.' *Psychonom. Monogr. Suppl.* **3** (Whole No. 35), 25–48.

Lehman, H. C. (1953). *Age and Achievement*. Princeton Univ. Press, Princeton, N.J.

Lenneberg, E. H., and Roberts, J. M. (1956). *The Language of Experience: A Study in Methodology*. Memoir 13, Indiana University Publications in Anthropology and Linguistics.

Levak, M. D. (1969). 'Eidetic images among the Bororo in Brazil.' *J. Soc. Psychol.*, **79**, 135–7.

Levine, M. (1959). 'A model of hypothesis behaviour in discrimination learning.' *Psychol. Rev.*, **66**, 353–66.

Lévi-Strauss, C. (1963). *Structural Anthropology*. Basic Books, New York. Penguin Books, Harmondsworth, 1972.

Lévi-Strauss, C. (1970). *The Raw and the Cooked*. Jonathan Cape, London.

Levy, D. M. (1943). *Maternal Overprotection*. Columbia Univ. Press.

Levy-Bruhl, C. (1910). *How Natives Think*. Washington Square Press, New York.

Lewis, B. M., Horabin, I. S., and Gane, C. P. (1967). 'Flow charts, logical trees and algorithms for rules and regulations.' *CAS Occasional Paper*, No. 2, H.M.S.O., London.

Lewis, O. (1959). *Five Families*. Basic Books, New York.

Lifton, R. J. (1961). *Thought Reform and the Psychology of Totalism: A Study of 'Brainwashing'*. Gollancz, London.

Light, R. J., and Smith, P. V. (1969). 'Social allocation models of intelligence: a methodological inquiry.' *Harvard Educ. Review*, **39**, 484–510.

Lindauer, M. S. (1969). 'Imagery and sensory modality.' *Percept. Motor Skills*, **29**, 203–15.

Loewenstein, L., and Gerhardi, W. A. (1942). *Meet Yourself as You Really Are*. Penguin Books, Harmondsworth.

Looft, W. R., and Bartz, W. H. (1969). 'Animism revived.' *Psychol. Bull.*, **71**, 1–19.

Lovejoy, E. P. (1965). 'An attention theory of discrimination learning.' *J. Math. Psychol.*, **2**, 342–62.

Lovell, K., and Ogilvie, E. (1960). 'A study of conservation of substance in the junior school child.' *Brit. J. Educ. Psychol.*, **30**, 109–18.

Luchins, A. S. (1942). 'Mechanization in problem solving: the effect of Einstellung.' *Psychol. Monogr.*, **54** (Whole No. 48).

Luria, A. R. (1961). *The Role of Speech in the Regulation of Normal and Abnormal Behaviour*. Tizard, J. (Ed.), Pergamon Press, Oxford.

Luria, A. R. (1966). *Human Brain and Psychological Processes*. Harper and Row, New York.

Luria, A. R. (1968). *The Mind of a Mnemonist*. Basic Books, New York.

Luria, A. R. (1969). 'The origin and cerebral organization of man's conscious action.' *Proc. XIX Int. Cong. Psychol. (London)*. Publ. Brit. Psychol. Soc., 1971.

Luria, A. R., and Yudovich, F. Ia. (1959). *Speech and the Development of Mental Processes in the Child*. Staples Press, London. Penguin Books, 1971. (Original Russian Publication, 1956).

410

Lyons, J. (1970). *Chomsky*. Fontana.

Lyons, J. (1970). *New Horizons in Linguistics*. Penguin Books, Harmondsworth.

MacCallum, D. M., and Smith, J. B. (1951). 'Mechanized reasoning.' *Electronic Engineering*, **23**, 126–33.

Maccoby, E. E., and Modiano, N. (1966). 'On culture and equivalence: I.' In Bruner, J. S. *et al. Studies in Cognitive Growth*. Wiley, New York.

Maccoby, E. E., and Rau, L. (1962). 'Differential cognitive abilities.' *U.S. Office of Education, Cooperative Research Project, No. 1040*.

Maccoby, E. E., Modiano, N., and Lander, P. (1964). 'Games and social character in a Mexican village.' *Psychiatry*, **27**, 150–62.

MacCorquodale, K., and Meehl, P. E. (1948). 'On a distinction between hypothetical constructs and intervening variables.' *Psychol. Rev.*, **55**, 95–107.

Mackay, D. M. (1967). 'Ways of looking at perception.' In Wathen-Dunn, W. (Ed.), *Models for the Perception of Speech and Visual Form*. M.I.T. Press.

MacKinnon, D. W. (1960). 'The highly effective individual.' *Teachers Coll. Rec.*, **61**, 367–78.

Mackintosh, N. J. (1965). 'Selective attention in animal discrimination learning.' *Psychol. Bull.*, **64**, 124–50.

Maier, N. R. F. (1930). 'Reasoning in humans: I. On direction.' *J. Comp. Psychol.*, **10**, 115–43.

Maier, N. R. F. (1931). 'Reasoning in humans: II. The solution of a problem and its appearance in consciousness.' *J. Comp. Psychol.*, **12**, 181–94.

Maloney, M. P., and Payne, L. E. (1969). 'Validity of the Draw-a-Person Test as a measure of body image.' *Percept. and Mot. Skills*, **29**, 119–22.

Maloney, M. P., Ball, T., and Edgar, C. (1969). 'An analysis of the generalizability of sensory-motor training.' Cited in Maloney, M. P. and Payne, L. E. (1969).

Malson, L., and Itard, J. (1972). *Wolf Children; The Wild Boy of Aveyron*. NLB, London. (French Edition, 1964).

Maltzman, I. (1960). 'On the training of originality.' *Psychol. Rev.*, **67**, 229–42.

Marbe, K. (1901). *Experimentell-psychologische Untersuchungen über das Urteil, eine Einleitung in die Logik*. Engelmann, Leipzig.

Marjoribanks, K. (1971). 'Environmental correlates of diverse mental abilities.' *J. Exp. Educ.*, **39**, 64–8.

Mayer, A., and Orth, J. (1901). 'Zur qualitativen Untersuchung der Associationen.' *Zeitschr. Psychol. and Physiol. d. Sinnesorg*, **26**, 1–13.

Mayman, M., Schafer, R., and Rapaport, D. (1951). 'Interpretation of the Wechsler-Bellevue Intelligence Scale in personality appraisal.' In Anderson, H. H. and Anderson, G. L. (Eds.), *An Introduction to Projective Techniques*. Prentice-Hall, Englewood Cliffs, N.J.

Mazer, M. (1951). 'An experimental study of the hypnotic dream.' *Psychiatry*, **14**, 265–77.

McClelland, D. C. (1953). *The Achievement Motive*. Appleton-Century-Crofts, New York.

McClelland, D. C. (1958). 'Methods of measuring human motivation.' In Atkinson, J. W. (Ed.), *Motives in Fantasy, Action and Society*. Van Nostrand, Princetown, N.J.

McClelland, D. C. (1961). *The Achieving Society*. Van Nostrand, Princetown, N.J.

McDougall, W. (1908). *Introduction to Social Psychology*. Methuen, London.

McGothlin, Cohen, and McGothlin (1967). Quoted by Barron, F. (1969). *Creative Person and Creative Process*. Holt, Rinehart and Winston, New York.

McGuigan, F. J. (1970). 'Covert oral behaviour during the silent performance of language tasks.' *Psychol. Bull.*, **74**, 309–26.

411

McKellar, P. (1957). *Imagination and Thinking.* Cohen and West, London.
McKellar, P. (1962). 'The method of introspection.' In Scher, J. (Ed.), *Theories of the Mind.* Free Press of Glencoe, New York.
McKellar, P. (1965). The investigation of mental images. In Barnett, S. A. and McLaren, A. (Eds.), *Penguin Science Journal.* Penguin Books, Harmondsworth.
McKellar, P. (1968). *Experience and Behaviour.* Penguin Books, Harmondsworth.
Mead, M. (1962). 'Where education fits in.' *Think, Nov-Dec,* 16–21.
Mednick, S. A. (1962). 'The associative basis of the creative process.' *Psychol. Rev.,* **69,** 220–32.
Mednick, S. A. (1971). Birth defects and schizophrenia. *Psychology Today,* **4,** 49–50, 80–1.
Mehrabian, A., and Williams, M. (1971). 'Piagetian measures of cognitive development for children up to age two.' *J. Psycholinguistic Research,* **1,** 113–26.
Meisels, M. and Guardo, C. J. (1969). 'Development of personal space schemata.' *Child Dev.,* **40,** 1167–78.
Meldman, M. J. (1970). *Diseases of Attention and Perception.* Pergamon Press, Oxford.
Merrifield, P. R. (1966). 'An analysis of concepts from the point of view of the structure of the intellect.' In Klausmeier, H. J. and Harris, C. W. (Eds.), *Analyses of Concept Learning.* Academic Press, London.
No. 259, 306–8.
Merton, R. K. (1961). 'The role of genius in scientific advance.' *New Scientist,* **No. 259,** 306–8.
Messer, A. (1906). 'Experimentell-psychologische Untersuchungen über das Denken.' *Arch. ges. Psychol.,* **8,** 1–224.
Michie, D. (1970). 'Future for integrated cognitive systems.' *Nature,* **228,** 717–22.
Miles, T. R. (1957). 'Contributions to intelligence testing and the theory of intelligence. I. On defining intelligence.' *Br. J. Educ. Psychol.,* **27,** 153–65.
Mill, J. (1829). *Analysis of the Phenomena of the Human Mind.* Longmans and Dyer, London.
Miller, G. A. (1956). 'The magical number seven, plus or minus two: some limits on our capacity for processing information.' *Psychol. Rev.,* **63,** 81–96.
Miller, G. A., Galanter, E., and Pribram, K. H. (1960). *Plans and the Structure of Behaviour.* Holt Rinehart and Winston, New York.
Milton, G. A. (1957). 'The effects of sex-role identification upon problem-solving skill.' *J. Abn. Soc. Psychol.,* **55,** 208–12.
Minsky, M. (Ed.), (1968). *Semantic Information Processing.* M.I.T. Press, Cambridge, Mass.
Mittler, P. (1971). *The Study of Twins.* Penguin Books, Harmondsworth.
Montague, W. E., and Kiess, H. O. 'Effect of mediation training on the acquisition and retention of paired associates.' Paper cited by Adams, J. A. (1967).
Montague, W. E., Adams, J. A., and Kiess, H. O. (1966). 'Forgetting and natural language mediation.' *J. Exp. Psychol.,* **72,** 829–33.
Mooney, R., and Razik, T. A. (1967). *Explorations in Creativity.* Harper and Row, New York.
Moore, O. K. (1961). 'Orthographic symbols and the pre-school child—a new approach.' *New Educational Ideas: Second Minnesota Conference on Gifted Children.* Torrance, New York.
Moray, N. (1969). *Attention: Selective Processes in Vision and Hearing.* Hutchinson Educational, London.
Morgan, J. J. B., and Morton, J. T. (1944). 'The distortion of syllogistic reasoning produced by personal convictions.' *J. Soc. Psychol.,* **20,** 39–59.

412

Morton, J., and Broadbent, D. E. (1967). 'Passive versus active recognition models, or is your homunculus really necessary?' In Wathen-Dunn, W. (Ed.), *Models for the Perception of Speech and Visual Form*. M.I.T. Press, Cambridge, Mass.

Moustakas, C. (1966). *The Authentic Teacher*. How and Doyle, Cambridge, Mass.

Mueller, R. E. (1967). *The Science of Art*. Rapp and Whiting, London.

Müller, G. E. (1917). *Zeitschr. für Ps. Ergänzbd*, 9.

Muller, M. (1887). *The Science of Thought* (2 vols). Appleton-Century-Crofts, New York.

Murphy, G. (1949). *An Historical Introduction to Modern Psychology*. Routledge and Kegan Paul Ltd., London.

Murray, F. B., and Johnson, P. E. (1969). 'Reversibility in Nonconservation of Weight.' *Psychon. Sci.*, 16, 285–7.

Murray, H. A. (1938). *Explorations in Personality*. Oxford Univ. Press.

Nachmansohn, M. (1925). 'Uber experimentell erzeugte Träume nebst kritischen Bemerkungen über die psychoanalytische Method.' *Zeitschr. Neurol. Psychiat.*, 98, 556–86.

Natsoulas, T. (1970). 'Concerning introspective knowledge.' *Psychol. Bull.*, 73, 89–111.

Neisser, U. (1963). 'Decision time without reaction time: experiments in visual scanning.' *Am. J. Psychol.*, 76, 376–85.

Neisser, U. (1967). *Cognitive Psychology*. Appleton-Century-Crofts, New York.

Neisser, U. (1968). 'The processes of vision.' *Scient. Amer.*, 219, 204–14.

Newell, A., and Simon, H. A. (1956). 'Problem-solving in humans and computers.' *RAND Corp. Paper P-987*, Santa Monica, Calif.

Newell, A., and Simon, H. A. (1972). *Human Problem Solving*. Prentice-Hall, Englewood Cliffs, N.J.

Newell, A., Shaw, J. C., and Simon H. A. (1958). 'Elements of a theory of human problem solving.' *Psychol. Rev.*, 65, 151–66.

Newell, A., Shaw, J. C., and Simon, H. A. (1962). 'The processes of creative thinking.' In Gruber, H. E. and Wertheimer, M. (Eds.), *Contemporary Approaches to Creative Thinking*. Atherton Press, New York.

Newman, E. A., and Evans, C. R. (1965). 'Human dream processes as analogous to computer programme clearance.' *Nature*, 206, 534.

Newman, H. H., Freeman, F. N. and Holzinger, K. J. (1937). *Twins: A Study of Heredity and Environment*. Univ. Chicago Press, Chicago.

Newman, R., Katz, J., and Rubenstein, R. (1960). 'The experimental situation as a determinant of hypnotic dreams.' *Psychiatry*, 23, 63–73.

Oden, M. H. (1968). 'The fulfilment of promise: 40-year old follow-up of the Terman gifted group.' *Genet. Psy. Monogr.*, 77, 3–93.

Olver, R. R. (1961). *A Developmental Study of Cognitive Equivalence*. Unpublished doctoral dissertation, Radford College.

Orth, J. (1903). *Gefühl und Bewusstseinslage*. Springer-Verlag, Berlin.

Osborn, A. F. (1957). *Applied Imagination*. Scribner, New York.

Osgood, C. E. (1953). *Method and Theory in Experimental Psychology*. Oxford Univ. Press, New York.

Oswald, I. (1966). *Sleep*. Penguin Books, Harmondsworth.

Owens, A. C. (1963). 'A study of mental imagery.' *Unpublished Ph.D. Thesis, Univ. of Liverpool*.

Paivio, A. (1968). 'Effects of imagery instructions and concreteness of memory pegs in a mnemonic system.' *Proc. 76th Ann. Conv. A.P.A.*, 3, 77–8.

Paivio, A. (1969). 'Mental imagery in associative learning and memory.' *Psychol. Rev.*, 76, 241–63.

Paivio, A. (1970). 'On the functional significance of imagery.' *Psychol. Bull.*, **73**, 385–92.

Paivio, A. (1971). *Imagery and Verbal Processes*. Holt, Rinehart and Winston, New York.

Paivio, A., and Csapo, K. (1969). 'Concrete image and verbal memory codes.' *J. Exp. Psychol.*, **80**, 279–85.

Paivio, A., Yuille, J. C., and Madigan, S. A. (1968). 'Concreteness, imagery and meaningfulness values for 925 nouns.' *J. Exp. Psychol. Monogr. Suppl.*, **76**, 1–25.

Panek, D. M. (1968). 'Is the basis of schizophrenia an associative disorder?' *J. of Schizophrenia*, **2**, 88–94.

Parnes, S. J. (1959). 'Effects of brain-storming instructions on creative problem solving.' *J. Educ. Psychol.*, **50**, 171–6.

Parnes, S. J. (1962). 'Do you really understand brainstorming?' In *A Source Book for Creative Thinking*. Parnes, S. J. and Harding, H. F. (Eds.), Scribner, New York.

Parnes, S. J., and Brunelle, E. A. (1967). 'The literature of creativity (Part 1).' *J. Creat. Behav.*, **1**, 52–109.

Patrick, C. (1935). 'Creative thought in poets.' *Arch. Psychol.*, **26**, 1–74.

Patrick, C. (1937). 'Creative thought in artists.' *J. Psychol.*, **4**, 35–73.

Payne, R. W. (1960). 'Cognitive abnormalities.' In Eysenck, H. J. (Ed.), *Handbook of Abnormal Psychology*, Pitman, London.

Peller, L. E. (1966). 'Freud's contribution to language theory.' *The Psychoanalytic Study of the Child*, **21**, 448–67.

Peluffo, N. (1962). 'Les notions de conservation et de causalité chez les enfants prévenant de differents milieux physiques et socio-culturels.' *Archiv. de Psychologie*, **38**, 75–90.

Penfield, W. (1966). 'Speech, perception and the cortex.' In Eccles, J. C. (Ed.), *Brain and Conscious Experience*. Springer-Verlag, New York.

Penrose, J. (1962). *An investigation into some aspects of problem solving behaviour*. Unpubl. Ph.D. Thesis, Univ. of London.

Perky, C. W. (1910). 'An experimental study of imagination.' *Amer. J. Psychol.*, **21**, 422–52.

Peters, R. S. (1953). *Brett's History of Psychology*. George Allen and Unwin Ltd., London.

Peterson, H. (Ed.), (1946). *Great Teachers*. Vintage Books, New York.

Peterson, J. (1920). 'The backward elimination of errors in mental maze learning.' *J. Exp. Psychol.*, **3**, 257–80.

Phillips, J. (1969). *The Origins of the Intellect*. W. H. Freeman, San Francisco.

Phillips, R. (1969). 'Psychological psychology: A new science?' *Bull. Br. Psychol. Soc.*, **22**, 83–7.

Piaget, J. (1926). *The Language and Thought of the Child*. Harcourt, Brace, New York.

Piaget, J. (1936). *The Origins of Intelligence in Children*. Translated by Cook, M. Internat. Univ. Press, New York, 1952.

Piaget, J. (1937). *The Construction of Reality in the Child*. Translated by Cook, M. Basic Books, New York, 1954.

Piaget, J. (1947). *The Psychology of Intelligence*. Translated by Piercy, M. and Berlyne, D. E. Routledge and Kegan Paul, London.

Piaget, J. (1953). *Logic and Psychology*. Manchester Univ. Press. Basic Books, New York, 1957.

414

Piaget, J. (1957). 'Logique et équilibre dans le comportements du sujet.' In Apostel, L., Mandelbrot, B. and Piaget, J. *Logique et équilibre. Études d'Epistém. Génét., II.* Presses Universitaires de France, Paris.

Piaget, J. (1962). 'The stages of the intellectual development of the child.' *Bull. Menning. Clinic*, **26**, 120–8.

Piaget, J. (1963). 'Le langage et les opérations intellectuelles.' In *Problems de psycholinguistique: Symposium de l'association de psychologie scientifique de langue francaise.* Presses Universitaires de France, Paris.

Piaget, J. (1964). *The Early Growth of Logic in the Child.* Routledge and Kegan Paul.

Piaget, J. (1966). *Mental Imagery in the Child.* Trans. 1971. Presses Universitaires de France, Paris. English Edn. Routledge and Kegan Paul, London.

Piaget, J. (1968). *On the Development of Memory and Identity.* Clark Univ. Press, Barre, Mass.

Piaget, J. (1968). *Six Psychological Studies.* (French Edn. 1964). Univ. London Press.

Piaget, J. (1969). In Furth, H. G. *Piaget and Knowledge,* Prentice-Hall. Reprinted from McGraw-Hill, *Modern Men of Science.* Vol. II. Suppl. to McGraw-Hill Encyclopedia of Science and Technology.

Piaget, J. (1971). *Structuralism.* Routledge and Kegan Paul, London.

Piaget, J., and Inhelder, B. (1962). *Le développement des quantités physiques chez l'enfant: conservation et atomisme.* (2nd revised edition) Delachaux et Niestlé, Neuchatel.

Piaget, J., and Inhelder, B. (1971). *Mental Imagery in the Child.* Routledge and Kegan Paul, London. (French Edn. Published 1966).

Piaget, J., and Szeminska, A. (1941). *The Child's Conception of Number.* Trans. by Cattegno, C. and Hodgson, F. M., 1952. Humanities Press, New York.

Piaget, J., and Szeminska, A. (1952). *The Child's Conception of Number.* Routledge and Kegan Paul, London.

Piaget, J., Inhelder, B., and Szeminska, A. (1948). *La Géométrie Spontanée chez l'Enfant.* Presses Univ. de France, Paris. *The Child's Conception of Geometry.* Basic Books, New York, 1960.

Ploog, D., and Melnechuk, T. (1969). 'Primate communication.' *Neurosci. Res. Prog. Bull.*, **7**, 419–510.

Popper, K. R. (1969). *Conjectures and Refutations.* Routledge and Kegan Paul, London (3rd Edn.).

Premack, D. (1970). 'A functional analysis of language.' *J. Exp. Anal. Behav.*, **14**, 107–25.

Premack, A. J., and Premack, D. (1972). 'Teaching language to an ape.' *Scient. Amer.*, **227**, 92–9 (October).

Price-Williams, D. R. (1961). 'A study concerning concepts of conservation of quantities among primitive children.' *Acta Psychologica*, **18**, 297–305.

Price-Williams, D. R. (1969) (Ed.). *Cross-Cultural Studies.* Penguin Books, Harmondsworth.

Prince, G. M. (1968). 'The operational mechanism of synectics.' *J. Creat. Behav.*, **2**, 1–13.

Pringle, M. K. (1965). *Deprivation and Education.* Longmans, London.

Quetelet, A. (1835). *Sur l'homme et le développement de ses facultés, ou essai de physique sociale.* Bachelier, Paris.

Quillian, M. R. (1969a). 'The Teachable Language Comprehender: A simulation program and theory of language.' *Communications of the A.C.M.*, **12**, 459–76.

Rankin, H. B. (1963). 'Language and thinking: positive and negative effects of naming.' *Science*, **141**, 48–50.

Ray, W. S. (1967). *The Experimental Psychology of Original Thinking.* Macmillan, New York.

Razik, T. A. (1965). *Bibliography of Creativity Studies and Related Areas.* Creative Education Foundation and State University of New York at Buffalo.

Razran, G. (1961). 'The observable unconscious, and the inferable conscious in current Soviet psychophysiology; interoceptive conditioning, semantic conditioning, and the orienting reflex.' *Psychol. Rev.,* **68**, 81–147.

Reader, A. V. (1958). 'The need for conversation for the mechanical learning of concepts.' *Mathematical Biosciences,* **3**, 275–87.

Reader, A. V. (1969). 'Steps towards genuine artificial intelligence.' *Acta Psychologica,* **29**, 279–89.

Reed, H. B. (1946a). 'Factors influencing the learning and retention of concepts. I. The influence of set.' *J. Exp. Psychol.,* **36**, 71–87.

Reed, H. B. (1946b). 'The learning and retention of concepts. II. The influence of length of series. III. The origin of concepts.' *J. Exp. Psychol.,* **36**, 166–79.

Reed, H. B. (1946c). 'The learning and retention of concepts. IV. The influence of complexity of the stimuli.' *J. Exp. Psychol.,* **36**, 252–61.

Reese, H. W. (1970). 'Imagery in children's learning: a symposium.' *Psychol. Bull.,* **73**, 383–4.

Reeves, J. W. (1965). *Thinking about Thinking.* Secker and Warburg, London.

Restle, F. (1962). 'The selection of strategies in cue learning.' *Psychol. Rev.,* **69**, 329–43.

Reynolds, P. C. (1968). 'Evolution of primate vocal-auditory communication systems.' *Amer. Anthropologist,* **70**, 300–8.

Richardson, A. (1962). Unpublished data cited by Richardson, A. (1969).

Richardson, A. (1969). *Mental Imagery.* Routledge and Kegan Paul, London.

Richardson, A. (1971). 'Voluntary control of the memory image.' *Bull. Brit. Psychol. Soc.,* **24**, 265.

Richardson, A., and Cant, R. (1970). 'Eidetic imagery and brain damage.' *Aust. J. Psy.,* **22**, 47–54.

Richardson, K., and Spears, D. (1972). *Race, Culture and Intelligence.* Penguin Books, Harmondsworth.

Richmond, P. G. (1970). *An Introduction to Piaget.* Routledge and Kegan Paul, London.

Roe, A. (1952). *The Making of a Scientist.* Dodd, Mead, New York.

Roffenstein, G. (1924). 'Experimentelle Symbolträume: ein Beitrag zur Diskussion über Psychoanalyse.' *Zeitschr. Neurol. Psychiat.,* **87**, 362–72.

Rosenbaum, C. P. (1968). 'Metabolic, physiological, anatomic and genetic studies in the schizophrenias: A review and analysis.' *J. Nerv. Ment. Dis.,* **146**, 103–26.

Rosenthal, R., and Jacobson, L. (1966). 'Teachers' expectancies: determinants of pupils' IQ gains.' *Psychol. Rep.,* **19**, 115–18.

Rubenstein, R., Katz, J., and Newman, R. (1957). 'On the sources and determinants of hypnotic dreams.' *Canad. Psychiat. Assoc'n. J.,* **2**, 154–61.

Russell, W. A., and Jenkins, J. J. (1954). 'The complete Minnesota norms for responses to 100 words from the Kent Rosanoff word association test.' *Tech. Report No. 11, Office of Naval Research* and University of Minnesota.

Russell, W. A., and Storms, L. H. (1955). 'Implicit verbal chaining in paired-associate learning.' *J. Exp. Psychol.,* **49**, 267–93.

Ryle, G. (1949). *The Concept of Mind.* Hutchinson, London.

Saugstad, P. (1955). 'Problem solving as dependent on availability of functions.' *Brit. J. Psychol.,* **46**, 191–8.

Saugstad, P. (1957). 'An analysis of Maier's pendulum problem.' *J. Exp. Psychol.*, **54**, 168–79.

Saugstad, P., and Raaheim, K. (1960). 'Problem solving, past experience and availability of functions.' *Brit. J. Psychol.*, **51**, 97–104.

Schaefer, C. E., and Anastasi, A. (1968). 'A biographical inventory for identifying creativity in adolescent boys.' *J. Appl. Psychol.*, **52**, 42–8.

Scheerer, M. (1963). 'Problem solving.' *Sci. Amer.*, **208**, 118–28.

Schenk, H., Jr., 'Me,' in Heinlein, R. A. *et al.*, *The Best from Fantasy and Science Fiction* (Ninth Series). Victor Gollancz, 1962. Mercury Press, 1958.

Schiller, P. H. (1952). 'Innate constituents of complex response in primates.' *Psychol. Rev.*, **59**, 177–91.

Schon, D. A. (1963). *Displacement of Concepts*. Tavistock Publications, London.

Schultz, R. W. (1960). 'Problem solving behaviour and transfer.' *Harvard Educ. Rev.*, **30**, 61–77. Reprinted in Grose, R. F. and Birney, R. C. (Eds.), 'Transfer of Learning', Van Nostrand, Princeton, N.J., 1963.

Seder, J. A. (1955). 'The origin of differences in the extent of independence in children: developmental factors in perceptual field dependence.' Unpublished thesis. Radcliffe College. Cited by Witkin, H. A. (1960), in Kaplan, B. and Wapner, S. (Eds.), *Perspectives in Psychological Theory*. Internat. Univ. Press, New York.

Segall, M. H., Campbell, D. T., and Herskovits, M. J. (1963). 'Cultural differences in the perception of geometric illusions.' *Science*, **139**, 769–71.

Sells, S. B. (1936). 'The atmosphere effect: an experimental study of reasoning.' *Arch. Psychol.*, **29**, 3–72.

Selz, O. (1913). *Über die Gesetze des geordneten Denkverlaufs*. Spemann, Stuttgart.

Shallice, T., and Warrington, E. K. (1970). 'Independent functioning of verbal memory stores: a neuropsychological study. *Q.J. Exp. Psychol.*, **22**, 261–73.

Shapiro, D. L. (1970). 'The significance of the visual image in psychotherapy.' *Psychotherapy: Theory, Research and Practice*, **7**, 209–12.

Sheehan, P. W. (1966). 'Accuracy and vividness of visual images.' *Percept. Motor Skills*, **23**, 391–8.

Sheehan, P. W. (1967). 'A shortened form of Betts' questionnaire upon mental imagery.' *J. Clin. Psychol.*, **23**, 386–9.

Sheehan, P. W., and Neisser, U. (1969). 'Some variables affecting the vividness of imagery in recall.' *Brit. J. Psychol.*, **60**, 71–80.

Short, P. L. (1953). 'The objective study of mental imagery.' *Brit. J. Psychol.*, **44**, 38–51.

Short, P. L., and Walter, W. G. (1954). 'The relationship between physiological variables and stereognosis.' *EEG Clin. Neurophysiol.*, **6**, 29–44.

Shouksmith, G. (1970). *Intelligence, Creativity and Cognitive Style*. Batsford, London.

Shuey, A. M. (1966). *The Testing of Negro Intelligence*. Social Science Press, New York. 2nd Edn.

Siegel, L. S. (1969). 'Concept attainment as a function of amount and form of information.' *J. Exp. Psychol.*, **81**, 464–8.

Sigel, I. E., and Hooper, F. H. (1968). *Logical Thinking in Children: Research based on Piaget's Theory*. Holt, Rinehart and Winston, New York.

Siipola, E. M., and Hayden, S. D. (1965). 'Exploring eidetic imagery among the retarded.' *Percept. Motor Skills*, **21**, 275–86.

Simon, H. A., and Barenfeld, M. (1969). 'Information-processing analysis of perceptual processes in problem solving.' *Psychol. Rev.*, **76**, 473–83.

Simon, H. A., and Newell, A. (1971). Human problem solving: the state of the theory in 1970. *Amer. Psychologist*, **26**, 145–59.

Sinclair-de-Zwart, H. (1967). *Langage et opérations: sous-systèmes linguistiques et opérations concrètes.* Dunod, Paris.

Singer, J. L. (1966). *Daydreaming.* Random House, New York.

Singer, J. L., and Antrobus, J. S. (1965). 'Eye movements during fantasies.' *Arch. Gen. Psychiat.,* **12**, 71–6.

Skeels, H. M., and Dye, H. B. (1939). 'A study of the effects of differential stimulation on mentally retarded children.' *Proc. Addr. Amer. Assoc. Ment. Defic.,* **44**, 114–36.

Skinner, B. F. (1948). *Walden Two.* Macmillan, New York.

Skinner, B. F. (1953). *Science and Human Behaviour.* Macmillan, New York.

Skinner, B. F. (1966). 'An operant analysis of problem solving.' In Kleinmuntz, B. (Ed.), *Problem Solving: Research, Method, Theory.* Wiley, New York.

Skinner, B. F. (1972). *Beyond Freedom and Dignity.* Jonathan Cape, London.

Slamecka, N.J. (1968). 'A methodological analysis of shift paradigms in human discrimination learning.' *Psychol. Bull.,* **69**, 423–38.

Slatter, K. H. (1960). 'Alpha Rhythm and mental imagery.' *EEG Clin. Neurophysiol.,* **12**, 851–9.

Slobin, D. I. (1966). 'Grammatical transformations and sentence comprehension in childhood and adulthood.' *J.V.L.V.B.,* **5**, 219–27.

Smedslund, J. (1961). 'The acquisition of conservation of substance and weight in children.' *Scand. J. Psychol.,* **2**, 11–20, 71–87, 153–60, 203–10.

Smedslund, J. (1962). 'The acquisition of conservation of substance and weight in children: VII. Conservation of discontinuous quantity and the operations of adding and taking away.' *Scand. J. Psychol.,* **3**, 69–77.

Smith, R. M. (1968). 'Characteristics of creativity research.' *Perc. Motor Skills,* **26**, 698.

Smoke, K. L. (1933). 'Negative instances in concept learning.' *J. Exp. Psychol.,* **16**, 583–8.

Sokolov, E. N. (1960). In *CNS and Behaviour,* Vol. III. Brazier, M.A.B. (Ed.), Josiah Macy Jr. Foundation, New York.

Sokolov, E. N. (1963). *Perception and the Conditional Reflex.* English translation. Pergammon Press, London.

Sokolov, E. N. (1972). *Inner Speech and Thought.* Plenum Press, New York, revised edition.

Spearman, C. (1904). 'General intelligence': objectively determined and measured. *Amer. J. Psychol.,* **15**, 201–92.

Spearman. C. (1923). *The Nature of Intelligence and the Principles of Cognition.* Macmillan, London.

Spence, K. W. (1936). 'The nature of discrimination learning in animals.' *Psychol. Rev.,* **43**, 427–49.

Spitz, R. A. (1945). 'Hospitalism: an inquiry into the genesis of psychiatric conditions in early childhood.' *The Psycho-analytic Study of the Child,* **1**, 53–74.

Spitz, R. A. (1946). 'Hospitalism: a follow-up report.' *The Psycho-analytic Study of the Child,* **2**, 113–17.

Spotts, J. V., and Mackler, B. (1967). 'Relationships of field dependent and field independent cognitive styles to creative test performance.' *Perc. Motor Skills,* **24**, 239–68.

Stevens, K. N., and Halle, M. (1967). 'Remarks on analysis by synthesis and distinctive features.' In Wathen-Dunn, W. (Ed.), *Models for the Perception of Speech and Visual Form.* M.I.T. Press, Cambridge, Mass.

Stone, A. A., *et al.* (1968). 'Simple schizophrenia: syndrome or shibboleth.' *Amer. J. Psychiat.,* **125**, 305–12.

Storms, L. A., and Broen, W. E. (1968). 'A theory of schizophrenic behavioral disorganization.' *Arch. Gen. Psychiat.*, **20**, 129–44.

Strauss, S., and Langer, J. (1970). 'Operational thought inducement.' *Child Dev.*, **41**, 163–75.

Stromeyer, C. F., and Psotka, J. (1970). 'The detailed texture of eidetic images.' *Nature*, **225**, 346–9.

Sutherland, N. S. (1959). 'Stimulus analysing mechanisms.' In *Proc. Symposium of the Mechanization of Thought Processes. Vol II.* HMSO, London 575–609.

Sutherland, N. S. (1964). 'The learning of discrimination by animals.' *Endeavour*, **23**, 140–52.

Sutherland, N. S., and Holgate, V. (1966). 'Two-cue discrimination learning in rats.' *J. Comp. Physiol. Psychol.*, **2**, 198–207.

Sutherland, N. S., and Mackintosh, N. J. (1964). 'Discrimination learning: non-additivity of cues.' *Nature*, **201**, 528–30.

Suchman, R. G., and Trabasso, T. (1966). 'Stimulus preference and cue functions in young children's concept attainment.' *J. Exp. Child Psychol.*, **3**, 188–98.

Sweetland, A., and Quay, H. (1952). 'An experimental investigation of the hypnotic dream.' *J. Abn. Soc. Psychol.*, **47**, 678–82.

Tambiah, S. J. (1968). 'The magical power of words.' *Man*, **3**, 175–208.

Tart. C. T. (1964). 'A comparison of suggested dreams occurring in hypnosis and sleep.' *Internat. J. Clin. Exp. Hyp.*, **12**, 263–89.

Tart, C. T. (Ed.), (1969). *Altered States of Consciousness.* Wiley, New York.

Tawney, R. H. (1926). *Religion and the Rise of Capitalism.* J. Murray, London.

Taylor, I. A. (1959). 'The nature of the creative process.' In Smith, P. (Ed.), *Creativity.* Hastings, New York.

Taylor, C. W., and Barron, F. (1963). *Scientific Creativity: its Recognition and Development.* Wiley, New York.

Terman, L. M. (Ed.) (1925–57). *Genetic Studies of Genius.* Vol. 1. 1925. Vol. 2. 1926. Vol. 3. 1930. Vol. 4. 1957. Stanford Univ. Press, Stanford, Calif.

Terman, L. M., and Chase, J. M. (1920). 'The psychology, biology and pedagogy of genius.' *Psychol. Bull.*, **17**, 397–409.

Teuber, H. L., and Milner, B. (1968). 'Alteration of perception and memory in man: reflections on methods.' In *Analysis of Behavioural Change.* Weiskrantz, L. (Ed.), Harper and Row.

Thomson, R. (1968). *The Pelican History of Psychology.* Penguin Books, Harmondsworth.

Thorndike, E. L. (1898). 'Animal intelligence: an experimental study of the associative processes in animals.' *Psychol. Rev., Monogr. Suppl.* **2**, No. 8.

Thorndike, E. L. (1911). *Animal Intelligence: Experimental Studies.* Macmillan, New York.

Thorson, A. M. (1925). 'The relation of tongue movements to internal speech.' *J. Exp. Psychol.*, **8**, 1–32.

Thurstone, L. L. (1938). 'Primary mental abilities.' *Psychometr. Monogr. No. 1.*

Tichomirov, O. K., and Poznayanskaya, E. D. (1966). 'An investigation of visual search as a means of analysing heuristics.' *Soviet Psychology*, **5**, 2–15 (Winter 1966–67). Trans. from *Voprosy Psikhologii*, **2**, 39–53.

Tighe, T. J., and Tighe, L. S. (1966). 'Overtraining and optional shift behaviour in rats and children.' *J. Comp. Physiol. Psychol.*, **62**, 49–54.

Torda, C. (1968). 'Contribution to serotonin theory of dreaming (LSD infusion).' *N.Y. State J. Medicine*, **68**, 1135–8.

Torrance, E. P. (1965). *Rewarding Creative Behaviour.* Prentice-Hall, Englewood Cliffs, N.J.

Torrance, E. P. (1967). 'The Minnesota studies of creative behaviour: national and international extensions.' *J. Creat. Behav.*, **1**, 137–54.

Torrance, E. P., and Hansen, E. (1965). 'The question-asking behaviour of highly creative and less creative basic business teachers identified by a paper-and-pencil test.' *Psychol. Rep.*, **17**, 815–18.

Trabasso, T., and Bower, G. H. (1968). *Attention in Learning: Theory and Research.* Wiley, New York.

Trabasso, T., Rollins, H., and Shaughnessy, E. (1971). 'Storage and verification stages in processing concepts.' *Cognitive Psychol.*, **2**, 239–89.

Treisman, A. (1969). 'Strategies and models of selective attention.' *Psychol. Rev.*, **76**, 282–99.

Turing, A. M. (1948). 'Intelligent machinery (Nat. Physic. Lab. Rep.).' In Evans, C. R. and Robertson, A. D. J. (Eds.), *Cybernetics.* Butterworth, 1968.

Turing, A. M. (1950). 'Computing machinery and intelligence.' *Mind*, **59**, 433–60.

Valentine, C. W. (1939). *An Introduction to Experimental Psychology.* University Tutorial Press, London. 3rd Edn.

Van de Castle, R. L. (1968). 'Dreams and menstruation.' *Psychophysiology*, **4**, 374–5.

Van de Castle, R. L., and Kinder, P. (1968). 'Dream content during pregnancy.' *Psychophysiology*, **4**, 375.

Vandenburg, S. G. (1966). 'Contributions of twin research to psychology.' *Psychol. Bull.*, **66**, 327–52.

Van Zelst, R. H., and Kerr, W. A. (1954). 'Personality self-assessment of scientific and technical personnel, *J. Appl. Psychol.*, **38**, 145–7.

Vernon, M. (1967). Relationship of language to the thinking process. *Arch. Gen. Psychiat.*, **16**, 325–33.

Vernon, M. D. (1937). *Visual Perception.* Cambridge Univ. Press, London.

Vernon, P. E. (1950). *The Structure of Human Abilities.* Methuen, London.

Vernon, P. E. (1964). 'Creativity and intelligence.' *Educ. Res.*, **6**, 163–9.

Vernon, P. E. (1965). 'Ability factors and environmental influences.' *Amer. Psychologist*, **20**, 723–33.

Vernon, P. E. (1965). 'Environmental handicaps and intellectual development.' *Brit. J. Educ. Psychol.*, **35**, 117–36.

Vernon, P. E. (1969). *Intelligence and Cultural Environment.* Methuen, London.

Vernon, P. E. (1971). 'Analysis of cognitive ability.' *Brit. Med. Bull.*, *Cognitive Psychology*, **27**, 222–6.

Voss, J. F. (Ed.) (1969). *Approaches to Thought.* Merrill, Ohio.

Vygotsky, L. S. (1962). *Thought and Language.* M.I.T. Press, Cambridge, Mass. (Original Russian Publication 1934).

Wallach, M. A., and Kogan, N. (1965). *Modes of Thinking in Young Children: A Study of the Creativity—Intelligence Distinction.* Holt, Rinehart and Winston Inc., New York.

Wallach, L., and Sprott, R. L. (1964). 'Inducing number conservation in children.' *Child Dev.*, **35**, 1057–71.

Wallach, L., Wall, A. J., and Anderson, L. (1967). 'Number conservation: the roles of reversibility, addition-subtraction, and misleading perceptual cues.' *Child Dev.*, **38**, 425–42.

Wallas, G. (1926). *The Art of Thought.* Harcourt, New York.

Warburton, F. W. (1951). 'The ability of the Gurkha recruit.' *Br. J. Psychol.*, **42**, 123–33.

Ward, J. (1883). 'Psychology.' In *Encyclop. Brit. (9th Edn.)*, **20**, 37–85.

Warden, C. J., and Jackson, T. A. (1935). 'Imitative behaviour in the Rhesus monkey.' *Pedagog. Sem.*, **46**, 103–25.

420

Wason, P. C. (1960). 'On the failure to eliminate hypotheses in a conceptual task.' *Q. J. Exp. Psychol.*, **12**, 129–40.

Wason, P. C. (1961). 'Response to affirmative and negative binary statements.' *Brit. J. Psychol.*, **52**, 133–42.

Wason, P. C. (1965). 'The contexts of plausible denial.' *J.V.L.V.B.*, **4**, 7–11.

Wason, P. C. (1968). ' "On the failure to eliminate hypotheses"—a second look.' In Wason, P. C. and Johnson-Laird, P. N. (Eds.), *Thinking and Reasoning.* Penguin, Harmondsworth.

Wason, P. C. (1968). 'Reasoning about a rule.' *Q. J. Exp. Psychol.*, **20**, 273–81.

Wason, P. C. (1969). 'Regression in reasoning?' *Brit. J. Psychol.*, **60**, 471–80.

Wason, P. C. (1972). In *New Scientist*, **55**, 134–7.

Wason, P. C., and Johnson-Laird, P. N. (1969). 'Proving a disjunctive rule.' *Q. J. Exp. Psychol.*, **21**, 14–20.

Wason, P. C., and Johnson-Laird, P. N. (1970). 'A conflict between selecting and evaluating information in an inferential task.' *Brit. J. Psychol.*, **61**, 509–15.

Wason, P. C., and Johnson-Laird, P. N. (1972). *The Psychology of Reasoning: Structure and Content.* Batsford, London.

Wathen-Dunn, W. (Ed.) (1967). *Models for the Perception of Speech and Visual Form.* M.I.T. Press, Cambridge, Mass.

Watson, J. B. (1920). *Behaviourism.* W. W. Norton and Company Inc., New York.

Watson, J. B. (1928). 'The unconscious of the behaviourist.' In *The Unconscious: A Symposium.* Alfred A. Knopf, New York.

Watt, H. J. (1905). 'Experimentelle Beiträge zur einer Theorie des Denkens.' *Arch. ges. Psychol.*, **4**, 289–436.

Webb, W. B. (1970). Individual differences in sleep length. In Hartmann, E. (Ed.) *Sleep and Dreaming.* Little, Brown and Co., Boston.

Weiskrantz, L. (1968). Treatments, inferences and brain function. In *Analysis of Behavioural Change.* Weiskrantz, L. (Ed.), N.Y.: Harper & Row.

Weismann, A. (1902). *Vorträge über Descendenztheorie—die Keimplasmatheorie.* Fischer, Jena.

Welford, A. T., and Houssiadas, L. (Eds.) (1970). *Contemporary Problems in Perception.* Taylor and Francis, London.

Welsford, E. (1935). *The Fool: His Social and Literary History.* Faber, London.

Werner, H. (1948). *Comparative Psychology of Mental Development.* (Revised Edition). Follett, New York.

Wertheimer, M. (1945). *Productive Thinking.* Harper and Row, New York.

Wetherick, N. E. (1969). 'Bruner's concept of a strategy: an experiment and a critique.' *J. Gen. Psychol.*, **81**, 53–8.

Wetherick, N. E. (1970). 'On the representativeness of some experiments in cognition.' *Bull. Brit. Psychol. Soc.*, **23**, 213–14.

Whitehead, A. N., and Russell, B. (1927). *Principia Mathematica.* Cambridge Univ. Press, London.

Whiting, J. W. M. (1968). 'Methods and problems in cross-cultural research.' In Lindzey, G. and Aronson, E. (Eds.), *Handbook of Social Psychology.* Vol. II. Addison-Wesley, Reading, Mass. 2nd Edn.

Whorf, B. J. (1956). *Language, Thought and Reality.* M.I.T. Press, Cambridge, Mass.

Whyte, L. L. (1960). *The Unconscious before Freud.* Basic Books, New York (1962 Tavistock).

Wickens, D. D. (1970). 'Encoding categories of words: an empirical approach to meaning.' *Psychol. Rev.*, **77**, 1–15.

Winikoff, A. W. (1967). *Eye Movements as an Aid to Protocol Analysis of Problem Solving Behavior.* Unpubl. doctoral dissertation. Carnegie-Mellon Univ.

Wiseman, S. (1964). *Education and Environment.* Manchester Univ. Press, Manchester.

Wiseman, S. (1967). *Intelligence and Ability.* Penguin Books, Harmondsworth.

Witkin, H. A. (1960). 'The problem of individuality in development.' In Kaplan, B. and Wapner, S. (Eds.), *Perspectives in Psychological Theory.* International Universities Press.

Witkin, H. A. (1965). 'Psychological differentiation and forms of pathology.' *J. Abn. Psychol.*, **70**, 317–36.

Witkin, H. A. (1967). 'A cognitive-style approach to cross-cultural research.' *Int. J. Psychol.*, **2**, 233–50.

Witkin, H. A. Dyk, R. B., Faterson, H. F., Goodenough, D. R. and Karp, S. A. (1962). *Psychological Differentiation.* Wiley, New York.

Witkin, H. A., Lewis, H. B., Hertzman, M., Machover, K., Meissner, P. B. and Wapner, S. (1954). *Personality through Perception.* Harper and Row, New York.

Wodehouse, P. G. (1953). *Performing Flea.* Barrie and Jenkins, London.

Wolf, R. (1966). 'The measurement of environments.' In Anastasi, A. (Ed.), *Testing Problems in Perspective.* American Council on Education, Washington, D.C.

Wolff, J. L. (1967). 'Concept-shift and discrimination-reversal learning in humans.' *Psychol. Bull.*, **68**, 369–408.

Woodworth, R. S. (1913). *Contemporary Schools in Psychology.* Methuen, London.

Woodworth, R. S. (1931). *Contemporary Schools of Psychology.* Ronald Press, New York.

Woodworth, R. S. and Sells, S. B. (1935). 'An atmosphere effect in formal syllogistic reasoning.' *J. Exp. Psychol.*, **18**, 451–60.

Wundt, W. (1862). 'Beitr. z. Theorie der Sinneswahrnehmung.' Cited by Whyte, L. L. *The Unconscious before Freud.* Tavistock, London, 1962.

Wundt, W. (1911). *Einführung in die Psychologie. Voitländer*, Leipzig (English Trans. 1912).

Wundt, W. (1912). *An Introduction to Psychology.* Pädogogische Literatur Gesellschaft Neue Bahnen. English Edn., Allen and Unwin, 1924.

Yamamoto, K. (1965). 'Validation of tests of creative thinking: a review of some studies.' *Exceptional Children*, February, 281–90.

Zeaman, D. and House, B. J. (1963). 'The role of attention in retardate discrimination learning.' In Ellis, N. R. (Ed.), *Handbook of Mental Deficiency.* McGraw-Hill, New York.

Zegans, L. S., Pollard, J. C. and Brown, D. (1967). 'The effects of LSD-25 on creativity and tolerance to regression.' *Arch. Gen. Psychiat.*, **16**, 740–9.

Acknowledgements

The acknowledgements to the authorized copyright holders of diagrams and tables reproduced in the text are indicated in the appropriate captions to the respective tables and figures.

The authors also wish to acknowledge the co-operation of the following for granting permission to reproduce passages of text from their publications.

Academic Press, Inc.
Pages 5–6 (Kendler, 'The concept of the concept', in Melton (ed.), *Categories of Human Learning*, Academic Press, New York, 1964. Copyright Academic Press).
Pages 67–68 (Wason and Johnson-Laird, *Quarterly Journal of Experimental Psychology*, 1969, **21**, pp. 14–20).
Pages 75–76 (Johnson-Laird and Wason, *Quarterly Journal of Experimental Psychology*, 1970, **22**, pp 49–61).
Page 380 (Berger, 'Physiological correlates of dreaming', *'Experimental Neurology' Supplement 4*, 1967, pp. 15–28. Copyright Academic Press)

Akademische Verlagsgesellschaft
Page 364 (Bühler, *Archiv für die gesamte Psychologie*, 1907, **9**, pp. 297–365).

Aldine Publishing Company
Pages 340–341 (Newell et al, *Contemporary Approaches to Creative Thinking*, Atherton Press, New York, 1962).

George Allen & Unwin Ltd.
Page 70 (Bartlett, *Thinking: An Experimental and Social Study*, Allen & Unwin, London, 1958).
Pages 371, 372–373 and 373–375 (Freud, *The Interpretation of Dreams*, Allen & Unwin, London, Revised edition 1938).

American Council on Education
Page 147 (Wolf, 'The measurement of environments', in Anastasi (ed.), *Testing Problems in Perspective*, American Council on Education, Washington, D.C., 1966).

American Psychological Association
Page 112 (Cross, 'The relation of parental training conditions to conceptual level in adolescent boys', *Journal of Personality*, 1966, **34**, pp. 348–365. Copyright 1966 by the American Psychological Association, and reproduced by permission).
Page 302 (Paivio, 'Mental imagery in associative learning and memory', *Psychological Review*, 1969, **76**, pp. 241–263. Copyright 1969 by the American Psychological Association, and reproduced by permission).
Pages 389–396 (Radford, 'Reflections on introspection', *American Psychologist*, in press. Copyright 1974 by the American Psychological Association and reproduced by permission).
Page 393 (Boring, 'A history of introspection', *Psychological Bulletin*, 1953, **50**, pp. 169–189. Copyright 1953 by the American Psychological Association, and reproduced by permission).

inquiry', *Harvard Educational Review*, **39**, 1969, 484–510. Copyright © 1969 by President and Fellows of Harvard College).
Pages 163–164 and 166 (Jensen, A. R., 'Reducing the heredity–environment uncertainty', *Harvard Educational Review*, **39**, 1969, 209–243. Copyright © 1969 by President and Fellows of Harvard College).

Harvard University Press
Pages 303 and 304 (Bruner, *Toward a Theory of Instruction*, Harvard University Press, Cambridge Massachusetts, 1966).

William Heinemann Ltd.
Pages 121–122 (Sir Max Beerbohm, *Mainly on the Air*, Heinemann, London, 1923).

Her Majesty's Stationery Office
Pages 339–340 (Turing, *Intelligent Machinery*, 1948, National Physical Laboratory Report 1–20).

The Hogarth Press Ltd.
Pages 365 and 369 (Freud, 'An Autobiographical Study' (1935) in *The Standard Edition of the Complete Psychological Works of Sigmund Freud*, revised and edited by James Strachey, Hogarth Press, London, 1963).
Page 372 (Breuer and Freud, 'Studies in Hysteria' (1895) in *The Standard Edition of the Complete Psychological Works of Sigmund Freud*, revised and edited by James Strachey, Hogarth Press, London, 1963).

Holt, Rinehart and Winston, Inc.
Page 88 (Wallach and Kogan, *Modes of Thinking in Young Children: A Study of the Creativity-Intelligence Distinction*, Holt, Rinehart and Winston, New York, 1965).
Page 105 (Barton, *Creative Person and Creative Process*, Holt, Rinehart and Winston, New York, 1969).
Page 280 (Jensen, 'Social class and verbal learning', in Deutsch, Katz and Jensen (eds.), *Social Class, Race and Psychological Development*, Holt, Rinehart and Winston, New York, 1968).

Humanities Press, Inc.
Pages 42 and 45–46 (Köhler, *The Mentality of Apes*, Humanities Press, Inc., New York, 1925).
Pages 189–190 and 193–194 (Piaget and Szeminska, *The Child's Conception of Number*, Humanities Press, Inc., New York, 1941).
Pages 257–258 (Piaget, *The Language and Thought of the Child*, Humanities Press, Inc., New York, 1926).

Hutchinson Publishing Group Ltd.
Pages 26–27 and 28–29 (Dienes and Jeeves, *Thinking in Structures*, Hutchinson Educational Ltd., London, 1965).
Pages 127–129 (Ryle, *The Concept of Mind*, Hutchinson, London, 1949).
Page 338 (Apter, *The Computer Simulation of Behaviour*, Hutchinson, London, 1970).

International Universities Press, Inc.
Pages 95–96 (Kris, *Psychoanalytic Interpretations in Art*, International Universities Press, New York, 1953).
Pages 184 and 185–186 (Piaget, *The Origins of Intelligence in Children*, International Universities Press, New York, 1952).

The Journal Press
Page 57 (Asher, *Journal of General Psychology*, 1963, **68**, pp. 3–8).

Allen Lane, The Penguin Press
Page 238–239 (Lévi-Strauss, *Structural Anthropology*, Allen Lane, The Penguin Press, Harmondsworth, 1972).

North-Holland Publishing Company
Page 211 (Green and Laxon, 'The conservation of number, mother, water and a fried egg chez l'enfant', *Acta Psychologica*, 1970, **32**, pp. 1–30).

W. W. Norton & Company, Inc.
Pages 102 and 109 (Reprinted from *Frames of Mind* by Liam Hudson. By permission of W. W. Norton & Company, Inc. Copyright © 1968 by Liam Hudson).
Pages 365, 369 and 372 (Reprinted from *The Standard Edition of the Complete Psychological Works of Sigmund Freud*, revised and edited by James Strachey. By permission of W. W. Norton & Company, Inc. (1952). Copyright renewed 1963 by James Strachey).

Oxford University Press
Page 12 (Osgood, *Method and Theory in Experimental Psychology*, Oxford University Press, New York, 1953).
Page 112 (Murray, *Explorations in Personality*, Oxford University Press, New York, 1938).

Penguin Books Ltd.
Page 159 (From Peter Mittler: *The Study of Twins* (Penguin Education 1971), copyright © Peter Mittler, 1971).
Pages 382–383 (From Ian Oswald: *Sleep* (Pelican Original 1966: Revised edition 1970), copyright © Ian Oswald, 1966, 1970. Reprinted by permission of the author and Penguin Books Ltd.).

A. D. Peters and Company
Page 264 (John Lyons, *Chomsky*, William Collins Sons & Co. Ltd., 1970. Reprinted by permission of A. D. Peters and Company).
Page 93 (Arthur Koestler, *Drinkers of Infinity*, Hutchinson & Co. Ltd., 1968. Reprinted by permission of A. D. Peters and Company).

Prentice-Hall, Inc.
Page 173 (Hans G. Furth, *Piaget and Knowledge: Theoretical Foundations*, © 1969. By permission of Prentice-Hall, Inc., Englewood Cliffs, New Jersey).
Pages 335. (Allen Newell and Herbert A. Simon, *Human Problem Solving*, © 1972. By permission of Prentice-Hall, Inc., Englewood Cliffs, New Jersey).
Pages 341–342 (L. A. Hiller and R. Baker, 'Computer music', in Harold Borko, Ed., *Computer Applications in the Behavioural Sciences*, © 1962. By permission of Prentice-Hall, Inc., Englewood Cliffs, New Jersey).

Princetown University Press
Pages 376–378 and 379 (*The Collected Works of C. G. Jung*, ed. by G. Adler, Mr. Fordham, and H. Read, trans. by R. F. C. Hull, Bollingen, Series XX, vol. 5, *Symbols of Transformation* (copyright © 1956 and 1967 by Bollingen Foundation, pp. 11, 12, 16–18; vol. 7, *Two Essays on Analytical Psychology* (copyright © 1953 and 1966 by Bollingen Foundation), p. 69; reprinted by permission of Princetown University Press).

Psychological Association for Scandinavia/Almqvist & Wiksell Periodicals
Page 222 (Smedslund, *Scandinavian Journal of Psychology*, 1961, **2**, 11–20, 71–87, 153–160, 203–210; 1962, **3**, 69–77.

Psychological Reports/Perceptual and Motor Skills
Pages 144–145 (Reprinted with permission of author and publisher: Rosenthal, R., and Jacobsen, L. 'Teacher's expectancies: determinants of pupils' IQ gains.' *Psychological Reports*, 1966, **19**, 115–118).
Page 226 (Reprinted with permission of author and publisher: Albert, R. S. 'Cognitive development and parental loss among the gifted, the exceptionally gifted and the creative.' *Psychological Reports*, 1971, **29**, 19–26).
Page 313 (Reprinted with permission of author and publisher: Haber, R. N., and Haber, R. B. 'Eidetic imagery: I. Frequency.' *Perceptual and Motor Skills*, 1964, **19**, 131–138).

428

Springer Publishing Company, Inc.
Pages 293–294, 299 and 312–313 (Richardson, *Mental Imagery*, Springer, New York, 1969).

Tavistock Publications Ltd.
Pages 96 and 107–108 (Schon, *Displacement of Concepts*, Tavistock Publications Ltd., London, 1963).

Taylor & Francis Ltd.
Page 323 (Gregory, *Ergonomics*, 1970, **13**, pp. 25–35).

Teachers College Record
Page 107 (MacKinnon, *Teachers College Record*, 1960, **61**, pp. 367–378).

University of London Press Ltd./The English Universities Press Ltd.
Pages 134–135 (Burt, *The Factors of the Mind*, University of London Press, London, 1940).
Pages 180–181 (Piaget, *Six Psychological Studies*, University of London Press, London, 1968. French edition 1964: Editions Gonthier S.A. with English translation 1967 by Random House Inc. and Random House of Canada Ltd.)

Author Index

432

436

Subject Index